Praise for *The Arabs*

"A rich, galloping narrative that spans the Arab world from Morocco to Yemen to Iraq."
—Simon Sebag Montefiore, *Financial Times*

"A fascinating [story], and exceedingly well told. . . . What makes [Rogan's] book particularly useful is the way it situates [the Arab-Israeli conflict] within the wider context of the Arabs' long, and still unsuccessful, struggle to come to more equal terms with the West. Europeans in particular, and also Americans, need their memories jogged about just how arrogant, duplicitous, and frequently stupid their governments have been in dealing with the Middle East. [An] exemplary history."
—*Economist*

"Readable and reliable, this sweeping survey balances the unity of a coherent story with due attention to detail. As such, Rogan's contribution belongs in the company of the earlier classics by Hitti and Hourani."
—*Foreign Affairs*

"[Rogan] provides a prism through which the lay Westerner can view five centuries of tumult, zealotry, and complication. . . . Rogan consistently plays up (and never papers over) the bountiful East-West parallels."
—*Atlantic*

"I'm often asked what is the single best introduction to the Arab world. I haven't had a good answer until I read this book. Rogan does a superb job explaining how the past has shaped the modern Middle East. A sweeping survey, wonderfully written, and filled with insight and analysis."
—*Fareed Zakaria GPS,* Book of the Week, CNN

"[*The Arabs*], which starts with the Ottoman Turks' conquest of the Arab world in 1516–17, offers a strikingly vivid and authoritative account of its subsequent experience. . . . [Rogan's] rehearsal of recent Middle East history is impeccable."
—*Times* (UK)

"Very much a modern history. . . . Rogan gives a lucid account of political developments throughout the Arab lands, unpicking messy tangles such as the Lebanese civil war or the fragmentation of Palestinian political movements."
—*Sunday Telegraph* (UK)

"Rogan's brilliant book is clear-eyed and balanced. Mixing academic rigour with a lively narrative style, *The Arabs: A History* is required reading for anyone seeking to understand the background to the mess that the Arabs find themselves in."
—*Spectator* (UK)

"An incredibly ambitious book . . . wonderfully inclusive and articulate and knowledge-able, pretty much indispensable."

—*Scotsman* (UK)

"Rogan manages the somewhat staggering feat of outlining nearly 500 years of history in a way that is neither cursory nor overwhelming—and is based in the experiences of the people themselves. . . . [Rogan's] ability to gather and synthesize such a wealth of infor-mation, showing both the humanity and malice present on all sides, while neither bowing to nor accepting conventional wisdom, is truly remarkable. It's to be hoped that America's decision makers get their hands on a copy of *The Arabs*—and take very good notes."

—*Dallas Morning News*

"A perceptive narrative of the past 500 years of Arab history. . . . This is a book for the general reader with little or no detailed knowledge of the Arab world. The writing is fluid and avoids academic theorizing and jargon. . . . However, even specialists should find this book a valuable guide to major events across the Arab world from Iraq to Mo-rocco over an extensive period of time."

—*Middle East Policy Journal*

"An eloquent grand narrative of optimism and despair. . . . Rogan's book is evocative, timely, and illuminating for the general reader. The individual Arab voices that he uses to structure the narrative—ordinary people, intellectuals, activists, and political leaders—provide a much-needed insider perspective, which nuances stereotypical images of the Arab world in the media. Moreover, *The Arabs* discloses unfamiliar and unsettling truths on the vexed and often over-simplified relationship between the Arab world and its his-torical 'others,' Europe, the West and Israel. Compelling as it is in its own right, this is indeed food for thought also for its relevance to world affairs at large."

—*BBC History Magazine* (UK)

"A straightforward, careful primer on Arab political history from the rise of the Ottoman Empire to the forging of modern fundamentalist Islamic entities. . . . A sweeping history."

—*Kirkus Reviews*

"Framing modern history as viewed from the Arab world, Rogan eruditely furnishes Western readers with a background to current events."

—*Booklist*

"An entertaining, gracefully written, and eye-opening look at a diverse people whose history, culture, and character are often badly misunderstood (if not actively distorted) here in the United States. Read it. You'll learn a lot."

—Stephen M. Walt, ForeignPolicy.com

"A masterful, thorough, and well-written survey of the entire sweep of modern Arab his-tory. Full of lively vignettes but comprehensive at the same time, this book will be of great interest both to general readers and students of the Arab world."

—Rashid Khalidi, Edward Said Professor of Arab Studies, Columbia University

"No better guide to the modern history of the Arab world could be found than Eugene Rogan. He is attentive as much to the insider accounts in Arab memoirs as to the imperial schemes hatched in drawing rooms in Paris and London, as concerned with popular movements and uprisings as with elite reformism, and unafraid to confront directly and with the best evidence and documentation available the vexed issues of colonialism, Orientalism, and the Arab-Israeli conflict. Rogan achieves a rare and realistic synoptic vision of the way in which Arabness has been shaped by both indigenous forces and Western imperial ones. In recent years, the United States has attempted to rule Arabs while carefully avoiding knowing anything about them, a strategy that has yielded all too predictable results. Those in the West who aspire to engage the Arab world in more productive ways in the future will find Rogan an indispensable companion."

—Juan Cole, Richard P. Mitchell Collegiate Professor of History, University of Michigan, and author of *Engaging the Muslim World*

"Eugene Rogan writes about the Middle East with exceptional empathy, wisdom, and insight. His book is a landmark in scholarship on this complex and controversial region. Western scholars have written extensively about the Middle East but mostly from the outside looking in. The Arabs often feature in their accounts as mere driftwood on the sea of international affairs. Rogan, by contrast, has narrated the history of the region over the last five centuries from the inside looking out. He tells the history of the Arabs from their own perspective, using an impressive range of Arabic sources. It is a fascinating story and in Eugene Rogan it has found its most gifted chronicler."

—Avi Shlaim, author of *The Iron Wall: Israel and the Arab World*

"Anyone who seeks to understand why the Islamic world bears a grudge against the West should read *The Arabs*. Few scholars know their subject better than Eugene Rogan, while even fewer are capable of rendering so complex a subject so engagingly readable. It is a joy to open, and a deprivation to put down."

—Sir Alistair Horne, author of *A Savage War of Peace*

"With eloquence, verve, and understanding, Eugene Rogan rightly reminds us that the world, and the Arabs themselves, need to remember the past if we are to build a better relationship between the Arab world and the West. If we are to avoid making the same mistakes again and again, we need to know Arab history from its many high points to its low ones. I can think of no better guide on this crucially important journey than *The Arabs*."

—Margaret MacMillan, author of *Paris 1919* and *Nixon and Mao*

The Arabs

A History

EUGENE ROGAN

BASIC BOOKS
New York

Basic Books
Hachette Book Group
1290 Avenue of the Americas, New York, NY 10104
www.basicbooks.com

Printed in the United States of America

First Hardcover Edition published in hardcover by Basic Books in November 2009.
2017 Trade Paperback Edition: November 2017

Published by Basic Books, an imprint of Perseus Books, LLC, a subsidiary of Hachette Book Group, Inc.

The publisher is not responsible for websites (or their content) that are not owned by the publisher.

Print book interior design by Trish Wilkinson
Set in Adobe Garamond

The Library of Congress has catalogued the hardcover as follows:
Rogan, Eugene L.
   The Arabs : a history / Eugene Rogan.
      p.   cm.
   Includes bibliographical references and index.
   ISBN 978–0-465–07100–5 (hardcover)
   1. Arab countries—History—1517–1918. 2. Arab countries—History—20th century. 3. Palestine—History—Partition, 1947. 4. Arab nationalism. 5. Petroleum industry and trade—Arab countries. 6. Islam and politics—Arab countries. 7. Imperialism. I. Title.
DS37.7.R64 2009
909'.04927—dc22   2009028575

ISBNs: 978-0-465-09421-9 (2017 paperback); 978-0-465-02504-6 (2011 paperback); 978-0-465-03248-8 (e-book)

LSC-C

10   9   8   7   6   5   4   3   2   1

This book is dedicated to
Richard Huia Woods Rogan

Contents

Introduction

Fayda Hamdy learned of the downfall of Tunisia's autocratic president from her jail cell. The date was January 14, 2011, and Zine el-Abidine Ben Ali had ruled Tunisia for over twenty-three years. Though she didn't dare acknowledge it to her cellmates, Hamdy had played no small part in the dictator's overthrow. A council inspector from the small town of Sidi Bouzid, Hamdy stood accused of humiliating a street vendor whose self-immolation provoked nationwide demonstrations in Tunisia that ultimately sparked the string of popular revolutions across North Africa and the Middle East known as the Arab Spring.

Four weeks earlier, on December 17, 2010, Fayda Hamdy was making the rounds of the vegetable market in her hometown. Sidi Bouzid is one of those provincial small towns in Tunisia neglected by tourists and the government alike. A woman in her forties dressed in an official blue uniform, her authority reinforced by epaulets and stripes, Hamdy was accompanied by two male colleagues. Most of the unlicensed hawkers fled on the inspectors' approach, but Mohamed Bouazizi, a twenty-six-year-old street vendor, refused to budge. Hamdy knew Bouazizi and had already cautioned him against selling fruit in the vicinity of the market without a license. On December 17, Bouazizi stood his ground and accused the inspectors of harassment and corruption. The altercation turned into a shouting match, with Bouazizi defending his cart and the inspectors seizing the young man's wares.

There is no agreement on what precisely happened in the fateful scuffle between the inspectors and Mohamed Bouazizi. The young vendor's friends and family insisted that Fayda Hamdy insulted and slapped Mohamed Bouazizi—"a grave insult in Middle Eastern societies"—before ordering her colleagues to confiscate his fruit and scales. Fayda Hamdy denied ever laying a hand on the street vendor, claiming, "Bouazizi attacked us and cut my finger" when the inspectors went to appropriate his goods. The details matter, for Bouazizi's response was so extreme that both friends and strangers still struggle to explain his subsequent actions.[1]

1

Mohamed Bouazizi emerged from his encounter with the inspectors in a fury. Immediately after the confrontation, Bouazizi first sought justice from the municipal offices of Sidi Bouzid, but instead of a sympathetic hearing he received the humiliation of a further beating. He turned next to the office of the governor, which refused him an audience. At that point, something snapped. His sister, Basma Bouazizi, explained, "What my brother experienced, from the confiscation of his fruit-cart to being insulted and slapped by a woman . . . was enough to make him lose his mind, especially after all municipal officials refused to meet with him, and he was unable to complain about this abuse."

It was now midday, and the streets around the governor's office were crowded with townspeople when Mohamed Bouazizi doused his clothes with paint thinner and set himself alight. Bystanders photographed the terrible scene, as others rushed to try to put out the flames that left Bouazizi with burns covering 90 percent of his body. He collapsed and was taken to hospital in the nearby town of Ben Arous.

Bouazizi's desperate act of self-violence left the townspeople of Sidi Bouzid stunned. They shared his sense of injustice, that the government seemed to be working against the common people in their struggle to get by. That same afternoon, a group of Bouazizi's friends and family held an impromptu demonstration outside the governor's office where Mohamed had set himself on fire. They threw coins at the metal gates, shouting, "Here is your bribe!" The police dispersed the angry crowd with batons, but the demonstrators came back in greater numbers the next day. By the second day, the police were using tear gas and firing into the crowd. Two men shot by the police died of their wounds. Mohamed Bouazizi's condition deteriorated.

News of the protests in Sidi Bouzid reached Tunis, the country's capital, where a restive young population of graduates, professionals, and the educated unemployed spread the word of Bouazizi's ordeal via social media. They appropriated him as one of their own, erroneously claiming that Bouazizi was an unemployed university graduate (though he never completed high school, Bouazizi helped pay for his sisters to go to university) reduced to selling vegetables to make ends meet. They created a Facebook group, and the story went viral. A journalist working for the Arab satellite TV station Al-Jazeera picked up the story. The state-controlled Tunisian press did not report on the troubles in Sidi Bouzid, but Al-Jazeera did. The story of the underprivileged in Sidi Bouzid standing up for their rights against corruption and abuse began to air nightly on that network, reaching a global Arab audience.

The self-immolation of Mohamed Bouazizi galvanized public opinion against everything that was wrong in Tunisia under President Zine el-Abidine Ben Ali's reign: corruption, abuse of power, indifference to the plight of the ordinary men and women, and an economy that failed to provide opportunities for the young. The Tunisian protest movement electrified citizens familiar with these problems across the Arab world as they followed the story on TV. After twenty-three years in power, Ben Ali had no solutions. Demonstrations spread from Sidi Bouzid to other poor inland towns—Kasserine, Thala, Menzel Bouzaiene—before erupting in Tunis itself.

Escalating tensions in Tunisian cities forced Ben Ali to respond. On December 28, eleven days after Bouazizi's self-immolation, the Tunisian president paid a visit to the dying man in his hospital room. The state-controlled Tunisian media, which had downplayed reports of nationwide demonstrations, gave prime-time coverage to the president's visit, plastering newspapers and television with images of a solicitous Ben Ali consulting with doctors caring for the unconscious Bouazizi, his burned body wrapped in gauze. Ben Ali invited Bouazizi's family to the presidential palace, promising to do all he could to save their son. And he ordered the arrest of Fayda Hamdy, the municipal inspector accused of the slap that provoked Mohamed Bouazizi's self-immolation.

On January 4, 2011, Mohamed Bouazizi died of his injuries. The Tunisian protesters declared the street vendor a martyr, and the municipal inspector became the Ben Ali regime's scapegoat. She was imprisoned in Gafsa with common criminals, and because the public reviled her widely for her role in Bouazizi's death, lawyers refused to represent her. Hamdy kept her identity a secret from her fellow inmates, claiming to be a teacher detained "for slapping a little boy." "I was afraid to tell them the truth," she later admitted.[2]

In the first two weeks of January, the demonstrations spread to all the major towns and cities of Tunisia. The police responded with violence, leaving two hundred dead and hundreds more wounded. The country's professional army, however, refused to intervene on behalf of Ben Ali's regime. When Ben Ali realized that he no longer commanded the loyalty of the army and that no concessions would mollify the demonstrators, he stunned his nation and the entire Arab world by abdicating and fleeing Tunisia for Saudi Arabia on January 14, 2011. Fayda Hamdy watched the extraordinary events on television with her cellmates. The Tunisian people had achieved the seemingly impossible: through popular protest they had toppled one of the Arab world's deeply entrenched dictators.

The impact of the Tunisian revolution reverberated around the Arab world. Presidents and kings watched nervously as citizens' action unseated one of their peers. As a "president for life," Ben Ali was hardly unique. Libya's dictator Muammar al-Qadhafi had been in power since 1969, Yemeni president Ali Abdullah Saleh since 1978, and Egyptian president Husni Mubarak since 1981, and each was grooming a son to succeed him. Syria, under the Asad family's rule since November 1970, became the first Arab republic to complete a dynastic succession, with the elevation of Bashar al-Asad to the presidency upon the death of his father, Hafiz al-Asad, in 2000. If a deeply entrenched dictator could fall in Tunisia, analysts across the region speculated, it could happen anywhere.[3]

People living under autocratic regimes across the Arab world shared the Tunisian experience of frustration and repression. The late Samir Kassir, a Lebanese journalist assassinated in June 2005, diagnosed an "Arab malaise" years before the Arab Spring. "It's not pleasant being Arab these days," he observed. "Feelings of persecution for some, self-hatred for others; a deep disquiet pervades the Arab world." The unease took root in all layers of society and spread across the Arab world before exploding in the revolutionary year of 2011.[4]

Egyptian citizens had been mobilizing for change years before the outbreak of the Arab Spring revolutions. In 2004, a group of activists formed the Egyptian Movement for Change, better known as Kifaya (literally, "Enough!"), to protest the continuation of Mubarak's rule over Egypt and moves to groom his son Gamal to succeed him as president. Also in 2004, Ayman Nour, an independent member of the Egyptian parliament, formed the Ghad ("Tomorrow") Party. His audacity in challenging Mubarak in the 2005 presidential election captured the public's imagination, but Nour paid a high price: he was convicted on dubious charges of election fraud and jailed for over three years. In 2008, younger, computer-literate opponents of the regime established the April 6 Youth Movement, whose Facebook page voiced support for workers' rights. By year's end, the group numbered in the tens of thousands, including many who had never previously engaged in political activity.

Whatever their appeal to a younger generation, prior to 2011 Egypt's grassroots movements were no match for the Mubarak regime. In parliamentary elections concluded in December 2010, the ruling National Democratic Party secured over 80 percent of seats in elections widely condemned as the most corrupt in Egypt's history. The populace widely assumed that the elder Mubarak was paving the way for his son Gamal's succession by rigging a totally compliant parliament. Disenchanted, most Egyptians had opted to boycott elections to deny the new legislature any glimmer of a popular mandate. Yet within two months of the election, the Egyptians shifted from boycott to active calls for the fall of the Mubarak regime.

Inspired by the Tunisian example, Egyptian activists organized a mass demonstration in central Cairo's Tahrir Square on January 25, 2011. Protesters descended on the square in unprecedented numbers, swelling to the hundreds of thousands. Waves of protests known as the January 25 Movement swept through other major cities of Egypt—Alexandria, Suez, Ismailiyya, Mansoura, across the delta and upper Egypt alike—and brought the country to a standstill.

For eighteen days the whole world watched transfixed as Egypt's reform movement challenged the Mubarak regime—and won. The government resorted to dirty tactics. It released convicted prisoners from jail to provoke fear and disorder. Policemen in civilian clothes assaulted the protesters in Tahrir Square, posing as pro-Mubarak counterdemonstrators. The president's men went to theatrical lengths, mounting a horse-and-camel charge against the protesters. Over eight hundred were killed and thousands wounded in the course of the demonstrations. Yet protesters repelled with determination the Mubarak regime's every attempt at intimidation, and their numbers only grew. Throughout it all, the Egyptian army refused to support the government and declared the protesters' demands legitimate.

Like Ben Ali before him, Mubarak recognized his position was untenable without the army's support. Its reticence was all the more surprising, given that Mubarak was himself a former air force general. On February 11, 2011, the Egyptian president stood down, sparking jubilation in Tahrir Square and nationwide celebrations. After nearly thirty years in power, Husni Mubarak had seemed unassailable. His fall confirmed that the Arab revolutions of 2011 would spread from Tunisia and Egypt across the Arab world as a whole.

Demonstrations erupted in Benghazi on February 15, marking the beginning of the Libyan revolution against the forty-one-year dictatorship of Muammar al-Qadhafi. That same month, demonstrators massed in Sanaa, Aden, and Ta'iz to call for the fall of Yemeni dictator Ali Abdullah Saleh. On February 14, protesters descended on Manama's Pearl Roundabout, taking the Arab Spring to Bahrain. And in March, nonviolent demonstrations in the southern Syrian town of Deraa provoked violent repression from the brutal regime of President Bashar al-Asad, opening the most tragic chapter of the Arab Spring.

By the time Fayda Hamdy emerged from prison, Tunisia and the Arab world at large had changed beyond recognition. Hamdy finally secured a lawyer—a female relation—and was acquitted of all charges in a single court hearing on April 19, 2011. Her release came as Tunisia moved beyond the tragic events of Mohamed Bouazizi's death to address the hopes and challenges of a new political era following the toppling of the Ben Ali regime. She returned to Sidi Bouzid to work for the municipality, though she no longer patrolled the markets. In place of her uniform and peaked cap, she donned civilian clothes and an Islamic head scarf. In her new dress, she personified an Arab world transformed from military autocracy to a new experiment in Islamic democracy.[5]

The Arab revolutions of 2011 took the world by surprise. After decades of stability under autocratic rulers, a seemingly unprecedented period of rapid and dramatic change engulfed states across the Arab world. It was as though the tectonic plates of Arab politics had shifted from geological to real time. In the face of an uncertain future, there is no better guide than the past—a simple truth often lost on political analysts. All too often in the West, we discount the current value of history. As political commentator George Will has written, "When Americans say of something, 'That's history,' they mean it is irrelevant."[6] Nothing could be further from the truth. Western policymakers and intellectuals need to pay far more attention to history if they hope to understand the roots of the Arab Spring and address the terrible challenges confronting the Arab world after 2011.

The Arab peoples in modern times have grappled with major challenges at home and abroad. They have sought to escape the domination of foreign powers and pressed for reforms to make their governments less autocratic and more accountable to their citizens. These are the great themes of modern Arab history, and they have shaped the writing of this book.

The Arabs are immensely proud of their history, particularly the first five centuries after the emergence of Islam, spanning the seventh to the twelfth centuries of the Current Era. This was the age of the great Islamic empires based in Damascus, Baghdad,

Cairo, and Cordoba that dominated world affairs. You could argue that the early Islamic centuries defined the Arabs as a people who shared a language (Arabic), ethnic origins among the tribes of the Arabian Peninsula, and, for the majority, a common faith in Sunni Islam. All Arabs look back on the early Islamic period as a bygone age when the Arabs were the dominant power in the world; it resonates particularly, however, with Islamists, who argue that the Arabs were greatest when they adhered most closely to their Muslim faith.

Starting at the end of the eleventh century, foreign invaders laid waste to Islamic lands. In 1099 the Crusaders seized Jerusalem after a bloody siege, initiating two centuries of foreign rule by Crusader kingdoms. In 1258 the Mongols sacked Baghdad, the seat of the Abbasid caliphate, and the Tigris flowed red with the blood of its inhabitants. In 1492, the Catholic Reconquista expelled the last of the Muslims from the Iberian Peninsula. Yet still Cairo held out as a seat of Islamic power under the Mamluk sultanate (1250–1517), ruling over all of modern Egypt, Syria, Lebanon, Israel, Palestine, Jordan, and the Red Sea provinces of Saudi Arabia.

Only after the sixteenth-century Ottoman conquests did the Arabs come to be ruled from a foreign capital. Since Mehmed the Conqueror seized the Byzantine capital Constantinople in 1453, the Ottoman Turks had governed their growing empire from the city they renamed Istanbul. Straddling the straits of the Bosporus, Istanbul spans Europe and Asia, with city quarters on both continents. Though the seat of a Sunni Muslim empire, Ottoman Istanbul was far from Arab lands—1,500 kilometers (940 miles) from Damascus, 2,200 kilometers (1,375 miles) from Baghdad, and 3,800 kilometers (2,375 miles) overland from Cairo. Moreover, the administrative language of the Ottoman Empire was Turkish, not Arabic. The Arabs began navigating the modern age by other people's rules.

The Ottomans ruled the Arabs for four of the past five centuries. Over this expanse of time the empire changed, and the rules changed accordingly. In the first century after the conquest, the Ottoman rules were none too demanding: the Arabs had to recognize the authority of the sultan and respect both his laws and God's (sharia, or Islamic law). Non-Muslim minorities could organize their own affairs, under their own communal leadership and religious laws, in return for payment of a poll tax to the state. All in all, most Arabs seemed to view their place in the dominant world empire of the age with equanimity, as Muslims in a great Muslim empire.

In the eighteenth century, the rules changed significantly. The Ottoman Empire had reached its zenith during the seventeenth century but in 1699 suffered its first loss of territory—Croatia, Hungary, Transylvania, and Podolia, in the Ukraine—to its European rivals. The cash-strapped empire began to auction both state offices and provincial agricultural properties as tax farms to generate revenues. This allowed powerful men in remote provinces to amass vast territories through which they accumulated sufficient wealth and power to challenge the authority of the Ottoman government. In the second half of the eighteenth century, a string of such local leaders posed a grave challenge to Ottoman rule in Egypt, Palestine, Lebanon, Syria, Iraq, and Arabia.

By the nineteenth century the Ottomans had initiated a period of major reforms intended to quell the challenges from within the empire and to hold at bay the threats of their European neighbors. This age of reforms gave rise to a new set of rules, reflecting novel ideas of citizenship imported from Europe. The Ottoman reforms tried to establish full equality of rights and responsibilities for all Ottoman subjects—Turks and Arabs alike—in such areas as administration, military service, and taxes. They promoted a new identity, Ottomanism, which sought to transcend the different ethnic and religious divides in Ottoman society. The reforms failed to protect the Ottomans from European encroachment but did allow the empire to reinforce its hold over the Arab provinces, which took on greater importance as nationalism eroded the Ottoman position in the Balkans.

Yet the same ideas that inspired the Ottoman reforms gave rise to new ideas of nation and community, which generated dissatisfaction among some in the Arab world with their position in the Ottoman Empire. They began to chafe against Ottoman rules, increasingly blaming them for the relative backwardness of the Arabs at the start of the twentieth century. Contrasting past greatness with present subordination within an Ottoman Empire that was retreating before stronger European neighbors, many in the Arab world called for reforms within their own societies and aspired to Arab independence.

The fall of the Ottoman Empire in 1918 at the end of World War I seemed to many in the Arab world like the threshold of a new age of independence and national greatness. They hoped to resurrect a greater Arab kingdom from the ashes of the Ottoman Empire and took heart from U.S. president Woodrow Wilson's call for national self-determination as set out in his famous Fourteen Points. They were to be bitterly disappointed, as they found that the new world order rested on European rather than Wilsonian rules.[7]

The British and French used the Paris Peace Conference of 1919 to apply the modern state system to the Arab world, with all Arab lands, bar central and southern Arabia, falling under some form of colonial rule. In Syria and Lebanon, newly emerging from Ottoman rule, the French gave their colonies a republican form of government. The British, in contrast, endowed their Arab possessions in Iraq and Transjordan with the trappings of the Westminster model of constitutional monarchy. Palestine was the exception, where the promise to create a Jewish national home against the opposition of the indigenous population undermined all efforts to form a national government.

The colonial powers gave each new Arab state a national capital, which served as the seat of government, and pressed rulers to draft constitutions and create parliaments elected by the people. Borders, in many cases quite artificial, were negotiated between neighboring states, often with some acrimony. Many Arab nationalists opposed these measures, which they believed divided and weakened an Arab people that could only regain its rightful status as a respected world power through broader Arab unity. Yet, in keeping with the European rules, only recognized nation-states, no matter how imperial their origins, were legitimate political actors.

An enduring legacy of the colonial period is the tension between nation-state nationalism (e.g., Egyptian or Iraqi nationalism) and pan-Arab nationalist ideologies. By the time the Arab states began to secure their independence from colonial rule in the 1940s and 1950s, the divisions between them had become permanent. The problem was that most Arab citizens believed smaller nationalisms based around colonial creations were fundamentally illegitimate. For those who aspired to Arab greatness in the twentieth century, only the broader Arab nationalist movement offered the prospect of achieving the critical mass and unity of purpose necessary to restore the Arabs to their rightful place among the powers of the day. The colonial experience left the Arabs as a community of nations rather than a national community, and the Arabs remain disappointed by the results.

World War II shattered European influence in world affairs. The postwar years were a period of decolonization as the states of Asia and Africa secured independence from their colonial rulers, often by force of arms. The United States and the Soviet Union emerged as the dominant powers in the second half of the twentieth century, and the rivalry between them, which came to be called the Cold War, defined the new age.

Moscow and Washington entered into an intense competition for global dominance. As the United States and the USSR attempted to integrate the Arab world into their respective spheres of influence, the Middle East became one of several arenas of superpower rivalry. Even in that age of national independence, the Arab world found its room to maneuver constrained by foreign rules—the rules of the Cold War—for nearly half a century (from 1945 to 1990).

The rules of the Cold War were straightforward: a country could be an ally of the United States or of the Soviet Union but could not have good relations with both. The Arab people generally had no interest in American anticommunism or Soviet dialectical materialism. Their governments tried to pursue an intermediate path through the Non-Aligned Movement—to no avail. Eventually, every state in the Arab world was forced to take sides.

Those Arab states that entered into the Soviet sphere of influence called themselves "progressives," but the West described them as "radical." This group included every Arab country that had undergone a revolution in the second half of the twentieth century: Syria, Egypt, Iraq, Algeria, Yemen, and Libya. Those Arab states that sided with the West—the liberal republics of Tunisia and Lebanon and the conservative monarchies such as Morocco, Jordan, Saudi Arabia, and the Gulf states—were dubbed "reactionaries" by the progressive Arab states but considered "moderates" in the West. The result was patron-client relations between the superpowers and the Arabs, in which Arab states secured from their respective superpower patrons arms for their militaries and development aid for their economies.

So long as there were two superpowers, the system contained checks and balances. Neither the Soviets nor the Americans could afford to take unilateral action in the region, for fear of provoking a hostile reaction from the other superpower. Government officials in Washington and Moscow lived in fear of a third world war and worked day and night to prevent the Middle East from sparking such a conflagration. Arab leaders also learned how to play the superpowers off each other by using the threat of defection to the other side to secure more arms or development aid from their patron state. Even so, by the end of the Cold War the Arabs well understood that they were no closer to achieving the degree of independence, development, and respect they had aspired to at the start of the era. With the collapse of the Soviet Union, the Arab world entered a new age—on even less favorable terms.

The Cold War came to an end shortly after the fall of the Berlin Wall in 1989. For the Arab world, the new unipolar age began with the Iraqi invasion of Kuwait in 1990. When the Soviet Union voted in favor of a UN Security Council resolution authorizing a U.S.-led war against the Kremlin's old ally Iraq, the writing was on the wall. The certainties of the Cold War era had given way to an age of unconstrained American power, and many in the region feared the worst.

American policies toward the Middle East have been highly inconsistent in the post–Cold War era. U.S. presidents have pursued very different policies since the 1990s. For President George H. W. Bush, who was in office as the Soviet Union collapsed, the end of the Cold War marked the beginning of a new world order. Under Bill Clinton, internationalism and engagement remained the hallmarks of U.S. policy. With the rise of the neoconservatives to power following the election of George W. Bush in 2000, the United States turned to unilateralism. In the aftermath of the September 11, 2001, attacks in the United States, the Bush administration's foreign policies had a devastating impact on the region as a whole, leading to a war on terrorism that focused on the Muslim world, with Arabs as prime suspects. Barack Obama sought to reverse many of the Bush administration's policies and reduce America's military presence in the region—lessening American influence in the process.

The rules of the unipolar age of American dominance have proved the most disadvantageous to the Arab world in modern times. With no alternate power to constrain American action, Arab governments found themselves facing actual invasion and the threat of regime change. It would be no exaggeration to describe the years since the 9/11 attacks as the worst in Arab history, with the Arab Spring serving as a brief if tragic hiatus. What Samir Kassir observed in 2004 holds ever truer today: "It's not pleasant being Arab these days."

For most of the past two centuries the Arabs have struggled for their independence from foreign powers. At the same time, the Arab peoples have sought to constrain the autocratic power of their rulers at home. The Arab Spring revolutions represent the latest chapter in a century-old struggle for accountable government and the rule of law.

Until the end of the eighteenth century, absolutism was the norm in Europe and the Mediterranean world. Only Great Britain and the Dutch Republic had subordinated the powers of the monarch to an elected body before the French Revolution in 1789. After that date, constitutions began to proliferate across the West—in the United States in 1789, in Poland and France in 1791, in Norway in 1814, and in Belgium in 1831. A new political order was emerging in which law constrained rulers' powers and subjects attained the higher legal status of citizens.

Arab visitors to Europe in the first quarter of the nineteenth century returned captivated by the novel political ideas they encountered in Paris and London. The Egyptian cleric Rifa'a al-Tahtawi translated all seventy-four articles of the French Charter of 1814 into Arabic upon his return from Paris in 1831. Living under the autocratic rule of Egyptian governor Muhammad 'Ali, Tahtawi marveled at the constraints the French constitution imposed on its king and the protections it extended to its citizens. Tunisian reformer Khayr al-Din al-Tunisi, inspired by Tahtawi's writings, advocated for a constitution to contain the arbitrary rule of the Tunisian governors. Perhaps uncoincidentally, the first two Arab states to introduce constitutions—Tunisia in 1861 and Egypt in 1882—were the first to undergo Arab Spring revolutions.

The next wave of constitutional reform coincided with the introduction of European colonial rule in the aftermath of World War I. The Egyptian Constitution of 1923, the Iraqi Constitution of 1925, the Lebanese Constitution of 1926, and the Syrian Charter of 1930 each expressed the Arab struggle for independence from European colonial powers on the basis of legitimate government and the rule of law. While these constitutions endowed Arab states with elected multiparty legislatures, the colonial authorities did their utmost to undermine Arab sovereignty. Liberal constitutional government became compromised as an extension of European colonial rule.

The rejection of Arab liberalism followed defeat in the 1948 Palestine War, when the Israeli army trounced the Arab states to secure 78 percent of Mandate Palestine for the new Jewish state. The lack of military preparedness alienated patriotic officers from their kings and presidents, and defeat at the hands of the armed forces of the new state of Israel, dismissed in Arab propaganda as mere "Jewish gangs," undermined citizen confidence in the newly independent governments of the Arab nations. The Arab world entered a new revolutionary age with military coups in Syria (1949), Egypt (1952), Iraq (1958), Yemen (1962), and Libya (1969) that brought decisive men of action to power at the head of technocratic governments. Intensely nationalist, and Arab nationalist, the military regimes promised a new age of social justice, economic development, military strength, and independence from outside influence. The new military rulers demanded only total obedience from their citizens in return. It was a social contract of sorts, and for over half a century Arab citizens willingly suspended their efforts to constrain autocratic rule in return for governments that promised to provide for their needs.

By the start of the twentieth-first century, the old Arab social contract was broken. By 2000, all but the oil rich states had proved incapable of living up to their promises. Increasingly only a narrow band of friends and family of the region's rulers benefited from any economic opportunities. The level of inequality between rich and poor rose alarmingly. Rather than address their citizens' legitimate grievances, Arab states responded to growing discontent by becoming ever more repressive. Worse, these repressive regimes actively sought to preserve their families' control over politics by dynastic succession, as aging presidents groomed their sons to follow them into office. Not only was the Arab social contract broken, but these failing regimes threatened to perpetuate themselves.

In 2011, the Arab peoples rose up in popular movements seeking to reimpose checks on their rulers. "The people should not fear their government," read a placard in Cairo's central Tahrir Square. "Governments should fear their people." For one brief moment, the Arab Spring revolutions succeeded in making Arab rulers fear their citizens. Unfortunately, the moment did not last, as revolution gave way to counter revolution and strongmen returned to power—except in Tunisia, where the movement first erupted with the fateful confrontation between Fayda Hamdy and Mohamed Bouazizi in December 2010. It is too early to know if the fragile constitutional order that has since emerged in that country will prove a harbinger of a future Arab social order or the unique success story of the Arab Spring.

It would be wrong to emphasize the tensions in Arab history to the detriment of all that makes the Arab world so fascinating. As a lifelong student of the Middle East, I was drawn to Arab history because it is so rich and diverse. Following my childhood in Beirut and Cairo, I took my interests in the Middle East to university in the United States, where I studied Arabic and Turkish so that I could read the primary sources of Arab history. Perusing court records and chronicles, archival documents and manuscripts, diaries and memoirs, I was equally struck by the familiar and the exotic in Arab history.

So much of what the Arab world has undergone in the past five centuries is common to human experience around the globe. Nationalism, imperialism, revolution, industrialization, rural-urban migration, the struggle for women's rights—all the great themes of human history in the modern age have played out in the Arab world. Yet much distinguishes the Arabs: the shape of their cities, their music and poetry, their special position as the chosen people of Islam (the Qur'an stresses no fewer than ten times that God bestowed his final revelation on humankind in Arabic), and their notion of a national community stretching from Morocco through Arabia.

Bound by a common identity grounded in language and history, the Arabs are all the more fascinating for their diversity. They are at once one people and many peoples. As the traveler moves across North Africa from Morocco to Egypt, the dialect, calligraphy, landscape, architecture, and cuisine, as well as the forms of government and types of economic activity, transform kaleidoscopically. If the traveler continues through the Sinai Peninsula into the Fertile Crescent, similar differences arise between Palestine and Jordan, Syria and Lebanon, and Iraq. Moving south from Iraq to the Gulf states, the Arab world shows the influences of nearby Iran. Oman and Yemen reflect the influences of East Africa and South Asia. All these peoples have distinct histories, but all see themselves bound by a common Arab history.

In writing this book, I have tried to do justice to the diversity of Arab history by balancing the experiences of North Africa, Egypt and the Fertile Crescent, and the Arabian Peninsula. At the same time, I have tried to show the linkages between the histories of these regions—for example, how French rule in Morocco influenced French rule in Syria, and how rebellion against French rule in Morocco influenced rebellion against French rule in Syria. Inevitably, some countries take up more than their fair share of the narrative, and others are woefully neglected, which I regret.

I have drawn on a wide range of Arab sources, using eyewitness accounts of those who lived through the tumultuous years of Arab history: chroniclers in the earlier periods give way to a wide range of intellectuals, journalists, politicians, poets, and novelists, men and women famous and infamous. It has seemed only natural to me to privilege Arab sources in writing a history of the Arabs, much as one might privilege Russian sources to write a history of the Russians. The authoritative foreigners—statesmen, diplomats, missionaries, and travelers—have valuable insights to share on Arab history. But I believe Western readers would view Arab history differently were they to see it through the eyes of Arab men and women who described the times through which they lived.

CHAPTER 1

From Cairo to Istanbul

The hot summer sun beat down upon al-Ashraf Qansuh al-Ghawri, forty-ninth sultan of the Mamluk dynasty, as he reviewed his troops for battle. Since the founding of the dynasty in 1250, the Mamluks had ruled over the oldest and most powerful Islamic state of its day. The Cairo-based empire spanned Egypt, Syria, and Arabia. Qansuh, a man in his seventies, had ruled the empire for fifteen years. He was now in Marj Dabiq, a field outside the Syrian city of Aleppo, at the northern-most limits of his empire, to confront the greatest danger the Mamluks had ever faced. He would fail, and his failure would set in motion the demise of his empire, paving the way for the conquest of the Arab lands by the Ottoman Turks. The date was August 24, 1516.

Qansuh wore a light turban to protect his head from the burning sun of the Syrian desert. He wore a regal blue mantle over his shoulders, on which he rested a battle axe, as he rode his Arabian charger to review his forces. When a Mamluk sultan went to war, he personally led the troops in battle and took most of his government with him. It was as if an American president took half his cabinet, leaders of both houses of Congress, Supreme Court justices, and a synod of bishops and rabbis, all dressed for battle alongside the officers and soldiers.

The commanders of the Mamluk army and the four chief justices stood beneath the sultan's red banner. To their right stood the spiritual head of the empire, the caliph al-Mutawakkil III, under his own banner. He too was dressed in a light turban and mantle, with a battle axe resting on his shoulder. Qansuh was surrounded by forty descendants of the Prophet Muhammad, who wore copies of the Qur'an enveloped in yellow silk cases wrapped around their heads. The descendents were joined by the leaders of the mystical Sufi orders under green, red, and black banners.

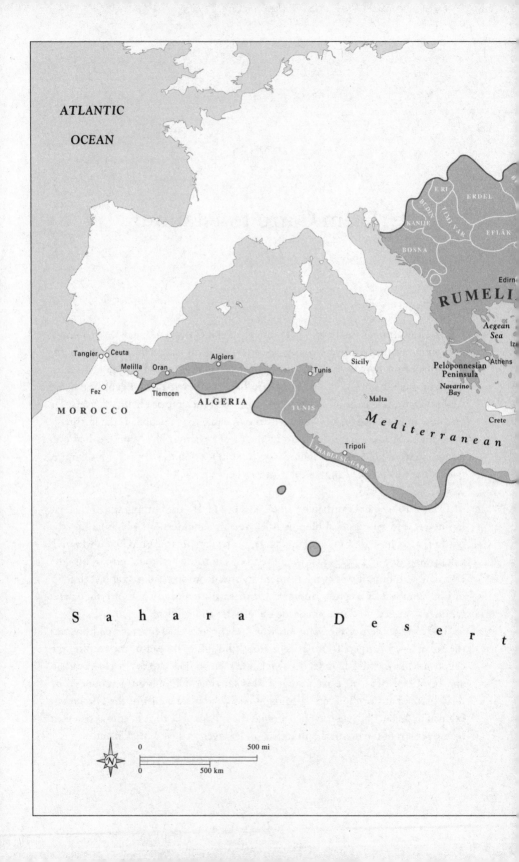

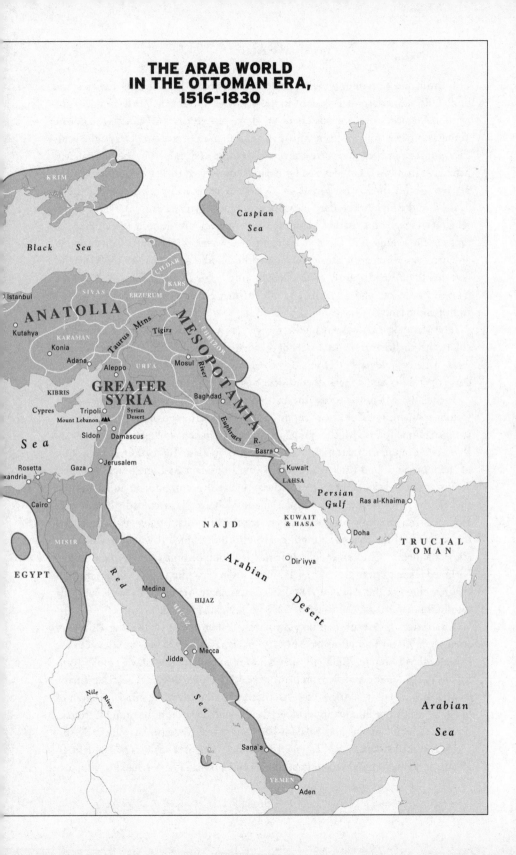

THE ARAB WORLD
IN THE OTTOMAN ERA,
1516-1830

Caspian Sea

Black Sea

KRIM

Istanbul

SIVAS
ERZURUM
CILDAR
KARS

ANATOLIA

Kutahya

KARAMAN

Taurus Mtns

Tigirs

MESOPOTAMIA

DEIRZOR

Konia

Adana

Aleppo

URFA

Mosul

Tigris River

KIBRIS

GREATER
SYRIA

Baghdad

Cypres

Tripoli

Syrian
Desert

Mount Lebanon ▲▲▲

Euphrates

Sidon

Damascus

R.
Basra

Sea

Jerusalem

Kuwait

Rosetta

Gaza

LAHSA

*Persian
Gulf*

Ras al-Khaima

xandria

Cairo

KUWAIT
& HASA

Doha

MISIR

N A J D

TRUCIAL
OMAN

EGYPT

Arabian

Dir'iyya

Red

Medina

HIJAZ

Desert

Jidda

Mecca

Nile River

Sea

*Arabian

Sea*

Sana'a

YEMEN

Aden

Qansuh and his retinue would have been impressed and reassured by the spectacle of 20,000 Mamluk soldiers massed in the plains around them. The Mamluks—the word in Arabic means "one possessed" or "slave"—were a caste of elite slave soldiers. Young men were brought from Christian lands in the Eurasian steppe and the Caucasus to Cairo, where they were converted to Islam and trained in the martial arts. Separated from their families and homelands, they owed their total loyalty to their masters—both those who physically owned them and those who taught them. Trained to the highest standard in warfare and indoctrinated into total devotion to religion and state, the mature Mamluk was then given his freedom and entered the ranks of the ruling elite. They were the ultimate warriors in hand-to-hand combat and had overpowered the greatest armies of the Middle Ages: in 1249 the Mamluks defeated the Crusader army of the French king Louis IX, in 1260 they drove the Mongol hordes out of Arab lands, and in 1291 they expelled the last of the Crusaders from Islamic lands.

The Mamluk army was a magnificent sight. Its warriors wore silk robes of brilliant colors, their helmets and armor were of the highest craftsmanship, and their weapons were made of hardened steel inlaid with gold. The show of finery was part of an ethos of chivalry and a mark of confidence of men who expected to carry the day.

Facing the Mamluks across the battlefield were the seasoned veterans of the Ottoman sultan. The Ottoman Empire had emerged at the end of the thirteenth century as a minor Turkish Muslim principality engaged in holy war against the Christian Byzantine Empire in Anatolia (the Asian lands of modern Turkey). Over the course of the fourteenth and fifteenth centuries, the Ottomans had integrated the other Turkish principalities and conquered Byzantine territory in both Anatolia and the Balkans. In 1453 the seventh Ottoman sultan, Mehmed II, succeeded where all previous Muslim attempts had failed when he seized Constantinople and completed the conquest of the Byzantine Empire. Henceforth Mehmed II would be known as "the Conqueror." Constantinople, renamed Istanbul, became the Ottoman capital. Mehmed II's successors proved no less ambitious in expanding the territorial reach of their empire. On this day in 1516, Qansuh was about to engage in battle with the ninth Ottoman sultan, Selim I (r. 1512–1520), nicknamed "the Grim."

Paradoxically, Qansuh had hoped to avoid going to war by making a show of strength on his northern frontier. The Ottomans were engaged in hostilities with the Persian Safavid Empire. Ruling in what is now modern Iran, the Safavids spoke Turkish like the Ottomans and were probably of Kurdish ethnic origins. Their charismatic leader, Shah Ismail (r. 1501–1524), had decreed Shiite Islam the official religion of his state, which put him on an ideological collision course with the Sunni Ottoman Empire.[1] The Ottomans and Safavids had fought over Eastern Anatolia in 1514–1515, and the Ottomans had emerged victorious. The Safavids urgently sought an alliance with the Mamluks to contain the Ottoman threat. Qansuh had no particular sympathy for the Safavids, but he wanted to preserve the balance of power in the region and hoped that a strong Mamluk military presence in northern Syria would confine Ottoman ambitions to Anatolia, leaving Persia to the Safavids and the Arab world to the Mamluks. Instead, the Mamluk deployment posed a strategic threat to the Ottoman flank. Rather than run the risk of a two-front war, the Ottoman sultan suspended hostilities with the Safavids to deal with the Mamluks.

The Mamluks fielded a great army, but the Ottoman force was greater by far. Its disciplined ranks of cavalry and infantry outnumbered the Mamluks by as much as three to one. Contemporary chroniclers estimated Selim's army to number 60,000 men in all. The Ottomans also enjoyed a significant technological advantage over their adversaries. Whereas the Mamluks were an old-fashioned army that placed much emphasis on individual swordsmanship, the Ottomans fielded a modern gunpowder infantry armed with muskets. The Mamluks upheld medieval military values while the Ottomans represented the modern face of sixteenth-century warfare. Battle-hardened soldiers with extensive combat experience, the Ottomans were more interested in the spoils of victory than in gaining personal honor through hand-to-hand combat.

As the two armies engaged in battle at Marj Dabiq, Ottoman firearms decimated the ranks of the Mamluk knights. The Mamluk right wing crumbled under the Ottoman offensive, and the left wing took flight. The commander of the left wing was the governor of the city of Aleppo, a Mamluk named Khair Bey who, it transpired, had been in league with the Ottomans before the battle and had transferred his allegiance to Selim the Grim. Khair Bey's treachery delivered victory to the Ottomans shortly after the start of battle.

The Mamluk sultan, Qansuh al-Ghawri, watched in horror as his army collapsed around him. The dust on the battlefield was so thick that the two armies could hardly see each other. Qansuh turned to his religious advisors and urged them to pray for a victory he no longer believed his soldiers could deliver. One of the Mamluk commanders, recognizing the hopelessness of the situation, took down the sultan's banner, folded it, and turned to Qansuh, saying: "Our master the Sultan, the Ottomans have defeated us. Save yourself and take refuge in Aleppo." As the truth of his officer's words sunk in, the sultan suffered a stroke that left him half paralyzed. When he tried to mount his horse, Qansuh fell and died on the spot. Abandoned by his fleeing retinue, the sultan's body was never recovered. It was as though the earth had opened and swallowed the fallen Mamluk's body whole.

As the dust of battle settled, the full horror of the carnage became apparent. "It was a time to turn an infant's hair white, and to melt iron in its fury," the Mamluk chronicler Ibn Iyas reflected. The battlefield was littered with dead and dying men and horses whose groans were cut short by the victorious Ottomans in their eagerness to rob their fallen adversaries. They left behind "headless bodies, and faces covered with dust and grown hideous" to be devoured by crows and wild dogs.² It was an unprecedented defeat for the Mamluks, and a blow from which their empire would never recover.

Victory at Marj Dabiq left the Ottomans masters of Syria. Selim the Grim entered Aleppo unopposed and went on to occupy Damascus without a fight. News of the defeat reached Cairo on September 14, some three weeks after the battle. The surviving Mamluk commanders gathered in Cairo to elect a new sultan. They chose Qansuh's deputy, al-Ashraf Tumanbay, as his successor. Tumanbay was to be the last Mamluk sultan, his reign lasting only three and a half months.

Selim the Grim wrote Tumanbay from Damascus, offering him two options: to surrender, and rule over Egypt as a vassal of the Ottomans, or to resist and face total annihilation. Tumanbay wept with terror when he read Selim's letter, for surrender was not an option. Fear began to grip the Mamluk sultan's soldiers and subjects alike. In a bid to preserve discipline, Tumanbay issued a proclamation forbidding the sale of wine, beer, or hashish, under penalty of death. However, the chroniclers claim, the anxious inhabitants of Cairo paid no attention to his orders and sought relief from the imminent threat of invasion in drugs and alcohol.³ When news reached Cairo of the conquest of the coastal town of Gaza, where the Ottomans had put to death 1,000 townspeople, the smell of fear swept through the city. In January 1517, the Ottoman army entered Egypt, heading for the Mamluk capital.

When Selim reached the northern outskirts of Cairo on January 22, Tumanbay's soldiers showed little enthusiasm for the fight. Many troops had failed to report for duty. Town criers were sent through the streets of Cairo threatening to hang any deserters before their own front doors. By such means Tumanbay assembled all the soldiers he could muster—a force of some 20,000 horsemen, infantry, and Bedouin irregulars. Learning from the experience of Marj Dabiq, Tumanbay dispensed with the chivalric prohibition on firearms and armed a large number of his soldiers with muskets. He also lined up 100 wagons bearing light cannon to confront the attackers. The men and women of Cairo came to the battlefield to cheer on the army and to offer prayers for their success. Unpaid, lacking in confidence, and largely unreliable, the Mamluk army approached the day of battle as a group of men fighting for their own survival rather than victory.

The battle took place on January 23, 1517, "a tremendous engagement," wrote Ibn Iyas, "the mere mention of which is enough to strike terror into the hearts of men and its horrors to unhinge their reason." The drums beat for battle, and the Mamluk cavalry mounted their horses and set off across the field. They ran into a much larger Ottoman force that "came on like locusts." Ibn Iyas claimed that the ensuing battle was yet worse than the earlier defeat at Marj Dabiq, the Turks "coming up from every direction like clouds," the "noise of their musketry deafening, and their attack furious." Within one hour the Mamluk defenders had suffered heavy casualties and were in full retreat. Tumanbay fought on longer than most of his commanders before he too retreated from the battle, vowing to fight again another day.[4]

The victorious Ottoman troops stormed Cairo and pillaged the city for three days. The helpless civilian population, left to the mercy of the invading army, could do nothing but watch as their homes and possessions were plundered. The only refuge against the violence of the Ottoman soldiers was the Ottoman sultan himself, and the people of Cairo bent over backward to honor their new master. The Friday prayers in mosques, which had traditionally been recited in the name of the Mamluk sultan, were now delivered in Sultan Selim's honor, one of the traditional means of acknowledging sovereignty. "God save the Sultan," the preachers intoned, "son of the Sultan, King of the two continents and the two seas; conqueror of the two armies, Sultan of the two Iraqs, servant of the two sacred cities, the victorious King Selim Shah. O Lord of both worlds, grant that he may ever be victorious." Selim the Grim responded to Cairo's submission and instructed his ministers to announce a public pardon and the restoration of security.

Sultan Selim waited nearly two weeks after defeating the Mamluk army to enter the city of Cairo. This was the first chance most of Cairo's residents had to scrutinize their new master. Ibn Iyas gives a graphic portrait of the Ottoman conqueror:

> As the Sultan passed through the city he was cheered by all the populace. He was described as having a fair complexion, a clean-shaven chin, and large nose and eyes, as being short in stature, and wearing a small turban. He showed levity and restlessness, turning his head from side to side as he rode along. He was said to be about forty years of age. He had not the dignity of former Sultans. He was of an evil disposition, blood-thirsty, violent-tempered, and intolerant of being answered.[5]

Selim did not rest easily in Cairo while the Mamluk sultan was still at large. So long as Tumanbay lived, the Ottomans knew that his partisans would plot his restoration. Only a very public death would dash those hopes forever. Selim the Grim was given the opportunity in April 1517, when the fugitive Tumanbay was betrayed by Bedouin tribesmen and handed over to the Ottomans. Selim forced Tumanbay to march through the center of Cairo to dispel any doubt that he was in fact the deposed Mamluk sultan. Tumanbay's procession ended at Bab Zuwayla, one of the main gates of the walled city of Cairo, where he was taken by his executioners and hanged before the horrified crowd. The hanging rope broke—some say it broke twice—as if reflecting divine reluctance to permit regicide. "Once he surrendered his soul, a loud cry went up from the crowd," the chronicler recorded, capturing the sense of public shock and horror at this unprecedented spectacle. "Never in the past have we witnessed such an event as the hanging of a sultan of Egypt at Bab Zuwayla, never!"[6]

For Sultan Selim, the death of Tumanbay was cause for celebration. With the termination of the Mamluk dynasty, Selim completed his conquest of their empire and the transfer of all their wealth, lands, and glory to his own dynasty. He could now return to Istanbul having added Syria, Egypt, and the Arabian province of the Hijaz to the Ottoman Empire. The Hijaz carried particular importance as the birthplace of Islam. It was here, in the city of Mecca, that Muslims believe God first revealed the Qur'an to the Prophet Muhammad, and it was in nearby Medina that the Prophet established the first Muslim community. Selim now added the religious legitimacy of being Servant and Protector of the Two Holy Places of Mecca and Medina to the sultan's imperial title. These gains confirmed Selim as sultan of the greatest Islamic empire in the world.

Before leaving Cairo, Selim asked to see one of the famous Egyptian shadow plays, a puppet theater performed with silhouette figures before a lit screen. He sat in private to enjoy the spectacle. The puppet master made a model of Bab Zuwayla and a figure of Sultan Tumanbay at the moment of his hanging. When the cord broke twice, the Ottoman sultan "found the spectacle very funny. He gave the artist 200 dinars and a velour cloak of honour. 'When we leave for Istanbul, come with us so that my son can see this,' Selim told him."[7] His son, Süleyman, would succeed to the Ottoman throne three years later and inherit all Selim had conquered from the Mamluks.

The Ottoman conquest of the Mamluk Empire was a major turning point in Arab history. The fateful clash of arms between Mamluk swordsmen and Ottoman riflemen marked the end of the medieval era and the beginning of the modern age in the Arab world. The Ottoman conquest also meant that for the first time since the rise of Islam, the Arab world was ruled from a non-Arab capital. The Umayyads, Islam's first dynasty, ruled their rapidly expanding empire from Damascus between AD 661 and 750. The Abbasid caliphate (750–1258) ruled the greatest Muslim empire of its day from Baghdad. Cairo, founded in 969, served as capital to no less than four dynasties before the advent of the Mamluks in 1250. From 1517 onward, the Arabs would negotiate their place in the world through rules set in foreign capitals, a political reality that would prove one of the defining features of modern Arab history.

That said, the shift from Mamluk to Ottoman rule had proved easier than many had initially feared at the time of Selim the Grim's bloody conquests. The Arabs had been ruled by Turkish-speaking foreigners since the thirteenth century, and the Ottomans were in many ways similar to the Mamluks. Elites in both empires came from Christian slave origins. Both empires were bureaucratic states that observed religious law and protected Islamic domains from foreign threats with strong armies. Moreover, it was too early to speak of a distinct Arab identity that would object to "foreign" rule. Before the age of nationalism, identity was linked to either one's tribe or town of origin. If Arabs thought in terms of a broader identity, it was more likely to be based on religion than ethnicity. For the majority of Arabs, who were Sunni Muslims, the Ottomans were perfectly acceptable rulers. The fact that the administrative center had moved from Arab lands to Istanbul, a city straddling the continents of Europe and Asia, seems not to have been problematic to people at the time.

The Arab peoples seem to have been pragmatic rather than ideological in assessing the change from Mamluk to Ottoman rule. They were far more concerned about questions of law and order, and reasonable taxation, than what it meant for Arabs to be ruled by Turks. The Egyptian historian 'Abd al-Rahman al-Jabarti, writing in the early nineteenth century, captured this respect for early Ottoman rule:

> At the outset of their reign, the Ottomans were among the best to rule the [Islamic] community since the Rightly-Guided Caliphs.[8] They were the strongest defenders of religion and opposers of unbelievers, and for this reason their dominions expanded through the conquests which God gave to them and to their deputies. They controlled the best inhabited regions on earth. Kingdoms far and wide submitted to them. They did not neglect the state, but guarded its territory and its frontiers. They upheld the performance of Islamic rites and . . . honoured the religious leaders, supported the maintenance of the Two Holy Cities, Mecca and Medina, and upheld the rules and principles of justice by observing Islamic laws and practices. Their reign was secure; their sway endured; kings stood in awe of them; free men and slaves obeyed them.[9]

The villagers and townspeople of Syria did not mourn the passing of the Mamluk Empire. Ibn Iyas relates that the residents of Aleppo, who had suffered from overtaxation and arbitrary rule, barred the retreating Mamluks from entering the city and "treated them worse than the Ottomans had" after their defeat in Marj Dabiq. When Selim the Grim entered the city of Aleppo, "the town was illuminated in celebration, candles lighted in the bazaars, voices were raised in prayer for him and the people rejoiced" at their deliverance from their former Mamluk overlords.[10] The people of Damascus were also unperturbed by the change in political masters, according to the Damascene chronicler Muhammad ibn Tulun (1475–1546). His account of the last years of Mamluk rule is replete with references to overtaxation, the greed of officials, the powerlessness of the central government, the unscrupulous ambition of the Mamluk amirs, the lack of security in the countryside, and the economic woes that resulted from such maladministration.[11] By comparison, Ibn Tulun had favorable things to say about Ottoman rule, which brought law and order and regular taxation to the province of Damascus.

The fall of the Mamluks probably changed the Ottoman Empire more dramatically than it affected the Arab world. The Ottoman heartlands were in the Balkans and Anatolia, and the capital—Istanbul—straddled the European and Asian provinces of the empire. The Arab lands were far from the Ottoman center, and the Arab peoples were a novel addition to the heterogeneous population of the empire. The Arabs were themselves a diverse people, their common Arabic language divided into dialects that grew mutually incomprehensible as one moved from the Arabian Peninsula through the Fertile Crescent to North Africa. Whereas most Arabs were (and are) Sunni Muslims like the Ottoman Turks, there were sizable minority communities of splinter Muslim sects, Christian communities, and Jews. There was also tremendous cultural diversity across the Arab world, with distinct cuisine, architecture, and musical traditions in different Arab regions. History too had divided the Arab peoples, as different regions had been ruled by separate dynasties over the Islamic centuries. The integration of the Arab lands fundamentally changed the geographic reach and the culture and demography of the Ottoman Empire.

The Ottomans faced a real challenge to devise viable administrative structures for their new Arab possessions. The Arabs entered the Ottoman Empire at a time of rapid expansion in Persia, the Black Sea region, and the Balkans. The territorial reach of the empire expanded much faster than the government's ability to train and post qualified administrators for these new acquisitions. Only those regions closest to the Ottoman heartlands—like the northern Syrian city of Aleppo—came under standard Ottoman rule. The farther one traveled from Anatolia, the more the Ottomans sought to preserve the preexisting political order to ensure the smoothest transition to their rule. Pragmatists rather than ideologues, the Ottomans were more interested in preserving law and order and collecting regular taxes from their new possessions than imposing their own ways on the Arabs. As a result, Ottoman rule in the Arab provinces was marked by great diversity and extensive autonomy in the early years after the conquest.

The first challenge facing the Ottomans in Syria and Egypt was to shape a loyal government from Mamluk administrators. Only the Mamluks had the knowledge and experience to rule Syria and Egypt on the Ottomans' behalf. Yet the Ottomans could not count on the loyalty of the Mamluks. The first decade of Ottoman rule was marked by a number of violent rebellions as key Mamluks sought to break from the Ottoman Empire and restore Mamluk rule in Syria and Egypt.

For the first few years after the conquest of the Mamluk Empire, the Ottomans left the institutions of the former state more or less intact, under Mamluk amirs, or "commanders." They divided the former Mamluk domains into three provinces based around the cities of Aleppo, Damascus, and Cairo. Aleppo was the first to come under the full instruments of Ottoman rule. An Ottoman governor was appointed over the province, which was closely integrated into the political and economic life of the Ottoman Empire. Though the populace could not have known it then, the Ottoman conquest would initiate a real golden age in Aleppo lasting through the eighteenth century, in which the city would emerge as one of the great centers of the overland trade between Asia and the Mediterranean. Though it lay some 50 miles from the coast, Aleppo attracted the offices of the Dutch, British, and French Levant companies and became one of the most cosmopolitan cities in the Arab world.[12] When William Shakespeare had the first witch in *Macbeth* say of a sailor's wife "Her husband's to Aleppo gone, master o' the Tiger" (act I, scene 3), his audiences in the Globe knew of where she spoke.

Sultan Selim chose Mamluks to serve as his governors in Damascus and Cairo. The two men he appointed could not have been more different. He named Janbirdi al-Ghazali as his governor in Damascus. Janbirdi had been a Mamluk governor in Syria and had fought valiantly against the Ottomans at Marj Dabiq. He led the Mamluk attack on Selim's forces in Gaza, where he was wounded. He retreated to Cairo with the remainder of his army to stand by Tumanbay in the defense of Cairo. Clearly Selim respected the integrity and loyalty Janbirdi had shown to his Mamluk sovereigns and hoped to turn that sense of loyalty to his new Ottoman master. In February 1518 Selim invested Janbirdi with all of the functions exercised by the former Mamluk governors of Damascus, in return for an annual tribute of 230,000 dinars.[13] There were clear risks in transferring so much power to one person without checks or balances on his authority.

In Cairo, Selim chose Khair Bey, the former Mamluk governor of Aleppo. Khair Bey had corresponded with Selim before the battle of Marj Dabiq and transferred his loyalty to the Ottoman sultan. It was Khair Bey who broke ranks in the Battle of Marj Dabiq and left the field to the Ottomans. He was later arrested by Tumanbay and placed in prison in Cairo. Selim released Khair Bey when he captured Cairo, and then honored the former governor of Aleppo for his services. However, Selim never forgot that Khair Bey had betrayed his former Mamluk sovereign and, according to Ibn Iyas, used to pun on his name, calling him "Khain Bey," or "Sir Traitor."[14]

For so long as Sultan Selim lived, these administrative arrangements held without challenge. In October 1520, news spread of Selim's death and the ascension of the young prince Süleyman to the Ottoman throne. Some Mamluks believed they had given their allegiance to Sultan Selim as their conqueror rather than to his dynasty as a whole. With the Ottoman succession, the new Sultan Süleyman faced a number of revolts in his Arab provinces.

The first Mamluk revolt broke out in Damascus. Janbirdi al-Ghazali sought to restore the Mamluk Empire and declared himself sultan, taking the regal name al-Malik al-Ashraf ("the most noble king"). He donned the clothes and light turban of a Mamluk and banned the people of Damascus from wearing Ottoman fashions. He forbade preachers in the mosques from reciting the Friday prayers in Sultan Süleyman's name. And he set about purging Ottoman soldiers and officials from Syria. The towns of Tripoli, Homs, and Hama rallied to his cause. He raised an army and set out to seize Aleppo from the Ottomans.[15]

The people of Aleppo remained faithful to the Ottoman sultanate. They mourned the death of Selim and recited the Friday prayers in Süleyman's name. When the governor learned of the approach of the rebel army, he set about strengthening Aleppo's defenses. In December, Janbirdi's force laid siege to the city. The rebels fired cannons at the gates of Aleppo and sent burning arrows flying over the city walls, but the defenders repaired the damage and kept Janbirdi's forces at bay. The Damascenes maintained the siege for fifteen days before withdrawing. Some 200 residents of Aleppo had been killed in the course of the siege, as well as a number of soldiers.[16]

As Janbirdi watched his rebellion falter, he returned to Damascus to consolidate his position and rally his forces. In February 1521, he set out to fight an Ottoman army on the outskirts of Damascus. His army was quickly routed, and Janbirdi was killed in battle. Panic swept Damascus. In supporting Janbirdi's futile bid to secede from the Ottoman Empire and to reestablish Mamluk rule, the Damascenes had forfeited the benefits of a peaceful submission to Ottoman rule.

The army that had just defeated Janbirdi's forces now turned to sack the city of Damascus. According to Ibn Tulun over 3,000 people were killed, the town quarters and neighboring villages were plundered, and women and children were taken into captivity. Janbirdi's head and the severed ears of 1,000 fallen soldiers were sent to Istanbul as trophies.[17] Mamluk influence in Damascus was now at an end. Henceforth Damascus would be placed under an Ottoman governor appointed from Istanbul.

In Egypt, the Ottomans faced repeated challenges to their rule. Although Selim had questioned the integrity of his Mamluk governor in Cairo and called him "Sir Traitor," Khair Bey preserved the Ottoman order in Egypt until his death in 1522. It took the Ottoman authorities the better part of a year to name a new governor to replace him. Two provincial governors from Middle Egypt took advantage of the interregnum to launch a rebellion in May 1523, supported by a number of Mamluks and Bedouin leaders. The revolt was quelled swiftly by Ottoman troops in Egypt, with many of the Mamluk insurgents subsequently imprisoned or killed.

The next challenge came from the new Ottoman governor himself. Ahmad Pasha had aspired to be grand vezir, or prime minister of the Ottoman government. Frustrated by his appointment as a mere provincial governor in Egypt, Ahmad Pasha sought to satisfy his ambitions by establishing himself as an independent ruler in Egypt. Shortly after his arrival in September 1523, he began to disarm the Ottoman troops posted to Cairo and shipped many of the infantrymen back to Istanbul. He released the Mamluks and Bedouins that had been imprisoned for taking part in the previous year's uprising. Ahmad Pasha then declared himself sultan and ordered his supporters to kill the remaining Ottoman troops in the Citadel. Like Janbirdi, Ahmad Pasha had Friday prayers recited and coins struck in his name. His rebellion, however, was short-lived. His opponents attacked him and forced him to retreat to the countryside, where he was captured and beheaded in March 1524. Istanbul dispatched a new governor to Cairo with clear instructions to bring Mamluk influence to an end and to draw Egypt more fully under the central government's rule. Thereafter, Sultan Süleyman proved more than capable of commanding the loyalty of his Arab subjects, and no further rebellions threatened Ottoman rule for the rest of his reign.

Within a decade of Selim's conquest, Egypt, Syria, and the Hijaz were firmly under Ottoman rule. Istanbul, the imperial capital, was home to both the decision takers and the law makers of the empire as a whole. At the top of the hierarchy was the sultan, an absolute monarch whose word was writ. He lived in the Topkapi Palace, behind great walls overlooking the imperial capital, the Straits of the Bosporus, and the Golden Horn. Downhill from the palace walls, behind an imposing set of gates, lay the offices of the grand vezir and his ministers. This center of government came to be known by its most distinctive feature—its gates. Referred to in Turkish as the *Bab-i Ali*, or "High Gate," the expression was rendered *La Sublime Porte* in French and anglicized as the Sublime Porte, or just "the Porte." These two institutions—the royal court and the Sublime Porte—set the new terms of government for the Arab provinces, as for the empire as a whole.

With Ottoman rule came new administrative practices. Ottoman provincial government in the sixteenth century was a form of feudalism in which military commanders were awarded territory by the central government. The post holder would oversee the administration of justice and tax collection from his lands. He would also maintain a certain number of cavalrymen from the revenues of his lands and pay a fixed sum in taxes to the central treasury. Unlike feudalism in Europe, the Ottoman system was not hereditary and so did not produce an aristocracy to rival the power of the sultan. The system was ideally suited for a rapidly expanding empire, where territory was conquered faster than the state's ability to produce a trained bureaucracy to administer it. The bureaucrats were left to bookkeeping, making an inventory of the wealth of the empire. Detailed tax registers were compiled listing the number of taxable men, households, fields, and revenues for each village of a given province. These registers were supposed to be updated every thirty years, though in the course of the sixteenth century the state began to neglect its bookkeeping; the practice died out altogether in the seventeenth century.[18]

The new Ottoman provinces in Syria—Aleppo, Damascus, and later the coastal province of Tripoli (in modern Lebanon)—were divided into smaller administrative units and placed under commanders. The provincial governor was given the largest fief, with a set number of troops and fixed taxes to deliver to the sultan for his campaigns and treasury. The military commander of the province was given the next largest fief, with lower-ranking commanders allotted lands in proportion to their rank and the number of troops they were expected to present for the sultan's military campaigns.[19] This modified feudal system was never applied to Egypt, which continued to be ruled in an uneasy partnership between Ottoman governors and Mamluk commanders.

The men who came to fill the posts in the Arab provincial administration were appointed by the central government in Istanbul, and they tended to come from outside the Arab lands. Like the Mamluks, the Ottomans operated their own system of slave recruitment, primarily in their Balkan provinces. Young Christian boys were taken from their villages in an annual conscription known in Turkish as the *devshirme*, or "boy levy." They were sent to Istanbul, where they were converted to Islam and trained to serve the empire. Athletic boys were sent for military training, to fill the ranks of the crack Janissary infantry regiments. Those with intellectual promise were sent to the palace to be trained for civil service in either the palace itself or the bureaucracy.

By modern standards, the boy levy appears nothing short of barbaric: children sent into slavery to be raised far from their families and forcibly converted to Islam. At the time, however, it was the only means for upward mobility in a fairly restrictive society. Through the boy levy, a peasant's son could rise to become a general or grand vizier. Indeed, entry to the elite ranks of the Ottoman military and government was more or less restricted to *devshirme* recruits. The fact that the Arabs, who in their great majority were free-born Muslims, were excluded from this practice meant that they were greatly underrepresented among the power elite of the early Ottoman Empire.[20]

One of the great innovations of Sultan Süleyman II's reign was to define the administrative structure of each Ottoman province in law. Known in the West as "the Magnificent," Süleyman was known locally by the Turkish nickname Kanuni, or "the law-giver." More than two centuries after Süleyman's death, the Egyptian chronicler al-Jabarti extolled the virtues of his legal and administrative reforms: "Sultan Süleyman al-Kanuni established the principles of government administration, completed the establishment of the empire, and organized the provinces. He shone in the darkness, lifted up the shining light of religion, and extinguished the fire of the infidels. The country [i.e., Egypt] has continued to be part of their empire and obedient to Ottoman rule from that time until now."[21] The rules of government were set out for each province in a constitutional document known as a *kanunname,* or "book of laws." These provincial constitutions made clear the relationship between governors and tax-payers and set down the rights and responsibilities of both sides in black and white. For its age, it represented the height of government accountability.

The first provincial constitution was drafted in Egypt in the immediate aftermath of Ahmed Pasha's rebellion in 1525. Sultan Süleyman II's grand vizier, Ibrahim Pasha, introduced the kanunname as a central part of his mission to restore the Sultan's authority over Egypt. The document is remarkably comprehensive, setting out the administrative framework down to the village level. It establishes the responsibilities of office holders in the maintenance of security, the preservation of the irrigation system, and the collection of taxes. The rules for land surveys, for pious endowments, for the maintenance of granaries, and for the running of seaports are clearly explained. The constitution even notes how often the governor should meet with his advisory council of state (four times each week, just like imperial council in Istanbul).[22]

In order to enforce the law, Ottoman administrators needed disciplined and reliable troops. The provincial governors had under their command military forces composed of both Ottoman regulars and locally recruited irregular troops. The elite of the military were the Janissaries, whose commander was appointed by Istanbul. A city like Damascus would have an infantry consisting of between 500 and 1,000 Janissaries to uphold local order. There were also a number of cavalry forces, whose ranks were supported by the revenues of the province. According to Ottoman sources there were over 8,000 cavalrymen in the three provinces of Aleppo, Tripoli, and Damascus combined in the last quarter of the sixteenth century.[23] These forces were supplemented with locally recruited infantrymen and North African mercenaries.

The judiciary was, along with the governors and the military, the third element of Ottoman administration. The central government in Istanbul dispatched a chief justice to each provincial capital, where he would preside over the Islamic courts. Though Christians and Jews were entitled to settle their differences in their own communities' religious tribunals, many chose to pursue their complaints or to record their transactions in the Muslim courts. All imperial decrees from Istanbul were read publicly in court and inscribed in the court registers. In addition to criminal cases, the courts provided arbitration between disputing parties, served as notary public to record commercial contracts and the exchange of land, and registered the major transitions in life—marriages and divorces, settlements for widows and orphans, and the distribution of the personal effects of the deceased. All cases and transactions were duly inscribed in the court registers, many of which still survive, providing an invaluable window into the daily life of the towns and cities of the Ottoman Empire.

Sultan Süleyman II proved one of the most successful rulers of the Ottoman Empire. In his forty-six-year reign (1520–1566) Süleyman completed the conquest of the

Arab world started by his father. He took Baghdad and Basra from the Persian Safavid Empire in 1533–1538, where the Ottoman army was received by the Sunni population as liberators after years of persecution by the Shiite Safavids. The conquest of Iraq was very significant in both strategic and ideological terms. Süleyman II had consolidated his empire, adding the ancient Arab capital of Baghdad to his conquests, and halted the advance of Shiite dogma into Sunni lands.

Süleyman II's forces moved south from Egypt to occupy the southern Arabian lands of Yemen in the 1530s and 1540s. In the Western Mediterranean, Süleyman added the North African coastal regions of Libya, Tunisia, and Algeria to Ottoman domains as tribute-paying vassal states between 1525 and 1574. By the end of the sixteenth century, all Arab lands were under some form of Ottoman control except Central Arabia and the sultanate of Morocco, territories that were to remain outside the Ottoman Empire.

Each of the Arab lands came into the Ottoman Empire at a different point in time, under particular circumstances, with distinct historical and administrative backgrounds. The story of Ottoman rule in every one of these provinces is unique, shaped by the conditions under which they entered the empire.

The Ottoman conquest of North Africa was achieved more through piracy than traditional warfare—though, of course, one man's pirate is another's admiral. Sir Francis Drake used piracy to great effect in fighting England's wars against the superior Spanish fleet in the sixteenth century, yet as a knight of Elizabeth I's realm and one of her most trusted advisors he hardly conjures the image popularly held of maritime brigands. So it was with Khayr al-Din "Barbarossa"—so called by European contemporaries for his red beard—one of the greatest admirals in Ottoman history. To the Spanish he was a ruthless pirate, the scourge of their Mediterranean shipping, who sold thousands of Christian sailors captured in battle into slavery. To the inhabitants of the North African coastline he was a holy warrior carrying the jihad against the Spanish occupiers, whose war booty was an important component of the local economy. And to the Ottomans he was a native son, born around 1466 on the Aegean island of Mytilene just off the coast of Turkey.

At the turn of the sixteenth century the Western Mediterranean was the arena of an intense conflict between Christian and Muslim forces. The Spanish conquest of the Iberian Peninsula culminated in the fall of Granada in 1492, bringing to an end nearly eight centuries of Muslim rule in Spain (711–1492). Faced with life in Catholic Spain, where religious proselytism soon gave way to forced conversion, most Iberian Muslims left their native land to seek refuge in North Africa. These Muslim refugees, known as *Moriscos*, never forgot their homeland or forgave Spain. The Spanish monarchs, Isabella of Castile and Ferdinand of Aragon, relentlessly pursued their holy war across the Mediterranean to the Muslim kingdoms in which the

Moriscos took refuge. They established a string of fortress colonies, or *presidios*, along the North African coast from Morocco to Libya and forced local leaders in the inland towns to pay tribute to Spain. Two of these colonies—Ceuta and Melilla—still survive as Spanish possessions on the Moroccan coastline.

The Spanish faced little opposition to their aggressive expansion from the Muslim mini-states of North Africa. Three local dynasties based in Fez (in modern Morocco), Tlemcen (in Algeria), and Tunis ruled in Northwest Africa. They paid tribute to the Spanish crown and dared raise no challenge to the Spanish fortresses that dominated their main ports and harbors. The Muslim rulers' cooperation with the Spanish invaders discredited them in the eyes of their subjects, and soon local zealots began to organize their own forces to rebuff the invaders. Because the presidios were resupplied by sea, Spanish shipping was more vulnerable to attack than the strong fortresses themselves. Local sailors who armed ships and took their jihad to sea came to be known in the West as the Barbary corsairs (the term *Barbary* derived either from the Greek for "barbarian" or, more charitably, from the indigenous Berber people of North Africa). While these corsairs took plunder and slaves from the Spanish shipping they attacked, they viewed their war as a religious conflict against Christian invaders. Their bold attacks against the Spanish made the corsairs local heroes and gained them the support of the Arab and Berber inhabitants of the coast.

Khayr al-Din was the most famous of the Barbary corsairs. He followed in the footsteps of his brother, 'Aruj, who created an independent ministate in the small port of Jijilli, to the east of Algiers. 'Aruj extended the area under his power across the Algerian coast to Tlemcen in the west, which he captured in 1517. He was killed by the Spanish the following year in a vain attempt to defend Tlemcen. Khayr al-Din understood that the corsairs would need the support of a powerful ally if they hoped to hold their gains against the might of the Spanish Empire, and he raised the corsairs' jihad to a successful war machine by entering into alliance with the Ottoman Empire.

In 1519 Khayr al-Din sent an envoy to the Ottoman court, bearing gifts and a petition from the people of Algiers, to request Sultan Selim's protection and offering to place themselves under his rule. Selim the Grim was near death as he agreed to add the Algerian coastline to the territories of the Ottoman Empire. He sent Khayr al-Din's envoy home with an Ottoman flag and a detachment of 2,000 Janissaries. The greatest Muslim empire in the world had now engaged battle with the fleet of Spain, shifting the balance of power in the Western Mediterranean decisively.

Encouraged by their new alliance with the Ottomans, the Barbary corsairs pressed their attacks far beyond the coast of North Africa. Khayr al-Din and his commanders struck against targets in Italy, Spain, and the Aegean Islands. In the 1520s he seized European ships carrying grain and, like a sea-faring Robin Hood, delivered the food to the people of the Algerian coast, who were suffering shortages from drought. His ships rescued Moriscos from Spain and brought them back to settle in the towns under his control to join the fight against Spain.

Yet Khayr al-Din and his men were best known for their exploits against Spanish shipping. They sunk galleys, freed Muslim slaves, and captured dozens of enemy ships. Barbarossa's name provoked fear all along the coasts of Spain and Italy—with reason. The number of Christians his men captured numbered in the thousands, with nobles held for high ransom and commoners sold into slavery. For the Muslim corsairs there was a sense of poetic justice: many of them had previously been held captive and sold as galley slaves by the Spanish.

The Spanish navy needed an admiral to match wits with Khayr al-Din. In 1528 the emperor Charles V engaged the celebrated commander Andrea Doria (1466–1560) to lead the fight against him. Doria, a native of Genoa who had commissioned his own fleet of war galleys and hired his services out to the monarchs of Europe, was no less a corsair than Khayr al-Din.

Doria was a great admiral, but Khayr al-Din was greater. In their eighteen years of dueling across the Mediterranean, Doria seldom got the better of his Ottoman adversary. Their first encounter, in 1530, was a case in point. Khayr al-Din's forces had taken the Spanish fortress in the Bay of Algiers after a short siege in 1529. The Spanish captives were reduced to slaves and made to dismantle the fort, whose stones were used to create a breakwater to shelter the harbor of Algiers. Charles V was outraged by the loss of the strategic fort and convened a council of state. Andrea Doria suggested an attack on the port of Cherchel, just west of Algiers. Doria's forces landed near Cherchel in 1530 and freed several hundred Christian slaves but met with stiff resistance from the Moriscos who inhabited the town, who were spoiling for a fight with the Spanish. Khayr al-Din sent a relief force, and Doria, who did not want to risk engaging the larger Ottoman fleet, withdrew his ships—abandoning the Spanish soldiers in Cherchel. Those Spaniards who fought were killed, and those who surrendered were enslaved. Khayr al-Din had dealt two humiliations to the Spanish and secured his position in Algiers.

Barbarossa had also raised his standing in the eyes of the sultan, and in 1532 he was invited to Istanbul to meet with Süleyman the Magnificent. He set off with a fleet of forty-four ships and ravaged the coast of Genoa and Sicily along the way, seizing eighteen Christian ships—which he robbed and burned. Finally he arrived in Istanbul, where the sultan invited him to the palace. When he was ushered into the sultan's presence, Khayr al-Din prostrated himself and kissed the ground, awaiting his sovereign's command. Süleyman bid his admiral to rise and promoted him to commander of the Ottoman navy, or Kapudan Pasha, and governor of the Maritime Provinces. Lodged in a royal palace for the duration of his stay in Istanbul, Khayr al-Din met regularly with the sultan to discuss naval strategy. In a final mark of favor, Süleyman pinned a golden medal to Khayr al-Din's turban during a palace ceremony, to demonstrate his gratitude to the Kapudan Pasha for his role in expanding the territory of the Ottoman Empire in North Africa and delivering victories against his Spanish foe.[24]

On his return from Istanbul, Khayr al-Din set about planning his next major campaign: the conquest of Tunis. He mounted an expedition of nearly 10,000 soldiers and took Tunis without a fight in August 1534. The Ottomans were now in control of the North African coast from Tunis to Algiers, placing Charles V's maritime supremacy in the Western Mediterranean in jeopardy. Andrea Doria advised the emperor to drive the corsairs from Tunis. Charles agreed, accompanying the fleet himself. He wrote of the vast assembly of "galleys, galleons, carracks, fusts, ships, brigantines, and other vessels" that carried the Spanish, German, Italian, and Portuguese troops—some 24,000 soldiers and 15,000 horses—to Tunis. "We left [asking] for the aid and guidance of our creator . . . and with divine assistance and favour, to do that which seems most effective and for the best against Barbarossa."[25]

As the massive fleet approached Tunis, Khayr al-Din withdrew his forces, knowing that he could not withstand the armada. Tunis now fell to Spanish forces. Charles V claimed in his letters home that the Spanish freed 20,000 Christian slaves. Arab accounts claim that the Spanish killed at least as many of the local inhabitants in the sack of Tunis. In strategic terms, the conquest of Tunis placed the Straits of Sicily, the gateway to the Western Mediterranean, firmly in Spanish hands. The only Muslim stronghold left was Algiers.

In 1541 the Spanish mounted a massive siege force to take Algiers and defeat Khayr al-Din once and for all. An armada of sixty-five galleys and over 400 transport vessels carrying 36,000 soldiers and siege machines set sail in mid-October. Sayyid Murad, the Algerian chronicler, wrote: "This fleet covered the entire surface of the sea, but I was unable to count all the vessels for they were so numerous." Against the Spanish, the Barbary corsairs raised a force of 1,500 Ottoman Janissaries, 6,000 Moriscos, and several hundred irregulars. Faced with an invasion force that outnumbered his own troops by a margin of more than four to one, Khayr al-Din's situation looked desperate. One of his officers tried to raise the morale of his troops, saying, "The Christian fleet is enormous . . . but do not forget the aid that Allah gives his Muslims against the foes of religion."[26] His words seemed prophetic to the local chronicler.

On the eve of the Spanish invasion, the weather suddenly turned and violent gales drove the Spanish ships onto the rocky shores. The soldiers who did manage to reach shore in safety were drenched by torrential rains, and their gunpowder was spoiled by water. The defenders' swords and arrows proved the more effective weapons in these conditions, as the drenched and demoralized Spanish were driven to retreat after 150 ships were lost and 12,000 men killed or captured. The Barbary corsairs had inflicted a decisive defeat on the Spanish and secured their position in

North Africa once and for all. It was Khayr al-Din's greatest triumph, celebrated each year in Algiers for the rest of the Ottoman era.

Five years later, in 1546, Khayr al-Din Barbarossa died at the age of eighty. He had succeeded in securing the coast of North Africa for the Ottoman Empire (though the final conquest of Tripoli and Tunis was achieved by his successors later in the sixteenth century). Ottoman rule in North Africa was unlike any other part of the Arab lands, reflecting its corsair origins. In the decades following Khayr al-Din's death, power was balanced between a governor appointed by Istanbul, an Ottoman admiral of the fleet, and the commander of Ottoman Janissary infantry. In the seventeenth century the commander of the Janissaries, who had settled and became permanent residents of Algiers, became governor of Algiers and ruled through a council, or *diwan*. Then in 1671 the power shifted again: the admiral of the fleet appointed a local civil ruler, or *dey*, who governed instead of the commander of the Janissaries. For a few years the dey exercised effective power, though Istanbul continued to appoint a pasha, or governor, whose powers were more ceremonial. After 1710, however, deys assumed the office of pasha as well, and Istanbul's control over North Africa grew ever weaker, as the deys enjoyed full autonomy in return for paying a small annual tribute to the Porte.

Long after the conclusion of the Ottoman-Spanish rivalry in the Western Mediterranean, the Porte was perfectly satisfied to leave the deys of Algiers to rule the North African coast on its behalf. Too far from Istanbul to administer more directly, and too thinly populated to cover the expense of a more elaborate administration, the Barbary Coast was typical of those Arab provinces the Ottomans chose to rule in collaboration with local elites. This allowed the Ottoman Empire to claim sovereignty over strategic Muslim territory, and to enjoy a small income stream, at little cost to the imperial treasury. The arrangement suited the deys of Algiers, who enjoyed Ottoman protection and extensive autonomy in their relations with the maritime powers of the Mediterranean. The arrangement would work to the advantage of both sides until the nineteenth century, when neither the deys nor the Ottomans were sufficiently strong to withstand a new era of European colonization in North Africa.

A very different system of autonomous rule developed in the Eastern Mediterranean. The mountains of Lebanon had long provided a refuge for unorthodox religious communities fleeing persecution. Two such communities—the Maronites and the Druzes—devised their own system of rule. Though the Lebanese highlands (known as Mount Lebanon) came under Ottoman rule along with the rest of Greater Syria at the time of Selim the Grim's conquest in 1516, the Porte preferred to leave the local inhabitants to rule themselves in their mountain fastness.

The Maronites had sought the safety of the northern Lebanese mountains in the late seventh century, fleeing persecution by rival Christian sects in what was then the Byzantine Empire. They were supporters of the Crusaders in the Middle Ages and enjoyed close relations with the Vatican thereafter. In 1584 a Maronite College was opened in Rome to teach theology to the most gifted young Maronites, cementing ties between the Maronites and the Roman Catholic Church.

The Druze trace their origins back to eleventh-century Cairo when a dissident group of Shiite Muslims fled persecution in Egypt. In the isolation of the southern Lebanese mountains, their beliefs took the form of a distinct and highly secretive new faith. The Druze emerged as a political community as well as a religious one, and they came to dominate the political order in Mount Lebanon, with the full participation of the Maronite Christians. A Druze amir, or prince, ruled over a rigid hierarchy of Druze and Christian hereditary nobles, each attached to a particular territory in Mount Lebanon.

When Mount Lebanon came under Ottoman rule, the sultans chose to preserve the region's particular feudal order, demanding only that the Druze prince recognize the sultan's authority and pay an annual tribute. The system worked, as the Druze were sufficiently divided among themselves so as not to pose a threat to Ottoman rule. All of that was to change with the rise of Amir Fakhr al-Din II.

Fakhr al-Din II (c.1572–1635), the prince of Mount Lebanon, was like a character from the pages of Machiavelli. His methods were certainly closer to those of Cesare Borgia than those of his Ottoman peers. Fakhr al-Din used a combination of violence and cunning to extend the territories under his control and preserve his position of power across the decades. He even appointed his own court historian to record the great events of his reign for all posterity.[27]

Fakhr al-Din came to power in 1591 following the assassination of his father by the rival Sayfa clan, a Kurdish family who ruled over northern Lebanon from the coastal city of Tripoli (not to be confused with the Libyan city of the same name). Over the next thirty years the Druze prince was driven by the twin motives of revenge against the Sayfa clan and the expansion of the lands under his family's rule. At the same time, Fakhr al-Din preserved good relations with the Ottomans. He paid the taxes on his territory in full and on time. He traveled to Damascus and lavished gifts and money on the governor, Murad Pasha, who later was promoted to grand vizier in Istanbul. Through these connections Fakhr al-Din succeeded in extending his rule over the southern port city of Sidon, the city of Beirut and the coastal plain, the northern districts of Mount Lebanon, and the Biqa' Valley to the east. By 1607 the Druze prince had consolidated his control over most of the territory of the modern state of Lebanon as well as parts of northern Palestine.[28]

Fakhr al-Din's troubles expanded in line with the growth of his mini-state. The territories under his control now extended well beyond the autonomous Mount Lebanon into areas under full Ottoman rule. This unprecedented expansion provoked concerns in government circles in Istanbul and jealousy among Fakhr al-Din's regional rivals. To protect himself from Ottoman intrigues, the Druze machiavel entered into a treaty of alliance with the Medici of Florence in 1608. The Medici offered guns and assistance with Fakhr al-Din's fortifications in return for a privileged position in the highly competitive Levantine trade.

News of Fakhr al-Din's treaty with Tuscany was met with dismay. Over the next few years, the Ottomans watched the deepening of Lebanese-Tuscan relations with mounting concern. Fakhr al-Din's stature in Istanbul had been undermined when his friend Murad Pasha had been succeeded as grand vizier by an enemy, Nasuh Pasha. In 1613 the sultan decided to act and dispatched an army to topple Fakhr al-Din and dismantle the Druze mini-state. Ottoman naval vessels were sent to block the Lebanese ports, both to prevent the Druze prince from escaping and to discourage Tuscan shipping from coming to his assistance. Fakhr al-Din deftly eluded his attackers and bribed his way past the Ottoman ships. Accompanied by an advisor and a number of servants, he hired two French galleons and a Flemish vessel to carry him to Tuscany.[29]

After a fifty-three-day journey from Sidon to Livorno, Fakhr al-Din landed on Tuscan soil. His five-year exile represented a rare moment when Arab and European princes met on equal footing and examined each other's customs and manners with respect. Fakhr al-Din and his retainers observed firsthand the working of the Medici court, the state of Renaissance technology, and the different customs of the people. The Druze prince was fascinated by all he saw, from the common household goods of the average Florentine to the remarkable art collection of the Medicis—including portraits of leading Ottoman figures. He visited the Duomo of Florence, climbing Giotto's campanile and the stairs up Brunelleschi's famous dome, completed the previous century and one of the greatest architectural achievements of its day.[30] Yet for all the marvels he witnessed in Florence, Fakhr al-Din never doubted the superiority of his own culture nor that the Ottoman Empire was the most powerful state of the age.

Fakhr al-Din returned to his native land in 1618. He chose his moment of return carefully: the Ottomans were at war with the Persians again and turned a blind eye to his return. Much had changed in the five years of Fakhr al-Din's absence. The Ottoman authorities had reduced his family's rule to the Druze district of the Shuf in the southern half of Mount Lebanon, and the Druze community had split into rival factions determined to prevent a single household from ever gaining such supremacy as Fakhr al-Din had enjoyed.

In no time, Fakhr al-Din confounded the plans of both the Porte and his regional rivals. From the moment he returned the Druze prince reestablished his authority over the people and the territory of Mount Lebanon to rebuild his personal empire from the northern port of Lattakia through the whole of the Lebanese highlands south to Palestine and across the Jordan River. In the past, Fakhr al-Din had secured his gains by consent of the Ottoman authorities. This time his seizure of territory represented a direct challenge to the Porte. He was confident that his fighters could defeat any army the Ottomans might field, and over the next five years Fakhr al-Din grew increasingly bold in confronting the Ottoman authorities.

Fakhr al-Din reached the height of his power in November 1623 when his forces defeated Ottoman troops from Damascus and captured the governor, Mustafa Pasha, in the battle of 'Anjar.[31] The Druze forces pursued their enemies up the Biqa' Valley to the town of Baalbek, with their prisoner, the governor of Damascus, in tow. While his forces laid siege to Baalbek, Fakhr al-Din received a delegation of notables from Damascus who negotiated for the release of their governor. The Druze amir dragged out the negotiations over the next twelve days and secured every one of his territorial objectives before releasing his prisoner.

When the Ottoman wars with Persia ended in 1629, however, Istanbul once again turned its attention to the rebellious Druze prince of Mount Lebanon, who had extended the borders of the lands under his control eastward into the Syrian desert and northward towards Anatolia. In 1631, in an act of pure hubris, Fakhr al-Din denied an Ottoman army rights to winter in "his" territory. From that point on, the Ottomans were determined to be rid of their insubordinate Druze vassal.

The aging Fakhr al-Din was facing significant challenges from other quarters, as well—from Bedouin tribes, his old enemies the Sayfas of Tripoli, and rival Druze families. Under the strong leadership of Sultan Murad IV, the Ottomans seized on Fakhr al-Din's growing isolation and dispatched a force from Damascus to overthrow the Druze leader in 1633. Perhaps his supporters were weary after years of constant fighting; perhaps they were losing confidence in Fakhr al-Din's judgment, as he flaunted Istanbul's writ ever more flagrantly. As the Ottoman army approached, the Druze warriors refused their leader's call to battle and left him and his sons to confront the Ottoman force on their own.

The fugitive prince took refuge in the mountain caves of the Shuf, deep in the Druze heartlands. The Ottoman generals followed him into the highlands and built fires to smoke him out of his hiding place. Fakhr al-Din and his sons were arrested and taken to Istanbul, where they were executed in 1635, bringing to an end a remarkable career and a dangerous threat to Ottoman rule in the Arab lands.

Once Fakhr al-Din had been eliminated, the Ottomans were pleased to restore Mount Lebanon to its indigenous political system. Its heterogeneous population of Christians and Druzes was ill-suited to a system of government intended for a Sunni Muslim majority. So long as local rulers were willing to work within the Ottoman system, the Porte was more than willing to accept diversity in the administration of its Arab provinces. The Lebanese feudal order would survive well into the nineteenth century without further trouble to Istanbul.

In the century following Selim II's conquest, a distinct political order developed in Egypt. Although their ruling dynasty had been destroyed, the Mamluks survived as a military caste to remain a central part of the ruling elite of Ottoman Egypt. They preserved their households, continued to import young slave recruits to renew their ranks, and upheld their military traditions. Unable to exterminate the Mamluks, the Ottomans had no choice but to draw them into the administration of Egypt.

Already in the 1600s Mamluk beys had come to take leading administrative positions in Ottoman Egypt. Mamluks were placed in charge of the treasury, were given command of the annual pilgrimage caravan to Mecca, were appointed as governors of the Arabian province of the Hijaz, and exercised a virtual monopoly over provincial administration. These posts conferred prestige and, more important, gave their post holder control over significant sources of revenue.

In the seventeenth century the Mamluk beys also came to hold some of the highest military positions in Egypt—putting them in direct rivalry with the Ottoman governors and military officers dispatched from Istanbul. The Porte, increasingly preoccupied with more pressing threats on its European frontiers, was more concerned to preserve order and to ensure a regular stream of tax revenues from its rich province than to redress the balance of power between Ottoman appointees and the Mamluks in Egypt. The governors were left to fend for themselves in the treacherous politics of Cairo.

Rivalries between the leading Mamluk households gave rise to fierce factionalism that made the politics of Cairo treacherous to Ottomans and Mamluks alike. Two main factions emerged in the seventeenth century—the Faqari and the Qasimi. The Faqari faction had links to the Ottoman cavalry, their color was white, their symbol the pomegranate. The Qasimi faction was connected to the native Egyptian troops, took red for their color, and had a disc as their symbol. Each faction maintained its own Bedouin allies. The origins of the factions have been lost in mythology, though by the late seventeenth century the division was well established.

Ottoman governors sought to neutralize the Mamluks by playing the factions against each other. This gave the disadvantaged Mamluk faction a real incentive to overthrow the Ottoman governor. Between 1688 and 1755, the years covered by the chronicler Ahmad Katkhuda al-Damurdashi (himself a Mamluk officer), Mamluk factions succeeded in deposing eight of the thirty-four Ottoman governors of Egypt.

The power of the Mamluks over the Ottoman governors is revealed in the factional intrigues of 1729. Zayn al-Faqar, leader of the Faqari faction, convened a group of his officers to plan a military campaign against their Qasimi enemies. "We'll ask the governor to furnish 500 purses to pay for the expedition," Zayn al-Faqar told his men. "If he gives them, he will remain our governor, but if he refuses, we will depose him." The Faqari faction sent a delegation to the Ottoman governor, who refused to pay the expense of a military campaign against the Qasimi faction. "We won't accept a pimp as our governor," the outraged Zayn al-Faqar told his followers. "Let's go and depose him." On their own initiative, without any other authority, the Faqari faction simply wrote to Istanbul to inform the Porte that the Ottoman governor had been deposed and that a deputy governor had been appointed to take his place. The Mamluks then strong-armed the deputy governor they had just installed to provide the funding for their campaign against the Qasimi faction, drawn from the customs revenues of the port of Suez. The payment was justified in terms of the defense of Cairo.[32]

The Mamluks used extraordinary violence against their rivals. The Qasimi faction knew all too well that the Faqaris were preparing for a major confrontation and took the initiative. In 1730 the Qasimis sent an assassin to kill the head of the rival faction, Zayn al-Faqar himself. The assassin was a turncoat who had fallen out with the Faqari faction and joined forces with the Qasimis. He disguised himself as a policeman and pretended to have arrested one of Zayn al-Faqar's enemies. "Bring him here," Zayn al-Faqar ordered, wanting to meet his enemy face to face. "Here he is," the assassin replied, and discharged his pistol into the Mamluk's heart, killing him instantly.[33] The assassin and his accomplice then fought their way out of Faqari leader's house and escaped, killing several men along the way. It was the beginning of a massive blood feud.

The Faqaris named Muhammad Bey Qatamish as their new leader. Muhammad Bey had risen to the top of the Mamluk hierarchy and held the title of *shaykh al-Balad*, or "commander of the city." Muhammad Bey responded to the assassination of Zayn al-Faqar by ordering the extermination of all Mamluks associated with the Qasimi faction. "You have among you Qasimi spies," Muhammad Bey warned, and pointed to an unfortunate man among his retainers. Before the man had a chance to defend himself, Muhammad Bey's officers dragged him under a table and cut off his head—the first man to be killed in retaliation for Zayn al-Faqar's murder. Many more would follow before the bloodletting of 1730 came to an end.

Muhammad Bey turned to the deputy governor appointed by Zayn al-Faqar and obtained a warrant to execute 373 persons he claimed were involved in the Faqari leader's assassination. It was his license to wipe out the Qasimi faction. "Muhammad Bey Qatamish annihilated the Qasimi faction entirely, except for those . . . who had escaped to the countryside," al-Damurdashi reports. "He even took the young Mamluks who hadn't reached puberty from their houses, sent them to an island in the middle of the Nile where he killed them, then threw their bodies into the river." Muhammad Bey closed all of the Qasimi households, swearing never to let the faction take hold in Cairo again.[34]

The Qasimi faction proved harder to eliminate than Muhammad Bey had imagined. In 1736 the Qasimis returned to settle scores with the Faqaris. They were assisted by Bakir Pasha, the Ottoman governor. Bakir Pasha's previous term as governor of Egypt had been cut short by the Faqaris, who had deposed him. He thus proved a natural ally to the Qasimi faction. Bakir Pasha invited Muhammad Bey and the other leading Mamluks of the Faqari faction to a meeting where a group of Qasimis lay in ambush, armed with pistols and swords. No sooner had Muhammad Bey arrived than the Qasimis emerged, shooting the leader of the Faqari faction in the stomach and butchering his leading commanders. In all, they killed ten of the most powerful men in Cairo and piled their severed heads in one of the main mosques of the city for public viewing.[35] It was by all accounts one of the worst killings in the annals of Ottoman Egypt.[36]

Years of factional fighting left both the Faqaris and the Qasimis too weak to preserve a commanding position in Cairo. The rival factions were overtaken by a single Mamluk household known as the Qazdughlis, who came to dominate Ottoman Egypt for the rest of the eighteenth century. With the rise of the Qazdughlis, the extreme factional violence abated, bringing a measure of peace to the strife-torn city. The Ottomans, for their part, never managed to impose their full authority over the rich but unruly province of Egypt. Instead, a distinct political culture emerged in Ottoman Egypt in which the Mamluk households continued to exercise political primacy over Istanbul's governor centuries after Selim the Grim had conquered the Mamluk Empire. In Egypt, as in Lebanon and Algeria, Ottoman rule adapted to local politics.

Two centuries after conquering the Mamluk Empire, the Ottomans had succeeded in extending their empire from North Africa to South Arabia. It had not been a smooth process. Unwilling, or unable, to standardize government in the Arab provinces, the Ottomans in many cases chose to rule in partnership with local elites. The diverse Arab provinces might have had very different relations with Istanbul and wide variations of administrative structures, but they were all clearly part of the same empire. Such heterogeneity was common to the multiethnic and multisectarian empires of the day, such as the Austro-Hungarian and Russian Empires.

Until the mid-eighteenth century, the Ottomans managed this diversity with some success. They had faced challenges—most notably in Mount Lebanon and Egypt—but had succeeded by a variety of strategies in entrenching Ottoman rule, ensuring that no local leader posed an enduring threat to the Ottoman center. The dynamics between this center and the Arab periphery changed, however, in the latter half of the eighteenth century. New local leaders emerged who began to combine forces and pursue autonomy in defiance of the Ottoman system, often in concert with the empire's European enemies. These new local leaders posed a real challenge to the Ottoman state that, by the nineteenth century, would put its very survival in jeopardy.

CHAPTER 2

The Arab Challenge
to Ottoman Rule

A barber comes to know everything that happens in his town. His day is taken up in conversations with people from all walks of life. Judging by the record of his diary, Ahmad al-Budayri "al-Hallaq" ("the Barber") was a great conversationalist who was well informed on the politics and society of Damascus in the mid-eighteenth century. The issues covered in his diary are familiar subjects of barbershop conversations everywhere: local politics, the high cost of living, the weather, and general complaints about how things were no longer as they were in the good old days.

Apart from what he wrote in his diary, we know very little about the life of Budayri, the barber of Damascus. He was too modest a man to feature in contemporary biographical dictionaries, the "who's who" of Ottoman times. His diary is all the more remarkable for that. It was unusual for tradesmen to be literate in the eighteenth century, let alone to leave a written record of their thoughts. He told us little about himself, preferring to write about others. We do not know when he was born or died, though it is clear that the diary, spanning the years 1741–1762, was written when he was a mature man. A pious Muslim, Budayri belonged to a mystical Sufi order. He was married, with children, but had little to say of his family life. He was proud of his profession, spoke with admiration of the teacher who inducted him into the trade, and recalled the prominent men whose heads he had shaved.

The barber of Damascus was a loyal Ottoman subject. In 1754 he noted the shock felt by the people of Damascus when they heard of the death of Sultan Mahmud I (r. 1730–1754). He recorded the public celebrations marking the ascension of the sultan's successor, Osman III (r. 1754–1757), when Damascus "was decorated more beautifully than ever in public memory. May God preserve this Ottoman State," he prayed, "until the end of time. Amen."[1]

The barber had good reason to pray for the preservation of the Ottoman state. According to Ottoman notions of statecraft, good government was a delicate balance of four interreliant elements conceived as a "circle of equity." First, the state needed a large army to exercise its authority. It took great wealth to maintain a large army, and taxes were the state's only regular source of wealth. To collect taxes, the state had to promote the prosperity of its subjects. For the people to be prosperous the state must uphold just laws, which brings us full circle—back to the responsibilities of the state. Most Ottoman political analysts of the day would have explained political disorder in terms of the neglect of one of these four elements. From all he saw going on in Damascus in the mid-eighteenth century, Budayri was convinced that the Ottoman Empire was in serious trouble. The governors were corrupt, the soldiers were unruly, prices were high, and public morality was undermined by the decline in the government's authority.

Arguably, the root of the problem lay with the governors of Damascus. In Budayri's time, Damascus was ruled by a dynasty of local notables rather than by Ottoman Turks dispatched from Istanbul to govern on the sultan's behalf, as was standard practice in the empire. The ruling Azm family had built their fortune in the seventeenth century by accumulating extensive agricultural lands around the Central Syrian town of Hama. They later settled in Damascus, where they established themselves among the rich and powerful of the city. Between 1724 and 1783, five members of the Azm family ruled Damascus—for a total of forty-five years. Several Azm family members were concurrently appointed to govern the provinces of Sidon, Tripoli, and Aleppo. Taken together, the Azm family's rule over the Syrian provinces represents one of the more significant local leaderships to emerge in the Arab provinces in the eighteenth century.

We might think today that Arabs would have preferred being governed by fellow Arabs rather than by Ottoman bureaucrats. However, Ottoman bureaucrats in the eighteenth century were still servants of the sultan who, at least in theory, owed their full loyalty to the state and ruled without self-interest. The Azms, in contrast, had clear personal and family interests at stake and used their time in high office to enrich themselves and to build their dynasty at the Ottoman state's expense. The circle of equity was broken, and things were beginning to fall apart.

Budayri discussed at length the strengths and weaknesses of Azm rule in Damascus. As'ad Pasha al-Azm ruled for most of the period covered by Budayri's diary. His fourteen-year reign (1743–1757) was to prove the longest of any governor in Ottoman Damascus. The barber could be quite lavish in his praise of As'ad Pasha, but he found a lot to criticize. He condemned the Azm governors for their plunder of the city's wealth and held them responsible for disorders among the military and the breakdown in public morality.

Under Azm rule, the army had degenerated from a disciplined force upholding law and order to a disorderly rabble. The Janissaries in Damascus were split into two groups—the imperial troops dispatched from Istanbul (the *kapikullari*), and the local Janissaries of Damascus (the *yerliyye*). There were also a number of irregular forces of Kurds, Turcomans, and North Africans. The different corps were in constant conflict and posed a real challenge to peace in the city. In 1756 the residents of the 'Amara quarter paid dearly for siding with the imperial Janissaries in their fight with the local Damascene Janissaries. The latter retaliated by putting the whole of the 'Amara quarter—homes and shops—to the torch.[2] Budayri recounts numerous instances of soldiers attacking and even killing residents of Damascus with complete impunity. In times of high anxiety, the townspeople responded by closing their shops and shutting themselves in their homes, bringing the economic life of the city to a standstill. The barber's diary captures a real sense of the menace posed by the "security forces" to the average Damascene's person and property.

Budayri also held the Azms responsible for the chronic high food prices in Damascus. Not only did they fail to regulate the markets and ensure fair prices, but as large landholders, Budayri alleged, the Azm governors actually abused their position to hoard and create artificial grain shortages to maximize their personal profits. Once, when the price of bread had fallen, As'ad Pasha sent his retainers to pressure the bakers to raise their prices in order to protect the wheat market, which was the source of his family's wealth.[3]

In his diary, Budayri railed against this accumulation of wealth by the Azm governors while the common folk of Damascus went hungry. As'ad Pasha's abuses of power were epitomized by the palace he built in central Damascus, which still stands in the city today. The project consumed all of the building materials and all of the trained masons and artisans of the city, driving up the cost of construction for common Damascenes. As'ad Pasha ordered his builders to strip precious building materials from older houses and buildings in the city, without regard for their owners or their historic value. The project was a testament to As'ad Pasha's greed. According to Budayri, As'ad Pasha constructed the palace with countless hiding places for his vast personal wealth "under the floors, in the walls, the ceilings, the water reservoirs and even the toilets."[4]

The collapse in military discipline, combined with the cupidity of the Azm governors, Budayri believed, had led to a grievous deterioration in public morals. The legitimacy of the Ottoman state rested in large part on its ability to promote Islamic values and to maintain the institutions necessary for its subjects to live within the precepts of Sunni Islam. A breakdown in public morality was thus a clear sign of a breakdown in the state's authority.

In Budayri's view, there was no greater proof of the decline of public morality than the brazen comportment of the prostitutes in his city. Damascus was a conservative town where respectable women covered their hair, dressed modestly, and had few opportunities to mix with men outside their own families. The prostitutes of Damascus observed none of these niceties. The barber frequently complained about drunken prostitutes, carousing with equally drunken soldiers, who strode through the streets and markets of Damascus with their faces unveiled and their hair uncovered. The governors of Damascus tried several times to ban prostitution in the city, with no effect. Emboldened by the support of the city's soldiers, the prostitutes refused to comply.

It would seem that the common people of Damascus came to accept, even admire, the city's prostitutes. One beautiful young woman named Salmun completely captivated the people of Damascus in the 1740s, her name becoming a byword in the local slang for all that was trendy and beautiful. A particularly smart dress would be called a "Salmuni dress," or a novel piece of jewelry a "Salmuni bauble."

Salmun was a reckless young woman defiant of authority. In a scene reminiscent of Bizet's *Carmen*, Salmun crossed paths with a *qadi* (judge) in downtown Damascus one afternoon in 1744. She was drunk and carrying a knife. The judge's retainers shouted at her to clear the path. Salmun only laughed at them and launched herself at the qadi with her knife. The judge's men barely managed to restrain her. The qadi had her arrested by the authorities, who executed Salmun for the outrage. A town crier was then sent through the streets of Damascus ordering all prostitutes to be killed. Many women fled, and others went into hiding.[5]

The prohibition proved short-lived, and the prostitutes of Damascus were soon back on the streets, unveiled and uninhibited. "In those days," the barber wrote in 1748, "corruption increased, the servants of God were oppressed, and prostitutes proliferated in the markets, day and night." He described a parade of the prostitutes held in honor of a local saint with outrage at both the profanation of religious values and at the fact that the Damascene public seemed to accept it. A prostitute had fallen in love with a young Turkish soldier who had fallen ill. She vowed to hold a prayer session in homage to the saint if her lover regained his health. When the soldier recovered, she fulfilled her vow:

> She walked in a kind of procession with the other sinful girls of her kind. They went through the bazaars carrying candles and incense burners. The group was singing and beating on tambourines with their faces unveiled and their hair over their shoulders. The people looked on without objecting. Only the righteous raised their voices, shouting "*allahu akbar*" ["God is great"].[6]

Soon after the parade, city authorities tried once again to ban prostitution. The heads of the town quarters were told to report anyone suspicious, and town criers were sent round to urge women to wear their veils properly. Yet within days of these new orders, the barber claimed, "we saw the very same girls walking the alleys and markets as was their custom." At that point, the governor, As'ad Pasha al-Azm, abandoned all efforts to expel the bold prostitutes and chose to tax them instead.

The Azm governors abused their powers of office to enrich themselves at the people's expense, yet they could not curb vice or control the soldiers nominally under their command. The barber of Damascus was deeply dismayed. Could a state governed by such men long survive?

By the middle of the eighteenth century, the Ottomans and the Arabs had come to a crossroads.

On the face of it, the Ottomans had succeeded in absorbing the Arab world into their empire. Over the course of two centuries the Ottomans had extended their rule from the southernmost tip of the Arabian peninsula to the frontiers of Morocco in northwestern Africa. The Ottoman sultan was universally accepted by the Arabs as their legitimate sovereign. They prayed in the sultan's name each Friday, they contributed soldiers for the sultan's wars, and they paid their taxes to the sultan's agents. The great majority of Arab subjects, those who farmed the land in the countryside and the city-dwellers who worked as craftsmen and merchants, had accepted the Ottoman social contract. All they expected in return was safety for themselves, security for their property, and the preservation of Islamic values.

Yet, an important change was taking place in the Arab lands. Whereas in the early Ottoman centuries the Arabs, as free-born Muslims, were excluded from high offices reserved to the servile elites recruited through the *devshirme*, or "boy levy," by the mid-eighteenth century local notables were rising to the highest ranks of provincial administration and awarded the title "pasha." The Azms of Damascus were but one example of a broader phenomenon that extended from Egypt through Palestine and Mount Lebanon to Mesopotamia and the Arabian Peninsula. The rise of local leaders came at the expense of Istanbul's influence in the Arab lands, as more tax money was spent locally on the armed forces and the building projects of local governors. The phenomenon spread across a number of Arab provinces, with the cumulative effect being a growing threat to the integrity of the Ottoman Empire. For, in the second half of the eighteenth century, the proliferation of local leaders led many Arab provinces to rebel against Istanbul's rule.

Local leaders in the Arab provinces came from diverse backgrounds, ranging from heads of Mamluk households to tribal shaykhs and urban notables. They were driven by ambition more than any specific grievance with the Ottoman way of doing things. They did have wealth in common: they were, without exception, large landholders who had taken advantage of changes in Ottoman land practices to build up huge estates, which they held for life and in some cases passed on to their children. They diverted the revenues of their estates away from the government's treasury to meet their own needs. They built lavish palaces and maintained their own armies to re-inforce their power. Istanbul's loss was a real gain to the local economy in the Arab provinces, and the authority to extend patronage to artisans and militiamen only enhanced the power of local lords.

Though such local notables were not unique to the Arab provinces—similar lead-ers emerged in the Balkans and Turkish Anatolia—the Arab lands were less central to Istanbul, in every sense of the word. The Ottomans relied less on revenues and troops from the Arab provinces than they did from the Balkans and Anatolia. More-over, the Arab lands were much farther from Istanbul, and the central government was unwilling to spare the troops and resources to put down minor rebellions. Is-tanbul was more concerned with challenges from Vienna and Moscow than troubles posed by local leaders in Damascus and Cairo.

By the eighteenth century, the Ottoman Empire was facing far greater threats from its European neighbors than anything the Arab provinces might produce. The Habsburgs in Austria were rolling back the Ottoman conquests in Europe. Until 1683 the Ottomans were pressing at the gates of Vienna. By 1699 the Austrians had defeated the Ottomans and were awarded Hungary, Transylvania, and parts of Poland in the Treaty of Karlowitz—the first territorial losses the Ottomans had ever suffered. Peter the Great of Russia was pressing the Ottomans in the Black Sea region and in the Caucasus. Local notables in Baghdad or Damascus were of no consider-ation compared to threats of this order of magnitude.

Ottoman defeats by European armies emboldened local challengers inside Ot-toman domains. As local leaders grew more powerful, the Ottoman officials that were sent to the Arab provinces gradually lost the respect and obedience of their Arab subjects. Government officials also lost authority over the sultan's soldiers, who grew lawless and engaged in scuffles with local soldiers and the militias of local lead-ers. Insubordination in military ranks in turn undermined the authority of the Is-lamic judges and scholars, who traditionally served as the guardians of public order. Where the Ottomans were seen to be ineffectual, the people turned increasingly to local leaders to provide for their security instead. In Basra, a local Christian merchant wrote, "Respect and fear were given to the chiefs of the Arabs, and as for the Ot-toman, nobody goes in awe of him."[7]

A state that loses the respect of its subjects is in trouble. The chronicler 'Abd al-Rahman al-Jabarti, analyzing the breakdown of Ottoman authority over the Mam-luks in eighteenth-century Egypt, reflected: "If this age should urinate in a bottle, time's physician would know its ailment."[8] The emergence of local leaders lay at the heart of the Ottoman illness and could only be redressed by a strong reassertion of the state's authority. The Porte's dilemma was to secure enough stability on its Eu-ropean frontiers to free the necessary resources to address the challenges within its Arab provinces.

The nature of local rule differed from one region to the next and posed a variable threat to Istanbul's authority. Roughly speaking, those provinces closest to the Ottoman center were the most benign, with prominent families like the Shihabs in Mount Lebanon, the Azms in Damascus, and the Jalilis in Mosul establishing dynasties loyal to Ottoman rule but pressing for the greatest possible autonomy within those limits.[9] Further to the south, in Baghdad, Palestine, and Egypt, Mamluk leaders emerged who sought to expand the territory under their control in direct challenge to the Ottoman state. The emergence of the Sa'udi-Wahabi confederation in Central Arabia posed the gravest threat to the Ottoman government when it seized control of the holy cities of Mecca and Medina and prevented the annual Ottoman pilgrimage caravans from reaching the holy cities. In contrast, more remote provinces, such as Algiers, Tunis, and Yemen, were happy to remain vassals of the Ottoman sultan, paying an annual tribute in return for extensive autonomy.

These local leaders in no way comprised an Arab *movement*. Many were not ethnic Arabs, and several did not even speak Arabic. The challengers to Ottoman rule in the second half of the eighteenth century were instead ambitious individuals acting in their own interests with little concern for the Arab people under their rule. In isolation, they posed little threat to the Ottoman center. When they worked together, however—as when the Mamluks in Egypt entered an alliance with a local leader in Northern Palestine—they were capable of conquering whole Ottoman provinces.

Oil put the Middle East on the map in the twentieth century. In the eighteenth century, it was cotton that generated extreme wealth in the Eastern Mediterranean. European demand for cotton dates back to the seventeenth century. Whereas the British Lancashire mills drew primarily on cotton from the West Indies and the American colonies, the French relied on Ottoman markets for the bulk of their cotton imports. As spinning and weaving technology improved in the course of the eighteenth century, leading to the Industrial Revolution, European demand for cotton spiked. French cotton imports from the Eastern Mediterranean increased more than fivefold, rising from 2.1 million kg in 1700 to nearly 11 million kg by 1789.[10] The cotton most prized by European markets was produced in the Galilee region in Northern Palestine. The wealth generated by Galilee cotton was sufficient to feed the ambitions of a local dynast who grew powerful enough to challenge Ottoman rule in Syria.

The strongman of the Galilee was Zahir al-'Umar (c.1690–1775). Zahir was a leader of the Zaydanis, a Bedouin tribe that had settled in the Galilee in the seventeenth century and secured control of extensive agricultural lands between the towns of Safad and Tiberias. They enjoyed strong trade connections with Damascus and began to build a respectable family fortune through their control of cotton plantations in the Galilee. Zahir represented the third generation of Zaydani shaykhs in the Galilee. Though not particularly well known in the West, Zahir has been a celebrity in the Arab world for centuries. He is often—anachronistically—described as something of an Arab or Palestinian nationalist due to his history of confrontation with Ottoman governors. By the time of his death he was already the stuff of legend—and the subject of two near-contemporary biographies.

Zahir's long and remarkable career began in the 1730s when he entered into an alliance with a Bedouin tribe to seize the town of Tiberias, which was hardly more than a village at the time. He consolidated his gains by securing a formal appointment as tax collector for the Galilee region from the governor of Sidon. Zahir then set about fortifying Tiberias and built up a small militia of some 200 horsemen.

From his base in Tiberias, Zahir and his family began to extend their control across the fertile plains and highlands of northern Palestine, ordering the tenant farmers to plant their lands in cotton. He gave his brothers and cousins territories to run on his behalf. As Zahir began to carve out a small principality for himself, he grew increasingly powerful. The more territory he controlled, the more cotton revenues he accrued, allowing him to expand his army, which in turn made further territorial expansion possible.

By 1740 Zahir had emerged as the most powerful leader in northern Palestine. He had defeated the warlords of Nablus, he had taken control of Nazareth, and now he dominated the trade between Palestine and Damascus, which further contributed to his wealth and resources.

The rapid growth of the Zaydani principality put Zahir al-'Umar on a collision course with the governor of Damascus. One of the governor's primary duties was to provide for the needs and expenses of the annual pilgrimage caravan to Mecca. Zahir now controlled lands whose tax revenues traditionally were earmarked to pay the expenses of the pilgrimage caravan. By beating the governor of Damascus to the taxes of northern Transjordan and Palestine, Zahir was putting the finances of the pilgrimage caravan in jeopardy. When the government in Istanbul learned of the situation, the sultan sent orders to his governor in Damascus, Sulayman Pasha al-Azm, to capture and execute Zahir and destroy his fortifications around Tiberias.

Budayri, the barber of Damascus, noted in his diary that in 1742 Sulayman Pasha led a large army from Damascus to put down Zahir. The government in Istanbul had sent men and heavy munitions, including artillery and mines, to destroy Zahir and his fortifications. Sulayman Pasha also recruited volunteers from Mount Lebanon, Nablus and Jerusalem, and neighboring Bedouin tribes, all of whom saw Zahir al-'Umar as a rival and welcomed the chance to bring him down.

Sulayman Pasha laid siege to Tiberias for over three months, but Zahir's forces did not succumb. With help from his brother, who smuggled food and provisions across Ottoman lines, Zahir managed to hold out against far superior forces. The governor of Damascus was not amused, and when he managed to intercept a number of Zaydani retainers smuggling food to Tiberias he sent their heads to Istanbul as trophies. Yet the big trophy eluded Sulayman Pasha, and after three months he was forced to return to Damascus to prepare for the pilgrimage to Mecca. Unwilling to admit defeat, Sulayman Pasha spread the rumor that he had lifted the siege of Tiberias out of compassion for the defenseless civilians of the town. He also claimed to have taken one of Zahir's sons as hostage against a pledge to pay his back taxes to Damascus. The barber of Damascus duly reported these rumors, adding a disclaimer: "We have heard another version of the story," he wrote, "and God knows the truth of the matter."[11]

Once Sulayman Pasha returned from the pilgrimage in 1743, he resumed his war against Zahir al-'Umar in Tiberias. Once again, he mobilized a great army with support from Istanbul and all of Zahir's aggrieved neighbors in Palestine. Again the residents of Tiberias braced themselves for a terrible siege. But the second siege never came to pass. While traveling to Tiberias, Sulayman Pasha al-Azm stopped in the coastal town of Acre, where he succumbed to a fever and died. His body was brought back to Damascus for burial, and the siege army was disbanded. Zahir al-'Umar was left in peace to pursue his own ambitions.[12]

Between the 1740s and the 1760s, Zahir's rule went unchallenged and his powers expanded enormously. The governor in Sidon could never match the strength of Zahir's armed forces, and the new governor in Damascus, As'ad Pasha al-Azm, chose to leave the ruler of Tiberias to his own devices. In Istanbul, Zahir had cultivated influential supporters who protected him from the scrutiny of the Sublime Porte.

Zahir took advantage of his relative independence to extend his rule from Tiberias to the coastal city of Acre, which had emerged as the main port for the Levantine cotton trade. He petitioned the governor of Sidon repeatedly to be awarded the lucrative rights to collect the taxes of Acre, but was always refused. Finally, in 1746, he occupied the city and declared himself its tax-farmer. Over the course of the 1740s, he fortified Acre and established his base in the city. He now enjoyed control over the cotton trade from the field to the market. Letters from French cotton merchants in Damascus reveal their frustration with Zahir al-'Umar, who had grown "too powerful and too rich . . . at our expense."[13] By the 1750s Zahir was setting the price for the cotton he sold. When the French tried to force their terms on Zahir, he simply forbade the cotton farmers of the Galilee to sell to the French to force them back to the negotiating table and agree to his terms.

In spite of his many confrontations with the Ottoman state, Zahir al-'Umar was constantly trying to secure official recognition; he was a rebel who ultimately wanted to be a member of the establishment. He strove to achieve the same standing the

Azms had in Damascus: the ministerial rank of Pasha and the governorship of Sidon. To this end, his every act of rebellion was followed by a loyal payment of taxes. Yet throughout his years in power, Zahir never rose above the status of a tax-farmer subordinate to the governor in Sidon. It was a source of constant frustration for the strongman of the Galilee. The Ottomans, tied up in a devastating war with Russia between 1768 and 1774, tried to preserve Zahir's loyalty and meet him halfway. In 1768 the Porte recognized him as the *"shaykh* of Acre, *amir* of Nazareth, Tiberias, Safed, and *shaykh* of all of Galilee."[14] It was a title, but not enough to satisfy Zahir's great ambitions.

After nearly two decades of relative peace, Zahir faced renewed threats from the Ottoman provincial government. In 1770 a new governor in Damascus sought to bring Zahir's rule over northern Palestine to a close. 'Uthman Pasha had managed to get his own sons appointed as governors in Tripoli and Sidon and had entered into an alliance with the Druze community of Mount Lebanon against Zahir. The notables of Nablus were also keen to see the end of their belligerent neighbor to the north. Suddenly, Zahir found himself surrounded by hostile forces.

In a life-or-death struggle with 'Uthman Pasha, Zahir could only survive by entering into partnership with another local leader. The only regional power strong enough to offset the combined forces of Damascus and Sidon was the ruling Mamluk in Cairo, a remarkable leader named 'Ali Bey. When Zahir and Àli Bey combined forces, they mounted the greatest challenge the Arab provinces had yet posed to Istanbul's rule.

The Mamluk leader 'Ali Bey had a number of nicknames. Some of his contemporaries called him *Jinn* 'Ali, or 'Ali the Genie, as though he used magic to achieve the seemingly impossible. His Turkish nickname was *Bulut Kapan*, or "cloud-catcher," for his repression of the Bedouin, whom the Ottomans believed to be harder to capture than clouds. He is best known as 'Ali Bey al-Kabir, or "the great," and indeed between 1760 and 1775 he achieved more greatness than any Mamluk in the history of Ottoman Egypt.

'Ali Bey came to Egypt in 1743 as a fifteen-year-old military slave in the leading Qazdughli Mamluk household. He rose through the ranks and gained his freedom and promotion to the rank of *bey* on the death of his master in 1755. The beys were the top of the Mamluk hierarchy, whose leader was the *shaykh al-Balad*, or "commander of the city." 'Ali Bey first attained primacy in 1760, and he held the office with brief exceptions until his death in 1773.

'Ali Bey was a warlord who engendered respect through fear. His contemporary, the great Egyptian historian al-Jabarti, described him as "a man of great strength, obstinate and ambitious, and satisfied only with supremacy and sovereignty. He showed inclination only for the serious, never for the playful, a joke or fun." [15] He is said to have had a physical effect on those who met him: "He was so awe-inspiring that some people actually died in awe of him, and many men would tremble at his mere presence."[16] He was utterly ruthless in the suppression of his rivals, and he showed loyalty to no one. Nor, as subsequent events would demonstrate, did he engender loyalty in others. He broke the bonds of collegiality and turned against fellow Mamluks of his own household, just as he eliminated rival Mamluk households.

'Ali Bey was the first person to rule Egypt single-handedly since the fall of the Mamluk Empire. He literally monopolized the wealth of Egypt by seizing the land revenues, controlling all external trade, and demanding extraordinary sums from the European merchant community. He extorted the wealth from the local Christian and Jewish communities and withheld payment of all taxes to Istanbul. 'Ali Bey's riches allowed him to expand his military power. Having broken the existing Mamluk factions in Egypt, 'Ali Bey set about establishing a new Mamluk household of his own. He bought and trained his own slaves, who were the only people he felt he could trust. His household numbered some 3,000 Mamluks at its height, many of them commanders of vast armies that numbered in the tens of thousands.

Having established paramount control over Egypt, 'Ali Bey sought his independence from Ottoman rule altogether. Inspired by the Mamluks of old, he tried to re-create their empire in Egypt, Syria, and the Hijaz. According to Jabarti, 'Ali Bey was an avid reader of Islamic history who used to lecture his retainers on how Ottoman rule in Egypt was fundamentally illegitimate. "The kings of Egypt—Sultan Baybars and Sultan Qalawun and their children—were Mamluks like us," he argued. "As for these Ottomans, they seized the country by force, taking advantage of the duplicity of the local people."[17] The implication was that land taken by force could be redeemed legitimately by force.

'Ali Bey's first targets were the governors and troops sent by Istanbul to uphold the law in Egypt. The governors had long since given up trying to rule Egypt—the rival Mamluk households did that. Instead, they sought to uphold Istanbul's nominal sovereignty by observing ceremonies of power and trying to collect the treasury's due. Powerless in their own right, the governors tried to play the rival Mamluk households against each other. This was no longer possible under 'Ali Bey, who had eliminated his rivals and ruled unchallenged. Now 'Ali Bey deposed and, it was rumored, even poisoned governors and commanding officers with impunity. The threat to Ottoman interests in their rich but rebellious Egyptian province could not be more acute.

'Ali Bey next deployed his military power against the Ottoman Empire in an open bid for territorial expansion. "He was not content with what God had granted him," al-Jabarti wrote, "the rule over Lower and Upper Egypt, the kingdom of which kings and pharaohs had been proud. His greed pushed him to extend the territory of the kingdom."[18] 'Ali Bey first seized the Red Sea province of the Hijaz, formerly part of the Mamluk Empire, in 1769. Following this success, he began to strike coins bearing his name rather than that of the reigning Ottoman sultan, signaling his rebellion against Ottoman sovereignty. 'Ali Bey had embarked on his project for the restoration of the Mamluk Empire of old. The Ottomans, tied up with their wars with Russia, were powerless to stop him.

'Ali Bey's revolt against the Ottomans was in full swing when Zahir al-'Umar first approached him in 1770 with the offer of an alliance against the governor of Damascus. His timing could not have been better. "When 'Ali Bey received this news," a contemporary chronicler noted, "he viewed it as the fulfillment of his greatest aspirations. He resolved to rebel against the Ottoman state, and to extend his rule over the lands from 'Arish in Egypt to Baghdad."[19] 'Ali Bey concluded an alliance with Zahir al-'Umar and agreed to unseat the Ottoman governor in Damascus.

'Ali Bey escalated the crisis in the Eastern Mediterranean when he wrote to the sultan's nemesis, the empress Catherine the Great of Russia, to seek her assistance in his war against the Ottomans. He asked Catherine for Russian ships and cavalry to drive the Ottomans out of Greater Syria, in return promising to help the Russians conquer territory in southern Persia. Although the empress refused to provide cavalry, she agreed to the assistance of the Russian fleet, which was then roaming the Eastern Mediterranean. 'Ali Bey's treason had not escaped the notice of the Ottoman government. However, pinned down by Russian forces in the Black Sea and Eastern Europe, the Ottomans were in no position to stop him.

Encouraged by his alliances with Catherine and Zahir, 'Ali Bey began to mobilize his forces. He raised an army of some 20,000 men to invade Syria under the command of one of his most trusted generals, a Mamluk named Isma'il Bey. In November 1770 the Mamluk force swept through Gaza; following a four-month siege, it occupied the port of Jaffa. Zahir and his men joined forces with Isma'il Bey and accompanied the Mamluk army on its march through Palestine. They crossed the Jordan Valley and headed east to the Pilgrimage Road along the desert's edge. The rebel army then made haste toward Damascus, intent on seizing the city from its Ottoman governor. They got as far as the village of Muzayrib, one day's march south of Damascus.

When Isma'il Bey entered Muzayrib he came face to face with the governor of Damascus—and he completely lost the will to fight. It was then the pilgrimage season, when pious Muslims were fulfilling one of the pillars of Islam and making the perilous journey through the desert from Damascus to Mecca. 'Uthman Pasha, the governor, was carrying out his duties as commander of the pilgrimage. Isma'il Bey was a pious man who had received more religious education than most Mamluks. To attack the governor at that moment would have been a crime against religion. Without warning or explanation, Isma'il Bey ordered his soldiers to withdraw from Muzayrib and return to Jaffa. The astonished Zahir al-'Umar protested in vain, and the rebel campaign came to a complete halt for the rest of the winter of 1770–1771.

'Ali Bey must have been furious with Isma'il Bey. In May 1771 he sent a second force to Syria, headed by Muhammad Bey, nicknamed "Abu al-Dhahab," or "the father of gold." He had earned his nickname through a flamboyant gesture: when 'Ali Bey promoted Muhammad to the rank of bey and gave him his freedom, Muhammad Bey threw gold coins to the crowds that lined the street between the Citadel and the center of town. It was a public relations coup that made Muhammad Bey a household name.

Muhammad Bey set off at the head of 35,000 troops. They swept through southern Palestine and in Jaffa united with the army commanded by Isma'il Bey. The combined Mamluk forces of Isma'il Bey and Muhammad Bey were unstoppable. They marched through Palestine and, after a minor engagement, drove the Ottoman governor out of Damascus in June. The Mamluks were now in control of Egypt, the Hijaz, and Damascus—'Ali Bey had nearly fulfilled his life's ambition to reconstruct the Mamluk Empire.

Then the unthinkable happened: without warning or explanation, Muhammad Bey abandoned Damascus and set course for Cairo at the head of his army. Once again it was the pious Mamluk general Isma'il who was to blame. No sooner did the Mamluk commanders find themselves in control of Damascus than Isma'il Bey confronted Muhammad Bey with the enormity of their crime—not just against the sultan but against their religion as well. Isma'il Bey had spent some time in Istanbul before entering 'Ali Bey's service, which instilled in him reverence for the sultan's position as head of the greatest Islamic empire of his day. He warned Muhammad Bey that the Ottomans would not allow such a major rebellion go unpunished in this life and that God would hold them accountable in the afterlife. "For truly rebellion against the Sultan is one of the schemes of the Devil," Isma'il Bey warned Muhammad Bey.

Once Isma'il Bey had provoked Muhammad Bey's anxiety, he turned next to play upon the latter's ambition. 'Ali Bey, he argued, had left the path of Islam by entering into a pact with the Russian empress against the sultan. "Now any Muslim would be permitted by Islamic law to kill ['Ali Bey] with impunity, claim his harem and his wealth," Isma'il Bey argued.[20] Essentially, Isma'il Bey reasoned that Muhammad Bey would gain redemption before God and the sultan, and promotion to 'Ali Bey's position of primacy over Egypt, by turning against his master. Isma'il Bey's arguments carried the day, and two of 'Ali Bey's most trusted generals were now returning to Egypt at the head of a huge Mamluk army bent on the overthrow of their former master.

Shock waves reverberated around the Eastern Mediterranean after the Mamluks' conquest and rapid abandonment of Damascus. "The people of Damascus were completely astonished by this amazing event," a contemporary chronicler exclaimed, and so too were Zahir al-'Umar and his allies. While the Mamluk forces were attacking

Damascus, Zahir had taken the town of Sidon and had placed a 2,000-man garrison in Jaffa. Overextended, he had now lost his most important ally and risked facing the wrath of the Ottomans alone. For his part, 'Ali Bey recognized his situation was hopeless. He could only raise a token number of supporters, and these were scattered after a skirmish with the army led by Muhammad Bey. In 1772, 'Ali Bey fled Egypt to take refuge with Zahir in Acre.

'Ali Bey's dreams of a neo-Mamluk empire dissolved with his flight from Egypt. Muhammad Bey established himself as the ruler of Egypt and sent Isma'il Bey to Istanbul to secure for him the governorship of both Egypt and Syria. Not for him dreams of empire; Muhammad Bey instead sought recognition within the Ottoman framework.

'Ali Bey was impatient to reclaim his throne and acted in haste, before he had the chance to mobilize enough of an army to confront the formidable Mamluk household he himself had created. He set off for Cairo in March 1773, at the head of a small force in a hopeless bid to recover his kingdom. Muhammad Bey's army engaged him in battle and routed 'Ali Bey's forces. 'Ali Bey was wounded and taken prisoner. Muhammad Bey took his master back to Cairo and kept him in his own home, where 'Ali Bey died a week later. Inevitably, there were rumors of foul play. "Only God knows the manner of his death," the chronicler al-Jabarti concluded.[21]

The death of 'Ali Bey proved a disaster for Zahir. He was now a very old man—well into his eighties at a time when life expectancy was half that. He had no allies in the region and had entered into outright treason against his Ottoman sovereign. Improbably, Zahir still sought formal recognition from the authorities and, with the Ottomans mired in their wars with Russia and keen to secure peace in their troubled Syrian provinces, seemed to be on the verge of realizing his lifetime ambition. In 1774 the Ottoman governor of Damascus informed him that he would be appointed governor of Sidon, including northern Palestine and parts of Transjordan.

The imperial decree from Istanbul confirming Zahir's gubernatorial appointment never arrived. In July 1774, the sultan concluded a peace treaty with Russia, bringing the six-year war to an end. He was in no mood to reward traitors who had entered into alliance with his Russian foes. Instead of sending a decree of promotion, the sultan dispatched Muhammad Bey, at the head of a Mamluk army, to overthrow the aged strongman of Palestine. Egyptian troops overran the city of Jaffa in May 1775 and massacred the inhabitants. Panic spread to the other towns under Zahir's control. Zahir's administration and much of the population fled Acre by the end of the month. Muhammad Bey occupied Acre in early June.

Remarkably, Muhammad Bey, the hale and hearty Mamluk ruler of Egypt, took ill almost as soon as he occupied Acre. He died suddenly of a fever on June 10, 1775. Zahir reclaimed his city days later and restored order after the panic of the Egyptian occupation. But Zahir's reprieve proved short-lived. The Ottomans sent the admiral of their fleet, Hasan Pasha, with fifteen vessels to demand Zahir's submission and payment of back taxes. Zahir mounted no opposition. "I am an old man," he told his ministers, "and I don't have the nerve anymore for fighting." His battle-weary ministers agreed: "We are Muslim people, obedient to the Sultan. For the Muslim, believing in One God, it is not permitted to fight against the Sultan in any form."[22]

Zahir's plans for a peaceful retirement were shattered by his own family. He had agreed to withdraw from Acre with his family and retainers and take refuge with his Shi'ite allies in south Lebanon. He was betrayed by his son, 'Uthman, who suspected his father of feigning a retreat only to return to power at the first opportunity, as he had done time and again. 'Uthman called on one of Zahir's long-serving officers, a North African commander named Ahmad Agha al-Denizli, and told him that his father was fleeing the city of Acre. "If you wish to be [Admiral] Hasan Pasha's favourite person, carry out God's will on my father, for he is outside, alone with his family." Al-Denizli gathered a group of North African mercenaries and waited to ambush Zahir.

The assassins had to lay a trap to catch the elusive old shaykh. Fifteen minutes beyond the gates of Acre, Zahir noticed that one of his concubines was missing. The rest of his household had no idea where she was. "This is no time to leave a person behind," the old shaykh chided, and rode back to collect the abandoned woman. He found her near the spot where al-Denizli's band were hiding and reached down to pull her onto his horse. Age and anxiety had taken their toll. Zahir, now eighty-six years old, was pulled from his mount by the younger woman and fell to the ground. The assassins leapt out and struck down the old man with their daggers. Al-Denizli took out his sword and struck off Zahir's head as a trophy for the Otto-man admiral, Hasan Pasha.

If al-Denizli had hoped by this act to gain favor with Hasan Pasha, he was to be sorely disappointed. The Ottoman admiral had his men clean Zahir's severed head. He then placed it on a chair and meditated on the wizened face of the elderly shaykh. The admiral turned back to the mercenary. "May God not forgive me if I fail to avenge Zahir al-'Umar against you!"[23] He then ordered his men to take al-Denizli away, strangle him, and throw his body into the sea.

So ended the story of Zahir al-'Umar and 'Ali Bey al-Kabir. The Ottoman Empire had just withstood the most serious internal challenge to its rule after more than 250 years of dominion over the Arab world. Two local leaders, in league with a Christian power, had combined the wealth of two rich territories—Egypt and Palestine—to make common cause against the government of the sultan. Yet even at this critical juncture, when 'Ali Bey seemed on the verge of reestablishing the ancient Mamluk

Empire of Syria, Egypt, and the Hijaz under his personal rule, the Ottomans still exercised tremendous influence over their rebellious subjects in the Arab lands. Mamluk
generals like Isma'il Bey and Muhammad Bey crossed the threshold of rebellion only
to retrace their footsteps to the limits of legitimacy and seek the Porte's recognition.
Most local leaders still believed that "rebellion against the Sultan" was, in Isma'il
Bey's words, "one of the schemes of the Devil."

The fall of Zahir al-'Umar and 'Ali Bey did not signal the end of local rulers in
the Arab world. The Mamluks continued to dominate political life in Egypt, though
no single ruler emerged after the deaths of 'Ali Bey and of Muhammad Bey. Instead,
the Mamluk households reverted to factional fighting that left Egypt in a state of
instability for the remainder of the eighteenth century. The Ottomans reasserted
their hold over the Syrian provinces and appointed strong governors to Damascus,
Sidon, and Tripoli. More remote places, like Mount Lebanon, Baghdad, and Mosul,
continued to be ruled by local leaders, though none attempted to challenge Istanbul's
rule directly.

The next real challenge to Ottoman rule in the Arab world arose beyond the boundaries of the empire, in the heart of Central Arabia. The movement was all the more
threatening for its ideological purity, and it would menace Ottoman rule in an arc
stretching from Iraq through the Syrian Desert to the holy cities of Mecca and Medina in the Hijaz. Unlike Zahir al-'Umar and 'Ali Bey, the leader of this movement
now enjoys the distinction of being a household name in both the Middle East and
the West: Muhammad ibn 'Abd al-Wahhab, the founder of the Wahhabi reformist
movement.

Muhammad ibn 'Abd al-Wahhab was born in 1703 to a family of scholars in the
small oasis town of 'Uyayna in the Central Arabian region known as the Najd. He
traveled widely as a young man, pursuing his religious studies in Basra and Medina.
He was trained in the most conservative of the four legal traditions of Islam—the
Hanbali school—and was profoundly influenced by Ibn Taymiyya, a fourteenth-
century theologian. Ibn Taymiyya argued for a return to the practices of the early
Muslim community of the Prophet Muhammad and his first successors, or caliphs.
He condemned all mystical practices associated with Sufism as deviations from the
true path of Islam. Ibn 'Abd al-Wahhab returned home to the Najd with a clear set
of beliefs and the ambition to put them into practice.

At first the passionate young reformer enjoyed the support of the ruler of his
home town. However, his views soon proved controversial. When Muhammad ibn
'Abd al-Wahhab ordered the public execution of a woman for adultery, leaders in
neighboring towns and key trade partners of 'Uyayna were appalled—and alarmed.

This was not Islam as the townspeople of 'Uyayna had known and practiced their faith. They pressured their ruler to kill the radical theologian, but he chose to exile Ibn 'Abd al-Wahhab instead.

The exiled young theologian with the dangerous ideas did not have far to wander. Ibn 'Abd al-Wahhab was welcomed by the ruler of the nearby oasis of al-Dir'iyya, Muhammad ibn Sa'ud. Modern Saudis date the founding of their first state to this historic meeting in 1744–1745, when the two men agreed that the reformed Islam preached by Ibn 'Abd al-Wahhab would be observed by the Saudi ruler and his followers. The "Dir'iyya Agreement" set out the basic tenets of the movement that would come to be called Wahhabism.

At the time the movement was forming, the Wahhabis were widely misunderstood by the outside world. They were described as a new sect and accused of unorthodox beliefs. Quite the contrary, their beliefs were extremely orthodox, calling for a return to the pristine Islam of the Prophet and his successors, the caliphs. The Wahhabis sought to draw a line around the third century after the revelation of the Qur'an, and to ban all subsequent developments as "pernicious innovation."

The single most important tenet of Wahhabism was the unique quality of God, or, as they put it, the "oneness of God." Any association of lesser beings with God was denounced as polytheism (in Arabic, *shirk*), for if one believed God had partners or agents, one believed in more than one God. Islam, like many other religions, is a dynamic faith and has undergone significant changes over time. Over the centuries, a number of institutions had developed in Islam that fell foul of this absolute tenet of Wahhabism, the unity or oneness of God.

There was, for instance, a widespread veneration of saints and holy men in the Arab world, from the companions of the Prophet Muhammad to the humblest of local village holy men, each with his own shrine or sacred tree. (These shrines are still maintained in many parts of the Arab world today.) The Wahhabis objected to Muslims praying to holy men to intercede on their behalf with God, as this compromised God's oneness. They argued that greater reverence was shown to outstanding Muslims by following their example rather than worshiping at their graves. The shrines to saints, and the annual pilgrimages marking a given saint's day, were thus an early target of Wahhabi attack. Muhammad Ibn 'Abd al-Wahhab chopped down sacred trees and shattered the tombs of holy men with his own hands. This horrified mainstream Sunni Muslim society, which saw such desecration of tombs as a mark of disrespect to some of the most revered figures in Islam.

Along with his abhorrence of saint worship, Ibn 'Abd al-Wahhab was particularly intolerant of the mystical practices and beliefs associated with Sufism. Islamic mysticism takes many forms, from mendicant ascetics to the famous whirling dervishes.

Sufis use a wide range of techniques, from fasting to chanting and dancing to self-immolation, to reach the ecstasy of mystical union with the Creator. Organized into orders that convened regular prayer sessions, Sufism was a fundamental part of Ottoman religious and social life. Some orders built fine lodges and attracted the elites of society, and others called for complete abstinence and abandonment of worldly goods. Certain trades and professions were linked to particular Sufi orders. It is hard to think of a religious institution more closely connected to Ottoman society. Yet the Wahhabis believed that all who engaged in Sufism were polytheists for aspiring to mystical union with their Creator. It was a very serious charge.

By defining much of Ottoman Islam as polytheistic, the Wahhabis set themselves on a collision course with the empire. Although Orthodox Islam decrees tolerance of other monotheistic faiths, such as Judaism and Christianity, it is absolutely intolerant of polytheism, or the belief in many gods. Indeed, all good Muslims have a duty to persuade polytheists of the error of their ways and convert them to the true path of Islam. Failing that, Muslims have a duty of jihad to fight and eliminate polytheism. By characterizing mainstream practices such as Sufism and the veneration of saints as polytheistic, Wahhabism posed a direct challenge to the religious legitimacy of the Ottoman Empire.

The challenge of Wahhabism was easy for the Ottomans to overlook so long as the movement remained confined to the central Arabian region of the Najd, beyond Ottoman frontiers. Between 1744 and the death of Muhammad ibn Sa'ud in 1765, expansion of the Wahhabi movement was limited to the oasis towns of central Najd. It wasn't until the late 1780s that Wahhabism reached Ottoman frontiers in southern Iraq and the Hijaz.

In the 1790s the Ottomans took notice of the new threat to their Arab provinces and urged their governor in Baghdad to take action. The pasha of Baghdad delayed sending his troops into the hostile terrain of the Arabian peninsula for as long as he could. It was not until 1798 that he finally mustered a 10,000-man army to fight the Wahhabis. The Ottoman forces did not fare well in Wahhabi territory; they soon were surrounded and forced to negotiate a truce with Sa'ud ibn 'Abd al-'Aziz, the Saudi commander. In agreeing to the truce, the Wahhabis made no promises to respect the towns and villages of Ottoman Iraq in the future. The pasha of Baghdad had serious grounds for concern.

The Wahhabis pursued their crusade into Ottoman territory for the first time in 1802, when they attacked the southern Iraqi shrine city of Karbala. Karbala holds a special position in Shiite Islam, for it was here that Husayn ibn 'Ali, the grandson of the Prophet Muhammad, was killed by the forces of the Umayyad caliph in 680 AD. The martyred Husayn is venerated as the third of twelve infallible leaders, or imams, of Shi'ite Islam, and the mosque built on the site of his tomb was lavishly decorated with a gilt dome. Thousands of pilgrims would come each year to lay precious gifts on the tomb of the imam and undertake acts of devotion in his honour—just the sort of saint veneration that the Wahhabis found most abhorrent.

The Wahhabi attack on Karbala was chillingly brutal. The chronicler Ibn Bishr gives a contemporary description of the carnage:

> The Muslims [i.e., Wahhabis] surrounded Karbala and took it by storm. They killed most of the people in the markets and houses. They destroyed the dome above Husayn's grave. They took away everything they saw in the mausoleum and near it, including the coverlet decorated with emeralds, sapphires and pearls which covered the grave. They took away everything they found in the town—possessions, arms, clothes, fabric, gold, silver and precious books. One cannot count their spoils. They stayed there for just one morning and left after midday, taking away all the possessions. Nearly 2,000 people were killed in Karbala.[24]

The slaughter, the desecration of Husayn's tomb and mosque, and the plundering of the town established the Wahhabis' violent reputation in Arab public opinion. The brutality of the attack and the killing of so many unarmed men, women, and children in a place of worship provoked widespread revulsion across the Ottoman world. The residents of towns and villages in southern Iraq, eastern Syria, and the Hijaz turned to the Ottoman government to shield them from this grave threat.

The Ottomans faced great difficulty in confronting the Wahhabi challenge. The reform movement was based in Central Arabia, beyond some of the most remote Arab provinces of the Ottoman Empire. Ottoman troops had to march for months from Anatolia to reach the borderlands of the Najd. As the governor of Baghdad had already discovered, it was very difficult to fight the Wahhabis on their own terrain. Just keeping large armies supplied with food and water proved a tremendous challenge for the Ottomans in such a hostile environment. The Ottoman government found itself powerless to contain the Wahhabi menace.

The Wahhabis next struck at the very heart of Ottoman legitimacy by attacking the holy cities of Islam—Mecca and Medina. In March 1803, the Saudi commander Sa'ud ibn 'Abd al-'Aziz advanced on the Hijaz; by April, he entered the city of Mecca. His army met no resistance and promised no violence. They first explained their beliefs to the residents of Mecca and then imposed their new laws: silk clothes and smoking were banned, shrines were destroyed, domes on buildings were knocked down. After holding the holy cities for a number of months, the Wahhabis withdrew to the Najd. It was not until 1806 that the Wahhabis decided to strip the Hijaz from Ottoman domains and annex the province to their rapidly expanding state.

Once the Wahhabis were in control of Mecca and Medina, pilgrims from the Ottoman Empire were no longer admitted to Islam's holy cities to perform their religious duty of pilgrimage. Both of the official Ottoman pilgrimage caravans, from

Damascus and Cairo, were accompanied by a *mahmal,* a richly decorated litter carried by a camel. The mahmal contained a cover for the shrine holding the holy black
stone known as the Ka'ba, at the center of the mosque in Mecca, as well as copies
of the Qur'an and rich treasures. The mahmal was surrounded by musicians playing
drums and blaring horns. The use of music, the decoration of the Ka'ba shrine, and
the association of opulence with worship all offended Wahhabi strictures, and they
refused to admit the mahmal to Mecca, breaking with centuries of Sunni Muslim
veneration for Mecca's holiest shrine.

One of the officers accompanying the Egyptian caravan in 1806 related his experiences with the Wahhabis to the chronicler al-Jabarti:

> Pointing to the mahmal, the Wahhabi had asked him: "What are these gifts of
> yours that you bring and hold in such veneration among yourselves?"
>
> He had answered: "It is a custom which has been observed from ancient times.
> It is an emblem and a signal for the pilgrims to gather."
>
> The Wahhabi said: "Do not do so, and do not bring it after this time. If you
> ever bring it again, I shall smash it."[25]

In 1807 a Syrian caravan without the mahmal and musicians sought entry to
Mecca and was nevertheless denied. With or without the mahmal, the Wahhabis
believed Ottoman Muslims to be no better than polytheists and denied them entry
to Islam's holiest places.

The most important of the sultan's imperial titles emphasized his role as the de-
fender of the faith and protector of the holy cities of the Hijaz. The Wahhabis' annexation of the Hijaz and ban on the Ottoman pilgrimage caravans defied the
temporal powers of the Ottoman state in securing its territories as well as the sultan's
religious legitimacy as the guardian of Islam's holiest cities. The gravity of this threat
could not be more severe. The Ottomans would not survive if they failed to respond
to this challenge and reassert their authority.

Although the Ottomans were quick to dismiss the Wahhabis as savage Bedouins of
the desert, they knew it would be difficult to defeat the movement. As modern wars
in Kuwait and Iraq have shown, great powers face huge logistical problems in fighting wars in Arabia. Troops would have to be sent on sailing ships and marched great
distances overland, in terrible heat, with long and vulnerable supply lines. They
would be forced to fight on the Wahhabis' own terrain. And the Wahhabis were
zealots, convinced that they were doing God's work. There was always the risk that
Ottoman soldiers might respond to the Wahhabis' powerful message and cross over
to the other side.

There was no question of sending a campaign force all the way from Istanbul to the Hijaz. The Ottomans lacked both the financial and military resources for such an enterprise. Instead, they made repeated demands of their provincial governors in Baghdad, Damascus, and Cairo. The governor in Baghdad was fighting continued Wahhabi attacks in his southern provinces and had yet to succeed in repelling the raiders. The Kurdish governor in Damascus, Kanj Yusuf Pasha, promised Istanbul to reopen the pilgrimage route. However, he lacked the resources to undertake such a campaign. As the Syrian chronicler Mikhayil Mishaqa observed, Kanj Yusuf Pasha "could neither send enough soldiers nor supply them with enough ammunition to drive the Wahhabi from the Hijaz, which was a forty-day march away [from Damascus] through burning sands without food or water along the way for themselves or their beasts."[26]

There was only one person who could mobilize the necessary forces and had demonstrated sufficient ability to defeat the Wahhabis and restore the Hijaz to the Ottoman Empire. Since 1805, Egypt had been ruled by a governor of extraordinary ability. Yet the talent and ambition that so recommended him to address the Wahhabi challenge would soon be turned against the Ottoman state. Indeed, Muhammad 'Ali Pasha proved the culmination of a dangerous trend, of provincial leaders challenging Istanbul's rule in the Arab provinces. Muhammad 'Ali proved strong enough to threaten the overthrow of the Ottoman dynasty itself.

CHAPTER 3

The Egyptian Empire
of Muhammad 'Ali

In June 1798, British ships appeared without warning off the coast of Egypt. A landing party rowed ashore to be received by the governor and notables of what was then the modest port town of Alexandria. The British warned of an impending French invasion and offered their assistance. The governor was indignant: "This is the sultan's land. Neither the French nor anyone else has access to it. So leave us alone!"[1] The very suggestion that an inferior nation like France posed a threat to Ottoman domains, or that Ottoman subjects might turn to another inferior nation like Britain for assistance, clearly offended the notables of Alexandria. The British rowed back to their tall ships and withdrew. No one gave the matter any further thought—for the moment.

The people of Alexandria awoke on the morning of July 1 to find their harbor filled with men-o'-war and their shores invaded. Napoleon Bonaparte had arrived at the head of a massive invasion force, the first European army to set foot in the Middle East since the Crusades. Outnumbered and outgunned, Alexandria surrendered in a matter of hours. The French secured their position and set off for Cairo.

Mamluk horsemen engaged the French army at the southern outskirts of Cairo. In what seemed like a replay of the 1516 Mamluk battle against the Ottomans at Marj Dabiq, the gallant Mamluks drew their swords and charged the French invaders. They never even got within striking distance. The French moved in tight formations, with row upon row of infantrymen maintaining a rolling thunder of rifle fire that decimated the Mamluk cavalry. "The air darkened with gunpowder, smoke and dust from the wind," a contemporary Egyptian chronicler recorded. "The uninterrupted shooting was ear-deafening. To the people it appeared as if the earth were shaking and the sky were falling in."[2] According to Egyptian eyewitnesses, the fighting was over within three-quarters of an hour. Panic swept the streets as the army of Napoleon occupied the defenseless city of Cairo.

Over the next three years, the people of Egypt came face to face with the customs and manners of the French, the ideas of the Enlightenment, and the technology of the Industrial Revolution. Napoleon had intended to establish a permanent presence in Egypt, which meant winning her people over to the benefits of French rule. This was more than a military matter. Accompanying the French infantry was a smaller army of sixty-seven *savants*, or learned men, who came with the dual mission of studying Egypt and impressing the Egyptians with the superiority of French civilization. With a liberal sprinkling of the ideas of the French Revolution, the occupation of Egypt was the original French "civilizing mission."

A crucial eyewitness to the occupation was 'Abd al-Rahman al-Jabarti (1754–1824), an intellectual and theologian with access to the highest echelons of both French and Egyptian society. Al-Jabarti wrote extensively on the French occupation, detailing the Egyptian encounter with the French, their revolutionary ideas, and their astonishing technology.

The gulf separating French Revolutionary thought from Egyptian Muslim values was unbridgeable. Enlightenment values that the French held to be universal were deeply offensive to many Egyptians, both as Ottoman subjects and observant Muslims. This gulf in worldview was apparent from Napoleon's very first proclamation to the people of Egypt, when he asserted "that all men are equal before God; that wisdom, talents, and virtues alone make them different from one another."

Far from striking a chord of liberation, Napoleon's pronouncement provoked deep dismay. Al-Jabarti wrote a line-by-line refutation of the proclamation that rejected most of the "universal" values Napoleon vaunted. He dismissed Napoleon's claim that all men were equal as "a lie and stupidity" and concluded: "You see that they are materialists, who deny all God's attributes. The creed they follow is to make human reason supreme and what people will approve in accordance with their whims."[3] Al-Jabarti's statements reflected the beliefs of Egypt's Muslim majority, who rejected the exercise of human reason over revealed religion.

If the French failed to win the Egyptians over to the ideas of the Enlightenment, they were nevertheless confident that French technology would impress the natives. Napoleon's savants brought quite a bag of tricks to Egypt. In November 1798, the French organized the launch of a Montgolfier hot-air balloon. They posted notices around Cairo inviting the townspeople to witness the marvel of flight. Al-Jabarti had heard the French make incredible claims about their airship, "that people would sit in it travelling to distant countries to gather information and to send messages," and went to see the demonstration for himself.

Looking at the limp balloon on its platform, decorated in the red, white, and blue of the French tricolor, al-Jabarti had his doubts. The Frenchmen lit the Montgolfier's wick, filling the balloon with warm air until it took flight. The crowd gasped in amazement, and the French took evident pleasure in their reaction. All seemed to be going well until the balloon lost its wick. Without a source of hot air, the Montgolfier collapsed and fell to the ground. The crash of the balloon restored the Cairo audience's contempt for French technology. Al-Jabarti wrote dismissively, "It became apparent that it was like the kites which servants construct for holidays and weddings."[4] The natives were not impressed.

The French failed to appreciate just how proud the Egyptians were and how humiliating they found the experience of alien occupation. Napoleon's proclamations seem to cry out for gratitude from the Egyptians, but few Egyptian Muslims would concede their approval of the French or their institutions—at least not to their faces. The chemistry demonstration by Monsieur Bertholet (1748–1822), was a case in point.

Al-Jabarti, who was a regular at the French Institute in Cairo, was once again in attendance. He wrote openly about his amazement at the feats of chemistry and physics he witnessed. "One of the strangest things I have seen in [the Institute] was the following," he wrote. "One of the assistants took a bottle filled with a distilled liquid and poured a little of it into a cup. Then he poured something from another bottle. The two liquids boiled and coloured smoke rose from them until it ceased and the contents of the cup dried and became a yellow stone. He turned it out on the shelf. It was a dry stone which we took in our hand and examined." This transformation of liquids to solids was followed by demonstrations of the flammable properties of gasses and the volatility of pure sodium, which, when struck "gently with a hammer," made "a terrifying noise like the sound of a carbine." Al-Jabarti resented the savants' amusement when he and his Egyptian compatriots were startled by the bang.

The *pièce de resistance* was a demonstration of the properties of electricity using Leyden jars, first developed as electrostatic generators in 1746. "If one held its connections . . . and with his other hand touched the end of the revolving glass . . . his body would shake and his frame tremble. The bones of his shoulder would rattle and his forearms immediately tremble. Anyone who touched the person in contact, or any of his clothes, or anything connected to him, experienced the same thing— even if it were a thousand or more people."

No doubt the Egyptians present at the demonstration were very impressed by what they had seen. However, they did their best not to show their amazement. One of Napoleon's aides who witnessed the chemistry demonstration later wrote how "all of the miracles of the transformation of fluids, electrical commotions and experiments in galvanism caused them no surprise at all." When the demonstration was over, he claimed one of the Muslim intellectuals asked a question through an interpreter. "This is all well and good, but can they make it so that I would be in Morocco and here at the same time?" Bertholet replied with a shrug of the shoulders. "Ah, well," said the shaykh, "he isn't such a good sorcerer after all."[5] Al-Jabarti, reflecting on the demonstration in the privacy of his own study, begged to differ: "They had strange things in [the Institute], devices and apparatus achieving results which minds like ours cannot comprehend."[6]

Napoleon's real reasons for invading Egypt in 1798 were geostrategic, not cultural. France's main rival in the second half of the eighteenth century was Great Britain. The two European maritime powers struggled for ascendancy in a number of theaters, including the Americas, the Caribbean, Africa, and India. British and French commercial companies had fought a bitter campaign for supremacy in India that was only resolved in the Seven Years War (1756–1763), when the British defeated the French and secured their hegemony over the subcontinent. France was never reconciled to its losses in India.

With the outbreak of the French Revolutionary Wars in 1792, Britain and France resumed their hostilities. Napoleon, looking for ways to hurt British interests, turned back to India. By capturing Egypt, he hoped to dominate the Eastern Mediterranean and to close the strategic land-sea route to India that ran from the Mediterranean through Egypt to the Red Sea and the Indian Ocean beyond. The British were aware that Napoleon was assembling a major expedition force in Toulon and suspected a move against Egypt. Admiral Horatio Nelson was put in command of a powerful squadron to intercept the French fleet. They actually beat the French to Egypt, where they had their brief and discouraging encounter with the governor of Alexandria. Nelson withdrew his ships to search for Napoleon elsewhere in the Eastern Mediterranean.

The French succeeded in eluding the Royal Navy, and Napoleon's army made a quick conquest of Egypt. However, Nelson's squadron caught up with the French fleet one month later and succeeded in sinking or capturing all but two of the French warships in the Battle of the Nile, on August 1. Napoleon's flagship, *l'Orient*, was set ablaze in the battle and exploded in a spectacular fireball that lit the night sky. The French lost more than 1,700 men in the Battle of the Nile.

The British victory over the French fleet condemned the Napoleonic expedition to failure. The 20,000-man French army was now trapped in Egypt with no line of communication to France. The defeat dealt a terrible blow to the morale of French troops in Egypt. Their sense of isolation was compounded when Napoleon abandoned his army without warning to return to France in August 1799, where he seized power in November of that year.

Following Napoleon's flight, the French army in Egypt was left without a mission. Napoleon's successor entered into negotiations with the Ottomans for a full French evacuation from Egypt. The French and Ottomans struck agreement as early as January 1800, but their plans were scuttled by the British, who had no wish to see a large and experienced French army rejoin Napoleon's legions to fight the British on other fronts. In 1801 the British Parliament authorized a military expedition to secure a French surrender in Egypt. The expedition reached Alexandria in March 1801 and combined forces with the Ottomans in a pincer movement on Cairo. The French surrendered Cairo in June and Alexandria in August 1801. They then boarded British and Ottoman ships to be transported home to France, bringing the whole sorry episode to a close.

The French occupation of Egypt lasted just three years. It was a fascinating moment in human terms, where Egyptians and Frenchmen found points to admire and to condemn in each other. Both sides emerged wounded from the encounter. The French who withdrew from Cairo in the summer of 1801, driven out by an Anglo-Ottoman force, were no longer the self-confident agents of a new revolutionary order. Rather, their ranks were thinned by war and disease and their morale was low after years without relief in Egypt. Many Frenchmen had converted to Islam and taken Egyptian wives—hardly a sign of condescension toward the people under their occupation. But the Egyptians too had had their confidence shaken by the experience of occupation. Their sense of superiority had been upset by their confrontation with the French, their ideas, and their technology.

———————

The departing French left a power vacuum in Egypt. Their three-year occupation had broken the Mamluks' power base in Cairo and Lower Egypt. The Ottomans wanted to prevent the reestablishment of the Mamluk households at all costs—in the absence of the French, they had never faced a better opportunity to reassert their authority over the rebellious province of Egypt. The British feared Napoleon would attempt the reconquest of Egypt and were determined to leave a strong deterrent behind. They had more confidence in the Mamluks than in the Ottomans defending Egypt from future French attack, and so they worked to rehabilitate the most powerful Mamluks. They pressured the Ottomans to pardon key Mamluk beys, who began to reestablish their households and rebuild their influence. The Ottomans complied with British wishes against their better judgment.

No sooner had the British expeditionary force departed in 1803 than the Ottomans reverted to their own solutions for Egypt. The Sublime Porte ordered the governor in Cairo to exterminate the Mamluk beys and seize their wealth for the treasury.[7] The Mamluks, however, had regained enough of their former strength to withstand Ottoman attacks. What followed was a bitter power struggle between the Ottomans and the Mamluks that prolonged the misery of the war-weary civilians of Cairo. One

Ottoman commander emerged from the chaos to master the conflict with the Mamluks and to build public support for his bid to rule over Egypt. In fact, he would soon become one of the most influential figures in Egypt's modern history. His name was Muhammad 'Ali.

An ethnic Albanian born in the Macedonian town of Kavala, Muhammad 'Ali (1770–1849) rose to command a powerful and unruly 6,000-man Albanian contingent of the Ottoman army in Egypt. Between 1803 and 1805, through an ever-shifting set of alliances, Muhammad 'Ali enhanced his personal power at the expense of the Ottoman governor, the commanders of the other Ottoman regiments, and the leading Mamluk beys. He openly courted the support of the notables of Cairo, who had grown increasingly restive after five years of political and economic instability, first under the French and now under the Ottomans. By 1805 the commander of the Albanian detachment had emerged as a king-maker in Cairo. But Muhammad 'Ali aspired to be king himself.

Muhammad 'Ali's activities had not escaped the attention of the Ottoman authorities. The commander of the Albanians was seen as a troublemaker, but he had talent and ambition that could be put to the empire's advantage. The situation in Arabia remained critical. The Wahhabis had attacked Ottoman territory in Iraq in 1802 and took control of the holy city of Mecca in 1803. The Islamic reformers now imposed conditions on the Ottoman pilgrimage caravans from Cairo and Damascus and threatened to prohibit them entry to the holy cities of Mecca and Medina altogether (as they would do after 1806). This was an intolerable situation for the sultan, who claimed by imperial title to be the guardian of Islam's holiest cities. When the notables of Cairo first petitioned Istanbul to appoint Muhammad 'Ali as governor of Egypt in 1805, the Porte decided to name him governor of the Arabian province of the Hijaz instead, and to entrust him with the dangerous mission of crushing the Wahhabi movement.

As governor-designate of the Hijaz, Muhammad 'Ali was promoted to the rank of pasha, which made him eligible to serve as governor in any Ottoman province. Muhammad 'Ali accepted the appointment to the Hijaz for the title alone. He showed no interest in moving to the Red Sea province to take up his new post. Instead, he conspired with his allies among the civilian notables of Cairo to put pressure on the Ottomans to appoint him governor of Egypt. The notables had confidence that Muhammad 'Ali and his Albanian soldiers could impose order on Cairo. They also suffered from the illusion that Muhammad 'Ali would be beholden to them for their support and would allow the notables to exercise control over the governor they'd appointed. They hoped in this way to lessen the government's tax burden on the merchants and artisans of Cairo and to regenerate the economic vitality of the province to *their* benefit. But Muhammad 'Ali had other plans.

In May 1805 the townspeople of Cairo rose in protest against Khurshid Ahmad Pasha, the Ottoman governor. The common people of Cairo had reached a breaking point after years of instability, violence, overtaxation, and injustice. They closed their shops in protest and demanded the Ottomans appoint a governor of their choosing. Al-Jabarti, who lived through these troubled times, describes large demonstrations led by beturbaned shaykhs in the mosques of Cairo where young men chanted slogans against their tyrannical pasha and Ottoman injustice. The mob made its way to Muhammad 'Ali's house.

"And whom do you want to be governor?" asked Muhammad 'Ali.

"We will accept only you," the people replied. "You will be governor over us according to our conditions, for we know you as a just and good man."

Muhammad 'Ali modestly declined the offer. The mob insisted. In a show of reluctance, the crafty Albanian allowed himself to be persuaded. The leading notables then brought him a fur pelisse and a ceremonial gown in an improvised ceremony of investiture. It was an unprecedented event: the people of Cairo had imposed their own choice of governor on the Ottoman Empire.

The incumbent governor, Khurshid Ahmad Pasha, was not impressed. "I was appointed by the sultan and I will not be removed at the command of the peasants," he retorted. "I will leave the Citadel only on the orders of the imperial government."[8] The civilians of Cairo laid siege to the deposed governor in the Citadel for over a month, until orders came from Istanbul confirming the people's choice of governor, on June 18, 1805. Muhammad 'Ali was now master of Egypt.

It was one thing to be named governor of Egypt—scores of men had held the title since the Ottomans had conquered the territory in 1517—and quite another to actually govern Egypt. Muhammad 'Ali Pasha established his mastery over the province like no one before or after him. He succeeded in monopolizing the wealth of Egypt and used the revenues to establish a powerful army and a bureaucratic state. He used his army to expand the territory under his command, making Egypt the center of an empire in its own right. But unlike 'Ali Bey al-Kabir, who as a Mamluk had dreamed of rebuilding the Mamluk Empire, Muhammad 'Ali was an Ottoman, and he sought to dominate the Ottoman Empire.

Muhammad 'Ali also was an innovator who put Egypt on a path of reform, drawing on European ideas and technology in ways that the Ottomans themselves would later imitate. He created the first peasant mass army in the Middle East. He undertook one of the earliest industrialization programs outside Europe, applying the technology of the Industrial Revolution to produce weapons and textiles for his army. He dispatched education missions to European capitals and created a translation bureau to publish European books and technical manuals in Arabic editions.

He enjoyed direct relations with the great powers of Europe, who treated him more like an independent sovereign than a viceroy of the Ottoman sultan. By the end of his reign, Muhammad 'Ali had succeeded in establishing his family's hereditary rule over Egypt and the Sudan. His dynasty would rule Egypt until the 1952 revolution brought down the monarchy.

Though they had shifted Muhammad 'Ali's appointment from the Hijaz to Cairo, the Sublime Porte still expected him to lead a campaign against the Wahhabis to restore Ottoman authority in Arabia. The new governor found many excuses to ignore Istanbul's commands. He had come to power through disorder and knew that he too would fall unless he brought the Cairo public and the Ottoman soldiers to heel.

Muhammad 'Ali's Albanian soldiers gave him an independent power base to help him achieve mastery in Cairo by force. The fragmented Mamluk households were his first target, and he pursued them to Upper Egypt. Such campaigns soon proved expensive, however, and the pasha realized that soldiers were not enough to control Egypt. He needed money too. Agriculture was the province's primary source of revenues. Yet, one-fifth of Egypt's agricultural land had been endowed to support Islamic institutions, and the other four-fifths were leased out in tax farms held by the Mamluk households and other large landholders that brought little benefit to the treasury in Cairo. To control the revenues of Egypt, Muhammad 'Ali would have to control its land.

By putting the land of Egypt under a system of direct taxation, Muhammad 'Ali gained the necessary resources to impose his control over Egypt. In the process, he undermined the financial bases of his Mamluk opponents and his supporters among the notables of Cairo alike. The religious scholars were divested of their autonomous revenues, and the landed elites found themselves dependent on the governor they had hoped to control. In all, it took six years for Muhammad 'Ali to consolidate his position in Egypt before he finally accepted the sultan's commission to conduct a campaign against the Wahhabis in Arabia.

In March 1811, Muhammad 'Ali sent his son Tussun Pasha to lead the military operation against the Wahhabis. This was to be Muhammad 'Ali's first venture beyond the frontiers of Egypt. Before sending a large part of his army abroad, he wanted to ensure peace and stability in Egypt. He organized a ceremony of investiture for Tussun and invited all of the leading figures of Cairo to attend—including the most powerful Mamluk beys. The beys saw the invitation as a conciliatory gesture following several years of hostilities with Muhammad 'Ali's government. Clearly, they reasoned, the governor would find it easier to rule with Mamluk support than to continue fighting against them. Nearly all of the beys accepted the invitation and arrived in Cairo's Citadel dressed in their finery to take part in the ceremony. If any of the beys had misgivings, the fact that nearly all of the leading Mamluks were in attendance must have given them some sense of security. Besides, what sort of man would violate the laws of hospitality by committing treachery against his guests?

After the ceremony of investiture, the Mamluks paraded in a formal procession through the Citadel. As they made their way through one of its gated passageways, the gates suddenly closed. Before the confused beys realized what was happening, soldiers appeared on the walls overhead and opened fire. After years of fighting, the soldiers had come to hate the Mamluks and went about their work with relish, leaping down from the walls to finish off the beys. "The soldiers went berserk butchering the amirs and looting their clothing," al-Jabarti recorded. "Showing their hatred, they spared no one." They killed Mamluks and the supernumeraries the beys had dressed up to accompany their procession—most of whom were common citizens of Cairo. "These people were shouting and calling for help. One would say, 'I'm not a soldier or a Mamluk.' Another would say 'I'm not one of them.' The soldiers, however, did not heed these screams and pleas."[9]

Muhammad 'Ali's troops then went on a rampage through the city. They dragged out anyone suspected of being a Mamluk and took them back to the Citadel, where they were beheaded. In his report to Istanbul, Muhammad 'Ali claimed that twenty-four beys and forty of their men had been killed, and he dispatched their heads and ears to support the claim.[10] Al-Jabarti's account suggests the violence was far more extensive.

The massacre in the Citadel was the final blow to the Mamluks of Cairo. They had survived Selim the Grim's conquest and Napoleon's invasion, but after nearly six centuries in Cairo they were practically exterminated by Muhammad 'Ali. The few surviving Mamluk beys stayed in Upper Egypt, knowing that Cairo's governor would stop at nothing to secure his power, and that they lacked the means to challenge him. Confident that he no longer faced any domestic challenge to his rule, Muhammad 'Ali could now send his army to Arabia to earn the gratitude of the Ottoman sultan.

The Wahhabi campaign proved a tremendous drain on the resources of Muhammad 'Ali's Egypt. The battlefield was far from home, communication and supply lines were long and vulnerable, and Tussun Pasha was forced to fight in a harsh environment on the enemy's terrain. In 1812, taking advantage of their superior knowledge of the countryside, the Wahhabis drew the Egyptian force into a narrow pass and dealt the 8,000-man army a serious defeat. Many of the demoralized Albanian commanders quit the battlefield and returned to Cairo, leaving Tussun short-handed. Muhammad 'Ali sent reinforcements to Jidda, and over the next year Tussun managed to secure Mecca and Medina. Muhammad 'Ali accompanied the pilgrimage caravan in 1813 and dispatched the keys of the holy city to the sultan in Istanbul as a token of the restoration of his sovereignty over the birthplace of Islam. These victories had come at a high price: the Egyptian force had lost 8,000 men and the Egyptian treasury had spent the enormous sum of 170,000 purses (approximately $6.7 million in 1820 U.S. dollars).[11] Nor had the Wahhabis been fully defeated. They had merely withdrawn before the Egyptian army's advance and were bound to return.

Fighting continued between Tussun's Egyptian army and the Wahhabi force, commanded by Abdullah ibn Saud, until the two sides struck a truce in 1815. Tussun returned home to Cairo, where he contracted plague and died within days of his return. When word of Tussun's death filtered back to Arabia, Abdullah ibn Saud broke his truce and attacked Egyptian positions. Muhammad 'Ali appointed his eldest son, Ibrahim, as commander in chief of Egyptian forces. It was the beginning of a brilliant military career, for Ibrahim Pasha emerged as Muhammad 'Ali's generalissimo.

Ibrahim Pasha took up his command in Arabia early in 1817 and pursued a relentless campaign against the Wahhabis. He secured Egyptian control over the Red Sea province of the Hijaz before driving the Wahhabis back into the central Arabian region of the Najd. Even though the Najd lay outside Ottoman territory, Ibrahim Pasha was determined to eliminate the Wahhabi threat once and for all, and he drove his adversaries back to their capital of Dir'iyya. For six months the two sides fought a terrible war of attrition. The Wahhabis, trapped within the walls of their city, were slowly starved of food and water by the Egyptian siege. Egyptian forces suffered heavy losses to disease and exposure in the lethal summer heat of Central Arabia. In the end the Egyptians prevailed, and in September 1818 the Wahhabis surrendered, knowing they faced total destruction.

On Muhammad 'Ali's orders, the Egyptian forces destroyed the town of Dir'iyya and sent all of the leaders of the Wahhabi movement to Cairo as prisoners. Muhammad 'Ali knew he had earned Sultan Mahmud II's favor by suppressing a movement that had brought the very legitimacy of the Ottoman sultanate into question for over sixteen years. Moreover, he had succeeded where no other Ottoman governor or commander could, in prosecuting a successful campaign in Central Arabia. From Cairo, Abdullah ibn Saud and the leaders of the Wahhabi state were sent on to Istanbul to face the sultan's justice.

Mahmud II (r. 1808–1839) turned the execution of the Wahhabi leaders into a state occasion. He summoned the top government officials, the ambassadors of foreign states, and the leading notables of his empire to the Topkapi Palace to witness the ceremony. The three condemned men—the military commander, Abdullah ibn Saud, the chief minister, and the spiritual leader of the Wahhabi movement—were brought in heavy chains and publicly tried for their crimes against religion and state. The sultan concluded the hearings by sentencing all three to death. Abdullah ibn Saud was beheaded before the main gate of the Aya Sofia Mosque, the chief minister was executed before the main entrance to the palace, and the spiritual leader was beheaded in one of the main markets of the city. Their bodies were left on display, heads tucked under arms, for three days before their corpses were cast into the sea.[12]

With the expulsion of French forces from Egypt and the defeat of the Wahhabi movement, Sultan Mahmud II might be excused for believing the Ottoman Empire had withstood the most serious challenges to its position in the Arab world. Yet the governor in Egypt who delivered victory in Arabia would himself prove a far graver threat to Mahmud II. For while the Wahhabis attacked the fringes of his state— very important fringes on spiritual grounds, but fringes nonetheless—Muhammad 'Ali would pose a challenge to the very center of the Ottoman Empire and the ruling dynasty itself.

In recognition of Ibrahim's services to the Ottoman state in defeating the Wahhabis, Sultan Mahmud II promoted Muhammad 'Ali's son to the rank of pasha and named him governor of the Hijaz. In this way, the Red Sea province of the Hijaz became the first addition to Muhammad 'Ali's empire. Henceforth, the Egyptian treasury would benefit from the customs revenues of the port of Jidda, which, given its importance in the Red Sea trade and as a gateway for the annual pilgrimage to Mecca, were considerable.

Muhammad 'Ali substantially consolidated Egypt's grip over the Red Sea in 1820 when his forces invaded Sudan. He had hoped to find mythical gold mines in Sudan to enrich his treasury while he sought a new source of slave soldiers for his army in the upper reaches of the Nile. The Sudan campaign was marred by great brutality. When Muhammad 'Ali's son Ismail was killed by the ruler of Shindi, a region on the Nile to the north of Khartoum, the Egyptian expeditionary force retaliated by killing 30,000 of the local inhabitants. The gold never materialized, and the Sudanese quite literally preferred to die rather than serve in Muhammad 'Ali's army. Thousands of men who had been captured for military service became despondent when taken from their homes, fell ill, and perished in the long marches to training camps in Egypt: of 20,000 Sudanese enslaved between 1820 and 1824, just 3,000 survived to 1824.[13] The only real gains to Egypt of the Sudan campaign (1820–1822) were commercial and territorial. By adding Sudan to Egypt's empire, Muhammad 'Ali doubled the land mass under his control and dominated the trade of the Red Sea. Egypt's hegemony over Sudan would endure 136 years, until Sudan regained its independence in 1956.

Muhammad 'Ali faced a severe constraint in the shortage of new recruits for the Egyptian army. His original Albanian forces had been decimated by wars in Arabia and the Sudan, and by age as well. By the time of the Sudan campaign, the surviving Albanians in Muhammad 'Ali's army had been in Egypt twenty years. The Ottomans had placed an embargo on the export of military slaves from the Caucasus to Egypt in 1810, both to prevent a Mamluk revival and to contain the ambitions of Muhammad 'Ali himself. Nor were the Ottomans willing to send any of the empire's soldiers to serve Muhammad 'Ali when they were needed on the European fronts. With no external source of new soldiers, the governor of Egypt was forced back on his own population.

The idea of a *national* army—a conscript force that drew its ranks from the workers and peasants of the country—was still novel in the Ottoman world. Soldiers were seen as a martial caste taken from slave ranks. In the course of the seventeenth and eighteenth centuries, the famous Ottoman infantry known as the Janissaries did modify their recruitment procedures as the *devshirme* ("boy levy") fell out of practice. Soldiers took wives and enrolled their sons in the Janissaries' ranks. But the notion of a military caste distinct from the rest of the population persisted. Peasants were dismissed as too passive and dull for military service.

As the Ottomans began to lose wars to European armies in the eighteenth century, the sultans came to doubt the effectiveness of their own infantry. They invited retired Prussian and French officers to Istanbul to introduce modern European methods of warfare, such as square formation, bayonet charges, and the use of mobile artillery. Toward the end of the eighteenth century, Sultan Selim III (r. 1780–1807) created a new Ottoman army recruited from Anatolian peasant stock dressed in European-style breeches and drilled by Western officers. He called this new force the *Nizam-i Cedid*, or "New Order" army (its soldiers were known as Nizami troops).

Sultan Selim deployed a 4,000-man Nizami regiment to Egypt in 1801, where Muhammad 'Ali would have seen the discipline of the corps firsthand. As one Ottoman contemporary recorded, the Nizami troops in Egypt "bravely combated the infidels and defeated them incessantly; and the flight of a single individual of that corps was never seen nor heard of."[14] However, the Nizami forces were a more immediate threat to the powerful Janissary corps than to any European army. If the Nizamis were the "new order," the Janissaries were by implication the "old order," and they weren't going to accept redundancy while they still had the power to protect their own interests. In 1807 the Janissaries mutinied, overthrew Selim III, and disbanded the Nizami army. Though this first experiment in an Ottoman national army came to an inauspicious end, it still provided Muhammad 'Ali with a viable model to replicate in Egypt.

The Napoleonic army gave Muhammad 'Ali a second model to consider. The French *levée en masse* was a citizen's mass army that, when led by able commanders, had proven capable of conquering continents. However, Muhammad 'Ali viewed the people of Egypt as subjects rather than citizens, and he never tried to stir his troops with rousing ideological slogans as did French revolutionary commanders. He decided to draw on French military experts to train his recruit army, but otherwise he modeled the Egyptian Nizam-i Cedid on the Ottoman example. In 1822 he commissioned a veteran of the Napoleonic wars named Colonel Sève—a French convert to Islam known in Egypt as Sulayman Agha—to organize and train a Nizami army drawn entirely from Egyptian peasant recruits. Within a year he had raised a force of 30,000 men. By the mid-1830s, that number would reach 130,000.

The Egyptian Nizami army was not an overnight success. Egyptian peasants feared for their farms and the welfare of their families; their close attachment to their homes and villages made military service a real ordeal. Peasants avoided conscription by fleeing their villages when military recruitment teams approached. Others deliberately maimed themselves by chopping off fingers or striking out an eye to gain exemption on grounds of disability. Whole regions rose in revolt against the draft, and in Upper Egypt an estimated 30,000 villagers rebelled in 1824. Once pressed into military service, many peasants deserted. It was only through heavy punishment that Muhammad 'Ali's government was able to force the peasants of Egypt to serve in the army. The astonishing thing is how successful this reluctant army proved on the battlefield. It was first put to the test in Greece.

In 1821 the Greek provinces of the Ottoman Empire erupted in a nationalist uprising. The revolt was initiated by members of a secret society known as the Filiki Etairia, or the "Society of Friends," established in 1814 with the goal of Greek statehood and independence. The Greeks of the Ottoman Empire were a distinct community held together by their language, their Orthodox Christian faith, and a shared history spanning the classical period to the Hellenic Byzantine Empire. As the first overtly nationalist uprising in the Ottoman Empire, the Greek War posed a danger of much greater magnitude than the eighteenth-century revolts by local leaders. In previous revolts, movements had been driven only by the ambitions of individual leaders. The novelty of nationalism was that it was an ideology capable of inspiring a whole population to rise up against their Ottoman rulers.

The revolt broke out in the southern Peloponnesian Peninsula in March 1821 and quickly spread to central Greece, Macedonia, the Aegean islands, and Crete. The Ottomans found themselves fighting pitched battles on several fronts simultaneously, and they turned to Muhammad 'Ali for assistance. In 1824 his son Ibrahim Pasha set off for the Peloponnesian Peninsula at the head of an Egyptian army of 17,000 newly trained infantry, 700 cavalry, and four artillery batteries. As all of his soldiers were native-born peasants, it is the first time we can speak of a genuinely *Egyptian* army.

The Egyptians achieved complete success in the Greek War, and the new Nizami army proved its mettle. Following his conquests in Crete and the Peloponnese, Ibrahim Pasha was awarded the governorships of those provinces, expanding Muhammad 'Ali's empire from the Red Sea to the Aegean. Ironically, the better his forces fared on the battlefield against the Greeks, the more concerned the sultan and his government grew. The Egyptians were subduing insurgencies that had withstood the Ottomans and expanding the territory under Cairo's control. If Muhammad 'Ali were to rise in rebellion, it was not clear that the Ottomans would be able to withstand his troops.

Egyptian victory and Greek suffering provoked concern in European capitals as well. The Greek War captured the imaginations of educated elites in Britain and France. As the cities of the classical world became modern battlefields, European Philhellenic societies clamored for their governments to intervene to protect the Christian Greeks from the Muslim Turks and Egyptians. The poet Lord Byron drew international attention to the Greek cause when he sailed to Messolonghi in 1823 to support the independence movement. His death in April 1824—of a fever, not at the hands of Ottoman soldiers—elevated him to the status of a martyr for the cause of Greek independence. Public calls for European intervention redoubled in the aftermath of Byron's death.

The British and French governments were susceptible to public pressure but were more concerned with larger geostrategic considerations. France had developed a privileged relationship with Muhammad 'Ali's Egypt. In turn, the governor of Egypt made use of French military advisors for his army, drew on French engineers for his industrial needs and public works, and sent his students to France for advanced training. The French were keen to preserve their special relationship with Egypt as a means to extend their influence in the Eastern Mediterranean. The expansion of Egyptian power to Greece, however, posed a dilemma for the government in Paris. It would not serve France's interests to see Egypt grow stronger than France itself in the Eastern Mediterranean.

The situation was more clear-cut for the British government. London watched Paris extend its influence in Egypt with mounting concern. Since Napoleon's invasion, the British had sought to prevent France from dominating Egypt and the land-sea route to India. Britain had also been scarred by the continental wars of the Napoleonic era and worried that attempts by strong European powers to secure positions in Ottoman territory could reignite conflict between the European powers. The British government thus sought to preserve the territorial integrity of the Ottoman Empire to preserve the peace in Europe. It was clear that the Ottomans could not retain Greece on their own, and the British did not wish to see Egypt extend its power into the Balkans at the expense of the Ottoman Empire. Thus, British interests would best be served by assisting the Greeks to achieve greater autonomy within the Ottoman Empire and securing a withdrawal of both Ottoman and Egyptian troops from the disputed territories.

Muhammad 'Ali had nothing left to gain from his campaign in Greece. The war proved a tremendous drain on his treasury. His new Nizami army was overextended across Greece. The Ottomans were treating him with growing suspicion and clearly doing their best to deplete his army and his treasury. By the summer of 1827 the European powers had made clear their opposition to Egypt's position in Greece and had assembled a combined British, French, and Russian fleet to force an Ottoman and Egyptian withdrawal. The last thing the governor of Egypt wanted was to engage the European powers on the battlefield. As Muhammad 'Ali wrote to his political agent in Istanbul in October 1827, "We have to realize that we cannot stand up against the Europeans, and the only possible outcome [if we do so] will be sinking the entire fleet and causing the death of up to 30 or 40 thousand men." Though he was proud of his army and navy, Muhammad 'Ali knew they were no match for the British or the French. "Although we are men of war," he wrote, "yet we are still in the A-B-Cs of that art, whereas the Europeans are way ahead of us and have put their theories [about war] into practice."[15]

Though he had a clear vision of possible disaster, Muhammad 'Ali committed his navy to the cause and dispatched his fleet to Greece. The Ottomans were unwilling to concede independence to Greece, and the sultan decided to call the European powers' bluff and ignore their joint fleet. It was a fatal mistake. The allied fleet trapped the Egyptian ships in Navarino Bay and sank virtually all the seventy-eight Ottoman and Egyptian ships in a four-hour engagement on October 20, 1827. Over 3,000 Egyptian and Ottoman men were killed in the battle, along with nearly 200 men in the attacking allied fleet.

Muhammad 'Ali was furious at his losses and held Sultan Mahmud II responsible for the loss of his navy. Moreover, the Egyptians found themselves in the same position Napoleon had been in after the Battle of the Nile: thousands of soldiers were trapped, with no ships to provision or repatriate them. Muhammad 'Ali negotiated directly with the British to conclude a truce and repatriate his son Ibrahim Pasha and the Egyptian army from Greece without consulting the sultan. Mahmud II was outraged by his governor's insubordination, but Muhammad 'Ali no longer sought the sultan's favor. His days of loyal service were through. Henceforth, Muhammad 'Ali would pursue his own objectives at the sultan's expense.

Navarino was also a turning point in the Greek war of independence. Assisted by a French expeditionary force, Greek fighters drove Ottoman troops out of the Peloponnesian Peninsula and central Greece in the course of the year 1828. That December the governments of Britain, France, and Russia met and agreed to the creation of an independent Kingdom of Greece, then imposed their solution on the Ottoman Empire. After three more years of negotiations, the Kingdom of Greece was finally established in the London Conference of May 1832.

In the aftermath of the Greek debacle, Muhammad 'Ali trained his sights on Syria. He had aspired to rule over Syria since 1811, when he first agreed to lead the campaign against the Wahhabis. He petitioned the Porte for Syria both in 1811 and again after the defeat of the Wahhabis in 1818. The Ottomans rebuffed him both times, not wanting their governor in Egypt to become too powerful to serve the Porte's purposes. When Istanbul sought Egypt's assistance in Greece, the Porte held out the prospect of conferring Syria on Muhammad 'Ali. The Egyptian governor called this debt due after the loss of his fleet in Navarino, but to no avail: the Porte believed Muhammad 'Ali had been sufficiently weakened by his losses that it was no longer necessary to earn his goodwill.

Muhammad 'Ali recognized that the Porte had no intention of ever conceding Syria to him. He also knew the Ottomans had no force to prevent him from taking the territory for himself. No sooner had Ibrahim Pasha and his soldiers been repatriated to Egypt than Muhammad 'Ali set about building a new fleet and reequipping his army to invade Syria. He approached both the British and the French to gain their support for his ambitions. France showed some interest in entering into an agreement with the Egyptians, but Britain continued to oppose all threats to the territorial integrity of the Ottoman Empire. Undeterred, Muhammad 'Ali continued his preparations, and in November 1831 Ibrahim Pasha set off at the head of an invasion force to conquer Syria.

The Egyptian army was now at war with the Ottoman Empire. Ibrahim Pasha led his 30,000 men in the rapid conquest of Palestine. By the end of November his army had reached the northern stronghold of Acre. As reports of Egyptian movements reached Istanbul, the sultan sent a special envoy to persuade Muhammad 'Ali to call off his attack. When this had no effect, the Porte then called on its governors in Damascus and Aleppo to raise an army to repel the Egyptian invaders. They enjoyed a six-month window of opportunity while the Egyptian army laid siege to the near-impregnable fortress of Acre.

While the Ottomans prepared to repel the Egyptian invasion, some of the local leaders in Palestine and Lebanon chose to lend their support to Ibrahim Pasha to preserve their positions in the face of the new Egyptian threat. Amir Bashir II, the ruler of Mount Lebanon, entered into alliance with Ibrahim Pasha when the Egyptian army reached Acre. One of the members of Amir Bashir's ruling Shihabi family sent his trusted advisor, Mikhayil Mishaqa, to observe the Egyptian siege of Acre and report back to the rulers of Mount Lebanon.

Mishaqa spent nearly three weeks in Acre, following Egyptian operations first-hand. When he arrived, Mishaqa witnessed a fierce battle between the Egyptian navy and the Ottoman defenders in Acre. Muhammad 'Ali had committed twenty-two warships to the siege, and they fired more than 70,000 rounds into the citadel of Acre. The defenders put up a stiff fight and managed to disable many of the ships in heated exchanges. "Acre," Mishaqa wrote, "could not even be seen for the smoke of gunpowder" in shelling that lasted from morning to sunset. According to Mishaqa's sources, the

Egyptians fielded eight regiments of foot soldiers (18,000 men), eight cavalry regiments (4,000 men), and 2,000 Bedouin irregulars against "three thousand brave and experienced soldiers" defending Acre. Given the strength of Acre's sea walls and the earthworks protecting its land walls, Mishaqa warned his employers to expect a long siege.

For six months the Egyptians pummeled the fortress of Acre. By May 1832, the impregnable walls of the castle had been sufficiently reduced for Ibrahim Pasha to assemble his infantry to storm the citadel. He gave a rousing speech, reminding his veterans of their victories in Arabia and Greece. Retreat was not an option for the Egyptian army. To reinforce the point that there would be no turning back, Ibrahim Pasha warned that "cannons would be brought up behind them to blast any soldier who returned without having taken the walls." With these menacing words of encouragement, Ibrahim Pasha led his men in a charge on the shattered walls of Acre. They easily overran the ramparts and forced the surrender of the surviving defenders, reduced by months of fighting to just 350 men.[16]

With Acre now secured, Ibrahim Pasha set off for Damascus. The city's Ottoman governor mobilized 10,000 civilians in defense. Ibrahim Pasha knew that untrained civilians would not fight a professional army and ordered his troops to fire over their heads to frighten away the defenders. Sure enough, the sound of gunfire was enough to dispel the Damascenes. The governor retreated from the city to join Ottoman forces further north, and the Egyptians entered Damascus unopposed. Ibrahim Pasha ordered his soldiers to respect the townspeople and their property, and he declared a general amnesty for all the people of Damascus. As he intended to rule over the people of Syria, he had no wish to alienate them.

Ibrahim Pasha appointed a ruling council for Damascus and continued his relentless march to conquer Syria. The Egyptian commander took some of the notables of Damascus with him to ensure the townspeople would not revolt in his absence. Mikhayil Mishaqa once again followed the Egyptian campaign, gathering intelligence for the rulers of Mount Lebanon. As the Egyptians marched out of Damascus, he took a tally of their numbers: "eleven thousand foot soldiers, two thousand regular cavalry, three thousand [Bedouin] cavalry"—16,000 men in all, supported by forty-three cannons, and 3,000 transport camels for supplies and materiel. They marched to the town of Homs in central Syria, where they were joined by a further detachment of 6,000 Egyptian troops.

On July 8, the Egyptians engaged the Ottomans in their first major battle for control of Syria near the town of Homs. "It was a stirring sight," Mishaqa wrote. "When the regular Egyptian troops reached the battlefield, they were met by the more numerous regular Turkish troops. One hour before sunset the battle raged between the two sides with continuous fire of guns and cannon." From his hilltop, Mishaqa could not make out which way the battle would go. "It was a frightful hour, during which the very gates of hell were opened. At sundown the noise of guns was quieted, leaving only the pounding of cannon until an hour and a half after sunset, when total silence reigned." Only then did he learn that the Egyptians had secured total victory in the Battle of Homs. The fleeing Ottoman commanders had abandoned their camp in their haste. "Food was left burning over the fire, and medicine chests, rolls of dressing and shrouds [for the dead], a great number of furs and mantles for awards and much materiel were all left behind.[17]

The restless Ibrahim Pasha did not linger in Homs. One day after his victory, he drove his army northward to Aleppo to complete his conquest of Syria. Like Damascus, Aleppo surrendered without resisting the Egyptian army, and Ibrahim Pasha left behind a new administration to govern the city on Egypt's behalf. The Ottoman governor had withdrawn to join a large Ottoman army that included the surviving units from the Battle of Homs. On July 29 the Ottomans engaged the Egyptian army in the village of Belen, near the port of Alexandretta (now in modern Turkey, but at the time part of the province of Aleppo). Though outnumbered, the Egyptian forces inflicted heavy casualties on the Ottomans before accepting their surrender. Ibrahim Pasha then marched his forces to the port of Adana, where Egyptian ships could resupply his exhausted army. Ibrahim Pasha sent dispatches to Cairo detailing Egypt's victories and awaited further orders from his father.

Muhammad 'Ali moved from warfare to negotiations, trying to secure his gains in Syria either by the sultan's edict or through European intervention. The Ottomans, for their part, were unwilling to concede any gains to their renegade governor in Egypt. Rather than recognize his position in Syria, the Ottoman grand vizier (or prime minister) Mehmed Reshid Pasha began to mobilize a massive army of over 80,000 men to drive the Egyptians from the Turkish coast and out of Syria altogether. After rebuilding his army and his stores, Ibrahim Pasha set off into Central Anatolia in October 1832 to face down the Ottoman threat. He occupied the city of Konya that month, where he prepared for battle.

The Egyptian army would now have to fight in the most inhospitable environment imaginable. Used to the desert heat of summer and the temperate winters along the Nile, the Egyptian troops found themselves in the driving snow and subfreezing temperatures of winter on the Anatolian plateau. Yet even in such conditions, the unwilling conscripts proved the more disciplined army, and though outnumbered, they secured a total victory over Ottoman troops in the Battle of Konya (December 21, 1832). The Egyptians even managed to take the grand vizier prisoner, which strengthened their bargaining position enormously.

Upon receiving news of his army's defeat and the capture of his grand vizier, the sultan capitulated and agreed to most of Muhammad 'Ali's territorial demands. He had no military options following the defeat of his army at Konya, and he now faced an Egyptian army billeted in the western Anatolian town of Kütahya, just 200 kilometers (124 miles) from the imperial capital, Istanbul. In order to secure a complete withdrawal of Egyptian forces from Anatolia, Mahmud II reestablished Muhammad 'Ali as governor of Egypt (he had been stripped of the title and declared a renegade following his invasion) and conferred the provinces of Hijaz, Crete, Acre, Damascus, Tripoli, and Aleppo on Muhammad 'Ali and Ibrahim Pasha, with the right to collect taxes from the port city of Adana. These gains were confirmed in the May 1833 Peace of Kütahya, brokered by Russia and France.

Following the Peace of Kütahya, Ibrahim Pasha withdrew his troops to Syria and Egypt. Muhammad 'Ali had not achieved the independence to which he had aspired. The Ottomans had bound him firmly to their empire's rule. But he had secured most of the Arab provinces of the Ottoman Empire for his family's rule, creating an Egyptian empire that rivaled the Ottomans for the rest of the 1830s.

Egyptian rule proved very unpopular in Syria. A new tax laid a heavy burden on all layers of society, from the poorest worker to the richest merchant, and local leaders were alienated when they were stripped of their traditional powers. "When the Egyptians began to alter the customs of the clans and institute more taxation of the inhabitants than they were accustomed to pay," Mishaqa recorded, "the people began to despise them and, wishing for the rule of the Turks back again, manifested signs of rebellion." The Egyptians responded by disarming and conscripting the Syrians into their service, which only compounded the opposition. "A soldier had no fixed period of service after which he would be free to return to his family, but rather his service was as everlasting as hell," Mishaqa explained.[18] Many young men took flight to avoid conscription, further undermining productivity in the local economy. Rebellion spread from the Alawite Mountains on the Syrian coast to the Druze in Mount Lebanon and southern Syria, to Nablus in the Palestinian highlands. Between 1834 and 1839, Ibrahim Pasha found his troops pinned down in the suppression of an accelerating cycle of revolts.

Muhammad 'Ali was undeterred by popular unrest in the Syrian countryside and viewed Syria as a permanent addition to his Egyptian empire. He worked assiduously to gain European support for a plan to secede from the Ottoman Empire and to establish an independent kingdom in Egypt and Syria. In May 1838 he informed the Porte and the European powers of his determination to establish his own kingdom, offering the Ottomans a severance fee of £3 million ($15 million). British Prime Minister Palmerston responded with a stern warning that "the Pasha [Muhammad 'Ali] must expect to find Great Britain taking part with the Sultan in order to obtain redress for so flagrant a wrong done to the Sultan, and for the purpose of preventing the Dismemberment of the Turkish empire."[19] Even Muhammad 'Ali's French allies warned him against taking measures that would draw him into confrontation with both the sultan and Europe.

Buoyed by European support, the Ottomans decided to take immediate action against Muhammad 'Ali. Sultan Mahmud II mobilized another massive campaign force. Since the violent disbanding of the Janissaries in 1826, Mahmud had made great investments in a new Ottoman Nizami army. His top officers assured him that his modern German-trained infantry was more than a match for the Egyptians, battle-weary after five years of suppressing popular rebellions in Syria. The Ottomans marched to the Syrian frontiers near Aleppo and attacked Ibrahim Pasha's forces on June 24, 1839. Contrary to all expectations, the Egyptians routed the Ottomans in the Battle of Nezib, inflicting massive casualties and taking more than 10,000 prisoners.

Sultan Mahmud II never received word of his army's defeat. Suffering from tuberculosis, the sultan's health had been deteriorating for months, and he died on June 30 before learning of the disaster at Nezib. He was succeeded by his adolescent son, Sultan Abdulmecid I (r. 1839–1861), whose youth and inexperience did little to calm nerves among the commanders of the empire. The admiral of the Ottoman fleet, Ahmed Fevzi Pasha, sailed his entire navy across the Mediterranean and placed it under Muhammad 'Ali's command. The admiral feared the fleet might fall to Russian control if, as he expected, they intervened to prop up the young sultan. He also believed Muhammad 'Ali to be the leader most capable of preserving the Ottoman Empire; a virile rebel would make a better sultan than a callow crown prince. Panic spread across Istanbul. The young sultan faced the greatest internal threat in Ottoman history with no army or navy to defend him.

The European powers were no less concerned by the turmoil in Ottoman domains than the Ottomans themselves. Britain feared that Russia would take advantage of the power vacuum to seize the Straits of the Bosporus and Dardanelles to secure access for its Black Sea fleet to enter the Mediterranean. This would overturn decades of British policies designed to contain the Russian fleet in the Black Sea and deny it access to warm water ports, preserving the balance of maritime power to Britain's advantage. The British also hoped to frustrate French ambitions to extend its ally Egypt's rule over the Eastern Mediterranean. Britain headed a coalition of European powers (from which France abstained) to intervene in the crisis, both to shore up the Ottoman dynasty and to force Muhammad 'Ali to withdraw from Turkey and Syria.

Negotiations dragged on for one year, as Muhammad 'Ali tried to leverage his victory at Nezib to secure more territorial and sovereign privileges, while the British and the Porte pressed for Egypt's withdrawal from Syria. In July 1840 the European coalition—Britain, Austria, Prussia, and Russia—offered Muhammad 'Ali lifetime rule over Damascus and hereditary rule over Egypt if his soldiers withdrew from the rest of Syria immediately. With the British and Austrian fleet assembling in the Eastern Mediterranean to take action, it was their last offer. Believing he had the support of France, Muhammad 'Ali rejected the offer.

The allied fleet approached the port city of Beirut under the command of British Admiral Napier, and on September 11 they bombarded Egyptian positions. The

British used local agents to circulate pamphlets throughout Syria and Lebanon calling on the local people to rise up against the Egyptians. The people of Greater Syria had done so in the past, and were only too happy to do so again. The allied fleet meanwhile proceeded from Beirut to Acre to drive the Egyptians from the citadel. The Egyptians had assumed they could withstand any attack, but the joint Anglo-Austrian-Ottoman fleet took the citadel within three hours and twenty minutes, according to Mikhayil Mishaqa. The Egyptians had just taken delivery of gunpowder, which lay stacked and exposed in the center of the citadel. A shot from one of the allied ships detonated the powder "in such an unexpected fashion that the soldiers inside Acre fled, leaving no one to defend it."[20] The European and Ottoman forces retook Acre and established their control over the whole of the Syrian coast.

Ibrahim Pasha found his position increasingly untenable. Cut off from the sea, he had no means to resupply his troops, which were now constantly harassed by the local population. He withdrew his forces from Turkey and all parts of Syria to Damascus. As soon as his soldiers—some 70,000 in all—had assembled in Damascus, Ibrahim Pasha began an orderly withdrawal from Syria along the overland route to Egypt in January 1841.

The Egyptian menace had been contained, but the threat posed by the Second Egyptian Crisis to the survival of the Ottoman Empire required a formal settlement. In a deal brokered in London, the Ottomans conferred on Muhammad 'Ali lifetime rule over Egypt and Sudan and established his family's hereditary rule over Egypt. Muhammad 'Ali, for his part, recognized the sultan as his suzerain and agreed to make an annual payment to the Porte as a token of his submission and loyalty to the Ottoman state.

Britain also wanted assurance that troubles in the Eastern Mediterranean would never again threaten the peace of Europe. The best insurance against conflict among the European powers for strategic advantage in the Levant was to ensure the territorial integrity of the Ottoman Empire—long a preoccupation of Lord Palmerston, the British prime minister. In a secret appendix to the London Convention of 1840, the governments of Britain, Austria, Prussia, and Russia gave a formal commitment to "seek no augmentation of territory, no exclusive influence, [and] no commercial advantage for their subjects, which those of every other nation may not equally obtain."[21] This self-denying protocol provided the Ottoman Empire with nearly four decades of protection against European designs on its territory.

Between 1805 and 1841, Muhammad 'Ali's ambitions had gone full circle. He rose to rank of governor and made himself master of Egypt. Once he was secure in Egypt and had expanded the revenues of his province, he set about creating a modern military. He then expanded his territorial reach from Sudan and Hijaz in the Red Sea to include much of Greece for a while, and all of Syria. These gains were denied him by foreign intervention, and by 1841 he had been reduced to Egypt and Sudan. Egypt would have its own government and make its own laws, but it would remain bound by the foreign policy of the Ottoman Empire. Though the Egyptians could strike their own coinage, their gold and silver coins would bear the sultan's name, leaving the name of the Egyptian ruler for base copper. Egypt would have its own army, but its numbers were restricted to 18,000—a far cry from the massive army of 100,000–200,000 that Egypt formerly fielded. Muhammad 'Ali's accomplishments were great, but his ambitions had been greater.

Muhammad 'Ali's final years in office were marked by disappointment and ill health. The pasha was now an old man—seventy-one years old by the time his army had returned from Syria. He had grown alienated from his son Ibrahim. Over the course of the Syrian campaign, father and son communicated through palace officials. Both fought illness—Ibrahim was sent to Europe to combat tuberculosis, and Muhammad 'Ali was beginning to lose his mental faculties to silver nitrate treatments he was given to combat dysentery. In 1847 the sultan recognized that Muhammad 'Ali was no longer sufficiently competent to rule and appointed Ibrahim Pasha to succeed him. Ibrahim died six months later. By that time, Muhammad 'Ali was too far gone to notice. The succession passed to Muhammad 'Ali's grandson, Abbas, who officiated at Muhammad 'Ali's funeral after the pasha's death on August 2, 1849.

The age of local leaders had come to an end. As the Egyptians were divested of Crete, the Syrian provinces, and the Hijaz, the Ottoman government was careful to dispatch its own men to serve as governors in these provinces. The Azm family in Damascus, like the Jalilis in Mosul, lost their grip over the cities they had ruled for much of the eighteenth century. The autonomous government of Mount Lebanon collapsed as the Shihab family was overthrown for collaborating with Egyptian rule. Here too the Ottomans sought to impose their own governors, though with explosive consequences that would send Lebanon down the road to sectarian conflict. The bid for local autonomy from the Ottoman government had come at a high price for the working people of the Arab lands, who suffered through wars, inflation, political instability, and countless injustices at the hands of ambitious local leaders. They now wanted peace and stability.

The Ottomans too wanted to put an end to the internal challenges to their rule. While preoccupied by foreign threats and wars with Russia and Austria, they had seen the risks of leaving the Arab provinces unattended: the alliance between Ali Bey al-Kabir and Zahir al-Umar had threatened Ottoman rule in Syria and Egypt; the Wahhabis had ravaged southern Iraq and seized the Hijaz from Ottoman rule;

and Muhammad 'Ali used the wealth of Egypt to create an army that gave him control of an empire in his own right and the means to threaten the very survival of the Ottomans themselves. But for the intervention of the European powers, Muhammad 'Ali could have toppled the Ottomans in the Second Egyptian Crisis. These experiences had impressed on the Ottoman government the need for reform. It would require not just a gentle tinkering with the standing institutions of government but a complete overhaul of the ancient machinery of rule.

The Ottomans recognized that they could not reform their empire on their own. They would need to draw on the ideas and technologies that had made their European rivals strong. Ottoman statesmen had noted how Muhammad 'Ali succeeded in harnessing modern European ideas and technologies in creating his dynamic state. The dispatch of Egyptian missions to Europe, the import of European industrial and military technology, and the contracting of European technical advisors at all levels of the military and bureaucracy had played a large role in Muhammad 'Ali's achievements.

The Ottomans were entering a new and complex era in their relations with their European neighbors. Europe would serve as the role model, the ideal to be attained in military and technological terms. But Europe was also a threat to be kept at arm's length, both as a belligerent that coveted Ottoman lands and the source of dangerous new ideologies. Ottoman reformers would struggle with the challenge of adopting European ideas and technology without compromising their own cultural integrity and values.

The one thing the Ottomans could not do was ignore Europe's progress. Europe had emerged as the dominant world power in the nineteenth century, and the Ottoman Empire increasingly would be obliged to play by Europe's rules.

CHAPTER 4

The Perils of Reform

A young Muslim cleric approached the French sailing vessel *La Truite*, moored in Alexandria's harbor, on April 13, 1826. As he stepped onto the gangway to board, dressed in the robes and turban of a scholar of Cairo's ancient mosque university of al-Azhar (founded 969), Rifa'a al-Tahtawi's feet left Egyptian soil for the first time in his life. He was bound for France, appointed chaplain to Muhammad 'Ali's first major education mission to Europe. He would not see his native land for another five years.

Once aboard, al-Tahtawi examined the faces of the other delegates. They made for a very diverse group: forty-four men in all, ranging in age from fifteen to thirty-seven. Al-Tahtawi (1801–1873) was then twenty-four years old. Though ostensibly an Egyptian delegation, only eighteen of its envoys were actually native-born Arabic speakers. The rest of the group spoke Turkish and reflected the national diversity of the Ottoman Empire, of which Egypt was still a part—Turks, Circassians, Greeks, Georgians, and Armenians. These men had been chosen by the governor of Egypt to study European languages and sciences and, on their return, to apply what they learned in France to reforming their native land.

Born to a notable family of judges and theologians in a small village in Upper Egypt, al-Tahtawi had studied Arabic and Islamic theology since the age of sixteen. A gifted scholar, he was appointed to teach at al-Azhar before entering government service as a preacher in one of the new European-style Nizami infantry divisions in 1824. Through this post, and with the support of his patrons, al-Tahtawi was selected for this prestigious mission to Paris. It was the kind of posting that made a man's career.

Al-Tahtawi took with him a blank copybook in which to record his impressions of France. No detail seemed too trivial to interest him: the way the French built their houses, earned a living, observed their religion; their means of transport and the workings of their financial system; relations between men and women; how they dressed and danced; how they decorated their homes and set their tables. Al-Tahtawi wrote with curiosity and respect but also critical detachment. For centuries, Europeans had traveled to the Middle East and written books on the manners and customs of the exotic people they found there. Now, for the first time, an Egyptian had turned the tables and wrote on the strange and exotic country called France.[1]

Al-Tahtawi's reflections on France are full of contradictions. As a Muslim and an Egyptian Ottoman, he was confident of the superiority of his faith and culture. He saw France as a place of disbelief, where "not a single Muslim had settled" and where the French themselves were "Christians only in name." Yet his firsthand observations left him in no doubt of Europe's superiority in science and technology. "By God, during my stay in [France], I was grieved by the fact that it had enjoyed all those things that are lacking in Islamic kingdoms," he recalled.[2] To give some sense of the gulf that al-Tahtawi believed separated his readers from Western science, he judged it necessary to explain that European astronomers had proven that the earth was round. He realized how much the Islamic world had fallen behind Europe in the sciences and believed that the Islamic world had a duty and a right to recover this knowledge, given that Western advances since the Renaissance had been built on medieval Islam's progress in the sciences. He argued that the Ottomans were only calling due the West's debts to Islamic science by borrowing European advances in modern technology.[3]

Although al-Tahtawi's book is replete with fascinating reflections on what, in Egyptian eyes, made France of the 1820s tick, he made his most substantial contribution to political reform with his analysis of constitutional government. He translated all seventy-four articles of the 1814 French constitution, or *Charte constitutionelle*, and wrote a detailed analysis of its key points.[4] Al-Tahtawi believed the constitution to hold the secret of French advancement. "We should like to include this," he explained to his elite readership, "so that you may see how their intellect has decided that justice and equity are the causes for the civilization of kingdoms, the well-being of subjects, and how rulers and their subjects were led by this, to the extent that their country has prospered, their knowledge increased, their wealth accumulated and their hearts satisfied."

Al-Tahtawi's praise for constitutional government was courageous for its time. These were dangerous new ideas with no roots in Islamic tradition. As he confessed, most of the principles of the French constitution "cannot be found in the Qur'an nor in the *sunna* [practices] of the Prophet." He may have feared the reaction of his fellow Muslim clerics to these dangerous innovations, but he took the even greater risk of provoking the disfavor of his rulers. After all, the constitution applied to the king and his subjects alike, and it called for a division of powers between the monarch and an elected legislature. Muhammad 'Ali's Egypt was a thoroughly autocratic state, and the Ottoman Empire was an absolute monarchy. The very notion of representative government or constraints on the powers of the monarch would have been seen as alien and subversive by most Ottoman elites.

The reformist cleric was captivated by the way the French constitution promoted the rights of common citizens rather than reinforcing the dominance of elites. Among the articles of the constitution that most impressed al-Tahtawi were those asserting the equality of all citizens before the law and the eligibility of all citizens "to any office, irrespective of its rank." The possibility of such upward mobility, he maintained, would encourage "people to study and learn" so that they might "reach a higher position than the one they occupy," thereby keeping their civilization from stagnating. Here again, al-Tahtawi was treading a fine line. In a rigidly hierarchical society like Ottoman Egypt, ideas of social mobility would have struck the elites of his time as a dangerous notion.

Al-Tahtawi went further, praising French rights of free expression. The constitution, he explained, encouraged "everybody freely to express his opinion, knowledge and feelings." The medium by which the average Frenchman made his views known, Al-Tahtawi continued, was something called a "journal" or a "gazette." This would have been the first time many of al-Tahtawi's readers would have heard of newspapers, which were still unknown in the Arabic-speaking world. Both the powerful and the common people could publish their views in the newspapers, he explained. Indeed, he stressed the importance of commoners having access to the press "since even a lowly person may think of something that does not come to the mind of important people." Yet it was the power of the press to hold people to account for their actions that struck the cleric as truly remarkable. "When someone does something great or despicable, the journalists write about it, so that it becomes known by both the notables and the common people—to encourage the person who did something good, or to make the person who has done a despicable thing forsake his ways."

In his most daring breach of Ottoman political conventions, al-Tahtawi gave a detailed and sympathetic account of the July 1830 revolution that overthrew the Bourbon king Charles X. Sunni Muslim political thought asserted the duty of subjects to submit to rulers, even despotic rulers, in the interest of public order. Al-Tahtawi, who had observed the political drama firsthand, clearly sided with the French people against their king when Charles X suspended the charter and "shamed the laws in which the rights of the French people were enshrined." In his bid to restore the absolute power of the monarchy, Charles X ignored the deputies in the Chamber, forbade public criticism of the monarch and his cabinet, and introduced press censorship. When the people rose in armed rebellion against their ruler, the Egyptian

cleric took their side. Al-Tahtawi's extensive analysis of the July Revolution is all
the more remarkable for its implicit endorsement of the people's right to overturn a
monarch to preserve their legal rights.[5]

After five captivating years in Paris, al-Tahtawi returned to Egypt in 1831, his
impressions of France still confined to his copybook. Fluent in French, he was given
a high-level appointment to establish a government translation bureau, primarily to
provide Arabic editions of European technical manuals essential for Muhammad
'Ali's reforms. While he was busy setting up the translation bureau, al-Tahtawi found
time to revise his notes on Paris for publication. Perhaps to protect himself from
retribution for the dangerous political ideas his book contained, he paid lavish tribute to Muhammad 'Ali in his preface. The results, published in Arabic in 1834 and
subsequently translated into Turkish, were nothing short of a masterpiece. With its
clear exposition of European advances in science and technology, and its analysis of
Enlightenment political philosophy, al-Tahtawi's book proved the opening shot in
the nineteenth-century age of Ottoman—and Arab—reforms.

The Ottomans and their Arab citizens experienced increased interaction with
Europe throughout the nineteenth century, forcing the people of the Middle
East to recognize that Europe had surpassed them in military and economic might.
Although most Ottomans remained convinced of the cultural superiority of their
world, their reformers argued that they needed to gain mastery over the ideas and
technology of Europe if Europe was not to gain mastery over them.

The Ottomans and their autonomous Arab vassals in Egypt and Tunisia began by
reforming their armies. It soon became apparent that the revenue base of the state
had to expand to support the expense of a modern army. Administrative and economic practices thus were changed along European lines with the hope that prosperity
and increased tax revenues would follow. More and more European technology was
imported, pushed by European capitalists looking for foreign markets for their manufactured goods and machinery. The sultan and his viceroys in Tunis and Cairo were
keen to use the benefits of modern European technology—such as telegraphs, steam-
ships, and railways—as visible signs of progress and development. This technology
was expensive, however, and as the educated elite in Istanbul, Cairo, and Tunis grew
concerned about their rulers' extravagance, they began to call for constitutions and
parliaments as the missing element in the reform agenda.

Each phase of the reforms was intended to strengthen the institutions of the Ottoman Empire and its Arab vassal states and to protect them from European encroachment. In this, the reformers were to be disappointed, for the reform era left the
Ottoman world increasingly vulnerable to European penetration. Informal European

control through consular pressure, trade, and capital investment would be followed by formal European domination as first Tunisia, then the Ottoman government, and finally Egypt failed to meet their financial commitments to foreign creditors.

The era of Ottoman reforms began at the height of the Second Egyptian Crisis, in 1839. The death of Sultan Mahmud II and the accession of his teenage son Abdulmecid I was hardly an auspicious moment to announce a program of radical reform. Yet the Ottoman Empire, under imminent threat from Muhammad 'Ali's Egyptian army, needed European goodwill more than ever. To secure Europe's guarantees of its territory and sovereignty, the Ottoman government believed it needed to demonstrate to the European powers that it could adhere to European norms of statecraft as a responsible member of the community of modern states. Moreover, the reformers who had worked under Mahmud II were determined to consolidate the changes already undertaken under the late sultan's reign, and to commit his successor to the reform process.

These twin motives would characterize the era of Ottoman reforms: public relations gestures to win European support coupled with a genuine commitment to reform the empire in order to ensure its survival against both internal and external threats. On November 3, 1839, the Ottoman foreign minister, Mustafa Reshid Pasha, read a reform decree on behalf of Abdulmecid I to an invited group of Ottoman and foreign dignitaries in Istanbul. On that date the Ottomans entered a period of administrative reforms that, between 1839 and 1876, would transform their state into a constitutional monarchy with an elected parliament—a period known as the Tanzimat (literally, "reordering").

Three major milestones mark the Tanzimat: the 1839 Reform Decree; the 1856 Reform Decree, which restated and extended the agenda of 1839; and the Constitution of 1876. The decrees of 1839 and 1856 reveal the debt of Ottoman reformers to Western political thought. The first document set out a modest, three-point reform agenda: to ensure "perfect security for life, honour, and property" for all Ottoman subjects; to establish "a regular system of assessing taxes"; and to reform the terms of military service by regular conscription and fixed terms of service.[6]

The 1856 Decree reiterated the reforms set out in 1839 and expanded on the process to address reforms in the courts and penal system. Corporal punishment was to be curbed, and torture abolished. The decree sought to regularize the finances of the empire through annual budgets that would be open to public scrutiny. The decree also called for the modernization of the financial system and the establishment of a modern banking system "to create funds to be employed in augmenting the sources of wealth" in the empire through such public works as roads and canals. "To accomplish these objects," the decree concluded, "means shall be sought to profit by the science, the art, and the funds of Europe, and thus gradually to execute them."[7]

However, to view the Tanzimat in the light of the major decrees alone would be to overlook the full scope of reforms carried out between 1839 and 1876. The middle decades of the nineteenth century witnessed a major transformation in the chief institutions of Ottoman state and society. In order to reform the tax base and ensure its future prosperity, the government began to conduct a regular census and introduced a new system of land records that replaced the tax farms of old with individual title, which was more in line with Western notions of private property. The provincial administration was completely overhauled to provide a regular system of government reaching from provincial capitals like Damascus and Baghdad down to the village level.

These changes required thousands of new bureaucrats with a modern, technical education. To meet this need, the state established a network of new elementary, intermediate, and high schools styled on European curricula to train civil servants. Similarly, the laws of the empire were codified in an ambitious project to reconcile Islamic law with Western codes to make the Ottoman legal system more compatible with European legal norms.

So long as the reforms applied to the higher echelons of government, the subjects of the Ottoman Empire took little interest in the Tanzimat. In the course of the 1850s and 1860s, however, the reforms began to touch the lives of individuals. Ever fearful of taxation and conscription, Ottoman subjects resisted all state efforts to inscribe their names in the government's registers. Parents avoided sending their children to state schools, fearing that by registering their names for study they would end up in the army. Townsmen avoided census officials and farmers avoided land registration for as long as they could. Yet as the bureaucracy grew in size and efficiency, the people of the empire succumbed to one of the imperatives of modern government: to maintain accurate records on the state's subjects and their property.

The sultan was no less affected by the reform process than his subjects. The absolute power of the Ottoman sultan eroded as the center of political gravity shifted from the sultan's palace to the offices of the Ottoman government in the Sublime Porte. The Council of Ministers took on the principal legislative and executive roles in government, and the grand vizier emerged as the head of government. The sultan was reduced to the ceremonial and symbolic role of head of state. This evolution was capped by the promulgation of the constitution in 1876, which, while leaving great powers in the sultan's hands, broadened political participation through the establishment of a parliament. In the course of thirty-seven years, Ottoman absolutism had been replaced by a constitutional monarchy.

There are dangers inherent in any major reform program, particularly when foreign ideas are involved. Conservative Ottoman Muslims denounced the Tanzimat for introducing un-Islamic innovations into state and society. No issue proved more explosive than changes to the status of Christians and Jews as non-Muslim minority communities in Sunni Muslim Ottoman society.

Over the course of the nineteenth century, the European powers increasingly used minority rights as a pretext to intervene in Ottoman affairs. Russia extended its protection to the Eastern Orthodox Church, the largest Ottoman Christian community. France had long enjoyed a special relationship with the Maronite church in Mount Lebanon and in the nineteenth century developed formal patronage of all Ottoman Catholic communities. The British had no historic ties to any church in the region. Nonetheless, Britain represented the interests of the Jews, the Druze, and the tiny communities of converts that gathered around Protestant missionaries in the Arab world. So long as the Ottoman Empire straddled areas of strategic importance, the European powers would exploit any means to meddle with Ottoman affairs. Issues of minority rights provided the powers with ample opportunity to impose their will on the Ottomans—sometimes with disastrous consequences for both Europeans and Ottomans alike.

The "Holy Places Dispute" of 1851–1852 demonstrated the dangers of great-power intervention on all parties. Differences arose between Catholic and Greek Orthodox monks over their respective rights and privileges to Christian holy places in Palestine. France and Russia responded by putting pressure on Istanbul to confer privileges on their respective client communities. The Ottomans first conceded to French pressures, giving the keys to the Church of the Nativity in Bethlehem to the Catholics. The Russians were determined to secure a bigger trophy for the Greek Orthodox Church so as not to lose face to the French. But after the Ottomans made similar concessions to the Russians, the French emperor Napoleon III dispatched a state-of-the-art propeller-driven warship up the Dardanelles to deliver his ambassador to Istanbul and threatened to bombard Ottoman positions in North Africa if the Porte did not rescind the concessions to Russia's Orthodox clients. When the Ottomans caved in to the French, the Russians threatened war. What began as an Ottoman-Russian war in the autumn of 1853 degenerated into the Crimean War of 1854–1855, pitting Britain and France against Tsarist Russia in a violent conflict that claimed over 300,000 lives and left many more wounded. The consequences of European intervention on behalf of Ottoman minority communities were too serious for the Porte to allow the practice to continue.

The Ottomans had made a half-hearted attempt to reclaim the initiative over non-Muslim minority communities in the 1839 Reform Decree. "The Muslim and non-Muslim subjects of our lofty Sultanate shall, without exception, enjoy our imperial concessions," the sultan declared in his *firman*, or rescript. Clearly he and his administrators needed to make a stronger statement of equality between Muslims and non-Muslims if they were to persuade the European powers that their interventions were no longer needed to ensure the welfare of Christians and Jews in the

Ottoman Empire. The problem for the Ottoman government was to gain the consent of its own Muslim majority for a policy of equality between different faiths. The Qur'an draws clear distinctions between Muslims and the other two monotheistic faiths, and these distinctions had been enshrined in Islamic law. For the Ottoman government to disregard such distinctions would, in the view of many believers, go against God's book and God's law.

In the aftermath of the Crimean War the Ottoman government decided to risk public outrage at home to prevent further European interventions on behalf of the non-Muslim minority communities of the empire. The 1856 Reform Decree was timed to coincide with the Peace of Paris, concluding the Crimean War. Most of the provisions of the 1856 Reform Decree were concerned with the rights and responsibilities of Ottoman Christians and Jews. The decree established for the first time complete equality of all Ottoman subjects regardless of their religion: "Every distinction or designation pending to make any class whatever of the subjects of my empire inferior to another class, on account of their religion, language, or race, shall be forever effaced from administrative protocol." The decree went on to promise all Ottoman subjects access to schools and government jobs, as well as to military conscription, without distinction by religion or nationality.

The reform process had already been controversial for its European leanings. But nothing in the reforms prior to the 1856 Decree had directly contravened the Qur'an—revered by Muslims as the literal and eternal Word of God. To contradict the Qur'an was to contradict God, and not surprisingly the decree provoked outrage among pious Muslims when it was read in the cities of the empire. An Ottoman judge in Damascus recorded in his diary in 1856, "The decree conferring complete equality on Christians was read in Court, granting equality and freedom and other such violations of the eternal Islamic law. . . . It was ashes on [the heads of] all Muslims. We ask Him to strengthen the religion and make the Muslims victorious."[8] Ottoman subjects understood immediately the significance of this particular reform.

The reforms of the Tanzimat were taking the Ottoman Empire into dangerous territory. With the government promulgating reforms that contravened the religion and values of the majority of the population, the reform process risked provoking rebellion against the authority of the government and violence between its subjects.

The Ottomans were not the first Muslim rulers to decree equality between Muslims, Christians, and Jews. Muhammad 'Ali had done this in Egypt in the 1820s; however, this earlier decree had more to do with Muhammad 'Ali's wish to tax and conscript all Egyptians on an equal basis, without distinction by religion, than with any concern to liberate minority communities. Although objections undoubtedly were raised among pious Muslims when the principle of equality was applied during the Egyptian occupation of Greater Syria in the 1830s, Muhammad 'Ali was sufficiently strong to face down his critics and impose his will. Having observed Muhammad 'Ali's reforms, the Ottomans likely believed they could follow his precedent without provoking civil strife.

The Egyptian occupation had also opened the Arab provinces of the Ottoman Empire to European commercial penetration. Beirut emerged as an important port in the Eastern Mediterranean, and merchants gained access to new markets in inland cities formerly closed to Western merchants, such as Damascus. European merchants came to rely on local Christians and Jews to serve as their intermediaries—as translators and agents. Individual Christians and Jews grew wealthy through these connections to European trade and consular activity, and many gained immunity from Ottoman law by accepting European citizenship.

The Muslim community in Greater Syria was already growing dangerously resentful of the privileges enjoyed by some Arab Christians and Jews in the 1840s. The delicate communal balance was being upset by external forces. For the first time in generations, the Arab provinces witnessed sectarian violence. The Jews of Damascus were accused of the ritual murder of a Catholic priest in 1840 and were subsequently subject to violent repression by the authorities.[9] In October 1850, communal violence broke out in Aleppo when a Muslim mob attacked the city's prosperous Christian minority, leaving dozens killed and hundreds wounded. Such events were unprecedented in Aleppo's history and reflected the resentment of Muslim merchants whose businesses had suffered while their Christian neighbors were enriched through their commercial contacts with Europe.[10]

Greater trouble was brewing in Mount Lebanon. The Egyptian occupation in the 1830s had led to the collapse of the local ruling order and drove a wedge between the Maronites, who had allied with the Egyptians, and the Druze, who had resisted them. The Druze returned to Mount Lebanon after the Egyptian withdrawal to find the Maronites had grown wealthy and powerful in their absence—and claimed lands the Druze had abandoned when they fled Egyptian rule. The differences between the communities led to an outbreak of communal fighting in 1841, which continued intermittently over the next two decades, fueled by British support for the Druze and French support for the Maronites.

The Ottomans tried to take advantage of the power vacuum left by the retreating Egyptian forces to assert greater control over the administration of Mount Lebanon. They replaced the discredited Shihabi principality that had ruled since the end of the seventeenth century with a dual governorate, headed by a Maronite in the northern district and a Druze governor to the south of the Beirut-Damascus road. This sectarian split had no basis either in geography or in the demography of Mount Lebanon, as Maronites and Druze were to be found on both sides of the boundary.

As a result, the dual governorate seemed only to exacerbate tensions between the two communities. To make matters worse, the Maronites suffered from internal cleavages, with deep divisions between the ruling families, the peasants, and the clergy erupting in peasant revolts that further heightened tensions. By 1860 Mount Lebanon had become a powder keg as the Druze and Maronites formed armed bands and prepared for war.

On May 27, 1860, a Christian force of 3,000 men from the town of Zahleh marched toward the Druze heartland to avenge attacks on Christian villagers. They engaged a smaller force of some 600 Druze, who met them on the Beirut-Damascus road near the village of 'Ayn Dara. The Druze dealt the Christians a decisive defeat and went on the offensive, sacking a number of Christian villages. The battle of 'Ayn Dara marked the beginning of a war of extermination. The Maronite Christians suffered one defeat after another, as their towns and villages were overrun by the victorious Druze in what today would be characterized as ethnic cleansing. Eyewitnesses spoke of rivers of blood flowing through the streets of the highland villages.

Within three weeks the Druze had secured the south of Mount Lebanon and the whole of the Biqa' Valley. The town of Zahleh, to the north of the Beirut-Damascus road, was the last Christian stronghold to fall. On June 18, the Druze attacked and overran Zahleh, killing the defenders and putting its residents to flight. The Christian forces of Lebanon had been utterly destroyed, leaving the Druze in full mastery. At least 200 villages had been sacked and thousands of Christians killed, wounded, or left homeless.[11]

Events in Mount Lebanon heightened communal tensions throughout Greater Syria. Relations between Muslims and Christians had already been strained by the proclamation of the 1856 Reform Decree and the establishment of legal equality between Ottoman citizens of all faiths. Various Damascene chroniclers noted how the Christians had changed since gaining their legal rights. They no longer recognized the customary privileges of the Muslims, but began to wear the same colors and clothes that formerly had been reserved for Muslims. They grew increasingly assertive, too. "So it came about," one outraged Muslim notable recorded, "that when a Christian quarrelled with a Muslim, the Christian would fling back at the Muslim any insults the latter used, and even add to them."[12] The Muslims of Damascus found such behavior intolerable.

These views were echoed by a Christian notable. Mikhayil Mishaqa was a native of Mount Lebanon who had served the ruling Shihabi family at the time of the Egyptian occupation in the 1830s. He had since moved to Damascus, where he secured an appointment as the vice consul of a relatively minor power at the time, the United States of America. "As the Empire began to implement reforms and equality among its subjects regardless of their religious affiliation," he wrote, "the ignorant

Christians went too far in their interpretation of equality and thought that the small did not have to submit to the great, and the low did not have to respect the high. Indeed they thought that humble Christians were on a par with exalted Muslims."[13] By flaunting such age-old conventions, the Christians of Damascus unwittingly contributed to sectarian tensions that would prove their undoing.

The Muslim community within Damascus followed the bloody events of Mount Lebanon with grim satisfaction. They believed, with some justification, that the Christians of Lebanon had behaved arrogantly and had provoked the Druze. The Damascene Muslims were pleased to see the Christians defeated, and they showed no remorse over the bloodletting. When they heard of the fall of Zahleh, "there was such rejoicing and celebration in Damascus," Mishaqa recorded, that "you would have thought the Empire had conquered Russia." Faced with the growing hostility of the Muslims of the city, the Christians of Damascus began to fear for their own safety.

Following the fall of Zahleh, Druze bands began to raid Christian villages in the hinterlands of Damascus. The Christian peasants fled their exposed villages for the relative safety of Damascus's walls. The streets of the Christian quarters of Damascus began to fill with these Christian refugees, who, Mishaqa claimed, "slept in the lanes around the churches, with no bed save the ground and no cover save the sky." These defenseless people became the target of growing anti-Christian sentiment, their vulnerability and poverty diminishing their very humanity to those who were increasingly hostile to the Christian community. They looked to their fellow Christians and to the Ottoman governor to shelter them from harm.

Ahmad Pasha, the Ottoman governor of Damascus, was no friend to the city's Christian community. Mishaqa, who as a consular official had many interactions with the governor, became convinced that Ahmad Pasha was actively promoting intercommunal tensions. Ahmad Pasha believed the Christians had risen above their station since the 1856 reforms, Mishaqa explained, and that they had deliberately tried to elude the duties—particularly tax obligations—that accompanied their newfound rights. Though the Muslim community of Damascus outnumbered the Christians by a margin of five to one, Ahmad Pasha exacerbated Muslim fears by posting cannons to "protect" mosques from Christian attack. By such measures, Ahmad Pasha encouraged Damascene Muslims to believe they were threatened by attack from the town's Christians.

At the very height of the tensions Ahmad Pasha ordered a demonstration designed to provoke a riot. On July 10, 1860, he paraded a group of Muslim prisoners jailed for crimes against Christians through the streets of central Damascus—ostensibly to teach them a lesson. Predictably, a Muslim mob gathered around the men to break their chains and set them free. The spectacle of Muslims being gratuitously humiliated in this way only reinforced public views that Christians had risen above their

station since the 1856 decree. The mob turned to the Christian quarters determined
to teach them a lesson. With the recent events in Mount Lebanon still fresh in everyone's minds, extermination seemed a reasonable solution to the merciless mob.

Mishaqa found himself caught up in the violence he had long predicted. He described how the mob beat down his gates and flooded into his home. Mishaqa and
his youngest children fled through a back door hoping to take refuge in the house
of a Muslim neighbor. At each turn of the road, their path was blocked by rioters.
To divert them, Mishaqa threw handfuls of coins and fled with his children while
the crowd scrambled after his money. Three times he eluded the mob by this ruse,
but eventually he found his way blocked by a frenzied crowd.

> I had nowhere to run. They surrounded me to strip and kill me. My son and
> daughter were screaming, "Kill us instead of our father!" One of these wretches
> struck my daughter on the head with an ax, and he will answer for her blood.
> Another fired at me from a distance of six paces and missed, but I was wounded
> on my right temple by a blow with an ax, and my right side, face and arm were
> crushed by a blow with a cudgel. There were so many crowding around me that
> it was impossible to fire without hitting others.

Mishaqa was now the prisoner of the crowd. He was separated from his family
and taken through the back streets to an official's house. Mishaqa was, after all, the
consul of a foreign state. One of Mishaqa's Muslim neighbors gave his battered
Christian friend sanctuary and reunited him with his family, all of whom—including
his young daughter struck down by the crowd—miraculously survived the massacre.

Only those Christians who found such safe refuge escaped the carnage. Some
were rescued by Muslim notables, headed by the exiled hero of the Algerian resistance to French colonialism, the amir Abd al-Qadir. He and others risked their own
lives to rescue and give shelter to fleeing Christians. Other Christians took refuge
in the limited space of the British and Prussian consulates, whose guards succeeded
in holding back the mob. The majority of those who survived took precarious shelter
in the citadel of Damascus, fearful that the soldiers might let the mob through at
any moment. While the majority of the city's Christians did find safe refuge, thousands did not and suffered terrible violence at the hands of the mob in three days
of carnage.

Mishaqa later detailed the human and material costs of the massacres in a report
to the American consul in Beirut. He claimed that no less than 5,000 Christians
had been killed in the violence, one-quarter of a community that originally numbered 20,000. Some 400 women were abducted and raped, and many were left preg-
nant, including one of Mishaqa's own house servants. The material damages were
very extensive. More than 1,500 houses lay in ruins, all Christian-owned shops had

been looted, and some 200 shops in the Christian quarters were put to the torch. Churches, schools, and monasteries were plundered and destroyed.[14] The Christian quarters had been gutted by theft, vandalism, and fire in an irruption of communal violence unprecedented in the city's modern history.

The Ottoman government had established legal equality between its Muslim and non-Muslim citizens largely to prevent the European powers from intervening in its domestic affairs. The ensuing violence against Christians in Mount Lebanon and Damascus engendered the prospect of a massive European intervention. Upon learning of the massacre, the French government of Napoleon III immediately dispatched a military expedition headed by General Charles de Beaufort d'Hautpoul, a French aristocrat who had advised the Egyptian army during its occupation of Syria in the 1830s. De Beaufort was charged with the mission of preventing further bloodshed and bringing to justice the perpetrators of violence against the region's Christians.

The Ottomans had to act quickly. They dispatched one of their highest-ranking government officials, an architect of the Ottoman reforms named Fuad Pasha, to take all necessary measures to restore order before the French expedition reached the Syrian coast. Fuad fulfilled his mission with remarkable efficiency. He set in motion a military tribunal to mete out severe punishments to all responsible for the breakdown in order. The governor of Damascus was sentenced to death for his failure to prevent the massacre. Dozens of Muslims, from the nobility down to the poorest urban workers, were publicly hanged in the streets of Damascus. Scores of Ottoman soldiers faced the firing squad for having broken ranks and participated in the murder and looting. Hundreds of Damascenes were exiled or marched away in chains to serve long prison sentences with heavy labor.

The government set up commissions to address Christian claims for compensation for damaged and stolen property. Muslim quarters were emptied to provide temporary housing for homeless Christians while state-funded masons rebuilt the devastated Christian quarters. Basically, the Ottoman officials anticipated every grievance the European powers might raise and acted upon it before the Europeans had a chance to intervene. By the time General de Beaufort reached the Lebanese coast, Fuad had the situation under control. He thanked the French profusely for their services and provided them with a campsite on the Lebanese coast, far from any population center, where the soldiers would be on hand in case they were needed. The need never arose, and within a year the French withdrew their forces. The Ottomans had weathered the crisis, their sovereignty intact.

The Ottomans learned some important lessons from the experience of 1860. Never again would they pursue a reform measure that openly contravened Islamic doctrine. Thus, in the decades that followed, when the abolitionist movement and the British government combined forces to pressure the Ottoman Empire to abolish slavery, the Porte demurred. Verses of the Qur'an encourage owners to treat slaves well, to allow them to marry, and to give them their manumission, but slavery is in no way forbidden. How could the sultan outlaw that which God's book permits? In an effort to accommodate British pressure, the Porte agreed to work instead toward the abolition of the slave *trade*, on which the Qur'an is silent. In 1880 the Porte signed the Anglo-Ottoman Convention for the suppression of the black slave trade. It was a compromise intended to preserve peace within the empire rather than to curb the institution of slavery.[15]

The Ottomans also recognized the need to balance reforms with benefits to win public support for the Tanzimat. The population at large did not gain from an expanded bureaucracy designed to tax them better or conscript them more efficiently into Western-style military service. All of the legal changes designed to make the Ottoman Empire more compatible with European political thought and practice were alien to the average Ottoman. To encourage its subjects to accept such alien changes, the Ottoman government needed to invest more in the local economy and in promoting social welfare. Large-scale projects that gave the public pride and confidence in the sultan's government—such as gas lighting, steam-powered ferry boats, and electric trams—could generate support for the reformist government. The Porte needed to make such tangible, visible contributions to Ottoman society and the economy if the reform process were not to produce more disturbances.

The second half of the nineteenth century witnessed massive state investment in building projects and public works throughout the Ottoman Empire. Two Ottoman vassal states—Egypt and Tunisia—enjoyed sufficient autonomy to pursue their own development programs. Having adopted Enlightenment ideas, the Ottoman world began to acquire advanced European industrial technology in a wild spending spree. Industrial goods and products reached Arab markets in ever-increasing diversity as the Ottoman world was drawn into the global economy of the late nineteenth century.

Egypt led the way in modernization initiatives in the nineteenth century. Muhammad 'Ali had invested heavily in industry and technology, though his projects were always undertaken with the military in mind. It fell to his successors to invest in Egypt's *civilian* infrastructure.

Abbas Pasha (r. 1848–1854) made a modest start when he granted a concession to a British firm to build a railroad between Alexandria and Cairo. Concessions were the standard contract by which a government encouraged private companies to undertake major investments in its domains. The terms of a concession would set out the rights and benefits accruing to both the investors and the government for a fixed period of time. The more generous the terms of a concession, the easier it was to attract entrepreneurs to one's country. However, governments had to be careful not to concede too much to foreigners if they hoped for the enterprise to generate some profit for their own treasury. With governments in South America, Africa, and Asia vying for new technology, industrialists drove hard bargains. Abbas Pasha was a conservative man who preferred not to make many commitments to foreign investors.

The next ruler of Egypt, Said Pasha (r. 1854–1863), committed the country to far more ambitious plans. He laid a second railway line between Cairo and Alexandria and awarded a concession for a new line from Cairo to Suez, completing the overland link between the Mediterranean and the Red Sea route to the Indian Ocean. He fostered Euro-Egyptian partnerships to bring steam shipping to the Nile and the Red Sea. Yet nothing could compare with the 1856 concession Said gave his former French tutor, Ferdinand de Lesseps, to construct a waterway linking the Mediterranean to the Red Sea: the Suez Canal. It was to prove Egypt's greatest development project, and the biggest drain on Egypt's treasury, of the nineteenth century.

The granting of concessions was not in itself an expense to the treasury. If all of the ventures established by Egyptian concession-holders had succeeded, investors and governments alike would have profited. Unfortunately, many of these ventures were very risky and failed. This would have been bad enough for the host government, which had hoped to build stronger domestic economies through investment in European technology. Its losses were compounded by the demands of European consuls for indemnities when their citizens' investments failed.

As a matter of national pride, each consul took note of the indemnities received by the consuls of other states and sought to outdo them. Thus, when the Nile Navigation Company went bankrupt, the Egyptian treasury had to compensate European shareholders to the sum of £340,000.[16] The Austrians set a new benchmark for individual claims when their consul managed to squeeze 700,000 francs from the government of Egypt to compensate an Austrian investor on the spurious grounds that twenty-eight cases of silk cocoons had been spoiled by the late departure of the Suez-to-Cairo train. Said was reported to have interrupted a meeting with a European businessman to ask a servant to close the window. "If this gentleman catches cold," he quipped, "it will cost me £10,000."[17]

The Suez Canal project generated the greatest indemnity bill of all. The British had objected to French plans to create a canal linking the Mediterranean and the Red Sea. Given its empire in India, Britain would inevitably be more reliant on the canal than any other maritime power. The idea of placing such a strategic waterway under the control of a *French* company was completely unacceptable to the British.

They had no right to prevent the government of Egypt from offering concessions to its sovereign soil, but they could object to the terms of the concession. Specifically, the British objected to Egypt's promise to provide free labor to dig the canal as tantamount to slavery, and they demanded that Egypt rescind those articles conferring rights on the Suez Canal Company to develop both banks of the canal in a colonization scheme. The Egyptian government was too reliant on Britain's goodwill to refuse its objections, and it therefore notified the Suez Canal Company that it wished to renegotiate key terms of the original 1856 concession. The company turned the dispute over to the French government to defend its rights as a concession holder against British pressure.

Said's successor Ismail Pasha (r. 1863–1879) inherited the dispute and had to suffer the arbitration of the French emperor Napoleon III—hardly a disinterested party. In his settlement of 1864, Napoleon III demanded that the Egyptian government pay 38 million francs to the Suez Canal Company to compensate it for the loss of free labor, and 30 million francs for the land along the banks of the canal that was to be returned to Egypt. Additionally, he found reason to charge the Egyptian government an additional 16 million francs, making for a total indemnity of some 84 million francs (£3,360,000, about $33.5 million in 1864)—an unprecedented sum.[18]

In spite of its heavy losses to development projects, the government of Egypt remained optimistic about its economic future. Egypt's most important export crop was long-staple cotton, prized by European weavers. In 1861 the supply of American cotton was cut by the outbreak of the Civil War. Between 1861 and 1865, cotton prices quadrupled. Egypt's annual income from cotton rose dramatically from around £1,000,000 in the early 1850s to reach a peak of £11,500,000 by the mid-1860s. With cotton money flowing into Egypt's coffers, Ismail Pasha believed he could honor his commitments to the Suez Canal Company and still undertake ambitious new projects.

Ismail aspired to turn Egypt into a great power and to gain greater personal recognition as its ruler. In 1867 he sought Ottoman permission to change his gubernatorial title of "pasha" to *khedive*, a more impressive Persian title meaning "viceroy." As khedive, Ismail sought to remake his capital city—Cairo—and took Paris for his example. With an eye to the ceremonies marking the opening of the Suez Canal in 1869, Ismail put Cairo on a course of rapid, radical transformation. Modern quarters with European-style buildings lining broad, straight streets were built between Old Cairo and the Nile. A new bridge was built across the Nile, and Ismail built himself a new palace on the main island in the Nile (it would later be converted to a hotel when the Egyptian government went bankrupt). The streets were paved and lit with gas fittings. Landscape architects turned the old Nile flood ponds, such as the

Ezbekiyya pool, into public gardens with cafés and promenades. A national theater and an opera house were built.[19] The Italian composer Verdi was commissioned to write an opera with an Egyptian theme to inaugurate the opera house, but he took a bit too long to complete *Aida*, and the hall was opened to the strains of *Rigoletto* instead. The flurry of construction climaxed with the visit of the French empress Eugénie to celebrate the opening of the Suez Canal in November 1869.

The outrageous spending was part of Ismail's bid to secure Egypt's place among the civilized states of the world. Though the ceremonies were by all accounts most impressive, the new Cairo was a vanity project built on borrowed funds that left Ismail's government living on borrowed time. The irony of the situation was that Egypt had embarked on its development schemes to secure independence from Ottoman and European domination. Yet with each new concession, the government of Egypt made itself more vulnerable to European encroachment. Egypt was not alone. Another state in North Africa was also increasing its dependence on Europe through ambitious reforms and development projects.

Tunisia, like Egypt, enjoyed sufficient autonomy from the Ottoman Empire to pursue its own development projects in the nineteenth century. Its government, known as the Regency, had been headed by the Husaynid Dynasty since the early eighteenth century. Gone were the days of Barbary Coast piracy. Since 1830 the Regency had banned all piracy and sought to develop the economy of the country through industry and trade.

Between 1837 and 1855, Tunis was ruled by a reformer named Ahmad Bey. Heavily influenced by the example of Muhammad 'Ali in Egypt, Ahmad Bey created a Nizami army in Tunisia, along with a military academy and support industries to produce the weapons and uniforms needed to provision the new army. Among the military men trained for the new army was a young Mamluk named Khayr al-Din, who would prove one of the great reformers of the nineteenth century, eventually rising to be prime minister both in Tunis and in the Ottoman Empire itself.

As a Mamluk, Khayr al-Din was the last of his kind, a man who rose from slavery to the pinnacle of political power. In his autobiography, addressed to his own children, Khayr al-Din gave a rare insight into how it felt to be a Mamluk: "Though I know with certainty that I am a Circassian, I have no precise memory of my country or of my parents. I must have been separated from my family after some war or emigration, and lost trace of them forever." Despite repeated attempts, Khayr al-Din never succeeded in his quest to find his biological family. "My earliest memories of childhood," he wrote, "were in Istanbul, whence I passed into the service of the Bey of Tunis in 1839."[20]

After learning Arabic and receiving an Islamic education, Khayr al-Din was enrolled in the military and trained by French officers. A brilliant young officer, he rose to the top of the officer corps and reached the rank of general before entering into political life—all within fourteen years of arriving in Tunisia. Fluent in French, Arabic, and Turkish, Khayr al-Din traveled widely through Europe and the Ottoman Empire in the course of his career. His firsthand experience of European progress made him an ardent supporter of the Tanzimat reforms and of the need to draw on European experience and technology to enable Muslim states to realize their full potential. He set out his views in an influential political tract published in Arabic in 1867, and in an authorized French translation two years later.

Khayr al-Din addressed his reform agenda to both a European audience skeptical of the Muslim world's ability to adapt to the modern age and to a Muslim audience that rejected foreign innovations as somehow contrary to the religion and values of Islam. Here Khayr al-Din was building on an argument first pronounced by the Egyptian advocate of reform, al-Tahtawi (Khayr al-Din had read and admired his book on France), to which later Muslim reformers would return increasingly across the nineteenth century: that Muslim borrowings from modern European sciences were but the return they were due from Europe's debt to medieval Islamic sciences.[21]

Although Khayr al-Din was an outspoken advocate for political and economic reform, he was a fiscal conservative. He wanted to see Tunisia develop its economic base to be able to support the expense of modern technology. He believed the government should invest in factories to process its own cash crops into goods for the domestic market. He regretted how Tunisian laborers sold their raw cotton, silk, and wool "to the European for a cheap price, and then in a short time buy it back, after it has been processed [into manufactured cloth], at a price several times higher."[22] Far better, he argued, for Tunisian factories to spin and weave Tunisian fibers to produce fabrics for domestic consumption. In this way, the prosperity of the country would expand, allowing the government to invest in more infrastructural projects. Such financial sound management required intelligent government. Khayr al-Din watched with growing dismay as he saw the rulers of Tunisia take their country down the road to insolvency through vanity projects and bad investments.

Tunisia is a relatively small country, and its expenditures on reforms were modest when compared to the projects undertaken in Egypt. The greatest expenditures undertaken during the reign of Ahmad Bey were related to the Nizami army. Because Ahmad Bey aspired to maintain an infantry of 26,000 men, he imported from France all of the necessary technology and work force to create support industries—arsenals, foundries, textile factories for uniforms, tanneries for saddles and boots, and so on. However, like Ismail Pasha in Egypt, Ahmad Bey also had his vanity projects. His most wasteful extravagance was a palace complex in Muhammadia, 10 miles southwest of the capital city Tunis, which he described as Tunisia's Versailles. As expenditures increasingly outstripped resources, Ahmad Bey was forced to cut back on his ambitions. He ultimately abandoned many of the new factories at a total loss.

Ahmad Bey's successors continued the reform process, combining high expenditures on public projects with dwindling resources. A telegraph line was laid in 1859 to improve communications, and an aqueduct was built to provide fresh water to Tunis. A concession was given to a British firm to build a 22-mile railway linking Tunis with the port of La Goulette and the seaside town of al-Marsa. Gas lighting was introduced to Tunis, and the city streets were paved.[23] Like Ismail Pasha in Egypt, the rulers of Tunisia wanted to endow their capital city with all the trappings of European modernity.

The reform process proceeded at a different pace in Istanbul and the other Ottoman provinces. As the imperial center, with responsibility for provinces scattered across the Balkans, Anatolia, and the Arab world, Istanbul had to ensure the development of all its provincial capitals. The government undertook major urban projects in the Arab world, building new markets, government offices, and schools. In addition, it introduced gas lighting and trams and other trappings of modern life in many of the Empire's leading cities.

The Ottomans also gave concessions to European firms to build major infrastructural projects. They modernized ports in Istanbul and Izmir, Turkey, and in Beirut. They set up steamship companies in the Black Sea and the Marmara Sea. A British firm received the concession in 1856 to build the first railway in Turkey, a 130-kilometer (81-mile) line from the port of Izmir to the agricultural hinterland of Aydin. A French company received the concession for a second line from Smyrna to Kasaba (93 kilometers, or 58 miles), built between 1863 and 1865. As these lines were extended, government revenues from the railways increased significantly, encouraging further investment in Anatolian railways. A number of industrial ventures were established in the Tanzimat era, and mines were founded to extract coal and minerals. However, profits from successful ventures were matched by losses in those that failed, and the returns on Ottoman investments in European technology never offset the costs of new technology.

Reckless government spending alarmed reformers across the Ottoman Empire and North Africa. The acquisition of European technology achieved the opposite of the intended result; instead of making these states strong and independent, the development process led to the impoverishment and weakening of Middle Eastern governments, increasing their vulnerability to European intervention. Writing about Tunisia, Khayr al-Din claimed, "It is clear that the excessive expenses which burden the kingdom beyond its capability are the result of arbitrary rule, and that economy, which is the course of the kingdom's well-being, is attained by regulating all expenses within the bounds of the *tanzimat*."[24] For the development projects to bear fruit, Khayr al-Din argued, governments needed to stay within their means. The benefits of Tanzimat reforms were being undermined by arbitrary rule and excessive spending.

To reform-minded thinkers like Khayr al-Din, the solution to both reckless government spending and arbitrary rule lay in constitutional reforms and representative government. The echoes of al-Tahtawi's analysis of the French constitution could be heard very clearly in the second half of the nineteenth century. Under constitutional rule, a country would prosper, the people's knowledge would increase, their wealth would accumulate, and their hearts would be satisfied. At least that was the theory.

The Tunisian Constitution of 1861 fell well short of reformers' hopes. The text of the constitution drew on the Ottoman reform decrees of 1839 and 1856 and placed few limits on the executive power of the bey, who retained the right to appoint and dismiss his ministers. However, it did call for the establishment of a representative assembly, the Grand Council, composed of sixty members nominated by the ruler. Khayr al-Din, appointed president of the Grand Council, was soon disillusioned by the assembly's limited powers to curb the bey's excesses. He recognized that Ahmad Bey and his prime minister had only convened the council to rubber-stamp their decisions, and so in 1863 he tendered his resignation. The issue that provoked his resignation was the government's decision to contract its first foreign loan, which Khayr al-Din predicted would drag his adoptive country "to its ruin."[25]

The Egyptian constitutional movement took root in the 1860s as well. Following the lines of al-Tahtawi's analysis, many reformers believed constitutional government to be the basis of European strength and prosperity and the missing link in Egypt's own reforms. Yet, as in Tunisia, no change was possible without the consent of the ruler. It was the viceroy of Egypt, Ismail Pasha, who called for the creation of the first Consultative Council of Deputies in 1866. The council was composed of seventy-five members indirectly elected to three-year terms. Like the bey in Tunisia, the ruler of Egypt sought to implicate the landed notables in his controversial financial policies through the convening of the council, whose role was limited to a consultative capacity (deputies had no role in making the laws of Egypt). Though a creation of the ruler, the council became a forum for Egyptian elites to voice criticism of the policies of the ruler and his government, and it marked the beginning of broader participation in the affairs of state.[26]

The most significant constitutional movement in the Eastern Mediterranean emerged from Ottoman Turkey. Some of Turkey's leading intellectuals met in Paris and London in the late 1860s, where they mixed with European liberals and framed a set of demands for constitutional government, the sovereignty of the people, and an elected parliament to represent the people. Known as the Society of Young Ottomans, they criticized the government for the poverty of Ottoman society and the financial condition of the state. Its members lamented the Ottoman Empire's increasing dependence on the European powers as well as foreign intervention into Ottoman affairs, and they laid blame for Turkey's problems squarely on the irresponsible policies of the sultan and his government. The Young Ottomans published news-papers and lobbied foreign governments to gain support for their cause. Even so, they recognized that change could only come with the consent of the sultan. Namik Kemal, one of the great Turkish intellectuals of the nineteenth century, told his fellow Young Ottomans that "the Ottoman nation was loyal to its Ottoman rulers; with us nothing was done unless the [sultan] really wanted it."[27] The society dissolved in 1871 but returned to lobby its cause in Istanbul, where it found support among re-formist government officials. The Young Ottomans' efforts were rewarded in 1876 with the promulgation of the Ottoman Constitution and the convening of the first Ottoman Parliament.

If reformers in Tunisia, Egypt, and the Ottoman Empire had hoped to stave off economic collapse by instituting constitutional reforms, they were to be sadly dis-appointed. The early constitutional movements were too respectful of authority to impose constraints on their rulers. They seemed to hope that the bey in Tunis, the pasha in Cairo, or the sultan in Istanbul would accept constraints voluntarily and share power with representative assemblies as an act of enlightened benevolence. These were not realistic expectations. The bey, pasha, and sultan continued to rule as before, and there was no constraint to prevent them from spending their governments into insolvency.

The single greatest threat to the independence of the Middle East was not the armies of Europe but its banks. Ottoman reformers were terrified by the risks involved in accepting loans from Europe. In 1852, when Sultan Abdulmecid sought funds from France, one of his advisors took him aside and counseled strongly against the loan: "Your father [Mahmud II] had two wars with the Russians and lived through many campaigns. He had many pressures on him, yet he did not borrow money from abroad. Your sultanate has passed in peace. What will the people say if money is bor-rowed?" The advisor continued: "If this state borrows five piasters it will sink. For if once a loan is taken, there will be no end to it. [The state] will sink overwhelmed in debt." Abdulmecid was convinced and canceled the loan, though he would return to European creditors within two years.[28]

In 1863 Khayr al-Din chose to resign as Tunisia's president of the Grand Council rather than be party to the country's first foreign loan. He later wrote bitterly of the policies that led to Tunisia's bankruptcy in 1869. "After having exhausted all the re-sources of the Regency, [the prime minister] cast himself down the ruinous path of loans and in less than seven years . . . Tunisia, which had never owed anything to anyone, saw itself burdened with a debt of 240 million piasters [£6 million, $39 million] borrowed by the Government from Europe."[29] By Khayr al-Din's estimate, the annual revenues of the Tunisian state had remained constant, at about 20 million piasters, right through the reform era. The result was that for seven years, expenditures exceeded revenues by 170 percent per annum. The result was the surrender of Tunisia's sovereignty to an international financial commission.

The Ottoman central government was next to declare bankruptcy, in 1875. In the course of twenty years, the Ottomans had contracted sixteen foreign loans totaling nearly £220 million ($1.21 billion). With each loan, the Ottoman economy fell deeper into European economic dominion. Between discounts to attract increasingly skeptical investors and the various commissions and fees charged to float loans on European markets, the Ottoman government only received £116 million ($638 million)—the greater part of which was spent to service the Ottoman debt (some £19 million, or $104.5 million, in repayment and over £66 million, or $363 million, in interest). This left only £41 million ($225.5 million) for the Ottomans to invest in their economic objectives out of a total debt of £220 million ($1.21 billion). As Abdulmecid's advisor predicted, the Ottoman state sank, overwhelmed in debt.

Over the next six years, amid the tumult of another disastrous war with Russia (1877–1878) and territorial losses confirmed in the 1878 Treaty of Berlin concluding the war, the Ottomans finally came to an agreement with their European creditors in 1881 with the formation of the Ottoman Public Debt Administration (PDA). Headed by a seven-man council representing the main bondholder states (Britain, France, Germany, Austria-Hungary, Italy, the Netherlands, and the Ottoman Empire), the presidency of the PDA rotated between France and Britain. Whole sectors of the Ottoman economy were placed under the control of the PDA, with revenues from the salt monopoly, fish tax, silk tithes, stamp and spirit duties, as well as part of the annual tributes of several Ottoman provinces, dedicated to debt repayment. The lucrative tobacco trade also fell under the PDA, though a separate administration soon was created to oversee the monopoly over the purchase and sale of tobacco. The PDA gained tremendous power over the finances of the Ottoman Empire as a whole, which the European powers used not just to control the actions of the sultan's government but to open the Ottoman economy to European companies for railways, mining, and public works.[30]

Although Egypt held the distinction of being the last of the Middle Eastern states to declare bankruptcy, in 1876, the government's position would have been far stronger had it declared insolvency sooner rather than later. The parallels to the Ottoman case are striking. Between 1862 and 1873, Egypt contracted eight foreign loans, totaling £68.5 million ($376.75 million), which, after discounts, left only £47 million ($258.5 million), of which some £36 million ($198 million) were spent in payments on the principal and interest on the foreign loans. Thus, out of a debt of £68.5 million ($376.75 million), the government of Egypt gained only about £11 million ($60.5 million) to invest in its economy.

Faced with increased difficulty in raising funds to cover his debts, Khedive Ismail began to sell off the assets of the Egyptian state. He borrowed an estimated £28 million ($154 million) domestically. In 1872 the Egyptian government passed a law granting landholders who paid six years of their land tax in advance a future discount of 50 percent on future land taxes in perpetuity. As this desperate measure failed to staunch the hemorrhage, the viceroy sold the government's shares in the Suez Canal Company to the British government in 1875 for £4 million ($22 million)—recouping only one-quarter of the £16 million ($88 million) the canal is estimated to have cost the government of Egypt. Stripped of key assets, the treasury tried to postpone payment on the interest of the state's debt in April 1876. This was tantamount to a declaration of bankruptcy, and the repo men of the international economy descended on Egypt like a plague.

Between 1876 and 1880 the finances of Egypt were assumed by European experts from Britain, France, Italy, Austria, and Russia whose primary concern was foreign bondholder interests. As in Istanbul, a formal commission was established. One unrealistic plan followed the next in quick succession, placing terrible burdens on Egyptian taxpayers. With each plan, the foreign economic advisors managed to insinuate themselves deeper into the financial administration of Egypt.

European control over Egypt was firmly established in 1878, when two European commissioners were "invited" to join the viceroy's cabinet. British economist Charles Rivers Wilson was appointed minister of finance, and the Frenchman Ernest-Gabriel de Blignières was named minister of public works. Europe got to demonstrate its power over Egypt in 1879, when Khedive Ismail sought to dismiss Wilson and de Blignières in a cabinet reshuffle. The governments of Britain and France brought pressure to bear on the Ottoman sultan to dismiss "his" viceroy in Egypt. Overnight, the recalcitrant Ismail was overthrown and replaced by his more compliant son, Tawfiq.[31]

With the bankruptcies in Tunis, Istanbul, and Cairo, the Middle East reform initiatives had gone full circle. What had begun as movements to strengthen the Ottomans and their vassal states from outside interference had instead opened the Middle Eastern states to increasing European domination. Over time, informal imperial control hardened into direct colonial rule, as the whole of North Africa was partitioned and distributed among the growing empires of Europe.

CHAPTER 5

The First Wave of Colonialism: North Africa

Though the colonization of Arab lands was built on foundations laid earlier, European imperialism in the Arab world began in earnest in the last quarter of the nineteenth century. As was noted in the previous chapter, both the spread of European technology and the financing that allowed cash-strapped Middle Eastern governments to spend beyond their means enabled the European powers to extend their influence across Ottoman domains from North Africa to the Arabian Peninsula. Bankruptcy in the Ottoman Empire and its autonomous provinces in North Africa lowered the barriers to more direct forms of European control.

As Europe's interests in North Africa intensified, their incentives for outright imperial rule expanded accordingly. By the 1880s the European powers were more concerned about upholding their national interests in the Southern Mediterranean than to preserve the territorial integrity of the Ottoman Empire. The "self-denying protocol" of 1840 was a dead letter, and the partition of North Africa followed. France extended its rule over Tunisia in 1881, Britain occupied Egypt in 1882, Italy seized Libya in 1911, and the European powers consented to a Franco-Spanish protectorate over Morocco (the only North African state to have preserved its independence from Ottoman rule) in 1912. Before the outbreak of the First World War, the whole of North Africa had passed under direct European rule.

There were a number of reasons why European imperialism in the Arab world began in North Africa. The Arab provinces of North Africa were far from the Ottoman center of gravity and, in the course of the eighteenth and nineteenth centuries, had become increasingly autonomous of Istanbul. The Arab provinces of the Middle East—in Greater Syria, Mesopotamia, and the Arabian Peninsula—were closer to the Ottoman heartland and came to be more closely integrated to Istanbul's rule in

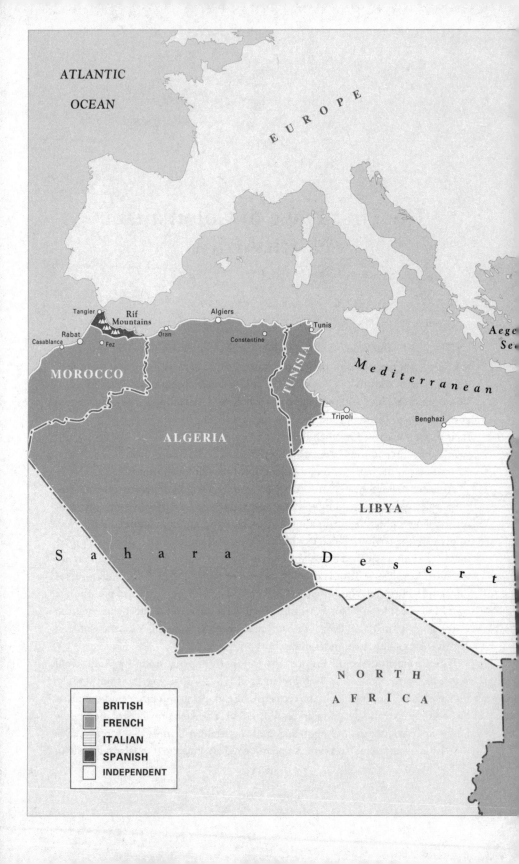

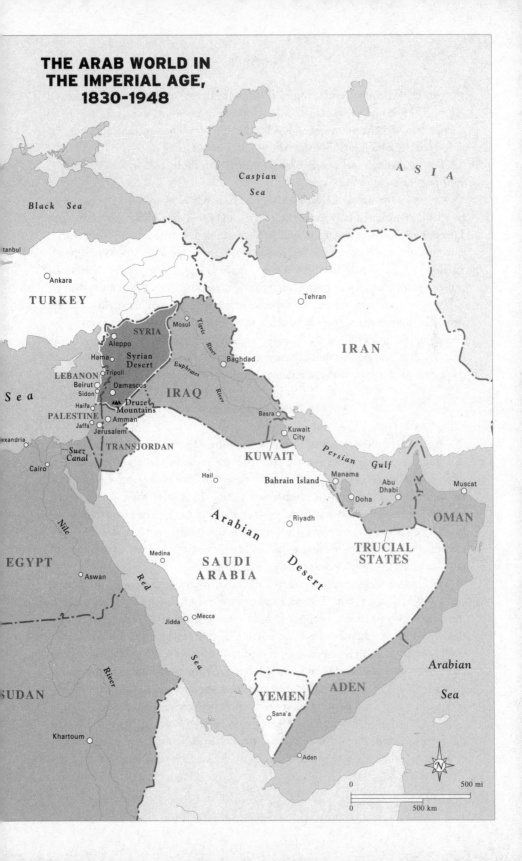

THE ARAB WORLD IN
THE IMPERIAL AGE,
1830-1948

ASIA

Black Sea

Caspian
Sea

tanbul

Ankara

TURKEY

Tehran

SYRIA
Mosul

Aleppo
Hama   Syrian
Desert   Baghdad
LEBANON   Tripoli
Beirut   Damascus
Sidon   IRAQ
Haifa   Druze
Palestine Mountains
Jaffa   Amman
Jerusalem
TRANSJORDAN

Tigris River
Euphrates
River

IRAN

Basra

Kuwait
City

Sea

axandria
Suez
Canal
Cairo

KUWAIT

Persian Gulf

Hail

Bahrain Island
Manama
Abu
Dhabi

Muscat

EGYPT

Nile

Aswan

Medina

Red

Jidda   Mecca

Sea

Doha

Riyadh

Arabian

Desert

SAUDI
ARABIA

TRUCIAL
STATES

OMAN

River

SUDAN

Khartoum

YEMEN

Sana'a

ADEN

Aden

Arabian

Sea

N

0   500 mi

0   500 km

the course of the nineteenth-century reforms (1839–1876). Places like Tunisia and Egypt had become vassal states of the Ottoman Empire, whereas Damascus and Aleppo were integral provinces of the Ottoman Empire. The very developments that enhanced the autonomy of North Africa—the emergence of distinct ruling families heading increasingly independent governments—left those states more vulnerable to European occupation.

Moreover, the states of North Africa were relatively close to Southern Europe—to Spain, France, and Italy in particular. Proximity had drawn these states closer to Europe's ambit: for military aid, industrial goods, and finance capital. North Africa was the Ottoman Empire's distant frontier but Europe's near abroad. As Europe expanded beyond its own frontiers in a new wave of imperialism at the close of the nineteenth century, it was only natural that it should turn to its near abroad first.

There was one other reason why the states of Europe colonized North Africa: precedent. The long-standing French presence in Algeria set an important precedent for French ambitions in Tunisia and Morocco and gave Italy grounds to seek imperial satisfaction in Libya. But for the accidents of history that led to the French invasion of Algiers in 1827, the partition of much of North Africa might never have happened.

Like Tunisia, the Regency of Algiers was nominally part of the Ottoman Empire and governed by a viceroy who enjoyed great autonomy in both domestic and international affairs. The ruling elites were Turkish military men, recruited from Istanbul and organized into an administrative council, electing their leader, or *dey*, who enjoyed direct relations with the governments of Europe. The sultan in Istanbul formally confirmed the elected dey and claimed a tribute from Algiers. The only Ottoman official posted to Algiers was the Islamic court judge. Otherwise, the sultan's authority over Algiers was strictly ceremonial.

The deys of Algiers exploited their autonomy to pursue their own commercial and political relations with Europe, independent of Istanbul's control. Yet without the weight of the Ottoman Empire behind them, the deys had little leverage over their European trade partners. Thus, when the deys provided grain to France on credit—to provision French military campaigns in Italy and Egypt between 1793 and 1798—their repeated pleas to the French government to honor their commitments fell on deaf ears. Decades passed without the French repaying their debts, and the deal became a growing source of friction between the two states.

By 1827, relations between the Algerian dey, Husayn Pasha (r. 1818–1830), and the French consul, Pierre Deval, reached the breaking point after the French government failed to respond to the dey's letters demanding repayment of the grain debt. In a private conversation with Deval, Husayn Pasha lost his temper and struck the French consul with his fly whisk.

In their reports to their respective superiors, Deval and Husayn Pasha gave very different accounts of their meeting.[1] To the French minister of foreign affairs, Deval claimed he found the dey in an agitated state when he called on Huseyn Pasha in his palace.

"Why has your Minister not replied to the letter I wrote him?" Husayn Pasha demanded. Deval claimed he replied in a measured tone: "I had the honour to bring you the reply as soon as I received it." At this point, Deval reported, the dey erupted:

"'Why did he not reply directly? Am I a clodhopper, a man of mud, a barefoot tramp? You are a wicked man, an infidel, an idolater!' Then, rising from his seat, with the handle of his fly-whisk, he gave me three violent blows about the body and told me to retire."

The Arab fly whisk is made from a knot of hair from a horse's tail, attached to a handle. It is not immediately evident how one might deal 'violent blows" with such an instrument. However, the French Consul was adamant that French honor was at stake. He concluded his report to the minister: "If Your Excellency does not wish to give this affair the severe and well-publicized attention that it merits, he should at least be willing to grant me permission to retire with leave."

In his own report to the Ottoman grand vezir, the dey acknowledged striking Deval with his whisk, though only after provocation. He explained that he had written three times to the French asking for repayment, without receiving the courtesy of a reply. He raised the matter with the French consul "in courteous terms and with a deliberately friendly attitude."

> "Why did no reply come to my letters written and sent to your [i.e., the French] Government?" The Consul, in stubbornness and arrogance, replied in offensive terms that "the King and state of France may not send replies to letters which you have addressed to them." He dared to blaspheme the Muslim religion and showed contempt for the honour of His Majesty [the sultan], protector of the world. Unable to endure this insult, which exceeded all bearable limits, and having recourse to the courage natural only to Muslims, I hit him two or three times with light blows of the fly-whisk which I held in my humble hand.

Whatever the truth of these two irreconcilable accounts, it was clear that by 1827 the French had no intention of honoring debts incurred three decades earlier—and the Algerians were unwilling to forgive the debts. After the fly-whisk incident, the French demanded reparations for the damage done to France's honor while the Algerians continued to insist on repayment of France's long-overdue debts. The dispute left the two sides on a collision course in which the Algerians refused to back down, and the French could not afford to.

The French responded to the dey's "insults" with ultimatums. They demanded the Algerians make a gun salute to the French flag, which the dey refused. The French then imposed a blockade on the port of Algiers, which did more harm to the merchants of Marseilles than to Algerian corsairs, whose swift ships easily slipped through the over-extended French line of ships enforcing the blockade. After a two-year stalemate, the French sought a face-saving solution and dispatched a diplomat to negotiate with the dey. The Algerians fired a few cannon at his flagship, preventing the negotiator from even disembarking. The Algerian imbroglio was turning into a major embarrassment for the beleaguered government of French king Charles X.

Charles X (r. 1824–1830) faced serious opposition at home as well as abroad. His efforts to restore some absolutism to the French monarchy, turning the clock back to pre-Revolutionary times, reached a crisis when he suspended the Constitutional Charter (described at length by Rifa'a al-Tahtawi in his study of France) in 1830. His premier, Prince Jules de Polignac, suggested that a foreign adventure might rally public opinion behind the throne. Polignac recognized that France had to overcome opposition from the other European powers—Britain in particular—to a measure that inevitably would alter the balance of power in the Mediterranean. He dispatched ambassadors to London and the other courts of Europe to set out the objectives of the impending invasion of Algeria as the complete destruction of piracy, the total abolition of Christian slavery, and the termination of all tribute paid by European states to the Regency to ensure the security of their shipping. Polignac hoped to gain international support for the French invasion of Algiers by claiming to uphold such universal interests.

In June 1830 a French expedition of 37,000 troops landed to the west of Algiers. It quickly defeated the dey's forces and entered the city of Algiers on July 4. This triumph was not enough to save Charles X, who was overthrown later that month in the July Revolution of 1830. The Egyptian scholar Rifa'a al-Tahtawi, who was living in Paris at the time, noted how the French showed far more satisfaction at overthrowing an unpopular king than in the conquest of Algiers, "which," he argued, "was based on specious motives."[2] Nonetheless, the French remained in possession of Algiers well after the fall of the Bourbon monarchy, one of the few enduring legacies of the undistinguished reign of Charles X. Husayn Pasha's capitulation on July 5, 1830, brought to a close three centuries of Ottoman history and marked the beginning of 132 years of French rule over Algeria.

Although the French had defeated the Turkish garrison at Algiers, this victory did not give them control over the country at large. So long as the French confined their ambitions to the main coastal towns, they were unlikely to encounter much organized resistance in Algeria. European powers had long held strategic ports on the North African coast. The French occupation of Algiers in July 1830 and of Oran in January 1831 was not so different from the Spanish position in their *presidios* in Ceuta and Melilla (which remain Spanish possessions today). But the French were not satisfied with holding the main towns. They hoped to colonize the fertile coastal plain with French settlers in a policy known as "restrained occupation." It was a policy that inevitably would alienate the indigenous people of Algeria.

The Algerian population was made up of fiercely independent Arabs and Berbers, a non-Arab ethnic community that converted to Islam after the seventh-century Islamic conquests. With their own language and customs, the Berber population is spread across North Africa, particularly in Algeria and Morocco. The Arabs and Berbers had preserved their independence from the deys of Algiers and resisted every attempt by the Turkish garrison to tax them or impose Ottoman rule outside the major cities of Algiers, Constantine, and Oran. Thus, they shed no tears over the fall of the Regency. Even so, the Berbers and Arabs in the Algerian countryside were no more amenable to the French than they had been to Turkish rule.

As the French began to colonize Algeria's coastal plains, the local tribes organized a resistance movement, beginning in the west of the country near Oran. The Arabs and Berbers turned to the charismatic leaders of their Sufi orders (mystical Muslim brotherhoods), which often combined religious legitimacy with a noble genealogy linking order members to the family of the Prophet Muhammad. The Sufi orders were organized into networks of lodges that spanned Algeria and commanded the loyalty of the leading men of the community. It was a natural framework within which to mount an opposition movement.

Among the most powerful Sufi communities in western Algeria was the Qadiriyya order. The head of the order was a wise old man named Muhi al-Din. Several of the leading tribes of the region petitioned Muhi al-Din to accept the title of sultan and lead the Arabs of western Algeria in a holy war against the French. When he refused, pleading age and infirmity, the tribes nominated his son Abd al-Qadir, who had already demonstrated courage in attacks on the French.

Abd al-Qadir (1808–1883) was acclaimed as amir, or leader of the tribes allied against French rule, in November 1832, at the age of twenty-four. It was the beginning of one of the most remarkable careers in the modern history of the Middle East. Over the next fifteen years, Abd al-Qadir united the people of Algeria in a sustained resistance movement against the French occupation of their country. It is no exaggeration to say he was a legend in his own lifetime—in the West and the Arab world alike.

To the French, Abd al-Qadir was the ultimate "noble Arab," a Saladin figure whose religious convictions and personal integrity placed his motives—defending his country against foreign military occupation—beyond reproach. He was bold and audacious in battle, pursuing a guerrilla style of warfare that brought his small forces victories against French armies more advanced than those that had routed Egypt's Mamluks. His exploits were captured in luscious oils by the Romantic artist Horace Vernet (1789–1863), the official recorder of the French conquest of Algeria. Victor Hugo eulogized Abd al-Qadir in verse as *le beau soldat, le beau prêtre*—literally, "the handsome soldier, the handsome priest."

To his Arab followers, Abd al-Qadir enjoyed religious legitimacy as a descendant of the Prophet Muhammad (a sharif) and as the son of one of the most respected heads of a leading Sufi order. They vowed their loyalty to him and were rewarded with victories against superior forces. Abd al-Qadir's exploits thrilled contemporaries across the Arab and Islamic world, as a "Commander of the Faithful" defending Muslim lands against foreign invaders.

Abd al-Qadir pursued a remarkably intelligent war. At one point, upon capturing some of his papers, the French were astonished to discover that he had obtained very reliable information on debates in the French Chamber of Deputies relating to the war in Algeria. He knew how unpopular the war was in French public opinion and was aware of the pressures on the government to come to terms with the Algerian insurgents.[3] Armed with this intelligence, Abd al-Qadir pursued a war designed to drive the French to seek peace.

Twice he forced French generals to conclude peace treaties on his terms, granting recognition of his sovereignty and clear limits to the territory that would remain under French control. The first treaty was agreed to in February 1834 with General Louis Desmichels, and the second—the Tafna Treaty of mutual recognition—was concluded in May 1837 with General Robert Bugeaud. The latter treaty granted Abd al-Qadir sovereignty over two-thirds of the land mass of Algeria.[4] Both treaties proved short-lived in the face of expansionist ambitions on both sides.

Abd al-Qadir and the French each sought to extend their authority over the eastern city of Constantine. The French argued that Constantine fell well outside the territories recognized in the 1837 treaty as part of Abd al-Qadir's state. The Algerians retorted that the treaty set clear boundaries on French territory, which the French had violated in the conquest of Constantine. Once again, the French and Algerian positions were irreconcilable. Abd al-Qadir accused the French of breaking their word and resumed his war. On November 3, 1839, he wrote to the French governor-general:

> We were at peace, and the limits between your country and ours were clearly determined. . . . [Now] you have published [the claim] that all of the lands between Algiers and Constantine should no longer receive orders from me. The rupture comes from you. However, so that you do not accuse me of betrayal, I warn you that I will resume the war. Prepare yourselves, warn your travellers, all who live in isolated places, in a word take every precaution as you see fit.[5]

Abd al-Qadir's forces descended on the vulnerable French agricultural colonies in the Mitija Plain, located east of Algiers. Provoking widespread panic, they killed and wounded hundreds of settlers, putting their homes to the torch. The government in Paris was faced with a clear choice: withdraw, or commit to a complete occupation of Algeria. It opted for the latter and dispatched General Bugeaud at the head of a massive campaign force to achieve the final "submission" of the Algerian resistance to French rule.

Bugeaud faced a daunting task in his attempt to achieve total victory in Algeria. The Algerians were well organized and highly motivated. Abd al-Qadir had organized his government in Algeria into eight provinces, each headed by a governor whose administration reached down to the tribal level. These governors were paid regular salaries and were charged with maintaining law and order and collecting taxes for the state. Judges were appointed to enforce Islamic law. Government was unobtrusive, operating within the constraints of Islamic law, which encouraged farmers and tribesmen to pay their taxes.

The Algerian government raised enough funds from taxes to support a volunteer army that proved highly effective in the field. By Abd al-Qadir's own estimate, his forces numbered 8,000 regular infantry, 2,000 cavalry, and 240 artillerymen with 20 cannons, spread equally across the eight governorates. These mobile forces were able to harass the French and withdraw from combat whenever French numbers threatened to overwhelm them in classic guerrilla war tactics.

Abd al-Qadir had also created a string of fortress towns along the ridge of the high plateau to provide his armies safe havens to escape French counterattacks. Speaking to his French captors in Toulon in 1848, Abd al-Qadir explained his strategy: "I was convinced, war having resumed, that I would be forced to abandon to you [i.e., the French] all of central inland towns, but that it would be impossible for you to reach the Sahara because the means of transport that encumbered your armies would prevent you from advancing so far."[6]

The Algerian leader's strategy was to draw the French into the interior, where the invaders would be overextended, isolated, and easier to defeat. Speaking with a French prisoner at the fortress town of Tagdemt, Abd al-Qadir warned: "You will die with disease in our mountains, and those whom sickness shall not carry off, my horsemen will send death with their bullets."[7] With both his government and his defenses better organized than ever, Abd al-Qadir was confident he would prevail once again over the French.

Abd al-Qadir did not anticipate, however, the extraordinary violence that the French would unleash on the Algerian people. General Bugeaud pursued a scorched-earth policy in the Algerian interior, designed to undermine popular support for Abd al-Qadir's resistance—burning villages, driving away cattle, destroying harvests, and uprooting orchards. Men, women, and children were killed, and officers were told to take no prisoners. Any of Abd al-Qadir's men who tried to surrender were simply cut down. Tribes and villages began to turn against Abd al-Qadir to avoid suffering the fate of his supporters. The measures also devastated the rural economy, cutting Abd al-Qadir's tax receipts.

The Algerians reeled under the French onslaught, and public support for Abd al-Qadir's resistance movement began to crumble. As the families of his soldiers came to fear attack by fellow Algerians, Abd al-Qadir brought all of their dependents—wives, children, and elderly folk—into a massive encampment called a *zimala*. By his own description, Abd al-Qadir's zimala was a mobile city of no less than 60,000. To give some sense of the size of the zimala, he claimed that "when an Arab lost track of his family, it sometimes took him two days to find them [within the crowd]." The zimala served as a mobile support unit for Abd al-Qadir's army, with armorers, saddle-makers, tailors, and all the workers needed for his organization.

Not surprisingly, Abd al-Qadir's zimala became a prime target of the French forces, keen to strike a blow against his soldiers' morale and the support base of the Algerian army. Through good intelligence on the position of the French army and knowledge of the terrain, Abd al-Qadir was able to keep the zimala safe for the first three years of the conflict. In May 1843, however, the location of the encampment was betrayed and the French army attacked the zimala. Abd al-Qadir and his men learned of the attack too late to intervene. "Had I been there," he reflected to his French captors, "we would have fought for our wives and our children and would have shown you a great day, no doubt. But God did not want it; I only learned of this misfortune three days later. It was too late!"[8]

The French attack on the zimala had the desired effect. By Abd al-Qadir's own estimate, the French killed one-tenth of the population of the mobile encampment. The loss of their elders, wives, and children dealt a severe blow to his troops' morale. The attack also dealt a severe material blow to Abd al-Qadir's war effort, as he lost most of his property and the wealth of his treasury. It was the beginning of the end of his war against the French. Abd al-Qadir and his forces went on the retreat, and in November 1843, the Algerian commander led his followers into exile in Morocco.

Over the next four years, Abd al-Qadir rallied his troops to attack the French in Algeria, falling back to Moroccan territory to elude capture. The sultan of Morocco, Moulay Abd al-Rahman, had no wish to be drawn into the Algerian conflict. However, for harboring their enemy, the French attacked the Moroccan town of Oujda near the Algerian border and sent their navy to shell the ports of Tangiers and Mogador. In September 1844, the French and Moroccan governments signed a treaty to restore friendly relations, which explicitly declared Abd al-Qadir outlawed throughout the empire of Morocco.[9] Denied a safe haven and cut off from his resource base, Abd al-Qadir found it ever harder to fight the French, and in December 1847, he surrendered his sword to the French.

France celebrated the defeat of Abd al-Qadir as a triumph over a major adversary. One of the Algerian leader's biographers (and admirers) reflected ironically: "The mind boggles when we think that it took seven years of combat and 100,000 men of the greatest army in the world to destroy that which the emir [prince] built in two years and five months."[10] The impact of the war on the people of Algeria was devastating. Estimates of Algerian civilian casualties number in the hundreds of thousands.

The French transported Abd al-Qadir back to France where he was imprisoned with his family. Abd al-Qadir was something of a celebrity, and the government of King Louis Philippe wanted to benefit from its prisoner's popularity to bestow a high-profile pardon on him. These plans were disrupted by the 1848 Revolution and Louis Philippe's overthrow. The Algerian leader was forgotten in the political turmoil of regime change in Paris. It was not until 1852 that the new president, Louis Napoleon (later crowned Emperor Napoleon III), restored Abd al-Qadir's freedom. The Algerian leader was invited as Louis Napoleon's guest of honor to tour Paris on a white charger and review the French troops with the president. Though he was never allowed to return to Algeria, the French gave him a pension for life and a steamship to take him to the place of exile of his choice. Abd al-Qadir set sail for Ottoman domains and settled in Damascus, where he was given a hero's welcome. He and his family were accepted into the circle of elite families of Damascus, where he was to play an important role in communal politics. In later life Abd al-Qadir dedicated himself to a life of scholarship and Islamic mysticism. He died in Damascus in 1883.

Victory over Abd al-Qadir was only the beginning of the French conquest of Algeria. Over the next decades France continued to extend its colonial sovereignty southward. By 1847, nearly 110,000 Europeans had settled in Algeria. The next year, the settler community won the right to elect deputies to the French parliament. In 1870, with nearly 250,000 French settlers, Algeria was formally annexed to France, its non-European residents made subjects (*not* citizens) of the French state. Aside from the Zionist colonization of Palestine, there was to be no settler-colonialism in all the Middle East to match what the French achieved in Algeria.

With the exception of France's violent imperial war in Algeria, the European powers abided by their commitment to preserve the territorial integrity of the Ottoman Empire from the 1840 London Convention for the Pacification of the Levant to the 1878 Treaty of Berlin. The formal colonization of North Africa resumed in 1881 with the French occupation of Tunisia.

Much had changed between 1840 and 1881—in Europe and the Ottoman Empire alike—as a powerful new idea from Europe took root: nationalism. A product of the eighteenth-century European Enlightenment, nationalism spread across Europe at a variable rate during the nineteenth century. Greece was an early convert, achieving its independence from the Ottoman Empire in 1830 after a decade of war. Other European states, such as Germany and Italy, took shape over decades due to nationalist-inspired unification movements, and only emerged into the community of nations in their modern form in the early 1870s. The Austro-Hungarian Empire began to face growing nationalist challenges from within, and it was only a matter of time until the Ottoman Empire's territories in Eastern Europe followed suit.

The Balkan nations—Romania, Serbia, Bosnia, Herzegovina, Montenegro, Bulgaria, Macedonia—began to seek their independence from the Ottomans in the 1830s. The European powers grew increasingly supportive of Ottoman Christians seeking to free themselves from the Turkish "yoke." Politicians in Britain and France tabled motions in support of Balkan nationalist movements. The Russian government gave full support to Orthodox Christians and fellow Slavs across the Balkans. The Austrians hoped to benefit from secessionist movements in Bosnia, Herzegovina, and Montenegro to extend their territory at the Ottomans' expense (and in the process integrated the very nationalist movements that by 1914 would lead to their downfall and set off a world war).

This outside support emboldened Balkan nationalists in their struggle with the Ottoman state. A major revolt broke out in Bosnia-Herzegovina in 1875. The following year, Bulgarian nationalists launched an uprising against the Ottomans. The Bulgarian conflict ravaged the countryside, as Christian and Muslim villages were caught up in the violence between nationalist fighters and Ottoman soldiers. The European newspapers, overlooking the higher casualty figures among Bulgarian Muslims, trumpeted the massacre of Christians as the "Bulgarian horrors." With the Ottomans pinned down by conflicts in Bosnia-Herzegovina and Bulgaria, Prince Milan of Serbia declared war on the Ottoman Empire in July 1876, and Russia followed suit in support of the Slavic peoples of the Balkans.

Ordinarily, Britain would have intervened at this point. Conservative prime minister Benjamin Disraeli had long advocated support for the Ottoman Empire as a buffer against Russian ambitions in Continental Europe. However, Disraeli found his hands tied by public opinion. The violence—and the press coverage of the atrocities—discredited his Turcophile policies and left Disraeli vulnerable to the barbs of his Liberal opponent, William Gladstone. In 1876 Gladstone published an influential pamphlet entitled *The Bulgarian Horrors and the Question of the East*. Gladstone's eloquent tirade condemned the Turks as "the one great anti-human specimen of humanity." His pamphlet advocated the expulsion of the Ottomans from their European provinces altogether. "Let the Turks now carry away their abuses," he wrote, "in the only possible manner, namely by carrying off themselves." Gladstone was more in tune with public opinion that Disraeli, and the British government was forced to abandon its support of Ottoman territorial integrity.

Once the principle of Turkish sovereignty over its provinces was breached, the European powers began to consider the dismemberment of the Ottoman Empire. Ottoman efforts at reform had not produced a stable or viable state, its European critics argued. They pointed to the Ottoman bankruptcy of 1875 as further evidence that Turkey was the "Sick Man of Europe." Better to agree a redistribution of Ottoman lands between the European Powers. Germany proposed the partition of the Ottoman Empire, dividing the Balkans between Austria and Russia, giving Syria to France, and awarding Egypt and key Mediterranean islands to Britain. Aghast, the British quickly proposed an international conference in Istanbul in November 1876, to resolve the Balkan crises and the Russo-Turkish conflict.

Diplomacy bought time, but the belligerent powers were bent on war and the volatile situation provided ample opportunities. Russia declared war again in April 1877 and proceeded to invade the Ottoman Empire from the east and the west simultaneously. Moving quickly into Eastern Anatolia and through the Balkans, the Russians inflicted heavy casualties on the Ottoman defenders. By early 1878 Ottoman defenses crumbled as Russian forces swept through Bulgaria and Thrace and pressed on to Istanbul itself, forcing an unconditional Ottoman surrender to prevent the occupation of their capital city.

Having suffered a total defeat to Russia, the Ottomans had little say over the terms imposed on them by the 1878 Congress of Berlin. The longstanding imperative of preserving the territorial integrity of the Ottoman Empire was abandoned as the European powers embarked on the first partition of Ottoman territory. In the course of the Berlin peace conference, Bulgaria received autonomy within the Ottoman Empire, whereas Bosnia and Herzegovina, though nominally still Ottoman territory, passed under Austrian occupation. Romania, Serbia, and Montenegro gained outright independence. Russia gained extensive territories in Eastern Anatolia. By these measures the Ottoman Empire was forced to surrender two-fifths of its territory and one-fifth its population (half of them Muslim).[11]

Unable to prevent the dismemberment of the Ottoman Empire, the British were intent on securing their own strategic interests in Ottoman domains before the Congress of Berlin even began. As a maritime power, Britain had long sought a naval base in the Eastern Mediterranean, from which it could oversee the smooth flow of navigation through the Suez Canal. The island of Cyprus would serve this purpose nicely. The beleaguered Ottoman sultan Abdul Hamid II (r. 1876–1909) needed an ally more than he needed the island, and so he concluded a treaty of defensive alliance with Britain in exchange for Cyprus on the eve of the Congress of Berlin.

It was the British claim to Cyprus that extended the partition of Ottoman domains from the Balkans to North Africa. Germany gave its consent to Britain's acquisition of Cyprus, though both the British and Germans recognized the need to compensate France to restore the balance of power in the Mediterranean. They

agreed to "offer" Tunisia to France to consolidate its empire in North Africa and secure its borders with Algeria. Germany, which had annexed the French province of
Alsace-Lorraine after the Franco-Prussian War of 1870–1871, was only too happy
to give its consent to this gift in the hope of fostering a rapprochement with Paris.
Only Italy, with its large settler population and significant investments in Tunisia,
raised objections—which the other powers were pleased to overlook, suggesting that
Italy might instead take satisfaction in Libya (which, in 1911, it did).

The French had permission to occupy Tunisia but had no grounds to justify a
hostile act against the compliant North African state. Since its bankruptcy in 1869,
the Tunisian government had cooperated fully with French financial advisors in honoring its external debts. The French government first proposed the establishment
of a protectorate over Tunisia in 1879, but its ruler, Muhammad al-Sadiq Bey
(r. 1859–1882), politely declined to deliver his country to foreign imperial rule.

To make matters more difficult, French public opinion had turned against colonial
ventures. A majority believed that Algeria had come at too high a price to France,
and there was little support for extending the French presence in North Africa. Without public support at home or a pretext from abroad, the French government was
stymied in its efforts to add Tunisia to its North African empire. Meanwhile, Italy
took advantage of every French delay to extend its own presence in Tunisia, where
the Italian settler community significantly outweighed the French. It was this Franco-
Italian rivalry that ultimately drove the French to action.

The French had to find grounds to justify invading Tunisia. In 1880 a French ad-
venturer defaulted on a concession and was expelled by the Tunisians for his pains.
The French consul protested, presenting the bey with an ultimatum demanding compensation for the Frenchman and the punishment of the Tunisian officials responsible
for the insolvent Frenchman's expulsion. It wasn't an insult on a par with the 1827
"fly-whisk" incident in Algeria, but it was deemed sufficient mistreatment of a French
national to warrant the mobilization of an invasion force to redeem national honor.
The unreasonably reasonable ruler of Tunisia deprived the French of a pretext for invasion by conceding to all of their outrageous demands. The troops were sent back
to their barracks to await a more propitious opportunity to invade Tunisia.

French troops were mustered again in March 1881 when a group of tribesmen were
alleged to have crossed into Algeria from Tunisia on a raid. Though the bey offered to
pay compensation for damages and to punish the tribesmen, the French insisted on
taking action themselves. A French cavalry detachment crossed the Tunisian border
and, bypassing the territory of the guilty tribe, made straight for Tunis. It met up with
a seaborne invasion force in the Tunisian capital in April 1881. Faced with French invasion forces by land and sea, Muhammad al-Sadiq Bey signed a treaty with the French
on May 12, 1881, that effectively severed his ties to the Ottoman Empire and ceded

his sovereignty to France. Tunisia's experience of reform and bankruptcy had led the country from informal European control to outright imperial domination.

While the French were occupied with integrating Tunisia into their North African empire, trouble was brewing to the east in Egypt. As was noted in the previous chapter, reform and bankruptcy in Egypt had led to European intervention in its finances and governance. Rather than restore stability, the measures undertaken by the European powers had so destabilized Egypt's internal politics that a powerful opposition movement had emerged to threaten the khedive's rule. What began as concerted action between Britain and France to reinforce the khedive's authority ended in Britain's accidental occupation of Egypt in 1882.

Egypt's new khedive, Tawfiq Pasha (r. 1879–1892), was caught between the demands of Europe and powerful interest groups within his own society. He came to the vice-regal throne suddenly, when Britain and France prevailed upon the Ottoman sultan to depose his predecessor (and father), Khedive Ismail, for obstructing the work of their financial controllers in Egypt. Tawfiq Pasha thus knew better than to cross the European powers. Yet compliance with British and French demands had exposed him to growing criticism within Egypt. Large landholders and urban elites, chafing under the economic austerity measures imposed to repay Egypt's foreign debts, grew increasingly outspoken against the khedive's misrule.

The Egyptian elites enjoyed a political platform in the Assembly of Delegates, the early Egyptian parliament established by Ismail Pasha in 1866. Their representatives in the Assembly began to demand a role in approving the Egyptian budget, increased ministerial responsibility to the Assembly, and a liberal constitution constraining the powers of the khedive. Tawfiq Pasha had neither the power nor the inclination to concede to such demands and, with the support of the European powers, suspended the Assembly in 1879. The landed elites responded by throwing their support behind a growing opposition movement in the Egyptian army.

Egypt's army had been hard hit by the austerity measures imposed after the country's bankruptcy—particularly the *Egyptians* in the army. There was a deep divide in the army between the Turkish-speaking elite in the officer corps and the Arabic-speaking native-born Egyptians. The Turkish-speaking officers, known as Turco-Circassians, traced their origins to the Mamluks as a martial class. They had strong ties to the khedive's household and to the Ottoman society of Istanbul. They held native-born Egyptians in low regard and spoke of them dismissively as peasant soldiers. When Egypt's financial controllers decreed sharp cut-backs in the size of the Egyptian army, the Turco-Circassian commanders protected their own and imposed the cuts onto native-born Egyptian ranks. Egyptian officers rallied to their men's cause and began to mobilize against unfair dismissal. They were led by one of the highest-ranking Egyptian officers, Colonel Ahmad Urabi.

Ahmad Urabi (1841–1911) was one of the first native-born Egyptians to enter the officer corps. Born in a village of the eastern Nile Delta, Urabi left his studies at the mosque university of al-Azhar in 1854 to enter the new military academy opened by Said Pasha. Urabi believed himself no less qualified to be an officer than any Turco-Circassian of his generation. He claimed descent from the family of the Prophet Muhammad on both his mother's and his father's side—in Islamic terms, a very illustrious lineage that no Mamluk could match, given their origins as Caucasian Christians converted to Islam as military slaves. A man of talent and ambition, Urabi achieved distinction, and his place in the history books, as a rebel, not as a soldier. Indeed, the revolt that bears his name was the event that precipitated the British occupation of Egypt in 1882.

In his memoirs Urabi idealized the army as a meritocracy, in which promotion was awarded through examination, "and those who excelled over their peers would be promoted to the appropriate rank."[12] Urabi clearly performed well in examination. In just six years, between 1854 and 1860, he rose from a common soldier to become, at the age of nineteen, Egypt's youngest colonel ever. Urabi was devoted to Said Pasha, the viceroy who had opened the oficer corps to native Egyptians.

With the accession of Ismail Pasha in 1863, the new viceroy reverted to the traditional bias that privileged Turkish-speaking officers in the Egyptian army. Henceforth, patronage and ethnicity would displace merit as the basis of advancement in the military. The ambitious Urabi ran into a glass ceiling imposed by the Turco-Circassian elites. Through the whole of the sixteen-year reign of Ismail (r. 1863–1879), Urabi did not receive a single promotion. The experience embittered him against his superiors in the military and the viceroys of Egypt.

Urabi's conflict with the Turko-Circassian elites began almost immediately after Ismail ascended to power. Placed under the command of a Circassian general named Khusru Pasha, Urabi complained, "He showed a blind favouritism for men of his own race, and when he discovered me to be a pureblood [Egyptian] national, my presence in the regiment distressed him. He worked to have me discharged from the regiment, to free my post to be filled by one of the sons of the Mamluks."[13]

Khusru Pasha's opportunity came when Urabi was posted to the examination board responsible for promotions—the one institution that ensured soldiers were advanced by their merit rather than their connections. Khusru Pasha ordered Urabi to falsify exam results to promote a Circassian, and when Urabi refused, the general reported him to the minister of war for disobeying orders. The case was referred up to Khedive Ismail himself and led to Urabi's temporary dismissal from the army and transfer to the civil service. Pardoned by the khedive in 1867, Urabi only returned to full military service at his former rank of colonel in the spring of 1870. Yet he still harbored deep resentments against his Turco-Circassian superiors and the injustice they had made him suffer.

The 1870s were years of frustration for the Egyptian army. Urabi took part in the disastrous Abyssinian Campaign, when Khedive Ismail attempted to extend Egypt's imperial rule over the modern territories of Somalia and Ethiopia. King John of Abyssinia dealt the Egyptians a decisive defeat in March 1876, driving the invaders from his lands. The demoralized army returned home having suffered heavy casualties and military disgrace abroad to face demobilization following the 1876 bankruptcy. As one of the economic measures imposed by the European financial controllers, the Egyptian army was to be trimmed from 15,000 to a token force of 7,000 men, and 2,500 officers were to be put on half pay. In January 1879, Urabi was ordered to move his regiment from Rosetta to Cairo for demobilization.

When Urabi reached Cairo he found the city awash in Egyptian soldiers and officers awaiting demobilization. Feelings ran high among men facing the sudden end of promising military careers and imminent unemployment. A group of Egyptian army cadets and officers staged a demonstration outside the Ministry of Finance on February 18, 1879, to protest their unfair dismissal. When Prime Minister Nubar Pasha and the British minister, Sir Charles Rivers Wilson, emerged from the Ministry, the angry officers rough-handled the politicians. Urabi, who did not take part in the protest, later recounted to a British sympathizer, "They found Nubar getting into his carriage, and they assaulted him, pulled his moustache, and boxed his ears."[14]

The military riot served Khedive Ismail's purposes so well that Urabi and his colleagues suspected the viceroy of having a hand in organizing the demonstration. Ismail wanted to be rid of the French and British ministers in his cabinet and wanted greater latitude over Egypt's budget. He argued that the stringent austerity the European financial advisors imposed were destabilizing Egypt's internal politics and put in jeopardy its ability to honor its debts to foreign bondholders. The day after the military demonstration, Ismail accepted the resignation of Nubar's mixed cabinet. However, the British and French were not about to indulge the khedive's bid to regain his powers, and in June 1879 Ismail was deposed.

Urabi and his fellow Egyptian officers were relieved to see Khedive Ismail depart. Yet the position of Egyptian officers only deteriorated under his successor, Khedive Tawfiq. The new minister of war, a Turco-Circassian named Uthman Rifqi Pasha, removed a number of native Egyptian officers from their posts and replaced them with men of his race. In January 1881, Urabi learned that he and a number of his colleagues were about to be dismissed in an operation he described in terms of a Mamluk restoration. "The Circassians were holding regular meetings of high and low ranking officers in the home of Khusru Pasha [Urabi's former Circassian commander], in the presence of Uthman Rifqi Pasha, in which they celebrated the history of the Mamluk state. . . . They believed they were ready to recover Egypt and all its possessions as those Mamluks had done."[15]

Urabi and his colleagues decided to take action. They drafted a petition to Khedive Tawfiq setting out their grievances and demands. This petition of January 1881 marked Urabi's entry into national politics, setting a dangerous precedent of military men intervening in politics that would recur through Arab history across the twentieth century.

Urabi and his fellow Egyptian officers had three main objectives: to increase the size of the Egyptian army, overturning the cuts in troop numbers imposed by the financial controllers; to revise the regulations and establish equality among all military men without distinction by ethnicity or religion; and to appoint a native-born Egyptian officer as minister of war. Urabi seemed unaware of the contradiction between these demands, for equality *and* the preference of a native Egyptian minister.

Urabi's demands were revolutionary for their time. When the officers' petition was submitted to the prime minister, Riyad Pasha, he openly threatened the officers. "This petition is destructive," he warned, "more dangerous than the petition submitted by one of your colleagues who was subsequently sent to the Sudan," Egypt's equivalent to Siberia.[16] Yet the officers refused to withdraw their petition and asked that it be brought to the khedive's attention.

When the khedive received Urabi's petition, he convened an emergency session in Abdin Palace with his top military commanders. They called for the arrest of Urabi and the two officers who had signed the petition on charges of sedition, and agreed to convene a special court-martial to try the men. Urabi and his fellow officers were summoned to the Ministry of War the following day, where they were told to surrender their swords. On their way to the prison, which was located inside the ministry, the Egyptians passed through two ranks of hostile Circassian officers, and they were taunted at their prison door by Urabi's old nemesis, Khusru Pasha. "He stood outside the cell and taunted us as 'peasants [suitable only for] working as fruit pickers,'" Urabi recalled with bitterness.[17]

The arrest of Urabi and his fellow officers provoked a mutiny in the Egyptian army. In February 1881 two units of the Khedivial Guard stormed the Ministry of War. The minister and the other Circassians fled the building. The soldiers released Urabi and his officers from their cell and led them back to Abdin Palace, where they held a noisy demonstration of loyalty to Khedive Tawfiq. The soldiers remained in Abdin Square until the unpopular Circassian minister of war, Uthman Rifqi, was dismissed and a man of their choice named his successor. The khedive also issued orders for changes in the military regulations to satisfy the soldiers' requests on pay and terms of service.

The demonstration then broke up, and the troops returned to their barracks. Calm had been restored, but the events had transformed Egyptian politics. Urabi emerged as a popular leader, and the military had forced the khedive and his government to accept their demands.

The large landholders and urban elites from the disbanded Egyptian Assembly of Delegates followed the army's successes with great interest. They recognized that they stood a much better chance of imposing their liberal constitutional reforms upon the unwilling khedive in partnership with the armed forces. Between February and September 1881, a mixed coalition of Egyptian army officers, large landholders, delegates from the Assembly, journalists, and religious scholars took shape, calling themselves the "National Party." As the Islamic reformer Shaykh Muhammad Abduh explained to a British observer, these "were months of great political activity, which pervaded all classes. [Urabi's] action gained him much popularity, and put him into communication with the civilian members of the National party . . . and it was we who put forward the idea of renewing the demand for a Constitution."[18]

The members of this coalition each had their own objectives and grievances. What held them together was a common belief that the Egyptians deserved a better deal in their own country. They took "Egypt for the Egyptians" as their slogan, and gave their support to each other's cause the better to promote their own. For Urabi and his fellow officers, the constitution represented constraints on the Khedive and his government that would protect them from arbitrary reprisals. It also enhanced their role as defenders of the interests of the Egyptian people rather than just the narrow interests of the military men.

To contemporary European observers the growing reform coalition appeared to be a nationalist movement, but this was not so. Urabi and his fellow reformers fully accepted Egypt's status as an autonomous Ottoman province. Urabi regularly declared his loyalty to both the khedive and the Ottoman sultan—and was decorated by Abdulhamid II for his services. The reformists objected to the power of European ministers and consuls over Egypt's politics and economy, and the dominance of the Turco-Circassians over the military and cabinet. When demonstrators took to the streets shouting, "Egypt for the Egyptians!" it was a call for freedom from European and Circassian interference, not for national independence.

This distinction, however, was lost on the Europeans, who interpreted the actions of the Egyptian military as the beginnings of a nationalist movement that threatened both their strategic and their financial interests. Britain and France began to discuss the best ways to respond to the Urabi threat.

The khedive followed the emergence of the opposition movement with growing concern. Already the European powers had whittled away his sovereignty, imposing European officials on his government and taking control of half of Egypt's budget. Now his own subjects sought to clip his wings further by imposing a constitution and recalling the Assembly. Tawfiq was isolated. He could only count on the support of the Turco-Circassian elites. In July 1881, Tawfiq dismissed the reformist cabinet and installed as minister of war his brother-in-law, a Circassian named Dawud Pasha Yegen, whom Urabi described as "an ignorant, fatuous, sinister man."

The officers responded by organizing another demonstration outside the khedive's palace in Abdin Square. Urabi notified the khedive on the morning of September 9, 1881, that "We will bring all of the soldiers present in Cairo to Abdin Square to present our demands to His Highness the Khedive at four in the afternoon" that same day.[19] Tawfiq Pasha was alarmed at the prospect of a new military mutiny and went with his prime minister and American chief of staff, Stone Pasha, to try to rouse loyal troops at the Abdin barracks and in the Citadel to intervene against Urabi—but to no effect. Urabi engendered more loyalty from the Egyptian military men than the khedive himself.

Tawfiq was forced to receive Urabi before Abdin Palace with only his courtiers and the foreign consuls behind him. The officers presented the khedive with their demands: a new cabinet, headed by the constitutional reformer Sharif Pasha; the reconvening of the Assembly; and the expansion of troop numbers to 18,000 men. Tawfiq had no choice but to concur. The military and their civilian supporters were in control.

The khedive succumbed to the reformers' pressures and reconvened the Assembly. In January 1882 the delegates submitted a draft constitution for the khedive's consideration. The constitution was promulgated in February, and a new reformist cabinet was appointed, with Ahmad Urabi named minister of war. Colonel Urabi, who had not seen a promotion since 1863, had finally overturned the Turco-Circassian hierarchy to secure control of the Egyptian military.

There is little doubt that the Egyptian officers took the opportunity to settle old scores with the Mamluks. Former minister of war Uthman Rifqi Pasha was accused of a plot to assassinate Urabi, and fifty of his officers—all Turco-Circassians—were found guilty of the conspiracy. Many of those detained were tortured, with Urabi's knowledge. He later confided: "I never went to the prison to see them tortured or ill-treated. I simply never went near them at all."[20]

Officials in Paris and London grew increasingly alarmed by Tawfiq's growing isolation in Cairo. The khedive's every concession to the reform movement reduced both his authority and the influence of the great powers over Egypt's economy. The British and French were concerned lest the khedive's concessions give rise to political disorder in Egypt. Urabi's presence in the government did little to assuage European concerns. Urabi forced the new prime minister, Mahmud Sami al-Barudi, to dismiss European officials appointed to the Egyptian civil service. These changes were too much, too fast, for the conservative European powers to accept. The Urabi movement was beginning to look like a revolution, and the British and French went into action to prop up the faltering khedive's regime. Ironically, their every action exacerbated Tawfiq's isolation and enhanced Urabi's standing.

In January 1882, the British and French governments drafted a joint communiqué, known as the Gambetta Note, in a bid to restore the khedive's authority. One might have expected better from two states that prided themselves on their mastery of diplomacy. The British and French hoped, by giving assurances of "their united efforts" against all internal or external threats to order in Egypt, that they might "avert the dangers to which the Government of the Khedive might be exposed, and which would certainly find England and France united to oppose them." Nothing could have weakened Tawfiq Pasha's position more than this poorly-veiled threat to protect the khedive from his own people.

The clumsy Gambetta Note was followed by European demands that Urabi be dismissed from the cabinet. Urabi's domestic standing was greatly reinforced when the unpopular European Powers sought to bring him down. Tawfiq, in comparison, became even more isolated. Urabi accused Tawfiq Pasha of acting on behalf of European interests and of betraying his own country. The prime minister resigned with most of his cabinet. Under the circumstances, no one was willing to form a new government. Urabi remained in office, which meant that the government was effectively under the control of its most popular and powerful minister. In seeking Urabi's dismissal, the European powers had unwittingly left him in control of the Egyptian government.

As the situation escalated, Britain and France resorted to gunboat diplomacy; in May 1882, the two powers dispatched a joint naval squadron to Egypt. This show of force left Khedive Tawfiq's position untenable. On May 31 he left Cairo for Ras al-Tin Palace in Alexandria to be closer to the protection of the British and French ships. Egypt was essentially being ruled by two men: the legally recognized head of state, Khedive Tawfiq, confined to his palace in Alexandria; and the popular leader, Ahmad Urabi, at the head of the acting government in Cairo.

With European warships cruising off the coast, tensions between Egyptians and Europeans exploded into violence in Alexandria on June 11, 1882. What began as a street fight between a British subject and an Egyptian coach driver turned into a riot against foreigners that claimed over fifty lives. Hundreds more were wounded, and thousands were left destitute by the destruction of homes and work places. The European press played up the Alexandria riots as a massacre of Christians and Europeans, putting pressure on the British and French governments to respond forcefully to the breakdown in order in Egypt.

Urabi knew that anti-European riots were likely to provoke the British and French to intervene. He even suspected Khedive Tawfiq of instigating the riots to precipitate foreign intervention, though there is no evidence to support this allegation. Urabi dispatched 12,000 troops to Alexandria to restore order—and to reinforce the city against the expected European response. Urabi placed Egypt on a war footing, turning to his supporters among the large landholders to ask for peasant recruits to bolster his armed forces. Emergency taxes were levied to provide Urabi's government with financial resources to withstand a European attack.

Sure enough, the commander of the British fleet, Sir Beauchamp Seymour, issued a series of escalating ultimatums, threatening to bombard Alexandria unless the city's sea defenses were dismantled. Undaunted, the Egyptian army set about reinforcing the defenses of Alexandria, extending the ramparts on the waterfront and building gun emplacements to face the threat of European ships. With neither the Europeans nor the Egyptians willing to back down, armed conflict was imminent.

The threat of military action had one unforeseen consequence: the withdrawal of the French fleet after months of concerted Anglo-French efforts. The French government was bound by its constitution to obtain the consent of parliament before entering into hostilities with any country. France was still recovering from its terrible defeat to Germany in 1870, the cost of subduing Algeria in 1871, and the expenses associated with the occupation of Tunisia in 1881. The French treasury was overextended, and the Chamber was unwilling to enter into any new foreign entanglements. On July 5 the French government explained its position to the British and withdrew its ships from Alexandria.

Now the British faced a momentous decision: either back down or go it alone. Britain did *not* want to occupy Egypt. A bankrupt state with a discredited ruler and an army in revolt is not an attractive proposition to any imperial power. Moreover, Britain's presence in Egypt would upset the balance of power in Europe that Whitehall had worked so long to preserve. Even more problematic was the exit strategy: once British troops had entered Egypt, when would they be in a position to withdraw? Given Britain's objectives of assuring the security of the Suez Canal and repayment of Egypt's debts to British creditors, the risks of military action seemed to outweigh the benefits.

Backing down, however, was never really an option. Victorian Britain would not have considered itself "Great" had it conceded to rebellious officers in less-developed countries. Admiral Seymour was given the government's approval, and on July 11 he opened fire on the ramparts and city of Alexandria. By sunset the city was ablaze, and the Egyptian forces were in retreat. A detachment of British soldiers occupied Alexandria on July 14. It was the beginning not just of a war but of a British occupation that would last three-quarters of a century.

Between June and September 1882, Ahmad Urabi served both as head of an insurrectionary government and commander in chief of Egypt's defenses against the British. Urabi enjoyed widespread support in both the cities and countryside for standing up to foreign invaders. While the khedive remained confined to his palace in Alexandria, many of the princes, attendants, and women of the royal household threw their support behind Urabi and contributed money, grain, and horses for the war effort.[21] He continued to enjoy the full support of the landed elites and the urban merchants, as well as of the religious establishment. Urabi's partisans did all they could to support the coming war, but the professional army was neither large nor confident enough to take on the British, and the peasant volunteers lacked the discipline and training to hold their ground under fire. Even as Urabi's numbers swelled, his chances remained slim.

The British were surprised by the stiff resistance they encountered from Urabi's irregular army. Sir Garnet Wolseley reached Alexandria at the height of summer at the head of a 20,000-man campaign force. He marched his troops from Alexandria to seize Cairo, but his progress was checked by Urabi's Egyptian defenders for five weeks, forcing the British to abandon the effort. Wolseley returned to Alexandria to ship his men to the Suez Canal zone, which the British were able to secure with extensive naval power in early September 1882. While in the canal zone, Wolseley received reinforcements from British India, after which he prepared to march westward toward Cairo. Urabi managed to surprise the British forces before they departed the zone and inflicted heavy casualties on the invaders before withdrawing in the face of superior numbers. The Egyptian forces fell back to a spot in the Eastern Desert halfway between the canal and the delta called Tall al-Kabir, to protect Cairo from invasion. Wolseley's forces attacked before the Egyptians had the time to lay down proper defenses. The British marched to within 300 yards of Egyptian lines in the predawn hours and surprised the defenders with a bayonet charge at sunrise on September 13. The battle was over within one hour as the exhausted Egyptian troops finally succumbed to superior British forces. The road to Cairo now lay clear before the invading forces.

The insurrectionary government of Ahmad Urabi collapsed with the Egyptian defenses at Tall al-Kabir. Urabi was captured in Cairo two days later. He and his colleagues were tried on charges of treason, found guilty, and had their death sentences commuted to a life in exile on the British colony of Ceylon (modern Sri Lanka). Khedive Tawfiq was restored to his throne, though he never recovered full sovereignty. With British troops occupying the country and British advisors posted to all levels of government, the real ruler of Egypt was the British Resident, Sir Evelyn Baring (later elevated to the peerage as Lord Cromer).

Urabi left behind a mixed legacy. Following the collapse of his movement, many criticized him for having provoked the British occupation of Egypt. Yet there is no denying the broad-based support he had enjoyed when standing up for the rights of native-born Egyptians. Some of his most outspoken supporters were women of the royal household. Urabi's lawyer, A. M. Broadley, recorded a conversation with one princess who enthused that they all "secretly sympathised from the first with Arabi [sic], because we knew he sought only the good of the Egyptians. . . . We saw in Arabi a deliverer, and our enthusiasm for him knew no bounds."[22] Princess Nazli, one of Muhammad 'Ali's granddaughters, explained Urabi's appeal in more universal terms:

> Arabi was the first Egyptian Minister who made the Europeans obey him. In his time at least the Mohammedans held up their heads, and the Greeks and Italians did not dare transgress the law. . . . Now there is nobody to keep order. The Egyptians alone are kept under by the police, and the Europeans do as they like.[23]

Urabi spent eighteen years in exile before being allowed to return to his native land by Tawfiq's successor, Khedive Abbas II (r. 1892–1914), in 1901. Granted a formal pardon by the Egyptian government, he pledged his loyalty to the khedive and forsook all political activity. A new generation of young nationalists hoped to gain his support for their fight against the British occupation, but Urabi kept his promise and stayed out of politics. An elderly man, Urabi wanted to see out his days in his beloved Egypt. His eyes were firmly fixed on the past, not the future. He spent the last decade of his life reading all of the books and newspaper accounts on the Urabi Revolt and dedicated his remaining years to clearing his name of all accusations of wrongdoing.[24] He wrote a number of autobiographical essays and circulated them widely to authors in Egypt and abroad.

In spite of his efforts, two charges stained Urabi's name for decades after his death in 1911: responsibility for provoking the British occupation of Egypt, and treason against the dynasty of Muhammad 'Ali, the legitimate rulers of Egypt. It was only after a new generation of young Egyptian colonels overthrew the last of Muhammad 'Ali's line in the 1952 revolution that Urabi was rehabilitated and was admitted to the pantheon of Egyptian national heroes.

The British occupation provoked upheaval well beyond the frontiers of Egypt. French dismay turned to hostility as they saw their British rivals establish an enduring imperial presence in Egypt, which since Napoleonic times had been an important French client state. The Egyptians had drawn upon French military advisors, sent their largest educational delegations to Paris, and imported French industrial technology; in addition, the Suez Canal was established as a French company. France refused to be reconciled to the loss of Egypt and sought by all means to settle scores with "perfidious Albion." The French took their revenge by securing strategic territories in Africa, both to restore their imperial glory and to put pressure on British overseas interests. What ensued came to be known as the "scramble for Africa," as Britain and France, followed closely by Portugal, Germany, and Italy, painted the map of Africa in their imperial colors.

Between 1882 and 1904, colonial rivalries led to a deep antagonism between Britain and France. The nadir of this competition came in 1898, when the two imperial powers very nearly went to war over rival claims to an isolated stretch of the Nile in Sudan. Neither side could allow the antagonism to fester and threaten open conflict. The only solution was to restore the imperial balance of power in the Mediterranean by conceding territory to France to compensate for Britain's position in Egypt. Given France's holdings in Tunisia and Algeria, the obvious solution lay in Morocco.[25]

The problem was that France wasn't the only European power with interests in Morocco. The Spanish held colonies on the Mediterranean coast, the British enjoyed significant trade interests, and the Germans were proving increasingly assertive in their own right. There was also the consideration that, after centuries of independent statehood, the Moroccans neither sought nor provoked invasion. The French foreign minister, Théophile Delcassé, set out his strategy in 1902, saying that he was interested "in distinguishing the international question from the French-Moroccan question, and to settle the former separately and successively with each power in order ultimately to enjoy full freedom to settle [with Morocco]."[26] Over the next ten years, France haggled with each of the European powers in turn before imposing its rule on Morocco.

The power with the least interest in Morocco was Italy, so Delcassé turned to Rome first, striking a deal in 1902 that recognized Italian interest in Libya in return for Italy's support of French ambitions in Morocco.

Britain was to prove more of a challenge. The British wished to preserve their commercial interests in Morocco and were unwilling to allow any maritime power to challenge the Royal Navy's domination of the Strait of Gibraltar. However, Britain had a genuine interest in settling its colonial differences with France. In April 1904, Britain and France came to an agreement—the *Entente Cordiale*—that served as a fresh start for their diplomatic relations. According to the terms of the agreement, France recognized Britain's position in Egypt and would not ask "that a limit of time be fixed for the British occupation." Britain, for its part, recognized France's strategic position "as a Power whose dominions are conterminous for a great distance with those of Morocco" and pledged not to obstruct French actions "to preserve order in that country, and to provide assistance for the purpose of all administrative, economic, financial, and military reforms which it may require."[27]

France moved swiftly to secure Spain's agreement to a future French occupation of Morocco. The French satisfied both British and Spanish concerns by conceding Morocco's Mediterranean coastline to Spain's sphere of influence. This provided the basis for a Franco-Spanish agreement on Morocco, concluded in October 1904.

The French had very nearly solved the "international question," paving the way to colonizing Morocco. All the European powers had now given their consent—except Germany. Delcassé had hoped to move on Morocco without involving Germany. After all, the German Empire had never extended to the Mediterranean. Moreover, Delcassé knew that Germany would demand French recognition of their annexation of Alsace-Lorraine, seized in the Franco-Prussian War of 1870–1871, in return for German recognition of France's ambitions in Morocco. This was more than France was willing to give for Germany's consent. However, the government of Kaiser Wilhelm II refused to be bypassed. Germany was emerging as an imperial power in its own right, with possessions in Africa and the South Pacific, and Morocco proved a point of competition between Germany and France.

The Germans began to assert their interests in Morocco to force France to the negotiating table. In March 1905 the German foreign minister, Prince Bernhard von Bülow, arranged for Kaiser Wilhelm II to visit the Moroccan sultan, Moulay Abd al-Aziz, in Tangier. Throughout his visit, the German emperor upheld respect for both Moroccan sovereignty and German interests in the sultan's domains, thereby raising the first obstacle to French ambitions in Morocco. The German demarche forced the French into negotiations with Germany, and the "Moroccan question" was reopened with the convening of the Algeciras Conference in January 1906.

The conference, in which eleven countries took part, was ostensibly aimed at helping the Moroccan sultan establish a reform program for his government. In reality, France hoped to use the meeting to bring broader European support to bear on Germany to overcome the kaiser's resistance to French ambitions in Morocco. Despite Germany's best efforts to turn the conference attendees against France, three of the states taking part—Italy, Britain, and Spain—had already given their consent to France's claims to Morocco, and the kaiser's government was forced to give ground. In 1909 Germany finally recognized France's special role in Morocco's security.

Having secured the consent of the other European powers to colonize Morocco, the French shifted their focus to French-Moroccan relations. The sharifs of Morocco had ruled independently of both the Ottoman Empire and the states of Europe in an uninterrupted line since 1511. From 1860 onward, however, the European powers increasingly interfered with the politics and economy of the ancient sultanate. Morocco had also undergone a series of state-led reforms during the reign of Moulay Hasan (r. 1873–1894), in a now-familiar bid to check European penetration by adopting European technology and ideas. Predictably, the results were greater European penetration and a weakening of the national treasury through expensive military and infrastructural projects.

The reforming sultan, Moulay Hasan, was succeeded by the fourteen-year-old Moulay Abd al-Aziz (r. 1894–1908), who lacked the maturity and experience to steer Morocco through rival European ambitions to preserve its sovereignty and independence. France was now actively exploiting the ill-defined boundary between Algeria and Morocco to send soldiers into Moroccan territory on the pretext of halting tribal incursions. While encroaching on the territory of Morocco, the French entangled the sultan's government in public loans. In 1904 the French government negotiated a 62.5 million francs loan ($12.5 million) from Parisian banks, furthering France's economic penetration of Morocco.

Moroccans resented the expanding French presence in their country, and they began to attack foreign commercial ventures. The French retaliated by occupying Moroccan towns—most notoriously, Casablanca was bombarded from the sea and occupied by 5,000 troops in 1907 after a violent attack on a French-owned factory. As the French encroached deeper into Morocco, the people began to lose confidence in their sultan. His own brother, Moulay Abd al-Hafiz, launched a rebellion against him, forcing him to abdicate and seek French protection in 1908.

Following his successful rebellion, Moulay Abd al-Hafiz (r. 1907–1912) succeeded his brother to the throne. However, Abd al-Hafiz was no more effective at staving off European encroachment than his brother had been. The sultan's last ally in Europe was Germany, which sent a gunboat to the Moroccan port of Agadir in July 1911 in a last bid to halt French expansion in Morocco. But the Agadir crisis was ultimately resolved at Morocco's expense. In return for France's agreement to cede territory in the French Congo to Germany, the kaiser's government acquiesced to French ambitions in Morocco.

The French occupation of Morocco was completed in March 1912, when Moulay Abd al-Hafiz signed the Fez Convention establishing a French protectorate over Morocco. Though the sharifs remained on the throne—indeed, the current king, Mohammad VI, is their lineal descendant—formal control over Morocco devolved to the French Empire for the next forty-four years. And France could finally forgive Britain for its occupation of Egypt.

Libya was the last territory in North Africa still under direct Ottoman rule, and by the time France had secured its protectorate over Morocco, Italy was already at war with the Ottoman Empire for its possession. While nominally part of the Ottoman Empire since the sixteenth century, the two Libyan provinces of Tripolitania and Cyrenaica had been under direct Ottoman control only since the 1840s—and the Porte ruled Libya with a very light touch. The two provincial capitals, Tripoli and Benghazi, were garrison towns in which the Ottoman presence was limited to a handful of officials and the soldiers needed to keep the peace.

After the French occupation of Tunisia and the British occupation of Egypt, however, the Ottomans placed growing strategic value on their Libyan provinces. Following the Young Turk Revolution of 1908, which brought a new group of nationalists to power in the Ottoman Empire, the government in Istanbul began to take active measures to limit Italian encroachment in Libya, blocking Italians from buying land or owning factories in Tripoli and Cyrenaica. The Ottomans sought by all means to avoid losing their last grip on North Africa to European imperial ambition.

For decades, the other European powers had been promising Libya to Italy—the British in 1878, the Germans in 1888, and the French in 1902. Clearly the other European states expected Italy to find a peaceful means of adding Libya to its possessions. Instead, the Italians chose to enter Libya with all guns blazing. They declared war on the Ottomans on September 29, 1911, on the pretext of alleged abuse of Italian subjects in the Libyan provinces. The Ottomans in Libya mounted a stiff resistance to the invaders, so the Italians decided to take their war to the Ottoman heartlands. Italian ships bombarded Beirut in February 1912, attacked Ottoman positions in the Straits of the Dardanelles in April, and occupied Rhodes and the other Dodecanese Islands in April–May 1912, wreaking havoc with the strategic balance in the Eastern Mediterranean.

The other European powers leaped into diplomatic action to contain the damage, fearing the Italians might set off a war in the volatile Balkans (indeed, they had been fanning the flames of the Albanian nationalist movement against the Ottomans). Italy was only too willing to allow the European conference system to settle the Libyan question. Its troops had been tied down by intense resistance from both the small Turkish garrisons and the local population in Libya and had not extended their control from the coastline to the inland regions.

Peace was restored at the price of the Ottomans' final North African territory. The European states served as mediators between the Ottomans and Italians, and a formal peace treaty was concluded in October 1912, conceding Libya to Italian imperial rule. Yet even after the Ottoman troops withdrew, the Italians faced sustained resistance from the Libyans themselves, who continued their fight against foreign rule into the 1930s.

By the end of 1912 the entire coast of North Africa, from the Strait of Gibraltar to the Suez Canal, was under European colonial domination. Two of the states— Algeria and Libya—were under direct colonial rule. Tunisia, Egypt, and Morocco were protectorates ruled by France and Britain through their own local dynasties. European rules came to replace Ottoman rules, with significant consequences for the societies of North Africa. So much of imperial history is written from the perspective of high politics and international diplomacy. Yet for the people of North Africa, imperialism changed their lives in very important ways. One person's experiences can shed light on what these changes meant for his society at large.

The intellectual Ahmad Amin (1886–1954) was born in Cairo four years after the British began their occupation of Egypt and died two years before the British withdrew. Colonial Egypt was all he ever knew. In the course of his education at al-Azhar and his early career as a school teacher, Ahmad Amin encountered many of the leading intellectual figures of his age. He met some of the most influential Islamic reformers of the day and witnessed the emergence of nationalist movements and political parties in Egypt. He saw the women of Egypt emerge from seclusion of veils and harems to enter public life. And he reflected on these tumultuous changes in his autobiography, written at the end of a successful life as a university professor and literary figure.[28]

Young Ahmad grew up in a rapidly changing world, and the generation gap separating him from his father, an Islamic scholar, was striking. His father, who passed between the academic life of al-Azhar and the demands of leading prayers in Imam al-Shafi'i mosque, lived in an age of Islamic certainties. Ahmad's generation was shaped by new ideas and innovations, including newspapers, for which journalists played a key role in shaping public opinion.

Ahmad Amin began reading newspapers as a young school teacher, frequenting a café that provided newspapers for its clientele. As Amin explained, each newspaper was known for its political orientation. Amin usually chose a conservative, Islamic-oriented paper in keeping with his own personal values, though he was familiar with both the nationalist and the pro-imperialist papers of his day.

Introduced to Egypt in the 1820s, printing presses were among the first industrial goods imported into the Middle East. Muhammad 'Ali sent one of his earliest technical missions to Milan, Italy, to acquire both the knowledge and technology of printing presses. Soon after, the Egyptian government began to publish an official gazette, which was the first periodical published in Arabic. Its primary objective was "to improve the performance of the honourable governors and other distinguished officials in charge of [public] affairs and interests."[29] Between 1842 and 1850, Rifa'a al-Tahtawi, author of the celebrated study of Paris, served as editor of this official newspaper, the Arabic title of which meant "Egyptian Events."

It took several decades before private entrepreneurs began to launch newspapers, though many of these papers came under indirect government control. Print runs were too small for newspapers to be viable without government support. One of the first Arabic newspapers, *al-Jawa'ib*, was published privately in Istanbul starting in 1861, until it ran into financial difficulties several months later. Sultan Abdul Aziz took the fledgling paper under his wing. "It has been decreed," the publisher informed his readers, "that the expenses of *al-Jawa'ib* from now on be covered by the [Ottoman] Ministry of Finance and that it be printed at the imperial press. Under these circumstances, we must pledge loyalty to our master, the great Sultan."[30] These constraints on press freedoms notwithstanding, *al-Jawa'ib* was remarkably influential, reaching an Arabic-reading audience from Morocco to East Africa and the Indian Ocean. Other papers were soon to follow.

Beirut and Cairo emerged as the two main centers for journalism and publishing in the Arab world, and they remain so today. Lebanon in the mid-nineteenth century was in the midst of a major literary revival, known in Arabic as the *nahda*, or "renaissance." Muslim and Christian intellectuals, encouraged by the power of the (often missionary-owned) printing press, were actively engaged in writing dictionaries and encyclopedias and publishing editions of the great classics of Arabic literature and thought.

The nahda was an exciting moment of intellectual rediscovery and of cultural definition, as the Arabs of the Ottoman Empire began to relate to the glories of their pre-Ottoman past. The movement embraced all Arabic-speaking peoples without distinction by sect or region and planted the seed of an idea that would prove hugely influential in Arab politics: that the Arabs were a nation, defined by a common language, culture, and history. In the aftermath of the violent conflicts of 1860 in Mount Lebanon and Damascus, this positive new vision was particularly important in healing deep communal divides. Newspapers played a key role in diffusing these ideas. One of the leading luminaries of the nahda, Butrus al-Bustani, declared in 1859 that newspapers were "among the most important vehicles in educating the public."[31] By the end of the 1870s, Beirut boasted no fewer than twenty-five newspapers and current affairs periodicals.

By the end of the 1870s, however, the Ottoman government had begun to exert new controls on the press, which developed into strict censorship during the reign of Sultan Abdul Hamid II (1876–1909). Many journalists and intellectuals moved from Syria and Lebanon to Egypt, where the khedive exercised far fewer constraints on the press. This migration marked the beginnings of the private press in Cairo and Alexandria. In the last quarter of the nineteenth century, over 160 Arabic-language newspapers and journals were established in Egypt.[32] One of the most famous papers in the Arab world today, *Al-Ahram* (literally, "the pyramids"), was founded by two brothers, Salim and Bishara Taqla, who moved from Beirut to Alexandria in the early 1870s. Unlike many of the contemporary papers that provided essays on cultural and scientific subjects, *Al-Ahram* was, from its first issue of August 5, 1876, a true *news* paper. The Taqlas took advantage of Alexandria's telegraph office to subscribe to the Reuters news wire service. Whereas the Beirut press, which had no access to the telegraph and was still reliant on the post, ran foreign stories months after the fact, *Al-Ahram* provided news from home and abroad within days, even hours, of the event.

As the Egyptian press grew more influential, the khedives sought to expand state control over the burgeoning media. The Egyptian government closed down those papers whose political views were deemed "excessive." Following the Egyptian bankruptcy in 1876 and the ensuing European encroachment into Egypt's political affairs, journalists were active in the coalition of reformers who threw their support behind Colonel Ahmad Urabi. The government responded by imposing a strict press law in 1881, setting a dangerous precedent of constraints on press freedoms.

The press restrictions were eased under British occupation, and by the mid-1890s, Lord Cromer no longer invoked the press law of 1881 at all. He continued to provide subventions for those newspapers most sympathetic to the British in Egypt— the English-language *Egyptian Gazette* and the Arabic *Al-Muqattam*—but took no action against papers that were openly critical of his administration. Cromer recognized that newspapers circulated among a very small circle of the literate elite, and that a free press was a useful pressure valve to allow the emerging nationalist movement to vent steam.

This was the world of newspaper publishing that Ahmad Amin encountered in the early 1900s: an Arab media that emerged from European technology to express the widest range of views, from pietism to nationalism and anti-imperialism.

The nationalism expressed in the newspapers of Ahmad Amin's day was a relatively new phenomenon. The idea of "the Nation" as a political unit—a community based in a specific territory with the aspiration of self-governance—was the product of European Enlightenment thought that took root in the Middle East, as in other parts of the world, in the course of the nineteenth century. Earlier in the century, many in the Arab world had frowned on nationalism when it was associated with Christian communities in the Balkans seeking to secede from the Ottoman Empire, usually with European support. Egyptian and North African soldiers had answered the sultan's call and fought in wars against Balkan nationalist movements from the 1820s through the 1870s.

However, once North Africa was removed from the Ottoman world, with the advent of European colonial rule, nationalism emerged as an alternative to foreign domination. Indeed, imperialism provided two important ingredients for nationalism to emerge in North Africa: frontiers that defined the national territory to be liberated, and a common enemy against which to unify the population in a common liberation struggle.

Mere resistance to foreign occupation does not constitute nationalism—for want of a clear ideological grounding, neither Abd al-Qadir's war in Algeria nor Urabi's revolt in Egypt can be considered nationalist movements. Without a background nationalist ideology, once the armies had been defeated and the leaders were exiled, there was no political movement to sustain the drive for independence from foreign rule.

It was only after the Europeans had occupied North Africa that the process of national self-definition began there in earnest. What did it mean to be an "Egyptian," a "Libyan," a "Tunisian," "Algerian," or "Moroccan"? These national labels did not correspond to any meaningful identity for most people in the Arab world. If asked who they were or where they were from, people either would claim a very local identity— a town ("an Alexandrian"), tribe, at most a region ("the Kabyle Mountains")—or else see themselves as part of a much larger community, such as the Muslim *umma*, or "community."

Only Egypt witnessed significant nationalist agitation in the years before the First World War. Reformist Muslim clerics, grappling with paradox of Muslims coming under European Christian rule, began to frame an Islamic response to imperialism. At the same time, a different group of reformers, influenced by the Islamic modernists, set out a secular nationalist agenda. Both the Islamic modernists and the secular nationalists influenced Arab thought and inspired later nationalist movements across the Muslim world.

Two men shaped the debate on Islam and modernity at the end of the nineteenth century: al-Sayyid Jamal al-Din al-Afghani (1839–1897), and Shaykh Muhammad Abduh (1849–1905). The two men were partners in an Islamic reform agenda that would shape Islam and nationalism well into the twentieth century.

Al-Afghani was a restless thinker who traveled widely across the Islamic world and Europe, inspiring followers and alarming rulers wherever he went. He spent eight years in Egypt, 1871 to 1879, where he taught at the influential mosque university of al-Azhar. Al-Afghani was a religious scholar by training but a political agitator by inclination. His travels through India, Afghanistan, and Istanbul had impressed on him the magnitude of the threat Europe posed to the Islamic world, and the impotence of the heads of Muslim states in addressing the threat. The central focus of al-Afghani's political philosophy was not that of how to make Muslim countries politically strong and successful, as was the case with Tanzimat reformers in Egypt, Tunisia, and the Ottoman Empire. Rather, he argued that if modern Muslims lived according to the principles of their religion, their countries would regain their former strength and overcome external threats from Europe.[33]

Although al-Afghani was convinced that Islam was fully compatible with the modern world, he believed that Muslims needed to update their religion to face the issues of the day. Like all observant Muslims, al-Afghani believed the message of the Qur'an was eternal and equally valid for all times. The part that had grown outdated was the *interpretation* of the Qur'an, a science that had been deliberately frozen by Islamic scholars in the eleventh century to prevent dissent and schism. Islamic scholars of the nineteenth century were taught theology by the same books as scholars of the twelfth century. Clearly a new interpretation of the Qur'an was called for, to bring Islamic strictures up to date and address the challenges of the nineteenth century—challenges that medieval theologians could never have foreseen. Al-Afghani hoped to constrain Muslim rulers with constitutions based on updated Islamic principles that would put clear limits on their powers, and to stimulate pan-Islamic unity of action among the global community of Muslims. These radical new ideas enflamed a talented generation of young scholars at al-Azhar, including nationalists Ahmad Lutfi al-Sayyid and Saad Zaghlul, and the great Islamic modernist, Shaykh Muhammad Abduh.

Born in a village of the Nile Delta, Abduh proved one of the greatest thinkers of his age. Islamic scholar, journalist, and judge, he ended his career as the grand mufti of Egypt, the country's highest religious functionary. He wrote for the famous *Al-Ahram* newspaper, and like al-Tahtawi he served as editor of the Egyptian government's official gazette. He was one of Ahmad Urabi's supporters in 1882 and was exiled by the British to Beirut for his pains.

While in exile, Abduh traveled to Western Europe and met up with al-Afghani in Paris, where they launched a reformist journal that called for an Islamic response to Western imperialism. Abduh built on Afghani's principles to pronounce a more rigorous course of action upon his return to Egypt later in the 1880s.

Abduh's call for a more progressive Islam, paradoxically, took the first community of Muslims—the Prophet Muhammad and his followers, known in Arabic as the *salaf*, or forefathers—as a role model. Abduh was thus one of the founders of a new line of reformist thought that came to be called Salafism, a term now associated with Osama bin Ladin and the most radical wing of Muslim anti-Western activism. It was not so in Abduh's time. By invoking the forefathers of Islam, Abduh was hearkening back to a golden age when Muslims observed their religion "correctly" and, as a consequence, emerged as the dominant world power. This period of Muslim dominance throughout the Mediterranean and extending deep into South Asia, lasted for the first four centuries of Islam. Thereafter, he argued, Islamic thought ossified. Mysticism crept in, rationalism waned, and the community fell into a blind observance of the law. Only by stripping Islam of these accretions could the *umma* return to the pure and rational practices of the forefathers and recover the dynamism that once made Islam the dominant world civilization.

As a student at al-Azhar, Ahmad Amin had to overcome his diffidence to attend classes given by the great Muhammad Abduh. His recollections of Abduh's teaching give a vivid sense of the Islamic reformer's impact on his students. "I attended two lessons, heard his beautiful voice, saw his venerable appearance, and understood from him what I had not understood from my Azharite shaykhs." Muhammad Abduh's reformist agenda was never far from his teaching. "From time to time," Amin recalled, Abduh "digressed to discuss the conditions of Muslims, their crookedness, and the way to cure them."[34]

Al-Afghani and Muhammad Abduh made Islam an integral part of national identity as Egypt moved into the age of nationalism. In their concern for the state of Muslim society, Abduh and his followers began to debate social reforms along with the national struggle.

In their debates on "the conditions of Muslims," Muhammad Abduh's followers began to argue for changes in the position of women in Muslim society. Since their first encounter with Europeans at the time of the Napoleonic invasion, Egyptian intellectuals had been confronted by a very different model of gender relations—and disapproved of what they saw. The Egyptian chronicler al-Jabarti was appalled by the impact Napoleon's men had on Egyptian women. "French local administrators, together with their Muslim wives dressed like French women, would walk in the streets, take interest in public affairs and current regulations," he noted disapprovingly. "Women commanded and forbade."[35] This was nothing short of an inversion of the natural order, as al-Jabarti understood it, of a world in which *men* commanded and forbade.

Al-Tahtawi, observing relations between the sexes in Paris thirty years later, also complained about this inversion of the "natural order." "The men are slaves to the women here and under their command," he wrote, "irrespective of whether they are pretty or not."[36] Al-Jabarti and al-Tahtawi came from a society where respectable women were confined to separate quarters at home and glided anonymously through public places under layers of clothes and veils. This was still the case in the Cairo of Ahmad Amin's childhood. Amin described his mother and sisters as "veiled, never seeing people or being seen by them except from behind veils."[37]

In the 1890s Egyptian reformers were beginning to articulate a different role for women, none more forcefully than the lawyer Qasim Amin (1863–1908), who argued that the foundation of the national struggle for independence had to begin with improving the position of women in society.

Qasim Amin (no relation to Ahmad Amin) was born into privilege. His Turkish father had served as an Ottoman governor and attained the rank of pasha before moving to Egypt. Qasim was sent to the best private schools in Egypt and went on to study law in Cairo and Montpelier. He returned to Egypt in 1885 and was soon caught up in the reformist circles around Muhammad Abduh.

While his colleagues debated the role of Islam and of the British occupation in Egypt's national revival, Qasim Amin focused on the status of women. In 1899 he wrote his pioneering work, *The Liberation of Women*. Writing as a Muslim reformer to a Muslim audience, Qasim Amin connected his arguments to a secular nationalist agenda of liberation from imperialism.

Denied access to education, let alone to the workplace, only 1 percent of women could read and write in Egypt in 1900.[38] As Qasim Amin argued then, and as the authors of the Arab Human Development Report still argue today, the failure to empower women disempowers the Arab world as a whole. In Qasim Amin's words, "Women comprise at least half the total population of the world. Perpetuating their ignorance denies a country the benefits of the abilities of half its population, with obvious negative consequences."[39] His critique, written in classical Arabic, was biting:

> Throughout the generations our women have continued to be subordinate to the rule of the strong and are overcome by the powerful tyranny of men. On the other hand, men have not wished to consider women other than as beings fit only to serve men and be led by men's will! Men have slammed shut the doors of opportunity in women's faces, thus hindering them from earning a living. As a consequence, the only recourse left to a woman was to be a wife or a whore.[40]

Qasim Amin drew a contrast between the progress of women's rights in Europe and America and the contribution of women to civilization in the West, and the relative underdevelopment of Egypt and the Muslim world. "The inferior position of Muslim women is the greatest obstacle that prevents us from advancing toward what is beneficial to us," he argued.[41] He then connected the position of women to the national struggle. "In order to improve the condition of the nation, it is imperative we improve the condition of women."[42]

The Liberation of Women provoked intense debate among reformers, conservatives, nationalists, and intellectuals. Conservatives and nationalists condemned Amin's work as subversive to the fabric of society while religious scholars accused him of subverting God's order. Qasim Amin responded to his critic with a sequel published the following year under the title *The New Woman*, in which he abandoned religious rhetoric and argued for women's rights in terms of evolution, natural rights, and progress.

Qasim Amin's work does not live up to the expectations of modern feminist thought. This was an argument among men, debating the benefits they should confer on women. In his call to improve education and the general position of women in

Egyptian society, Amin fell short of demanding full equality between the sexes. Yet for his time and place, Qasim Amin pushed the agenda of women's rights farther than had ever been done before. The debates provoked by his work set change in motion. Within twenty years, the initiative would be taken up by elite women in Egypt, who entered the nationalist movement and began to demand their own rights.

Under the impact of the great debates of the day—on national identity, Islamic reform, and social issues like gender equality, a distinct Egyptian nationalism began to emerge by the end of the nineteenth century. Two men proved most influential in shaping early Egyptian nationalism: Ahmad Lutfi al-Sayyid, and Mustafa Kamil.

Ahmad Lutfi al-Sayyid (1872–1963) was the son of a rural notable who attended a modern secondary school and, in 1889, entered law school. Though he is acknowledged as one of the disciples of Muhammad Abduh, Lutfi al-Sayyid did not privilege Islam as the basis of national regeneration. Rather, Egypt as a nation was the focus of Lutfi al-Sayyid's political vision. In this sense, he was one of the very first nation-state nationalists in the Arab world. He differed with those who gave their primary allegiance to the Arabs, or the Ottomans, or to pan-Islamic ideals. As a founding member of the People's Party, established by the circle of Muhammad Abduh, and through his writings in the newspaper he edited, *al-Jarida*, he promoted the ideal of an Egyptian nation with a natural right to self-rule.

Lutfi al-Sayyid objected to the British and the khedives as two forms of autocracy denying the Egyptian people legitimate government. Yet he recognized the benefits of sound administration and financial regularity that came with British rule. He also believed that, under the circumstances, it was unrealistic to hope for independence from Britain. The British had vested interests in Egypt and the military strength to uphold them. Rather, Lutfi al-Sayyid argued, the Egyptian people should use the British to change the Egyptian government by imposing a constitution on the khedive and to build up the institutions of indigenous rule—both the Legislative Council and the Provincial Councils.

Ahmad Amin was a regular at Lutfi al-Sayyid's office at the *Jarida* newspaper, where Egyptian nationalists would gather to debate the issues of the day. Here Ahmad Amin received his social and political education, "thanks to the lectures of our Professor Lutfi [al-Sayyid] and others, and my contact with a select group of the best intellectuals."[43]

Lutfi al-Sayyid represented the moderate wing of the nationalist movement in Egypt, a man who was willing to work with the imperialists to bring Egypt up to a standard where it could achieve independence. There was, however, a more radical version of Egyptian nationalism, and its champion was Mustafa Kamil (1874–1908). Like Lutfi al-Sayyid, he received a modern education in law, in Cairo and in France.

He was a founding member of the National Party. While in France, Kamil connected with a number of French nationalist thinkers, who were every bit as hostile toward British imperialism as was the young Egyptian. Kamil returned to his homeland in the mid-1890s to agitate for the end of the British occupation. In 1900 he founded a newspaper, *al-Liwa'* ("the banner"), which proved an influential voice piece for the nascent nationalist movement.

Kamil was a brilliant orator and a charismatic young man. He provided the national movement with broad support among students and the street. For a while, he also enjoyed the clandestine support of the khedive Abbas II Hilmi (r. 1892–1914), who hoped to exploit the nationalist movement to put pressure on the British. Yet the young religious scholar Ahmad Amin was not at first won over by Kamil's radical nationalism, which he dismissed as emotional rather than rational.[44]

In a sense, the great challenge facing nationalists in Egypt at the start of the twentieth century was that the British had done so little to provoke the Egyptian people to revolt against them. Though the people of Egypt resented the idea of foreign rule, the British brought regular government, stability, and low taxes. Few Egyptians ever came into contact with their British occupiers, who were a remote and self-contained people little given to mixing with the common people of Egypt. Thus, while the Egyptians did not like being under British rule, the British had done nothing to provoke them out of a complacent acceptance of colonial rule.

Until the Dinshaway Incident.

In 1906 a British hunting party entered lands of the village of Dinshaway in the Nile Delta on a pigeon shoot. A group of outraged peasants surrounded the British to stop them from killing their pigeons, which they raised for food. In the fracas that followed, one British officer was injured and died seeking help. Lord Cromer was out of the country at the time, and his caretakers grossly over-reacted. British soldiers arrested fifty-two men from the village and convened a special tribunal, as the Egyptian public followed developments avidly through the newspapers.

Ahmad Amin's politics and reading habits changed dramatically after the Dinshaway Incident. He remembered the date precisely—June 27, 1906—when he and his friends were having dinner on a roof terrace in Alexandria. "When the newspapers came, we read that four of Dinshaway's people were sentenced to death, two to hard labor for life, one to fifteen years in prison, six to seven years in prison, and five to fifty lashes each. We were [overcome with grief], the banquet turned into a funeral, and most of us wept."[45] Henceforth, Amin claimed, he only read Mustafa Kamil's radical nationalist newspaper in his local coffee shop.

Amin's conversion to nationalism was repeated across Egypt. Newspapers conveyed the tragedy to people in the cities, and folk poets spread the news from village to village with the songs they composed recounting the tragedy of Dinshaway and the injustice of British rule.

Calm eventually returned to Egypt, though Dinshaway was not forgotten nor were the British forgiven. In 1906 the foundations for a nationalist movement were all in place. Yet nationalists in Egypt found themselves confronting a British Empire that was looking to expand its presence in the Arab world rather than retreat. Indeed, Britain's moment in Egypt and the rest of the Middle East was just beginning.

CHAPTER 6

Divide and Rule:
World War I and the
Postwar Settlement

Nationalism emerged in the Arab provinces of the Ottoman Empire at the start of the twentieth century. It was at first difficult for the Arab peoples of the empire to imagine themselves in a separate state after nearly four centuries under Ottoman rule. The early nationalists grappled with conflicting notions of what an Arab state might look like. Some imagined a kingdom centered in the Arabian Peninsula whereas others aspired to statehood in discrete parts of the Arab world, like Greater Syria or Iraq. Nationalists before their time, they were marginal in their own society and faced such repression from the Ottoman authorities as to discourage others from following their lead. Those who wished to pursue their political dreams were forced into exile. Some went to Paris, where their ideas were nourished by European nationalists; others traveled to Cairo, where they were inspired by the Islamic reformers and the secular nationalists agitating against British rule.

Arab disenchantment with Ottoman rule grew more widespread after the 1908 Young Turk Revolution. The Young Turks were ardent nationalists who instigated the revolution to force the sultan to restore the 1876 Constitution and to reconvene the Parliament. These measures met with widespread support among the Arab subjects of the empire, who believed the Young Turks would liberalize Ottoman rule. They soon learned, however, that the new regime in Istanbul was determined to strengthen its hold over the Arab provinces through a more rigorous application of Ottoman rule.

The Young Turks introduced a series of measures they viewed as centralizing, but which many Arabs saw as repressive. In particular, they promoted the use of Turkish

as the official language of the empire over Arabic in the schools and public administration of the Arab provinces. This policy alienated Arab ideologues, for whom
the Arabic language was an integral part of their national identity. The very measures
the Young Turks imposed to reinforce the Arabs' attachment to the empire had the
unintended consequence of encouraging a nascent nationalist movement. By the
1910s, groups of intellectuals and army officers had begun to organize secret nationalist societies to pursue Arab independence from Ottoman rule. Some of these
nationalists entered into correspondence with the European powers through their
local consulates, hoping to secure outside support for their aims.

The difficulties faced by the early Arab nationalists were nearly insurmountable.
The Ottoman state was omnipresent, and it cracked down ruthlessly on illegal political activity. Those seeking independence for the Arab lands lacked the means to
achieve their goals. Gone were the days when a strong man from the Arab provinces
might rise up to defeat Ottoman armies, like Muhammad 'Ali had done. If the Ottoman reforms of the nineteenth century had achieved anything, it was to make the
central government stronger and the Arab provinces more subordinate to Istanbul's
rule. It would take a major cataclysm to shake the Ottoman grip on the Arab world.

The First World War was to prove that cataclysm.

The Ottoman Empire entered the First World War in alliance with Germany in
November 1914. It was a war that the Ottomans would have preferred to avoid.
The empire was battle weary after fighting the Italians in 1911 over Libya and the
Aegean Islands, and after two devastating wars with the Balkan states in 1912 and
1913. As a major European war loomed in the summer of 1914, the Ottoman government hoped to stay out of the fight and secure a defensive alliance with Britain
or France. However, neither Britain nor France was willing to enter into binding
commitments against their Entente partner, Russia, whose territorial ambitions the
Ottoman Empire feared most of all.

One of the leaders of the Young Turk government, Enver Pasha, was a great admirer of Germany. He believed Germany, as the only European power without territorial ambitions in the Middle East, could be trusted. Russia, France, and Britain
had enlarged their own empires at the Ottomans' expense in the past and were likely
to try to do so again. Enver was impressed by Germany's military prowess, and he
argued forcefully that Germany alone could provide the protection the Ottomans
needed against further European encroachment into Ottoman domains. Enver led
the secret negotiations with the German government and secured a treaty of alliance
shortly after the outbreak of war in Europe, on August 2, 1914. The treaty promised

German military advisors, war materiel, and financial assistance in return for an Ottoman declaration of war in support of the Central Powers.

The Germans had hoped to exploit the Ottoman sultan's titular role as caliph, or leader of the global Muslim community, to foment a jihad against Britain and France. Given the millions of Muslims in British and French colonies in South Asia and North Africa, German war planners believed that such a jihad would have devastating consequences on their enemies' war effort. When the Ottomans finally declared war on the Entente Powers, on November 11, 1914, the sultan called on Muslims around the world to join in jihad against Britain, Russia, and France. Though the sultan's call had little effect on the international community of believers, who were preoccupied with their own daily concerns far from the European theaters of war, it did raise serious concern in Paris and London. Long after the outbreak of war, British and French strategists actively courted the support of high Muslim officials for their war effort in a bid to counter the sultan-caliph's jihad.

At war once again, the Ottoman authorities clamped down ruthlessly on anyone suspected of separatist tendencies. Arab nationalists came under particular attack. One of the three leaders of the Young Turks government, Cemal Pasha, took control of Greater Syria and led the suppression of Arab nationalists there. Drawing on papers confiscated from the French consulate that implicated some of the most prominent Arabists in Beirut and Damascus, Cemal charged scores of Syrians and Lebanese with high treason. A military tribunal was established in Mount Lebanon in 1915 that, over the course of the year, sentenced dozens to be hanged in Beirut and Damascus and condemned hundreds more to long prison sentences, and thousands to exile. These draconian punishments earned Cemal Pasha the nickname *al-Saffah*, or "the blood-shedder," and convinced a growing number of Arabs to seek independence from the Ottoman Empire.

Yet the hardships of the war years affected everyone in the Arab provinces, not just those engaged in illicit political activities. The Ottoman army conscripted thousands of young men into active service, many of whom over time were wounded, succumbed to disease, or killed in action. Peasants lost their crops and livestock to the government's requisition officers, who paid for these goods in freshly printed paper money that had no real value. Poor rains, and a locust plague, compounded the farmers' problems and led to a terrible famine that claimed nearly half a million lives in Mount Lebanon and the Syrian coastal regions.

Nevertheless, and to the surprise of the European powers, the Ottomans proved a tenacious ally. Ottoman forces attacked British positions in the Suez Canal zone at the start of the war. They defeated the French, British, and Commonwealth forces at Gallipoli in 1915. They secured the surrender of the Indian Expeditionary Force in

Mesopotamia in 1916. They contained an Arab revolt along the Hijaz Railway line from 1916 to 1918. And they forced the British to fight for every inch of Palestine until the autumn of 1918.

After that, the Ottoman war effort collapsed. British forces completed their conquest of Mesopotamia, Palestine, and—with the help of their allies in the Arab Revolt—Syria. The Ottomans retreated to Anatolia, never to return to Arab lands. In October 1918, the last Turkish troops slipped over the border north of Aleppo, near the spot where Selim the Grim had begun his conquest of Arab lands 402 years earlier. Four centuries of Ottoman rule over the Arab lands came to an abrupt end.

When the defeated Ottomans withdrew from their Arab provinces, there were few who mourned their passing. With the end of Ottoman rule, people in the Arab world entered a period of intense political activity. They looked back on the Ottoman era as four centuries of oppression and underdevelopment. They were electrified by a vision of a renascent Arab world emerging into the community of nations as an independent, unified state. At the same time, they were aware of the danger posed by European imperialism. Having read in their newspapers about the hardships of French rule in North Africa and of British rule in Egypt, the other Arab peoples were determined to avoid foreign domination at all costs. And, for a brief, heady moment between October 1918 and July 1920, it seemed as though Arab independence might be achieved. The greatest obstacles they faced were the territorial ambitions of the victorious Entente Powers.

No sooner had the Ottomans entered the world war on Germany's side than the Entente Powers began to plan for the postwar partition of the empire. The Russians were first to stake a claim, informing their Entente allies in March 1915 that they intended to annex Istanbul and the straits linking the Russian Black Sea coast to the Mediterranean. France accepted Russia's claim and set out its own plans to annex Cilicia (the southeastern Turkish coast, including the cities of Alexandretta and Adana) and Greater Syria (roughly equivalent to modern Lebanon, Syria, Palestine, and Jordan), including the holy places in Palestine.

In considering their allies' demands, Britain was forced to weigh its own strategic interests in Ottoman territory. On April 8, 1915, Prime Minister Herbert Asquith convened a committee to consider postwar scenarios for a defeated Ottoman Empire. The interdepartmental committee, named after its chairman, Sir Maurice de Bunsen, aimed to balance "the prospective advantages to the British Empire by a readjustment of conditions in Asiatic Turkey, and the inevitable increase of Imperial responsibility." At the end of June 1915, the de Bunsen Committee presented its findings.

In the event of a partition of the Ottoman Empire, Britain sought to preserve its position in the Persian Gulf, from Kuwait to the Trucial States (the modern United Arab Emirates), as an exclusive sphere of influence. Furthermore, Britain sought to bring all of Mesopotamia—Basra, Baghdad, and Mosul—under its control. Britain also sought a land bridge linking Mesopotamia to the Mediterranean port of Haifa, with a railway line to ensure imperial communications.[1] What is striking is how closely the eventual postwar settlement corresponded to the recommendations of the de Bunsen Committee—particularly given the tangled web of promises that Britain subsequently concluded with its wartime allies.

The British concluded three separate agreements between 1915 and 1917 for the postwar partition of Ottoman Arab lands: an agreement with the sharif of Mecca for the creation of an independent Arab Kingdom; a European pact for the partition of Syria and Mesopotamia between Britain and France; and a pledge to the Zionist movement to create a Jewish national home in Palestine. One of the challenges of British postwar diplomacy was to find a way to square what were, in many ways, contradictory promises.

The first promise was the most extensive. Shortly after the de Bunsen Report was filed, Lord Kitchener, Britain's secretary of state for war, authorized British officials in Cairo to negotiate an alliance with the sharif of Mecca, the Ottoman-appointed chief religious authority of Islam's holiest city. It was early in the war, and the British were concerned that the Ottoman call to jihad might indeed have the impact the Germans had hoped for—a general uprising in the Muslim world that would destabilize Britain's colonies. The British hoped to turn the tables on the Ottomans with a counter-declaration of jihad by the highest Islamic official in the Arab world—in essence, turning the budding Arab nationalist movement against the Ottomans. Such an Arab revolt would also open an internal front against Germany's eastern ally.

By the summer of 1915, British and Commonwealth troops were in dire need of relief, pinned down by fierce Ottoman and German resistance in Gallipoli. In July 1915, Sharif Husayn ibn 'Ali of Mecca entered into correspondence with the British High Commissioner in Egypt, Sir Henry McMahon. In the course of their eight-month correspondence, which ran until March 1916, McMahon promised British recognition of an independent Arab kingdom, to be ruled by Sharif Husayn and his Hashemite dynasty, in return for the Hashemites leading an Arab revolt against Ottoman rule. Britain promised to support the Arab revolt with funds, guns, and grain.

Most of the negotiations between Husayn and McMahon concerned the boundaries of the putative Arab kingdom. Sharif Husayn was very specific in his territorial demands: all of Syria, from the Egyptian border in the Sinai up to Cilicia and the Taurus Mountains in Turkey; all of Mesopotamia to the frontiers of Persia; and all of the Arabian peninsula, except for the British colony of Aden.

In his famous letter of October 24, 1915, Sir Henry McMahon confirmed the boundaries proposed by Sharif Husayn, with two exclusions. He ruled out Cilicia and those "portions of Syria lying to the west of the districts of Damascus, Homs, Hama and Aleppo" in which France had declared its interests, and upheld British claims to the provinces of Baghdad and Basra, which could be satisfied by a joint Anglo-Arab administration. "Subject to [these] modifications," McMahon assured Husayn, "Great Britain is prepared to recognize and support the independence of the Arabs in all the regions within the limits demanded by the Sherif of Mecca." Husayn grudgingly accepted these exclusions, warning that "at the first opportunity after this war is finished, we shall ask you . . . for what we now leave to France in Beirut and its coasts."[2]

On the basis of this understanding with Great Britain, Sharif Husayn called for an Arab uprising against Ottoman rule on June 5, 1916. The Arab Revolt began with attacks on government positions in the Hijaz. Mecca fell to the Hashemite forces on June 12, and the Red Sea port of Jidda surrendered four days later. The large Ottoman garrison in Medina was able to withstand the Arab attack and was resupplied by the Hijaz Railway line. The Hashemites were determined to cut this vital line of communications with Damascus to force the surrender of Medina and complete their conquest of the Hijaz. They moved northward to sabotage the 1,300-kilometer-long (or 810-miles long) railway in more exposed parts of the Syrian Desert. This was where T. E. Lawrence came into his own, setting charges under culverts and trestles to disrupt the trains heading to Medina.

In July 1917, the Arab Army, commanded by Sharif Husayn's son, Amir Faysal, took the Ottoman fortress in the small port of al-'Aqaba (in modern Jordan). Faysal established his headquarters in Aqaba, from which point his forces harassed Ottoman strongholds in Ma'an and Tafila while keeping up a steady stream of attacks on the Hijaz Railway. However, the Arab Army never managed to overcome Ottoman defenses and take the town of Ma'an. Moreover, they encountered resistance from Arab tribes and townsmen allied with the Ottomans.

In the nearby town of Karak, the tribesmen and townspeople formed a 500-man militia and set off "fired with enthusiasm to fight Faysal and his band" on July 17, 1917. The Karak volunteers fought a three-hour battle against the Hashemite-led forces and declared victory after killing nine men from the Arab Army and capturing two of their horses. This minor engagement revealed the extent to which the Arab Revolt divided local loyalties between supporters of the Ottomans and of the Hashemites. In August 1917, British and French intelligence concurred that the tribes of Transjordan were firmly in the Ottoman camp.[3] Sharif Husayn's counter-jihad had failed to win over the Arabs as a whole.

Faced with stubborn Ottoman resistance in Ma'an and fighting on what was sometimes hostile territory, the Hashemites raced northward to the oasis town of al-Azrak in August 1918. From this new base, the Arab Army, which had expanded to a force of 8,000 men, set off in a pincer movement with General Edmund Allenby's army in Palestine, to take the city of Damascus. With the fall of Damascus on October 2, 1918, the Arab Revolt had secured its greatest ambition—and Sharif Husayn expected Britain to honor its commitments.

Britain's second wartime agreement for the disposition of Ottoman territory was the most complex. Britain was aware of France and Russia's territorial ambitions in Ottoman lands, though the three wartime allies had not yet struck a formal agreement. While McMahon was still in negotiations with Sharif Husayn, the British and French governments appointed delegates to conclude a formal agreement on the postwar division of Ottoman territory. The French were represented by Charles François Georges-Picot, the former consul general in Beirut, and the British by Lord Kitchener's Middle East advisor, Sir Mark Sykes. The two sides reached an agreement in early 1916, to which Russia subscribed on condition that its territorial claims be accepted by Britain and France.

The final accord, which came to be known as the Sykes-Picot Agreement, was concluded in October 1916. It painted the map of the Middle East in shades of red and blue: the red zone corresponded to the provinces of Baghdad and Basra, in which the British would have the right "to establish such direct or indirect administration or control as they desire," and the blue zone covered Cilicia and the Syrian coastal region, where the French enjoyed the same prerogatives. Palestine was the exception, shaded in brown as an area under "an international administration," whose ultimate form remained to be determined. In addition, Britain claimed an area of informal control stretching across northern Arabia from Kirkuk in central Iraq to Gaza, and the French claimed informal control over a vast triangle running from Mosul to Aleppo and Damascus.[4] The agreement also confirmed the boundaries of those territories claimed by Russia in eastern Anatolia.

The Sykes-Picot Agreement created more problems than it resolved. The British later regretted offering France trusteeship over Mosul and northern Mesopotamia, and they had second thoughts about internationalizing the whole of Palestine. Moreover, the Sykes-Picot Agreement respected neither the spirit nor the letter of the Husayn-McMahon correspondence. It was, in the words of one Palestinian observer, "a startling piece of double-dealing."[5]

Of all the wartime promises made by the British government, the third proved the most enduring. After centuries of anti-Semitism in Europe and Russia, a group of European Jewish thinkers had united around the dream of establishing a homeland in Palestine. Starting in 1882, waves of Jewish immigrants had fled persecution in Russia, and a small minority—some 20,000–30,000 in all—settled in Palestine. From

1882–1903 most of this first wave settled in the cities of Palestine, but some 3,000 lived in a series of agricultural colonies along the coastal plane and the northern highlands of Mount Carmel, supported by European Jewish philanthropists like Moses Montefiore and Baron Edmond de Rothschild.

This movement gained momentum in 1896 with the publication of Theodore Herzl's landmark book, *The Jewish State*. Herzl, a Viennese journalist, encouraged the spread of a new Jewish nationalist movement that came to be known as Zionism. Herzl convened the First Zionist Congress in the summer of 1897, in which the World Zionist Organization was established and set out its aims, "to create for the Jewish people a home in Palestine secured by public law."[6]

The World Zionist Organization needed to gain international support for its project. With the outbreak of World War I, the organization moved its headquarters from Berlin to London. The leader of the organization was Chaim Weizmann, a chemistry professor whose contributions to the war effort (he made a discovery of direct application to the production of artillery shells) gave him access to the highest levels of British government. Weizmann took advantage of his connections to seek the government's formal support of Zionism.[7] After more than two years' active lobbying with Prime Minister David Lloyd George and Foreign Minister Arthur Balfour, Weizmann secured the endorsement he sought. In a letter dated November 2, 1917, Balfour reported to Weizmann:

> His Majesty's Government view with favour the establishment in Palestine of a national home for the Jewish people, and will use their best endeavours to facilitate the achievement of this object, it being clearly understood that nothing shall be done which may prejudice the civil and religious rights of existing non-Jewish communities in Palestine, or the rights and political status enjoyed by Jews in any other country.[8]

Such a sweeping pronouncement clearly had British interests at heart. By extending their support to Zionist aspirations in Palestine, Balfour told the war cabinet, "we should be able to carry on extremely useful propaganda both in Russia and America" where "the vast majority of Jews . . . appeared to be favourable to Zionism." Moreover, the Zionists returned the favor and, following the Balfour Declaration, lobbied for Palestine to be placed under British rule, resolving one of Britain's misgivings with the Sykes-Picot Agreement, which left Palestine under an ill-defined international administration.

The moment of truth, when Britain was forced to confront its conflicting promises, came in December 1917. The Balfour Declaration was a public statement, openly discussed by the British government. The Sykes-Picot Agreement, in contrast, was concluded in secret between the three Entente partners. Following the Russian Revolution in October 1917, the Bolsheviks began to publish confidential documents from the foreign ministry to discredit the secret diplomacy of the tsarist government—among them the exchange of letters that constituted the Sykes-Picot Agreement. News of the secret agreement for the partition of the Ottoman Empire reached Istanbul before the Arab world. The Ottomans and Germans saw an opportunity to drive a wedge between the Hashemites and the British.

The Ottomans, besieged by the British army in Palestine, seized on British perfidy to approach the Hashemites with a peace offer. The Ottoman commander, Cemal Pasha, elaborated on the theme of the British duping the Arabs in a speech he gave in Beirut on December 4, 1917:

> Were not the liberation promised to the Sharif Husain by the British a mirage and a delusion, had there been some prospect, however remote, of his dreams of independence being realised, I might have conceded some speck of reason to the revolt in the Hejaz. But, the real intentions of the British are now known: it has not taken them so very long to come to light. And thus will the Sharif Husain . . . be made to suffer the humiliation, which he has brought upon himself, of having bartered the dignity conferred upon him by the Caliph of Islam [i.e., the Ottoman sultan] for a state of enslavement to the British.[9]

Cemal Pasha offered generous terms to the Hashemites with the hope that they might abandon their alliance with Britain and return to the Ottoman fold. Sharif Husayn and his sons faced a difficult decision, but they opted to preserve their alliance with Britain in order to seek their independence from the Ottomans. Arab trust in British promises, however, had been shaken—and with good grounds. Between the Husayn-McMahon correspondence, the Sykes-Picot Agreement, and the Balfour Declaration, the British government had promised most of Greater Syria and Mesopotamia to at least two parties, and in the case of Palestine, to no less than three.

To reassure their Arab allies of their good intentions, in November 1918, after the final Ottoman retreat from Arab territory, the British and French issued a palliative public statement. In their joint declaration, the countries set out their war aims in Arab lands as "the complete and definite emancipation of the peoples so long oppressed by the Turks and the establishment of national governments and administrations deriving their authority from the initiative and free choice of the indigenous populations."[10] The British and French took pains to reassure the Arabs that they sought no gain from their actions. Such disingenuous statements calmed Arab public opinion in the short run but had little bearing on Anglo-French imperial interests that underlay their partition agreements.

As the Great War came to an end, the victorious Entente Powers set themselves the daunting task of restoring order—their vision of it, that is—to a world troubled by war. In the great queue of postwar issues to be resolved, the impatient leaders of the Arab world were told to take a number and have a seat. The peacemakers would address their concerns, and the conflicts of interest arising from British wartime promises, in due course.

In more than 100 meetings between January and June 1919, the leaders of the victorious Entente met in Paris to impose terms on their vanquished foes—Germany, Austria-Hungary, and the Ottoman Empire. A serving American president left the United States for the very first time to play a role in world diplomacy. David Lloyd George and Georges Clemenceau, the prime ministers of Britain and France, took the lead in setting the agenda. Together with Italy, these states comprised the Council of Four that would make most of the decisions in Paris. After four years of "the war to end all wars," France and Great Britain were determined to use the Paris Peace Conference to ensure Germany would never rise to pose a threat to the peace of Europe again. They would use the conference to redraw the maps of Europe, Asia, and Africa, including the Arab world. And they would reward their own war efforts with the territory and colonial possessions of the defeated powers.

Among the peacemakers at the Paris Peace Conference of 1919, U.S. president Woodrow Wilson spoke with an idealism that electrified people under foreign domination around the world. In his address to a joint session of Congress delivered on January 8, 1918, Wilson set out a vision of America's postwar policies in fourteen famous points. He declared an end to "the day of conquest and aggrandizement" and asserted the radical view that in colonial matters the interests of the populations concerned must have equal weight with the claims of the imperial power. Wilson addressed Arab aspirations in his twelfth point, assuring Arabs "an absolutely unmolested opportunity of autonomous development." For many in the Arab world, this was their first encounter with the emerging American superpower that would come to dominate world affairs in the twentieth century. As the world assembled in Paris to work out the terms of peace, the Arabs looked to Woodrow Wilson as the standard-bearer of their aspirations.

Among the Arab delegations to present their case in Paris was the commander of the Arab Revolt, Amir Faysal. Born in the Arabian highlands of Taif, Faysal (1883–1933) was the third son of Sharif Husayn ibn 'Ali of Mecca (served 1908–1917). Faysal spent much of his childhood in Istanbul, where he received an Ottoman education. He was elected in 1913 to the Ottoman Parliament to represent the Hijazi port of Jidda. Faysal visited Damascus in 1916 and was appalled by Cemal Pasha's repressive measures against Arab nationalists. While in Damascus, Faysal met with members of secret Arab nationalist societies and took the leading role in commanding operations during the Arab Revolt of 1916–1918.

Following the Ottoman retreat in 1918, Amir Faysal established an Arab government in Damascus with the aim of redeeming Britain's pledge to support the creation of an Arab Kingdom. At the Versailles Peace Conference, Faysal sought to consolidate his position in Syria and to force the British to honor their commitments to his father, as set out in the Husayn-McMahon correspondence of 1915–1916, over Britain's other wartime promises. He came to terms with the Balfour Declaration and even signed an agreement with Zionist leader Chaim Weizmann in January 1919 conceding Palestine to the Zionist movement on condition that the remainder of his demands for an Arab kingdom be fulfilled in full by the Allies. "But if the slightest modification or departure were to be made" to Hashemite demands for an Arab kingdom, Faysal penned at the bottom of his agreement with Weizmann, "I shall not then be bound by a single word of the present Agreement."[11] Faysal had good reason to doubt that he would ever have to honor his agreement with Weizmann.

In January 1919, Faysal presented the Supreme Council of the Paris Peace Conference with a memorandum setting out Arab aspirations. He intended to be realistic, going so far as to tone down many of his father's original demands set out in his correspondence with McMahon three years earlier. In his memo, Faysal wrote that "the aim of the Arab nationalist movements . . . is to unite the Arabs eventually into one nation." He based his claim on Arab ethnic and linguistic unity, on the alleged aspirations of prewar Arab nationalist parties in Syria and Mesopotamia, and on Arab service to the Allies' war effort. He acknowledged that the different Arab lands were "very different economically and socially" and that it would be impossible to integrate them into a single state at once. He sought immediate and full independence for Greater Syria (including Lebanon, Syria, and Transjordan) and the western Arabian province of Hijaz; accepted foreign intervention in Palestine to mediate between Jewish and Arab demands, and in Mesopotamia, where Britain had declared its interest in oil fields; and declared the Yemen and the central Arabian province of Najd (with whose Saudi rulers Britain had concluded a formal agreement) outside the scope of the Arab kingdom. Yet he maintained a commitment to "an eventual union of these areas under one sovereign government." He concluded, "If our independence be conceded and our local competence established, the natural influences of race, language, and interest will soon draw us into one people."[12]

This vision of a unified Arab state was the last thing that the Allies wanted. Faysal's presence in Paris was an embarrassment to the British and French alike. He was holding the British to their word and getting in the way of French imperial ambitions. The Americans provided a way out for what was becoming an awkward situation for Britain, France, and the Hashemites. Wilson suggested the formation of a multinational commission of enquiry to determine the wishes of the Syrian people firsthand. For Wilson, the commission would set a precedent for national self-determination, putting the principles of his Fourteen Points to work. For Britain and France, the fact-finding commission would defer consideration of Hashemite claims for months, during which time they would be free to dispose of Arab lands as they saw fit. Faysal took the suggestion at face value and thanked Wilson for giving the Arabs the opportunity to express "their own purposes and ideals for their national future."[13]

In hindsight, it is easy to see that the American-led King-Crane Commission was a fool's mission. The British and French declined to nominate officials to take part in the study, thereby undermining the validity of what had become an American, rather than a multinational, delegation. As they had no intention of being bound by the commission's findings, they did not wish to commit their own diplomats to the process. And yet the King-Crane Report is a unique document, providing in the words of its authors "a fairly accurate analysis of present political opinion in Syria"—a glimpse into the aspirations and fears of rural and urban communities in that brief moment between Ottoman and European rule.[14]

In March 1919, President Wilson named Oberlin College president Henry Churchill King and Chicago businessman Charles R. Crane to head the commission. Both men had extensive knowledge of the Middle East—King as a scholar of biblical history and Crane through his travels in Ottoman lands, dating back to 1878. The Americans set out for Syria in May 1919 with instructions to meet with local representatives and report back on the aspirations of the Arab peoples in Syria, Iraq, and Palestine. The King-Crane Commission proved to be much more than just a fact-finding mission. The two men's presence in Greater Syria set in motion intense nationalist activity involving a broader swath of the Syrian population than any political movement up to that point.

When Amir Faysal returned to Syria from Paris empty-handed, he presented the imminent arrival of the King-Crane Commission to his followers as a favorable development and a serious step toward achieving Syrian national aspirations. He gave a speech to an assembly of notables from across Greater Syria to brief them on his experiences. He could not tell them the whole truth, of how he had been kept waiting and was humiliated by the peacemakers in Paris, who seemed intent on rejecting his claims to uphold their own imperial interests in Greater Syria. Now that he was back on Arab territory, speaking his own language to his own supporters, he turned the condescension back on the Europeans. "I went . . . to claim our due at the Conference which was meeting in Paris," he explained. "I soon realized that the Westerners were profoundly ignorant about the Arabs and that their information was derived entirely from the tales of the *Arabian Nights*." In many regards, Faysal was right. Aside from a handful of experts, the average politician in Britain and France would have known very little about the Arab world. "Naturally this ignorance of theirs made me spend a good deal of time in simply giving basic facts," Faysal explained.

Looking out over the faces of his supporters, who frequently interrupted his speech to pledge their devotion, he could not admit to failure. However, he stretched the truth beyond recognition when he asserted that the Allies had recognized the independence of the Arab people in principle. He tried to present the King-Crane Commission as an extension of great power recognition of Arab aspirations. "The international committee," he said, "will ask you to express yourselves in any way you please, for the nations today do not want to govern other peoples except with their consent."[15]

Buoyed by Faysal's words, Syrian nationalists set to work to unite the people of Syria behind a common agenda. The Arab government distributed sermons to be read in Friday prayers in Syrian mosques, political and cultural associations were enlisted to prepare petitions for the King-Crane Commission, and the headmen of villages and town quarters were mobilized to encourage an enthusiastic response to the commission. Thousands of leaflets were printed and distributed in towns and villages. For people new to nationalist politics, the leaflets provided straightforward ideas in the form of slogans. "We demand absolute independence," asserted one leaflet in bold Arabic and English. Another leaflet exhorted all Syrians to defend their freedom and used parentheses to set out nationalist slogans within the longer text.

Let no one mislead you into betraying the land of your grandfathers, or your children and grandchildren will curse you. Live free! Liberate yourself from the yoke of oppression. Seek your own benefit and make your demands the following:

First: Demand (Complete Political Independence) without restriction or condition or protection or trusteeship.

Second: Accept no partition of your people's land and your fatherland, in other words (Syria in its entirety is one and indivisible).

Third: Demand your country's borders, the Taurus Mountains in the north, the Sinai Desert in the south, the Mediterranean to the West.

Fourth: Seek for the other liberated Arab lands independence and union [with Syria].

Fifth: When necessary, show preference in financial or technical insistence to America on condition that it not compromise our complete political independence.

Sixth: Protest Article 22 of the League of Nations setting out the necessity of trusteeship over people seeking independence.

Seventh: Refuse absolutely any claim made by any state to historic or preponderant rights in our lands.

(signed) An informed Arab nationalist[16]

Even in the Arabic original the language is awkward, but the message was unam-
biguous. As local communities prepared to meet with the King-Crane Commission,
these demands were frequently repeated in the petitions they submitted and in the
slogans chanted and painted on signs and banners.

Having mobilized Syrian public opinion, Faysal and his advisors convened a
makeshift parliament to present the Syrian people's views to the international commission. The Hashemites knew enough about European statecraft to recognize that
according to their rules, a nation expressed its legitimate aspirations through an
elected assembly. They relied on Ottoman electoral procedures to select delegates
from the inland towns of Syria. They had to resort to other methods in Lebanon
and Palestine, where the British and French occupation authorities obstructed all
political action.[17] Leading members of notable families and tribes in Palestine and
Lebanon were invited to Damascus to join the Syrian General Congress. Nearly one
hundred delegates had been selected to take part in the Congress, though only sixty-
nine actually managed to reach Damascus in time to participate in its deliberations.
They were working against the clock to produce a statement of national aspirations
before the King-Crane Commission reached Damascus.

The King-Crane Commission arrived in Jaffa on June 10, 1919, and spent six weeks
touring towns and villages in Palestine, Syria, Transjordan, and Lebanon. The commissioners kept statistics on all aspects of their trip. They held meetings in more
than forty towns and rural centers and met with 442 delegations, representing people
from all walks of life, such as municipal and administrative councils, village chiefs,
and tribal shaykhs. They received farmers and tradesmen, and representatives of over
a dozen Christian denominations, Sunni and Shiite Muslims, Jews, Druze, and other
minority groups. They met with eight different women's delegations and marveled
at "the new role women are playing in the nationalistic movements in the Orient."
In the course of their travels they collected 1,863 petitions, with a total of 91,079
signatures—representing nearly 3 percent of the total population of Greater Syria
(which they estimated at 3.2 million). The commissioners could not have been more
thorough in sounding out public opinion in Greater Syria.

King and Crane reached Damascus on June 25. Yusif al-Hakim, a minister in
Amir Faysal's government, recalled:

> They paid an official visit to the Royal Palace and to the head of the government.
> They then returned to their hotel, where the first people to greet them were the men
> of the press. In brief, they told the journalists that they had merely come to assess
> the will of the people in their political future, and to learn which state they would
> choose to serve as a mandatory over them for a period to provide technical and eco-
> nomic assistance, in accordance with previous statements of President Wilson.[18]

On July 2 the Syrian Congress presented the commission with a ten-point resolution that, they maintained, represented both the views of the Syrian people and
the government of Amir Faysal.[19] The resolution revealed a surprising degree of
knowledge on the part of the drafters about international affairs; the text was replete
with quotes from President Wilson and the Covenant of the League of Nations as
well as references to the conflicting promises of Britain's wartime diplomacy and the
aims of Zionism. King and Crane claimed the resolution was the most important
document of their mission.

In their resolution, the delegates of the Syrian Congress demanded complete political independence for Syria within geographic boundaries separating it from
Turkey, Iraq, Najd, Hijaz, and Egypt. They wanted their country to be ruled as a
constitutional monarchy, with Amir Faysal as their king. They rejected the mandate
principle set out in Article 22 of the Covenant of the League of Nations outright,
arguing that the Arabs were no less gifted than the Bulgarians, Serbians, Greeks,
and Romanians, all of whom had secured full independence from the Ottomans
without such European tutelage. The Syrian delegates expressed their full willingness
to come under a mandate that was restricted to providing technical and economic
assistance. They most trusted the Americans to fulfill this role, "believing that the
American Nation is farthest from any thought of colonization and has no political
ambition in our country." Should America refuse to serve, the Syrian people would
accept a British mandate, but they rejected any role for France whatsoever. The resolution also called for the independence of Iraq, then under British occupation.

The Syrian Congress took a strong stand against the secret wartime diplomacy.
In a swipe against both the Sykes-Picot Agreement and the Balfour Declaration, its
members wrote: "The fundamental principles laid down by President Wilson in
condemnation of secret treaties impel us to protest most emphatically against any
treaty that stipulates the partition of our Syrian country and against any private engagement aiming at the establishment of Zionism in the southern part of Syria;
therefore we ask the complete annulment of these conventions and agreements."
They ruled out any separation of Lebanon or Palestine from the Syrian kingdom,
and went on to reject the aims of Zionism as inimical to their national interests.
"We oppose the pretensions of the Zionists to create a Jewish commonwealth in the
southern part of Syria, known as Palestine, and oppose Zionist migration to any
part of our country; for we do not acknowledge their title but consider them a grave
peril to our people from the national, economical, and political points of view."

There was a tone of moral indignation to the Resolution of the Syrian Congress.
Many in the provisional Syrian government had fought with Amir Faysal in the Arab
Revolt. They believed they were wartime allies of Britain and France, and had contributed significantly to the victory on the Ottoman front. Faysal and his Arab Army
had entered Damascus on October 2, 1918, and liberated the city from Ottoman

rule. The people of Syria, they believed, were now entitled to determine their own political future by rights earned on the battlefield. The Syrian General Congress expected basic justice from its wartime allies, "in order that our political rights may not be less after the war than they were before, since we have shed so much blood in the cause of our liberty and independence."

In August 1919, after six weeks in Syria, King and Crane withdrew to Istanbul to draft their report. The commissioners subjected all of the materials they had gathered to extensive analysis. In their recommendations to the Peace Conference, King and Crane largely endorsed the Syrian Congress's resolution. They called for a single Syrian state, undivided, with Amir Faysal as head of a constitutional monarchy. They recommended that Syria as a whole be placed under a single mandatory power, preferably American (though with Britain as second choice), for a limited period, to provide support. And they urged major modifications to the Zionist project, with limits on Jewish immigration. King and Crane argued that the Balfour Declaration's promises, both to establish a Jewish national home in Palestine *and* to respect "the civil and religious rights of existing non-Jewish communities in Palestine," could not be reconciled. "The fact came out repeatedly in the Commission's conference with Jewish representatives," the King-Crane report noted, "that the Zionists looked forward to a practically complete dispossession of the present non-Jewish inhabitants of Palestine, by various forms of purchase."[20] Not surprisingly, the commissioners found that nine-tenths of the non-Jewish population of Palestine were "emphatically against the entire Zionist program" and that 72 percent of the petitions they received in Greater Syria were directed against Zionism.

The commission submitted its report to the American delegation in Paris at the end of August 1919. Though Amir Faysal was not privy to the report, he could not have asked for more. For the Europeans, however, the King-Crane report was a very inconvenient document. The report was received by the Peace Conference secretariat and shelved without further consultation. It was only made public three years later, by which time Britain and France had concluded a division of the Arab world that they believed at the time better served their interests.

Britain declared its intention to withdraw its troops from Syria and Lebanon on November 1, 1919, with the transfer of authority to the French military to follow. The Syrian General Congress, faced with an imminent French occupation, decided to take matters into its own hands. Its members prepared a declaration of independence, based on the resolution delivered to the King-Crane Commission, which was read from the town hall of Damascus on March 8, 1920. Faysal was declared king of Syria, including Palestine and Lebanon.

The British and French governments refused to recognize the Syrian declaration of independence. The British looked the other way as the French prepared to occupy

Damascus and unseat their wartime ally, Amir—now King—Faysal. Increasingly isolated at home for his failure to deliver on his promises of independence, Faysal could only rally a small band of supporters to confront the French army as it advanced from Lebanon toward Syria. The Damascenes did not believe Faysal's cause worth dying for.

At dawn on July 24, 1920, a group of 2,000 Arab volunteers assembled at an isolated caravansary named Khan Maysalun, in a mountain pass on the road from Beirut to Damascus. They faced a bizarre column of colonial soldiers in French uniforms: Algerians, Moroccans, and Senegalese troops under French commanders sent to secure French rule in Syria. It was a reflection of the power of the French Empire that Arab Muslim soldiers from its North African colonies were willing to serve their colonial masters against Arab Muslim irregulars in Syria. One of the members of the provisional Syrian government, and a committed Arab Nationalist, Sati al-Husri, recorded his memories of the "day of Maysalun" as he followed events from Damascus:

> Details of the battle began to trickle back. Although I couldn't entertain any hopes of victory in view of what I knew about our army and the equipment of the French, I kept wishing that the outcome would remain in doubt as long as possible for the sake of our military honour. By 10 o'clock, however, we received word that the army had been defeated and the front shattered. Yusuf al-Azmah [the Minister of War and commander of the armed forces] was reported to have been killed. I said no—he committed suicide at Maysalun, a true martyr![21]

French forces swept past the defenders at Maysalun to enter Damascus, marking the start of an unhappy colonial occupation that would last twenty-six years. Yet the symbolic significance of Maysalun spread far beyond the frontiers of Syria. To the Arabs, this small battle represented the betrayal of Britain's wartime promises, the bankruptcy of U.S. president Woodrow Wilson's vision of national self-determination, and the triumph of British and French colonial self-interest over the hopes and aspirations of millions of Arabs. Maysalun was equated with original sin, when the Europeans imposed their state system on the Middle East, dividing a people who aspired to unity and placing them under foreign rule against their will. The new Arab states and boundaries of the postwar settlement proved remarkably enduring. So too did the problems they engendered.

Nationalist politicians in Egypt also believed they could achieve their independence from Britain at the Paris Peace Conference. Misled by Woodrow Wilson's Fourteen Points, the Egyptian political establishment thought that Paris would inaugurate a new world order. They believed the age of empire would be replaced by a new community of nations created through the exercise of national self-determination. And, like Britain's Hashemite allies, the Egyptians believed they had earned their independence after the wartime hardship they had suffered for Britain.

Following thirty-six years of British rule, the First World War had served only to entrench Britain's imperial presence in Egypt. The British unilaterally declared Egypt a protectorate in December 1914, deposing the reigning khedive Abbas II for having "adhered to the King's enemies" (he was in Istanbul at the time). As Egypt was no longer an Ottoman vassal state, its ruler was no longer a viceroy. The deposed khedive was replaced by his uncle, Husayn Kamil, the eldest member of the line of Muhammad 'Ali, with the new title of sultan. The British hoped to undermine the influence of the Ottoman sultan by promoting the Egyptian sultan, just as they hoped Sharif Husayn's call for a revolt against the Ottomans would undermine the sultan's call to jihad against Britain and France. This stratagem had little impact on Muslims in Egypt or the broader Muslim community, who continued to revere the Ottoman sultan in his role as caliph, or leader of the global Islamic community.

Once war began, the burden of Egypt's support for the British fell most heavily on the working people of Egypt. Crops were requisitioned for the war effort, and peasants were recruited to serve in labor teams to provide logistical support on the western front. Inflation and shortage of goods had reduced living standards for all, and many Egyptians were left impoverished. Cairo and Alexandria were flooded with British and Commonwealth soldiers who assembled and trained in Egypt before being dispatched to conflict in Gallipoli and Palestine. The flood of soldiers raised tensions with the local population, who believed that the presence of more Britons inevitably meant less independence.

As the war drew to a close, Woodrow Wilson's message of national self-determination fell on fertile ground in the Nile Valley. The Egyptians believed that through their many contributions to a war not of their making, they had earned the right of self-determination. On November 13, 1918, only two days after the armistice ending the First World War, a group of respected Egyptian political figures called on the British high commissioner, Sir Reginald Wingate, to demand complete independence for their country. The group was headed by Sa'd Zaghlul, the Azhar-trained follower of Muhammad Abduh who served as minister of education and vice president of the Egyptian Legislative Assembly. Zaghlul, a member of the prewar People's Party, had emerged as the leader of the nationalist opposition to the British presence in Egypt. He was accompanied by two other nationalists, Abd al-Aziz Fahmi and Ali Sha'rawi.

Wingate received the men, heard their request, and refused out of hand. Not only were the Egyptians forbidden to send a delegation to Paris to press their claim before the Peace Conference, but he refused to recognize Zaghlul's right to speak on behalf of Egyptian national aspirations. After all, no one had elected Zaghlul to be Egypt's spokesman.

The Egyptian delegation did not take Wingate's refusal sitting down. Zaghlul and his colleagues left the High Commission and promptly set about securing their mandate to speak on behalf of Egyptian national aspirations. They drafted a petition asking that Zaghlul and his delegation be allowed to travel to Paris and present Egypt's case before the Peace Conference as Amir Faysal was doing for Syria. Activists traveled across the whole of Egypt securing signatures. In spite of official obstruction by British officials and the confiscation of signed copies of the petition, the nationalists succeeded in gathering impressive support for Zaghlul's movement. Copies of the petition were sent to local elected bodies, provincial councils, and other notables, and in a short time, hundreds of thousands of signatures poured in.[22]

People across Egypt rallied to Sa'd Zaghlul's cause, impatient to secure their independence from Britain at the Paris Peace Conference. As the movement gained ground, the British tried to put a stop to the nationalist agitation by making Paris irrelevant to the Egyptian question. Wingate announced that any change in the status of Egypt would be treated by His Majesty's government as "an imperial and not an international question." In other words, Zaghlul and his colleagues would have to discuss their ambitions with the British government in Whitehall, as an imperial question, rather than argue Egypt's case to the world in Paris. The British administration gave Zaghlul a direct warning to stop his agitation. When he disregarded the British warning, Zaghlul and his principal colleagues were arrested on March 8, 1919, and deported to Malta. The result was a nationwide uprising that marked the beginning of Egypt's Revolution of 1919.

The public response to the arrest of Sa'd Zaghlul and his colleagues was immediate and violent. The country rose up in a combination of spontaneous and planned revolts that spread from the urban centers to the countryside and involved all levels of Egyptian society. The demonstrations began on March 9 when a group of students rioted and vandalized the infrastructure they associated with British rule, such as trains, trams, and lamp posts. The anti-British demonstrations and their repression by British forces left many dead and wounded on both sides.

The ancient mosque university of al-Azhar became one of the nerve centers of the uprising. After British forces arrested a number of teachers and students from al-Azhar on March 13, the British chief of security, Joseph McPherson, visited the mosque to observe the political agitation firsthand. Wearing only a fez for a disguise and receiving unfriendly looks from the Egyptians around him, McPherson could not get through the front door of the mosque because the crowd was so large. Yet even from his limited vantage point he could see a religious shaykh inside the mosque "haranguing an audience of many hundreds from the top of a pile of stones, telling them that they must scorn death itself in their efforts to destroy the tyrant, and throw off his yoke, and promising Paradise to 'Martyrs' in the holy cause." McPherson saw money being collected by the Central Revolutionary Committee to raise the revolt in the countryside.[23]

Rural communities also struck against those things they associated with British rule—the produce depots and railway facilities through which their requisitioned crops were transported during wartime were sabotaged, along with the telegraph lines that provided administrators with efficient communications. In the cities themselves, the urban working classes resorted to industrial action. The Egyptian state railway went on strike. The Cairo tramways went on strike. McPherson, the British security chief, catalogued the participants in the uprising, from schoolboys to street sweepers, with mounting disdain: "howling lunatics in the streets, women emancipated for the occasion making stump orations, children and rapscallions of all sorts shouting ribald doggerels in contempt of the fallen tyrants."

The Egyptians remember 1919 differently. It was for many their first opportunity to take part in the political life of their nation. They were united in a common belief that the Egyptians should rule over their own country without foreign interference. It was the first real nationalist movement in Arab history, in which nationalist leaders enjoyed the full support of the masses, from the countryside to the cities.

The women of Egypt made their entry into national politics for the first time in 1919. Their leader was a woman named Huda Sha'rawi. The daughter of a Circassian mother and an elderly Egyptian notable, Huda Sha'rawi (1879–1947) was born into privilege and confinement. Raised in the harem of an elite Cairo household, she grew up surrounded by women, children, and eunuchs. In her memoirs, she writes of two mothers—her father's first wife, whom she called "Big Mother," and her own mother. She loved them both but felt particularly close to Big Mother, who "knew how I felt when people favoured my brother over me because he was a boy."[24]

As a child, Sha'rawi resented being given less education than her young brother. A devoted student, she pressed her tutor to bring her grammar books so that she might learn to read the Qur'an properly. "Take your book back," the children's eunuch told the tutor. "The young lady has no need of grammar as she will not become a judge!" Huda was despondent. "I became depressed and began to neglect my studies, hating being a girl because it kept me from the education I sought. Later, being a female became a barrier between me and the freedom for which I yearned."[25]

While still a teen, Huda learned to her dismay that she was to become the second wife of an elderly cousin named Ali Pasha Sha'rawi. "I was deeply troubled by the idea of marrying my cousin whom I had always regarded as a father or older brother deserving my fear and respect. I grew more upset when I thought of his wife and three daughters who were all older than me, who used to tease me saying, 'Good-day, stepmother!'"[26] She went to her bridal bed like "a condemned person approaching execution." Not surprisingly, the marriage was not a happy one and the couple was soon estranged. They spent seven years apart, which gave Huda a chance to mature and develop her own interests before returning to her husband and resuming her role as the wife of an influential man.

The years of her marital estrangement proved a period of political development for Huda Sha'rawi. She began to organize public activities for women. She invited a French feminist, Marguerite Clement, to give a lecture in the Egyptian University, comparing the lives of eastern and western women and discussing social practices such as veiling. This first lecture gave rise to a regular series in which Egyptian women began to speak, including the Egyptian feminist Malak Hifni Nasif (1886–1918), the first Egyptian woman to make public demands for the liberation of women.[27] In April 1914, Sha'rawi convened a meeting to establish the Intellectual Association of Egyptian Women, a literary society that brought together some of the pioneers of women's literature in the Arab world, including the Lebanese writer Mai Ziyada, and Labiba Hashim, the founder of one of the earliest women's magazines.

These activities marked the beginning of a distinct women's movement in Egypt, to which Sha'rawi would dedicate the rest of her life. Lectures and women's meetings broadened the scope of elite women's participation in cultural affairs in Cairo and provided forums for women to meet and discuss issues of their own choosing without having first to seek their husbands' permission. Such limited gains were significant in their own right, but the social conventions dictating gender roles had hardly been affected. To challenge such deeply entrenched customs as had long divided men and women in Arab and Ottoman society would take a revolution.

The uprising of 1919 proved as much a social as a political revolution. The spring of 1919 was a time when strict social divides were challenged and briefly overturned. The nationalist struggle provided the opportunity for women to emerge as political actors in Egypt, and left an enduring feminist movement as a legacy. At a more personal level, these events helped Ali Pasha Sha'rawi to reconcile with his wife Huda, and to turn their marriage into a political partnership united by the nationalist cause.

Ali Pasha Sha'rawi had been involved in the nationalist movement since Sa'd Zaghlul's fateful 1918 meeting with the British high commissioner, Sir Reginald Wingate, which he attended. With Zaghlul, he was a founding member of the nationalist party that came to be known as the Wafd, or "delegation," seeking to represent Egypt's aspirations before the Paris Peace Conference. When Zaghlul was exiled, Sha'rawi took over party leadership. Ali Pasha's relationship with his wife Huda changed dramatically in the course of the revolution. He kept Huda fully briefed on all political developments so that, in the event of his arrest, she could help fill the political vacuum. Furthermore, they soon learned that there were things women could do with impunity because the British did not dare to arrest them or fire upon them for fear of provoking public outrage.

The Wafd were quick to seize upon the advantages of mobilizing women for the nationalist cause. The first women's demonstration took place on March 16, just one week after the outbreak of the revolution. Black placards with slogans in Arabic and French painted in white letters—the colors of mourning—were prepared. The demonstrators then gathered in central Cairo, planning to march to the United States legation as if to claim the right of self-determination Woodrow Wilson promised in his Fourteen Points. Before they could reach their destination, the women demonstrators found their way blocked by British troops. "They blocked the streets with machine guns," Huda Sha'rawi wrote, "forcing us to stop along with the students who had formed columns on both sides of us. I was determined the demonstration should resume. When I advanced, a British soldier stepped toward me pointing his gun, but I made my way past him. As one of the women tried to pull me back, I shouted in a loud voice, 'Let me die so Egypt shall have an Edith Cavell' [an English nurse shot and killed by the Germans during the First World War, who became an instant martyr]." After a three-hour stand-off, the demonstration broke up without violence. Further demonstrations were to follow.

The symbolic power of Egyptian women facing down the British encouraged nationalists across the country. Once outside of their harems, Egyptian women threw themselves into public life with great energy and commitment. They raised funds for the needy, visited the wounded in the hospital, and attended rallies and protests, often exposing themselves to great danger. Women also began to cross the class barrier, as elite women made common cause with working-class women. Huda noted the deaths of six working-class women in the course of the nationalist movement as a "focus of intense national mourning." Women did all they could to encourage the civil servants' strike, standing outside government offices and urging workers to defy the British and stay away from work. When Britain sent a commission of enquiry under Lord Milner at the end of 1919, Egyptian women organized another round of demonstrations and drafted a resolution in protest. They began to hold mass meetings attended by hundreds of women of all classes.

At the end of 1919, Huda Sha'rawi and her colleagues consolidated their feminist gains by organizing the Wafdist Women's Central Committee, the first women's political body in the Arab world. Huda Sha'rawi was elected its president. Sha'rawi went on to cofound the Egyptian Feminist Union in 1923, and she shattered the conventions of women's confinement that same year when she and her colleagues removed their veils publicly at the Cairo Railway Station on their return from a feminist conference in Rome. Egypt's feminist movement long outlived the revolutionary moment of 1919.

The Wafd's struggle for Egypt's independence met only partial success. Though Zaghlul and his colleagues secured Britain's permission to present Egypt's case to the Peace Conference, they learned on their arrival in Paris that the American delegation had just issued a statement recognizing Britain's protectorate over Egypt. The hopes to which President Wilson's soaring rhetoric had given rise were now dashed. The Egyptians were forced to negotiate directly with the British in London, rather than securing their independence as part of the postwar settlement.

The years between 1919 and 1922 were punctuated with periods of civil disorder alternating with periods of negotiations between the British and the Wafd. In the end, the best the Egyptian nationalists could achieve was independence in name alone. In the interest of preserving order in Egypt, Britain unilaterally declared the end of the protectorate on February 28, 1922, and recognized Egypt as an independent sovereign state, subject to Britain retaining control over four key areas "of vital interest to the British Empire": the security of imperial communications, defense of Egypt against outside aggression, the protection of foreign interests and minority rights, and the Sudan. Both sides recognized the limits of independence when put in these terms, which would allow Britain to keep bases, control the Suez Canal, and interfere in Egyptian domestic matters with nearly as much frequency as it had under the protectorate. For the next thirty-two years, Egypt and Britain would be locked in regular negotiations to redefine this colonial relationship, with Egyptians seeking their sovereignty and Britain doing its all to preserve the imperial order.

E vents in Egypt were closely followed across the Arab world, nowhere more so than in Iraq. The three Ottoman provinces of Basra, Baghdad, and Mosul had come under British occupation in the course of the First World War. Though the British had given the people of Iraq many reassurances that they would enjoy self-government, their efforts to deny the Egyptians independence were grounds for concern.

Upon the outbreak of World War I, British forces from India occupied the southern city of Basra and secured their control over the province as a whole. The British were intent on protecting the Persian Gulf gateway to their empire in India from encroachment by the Ottomans' German allies. Once in Basra, the British extended their forces northward to engage the Ottoman Sixth Army. By November 1915, British forces had advanced to within 50 miles of Baghdad, whereupon they encountered superior Ottoman numbers. The British were driven back to Kut, where they withstood an Ottoman siege for four months before surrendering to the Turks in April 1916. The Ottomans had now scored two major victories against invading British forces—in Gallipoli and Mesopotamia. However, the British resumed their campaign in Mesopotamia, taking Baghdad in March 1917 and defeating the Ottoman Sixth Army in Kirkuk in late summer 1918. British troops occupied the province of Mosul in November 1918, even though technically it fell outside the territory conceded to British occupation by the terms of the armistice agreement. British control over Mesopotamia, as first recommended by the de Bunsen Report of 1915, had been secured.

It proved easier to conquer Mesopotamia than to impose a political order on the country—in 1918 as in 2003. The people of the three provinces—Kurds, Sunni Arabs, and Shiites—were divided in their aims and aspirations. Though the different communities of Mesopotamia were fairly unanimous in demanding the union of the three provinces into a single, independent state they called Iraq and placing it under a constitutional monarchy, they had very different views on what role Britain should play in that new state. Some large landowners and wealthy merchants put a higher premium on stability and economic growth than on full independence and openly supported British administration. Some Iraqi military officers, who had served with Amir Faysal in the Arab Revolt, saw Britain as a guarantor of Sunni political preeminence. However, the majority of Iraqis rejected the idea of foreign interference in their affairs.

At the start of their occupation over Mesopotamia, the British had reassured the people of Iraq of their honorable intentions. The Anglo-French Declaration of November 1918, promising Allied support for "the establishment of national governments and administrations" in the Arab lands through a process of self-determination, was widely reproduced in the local press and reassured many Iraqis that the Europeans did not seek to impose a colonial settlement on them. As the Najaf-based newspaper *al-Istiqlal* ("Independence") noted: "The two states, Britain and France, delighted us with their statement of intention to assist us towards complete independence and freedom."[28]

But Iraqis grew increasingly suspicious as months passed without any tangible progress toward Iraqi self-rule. Instead of helping the Iraqis set up their own government, the British seemed to be establishing their own administration over the country. When in February 1919 a group of Iraqis sought permission from the British authorities to send a delegation to Paris to secure recognition for their claims to national independence, the British authorities refused. When the Iraqis pressed the British to elaborate their plans for the political future of their country, they could not obtain a straight answer to their question.

The British were, in fact, of two minds themselves on how best to rule Iraq. Some, like Sir Arnold Wilson, who as civil commissioner headed the British administration in Iraq, sought to establish the instruments of direct colonial rule on the model of British India. He even encouraged a steady stream of immigrants from India into Mesopotamia as a ready work force for a colonial administration. Others, like Gertrude Bell, who served as Oriental Secretary in Baghdad, thought it in Britain's best interests to work with the Arab nationalists in Iraq. Bell argued that a Hashemite monarchy in Iraq would provide an ideal structure for informal empire, at far less cost to the British government and far less risk of confrontation with the growing Arab nationalist movement. The Iraqis did not know whom to believe—Bell, who seemed to support their wishes, or her boss, Sir Arnold Wilson, who seemed intent on the British ruling Iraq.[29]

By 1920 the Iraqis were convinced that the British intended to subject their country to colonial rule. They had witnessed the Egyptian Revolution of 1919 from afar. They had watched with growing concern as Britain abandoned Faysal's government in Damascus and evacuated their troops from Syria and Lebanon, paving the way for a French colonial occupation there. It seemed as though Britain and France intended to deny independence to the Arab lands and to divide those territories among themselves—as of course they did.

Iraqi suspicions were confirmed in April 1920, when the League of Nations assigned Iraq to Britain as a formal mandate. The Iraqis, who had always opposed the idea of a mandate as imperialism by another name, began to mobilize to confront British plans. The opposition was led by a new organization, the Guardians of Iraqi Independence, which had emerged in 1919 primarily among the Shiite community. The Guardians attracted many Sunni supporters with their demands for complete independence and a complete British evacuation from Iraq. They held their meetings in mosques to avoid British interference, alternating between Shiite and Sunni places of worship. This political collaboration between the Muslim communities of Iraq was unprecedented, and it laid the foundations for an Iraqi national community that transcended religious boundaries.

The first public demonstrations against the British mandate in Iraq were peaceful. Shiite clerics, tribal leaders, and members of nationalist organizations demonstrated en masse in Baghdad in May 1920. The British responded immediately with a crackdown on all peaceful demonstrations and arrested those suspected of inciting opposition to the occupation. Under British repression, the Iraqi nationalists were driven from Baghdad to continue their resistance in provincial towns and villages.

The Iraqi Uprising of 1920 broke out at the end of June, encouraged by the Shiite clerics of the shrine cities of Najaf and Karbala. The British made the mistake of arresting the son of the most prominent Shiite cleric, Ayatollah al-Shirazi, and he

responded with a fatwa, or legal opinion, that encouraged revolt against foreign occupation. Fearing an escalation of the crisis, the British administration in Baghdad
arrested a number of Shiite activists and tribal leaders they believed to be instigating
the ferment. Predictably, the crackdown hardened what had begun as peaceful opposition into violent confrontation.

The Iraqi resistance movement was both well-organized and disciplined. The
leadership drew up guidelines for common action, which they had printed and distributed through local printing presses. One leaflet printed in Najaf in July 1920
decreed the rules of engagement: "Each head of tribe must make all their members
understand that the goal of this uprising is the demand for complete independence."[30] The insurgent tribesmen were instructed to make "independence" their
battle cry. They were to ensure the smooth administration of all towns and villages
that fell under their control, they were to take good care of all English and Indian
prisoners, and most of all they were to preserve all weapons, ammunition, equipment, and medicines captured from the British, as such supplies were "among the
greatest means to achieve victory."

Initially, the uprising spread across all three provinces, though the principal area
of conflict lay in the Middle Euphrates region, between Baghdad and Basra, with
Najaf and Karbala at the center of the movement. Here, the British were forced to
withdraw their troops as the insurgents took control of towns and villages, established local government, and managed to collect taxes and preserve order. Although
the British managed to prevent any major outbreaks in the capital city, the areas
surrounding Baghdad were soon overrun by insurgents. The tribes to the northeast
of Baghdad raised a major revolt in August 1920 and, for one month, held Baquba
and the other towns to the north of the Diyala River. Another major uprising took
place to the west of Baghdad, in Faluja.[31] The British hastily withdrew their troops
to consolidate their forces before striking back—with a vengeance.

Faced with a nationwide insurgency, the British had no choice but to reinforce
their overstretched military in Iraq to regain authority over their new mandate. Fresh
troops from India raised the number of British forces in Iraq from 60,000 in July
1920 to over 100,000 that October. In the course of September and October, the
British completed their reconquest of Iraq with overwhelming force, using heavy
artillery and aerial bombardment. They regained Faluja in early September, inflicting
a heavy punishment on the local tribes. Later that month they proceeded against
the tribes of the Diyala River. They then moved on to the Middle Euphrates. A journalist in Najaf described the British onslaught: "They attacked the houses of tribal
shaykhs and burned them down, contents and all. They killed many men, horses
and livestock." The British were relentless in pursuing the insurgents and refused
all negotiations. "The officers had no other interest than our extermination, or put-

ting us on trial," he continued. "We agree to their request for a truce and they violate it. We allow them to withdraw with their arms when we have secured [territory] from them and they respond treacherously with attacks on us. In recent days there has been bloodshed and the destruction of populous towns and the violation of the sanctity of places of worship to make humanity weep."[32]

With the surrender of Najaf and Karbala at the end of October, the uprising came to an end. The costs—human and material—were high. According to British estimates, over 2,200 British and Indian soldiers and some 8,450 Iraqis were killed or wounded.[33] There are no estimates for the material losses of the Iraqi people.

The Uprising of 1920, referred to in Iraq as the "Revolution of 1920," has a special place in the nationalist mythology of the modern Iraqi state comparable to the American Revolution of 1776 in the United States. These were not social revolutions so much as popular uprisings against foreign occupiers, and they marked the starting point of nationalist movements in both countries. Whereas most westerners have no knowledge of the 1920 uprising, generations of Iraqi schoolchildren have grown up learning how nationalist heroes stood up against foreign armies and imperialism in towns like Faluja, Baquba, and Najaf—the Iraqi equivalents of Lexington and Concord.

The First World War and the postwar settlement together constituted one of the most momentous periods in modern Arab history. Four centuries of Ottoman rule came to a decisive end across the Arab world in October 1918. Few Arab contemporaries could have imagined a world without the Ottomans. The nineteenth-century reforms had extended Istanbul's hold on the Arab provinces by a more elaborate bureaucracy, communications infrastructure like railways and telegraphs, and by making an Ottoman education available to a growing number of Arab subjects through expansions in the school system. The Arabs probably felt more connected to the Ottoman world by the start of the twentieth century than they ever had before.

The links between the Arabs and the Ottomans only intensified after 1908, under the Young Turks. By that time, the Ottomans had lost nearly all their European provinces in the Balkans. The Young Turks had inherited a Turco-Arab empire and did all they could to intensify Istanbul's grip over the Arab provinces. Young Turk polices might have alienated Arab nationalists, but they succeeded in making Arab independence seem an unattainable goal.

With the collapse of the Ottoman Empire, Arab nationalists entered a period of intense activity, driven by aspirations to independent rule. For a brief, heady moment between 1918 and 1920, political leaders in Egypt, Syria, Iraq, and the Hijaz believed themselves on the threshold of a new age of independence. They looked to the Paris Peace Conference, and to the new world order promised by Woodrow Wilson, to confirm their ambitions. They were, without exception, to be disappointed.

The new age the Arabs faced would in fact be shaped by European imperialism rather than Arab independence. The European powers established their strategic imperatives and resolved all points of disagreement between themselves through the postwar peace process. France added Syria and Lebanon to its Arab possessions in North Africa. Britain was now master of Egypt, Palestine, Transjordan, and Iraq. Though there would be some tinkering with specific frontiers, the European powers drew up the boundaries of the modern states of the Middle East as we now know them (with the significant exception of Palestine). The Arabs were never reconciled to this fundamental injustice, and they spent the remainder of the interwar years in conflict with their colonial masters in pursuit of their long-standing aspiration for independence.

CHAPTER 7

The British Empire
in the Middle East

By the time of the postwar settlement conferring the mandates of Iraq, Transjordan, and Palestine on Great Britain, the British Empire in the Arab world was already a century old. The British East India Company had been drawn into the treacherous waters of the Persian Gulf in the early nineteenth century to combat the growing threat to merchant shipping posed by the seaborne tribes of Sharja and Ras al-Khaima, now part of the United Arab Emirates. The Persian Gulf was a vital land-and-sea link between the Eastern Mediterranean and India, and the British were determined to put a stop to Gulf piracy. In the process of subduing what they called the "pirate coast," the British transformed the Persian Gulf into a British lake.

The record of British grievances against the Qasimi confederation of tribes in Sharja and Ras al-Khaima dated back to 1797. The East India Company attributed a string of attacks on British, Ottoman, and Arab shipping to the Qawasim (plural of Qasimi). In September 1809, the East India Company dispatched a sixteen-ship punitive expedition to the pirate coast. The fleet was under instructions to attack the town of Ras al-Khaima and burn the ships and stores of the Qasimi raiders. Between November 1809 and January 1810, the British fleet inflicted significant damage on Ras al-Khaima and a string of four other Qasimi ports. The British burned sixty large and forty-three small vessels and seized some £20,000 in allegedly stolen property before returning home. Yet for failing to secure a formal agreement with the Qawasim, the British would continue to face attacks on their shipping in the Gulf.[1]

Within five years of the first British expedition, the Qasimis had rebuilt their fleet and resumed their seaborne raiding. In 1819 a second British expedition was dispatched from Bombay to subdue the Qasimis. With twice the forces, and a focus on Ras al-Khaima, the expedition not only succeeded in seizing and burning most of the Qasimi shipping but also achieved the political settlement that had eluded the first campaign. On January 8, 1820, the shaykhs of Abu Dhabi, Dubai, Ajman, Umm al-Qaiwain, and Bahrain, as well as the Qasimi family who ruled over Sharjah and Ras al-Khaima, signed a general treaty pledging a complete and permanent cessation to all attacks on British shipping. They also accepted a common set of maritime rules in return for trade access to all British ports in the Persian Gulf and Indian Ocean. By granting the seafaring shaykhdoms access to ports under British control, the agreement gave all parties an economic incentive to preserve the peace on the high seas and in-shore waters. These terms were confirmed in the Perpetual Treaty of 1853, which outlawed maritime hostilities between all of the states in the Gulf. The mini-states of the "pirate coast" now came to be known as the Trucial States, so called for the formal truce struck with Britain and among themselves.

It was the beginning of a nineteenth century *Pax Britannicus* during which the Persian Gulf developed into an out-and-out British protectorate. The British deepened their control over the Gulf through a series of bilateral agreements concluded with the rulers of individual shaykhdoms. In 1880 the shaykh of Bahrain signed an agreement that effectively placed his foreign relations under British control, promising "to abstain from entering into negotiations or making treaties of any sort with any State or Government other than the British without the consent of the said British Government." The British concluded similar agreements with the other Persian Gulf shaykhdoms.[2] In the 1890s the British went even further, obtaining from the Gulf rulers "nonalienation bonds," in which they pledged not to "cede, sell, mortgage or otherwise give for occupation any part of [their] territory save to the British Government."[3] Britain took these measures to ensure that neither the Ottoman Empire, which since the 1870s had sought to extend its sovereignty over the Persian Gulf, nor any of its European rivals might threaten Britain's paramount control over this strategic sea route to its empire in India. Kuwait and Qatar both sought British protection against Ottoman expansionism and joined the Gulf "protectorate" in 1899 and 1916, respectively.

Britain's growing reliance on oil gave the Persian Gulf added significance in the twentieth century. With the conversion of the Royal Navy from coal to oil in 1907, the Arab shaykhdoms of the Persian Gulf took on a new strategic role in British imperial thinking. In 1913 Winston Churchill, then first lord of the admiralty, confronted the House of Commons with Britain's new dependence on oil. "In the year 1907," he revealed, "the first flotilla of ocean-going destroyers wholly dependent upon oil was created, and since then, in each successive year, another flotilla of 'oil only' destroyers has been built." By 1913, he claimed, there were some 100 new oil-powered ships in the Royal Navy.[4] As a result, Britain's priorities in the Persian Gulf expanded from trade and communications with India to reflect this new strategic interest in oil.

The first major oil reserve in the Persian Gulf region was struck in May 1908 in central Iran. Geologists had every reason to believe that exportable quantities of oil remained to be discovered in the Arab states of the Gulf. The British began to conclude agreements with the gulf shaykhdoms for exclusive rights to explore for oil. The ruler of Kuwait gave the British a concession in October 1913, pledging to allow only persons or firms approved by His Majesty's government to prospect for oil in his territory. A similar agreement was concluded with the ruler of Bahrain on May 14, 1914. The prospect of oil, combined with commerce and imperial communications, made the Persian Gulf an area of particular strategic importance to Great Britain by the First World War. In 1915 a British government report defined "our special and supreme position in the Persian Gulf" as "one of the cardinal principles of our policy in the East."[5]

In 1913 a new Arab state burst upon the *Pax Britannica* in the Persian Gulf. The Al Sa'ud (whose eighteenth-century confederation challenged Ottoman rule from Iraq to the holy cities of Mecca and Medina until defeated by Muhammad 'Ali's forces in 1818) had reestablished their partnership with the descendants of Muhammad ibn Abd al-Wahhab to launch a new Saudi-Wahhabi confederation. At their head was a charismatic young leader named Abd al-Aziz ibn Abd al-Rahman al-Faysal Al Sa'ud (1880–1953), better known in the West as Ibn Saud.

Ibn Saud began his rise to power in 1902 when he led his followers to victory over their long-standing rivals, the Rashidi clan, to seize the Central Arabian oasis town of Riyadh. His fighters, known as the Ikhwan ("the brothers"), were zealots who sought to impose their austere Wahhabi interpretation of Islam across the Arabian Peninsula. They also reaped the rewards of religiously sanctioned plunder whenever they conquered a town that rejected their message. These incentives of faith and gain combined to make the Ikhwan the strongest fighting force on the peninsula. Ibn Saud declared Riyadh his capital, and over the next eleven years he deployed the Ikhwan to expand the territory under his rule from the Arabian interior to the Persian Gulf.

In 1913 Ibn Saud conquered the Hasa region of Eastern Arabia from the Ottoman Empire. The Ottomans had attempted to integrate this isolated Arabian region (known today as the Eastern Province of Saudi Arabia) to their empire in 1871 in a bid to extend their influence over the Persian Gulf—a bid the British were determined to stymie. By 1913 the Ottomans had all but abandoned their administration in the district. The Saudis took the main town of Hufuf unopposed and emerged as the dominant new power among the Arab Gulf states.

Faced with a powerful new Gulf ruler, the British concluded a treaty with Ibn Saud by the end of 1915. The treaty confirmed British recognition of Ibn Saud's leadership and extended British protection over the central and eastern Arabian territories then under his control. In return, the Saudis pledged not to enter into agreement with, or to sell any territory to, any other foreign power without prior British consent, and to refrain from all aggression against other Gulf states—in essence turning Ibn Saud's lands into another Trucial State. In concluding the agreement, Britain gave Ibn Saud £20,000, a monthly stipend of £5,000, and a large number of rifles and machine guns, intended to be used against the Ottomans and their Arab allies, who had sided with Germany against Britain in World War I.

But Ibn Saud had no interest in fighting the Ottomans in Arabia. Instead, he used British guns and funds to advance his own objectives, which increasingly led westward toward the Red Sea province of the Hijaz, in which lay Mecca and Medina, the holy cities of Islam. Here Saudi ambitions confronted the claims of another British ally— Sharif Husayn of Mecca, with whom Britain had concluded a wartime alliance in autumn 1915. Sharif Husayn, like Ibn Saud, aspired to rule all of Arabia. By declaring the Arab Revolt against Ottoman rule in June 1916, Sharif Husayn hoped to realize his ambitions in Arabia, Syria, and Iraq with British support. Yet by fighting the Ottomans and extending his forces along a 1,300-kilometer (810-mile) stretch of desert, the sharif had left his home province of Hijaz vulnerable to Ibn Saud's forces. The vast Arabian Peninsula was not big enough to accommodate the ambitions of both men. Between 1916 and 1918, the balance began to shift in Ibn Saud's favor.

Conflict between the Saudis and the Hashemites became inevitable when Sharif Husayn declared himself "king of the Arab Countries" in October 1916, following the outbreak of the Arab Revolt. Even his British allies, who had promised him an "Arab kingdom," were only willing to recognize him as "king of the Hijaz" in addition to sharif of Mecca. Ibn Saud was unlikely to let the self-proclaimed King Husayn's claim stand.

Throughout World War I Britain tried to keep the peace between its two Arab allies and to focus their energies on fighting the Ottomans. However, the Saudi-Hashemite battle for ascendancy broke into open conflict just months before the collapse of the Ottoman war effort. A remarkable exchange of unpublished letters written by the two desert monarchs captures the rivalry just as tempers rose with the summer heat in 1918.

With his forces fully engaged against the Ottomans all along the Hijaz Railway line, King Husayn was growing increasingly concerned by reports that the Saudi ruler had been distributing weapons among tribes that had recently pledged allegiance to the Wahhabi cause. These were no doubt arms that the British had provided Ibn Saud, and the Hashemite ruler was increasingly concerned that British arms would be used against his own forces. In February 1918, Husayn wrote to admonish Ibn Saud: "Do the [Wahhabi] tribesmen believe God will find them innocent of hostilities against the people of Islam," he wrote, "who trust in God to protect their lives and property?" Husayn warned his rival that it was an act against God's religion to arm Muslims to fight against fellow Muslims.[6]

Ibn Saud was outraged by Husayn's letter. After all, what went on in the Najd was no business of the sharif of Mecca. Ibn Saud's response provoked a fresh riposte from Husayn in May 1918. If Ibn Saud's actions had been limited to the Central Arabian province of the Najd, the Hashemites might not be so concerned. However, the Saudi ruler had recently secured the allegiance of one of King Husayn's own governors, a man named Khalid ibn Luway, in the oasis town of al-Khurma on the Najd-Hijaz frontier. "There is no cause for deceiving Khalid ibn Luway, or to use tricks and subterfuge on him," the old king complained.[7]

The oasis town of Khurma was strategically located between the rival Arab rulers' territories, and with a population of 5,000 it was an important settlement in its own right. Though he had been a subject of the sharif of Mecca, Khalid had declared his adherence to Wahhabi doctrine in 1918, placed his town under Ibn Saud's rule, and diverted its taxes from Mecca to the Saudi treasury. In his memoirs, King Husayn's son Amir Abdullah wrote that Khalid "killed innocent people, even putting his own brother to death because he did not share his religious convictions. He kept persecuting any of the Hashemite tribes who would not follow the Wahhabi movement."[8] King Husayn tried to persuade the wayward governor to return to the fold, but to no avail.

The dispute over Khurma led to the first armed conflict between the Hashemites and the Saudis. King Husayn dispatched a force of over 2,600 infantry and horsemen in June 1918 to retake Khurma but found the town reinforced by Ibn Saud's Ikhwan fighters.[9] The Hashemite troops were decimated by the Saudis in two separate engagements. The British, concerned lest their Arab allies succumb to internecine fighting before the Ottomans had been defeated, put pressure on Ibn Saud to seek peace with King Husayn.

Buoyed by his fighters' victories in Khurma, Ibn Saud drafted a condescending letter to Husayn in August 1918. The Saudi leader deployed titles as a way of asserting geographic sway. Whereas Ibn Saud claimed to be "amir of Najd, Hasa, Qatif and their dependencies," he only recognized Sharif Husayn as "amir of Mecca"—not "king of the Arab Lands," as Sharif Husayn wished, nor even king of the Hijaz, as the British acknowledged. He pointedly avoided making any reference to the Hijaz at all, as though the sovereignty of that vast Red Sea province had yet to be decided.

Ibn Saud acknowledged receipt of King Husayn's letter of May 7 with the reservation that "some of the things expressed in your letter were not appropriate." He also acknowledged British pressure to reconcile their differences, for the campaign against the Ottomans was reaching a critical stage and "the dispute is harmful to all," he explained. Yet Ibn Saud could not let prior Hashemite provocations go unchallenged.

"Your Eminence will undoubtedly have suspicions that I played a role in the matter of the people of al-Khurma," he wrote. However, he argued that the Hashemites themselves were to blame for the governor's defection and the townspeople's adherence to the Wahhabi cause. "I kept them in check as far as I could," he continued, "until your forces marched over them twice"—referring to the two Hashemite engagements at al-Khurma—"and that which God had ordained happened," a smug reference to the defeat the Saudis dealt the Hashemite forces.[10]

Looking to the future, Ibn Saud proposed a truce with the Hashemites based on the status quo. Khurma would stay under Saudi rule, and King Husayn would write to the governor of the oasis town to reassure him that there were no differences between the Saudis and the Hashemites. Ibn Saud and King Husayn would preserve the peace between their followers, guaranteeing the compliance of the tribes of Najd and Hijaz to the truce. In hindsight, it was the best offer Husayn would ever get from the Saudis—mutual recognition of borders and territories with the Hashemites left in control of the Hijaz.

King Husayn did not even consider Ibn Saud's offer; he returned the letter unopened, telling the messenger: "Ibn Saud has no claim on us and we have no claim on him." Instead of pursuing a truce, King Husayn dispatched another force to al-Khurma in August 1918 in a bid to restore his authority over the oasis. He assigned one of his most trusted commanders, Sharif Shakir bin Zayd, to command the expedition. The king reassured his commander that he had dispatched sufficient camels and supplies "for you to do great things with."[11] Shakir's expedition, however, was easily repelled by Saudi forces before even reaching the contested oasis.

Infuriated and humiliated by his repeated defeats to Ibn Saud's forces, King Husayn ordered his son Amir Abdullah to lead a new campaign against Khurma. Abdullah had no stomach for such a fight. He and his soldiers had maintained the siege of the Ottoman garrison in Medina until their commander finally surrendered in January 1919. Abdullah's troops were battle-weary after years of fighting the Ottomans. He also recognized that the Wahhabi soldiers were zealous warriors. "The Wahhabi fighter," he wrote, "is anxious to attain Paradise which, according to his faith, he will enter if he be killed."[12] But Abdullah could not defy his father, and in May 1919 he took up his commission and led his force to battle with the Wahhabis.

The Hashemite army met with initial success in its final campaign against the Saudis. In May 1919, on the way to Khurma, Amir Abdullah captured the oasis of Turaba, which had also pledged allegiance to Ibn Saud. Rather than seek the goodwill of the 3,000 inhabitants of the oasis, Abdullah allowed his troops to plunder the rebellious town. No doubt he intended to make an example of Turaba, to discourage other frontier oases from siding with the Saudis. However, the behavior of Abdullah's troops only served to increase Turaba's loyalty to Ibn Saud. While Amir Abdullah was still in Turaba, some of the townspeople must have sent word to Ibn

Saud to come to their assistance. Abdullah himself drafted a letter to the Saudi leader from Turaba in an attempt to leverage his conquest of the oasis to secure a peace agreement with Ibn Saud on terms more favorable to the Hashemites.

The Saudi fighters had no interest in coming to terms with the Hashemites. Having defeated every Hashemite army they had encountered, they were confident of carrying the day against Amir Abdullah's force. Some 4,000 Ikhwan fighters surrounded Turaba from three sides. They struck Abdullah's positions at dawn and nearly wiped out his forces. By his own account, Abdullah claimed that only 153 men from his detachment of 1,350 troops survived. "I personally escaped through a miracle," he later recalled. Abdullah and his cousin, Sharif Shakir bin Zayd, cut through the back of their tent and sustained wounds as they fled the fighting.[13]

The repercussions of the battle reached far beyond the carnage at the oasis. Turaba demonstrated that the Wahhabis were the dominant force in the Arabian Peninsula and that the Hashemites' days in the Hijaz were numbered. Amir Abdullah recalled: "After the battle there began a period of unrest and anxiety as to the fate of our movement, our country and the person of our King." Indeed, his father, King Husayn, seemed to be suffering from a mental breakdown. "On returning to headquarters I found my father ill and nervous," Abdullah wrote. "He was now bad tempered, forgetful and suspicious. He had lost his quick grasp and sound judgment."[14]

The result of the battle came as a surprise to the British too, many of whom had underestimated the fighting power of Ibn Saud's forces. They did not wish to see their Saudi ally overwhelm their Hashemite ally, upsetting the balance of power they had carefully established in Arabia. The British resident (or chief colonial administrator under the Political Service of British India) in Jidda sent a message to Ibn Saud in July 1918 demanding he withdraw from the oasis towns immediately, leaving Turaba and Khurma as neutral zones until both sides had agreed on their frontiers. "If you fail to retreat after receiving my letter," the resident warned, "the Government of His Majesty will consider the treaty they have concluded with you null and void and take all necessary steps to hinder your hostile action."[15] Ibn Saud complied with the request and ordered his troops to withdraw to Riyadh.

To restore the balance of forces in Arabia, the British also needed to conclude a formal treaty with the Hashemites in the Hijaz. The exchange of correspondence between the then Sharif Husayn and Sir Henry McMahon had established a wartime alliance, but this did not constitute the sort of treaty such as Britain had concluded with the Persian Gulf rulers, including Ibn Saud. Without a formal treaty, Britain would have no grounds to preserve its Hashemite allies from the Saudis. And Britain preferred to see many states balancing each other in Arabia to having a single dominant power emerge that straddled both the Red Sea and the Persian Gulf. It was thus convenient for British imperial interests to preserve the Hashemites as a buffer against the growing power of the Saudi state.

As World War I drew to an end, the British government was anxious to conclude a formal alliance with King Husayn and his Hashemite family. They sent Colonel T. E. Lawrence, the famous "Lawrence of Arabia," who had served as British liaison with the Hashemites during the Arab Revolt, to open negotiations with Husayn.

Between July and September 1921, Lawrence tried in vain to persuade King Husayn to sign a treaty that recognized the new realities of the postwar settlement. Husayn rejected nearly every feature of the postwar Middle East as a betrayal of Britain's promises to him: he refused to limit his kingdom to the Hijaz; he objected to the expulsion of his son, King Faysal, from Damascus and the establishment of a French mandate in Syria; he rejected Britain's mandates over Iraq and Palestine (which then included Transjordan); and he objected to the policy of a Jewish national home in Palestine. The British ventured one last attempt to reach a treaty in 1923, but the bitter old king refused to sign. As a result, he forfeited British protection just as Ibn Saud began to mount his campaign to conquer the Hijaz.

In July 1924, Ibn Saud gathered his commanders in Riyadh to plan the conquest of the Hijaz. They began with an attack on Taif, a mountain town near Mecca, to test Britain's reaction. In September 1924 the Ikhwan seized the town and plundered it for three days. The townspeople of Taif resisted the Wahhabis, who responded with great violence. An estimated 400 people were killed, and many others fled. The fall of Taif sent a shock wave through the Hijaz. The notables of the province gathered in Jidda and forced King Husayn to resign his throne. They believed Ibn Saud was attacking the Hijaz because of his antagonism toward King Husayn, and that a change in monarch might change Saudi policy. On October 6, 1924, the old king complied with his people's wishes, declared his son Ali king, and went into exile. However, these measures did not halt Ibn Saud's advance.

In mid-October 1924, the Ikhwan captured the holy city of Mecca. They met with no resistance and refrained from all violence toward the townspeople. Ibn Saud sent messengers to sound out Britain's reaction to the conquest of Taif and Mecca. He was reassured of Britain's neutrality in the conflict. The Saudi ruler then proceeded to complete his conquest of the Hijaz. He laid siege to the port of Jidda and the holy city of Medina in January 1925. The Hashemites held out for nearly a full year, but on December 22, 1925, King Ali surrendered his kingdom to Ibn Saud and followed his father into exile.

Having conquered the Hijaz, Ibn Saud was proclaimed "sultan of Najd and king of the Hijaz." The vast extent of territory under his control placed Ibn Saud in a different category from the other Gulf rulers of the Trucial States. Britain recognized the change in his status and concluded a new treaty with King Abdul Aziz in 1927 that recognized his full independence and sovereignty, without any of the restrictions on external relations accepted by the Trucial States. Ibn Saud continued to extend the territory under his rule, and renamed his kingdom Saudi Arabia in 1932.

1 and 2. Portraits of Ottoman sultan Selim I, who conquered the Arab lands of the Mamluk Empire in 1516–1517, and of Khayr al-Din Barbarossa, the Barbary Coast corsair who brought the North African coast under Ottoman rule in 1519. These fanciful Florentine paintings, composed around 1550 after the death of both subjects, were probably part of the Medici collection that Druze prince Fakhr al-Din II viewed while on exile in Florence between 1613 and 1618. "They had portraits of all the sultans of Islam and all the Arab shaykhs," Fakhr al-Din's court chronicler noted in amazement.

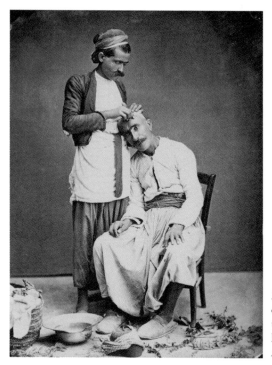

3. This nineteenth-century barber of Damascus would have plied his trade in much the same way as his colleague of one century earlier, Ahmad al-Budayri al-Hallaq.

4. French troops under Napoleon Bonaparte inflicted a decisive defeat on Egypt's ruling Mamluk Amirs in the Battle of the Pyramids (July 21, 1798) before entering Cairo in triumph. This painting by Louis-François Lejeune (1775–1848) was composed in 1806 from sketches taken on the battlefield. Lejeune captured the unequal clash between Mamluk cavalry and the disciplined ranks of French infantry whose "uninterrupted shooting was ear-deafening," in the words of Egyptian chronicler al-Jabarti.

5. The aged ruler of Mount Lebanon, Amir Bashir II Shihab (standing in the centre with cane), rendering homage to Egyptian general Ibrahim Pasha (on horseback) outside the gates of Acre in 1831, in this painting by Georg Emanuel Opitz (1775–1841). Ibrahim, son of the ruler of Egypt, Muhammad Ali Pasha, laid siege to Acre for six months before conquering the strategic fortress and completing his conquest of Syria.

6. Medical doctor and chronicler Mikhayil Mishaqa observed the Egyptian siege of Acre firsthand in 1831–1832 and reported back to the ruling Shihabi family of Mount Lebanon. Mishaqa later served as U.S. consular agent in Damascus, where he and his family survived mob violence in the 1860 massacres. This portrait by Bonfils was taken towards the end of Mishaqa's life in the early 1870s.

7. Muhammad Ali Pasha, an ethnic Albanian from Kavala, ruled Egypt from 1805 to 1849 and created an empire that embraced Sudan, the Hijaz, Greater Syria, and Crete. The Pasha sat for this portrait by Louis Charles Auguste Couder (1790–1873) in 1840, when his troops had been forced out of Syria by a joint Anglo-Ottoman force. He established a dynasty that would rule over Egypt until 1952.

8. The amir Abd al-Qadir led the Algerian resistance to French rule from 1832 until his final surrender in 1847 to the Duke of Aumale, captured here by French artist Augustin Regis (1813–1880). The Algerian earned widespread admiration in France for his determined resistance and was later received with honor by French president Louis Napoleon before being sent in honorable exile to Ottoman domains on a French pension. Abd al-Qadir settled in Damascus where he played an important role in saving many of the city's Christians from the 1860 massacres.

9. Portrait of Amir Faysal, son of Sharif Husayn of Mecca and commander of the Arab Army in the 1916–1918 Arab revolt against the Ottomans. This autochrome photograph by Paul Castelnau was taken at the Red Sea port of Aqaba on February 28, 1918. Faysal went on to become King of Syria in 1920, was deposed by the French that same year, and was crowned king of Iraq in 1921.

10. A group of Bedouin soldiers from Faysal's Arab Army among the palm groves of Aqaba, March 28, 1918. This autochrome image by Paul Castelnau captures the faces of some of the men who took part in the raids on the Hijaz Railway and Ottoman desert fortresses between Mecca and Damascus, celebrated by British officer T. E. Lawrence, the famous "Lawrence of Arabia," in his classic *Seven Pillars of Wisdom*.

11. Portrait of the first French Resident General to Morocco, Marshal Louis-Hubert Lyautey, an innovator whose compassionate form of imperial rule was to prove influential in later French colonial administration in Syria. Lyautey's rule was undermined by the Rif War led by Abd el-Krim al-Khattabi (1921–1926). This autochrome photograph was taken by Georges Chevalier in 1927, two years after Lyautey left Morocco.

الحرب في مراكش : هجوم جيوش مولاي الأمير محمد عبد الكريم على الخطوط الفرنسوية حول مدينة فاز

12. Such stirring images of Abd el-Krim al-Khattabi fighting the French in Morocco captured the imagination of nationalists across the Arab world in 1925. From his mountain stronghold in the northern Rif region, Abd el-Krim led his Berber irregulars to victory, first over the Spanish and then the French, before the Europeans combined forces to besiege and defeat the Rifis in 1926. In this lithograph, the French with modern aircraft and artillery are driven in full retreat by mounted Moroccan fighters led by Abd el-Krim under an Islamic banner reading "There is no god but Allah and Muhammad is His prophet."

13. Autochrome portrait of the first French High Commissioner of Syria, General Henri Gouraud taken by Auguste Léon in Beirut on October 3, 1919. Gouraud had been Lyautey's assistant in Morocco and tried to apply many of Lyautey's measures to facilitate French rule in Syria . . . and failed. His divide-and-rule tactics ultimately provoked a nationwide rebellion in Syria that raged from 1925 to 1927 before its ultimate suppression.

14. Beirut under French rule, November 22, 1919. The French tricolour festooned the Ottoman clock tower and the balconies of the main administrative centre, with troops bivouacked in the parade ground below. While some Lebanese had actively sought a French mandate in the Paris Peace Conference in 1919, they had hoped France would play a more disinterested role in assisting their country achieve institutions of independent statehood.

15. Damascus devastated by French bombardment in 1925. In October 1925, the city rose in revolt against French colonial rule. Insurgents overran the eighteenth-century Azm Palace in a bid to capture the French high commissioner, Maurice Sarrail. Though the French administrators had already evacuated the palace, they trained artillery on the quarter surrounding the palace for over 48 hours. As one eyewitness reported, "the shells of destruction and fire consumed more than six hundred of the finest homes" in Damascus. The ruins of the Azm Palace are in the foreground.

16. Sa'd Zaghlul and the other delegates of the Wafd return from exile in Malta. The arrest of Zaghlul on March 8, 1919, sparked nationalist demonstrations across Egypt. Public pressure forced Britain to reverse its policies, allowing Zaghlul and the Wafd to return to Cairo and present Egypt's case to the Paris Peace Conference. In vain: the great powers had already granted recognition to Britain's protectorate over Egypt. Zaghlul is seated in the centre of the photograph, holding a cane. To his right is Ismail Sidqi, the villain of Egypt's "Liberal Age," before the two men fell out.

17. Women entered national politics in Egypt for the first time in 1919—and made headlines across the world. This French weekly trumpeted the "feminist demonstration in Egypt," portraying a group of heavily veiled women surrounded by a phalanx of men, under the noses of a group of mounted British police. Huda Sha'rawi, whose husband Ali was exiled with Zaghlul and the other members of the Wafd, was one of the leaders of this movement.

Not only had Ibn Saud succeeded in establishing his kingship over most of the Arabian Peninsula, but he had managed to preserve his independence from all forms of British imperial rule. In this he was assisted by a critical British miscalculation: they did not believe that there was any oil in Saudi Arabia.

The exiled King Husayn of the Hijaz was within his rights to feel betrayed by the British. Not only had Britain failed to fulfill Sir Henry McMahon's written commitments to the Hashemites, but the British had stood by and watched as the French drove his son King Faysal from Syria in 1920, and the Saudis drove his eldest son King Ali from the Hijaz in 1925.

The British, for their part, were not entirely satisfied they had discharged their commitments to their wartime ally, and they looked for a way to redeem their promises in part, if not in full. As the colonial secretary, Winston Churchill, explained to the House of Commons in June 1921, "We are leaning strongly to what I may call the Sherifian Solution both in Mesopotamia to which the Emir Feisal [Amir Faysal] is now proceeding, and in Trans-Jordania, where the Emir Abdullah is now in charge."[16] Churchill hoped that by putting Husayn's sons on British mandate thrones he would go some way toward redeeming Britain's broken promises to the Hashemites while providing Britain with loyal and dependent rulers in their Arab possessions.

Of all the British imperial possessions in the Middle East, Transjordan would prove the easiest to rule. However, the new state of Transjordan got off to a difficult start. With a land mass the size of Indiana or Hungary, Transjordan had a population of only 350,000, divided between the townspeople and villagers living in the high plateau overlooking the Jordan Valley and the nomadic tribesmen who made their home between the desert and the steppe. Its subsistence economy was based on agricultural and pastoral products that provided a modest tax base for a very small state. The politics of Transjordan were also fairly basic. The country was divided into distinct regions, each with its own local leadership whose view of politics was very local. A small British subsidy—£150,000 per annum—went a long way in such a place.

The British did not initially conceive of Transjordan as a separate state in its own right. The territory initially was awarded to Great Britain as part of the Palestine mandate. The decision to sever Transjordan from Palestine, formalized in 1923, was driven by two considerations: Britain's wish to confine the Balfour Declaration's promise of a Jewish national home to the lands *west* of the Jordan River; and Britain's wish to confine Amir Abdullah's ambitions to territory under British control.

Amir Abdullah first entered Transjordan uninvited, in November 1920. He was surrounded by a group of Arab nationalists, political refugees from his brother

Faysal's defunct Arab Kingdom in Damascus. Abdullah announced he would lead Arab volunteers to liberate Syria from French rule and to restore his brother Faysal to his rightful throne in Damascus (Abdullah himself aspired to the throne of Iraq). The last thing the British government needed was for Transjordan to become a launching pad for hostilities against the neighboring French mandate of Syria. British officials scrambled to deal with the situation before things got out of hand.

Winston Churchill and T. E. Lawrence invited Amir Abdullah to a meeting in Jerusalem in March 1921, at which point they updated him on Britain's plans for its empire in the Middle East. Faysal would never return to Damascus, which was securely in French hands; instead, he was to be king of Iraq. The best they could offer Abdullah was to place him at the head of the new state of Transjordan. Land-locked Transjordan (the territory did not yet include the Red Sea port of Aqaba) fell well short of Abdullah's ambitions, but Churchill suggested that if Abdullah kept the peace in Transjordan and established good relations with the French, they might one day invite him to rule over Damascus for them.[17] It was a long shot, but Abdullah agreed to these proposals, and the Sharifian Solution became British imperial reality in Transjordan.

When Amir Abdullah established his first government in Transjordan in 1921, he drew heavily on the Arab nationalists who had served with his brother Faysal in Damascus. The British and the people of Transjordan had a common dislike of Abdullah's entourage. The British saw them as firebrands and troublemakers whose attacks against the French in Syria were a constant irritant. For the Transjordanians, the Arab nationalists, who came to form a new party called the Istiqlal, or "Independence," represented a foreign elite who dominated the government and bureaucracy to the exclusion of the indigenous people of the land.

One of the most outspoken opponents of the Istiqlalis in Transjordan was a local judge named Awda al-Qusus (1877–1943). Qusus was a Christian from the southern town of Karak who had served in the Ottoman court system before the First World War. Fluent in Turkish, with a spattering of English learned from Methodist missionaries, al-Qusus had traveled widely throughout the Ottoman Empire and had worked with high government officials. He firmly believed that Amir Abdullah should form his government from Transjordanians like himself, who had a real interest in the welfare of their new country. His greatest objection to the Istiqlalis was that they were only concerned with liberating Damascus. The first article of their party's constitution, Al-Qusus wryly remarked, was "to sacrifice Transjordan and its people on the road to Syria's betterment."[18] Certainly his own persecution at the hands of the Istiqlalis would only confirm this view.

Al-Qusus openly criticized the Istiqlalis in articles he wrote for the local newspaper. He accused government ministers of corruption and the misappropriation of treasury funds for their own projects, without Abdullah's knowledge. The native Transjordanians responded to the judge's criticisms by refusing to pay taxes to an "alien" government that was seen to be squandering their country's limited funds. In June 1921 the villagers of northern Transjordan declared a tax strike that quickly escalated into a serious rebellion. The British had to resort to air strikes by Royal Air Force planes to quell the uprising.

The troubles between Amir Abdullah's government and the natives of Transjordan only worsened after the 1921 tax revolt. Al-Qusus met regularly with a group of professional townsmen to discuss the cronyism and corruption they deplored in the amir's government. These Transjordanian dissidents compared notes on government maladministration and openly discussed the need for reform. When Amir Abdullah faced a major tribal uprising in the summer of 1923, the Istiqlalis accused al-Qusus and the dissident townsmen of provoking the revolt, and they urged Abdullah to crack down on their domestic opponents. That very night, September 6, 1923, the police pounded on Justice Awda al-Qusus's door and took him away.

Al-Qusus would not return home for seven months. Stripped of his official rank by order of the amir, he was exiled to the neighboring Kingdom of the Hijaz (which was still under Hashemite rule). He was joined by four other natives of Transjordan: an army officer, a Circassian, a Muslim cleric, and a rural notable who would later be celebrated as the national poet of Jordan, Mustafa Wahbi al-Tall. The five were accused of creating a "secret society" that sought to overturn the amir's government and replace it with natives of Transjordan. They were falsely accused of being in league with the head of the Adwan tribe and encouraging the tribal revolt to facilitate their coup. The charge was high treason, and the severity of the charge was reflected in the harshness of the treatment meted out to al-Qusus and his fellows.

As they arrived at the railway station in Amman to take the train into exile, the five were in a defiant mood. Mustafa Wahbi, the poet, was singing nationalist songs and stirring the men's defiance. "Before God and history, Awda!" he shouted. The men had no sense of the ordeal that lay before them. When they arrived in Maan, now a city in Jordan but then a town on the frontier of the Hijaz, they were taken to a dank and fetid cell in the basement of the old castle. Al-Qusus grabbed his guard and screamed: "Have you no fear of God? A place like this is not suitable for animals, let alone for people."

The guards and their commanders, who knew their prisoners were respectable men, were embarrassed. Everything about their culture and society dictated that they should show hospitality to men entrusted to their care. Yet they were military men who had to obey orders. Their behavior toward their prisoners alternated radically between great kindness—finding clean bedding, providing tea and company—and great cruelty, torturing the detainees to secure their signed confessions to the

charges leveled against them by the government. The officials who ordered the torture and dictated the confessions were of course men from Amir Abdullah's foreign
retinue. Al-Qusus and his companions were then formally indicted in absentia of
"plotting against the government of His Highness the Amir with intent to overthrow
the government by armed insurrection."[19] They were then sent to prison in the Hijaz,
first in Aqaba and then in Jidda.

The exiles were allowed to return to their homeland as part of a general amnesty
issued on the occasion of King Husayn's assumption of the caliphate in March 1924.
The new Turkish president, Mustafa Kemal Ataturk, had just abolished the institution
of the caliphate as a final measure to eradicate the influence of the Ottoman sultanate,
and King Husayn, now in exile from the Hijaz, was quick to seize the honor for the
Hashemite family. As was customary on high state occasions, prisoners were released
as part of the celebrations.

Their prison ordeal now at an end, the five men were given first-class berths on
a steamship from Jidda to the Egyptian port of Suez, whence they made their way
to Transjordan. Al-Qusus sent a telegram of thanks to King Husayn and congratulated him on his (ultimately unsuccessful) assumption of the caliphate. He received
a quick reply from the exiled monarch, wishing al-Qusus a safe and speedy return
to his homeland, "which is in need of people like you with patriotism and friendship
towards the fatherland and true adherence to the great Hashemite household." Was
the old king being ironic, or was he admonishing the political prisoners to mend
their ways and prove more loyal in future? The truth of the matter was that al-Qusus
had never shown disloyalty to Amir Abdullah; he had only objected to the Istiqlalis
the amir put into positions of authority over native Transjordanians.

Though he did not know it, the British colonial authorities fully shared Awda
al-Qusus's concerns. The British resident in Amman, Lieutenant-Colonel Charles
Cox, invited al-Qusus to visit him shortly after his return from exile in the Hijaz.
He asked the judge to explain the reasons for his imprisonment, and to share his
views on Amir Abdullah's government. Cox took careful notes on their discussion,
thanked al-Qusus, and saw him out.

In August 1924, Cox delivered an ultimatum from the acting high commissioner
in Palestine, Sir Gilbert Clayton, to Amir Abdullah. In his letter, Clayton warned
Abdullah that the British government viewed his administration "with grave displea-
sure" for its "financial irregularities and unchecked extravagance" and for allowing
Transjordan to become a focus of disorder to neighboring Syria. Abdullah was asked
to commit in writing to six conditions to reform his administration, chief among
them the expulsion of leading Istiqlalis within five days' time.[20] Abdullah dared not
refuse. The British had sent 400 cavalrymen to Amman and 300 troops to the northern town of Irbid to back up their ultimatum. Fearing the British would depose him
as quickly as they had installed him, Amir Abdullah signed the ultimatum.

After this confrontation Amir Abdullah expelled the Istiqlali "undesirables," re-formed the finances of his government, and drew natives of Transjordan into his administration. Awda al-Qusus returned to service in the Jordanian judiciary, rising to the office of attorney general in 1931. Once he had thrown in his lot with the elites of Transjordan, Amir Abdullah enjoyed the support and loyalty of his people. Transjordan went on to be a model colony of peace and stability, at very little cost to the British taxpayer until its independence in 1946.

A lthough Transjordan proved the easiest to manage of Britain's Middle East pos-sessions, Iraq was for a time viewed as the most successful mandate. King Faysal was installed in 1921, a Constituent Assembly was elected beginning in 1924, and a treaty regulating relations between Britain and Iraq was ratified later that same year. By 1930 Iraq was a stable constitutional monarchy and Britain's work as mandatory power was complete. A new treaty was negotiated between Britain and Iraq, paving the way to Iraq's independence in 1932. The League of Nations recog-nized Iraq's independence and admitted the new state to its ranks—the only mandate to become a full member of the league in its twenty-six-year history. Iraq was the envy of all the other Arab states left under British or French rule, and its accom-plishments became the goals of nationalists across the Arab world: independence and membership in the League of Nations.

As Britain ushered the young kingdom of Iraq into statehood, behind a facade of success lay a very different reality. Many Iraqis had never accepted Britain's posi-tion in their country. Their opposition did not end with the 1920 uprising but con-tinued to plague the British project in Iraq to the end. Though Faysal was in many ways a popular king, his own position was undermined by his reliance on the British. Iraqi nationalists increasingly came to see Faysal as an extension of British influence and to criticize him in the same breath as they condemned their imperial masters.

When Faysal arrived in Iraq in June 1921, the British went to work in promoting their candidate to the Iraqi throne. A number of local contenders threw their hats in the ring but encountered stiff British resistance. An influential notable from Basra who had made a bid for the throne, Sayyid Talib al-Naqib, went for tea with the British high commissioner's wife, Lady Cox, and found himself arrested and exiled to Ceylon on the way home. The high commissioner, Sir Percy Cox, and his staff or-ganized an exhausting tour for Faysal to visit towns and tribes across Iraq in advance of a national referendum intended to confirm Britain's choice for Iraq's throne. By all accounts, Faysal played his part well, traveling around the country meeting Iraq's diverse communities and winning their allegiance. Even without British tampering, he probably would have won the consent of a majority of Iraqis to be their king. But the British left nothing to chance. Gertrude Bell, the Oriental secretary in Baghdad, famously remarked that she would "never engage in creating kings again; it's too great a strain."[21]

Faysal was crowned king of Iraq on August 23, 1921. The ceremony was held in the early morning hours to take advantage of the coolest time of day in the prodigious heat of the Baghdad summer. Over 1,500 guests were invited to witness the coronation. Sulayman al-Faydi, a notable from Mosul, described the "great splendour" of the coronation, which was "attended by thousands of guests, the roads leading to it crowded with tens of thousands of people."[22] Faysal stood on a dais flanked by the British high commissioner and members of the Iraqi Council of Ministers. The secretary of the council rose to read Sir Percy's proclamation announcing the results of the referendum. Faysal had been elected king by 96 percent of the Iraqi voters. The assembled guests and dignitaries stood and saluted King Faysal while the Iraqi flag was raised to the strains of "God Save the King"—the Iraqis had yet to compose their own national anthem.[23] The music could only have reinforced the belief that Faysal was Britain's choice of king—as indeed he was.

Faysal's honeymoon with his new subjects proved short-lived. Most Iraqis believed Faysal to be an Arab nationalist and expected him to free their country from British rule. They were quickly disappointed. Muhammad Mahdi Kubba, a student in a Shiite theological college in Baghdad at the time of Faysal's coronation, captured the public's mood in his memoirs. The British, he explained, "brought Amir Faysal, and crowned him king of Iraq, and charged him with the task of implementing their policies. At first the Iraqis welcomed the installation of Faysal, and they pinned their hopes on him, that his presence at the head of the government would open a new age of independence and national sovereignty." Indeed, some leading notables gave their allegiance to Faysal on condition that he defend Iraq's sovereignty and independence. One such skeptic was an influential cleric named Ayatollah Mahdi al-Khalisi, the head of Kubba's theological school in Baghdad. Kubba witnessed al-Khalisi's pledge of allegiance before a school assembly convened to welcome King Faysal. "Khalisi said prayers for King Faysal . . . [and] took [him] by the hand saying: 'We give you our allegiance as King of Iraq, so long as you govern with justice, that the government is constitutional and parliamentary, and that you do not entangle Iraq in any foreign commitments.'"[24] King Faysal promised to do his best, saying he had only come to Iraq to serve its people. Faysal knew full well that he would not be able to rule Iraq independent of Britain. As was mandated by the League of Nations, he was condemned to rule under British tutelage until Britain saw fit to concede Iraq its independence. Moreover, he was a stranger in Iraq, with only a handful of army officers who had served with him in the Arab Revolt and the short-lived Kingdom of Syria, for allies. Until he had established his position in Iraq, Faysal would need Britain's support to survive. The problem for Faysal was that his dependence on Britain cost him the support of Iraqi nationalists. The irony was that it was his dependence on Britain that undermined his ability to develop the loyalty of his own countrymen—right until his death in 1933.

Faysal's predicament became apparent in 1922 when Britain drafted a treaty to regularize its position in Iraq. The Anglo-Iraqi Treaty scarcely veiled the degree of British domination over the Hashemite Kingdom—in the economy, diplomacy, and law. "His Majesty the King of Iraq," the treaty stipulated, "agrees to be guided by the advice of His Britannic Majesty tendered through the High Commissioner on all important matters affecting the international and financial obligations and interests of His Britannic Majesty for the whole period of this Treaty."[25] Most revealing of British intentions was the duration of the treaty—twenty years—after which the situation would be reviewed and the treaty either renewed or terminated, according to the views of the "High Contracting Parties." This was a formula for extended British colonial rule, not Iraqi independence.

The draft treaty faced widespread condemnation in Iraq. Even King Faysal discretely encouraged opposition to the treaty, both because of the limits it imposed on his power as king and to distance himself from British imperial policy. Some ministers resigned in protest. The Council of Ministers, unwilling to bear responsibility for so controversial a document, insisted on convening an elected constituent assembly to ratify the treaty. The British agreed to elections but wanted to ensure that the resulting assembly would endorse their treaty. Nationalist politicians opposed both the treaty and the elections, recognizing that the constituent assembly would serve only to rubber stamp an agreement designed to perpetuate British control.

Inevitably, Faysal's credibility was compromised by the treaty crisis. Ayatollah al-Khalisi addressed another assembly of the students and teachers of his theological school. "We gave our allegiance to Faysal to be king of Iraq on condition," the ayatollah intoned, "and he failed to fulfill these conditions. Consequently, neither we nor the Iraqi people owe him any allegiance." Al-Khalisi threw in his lot with the nationalist opposition and began to issue fatwas (Islamic legal rulings) declaring the treaty unlawful and forbidding all participation in the constituent assembly elections as "tantamount to an act against religion, as a step that assisted non-believers to rule over Muslims."[26] The clerics made common cause with secular nationalists and organized a boycott campaign against the upcoming elections.

In the end, the British had to impose their treaty by force. The British authorities prohibited all demonstrations. Al-Khalisi and other opposition leaders were arrested and exiled. The Royal Air Force was dispatched to bomb tribal insurgents in the

Middle Euphrates region who had risen in protest. With the opposition quelled, the authorities proceeded with the elections. Despite the fatwas and the nationalists' campaigning, the elections did proceed and a constituent assembly was convened in March 1924 to debate and ratify the treaty.

The Constituent Assembly met and debated the terms of the treaty in earnest from March to October 1924. In the end, the treaty was ratified by a slim majority. It remained hugely unpopular with the Iraqi public, though it set in motion a number of important developments: the Assembly approved a constitution for the new state and passed an electoral law that lay foundations for both a constitutional monarchy and a multiparty democracy. However, the means used by the British to get the treaty passed tainted the instruments of constitutional and parliamentary government with imperial associations that would ultimately undermine democracy in Iraq. The new state was not seen by Iraqi nationalists as a government "of the people, by the people, for the people," but as an institution implicating Iraqis in British rule over their country.

If the British hoped things would go smoothly after the passage of the Anglo-Iraqi Treaty, they were to be sorely disappointed. Indeed, British and American war planners of 2003 would have found many relevant lessons to be learned from British experiences in the 1920s.

Divisions quickly emerged between the different regions and communities of the new Iraqi state, which had been forged from three very different Ottoman provinces. The problem was immediately apparent in the formation of a national army, one of the key institutions of independent sovereign states. King Faysal was surrounded by military men who had served with him in the Arab Revolt and were keen to establish an army in Iraq that would unite Kurds, Sunnis, and Shiites through national military service. The project foundered in the face of active opposition from the Shiite and Kurdish communities, however, who objected to conscription as to any government initiative they believed gave disproportionate power to the minority Sunni Arab community.

The Kurds presented a particular challenge to the integrity and identity of the Iraqi state. Unlike the Sunnis and Shiites, the Kurds are not ethnic Arabs and they resented government efforts to cast Iraq as an Arab state. They believed this denied the Kurds their distinct ethnic identity. Some in the Kurdish community did not resist Iraqi claims to Arabness but used this as a pretext to demand greater autonomy in those parts of northern Iraq in which they represented an absolute majority.

At times it seemed that the only thing uniting the people of Iraq was their opposition to the British presence. King Faysal himself despaired of his subjects. Shortly before his death in 1933, the first king of Iraq observed in a confidential memo that "there is still—and I say this with a heart full of sorrow—no Iraqi people but unimaginable masses of human beings, devoid of any patriotic idea, imbued with religious traditions and absurdities, connected by no common tie, giving ear to evil, prone to anarchy, and perpetually ready to rise against any government whatever."[27]

For the British, the cost of maintaining order soon began to exceed the benefits of perpetuating the mandate in Iraq. By 1930 the British reassessed their position. They had secured their interests in Mesopotamian oil through the 1928 Red Line Agreement, which awarded Britain a 47.5 percent share in the Turkish (Iraq) Petroleum Company—the French and Americans had only secured 23.75 percent of the shares each. They had established a friendly and dependent government in Iraq, headed by a "reliable" king, to protect British interests. British officials in Iraq increasingly came to the view that they would better assure their strategic interests by treaty than by continued direct control.

In June 1930, the British government concluded a new agreement to replace the controversial Anglo-Iraqi Treaty of 1922. The terms of the new pact stipulated that Britain's ambassador would enjoy preeminence among foreign representatives in Iraq. The Royal Air Force would retain two air bases in the country, and British troops would be assured transit rights through Iraq. The Iraqi military would be reliant on Britain for its training and provision of arms and ammunition. This still was not full independence, but it was enough to secure the country's admission to the League of Nations. It also satisfied one of the main demands of Iraqi nationalists, who hoped the treaty would prove a first step toward independence.

Upon ratification of the 1930 Treaty of Preferential Alliance, the British and Iraqis agreed to the termination of the mandate. On October 3, 1932, Iraq was admitted to the League of Nations as an independent, sovereign state. Yet it was an ambiguous independence in which British civil and military officials continued to exercise more influence than was compatible with true Iraqi sovereignty. Such informal British controls would undermine the legitimacy of the Hashemite monarchy until its ultimate overthrow in 1958.

E gyptian nationalists looked on Iraq's accomplishments with great envy. Though the 1930 Anglo-Iraqi Treaty was not so different in content from Egypt's 1922 treaty with Britain (which conceded nominal independence to Egypt), the Iraqis had secured Britain's nomination for admission to that exclusive club of independent states, the League of Nations. This became the benchmark of success by which nationalists in other Arab countries would measure their own accomplishments. As the Arab country with the longest tradition of nationalist activity, Egypt should have led the way toward independence from European colonial rule—or so thought the political elite. In the course of the 1930s, the Wafd, Egypt's leading nationalist party, came under growing public pressure to secure independence from Britain.

During the interwar years, Egypt achieved the highest degree of multiparty democracy in the modern history of the Arab world. The Constitution of 1923 introduced political pluralism, regular elections to a two-chamber legislature, full male suffrage, and a free press. A number of new parties emerged on the political stage. Elections attracted massive turnout at the polls. Journalists plied their trade with remarkable liberty.

This liberal era is remembered more for its divisive factionalism than as a golden age of Egyptian politics. Three distinct authorities sought preeminence in Egypt: the British, the monarchy, and, through Parliament, the Wafd. The rivalry between these three proved very disruptive to politics in Egypt. In his efforts to protect the monarchy from parliamentary scrutiny, King Fuad (r. 1917–1936) tended to oppose the nationalist Wafd party even more than the British. The Wafd, for their part, alternated between fighting the British for independence and promoting the powers of Parliament over the monarchy. The British alternately worked with the king to undermine the Wafd when they were in power, and with the Parliament to undermine the king when the Wafd was out of power. The political elites were a fractious bunch whose internecine squabbles played into the hands of both the king and the British. Under the circumstances, it is not surprising that little progress was made in securing Egypt's independence from Britain.

Egyptians first went to the polls in 1924. Sa'd Zaghlul (1859–1927), hero of the nationalist movement of 1919, led his Wafd party to a sweeping victory and took 90 percent of the seats in the Chamber of Deputies. King Fuad named Zaghlul prime minister and invited him to form a government, which took office in March 1924. Buoyed by the public mandate of his election returns, Zaghlul immediately entered into negotiations with the British to secure Egypt's complete independence, compromised only by the four "reserved points" of the 1922 treaty: British control over the Suez Canal, the right to base British troops in Egypt, preservation of the foreign legal privileges known as the Capitulations, and British dominance in Sudan.

Sudan was a particular sticking point. The Egyptians had first conquered Sudan during the reign of Muhammad 'Ali in the 1820s. Driven from the territory by the Mahdi's Revolt (1881–1885), the Egyptians joined forces with the British to reconquer Sudan in the late 1890s. In 1899 Lord Cromer devised a novel form of colonialism called a "condominium," which allowed Britain to add Sudan to its empire in collaboration with the Egyptians. Since then, both Britain and Egypt claimed Sudan was actually their own. Egyptian nationalists rejected Britain's claim to absolute discretion over Sudan in the 1922 treaty and demanded preservation of the "unity of the Nile Valley." This issue, more than any other of the four reserved points, provoked greatest tension between the Egyptians and the British.

Tensions led to violence on November 19, 1924, when a band of Egyptian nationalists shot and killed the governor-general of Anglo-Egyptian Sudan, Sir Lee Stack, as he drove through downtown Cairo. The stunned British government nonetheless used the assassination to secure their objectives in Sudan. Egypt's high commissioner, Lord Allenby, presented Prime Minister Zaghlul with a punitive seven-point ultimatum, including changes to the status quo in Sudan. When Zaghlul refused to comply with British demands in Sudan (to withdraw all Egyptian soldiers and to allow Nile irrigation for a British agricultural scheme), Allenby gave orders to the Sudan government to implement Britain's demands over the Egyptian prime minister's objections. Zaghlul's position was untenable, and he tendered his resignation on November 24. King Fuad named a royalist to form the next government and dissolved the Parliament, effectively sidelining the nationalists in the Wafd. As Zaghlul watched the British and the king enhance their powers at the Wafd's expense, he famously remarked: "The bullets that were fired were not targeted at the chest of Sir Lee Stack; they were targeted at mine."[28] In fact, Zaghlul never did return to power, dying on August 23, 1927, at the age of sixty-eight. Zaghlul would be replaced by lesser men, whose factionalism and in-fighting eroded public confidence in their political leaders.

If the Wafd's Sa'd Zaghlul was the hero of Egypt's liberal age, then Ismail Sidqi was certainly its villain. Sidqi had gone to the Paris Peace Conference with the Wafd delegation in 1919, only to fall out with Zaghlul and be expelled from the party on his return to Egypt. He was one of the architects of the 1922 treaty conferring limited independence on Egypt—which Zaghlul had always opposed. The further Sidqi fell from Zaghlul's graces, the greater he grew in King Fuad's esteem. By 1930 Sidqi and his monarch were united by a common goal of destroying the Wafd party under its new leader, Mustafa al-Nahhas.

The Wafd swept to power once again in January 1930 after a landslide victory in the 1929 elections in which the nationalist party secured a record 212 of 235 parliamentary seats. The king invited al-Nahhas to form a government. Given his electoral mandate, al-Nahhas entered into a new round of negotiations with British Foreign Secretary Arthur Henderson to secure Egypt's illusive independence. Between March 31 and May 8, the governments of Egypt and Britain engaged in extensive negotiations. The two sides came to a deadlock over Sudan, with Britain insisting on separating discussion of Egypt's independence and Sudan's future, and the Egyptians refusing independence exclusive of Sudan. The breakdown in Anglo-Egyptian negotiations provided an opportunity for the Wafd's enemies—the king and rival parties—to call for a new government. Al-Nahhas tendered his government's resignation in June 1930.

In the summer of 1930 the king and the British were in agreement: the government had to be placed in a "safe pair of hands." Sidqi was the obvious candidate.

The king's chamberlain called on Sidqi at his gentleman's club in Cairo to sound out his willingness to form a minority government. "I am honoured by His Majesty's confidence in me," Sidqi replied, "but I wish to inform him, should he decide to appoint me at this critical juncture, that my policies would start from a clean slate and that I would reorganize parliamentary life in accordance with my views on the Constitution and the need for stable government."[29]

Sidqi's response only confirmed the king's high opinion of the man. Sidqi had already declared his hostility to liberal democracy, denouncing the "parliamentary autocracy which the 1923 Constitution afforded, with the tyranny of the majority over the minority." He wanted to free government from constitutional bonds and rule by decree in partnership with the king. The king sent his chamberlain to inform Sidqi that he was "very comfortable with his policies" and invited him to form a cabinet.

Taking the helm of government for the first time in June 1930, Sidqi consolidated his grip over government by claiming three cabinet portfolios. In addition to the premiership, he assumed control of the ministries of finance and the interior. Fuad and Sidqi worked together to dissolve the Parliament, postpone elections, and draft a new constitution conferring yet more power on the king. For the next three years, Egypt's parliamentary democracy was overthrown and the country ruled by royal decree.

Sidqi made no attempt to hide his autocratic politics and his disregard for the democratic process. "It was inevitable that I would suspend the Parliament" at the end of June 1930, Sidqi confided in his memoirs, "in order to proceed to the reorganization that I had come to initiate." When al-Nahhas and his colleagues called for mass demonstrations protesting the suspension of the Parliament, Sidqi did not hesitate to crush the movement. "I did not wait until this opposition turned to a civil war" before taking action, Sidqi explained. He sent out the army to break up the demonstrations, and violence ensued. Three days after the royal decree that terminated the parliamentary session, twenty-five demonstrators were killed in Alexandria; nearly 400 were wounded. "Unfortunately," Sidqi continued, with the moustache-twirling panache of a vaudeville villain, "painful events occurred in Cairo, Alexandria and some rural cities. The government had no alternative but to preserve order and prevent the offenders from disturbing public order and breaking the law."[30] The British cautioned both Prime Minister Sidqi and nationalist leader al-Nahhas but did not interfere in a fight that would divert the Egyptians from their pursuit of greater freedom from British rule.

Sidqi justified his political philosophy on grounds that, in a time of economic troubles, leaders could only achieve progress and prosperity through peace and order. The crash of 1929 had ushered in a global depression that had left its mark on the Egyptian economy, and in the face of economic disruption, Sidqi viewed the Wafd and its brand of mass politics as a grave threat to public order. In October 1930, Sidqi introduced a new constitution that expanded the powers of the king at the expense of the Wafd. It reduced the number of deputies in the Parliament from 235 to 150 and gave the king control over the upper chamber by expanding the proportion of appointed senators from 40 to 60 percent, leaving only a minority to be chosen by popular vote. Sidqi's constitution reduced universal suffrage, replacing the system of direct elections to a more complex two-stage voting process, in which the voting age was increased for the first round and introducing restrictions to the second round of voting based on financial criteria or levels of education. These measures served to take voting power from the masses (on whose support the Wafd relied) and concentrate electoral authority in the propertied elite. The powers of the legislature were reduced, as the length of the parliamentary session was reduced from six to five months, and the king's powers to defer bills were expanded.

The new constitution was blatantly autocratic and provoked nearly unanimous opposition from politicians across the political spectrum and the general public. When the press criticized Sidqi and the 1930 Constitution, he simply closed the papers down and locked the journalists up. Even those who initially supported Sidqi found their papers closed. The journalists responded by printing underground leaflets that made virulent attacks against the autocratic government and its authoritarian constitution.

Sidqi formed his own party in 1931, when parliamentary elections loomed under the terms of the new constitution. Ever the political loner who had consistently eschewed party affiliation, Sidqi knew that he needed a party behind him to secure a parliamentary majority. He called his new party the People's Party, an inversion of reality worthy of George Orwell's *1984*. Sidqi attracted ambitious defectors from the Liberal Constitutional Party, and from the palace's own Unity Party—men of the elite, not of the people. The party's program gave ample material for satirists in the opposition press, pledging "assistance to the constitutional order," the "preservation of the people's sovereignty" and upholding "the rights of the throne" (King Fuad *had* chosen well).[31] The Wafd and the Liberal Constitutional Party both boycotted the elections of May 1931, and Sidqi's People's Party achieved an outright majority. His autocratic revolution seemed on the verge of success.

Yet ultimately Sidqi failed. His autocratic reforms provoked opposition from the real people's party, the Wafd, and the other major political parties. The press, refusing to be silenced, kept up a steady barrage to turn public opinion against Sidqi's government. Security conditions began to deteriorate as the public grew more outspoken against Sidqi's government. Sidqi had always justified autocratic rule in terms of providing law and order. Faced with growing disorder, the British began to pressure for a new government to restore public confidence and curb political violence. Sidqi's revolution had stalled and was now coming undone. In September 1933 the king dismissed his prime minister. Down but not out, Sidqi would remain one of Egypt's most influential politicians until his death in 1950.

King Fuad made a brief stab at absolute rule. He repealed Sidqi's 1930 Constitution by royal decree without restoring the earlier 1923 Constitution, and he dissolved the Parliament elected in 1931 without calling for new elections. The king assumed full power over Egypt for a transition period of unspecified duration. Needless to say, these measures were no more successful in restoring public confidence in the Egyptian government, and King Fuad came under pressure from both the British and the Wafd to restore Egypt's 1923 Constitution and prepare for new elections. On December 12, 1935, King Fuad conceded defeat and decreed the restoration of the original constitution.

The political deadlock between the British, the palace, and the Wafd was finally broken in 1936. In April of that year, King Fuad died and was succeeded by his handsome young son, Faruq. Elections were held in May and returned a Wafd majority. These two developments—the return of the Wafd to power and Faruq's coronation—were greeted with a great sense of optimism, a sort of Cairo spring. This was matched by a new British openness to renegotiate the terms of its relations with Egypt. The rise of fascism in Europe, and Mussolini's 1935 invasion of Ethiopia, gave new urgency to securing Egyptian consent to Britain's position. German and Italian propaganda against British colonialism had begun to turn some heads in Egypt. Ultra nationalist new parties like Young Egypt espoused openly fascist ideologies.

To counter these dangers, the British high commissioner, Sir Miles Lampson, opened new negotiations in Cairo in March 1936. A new treaty was concluded between an all-party Egyptian delegation and the British government and signed into law in August 1936. The Treaty of Preferential Alliance expanded Egypt's sovereignty and independence, though like the Iraqi treaty it gave Britain preferential standing among foreign nations and the right to keep military bases on Egyptian soil. It also left Sudan under British control. The gains were enough to secure Egypt's admission to the League of Nations in 1937, five years after Iraq's entry and the only other Arab state to join the international organization. But the compromises made, and the twenty-year duration of the treaty, pushed Egyptian aspirations for complete independence beyond the political horizon.

The experiences of the 1930s left many Egyptians disenchanted with the party politics of liberal democracy. Though the Egyptians rejected Sidqi's autocracy, they were never satisfied with the results the Wafd obtained. Zaghlul had promised to deliver Egypt from British rule in 1922, and al-Nahhas promised the same in 1936, yet the elusive promise of independence remained a generation away.

The British mandate in Palestine was doomed from the outset. The terms of the Balfour Declaration were written into the preamble of the mandatory instrument issued by the League of Nations to formalize Britain's position in Palestine. Unlike all of the other postwar mandates, in which a great power was charged with establishing the instruments of self-rule in a newly emerging state, the British in Palestine were required to establish both a viable state from among the indigenous people of the land and a national home for the Jews of the world.

The Balfour Declaration was a formula for communal conflict. Given Palestine's very limited resources, there simply was no way to establish a national home for the Jewish people in Palestine without prejudice to the civil and religious rights of existing non-Jewish communities in Palestine. Inevitably the mandate engendered conflict between rival nationalisms—the highly organized Zionist movement, and a new Palestinian nationalism forged by the dual threats of British imperialism and Zionist colonialism. Palestine would prove Britain's gravest imperial failure in the Middle East, a failure that would condemn the whole of the Middle East to conflict and violence that persist to the present day.

Palestine was a new country in an ancient land, cobbled together from parts of different Ottoman provinces to suit imperial convenience. The Palestine mandate originally spanned the Jordan River and stretched from the Mediterranean to the frontiers of Iraq through vast, inhospitable desert territory. In 1923 the lands to the east of the Jordan were formally detached from the Palestine mandate to form a separate state of Transjordan under Amir Abdullah's rule. The British also ceded a part of the Golan Heights to the French mandate in Syria in 1923, by which point Palestine was a country smaller than Belgium, roughly the size of the state of Maryland.

The population of Palestine was already quite diverse in 1923. Palestine was a land holy to Christians, Muslims, and Jews, and for centuries had attracted pilgrims from around the world. Starting in 1882 a new wave of visitors—settlers rather than pilgrims—began to arrive. Pushed by the pogroms of Tsar Alexander III's Russia and pulled by the appeal of a powerful new ideology, Zionism, thousands of Eastern European and Russian Jews sought refuge in Palestine. They entered a society that had an 85 percent Muslim majority, a Christian minority representing some 9 percent of the population, and an indigenous Jewish community. The original Yishuv (as the Jewish community of Palestine was known) did not exceed 3 percent of the population of Palestine in 1882 and lived in the four towns of rabbinical learning: Jerusalem, Hebron, Tiberias, and Safad.[32]

Two distinct waves of Zionist settlers reached Palestine before the First World War. The First Aliya, or wave of Jewish immigrants, entered Palestine between 1882–1903 and doubled the size of the Yishuv from 24,000 to 50,000. The Jewish community expanded yet more rapidly under the Second Aliya (1904–1914), and by 1914 the total Jewish population of Palestine was estimated to have reached 85,000.[33]

The Arab population of Palestine had watched the expansion of Jewish immigration after 1882 with mounting concern. The Arab press began to condemn Zionism during the 1890s, and leading Arab intellectuals openly criticized the movement in the early years of the twentieth century. Legislation was drafted in 1909 to stop Jewish settlement in Palestine, and Zionist activity was twice debated in the Ottoman Parliament in 1911, though no bills ultimately were passed.[34]

These concerns intensified after support for Zionism became official British policy with the 1917 Balfour Declaration. The King-Crane Commission, which traveled the length and breadth of Palestine in June 1919, was overwhelmed by petitions opposed to Zionism. "The anti-Zionist note was especially strong in Palestine," explained the commissioners in their report, "where 222 (85.3 per cent) of the 260 petitions declared against the Zionist program. This is the largest percentage in the district for any one point."

The message from Palestine was clear: the indigenous Arab people, who had opposed Zionist immigration for years, did not accept Britain's commitment to build a Jewish national home in their land. Yet the message seemed to fall on deaf ears, as Britain and the international community determined Palestine's future without consultation or the consent of its people. Where peaceful means failed, desperate people soon turned to violence.

Jewish immigration and land purchase provoked growing tension in Palestine from the beginning of the mandate. Opposed to British rule and to the prospect of a Jewish national home in their midst, the Arab population viewed the expansion of the Jewish community as a direct threat to their political aspirations. Moreover, Jewish land purchase inevitably led to Arab farmers being displaced from lands they had tilled as sharecroppers, often for generations.

Between 1919 and 1921, Jewish immigration to Palestine accelerated dramatically, as over 18,500 Zionist immigrants moved to the country. Major riots broke out in Jerusalem in 1920 and in Jaffa in 1921, which left 95 Jews and 64 Arabs dead and hundreds wounded. Some 70,000 Zionist immigrants reached Palestine between 1922 and 1929. In the same period, the Jewish National Fund bought 240,000 acres of land in the Jezreel Valley in northern Palestine. The combination of high immigration and extensive land purchase was blamed for the next round of violence, which erupted in Jerusalem, Hebron, Safad, and Jaffa in 1929, claiming 133 Jewish and 116 Arab lives.[35]

After each instance of violence, British investigations led to new policies designed to assuage the fears of the Palestinian majority. In July 1922, following the first wave of riots, Winston Churchill issued a White Paper that sought to calm Arab fears that Palestine would become "as Jewish as England is English." He claimed that the terms of the Balfour Declaration did not "contemplate that Palestine as a whole should be converted into a Jewish National Home, but that such a Home should be founded *in Palestine*."[36] Similarly, the gravity of the 1929 riots led to a number of new reports and recommendations. The 1930 Shaw Report identified Jewish immigration and land purchase as the primary cause of Palestinian unrest and called for limits on Zionist immigration to prevent future problems. This was followed in October 1930 by the Passfield White Paper, which called for restrictions on Jewish land purchase and immigration.

Following the publication of each British White Paper sympathetic to Palestinian Arab concerns, the World Zionist Organization and the Jewish Agency of Palestine worked the halls of power in London and Jerusalem to overturn policies deemed inimical to their aims. By bringing great pressure to bear on Prime Minister Ramsay MacDonald's minority government, the Zionists succeeded in getting MacDonald to repudiate the Passfield White Paper. Chaim Weizmann and his advisors more or less wrote the letter for MacDonald, which he signed on February 13, 1931. In his letter, MacDonald confirmed that the British government "did not prescribe and [does] not contemplate any stoppage or prohibition of Jewish immigration," nor would it prevent Jews from acquiring more land in Palestine. Arab expectations for an improvement in their situation were dashed by the MacDonald letter, which they called "the Black Letter" (in contrast to the White Paper).

A vicious cycle then dragged the Palestine mandate into chronic violence: ever-increasing Zionist immigration and land purchase provoked communal conflict, which in turn led to British attempts to introduce limits on the Jewish national home, and Zionist politicking to reverse those limits. As long as this process persisted, no progress was possible in establishing institutions of government or self-rule. The Palestinians did not wish to legitimate the mandate and its commitment to create a Jewish national home; the British did not wish to confer proportional representation, let alone self-rule, on the Palestinian majority who were hostile to the aims of the mandate; and the Zionists cooperated with every aspect of the mandate that advanced their national aims. With each round of violence, the difficulties grew more profound.

The problems of the Arab community of Palestine were compounded by divisions within their own leadership. The two leading families of Jerusalem—the Husaynis and Nashashibis—vied for ascendancy over Arab politics in Palestine. The British played upon the divisions between the two families from the outset. In 1920 the notables of Palestine created an Arab Executive to represent their demands to the British authorities, headed by Musa Kazim al-Husayni. A second representative body, the Supreme Muslim Council, was headed by Hajj Amin al-Husayni, the grand mufti of Jerusalem. The Nashashibis boycotted these Husayni-dominated bodies and tried to work directly with the British. With their leadership divided, the Palestinians were disadvantaged in their relations with both the British and the Zionists.

By 1929 the shortcomings of the Palestinian nationalist leadership encouraged a host of new actors to take to the national stage. As in Egypt in 1919, nationalism provided a window of opportunity for the emergence of women into public life for the first time. Elite women, inspired by Huda Sha'rawi and the Wafdist Women's Association, responded to the 1929 riots by convening the First Arab Women's Congress in Jerusalem in October 1929. Two hundred women attended the congress from the Palestinian Muslim and Christian communities. They passed three resolutions: a call for the abrogation of the Balfour Declaration, an assertion of Palestine's right to a national government with representation for all communities in proportion to their numbers, and the development of Palestinian industries. "The Congress urges every Arab to buy nothing from the Jews but land, and to sell them everything but land."[37]

The delegates then began to break with tradition. Contrary to Palestinian custom, which frowned on women meeting with men in public, they decided to call on the British high commissioner, Sir John Chancellor, to present him with their resolutions. Chancellor received them and promised to communicate their message to London, to be shared with the government's Commission of Enquiry into the troubles in Palestine. After their meeting with Chancellor, the delegation returned to the Women's Congress, which was still in session, and held a public demonstration, further departing from accepted standards of female decorum. The demonstration turned into a 120-car parade starting at Damascus Gate and passing through the main streets of Jerusalem to distribute their resolutions to the foreign consulates in the city.

Following the congress, the delegates created an Arab Women's Association with both a feminist and a nationalist agenda: "to assist the Arab woman in her endeavours to improve her standing, to help the poor and distressed, and to encourage and promote Arab national enterprises." The society raised money to help the families of Palestinians who were imprisoned or executed for anti-British or anti-Zionist attacks. They sent repeated petitions and memoranda to the high commissioner seeking clemency for political prisoners, protesting Jewish arms purchases, and condemning British failures to reach a political agreement with the men of the Arab Executive—to whom they were bound by marriage and family ties.

The Arab Women's Association was a strange hybrid of the politics of Palestinian nationalism and the upper-middle-class culture of British county ladies. They addressed each other by their husbands' names—Madame Kazem Pasha al-Husayni, Madame Awni Abd al-Hadi—and met to strategize over tea. Yet, as in Egypt in 1919, women's participation in the national movement was of powerful symbolic value. These well-educated and eloquent women added a powerful voice to the nascent Palestinian nationalist movement. Take, for example, the speech of Madame Awni Abd al-Hadi berating Lord Allenby in the association's second public demonstration in 1933: "The Arab women have seen the extent to which the British have violated their pledges, divided their country and enforced a policy on the people during the last fifteen years, which will inevitably result in the annihilation of the Arabs and in their supplantation by the Jews through the admission of immigrants from all parts of the world."[38] Her message was clear: the whole of the Palestinian nation, not just its men, was holding Britain accountable for the policies of the mandate.

The Arab elites of Palestine were eloquent, but talk was cheap. For all their fiery nationalist rhetoric and repeated negotiations with the British authorities, Zionist immigration continued apace, and the British showed no signs of granting independence to the Palestinian Arabs. Following the Passfield White Paper, between 1929 and 1931 Zionist immigration had slowed to 5,000–6,000 each year. However, the MacDonald letter of 1931 reversed British policy, and with the Nazi seizure of power in Germany, a massive new influx of Jewish immigrants began to flood into Palestine. In 1932 nearly 10,000 Jewish immigrants entered Palestine, in 1933 over 30,000, in 1934 over 42,000. The peak of immigration came in 1935, when nearly 62,000 Jews entered the country.

Between 1922 and 1935 the Jewish population of Palestine had increased from 9 percent to nearly 27 percent of the total population.[39] Jewish land purchases had begun to displace significant numbers of Palestinian agricultural workers—already a concern addressed in the Passfield White Paper, when the Jewish population of Palestine was half its 1935 size. The failings of the Palestinian leadership, composed exclusively of urban elites, were falling squarely on the shoulders of the rural poor.

In 1935 one man decided to channel the anger of the rural communities into armed rebellion. In the process, he provided the spark that revealed Palestine for the powder keg it had become.

Izz al-Din al-Qassam, a native of Syria, had fled the French mandate in the 1920s to take refuge in Palestine. He was a Muslim cleric who had become a preacher in the popular Istiqlal ["independence"] mosque in the northern port of Haifa. He also headed the Young Men's Muslim Association, a nationalist and anti-Zionist youth group. Shaykh al-Qassam used the pulpit to rouse opposition to both the British and Zionism. His popularity quickly grew among those poorer Palestinians most directly affected by Jewish immigration, who looked to al-Qassam rather than the fractious and ineffectual urban notables for leadership.

In the aftermath of the 1931 MacDonald Black Letter, al-Qassam began to promote the idea of an armed struggle against the British and the Zionists. His appeal met with an enthusiastic response from the congregants at his mosque. A number of men volunteered to fight, and others contributed funds for guns and ammunition. Then, without warning, al-Qassam suddenly disappeared in the autumn of 1935. His supporters were concerned. Some feared he had come to grief; others suspected him of running off with their money. In November 1935, a journalist named Akram Zuaytir was discussing al-Qassam's mysterious disappearance with a mason who was friends with the shaykh. Zuaytir said it was shameful for people to make such accusations against al-Qassam. "I agree, brother," the builder replied, "but why then has he gone into hiding like this?"[40]

Their conversation was interrupted when a man ran up to tell them that there had been a major engagement between an Arab gang and British forces in the hills above Jenin. The bodies of the rebels and the policemen they had killed were being taken to the British fort in Jenin. The young Zuaytir recognized a scoop and called the head of the Arab press bureau in Jerusalem to alert him. The bureau chief set out immediately for Jenin, leaving Zuaytir to watch over the office and to notify the Palestinian newspapers that a big story was brewing.

The shocked bureau chief returned from Jenin three hours later, his speech reduced to headlines. "Important events," he gasped breathlessly. "Very dangerous news. Shaykh Izz al-Din al-Qassam and four of his brethren in the gang were martyred." In the Jenin police station, the bureau chief had interviewed a wounded survivor of al-Qassam's band. Though the man was in great pain, he managed to give a concise account of al-Qassam's movement.

Al-Qassam had created his armed band in 1933, the wounded man explained. He only recruited devout Muslims prepared to die for their country. They collected funds to buy rifles and ammunition and began to prepare for an armed struggle "to kill the English and the Jews because they were occupying our nation." In October 1935, al-Qassam and his men left Haifa in secret—prompting the rumors Zuaytir and the mason had been discussing earlier in the day.

Al-Qassam's armed band ran into a police patrol in the plain of Baysan and killed a Jewish sergeant. The British scoured the hills and surprised one of al-Qassam's men on the roads between Nablus and Jenin. They exchanged fire, and the Arab insurgent was killed. "We learned of his martyrdom," the survivor of al-Qassam's band explained, "and decided to attack the police the following morning." The insurgents found themselves outnumbered by a joint force of British police and soldiers and took refuge in the caves near the village of Ya'bad, close to Jenin. While a Royal Air Force plane circled overhead, the British engaged the Arabs in a two-hour gunfight in which Izz al-Din al-Qassam and three other men were killed. Four survivors were taken prisoner. One British soldier was killed and two others wounded.

Though he was shocked by these events, Zuaytir's first thoughts were of the funeral. In accordance with Islamic practice, al-Qassam and his men would normally be buried before sundown. However, the bodies of the "martyrs" were still in police custody. Zuaytir called one of his colleagues in Haifa to enter into negotiations with the British for the bodies to be delivered to their families, who would need to make arrangements for their funerals. The British agreed to cooperate, on two conditions: the funeral was to be held at ten o'clock the following morning, and the funeral cortege had to proceed directly from al-Qassam's home eastward to the cemetery, without entering Haifa's city center. The British were all too aware of the volatility of the situation and wanted to avoid any outbreak of violence. Zuaytir, in contrast, wanted to ensure that the funeral would be a political event, to galvanize Palestinian opposition to the mandate. At the end of the day, he filed an article in an Islamic newspaper, *al-Jami'a al-Islamiyya* ("Islamic Society"), which called on all Palestinians to converge on Haifa to march in the funeral procession. He posted the challenge directly to the nationalist leadership: "Will the leaders of Palestine march with its young men in the cortege of a great religious scholar, accompanied by the faithful?"[41]

Zuaytir awoke early the next morning to check the coverage in the Arabic press and to prepare for his trip to Haifa. "When I read the newspapers and the descriptions of the battle, and saw my call to march in the funeral procession, I thought today would be a day of great historic importance in Haifa," he wrote. "It is the martyrs' day." He was right—thousands had flocked to Haifa to share in a day of national mourning. Contrary to British wishes, the funeral was held in the central mosque of Haifa and the funeral procession passed through the city center. "With great effort the martyrs were carried through the crowd from the mosque to the great square outside. Here the pen falters in describing the scene. Thousands accompanied the procession, with the bodies carried at shoulder height, shouting *Allahu akbar, Allahu akbar* [God is great], while the women ululated from the roof tops and the windows." The mourners sung fiery songs of resistance. "Then, while the bodies were raised, a voice cried out: Revenge! Revenge! The thousands responded with one voice like a roar of thunder: Revenge! Revenge!"

The enraged crowd stormed the Haifa police station, stoning the building and destroying police cars parked outside. They set upon every British soldier and policeman they found along the way, though the British withdrew to avoid casualties on either side. The crowd also attacked the railway station as another symbol of hated British rule.

The whole of the procession took three and one-half hours, at which point al-Qassam and his men were laid to rest. "Imagine the impact on the masses who witnessed the heroic martyrs buried in their blood-stained clothes of jihad," Zuaytir reflected. He also noted how all the towns and cities of northern Palestine were represented at the funeral—Acre, Jenin, Baysan, Tulkarm, Nablus, Haifa—"but I did not see the heads of the [nationalist] parties, for which they must be reviled."[42]

The short-lived revolt of Shaykh 'Izz al-Din al-Qassam changed Palestinian politics forever. The urban notables who had led the nationalist movement had lost the confidence of the population at large. They had negotiated with the British for fifteen years and had nothing to show for their efforts. The Palestinians were no closer to independence or self-rule, the British were still firmly in control, and the Jewish population was growing at a rate that would soon bring them to parity with the Arab population. The Palestinians wanted men of action who would confront the

British and Zionist threats directly. The result was three years of revolt that devastated the towns and countryside of Palestine.

In the aftermath of the Qassam revolt, the heads of the Palestinian political parties attempted to reassert their leadership over the nationalist movement. In April 1936 the leading parties united in a new organization called the Arab Higher Committee. They called for a general strike by all Arab workers and government employees, as well as a complete boycott on all economic exchanges with the Yishuv. The general strike was accompanied by violent attacks on British forces and Jewish settlers.

The nationalist leaders' strategy backfired badly. The Palestinian Arab economy suffered far worse than the Yishuv as a result of the boycott. Britain flooded the country with 20,000 new troops to put down the rebellion. Britain also called on its allies in neighboring Arab states to persuade the Palestinian leadership to call off the general strike. On October 9, 1936, the kings of Saudi Arabia and Iraq joined the rulers of Transjordan and Yemen in a joint declaration calling on "our sons the Arabs of Palestine" to "resolve for peace in order to save further shedding of blood. In doing this," the monarchs claimed implausibly, "we rely on the good intentions of your friend Great Britain, who has declared that she will do justice."[43]

When the Arab Higher Committee responded to the kings' declaration and called for an end to the strike, the Palestinians felt betrayed by their own leaders and their Arab brethren alike. Their views were captured by the Palestinian nationalist poet Abu Salman, whose acerbic verses accused both the Palestinian leaders and British-backed Arab monarchs of selling out the Arab movement:

> You who cherish the homeland
>   Revolt against the outright oppression
> Liberate the homeland from the kings
>   Liberate it from the puppets
> I thought we had kings who could lead the men behind them[44]

Abu Salman spoke for the disenchanted Palestinian masses when he asserted that the liberation of Palestine would come from its people, not its leaders.

In the aftermath of the general strike the British responded once again with a commission of enquiry. The report of the Peel Commission, published July 7, 1937, sent shock waves through Palestine. For the first time, the British acknowledged that the troubles in Palestine were the product of rival and incompatible national movements. "An irrepressible conflict has arisen between two national communities within the narrow bounds of one small country," the report acknowledged. "About 1,000,000 Arabs are in strife, open or latent, with some 400,000 Jews. There is no common ground between them."

The solution proposed by the Peel Commission was partition. The Jews were to gain statehood in 20 percent of the territory of Palestine, including most of the coastline and some of the country's most fertile agricultural land, in the Jezreel Valley and the Galilee. The Arabs were allotted the poorest lands of Palestine, including the Negev Desert and the Arava Valley, as well as the hill country of the West Bank and the Gaza Strip.

The population of Palestine did not correspond to the geography of partition. This was particularly problematic as major Arab towns and cities were included in the proposed Jewish state. To iron out such anomalies, the Peel Commission held out the possibility of "population transfers" to remove Arabs from territories allocated to the Jewish state—something that in the later twentieth century would come to be called ethnic cleansing. Britain's recommendation of forced transfer won the chairman of the Jewish Agency, David Ben-Gurion (1886–1973), over to the partition plan. "This will give us something we never had, even when we were under our own authority" in antiquity, he enthused—namely, a "really Jewish" state with a homogenously Jewish population.[45]

To compound Arab grievances, the partition plan did not envisage an independent Palestinian state but called for the Arab territories to be appended to Transjordan, under Amir Abdullah's rule. The people of Palestine had grown deeply distrustful of Abdullah, seeing him as a British agent who was covetous of their lands. For the Palestinians, the Peel Commission's recommendations represented the worst possible outcome for their national struggle. Far from securing their rights to self-rule, their population was to be dispersed and ruled by hostile foreigners—the Zionists and Amir Abdullah.

The Jewish Agency accepted the terms, Amir Abdullah agreed with the Peel Commission, and the Palestinians went to war against both the British and the Yishuv.

The second phase of the Palestinian Arab Revolt lasted two years, from the autumn of 1937 through 1939. On September 26, 1937, Palestinian extremists murdered the district commissioner in Galilee, L. Y. Andrews. The British arrested 200 Palestinian nationalist leaders, deported many to the Seychelles, and declared the Arab Higher Committee illegal. Without central leadership, the revolt degenerated into an uncoordinated insurgency that ravaged the Palestinian countryside. The insurgents attacked British police and army patrols and Jewish settlements, assassinated British and Jewish officials, and killed Palestinians suspected of collaborating with the occupation authorities. They sabotaged railways, communications, and the oil pipelines that crossed through Palestine. Villagers found themselves caught between the insurgents, who demanded their support, and the British, who punished all those suspected of aiding the insurgents. The effects on the Palestinians were devastating.

Every Arab attack against the British and the Yishuv brought massive reprisals. The British, determined to suppress the revolt militarily, dispatched 25,000 soldiers and policemen to Palestine—the largest deployment of British forces abroad since the end of the First World War. They established military courts, operating under "emergency regulations" that gave the mandate the legal trappings of a military dictatorship. The British destroyed the houses of all persons involved in attacks, as well as all persons known or suspected of having aided insurgents, under the legal authority of the emergency regulations. An estimated 2,000 houses were destroyed between 1936 and 1940. Combatants and innocent civilians alike were interned in concentration camps—by 1939, over 9,000 Palestinians were held in overcrowded facilities. Suspects were subjected to violent interrogation, ranging from humiliation to torture. Younger offenders, of between seven and sixteen years, were flogged. Over 100 Arabs were sentenced to death in 1938 and 1939, and more than thirty were actually executed. Palestinians were used as human shields to prevent insurgents from placing land mines on roads used by British forces.[46]

The use of overwhelming force and collective punishments by the British degenerated into abuses and atrocities that would forever stain the mandate in the memory of the Palestinians. The most heinous atrocities came in retaliation for the killing of British troops by insurgents. In one well-documented case, British soldiers took revenge for comrades killed by a land mine in September 1938 by loading more than twenty men from the village of al-Bassa into a bus and forcing them at gun point to drive over a massive land mine the British themselves had buried in the middle of the village access road. All of the occupants were killed by the explosion, their maimed bodies photographed by a British serviceman before the villagers were forced to bury their men's remains in a mass grave.[47]

The Palestinian Arabs had been thoroughly defeated and by 1939 had no fight left in them. Some 5,000 men had been killed and 10,000 others wounded—in all, over 10 percent of the adult male population was killed, wounded, imprisoned, or exiled. However, the British could hardly claim victory. They could not sustain the cost of suppressing the revolt, and they could not impose their policies on the Palestinian Arabs. With war looming in Europe, Whitehall could no longer afford to deploy so many troops to suppress a colonial war. To restore peace to their troubled Palestine mandate, the British shelved the Peel Commission's partition plan of 1937. Once again, a royal commission was convened to reexamine the situation in Palestine, and once again, the commission published a White Paper that sought to address Palestinian Arab grievances.

The 1939 White Paper was the best deal Britain ever offered the Palestinian Arabs. The new policy capped Jewish immigration at 15,000 each year for five years, or 75,000 total. This would raise the population of the Yishuv to 35 percent of the total population of Palestine—a minority large enough to look after itself, but not so large as to take control of the country as a whole. There would be no further Jewish immigration without the consent of the Arab majority—which all parties acknowledged was unlikely to be forthcoming. Jewish land purchase was to be banned or severely restricted, depending on the region. Finally, Palestine would gain its independence in ten years under joint Arab and Jewish government "in such a way as to ensure that the essential interests of each community are safeguarded."[48]

The 1939 White Paper was unsatisfactory to both Arabs and Jews in Palestine. The Arab community rejected the terms because it allowed Jewish immigration to continue, if at a reduced rate, and because it preserved the political status quo and delayed independence by a further ten years. The Yishuv rejected the terms because it closed Palestine to Jewish immigration just as Nazi atrocities against Jews were escalating. (In November 1938, Nazi gangs had terrorized German Jewish citizens in *Kristallnacht*, or the "night of broken glass," Europe's worst pogrom to date.) The White Paper also ruled out the creation of a Jewish state in Palestine, relegating the Yishuv to a minority status in a future Palestinian Arab state.

The leadership of the Yishuv itself was divided by the 1939 White Paper. David Ben-Gurion made clear his opposition to the White Paper from the outset. However, he identified Nazi Germany as the greater threat to the welfare of the Jewish people and famously vowed to fight on Britain's side against Nazism as though there were no White Paper. The extremists in the Zionist movement—the Irgun and the Stern Gang—responded to the White Paper by declaring Britain the enemy. They fought against the British presence in Palestine as an illegitimate imperial state denying independence to the Jewish people, and they turned to terror tactics to achieve a Jewish state in Palestine. By the end of the Second World War, when Nazism had been eradicated, Britain would find itself combating a Jewish revolt of far greater magnitude than the Arabs had ever mounted against British rule.

At the end of the First World War, Britain's mastery over the Middle East was unrivaled. Its troops occupied the Arab world from Egypt to Iraq, and its control over the Persian Gulf was unassailable. Although few in the Arab world had wanted the British to rule over them, most viewed their colonial overlord with respect, however grudging. The British were efficient, inscrutable, orderly, technologically advanced, and militarily strong. Britain was truly great, a colossus that towered over its colonial possessions.

Two decades of colonial rule revealed the colossus to have clay feet. Across the region the British faced a gamut of opposition, from moderate nationalist politics to radical armed insurgency. In Iraq, Palestine, and Egypt, the British were forced to negotiate and renegotiate the terms of their unwelcome presence. Each British concession to Arab opposition, every reversal of policy, revealed the fallibility of the imperial power.

It was the rising threat of fascism in Europe, however, that turned Britain's Middle Eastern possessions into the vulnerable underbelly of the British Empire. At times, it looked as though the Arab colonies might slip from Britain's control. British actions in Iraq and Egypt during the Second World War demonstrated the weakness of their position in a way that presaged the end of Britain's dominion in the Middle East.

In Iraq, the British faced a pro-Axis coup d'état on April 1, 1941. Iraq was then ruled by an unpopular regent, Prince Abd al-Ilah (r. 1939–1953), who ruled on behalf of the child King Faysal II (r. 1953–1958). When Abd al-Ilah backed British calls for the resignation of the popular prime minister, Rashid Ali al-Kaylani, on grounds of his pro-Axis leanings, key Iraqi officers put their support behind the prime minister. The top military officers believed Germany and Italy would win the war and that Iraq's interests lay in fostering good relations with the Axis. The regent, fearful of a military coup, fled Iraq for Transjordan, leaving Rashid Ali and the Iraqi military in control.

Rashid Ali's continued exercise of political authority in the regent's absence was deemed by Britain to constitute a coup. In spite of Rashid Ali's every effort to demonstrate to the British that no fundamental change had occurred, the nationalist tone of his new cabinet (which included Palestinian leader Hajj Amin al-Husayni, the grand mufti exiled for his extreme nationalist views, who was a close advisor to Rashid Ali) served only to exacerbate Britain's fears. Invoking the terms of the 1930 Anglo-Iraqi Treaty, the British requested permission to land troops in Iraq. Rashid Ali and the nationalist officers demurred, as they mistrusted British intentions. Undaunted, the British began landing troops without official sanction. The Iraqis threatened to fire on unauthorized British aircraft, which the British warned would be grounds for war. Under the circumstances, neither side could afford to back down.

Britain and Iraq went to war in May 1941. Fighting began outside the British base at Habbaniyya and lasted several days until the Iraqi forces fell back on Falluja, where they regrouped to defend Baghdad. Fresh British troops were sent from India and Transjordan. Rashid Ali turned to Germany and Italy to request assistance against the British. The Axis powers managed to send thirty aircraft and some small arms but, under the time constraints, were unable to intervene more directly. As British forces closed in on Baghdad, Rashid Ali and his political allies, including Hajj Amin al-Husayni, fled the country. They left the mayor of Baghdad to negotiate an armistice with the British, and the country as a whole in a state of chaos.

It was the Jewish community of Baghdad that fell victim to the chaos after the fall of Rashid Ali's government in 1941. Anti-British sentiment combined with hostility to the Zionist project in Palestine and German notions of anti-Semitism to produce a pogrom unprecedented in Arab history, known in Arabic as the *Farhud*. The Jewish community of Baghdad was large and highly assimilated into all levels of society— from the elites to the bazaars to the music halls, in which many of Iraq's most celebrated performers were Jewish. Yet all of this was forgotten in two days of communal violence and bloodshed that claimed nearly 200 lives and left Jewish shops and houses robbed and gutted, before the British authorities decided to enter the city and restore order.

The fall of Rashid Ali's government led to the restoration of the Hashemite monarchy in Iraq. The regent, Abd al-Ilah, and those Iraqi politicians most sympathetic to the British were returned to power by their former colonial master. Iraqi nationalists were outraged. They argued that Rashid Ali enjoyed widespread support among the Iraqi people. Clearly the British would only allow the Iraqis a leadership that met with London's approval. Coming only nine years after Iraq had achieved its nominal independence, this intervention served to discredit both Great Britain and the Hashemite monarchy in the Iraqi people's eyes.

Britain, however, was the ultimate loser in Iraq. The mandate, which had once been a success story, was now left with a shaken monarchy, a dangerous military, and a population so hostile to Britain's role in the Middle East that they preferred to throw their lot in with Britain's Axis enemies.

The Axis had its supporters in Egypt as well. Egyptian nationalists were not satisfied with the partial independence achieved in the 1936 Anglo-Egyptian Treaty. Britain continued to exercise disproportionate control over Egypt's affairs and full control over Sudan. With the outbreak of the Second World War, Egypt was flooded with British troops, and the Egyptian government seemed more subordinate to Britain since independence than it had been before. This situation was intolerable to a new generation of Egyptian nationalists whose enmity for Britain made them look with favor on Britain's Axis enemies.

The Italians and the Germans played on nationalist sentiment to isolate the British in Egypt. The Italians launched a powerful new radio station to carry their propaganda to Egypt and the Eastern Mediterranean. Radio Bari trumpeted the accomplishments of the fascist government of Benito Mussolini. The combination of extreme nationalism, strong leadership, and the military might of fascism appealed to Egyptian nationalists far more than the petty squabbles of the multiparty democracy that Britain had imposed on their country. With Germany and Italy at war with Britain, many in Egypt hoped to see the Axis powers defeat the British and force them from Egypt once and for all.

With the launch of the North African campaign in 1940, some Egyptian nationalists believed the moment of deliverance was at hand. Italian forces crossed from Libya to attack British positions in Egypt. German forces joined the Italians in North Africa with the specially trained Afrika Korps, commanded by the brilliant field marshal Erwin Rommel. By the winter of 1942, Axis forces posed a real threat to Britain's position in Egypt. Some Egyptian political leaders, including even King Faruq himself, seemed quite receptive to the idea of Germany driving the British out of Egypt for them.

British mistrust of Egyptian prime minister Ali Mahir's fascist leanings led them to demand his resignation in June 1940. This sort of intervention revealed Britain's disregard for Egypt's sovereignty and independence and further soured Anglo-Egyptian relations. As German and Italian forces gained the upper hand in the battlefields of North Africa, the British sought to crush support for the Axis within Egypt's political circles. Ironically, the only Egyptian political party with reliable antifascist credentials was the nationalist Wafd party. On February 4, 1942, the British high commissioner Sir Miles Lampson presented King Faruq with an ultimatum either to name Mustafa Nahhas to form an entirely Wafdist government or to abdicate his throne. To back up his ultimatum, Lampson deployed British tanks around Faruq's Abdin Palace in central Cairo.

The Abdin Palace ultimatum shattered twenty years of Anglo-Egyptian politics by compromising the three pillars of the system: the monarchy, the Wafd, and the British themselves. King Faruq had betrayed his country by succumbing to British threats and allowing a foreign power to impose a government upon him. Many nationalists believe their king should have stood up to the British, even at the risk of death. As for the Wafd, the party that had won the support of the Egyptian people to struggle against imperialism had agreed to come to power by the bayonets of the British. Yet it was the hysteria behind the ultimatum that revealed how weak and threatened the British were in the face of Axis advances in the Western Desert. The British were on the defensive against the Axis and Egyptian nationalism alike, and had shown their fallibility. The three-way power struggle between the British, the palace, and the Wafd collapsed in February 1942. All three parties would be swept away a decade later in the revolutionary ferment of the 1950s.

The British entered the Middle East with the intention of integrating the Arab world into an empire they thought would last forever. They encountered stiff opposition from the outset—in Egypt, Iraq, and Palestine in particular. As nationalist opposition mounted and the cost of formal empire escalated, Britain tried to modify the terms of empire by conceding nominal independence and securing its strategic interests by treaty. Yet even this concession to their nationalist opponents failed to reconcile the Arabs to Britain's position in the Middle East. By the Second World War, internal opposition left Britain highly vulnerable in its Arab possessions. Italy and Germany were quick to exploit Britain's weakness and played on Arab national aspirations to the Axis powers' advantage. As the Arab world slipped from Britain's control, the British Empire in the Middle East proved more of a liability than an asset.

The only possible consolation for the British was that their imperial rival France had proven no more successful in its Arab possessions.

CHAPTER 8

The French Empire
in the Middle East

France long had coveted Greater Syria—that land mass embracing the modern states of Syria, Lebanon, Palestine, Israel, and Jordan—for its empire in the Arab world. Napoleon had invaded Syria from Egypt in 1799, though his progress was checked by stubborn resistance from the Ottoman defenders in Acre, and he was forced to withdraw. France gave its support to Muhammad 'Ali in his invasion of Syria in the 1830s, hoping to extend French influence over the region through their Egyptian ally. When Egypt withdrew from Syria in 1840, the French deepened their ties to the indigenous Catholic communities of Syria, particularly the Maronites of Mount Lebanon. When the Druzes massacred the Maronites of Mount Lebanon in 1860, France dispatched a campaign force of 6,000 men in a transparent bid to stake its claim to the Syrian coast. Again the French were frustrated, as the Ottoman government managed to reassert control over its Arab provinces for the next half century.

The First World War finally offered France the opportunity to secure its claim to Syria. At war with the Ottoman Empire, France and its Entente allies could openly discuss the division of Ottoman territories in the event of victory. The French government won Britain's support for its ambitions through intense negotiations between Sir Mark Sykes and François Georges-Picot over the years 1915–1916, culminating in the Sykes-Picot Agreement. Having already colonized Algeria, Tunisia, and Morocco, France was confident it had the knowledge and experience to rule Arabs successfully. What worked in Morocco, the French maintained, would work in Syria. Moreover, France had earned the loyalty and support of the Maronite Christian community of Mount Lebanon over the decades. Indeed, by the end of the First World War, Lebanon was probably the only country in the world with a significant constituency actively lobbying for a French mandate.

Late-Ottoman Lebanon was a strangely truncated land. In the aftermath of the Christian massacres of 1860, the Ottomans and the European powers conferred to establish a special province of Mount Lebanon in the highlands overlooking the Mediterranean to the west, and the Bekaa Valley to the east. The Ottomans had kept the strategic coastline, with its port cities of Tyre, Sidon, Beirut, and Tripoli, under their own direct administration. In 1888 the Syrian littoral was redesignated as the Province of Beirut. Mount Lebanon was for the most part cut off from the sea, and the Province of Beirut was at many points no more than a few miles wide.

One of the chief shortcomings of the autonomous province of Mount Lebanon was its geographic constraints. The territory was too small and infertile to support a large population, and many Lebanese were driven from their homeland in search of better economic opportunities in the last years of Ottoman rule. Between 1900 and 1914 an estimated 100,000 Lebanese—perhaps one-quarter the total population— left Mount Lebanon for Egypt, West Africa, and the Americas.[1] This was a cause of growing concern to the twelve-member Administrative Council that ruled Mount Lebanon, whose members were drawn proportionally from the territory's diverse communities. As the First World War came to an end, the members of the Administrative Council aspired to a larger country and looked to their long-time patron France to help achieve their ambitions.

The Administrative Council of Mount Lebanon met on December 9, 1918, and agreed on the terms it wished to present to the Paris Peace Conference. The council sought Lebanon's complete independence, within its "natural boundaries," under French tutelage. By "natural boundaries," the council members envisaged the expansion of Mount Lebanon to include the coastal cities of Tripoli, Beirut, Sidon, and Tyre as well as the eastern Bekaa Valley up to the western slopes of the Anti-Lebanon Mountains. A Lebanon within its "natural boundaries" would be framed between rivers to the north and south, mountains to the east and the Mediterranean to the west.

The people of Mount Lebanon knew that France had advocated such a "Greater Lebanon" since the 1860s, and they hoped to achieve this critical land mass through a French mandate. Consequently, the Administrative Council of Mount Lebanon was formally invited by the French government to present its case to the Paris Peace Conference—unlike such inconvenient Arab states as Egypt or Syria, which were snubbed or excluded because their nationalist aspirations conflicted with imperial ambitions at the conference.

The Administrative Council dispatched a five-man delegation to Paris headed by Daoud Ammoun, a leading Maronite politician.[2] Ammoun set out Mount Lebanon's aspirations in his address to the Paris Peace Conference's Council of Ten on February 15, 1919:

We want a Lebanon removed from all servitude, a Lebanon free to pursue its national destiny and reestablished in its natural frontiers—all indispensable conditions for it to live in its own freedom and to prosper in peace.

Yet we all know that it is not possible for us to develop economically and to organize our liberty without the support of a great power, as we lack the technicians trained in the workings of modern life and Western civilization. Always in the past, France has defended us, supported us, guided, instructed and secured us. We feel a constant friendship for her. We wish for her support to organize ourselves, and her guarantee of our independence.[3]

The Lebanese delegation was not seeking French colonialism in Lebanon but French assistance toward their ultimate goal of independence. However, the French seemed only to hear what they wanted to hear, and they were glad to use the Lebanese delegation to legitimate their own claims over Lebanon.

The Administrative Council, however, did not speak for all Lebanese. Over 100,000 Lebanese emigrants lived abroad—in Africa, Europe, and the Americas—and took a passionate interest in the political future of their homeland. Many of the Lebanese expatriate community had come to see themselves as members of a broader Syrian people that embraced émigrés from Palestine, inland Syria, and Transjordan. These "Syrians" included some of Lebanon's most celebrated men of letters, including Khalil Gibran, author of the mystical masterpiece *The Prophet*. They saw Lebanon as an integral if distinct part of Greater Syria and lobbied for the independence of Syria as a whole, under French tutelage. Given their support for French rule, the Lebanese advocates of Greater Syria were also invited to present their case at the Paris Peace Conference.

One of the most prominent of the Lebanese expatriates was Shukri Ghanim. President of the Syrian Central Committee, a nationalist network with branches in Brazil, the United States, and Egypt, Ghanim appeared before the Council of Ten in February 1919, calling for a federation of Syrian states under French mandatory rule. "Syria must be divided into three parts," he argued, "or four, if Palestine is not excluded. Greater Lebanon or Phoenicia, the region of Damascus, and that of Aleppo, [should be] constituted in independent, democratic states." Yet Ghanim did not believe all Syrians were created equal, concluding ominously, "France is there to guide, advise and balance all things, and—we should not fear to say this to our compatriots, who are reasonable men—will dose our liberties according to our different states of moral health."[4] While we can only guess what Ghanim meant by "moral health," it is clear he believed Lebanon was far more advanced than the other parts of Syria and better prepared to enjoy full political liberties under French protection than Damascus, Aleppo, and the like. In many ways, Ghanim's appeal was more in line with French thought than Daoud Ammoun's presentation on behalf of the Administrative Council of Mount Lebanon.

There was, however, a third trend in Lebanese politics that was overtly hostile to France's position in the Levant. The Sunni Muslims and Greek Orthodox Christians of coastal cities like Tripoli, Beirut, Sidon, and Tyre had no wish to be isolated from the mainstream of Syrian political society and find themselves reduced to a minority in a Christian-dominated Lebanese state. It was a clear divide between the French-oriented politics of Mount Lebanon and the Arabism of the coastal province of Beirut. Coming out of centuries of Ottoman rule, the nationalists in Beirut wished to be part of a larger Arab empire and threw their support behind Amir Faysal's government in Damascus. Faysal, who had led the Arab Revolt against Ottoman rule from the Hijaz to Damascus between 1916 and 1918, spoke on behalf of the political aspirations of the Lebanese of the coastal plain when he addressed the Council of Ten in Paris in February 1919. Lebanon, he argued, was an integral part of the Arab kingdom promised to his father, Sharif Husayn, by British High Commissioner Sir Henry McMahon and should come under Faysal's Arab government in Damascus, without any mandate at all.

Amir Faysal's plea to the great powers in Paris met with widespread support among Arab nationalists in Beirut. Muhammad Jamil Bayhum was a young intellectual who became one of Faysal's ardent supporters. In July 1919, Bayhum was elected to represent Beirut in the Syrian Congress convened in Damascus in advance of the King-Crane Commission. "The French authorities tried everything to prevent the election from taking place, applying pressure on both the electors and the candidates," Bayhum recalled. "However, their attempts to persuade and coerce were in vain."[5] Lebanon was well-represented in the Syrian Congress, with twenty-two delegates from all parts of the country.

Bayhum joined the Syrian Congress, which opened on June 6, 1919, in a state of heightened excitement. The delegates firmly believed they had assembled to communicate the political wishes of the Syrian people, through the King-Crane Commission, to the great powers at the Paris Peace Conference. They aspired to an Arab state in all of Greater Syria under Faysal's rule in Damascus, with little or no foreign interference. Bayhum described the political atmosphere in Damascus as charged with optimism and high ideals, comparing the city to the revolutionary Paris of 1789. "We participated in the Congress, with the representatives of Palestine, Jordan, Antioch, Alexandretta, and Damascus, all of us hoping that the allied states would hear our appeals, and deliver the freedom and independence that had been promised to us."[6]

Bayhum remained in Damascus to attend all of the sessions of the Syrian Congress, well after the King-Crane Commission had come and gone in July 1919. He watched in dismay as Britain withdrew its troops from Syria in October 1919 and French forces began to take their place. Over the winter of 1919–1920, France began to impose increasingly stringent terms on the isolated Amir Faysal that fragmented Greater Syria and stripped Faysal's government of its independence. In March 1920 the Congress declared the independence of Greater Syria, in a last-ditch attempt to prevent the imposition of mandates by presenting the European powers with a *fait accompli*. The Syrian Congress staked its claim to Lebanon as an integral part of Syria, asserting in its declaration of independence: "We will take into consideration all patriotic wishes of the Lebanese with respect to the administration of their country, within its pre-war limits, on condition that Lebanon distances itself from all foreign influences."

The Administrative Council of Mount Lebanon was quick to protest the Syrian Congress's declaration and insisted that Faysal's government had no right "to speak on behalf of Lebanon, to set its frontiers, to limit its independence and to forbid it to call for the collaboration of France."[7] Yet political leaders in Mount Lebanon were growing increasingly concerned over France's intentions. In April 1920, Britain and France confirmed the final distribution of the Arab provinces of the Ottoman Empire at the San Remo conference. Lebanon and Syria were awarded to France, and Palestine and Iraq passed to British rule. Though many in the Maronite community had sought French technical assistance and political support, they somehow expected France to act out of altruism rather than imperial self-interest. As France began to prepare for its mandate over Lebanon, its military administrators started to impose their policies on the Administrative Council in Mount Lebanon. In turn, politicians in Mount Lebanon began to question the wisdom of seeking French assistance in state-building.

In July 1920, seven of the Administrative Council's eleven members made a spectacular U-turn and sought an accommodation with King Faysal's administration in Damascus. They drafted a memorandum calling for joint action between Syria and Lebanon to achieve complete independence for both countries, and a negotiated resolution of territorial and economic differences between the two sides. The dissident Lebanese councilors called for the formation of a Syro-Lebanese delegation to present their claims to the European powers still gathered in Paris. However, when the French got wind of the initiative they arrested the seven councilors on their way to Damascus.

The arrest of some of Lebanon's most respected politicians sent shock waves throughout the region. Bishara al-Khoury (1890–1964) was a young Maronite lawyer who had worked closely with the French military administrators in Lebanon (he would later become independent Lebanon's first president). Late in the night of July 10, 1920, the French high commissioner, General Henri Gouraud, asked al-Khoury to come to his residence to discuss an urgent matter. Al-Khoury found Gouraud among his officers, pacing anxiously. The high commissioner informed al-Khoury that the French had just arrested the seven dissident councilors.

"They were traitors who were trying to unite with Amir Faysal and append Lebanon to Syria," Gouraud explained. "The Administrative Council has been dissolved."

Al-Khoury was stunned. "On what basis did you undertake this violent act?"

Gouraud replied that they were found with a memorandum setting out their objectives. "You are a Lebanese before all else," the Frenchman said to Khoury. "Do you agree with their actions?"

Al-Khoury, who had not been shown the text of the councilors' memorandum, responded cautiously: "I agree with all who seek independence, though I would not turn to anyone from outside Lebanon." "We are agreed," replied one of the French officers. Gouraud informed al-Khoury that the seven councilors would be brought before a military tribunal for their crimes.

The trial of the dissident councilors alienated some of France's strongest advocates in Lebanon. As a trained lawyer, al-Khoury was appalled that such an important trial could be concluded in just two days, and he described the proceedings taking place "in a climate of terrorism." He was offended when Lebanese witnesses were forced to declare "their love of France" as part of their testimony. The defendants were fined, forbidden to work in Lebanon, and exiled to Corsica. Worse yet, when al-Khoury finally got to read the text of the councilors' memorandum, he found himself in sympathy with most of their objectives.[8] The French were seriously undermining their support base in Lebanon by these high-handed actions.

Nevertheless, French plans for the new Lebanese state proceeded apace. On August 31, 1920, the frontiers of Mount Lebanon were extended to the natural boundaries sought by Lebanese nationalists, and the "independent" state of Greater Lebanon was established the following day under French assistance. Yet the more France assisted, the less independence Lebanon enjoyed. The defunct Administrative Council was replaced by an Administrative Commission, headed by a French governor who answered directly to High Commissioner Gouraud.

By imposing a new administrative structure on Lebanon, France began to shape the political culture of the new state in line with its own views of Lebanese society. The French saw Lebanon as a volatile mix of communities rather than as a distinct national community, and they shaped the political institutions of the country accordingly. Positions within the new Administrative Commission were allocated by religious community in keeping with a system known as confessionalism. This meant that political office was distributed among the different Lebanese religious communities (or *confessions,* in French), ideally in proportion to their demographic weight. Given its long history as patron of Lebanon's Catholics, France was determined to ensure that Lebanon would be a Christian state.

The challenge for France was to expand Lebanon's boundaries without making the Christians a minority in their own country. Although Christians represented 76 percent of the population of Mount Lebanon, they were a distinct minority in the newly annexed coastal cities and the eastern territories in the Bekaa and Anti-Lebanon Mountains. The proportion of Christians in Greater Lebanon was thus only 58 percent of the total population and, given differences in fertility rates, declining.[9] Ignoring the new demographic realities of Lebanon's population, the French favored their Christian clients and gave them disproportionate representation in the governing Administrative Commission: ten Christians to four Sunni Muslims, two Shiite Muslims, and one Druze representative.

Though the French experts believed this archaic system of government best fit the political culture of the country, many Lebanese intellectuals were increasingly uncomfortable with confessionalism and aspired to a national identity. In the newspaper *Le Réveil*, one journalist wrote: "Do we wish to become a nation in the real and whole sense of the word? Or to conserve ourselves as a laughable mix of communities, always separate from each other like hostile tribes? We must furnish ourselves a unique unifying symbol: a nationality. That flower can never thrive in the shadow of steeples and minarets, but only under a flag."[10] Yet the first flag that the French allowed independent Lebanon was the French Tricolour with a cedar tree at the center. France was beginning to show its true colors in Lebanon.

In March 1922, Gouraud announced that the Administrative Commission would be dissolved and replaced by an elected Representative Council. The measure angered Lebanese politicians both because the French had acted unilaterally and because the new elected assembly would have even fewer responsibilities than the former Administrative Commission. Far from being an elected legislature, the Representative Council was barred from discussing political matters and was to meet in session for only three months of the year. The decree gave legislative power to the French high commissioner, who could adjourn or dissolve the Representative Council at will. Even France's most ardent Lebanese supporters were outraged. "This decree of enslavement now gives [France] the image of a conquering power casting treaty and friendship beneath the boot of its victorious soldiers," wrote one disillusioned Francophile émigré.[11]

Undeterred by the growing Lebanese opposition to their rule, the French proceeded with elections for the Representative Council. They spared no effort to ensure that their supporters were elected and that their opponents were excluded.

Muhammad Jamil Bayhum, the Beirut delegate to the 1919 Syrian Congress, had opposed the mandate in principle and was outspoken in his criticism of French administrative measures in Lebanon. Though he had never considered running for office, close friends persuaded him to join an opposition slate. Bayhum met with the French administrator responsible for organizing the elections to see if the authorities would object to his candidacy. The official, Monsieur Gauthier, assured him that the elections would be free and that the French authorities would not intervene in the process at all. Encouraged by Gauthier's response, Bayhum announced his candidacy on a strong nationalist slate, which quickly rose to the top of the polls.

Despite Gauthier's assurances, it was soon clear that France had every intention of intervening in the electoral process. Once the French came to appreciate the electoral appeal of the nationalist list, they worked to undermine its candidates. Within weeks of their first meeting, Gauthier called Bayhum to his office and asked him to withdraw his candidacy, on "an order from the highest authority." Bayhum was outraged, having spent an intense month on the campaign trail. Gauthier was direct: "We will oppose you in the elections, and if you are elected we will expel you from the Council by force." When Bayhum refused to back down, he found himself in court facing charges of electoral fraud. During the court hearing, the judge called Gauthier himself as a witness.

"My good sir, do you not have many complaints against Monsieur Bayhum confirming that he bribed the secondary electors to buy their votes?" the judge asked.

"Indeed, indeed," replied Gauthier.

The judge turned to Bayhum and said, "I have an enormous file [on you]." He pointed to a folder. "It is overflowing with complaints against you for buying votes, which is something the law forbids."

Bayhum argued his case to no avail. The charges of electoral fraud were left hanging over Bayhum to pressure him to withdraw his candidacy for the council.

After his hearing, Bayhum retired to discuss strategy with the other members of the nationalist list. One of his friends was Gauthier's personal physician, and the doctor offered to call upon the French administrator to try to persuade him to drop the charges against Bayhum. The doctor returned from his interview laughing, much to the surprise of Bayhum and his friends. Gauthier had dismissed the doctor's efforts to speak on Bayhum's behalf, replying: 'You, my friend, have no experience in politics. I would say that it is Monsieur Bayhum himself who has obliged us to keep him out of the Assembly. What we want is this: if we place a glass on a window sill it will stay in its place, and not budge a hair's breadth."

The doctor understood Gauthier's message all too well: the French would tolerate no challenge to the institutions they put in place. Someone like Bayhum threatened to knock the "glass" of French colonial rule right off the Lebanese window sill. Bayhum recalled: "We all laughed with the doctor at this ridiculous policy, imposed on our country by the mandatory power. This was the same country that had promised to help us attain our independence." Bayhum withdrew his candidacy and chose not to stand for the council at all.[12]

The elections confirmed France's intention to rule Lebanon as a colony rather than assist it in achieving independence. These measures convinced some of France's strongest supporters to join the growing ranks of Lebanese nationalists struggling against French rule. It was an ominous beginning for the French Empire in the Middle East in the interwar years. If France couldn't make things work in Lebanon, how would it manage in its other Arab territories?

While the French faced electoral battles in Lebanon, colonial administrators in Morocco were confronted with a major armed uprising that targeted both Spanish and French rule. Between 1921 and 1926, the Rif War posed the greatest challenge yet to European colonialism in the Arab world.

France was given the green light by the European powers to add Morocco to its North African possessions in 1912. The Moroccan sultan, Moulay Abd al-Hafiz (r. 1907–1912), signed the Treaty of Fez in March 1912, preserving his family's rule in Morocco but conceding most of his country's sovereignty to France under a colonial arrangement known as a protectorate. In principle this meant that France would protect the government of Morocco from outside threats, though in practice France ruled absolutely, if indirectly, through the sultan and his ministers.

The first thing the French failed to protect was Morocco's territorial integrity. Spain had imperial interests in Morocco dating back to the sixteenth century, its coastal fortresses having long since evolved into colonial enclaves (Ceuta and Melilla remain under Spanish rule to the present day, fossils of an extinct empire). France had to negotiate a treaty with Spain setting out their respective "rights" in Morocco, a process concluded in November 1912 with the signing of the Treaty of Madrid. Under the terms of the treaty, Spain claimed a protectorate over the northern and southern extremities of Morocco. The northern zone comprised some 20,000 square kilometers (8,000 square miles) of the Atlantic and Mediterranean coastline and hinterlands, and the southern zone covered 23,000 square kilometers (9,200 square miles) of desert that came to be known as Spanish Sahara or Western Sahara. In addition, the port city of Tangier in the Strait of Gibraltar was placed under international control. After 1912 the Moroccan sultan ruled a very truncated state.

Though Morocco had enjoyed centuries of independent statehood before becoming a protectorate, its rulers had never succeeded in extending their authority over the whole of their national territory. The sultan's control had always been strongest in the cities and weakest in the countryside. This situation was only exacerbated when Morocco came under imperial rule. Soldiers mutinied, many returning to their tribes to foment rural rebellion. The Moroccan countryside was in turmoil when the first French governor arrived to take up his post in May 1912.

During his thirteen-year tenure in Morocco, Marshal Hubert Lyautey (1854–1934) would prove to be one of the great innovators of imperial administration. He arrived in Fez the day before a massive attack on the city by mutinous soldiers and their tribal supporters. He saw firsthand the limits of what French diplomats had achieved in securing European consent for French rule in Morocco.

Though trained as a military man, Lyautey did not wish to repeat the mistakes made in Algeria, where hundreds of thousands of Algerians and Frenchmen had perished in the decades it took to "pacify" the country by force. Instead of imposing European forms of administration, Lyautey hoped to win the Moroccans over by preserving local institutions and working through native leaders, starting with the sultan.

The French sought to control the cities of Morocco through the institutions surrounding the sultan's government, known as the *Makhzan* (literally, the land of the treasury). Lyautey made a great show of respect for the symbols of the sultan's sovereignty, playing the Moroccan anthem at state occasions and flying the Moroccan flag over public buildings. But such respect for the *office* of the sultan did not always extend to the office-holder. One of Lyautey's first acts was to force the abdication of the reigning sultan, Moulay Abd al-Hafiz, whom he found unreliable, and his replacement with a more compliant ruler, Moulay Youssef (r. 1912–1927).

Lyautey built his control over the countryside on three indigenous pillars: the "big *qa'ids*," or tribal leaders; the *tariqa*s, or mystical Islamic brotherhoods whose network of lodges spanned the country; and the indigenous Berber people. The big qa'ids commanded the loyalty of their fellow tribesmen and were capable of raising hundreds of armed men. Having witnessed a tribal attack on Fez immediately after his arrival, Lyautey recognized the importance of securing their support for French rule. The tariqas represented a network of faith that transcended tribal ties whose lodges had served to shelter dissidents and mobilize religious opposition to repel non-Muslim invaders. Lyautey knew that the Algerian tariqas had played an important role in Abdel Kader's resistance to the French in the 1830s and 1840s and was determined to co-opt their support for his government. The Berbers are a non-Arab minority community with a distinct language and culture. The French sought to play the Berbers of North Africa against their Arab neighbors in a classic divide-and-rule strategy. A law of September 1914 decreed that Morocco's Berber tribes henceforth would be governed in accordance with their own laws and customs under French supervision as a sort of protectorate within a protectorate.

This Lyautey system was no less imperial for preserving indigenous institutions. French administrators ruled in all departments of "modern" government: finance, public works, health, education, and justice, among others. Religious affairs, pious endowments, Islamic courts, and the like came under Moroccan authority. Yet Lyautey's system provided local leaders incentives to collaborate with, rather than subvert, the French colonial administration. The more Moroccan notables implicated in French rule, the fewer Lyautey had to "pacify" on the battlefield. Lyautey was feted as a great innovator, whose concern for preserving indigenous customs and traditions was seen by his contemporaries as a compassionate colonialism.

Even under the Lyautey system, however, a great deal of Morocco remained to be conquered. To reduce the drain on the French army, Lyautey recruited and trained Moroccan soldiers willing to deliver their own country to French rule. Though he aspired to total conquest, Lyautey focused on the economic heartland of Morocco, which he dubbed *le Maroc utile*, or "Useful Morocco," comprising those regions with greatest agricultural, mining, and water resources.

The conquest of Useful Morocco proceeded slowly against sustained resistance from the countryside. Between the establishment of the protectorate in 1912 and the outbreak of World War I in 1914, French control stretched from Fez to Marrakesh, including the coastal cities of Rabat, Casablanca, and the new port of Kénitra, which was renamed Port Lyautey. There matters were left to stand for the duration of the war years, when 34,000 Moroccan soldiers were called to fight France's war with Germany, suffering high casualties for their imperial overlord. Lyautey himself was recalled between 1916 and 1917 to serve as the French minister of war. Even so, the system held, with the big qa'ids proving France's greatest supporters in Morocco. The rural notables met in Marrakesh in August 1914 and acknowledged their dependence on France. "We are the friends of France," one of the leading notables declared, "and to the very end we shall share her fortunes be it good or bad."[13]

In the aftermath of the war and the Paris Peace Conference, Lyautey resumed the conquest of Morocco—and faced stronger opposition than ever. In 1923, over 21,000 French troops were fighting an estimated 7,000 Moroccan insurgents. Yet his biggest challenge would come from outside the territory of the French protectorate, from the Berber people of the Rif Mountains of the northern Spanish zone. His nemesis would be a small-town judge named Muhammad ibn Abd al-Karim al-Khattabi, better known as Abd el-Krim. From his native Rif Mountains, overlooking the Mediterranean coastline, Abd el-Krim mounted a five-year rebellion between 1921–1926 that claimed the lives of tens of thousands of Spanish soldiers in what has been called the worst defeat of a colonial army in Africa in the twentieth century.[14]

Conflict between the people of the Rif (known as Rifis) and the Spanish broke out in the summer of 1921. Inspired by debates about Islamic social and religious reform, Abd el-Krim rejected French and Spanish rule alike and aspired to an independent state in the Rif quite separate from the Kingdom of Morocco. "I wanted to make the Rif an independent country like France and Spain, and to found a free state with full sovereignty," he explained. "Independence which assured us complete freedom of self-determination and the running of our affairs, and to conclude such treaties and alliances as we saw fit."[15]

A charismatic leader, Abd el-Krim recruited thousands of Rifis into a disciplined and motivated army. The Rifis had the double advantage of fighting to protect their homes and families from foreign invaders and doing so on their own treacherous mountain terrain. Between July and August 1921, Abd el-Krim's forces decimated the Spanish army in Morocco, killing some 10,000 soldiers and taking hundreds prisoner. Spain sent reinforcements and, in the course of 1922, managed to reoccupy territory that had fallen to Abd el-Krim's forces. However, the Rifis continued to score victories against Spanish troops and managed to capture more than 20,000 rifles, 400 mountain guns, and 125 cannon, which were quickly distributed among their fighting men.

The Rifi leader ransomed his prisoners to get the Spanish to subsidize his war effort. In January 1923, Abd el-Krim secured over four million pesetas from the Spanish government for the release of soldiers taken prisoner by the Rifis since the start of the war. This enormous sum funded Abd el-Krim's ambitious plans to build on his revolt to establish an independent state.

In February 1923, Abd el-Krim laid the foundations of an independent state in the Rif. He accepted the Rifi tribes' pledges of allegiance and assumed political leadership as amir (commander or ruler) of the mountain region. The Spanish responded by mobilizing another campaign force to reconquer the Rif. Between 1923 and 1924 the Rifis dealt the Spaniards a number of defeats, crowned by the conquest of the mountain town of Chaouen in the autumn of 1924. The Spanish lost another 10,000 soldiers in the battle. Such victories gave Abd el-Krim and his Rifi legions more confidence than prudence. If the Spanish could be defeated so easily, why not the French?

The Rif War provoked grave concern in France. On a tour of his northern front in June 1924, Lyautey was alarmed to see how the defeat of Spanish forces left French positions vulnerable to attack by the Rifis. The Rif was a poor, mountainous land that was heavily reliant on food imports from the fertile valleys of the French zone. Lyautey needed to reinforce the region between Fez and the Spanish Zone to prevent the Rifis from invading to secure their food needs.

Lyautey returned to Paris in August to brief the premier, Edouard Herriot, and his government on the threat posed by Abd el-Krim's insurrectionary state. Yet the French were overstretched, in occupation of the Rhineland and setting up their administration in Syria and Lebanon, and could not spare the men and material Lyautey believed the absolute minimum to preserve his position in Morocco. Whereas he requested the immediate dispatch of four infantry battalions, the government could muster only two. A life-long conservative, Lyautey sensed that he did not have the support of Herriot's Radical government. Seventy years old, and in poor health, he returned to Morocco with neither the physical nor the political strength to contain the Rifis.

In April 1925, Abd el-Krim's forces turned south and invaded the French zone. They sought the support of the local tribes that claimed the agricultural lands to the south of the Rif. Abd el-Krim's commanders met with the tribal leaders to explain the situation as they saw it. "Holy war had been proclaimed by Abd el-Krim, the true Sultan of Morocco, to throw out the infidels, and particularly the French, in the name of the greater glory of regenerated Islam." The occupation of all of Morocco by Abd el-Krim's forces, they explained, "was no more than a question of days."[16] Abd el-Krim increasingly saw his movement as a religious war against non-Muslims who were occupying Muslim land, and he staked a claim to the sultanate of Morocco as a whole, and not just the smaller Rif Republic.

As Lyautey had feared, the Rifis swept rapidly through his poorly defended northern agricultural lands. The French were forced to evacuate all European citizens and to withdraw their troops from the countryside to the city of Fez, with heavy casualties. In just two months, the French had lost forty-three army posts and suffered 1,500 dead and 4,700 wounded or missing in action against the Rifis.

In June, with his forces encamped just 40 kilometers (about 25 miles) from Fez, Abd el-Krim wrote to the Islamic scholars of the city's famous Qarawiyyin mosque-university to win them over to his cause. "We tell you and your colleagues . . . who are men of good faith and have no relations with hypocrites or infidels, of the state of servitude into which the disunited nation of Morocco is sunk," he wrote. He accused the reigning sultan, Moulay Youssef, of having betrayed his nation to the French and of surrounding himself with corrupt officials. Abd el-Krim asked the religious leaders of Fez for their support as a matter of religious duty.[17]

It was a persuasive argument, put forward in sound, theological terms supported by many quotes from the Qur'an on the necessity of jihad. But the Arab religious scholars of Fez did not throw their support behind the Berber Rifis. When it reached the outskirts of Fez, Abd el-Krim's army came up against the solidly French-controlled "Useful Morocco" created by the Lyautey system. Faced with a choice between the aspiring national liberation movement from the Rif and the solidly established instruments of French imperial rule, the Muslim scholars of Fez clearly believed the Lyautey system was the stronger of the two.

Abd el-Krim's movement came to a halt at the walls of Fez in June 1925. If the three pillars of French rule in the countryside were the mystical Muslim brotherhoods, the leading tribal notables, and the Berbers, then Lyautey had secured two out of the three. "The greatest reason for my failure," Abd el-Krim later reflected, "was religious fanaticism." The claim is incongruous in light of Abd el-Krim's own use of Islam to rally support for a holy war against the imperial powers. But the Rifi leader was actually referring to the mystical Muslim brotherhoods. "The shaykhs of the tariqas were my bitterest enemies and the enemies of my country as it progressed," he believed. He had no more success with the big qa'ids. "At first I tried to win over the masses to my point of view by argument and demonstration," Abd el-Krim wrote, "but I met with great opposition from the main families with powerful influence." With one exception, he claimed, "the rest were all my enemies."[18] In their opposition to Abd el-Krim, the big qa'ids and the shaykhs of the brotherhoods had all upheld

French rule in Morocco as Lyautey intended. As for the Berbers—Abd al-Krim and his Rifi fighters were themselves Berbers. They took Lyautey's policy of Berber separatism further than Lyautey himself ever intended. It is of no doubt that the Rifis' Berber identity played a role in discouraging Moroccan Arabs from joining their campaign against the French.

Though his system of colonial government held, Lyautey himself fell to the Rifi challenge. To his critics in Paris, the overflow of the Rif War into the French protectorate proved the failure of Lyautey's efforts to achieve the total submission of Morocco. As major reinforcements from France flooded Morocco in July 1925, Lyautey—exhausted by months of campaigning against the Rifis compounded by ill health—asked for another commander to assist him. The French government dispatched Marshal Philippe Pétain, the hero of the World War I battle of Verdun, to assist. In August, Pétain took control of French military operations in Morocco. The following month, Lyautey tendered his resignation. He left Morocco for good in October 1925.

Abd el-Krim did not long survive Lyautey. The French and Spanish combined forces to crush the Rifi insurgency. The Rifi army had already withdrawn back to its mountain homeland in northern Morocco, where it came under a two-front siege by massive French and Spanish armies in September 1925. By October, the European armies had completely surrounded the Rif Mountains and imposed a complete blockade to starve the Rifis into submission. Abd el-Krim's efforts to negotiate a resolution were rebuffed, and in May 1926, the Rif Mountains were overrun by a joint European force of some 123,000 soldiers. Rifi resistance crumbled, and Abd el-Krim surrendered to the French on May 26. He was later exiled to the Indian Ocean island of Réunion, where he remained until 1947.

With the collapse of the Rif War, France and Spain resumed their colonial administration of Morocco unencumbered by further domestic opposition. Though the Rif War did not engender sustained resistance to the French or Spanish in Morocco, Abd el-Krim and his movement sparked the imagination of nationalists across the Arab world. They saw the Rifis as an Arab people (not as Berbers) who had led a heroic resistance to European rule and had inflicted numerous defeats on modern armies in defense of their land and faith. Their five-year insurgency (1921–1926) against Spain and France inspired some Syrian nationalists to mount their own revolt against the French in 1925.

———————

One young Syrian officer avidly followed newspaper accounts on the Rif War from the central town of Hama. Fawzi al-Qawuqji had once fought the French himself. A native of the city of Tripoli, in what would become Greater Lebanon, he had rallied to King Faysal's cause and joined the disorganized band that confronted the French colonial army at Khan Maysalun in July 1920. The magnitude of that defeat left al-Qawuqji convinced that the Syrians could not expel the French—for the moment.

Within weeks of Maysalun, al-Qawuqji chose pragmatism over idealism and accepted a commission in the new Syrian army the French were establishing, called the *Troupes Spéciales*, or the Syrian Legion. Yet he wasn't comfortable in his French uniform, collaborating with a foreign imperial power to run his country. Reading the newspaper in the barracks of Hama, al-Qawuqji and his fellow nationalists were inspired by the Rif War and took Abd el-Krim for their role model. "What we saw in the heroism of their fight convinced us that the distinct character of the Arabs had survived," al-Qawuqji wrote in his memoirs, "and a love of sacrifice spread among us. I obsessively followed events in Morocco, and found maps of the field of conflict."[19]

If the Rif War inspired nationalists in Syria, the imperial administrators took their inspiration from Lyautey's methods of imperial rule in Morocco. The French officials appointed to rule Syria were in large part graduates of the Lyautey "school": General Henri Gouraud, the first high commissioner in Syria, had been Lyautey's assistant in Morocco. Other prominent colonial officials appointed to Syria had served under Lyautey, including Colonel Catroux, Gouraud's delegate to Damascus; General de Lamothe, the delegate to Aleppo; and the two colonels who served as delegates to the Alawite territories. Many lower-ranking officials came to Syria from Morocco as well. Predictably, they sought to reproduce a modified Lyautey system in Syria.[20]

The French faced nationalist opposition in town and country alike from the outset of their occupation of Syria. In 1919, an anti-French uprising broke out in the Alawite Mountains in western Syria and took two years to quell. The Alawites, a religious community that trace their origins to Shiite Islam, only wanted to preserve their autonomy; they made no pretense of fighting for national independence. The French were able to satisfy Alawite wishes for local autonomy by creating a ministate based in the port city of Latakia and the Alawite highlands, in which local notables ruled in collaboration with French administrators.

A more serious nationalist revolt broke out in the countryside around the northern city of Aleppo in 1919, headed by a local notable named Ibrahim Hananu. A landowner who had served in the Ottoman bureaucracy before the First World War, Hananu was disenchanted with Ottoman wartime repression. He volunteered for Amir Faysal's army in the 1916–1918 Arab Revolt and took part in the Syrian General Congress of 1919. A man of action, Hananu viewed the Syrian Congress as little more than a talking shop and returned north to Aleppo to mobilize a guerrilla force to mount an effective deterrent against the French. He initiated a rural uprising against the threat of French rule that quickly turned into a nationalist insurgency

after the French occupied Aleppo in 1920. The number of insurgents expanded rapidly between the summer and autumn of 1920, from 800 to nearly 5,000 volunteers.[21] The Syrian nationalists received arms and funding from the neighboring
Turks, who were fighting their own war against a short-lived French occupation in
the southern coastal region of Anatolia. The French moved quickly to deploy troops
and reassert their control over Aleppo, lest Hananu's revolt provoke a broader nationalist uprising across Syria. In the autumn of 1921 Hananu fled to Jordan, where
he was captured by the British and delivered to French justice. The French put
Hananu on trial but had the wisdom to acquit the nationalist rather than turn him
into a martyr. For Fawzi al-Qawuqji, who was already enrolled in the Syrian Legion,
the collapse of Hananu's revolt only confirmed his view that the Syrians were not
yet ready to withstand the French.

The French were more concerned about their vulnerability to nationalist agitation
than Fawzi al-Qawuqji realized. To counter the threat of a unified nationalist movement, the French chose to employ a divide-and-rule scheme, splitting Syria into
four mini-states. Aleppo and Damascus were made the seats of two separate administrations to keep the urban nationalists in Syria's principal cities from making
common cause. The French also envisaged separate states for the two religious communities with long histories of territorial autonomy—the Alawites in western Syria,
and the Druzes to the south. On the model of Lyautey's Berber policies, France
hoped by these means to give the Alawites and Druzes a vested interest in the mandate that would insulate them from urban nationalism. High Commissioner
Gouraud justified this division of Syria into autonomous regions with local men
appointed to serve as governors with reference to the doctrine he had learned at the
school of Marshal Lyautey.[22]

While working to assure the goodwill of Syria's Druze and Alawite communities,
the French authorities made no concessions to nationalist leaders in Damascus. The
most influential Syrian nationalist in the early 1920s was Abd al-Rahman Shahbandar (1882–1940), a medical doctor who had trained at the American University of
Beirut. Fluent in English after his medical training, Shahbandar had served as guide
and translator to the King-Crane Commission in 1919 and had struck a personal
friendship with Charles Crane. He briefly served as foreign minister in King Faysal's
last cabinet in May 1920, taking refuge in Egypt following the fall of Faysal's government in July of that year. He returned to Damascus one year later when the
French announced a general amnesty in the summer of 1921.

On his return to Syria, Dr. Shahbandar resumed his nationalist activities and
founded a clandestine organization called the Iron Hand Society. The Iron Hand assembled veterans of the Ottoman-era secret Arabist societies and the supporters of
Faysal's Arab government in Damascus with a common agenda to expel the French
from Syria. The activities of the Iron Hand were held in check by strict French sur-

veillance. On April 7, 1922, the French arrested Shahbandar and four other leaders of the movement on suspicion of fomenting rebellion.

The French arrests only fanned the flames of Syrian dissent. The following day a group of nationalists used Friday prayers in the central Umayyad Mosque to rouse the 8,000 congregants to a mass demonstration. Iron Hand members led a diverse crowd of religious leaders, neighborhood bosses, merchants, and students. They marched through the central markets of Damascus toward the citadel, where they were dispersed by French security forces, who wounded dozens and arrested forty-six Damascenes.

French repressive measures failed to stem the protests, as ever more Damascenes responded to the nationalists' call. On April 11 a group of forty women headed by Shahbandar's wife led a massive demonstration. French soldiers fired into the crowd, killing three and wounding many more, including several women. A general strike was called, and shopkeepers in Damascus kept their shutters down for two weeks while the French tried Shahbandar and the other opposition leaders. Severe sentences were passed against all the men, with Shahbandar receiving twenty years and the others between five and fifteen years. The Iron Hand was broken, the nationalists were silenced, and calm prevailed—though only for the next three years.

By 1925, after three years of relative calm, the French began to reconsider their political arrangements in Syria. Running a number of mini-states was proving expensive. High Commissioner Gouraud had completed his tour of duty, and his successors decreed the union of Aleppo and Damascus into a single state, scheduling elections for a new Representative Assembly to be held in October 1925.

After three years of political tranquility, the French relaxed their grip on Syrian politics. General Maurice Sarrail, the new high commissioner, gave pardons to political prisoners and allowed the nationalists in Damascus to form a party in advance of the elections for the Representative Assembly. Shahbandar, who served two years of his sentence before being released as part of the general amnesty, formed a new nationalist organ called the People's Party in June 1925. Shahbandar recruited some of the most prominent Damascenes to his party. The mandate authorities responded by sponsoring a pro-French party—the Syrian Union Party. The Syrians feared France would rig the results of the elections, just as they had in Lebanon. However, the disruption to the political process came from the Druze Mountain rather than the high commissioner's office.

Trouble had been brewing between the French and the Druzes since 1921. General Georges Catroux, another product of the Lyautey school, had drafted the French treaty with the Druzes in 1921 on the model of French Berber policy in Morocco. According to the treaty, the Druze Mountain would constitute a special administrative unit independent of Damascus with an elected native governor and a representative council. In other words, the administration of the mountain ostensibly was to be under Druze control. In return, the Druzes had to accept the terms of the French mandate, the posting of French advisors to the mountain, and a garrison of French soldiers. Many of the Druzes had deep misgivings about the terms of the treaty and feared it gave the French far too much scope to interfere in their affairs. Most took a wait-and-see approach, to judge the French by their practices. They were not reassured by what they experienced over the years that followed.

To begin, France made the mistake of alienating the most powerful Druze leader, Sultan Pasha al-Atrash. In a transparent bid to undermine the authority of the most powerful person in the Druze Mountain, the French authorities named one of Sultan Pasha's subordinate relations, Salim al-Atrash, as governor over the mountain in 1921. This placed the French and Sultan Pasha on a collision course. When Sultan Pasha's men released a captive taken by the French in July 1922, the imperial authorities responded by sending troops and aircraft to destroy Sultan Pasha's house. Undaunted, Sultan Pasha led a guerrilla campaign against French positions in the mountain that lasted for nine months, until the Druze warlord was forced to surrender in April 1923. The French secured a truce with the Druze leader and avoided the dangers of putting such a powerful local leader on trial. Yet Salim Pasha, the nominal governor of the Druze Mountain, had already tendered his submission, and no other Druze leader would accept the poisoned chalice of becoming governor of the mountain over Sultan Pasha's opposition.

Left without any other suitable Druze candidates, the French broke one of the cardinal rules of the Lyautey system, as well as the terms of their own treaty with the Druzes, by naming a French officer as governor of the mountain in 1923. If that wasn't bad enough, the man they named as governor, Captain Gabriel Carbillet, was a zealous reformer who made it his mission to destroy what he referred to as the "ancient feudal system" of the Druze Mountain, which he considered "retrograde." Druze complaints against Carbillet multiplied. Shahbandar noted ironically that many of his fellow nationalists credited the French officer with promoting Syrian nationalism by driving the Druzes to the brink of revolt.[23]

The Druze leaders refused to accept French violations of their 1921 treaty and decided to put their complaints directly to the mandate authorities. In spring 1925 the leaders of the mountain assembled a delegation and set off to Beirut to meet the high commissioner and lodge a complaint against Carbillet. Rather than seize the opportunity to placate the disgruntled Druzes, High Commissioner Sarrail openly humiliated the great men of the mountain by refusing even to meet with them. The Druze leaders returned to the mountain in a fury, determined to revolt against the French, and looking for partners. They turned to the urban nationalists as natural allies.

Nationalist activity was gaining ground across the towns of Syria in 1925. In Damascus, Abd al-Rahman Shahbander gathered the leading nationalists in his new

People's Party. In Hama, Fawzi al-Qawuqji had created a political party with an overtly religious orientation, which he called the Hizb Allah, or "the Party of God." In this, al-Qawuqji proved one of the first to appreciate the *political* power of Islam to mobilize people against foreign rule. He grew a beard and visited the different mosques of Hama each night to gain support for an uprising. He established good relations with the Muslim preachers of the town and encouraged them to pepper their Friday sermons with Qur'anic references to jihad. He also gained financial support from some of the wealthy landowning families of Hama. Hizb Allah grew in manpower and financial resources. Early in 1925 al-Qawuqji sent emissaries to meet with Shahbandar in Damascus to encourage better coordination between Shahbandar's People's Party and Hizb Allah in Hama. Shahbandar had discouraged the emissaries from Hama, warning them "that the idea of a revolt in present circumstances was a clear danger harmful to the interests of the Nation."[24] With the Druzes entering the nationalist cause in May 1925, Shahbandar believed the movement had reached the critical mass to stand a chance of success.

That month the Druze leadership made contact with Shahbandar and the Damascus nationalists. The first meeting was convened in the home of a veteran journalist, where the conversation revolved around the means to launch a revolt. Shahbandar briefed the Druzes on Fawzi al-Qawuqji's activities in Hama and discussed opening several fronts against the French in a nationwide Syrian revolt. Subsequent meetings were held in Shahbandar's house, attended by leading members of the Atrash clan. Oaths were sworn and pacts concluded in secret, and all of the participants vowed to work toward national unity and independence.[25] It was an alliance of convenience for both sides. Shahbandar and his colleagues were only too happy to see the Druzes launch armed action in their own region, where they enjoyed far greater mobility than nationalists in Damascus and were heavily armed; in return, the Druzes would not have to face the French on their own. The Damascus nationalists promised to spread revolt nationwide, giving the Druzes the support they needed to make the first move.

The Druzes launched the revolt against French rule in July 1925. Sultan Pasha al-Atrash led a force of several thousand fighters against the French in Salkhad, the second largest town in the mountain, which they occupied on July 20. The next day, his band laid siege to Suwayda', the administrative capital of the Druze Mountain, pinning down a large contingent of French administrators and soldiers.

Caught by surprise, the French lacked the forces and the strategy to combat the Druze revolt. Over the next few weeks, the Druze army of between eight and ten thousand volunteers defeated every French force dispatched against them. High Commissioner Sarrail was determined to suppress the revolt in its infancy so as to prevent the nightmare scenario of a nationwide uprising. He redeployed French troops and Syrian Legion forces from northern and central Syria to confront the uprising in the southern Druze Mountain. The authorities cracked down on all the usual nationalist suspects in Damascus in August, arresting and deporting men without trial. Shahbandar and his closest collaborators fled Damascus to take refuge with the Atrash clan in the Druze Mountain. And despite France's best efforts, the revolt began to spread. The next outbreak came in Hama.

Fawzi al-Qawuqji had prepared the ground for revolt in Hama, waiting for the right moment to strike. Having watched as previous Syrian revolts against the French had surged and faltered, he believed the situation was different in 1925. There was a new degree of coordination among the opponents of French rule, between the Druzes, the Damascenes, and his own party in Hama. The Druzes had launched their revolt with devastating effect on the French. Al-Qawuqji still followed the news of the Rif War in Morocco and knew that France's position there was deteriorating: "The French army had gotten entangled in the fighting with the tribes of the Rif under Abd el-Krim's leadership. News of his victories began to reach us. We also began to receive news of French reinforcements sent to Marrakesh." Al-Qawuqji realized that with the French dispatching troops to Morocco, there would be no reinforcements available for the French army in Syria. "My preparations were complete," he concluded. "All that remained was to implement them."[26]

In September 1925, al-Qawuqji sent emissaries to Sultan Pasha al-Atrash in the Druze Mountain. Al-Qawuqji suggested that the Druzes escalate their attacks to draw all available French soldiers to the south. He would then launch an attack in Hama in early October. The Druze leader was willing to expose his fighters to heavy fighting against the French to secure a second front against the French in Hama, and he agreed to al-Qawuqji's plan.

On October 4 al-Qawuqji led a mutiny of the Syrian Legion, assisted by fighters from the surrounding Bedouin tribes, with the support of the town's population. They captured a number of French soldiers and laid siege to the town's administrators in the government palace. By midnight the town was in the hands of the insurgents.

The French were quick to respond. Though most of their soldiers were in the Druze Mountain, as al-Qawuqji had anticipated, the French still had their air force. The French began an aerial bombardment that struck residential quarters and leveled parts of the town's central markets, killing nearly 400 civilians, many of them women and children. The town's notables, who had initially pledged their support to al-Qawuqji's movement, were the first to break ranks and strike a deal with the French to bring both the revolt and the bombardment to a close. Within three days of launching their revolt, al-Qawuqji and his men had to withdraw to the countryside, leaving the French to reclaim Hama.

Undaunted by their failure in Hama, al-Qawuqji and his men carried the revolt to other towns and cities across Syria. "The gates of Syria's fields were opened before us for revolt. By these manoeuvres," al-Qawuqji boasted, "the intelligence and cunning of the French collapsed before the intelligence of the Arabs and their cunning."[27]

Within a matter of days, the revolt had spread to the villages surrounding Damascus. The French tried to stifle the movement with displays of extreme violence. Whole villages were destroyed by artillery or aerial bombardment. Nearly one hundred villagers in the hinterlands of the capital were executed. Corpses were brought back to Damascus as grisly trophies to deter others from supporting the insurgents. Predictably, violence begat violence. Twelve mutilated corpses of local soldiers serving the French were left outside the city gates of Damascus as a warning against collaboration with the colonial authorities.

By October 18, the insurgency had reached the Syrian capital, where men and women alike joined the resistance. The men who fought were reliant on their wives and sisters to smuggle food and arms to them in their hiding places. Beneath the watchful gaze of a French soldier, one Damascene wife carried food and weapons to her fugitive husband and his rebel friends. "It never occurred to [the French sentry] that women were helping the rebels to escape over the rooftops or that they were delivering weapons to them under the cloaks and plates of food to contribute their part to the revolution," Damascene journalist Siham Tergeman recalled in her memoirs.[28]

For the nationalist leaders in Damascus, the revolt had become a sacred jihad, and the combatants holy warriors. Some four hundred volunteers entered Damascus and managed to secure the Shaghur and Maydan quarters, driving the French administrators to seek refuge in the citadel. One detachment of insurgents made their way to the Azm Palace, the eighteenth-century vanity project of As'ad Pasha al-Azm that had been taken over by the French as a governor's mansion, in an attempt to capture the high commissioner, General Maurice Sarrail. Though Sarrail had in fact already left his quarters, a fierce gun battle ensued, which left the old palace in flames. It was but the beginning.

The French used *force majeure* to defeat the revolt in Damascus. They shelled the quarters of Damascus indiscriminately with artillery from the citadel. "At the appointed time," the Damascene nationalist leader Dr. Shahbandar wrote, "those hellish instruments opened their mouths and belched their ashes upon the finest quarters of the city. Over the next twenty-four hours, the shells of destruction and fire consumed more than six hundred of the finest homes." This was followed by days of aerial bombardment. "The bombardment lasted from midday Sunday until Tuesday evening. We will never know the precise number of those who died under the rubble," Shahbandar recorded in his memoirs.[29] Subsequent estimates put the number of dead at 1,500 in three days' violence.

The impact on the civilian population made the insurgents bring their operations in Damascus to a close. "When the rebels saw the terror that gripped the women and children from the continuous shelling of the quarters, and the circling of aircraft dropping bombs indiscriminately on houses, they left the city," Shahbandar recounted. Though they had been driven from Hama and Damascus, the insurgents had succeeded in relieving the Druze Mountain, which for three months had borne the brunt of French repression. If the French had hoped to discourage the spread of the revolt through the use of indiscriminate violence against Hama and Damascus, they were to be disappointed. French troops had to be dispatched to all corners of Syria as the revolt spread across the country in the winter of 1925–1926.

Only after they had quelled revolts in northern and central Syria were the French able to return to the Druze Mountain, where Sultan Pasha al-Atrash still led an active resistance movement. In April 1926 the French retook Suwayda', the Druze regional capital. After May 1926, when Abd el-Krim finally surrendered in Morocco, the French were able to divert a large number of soldiers to Syria, bringing the total French force up to 95,000 men, according to Fawzi al-Qawuqji. The Syrian resistance was overwhelmed by the French, and their leaders went into exile. On October 1, 1926, Sultan Pasha al-Atrash and Dr. Abd al-Rahman Shahbandar crossed the border into neighboring Transjordan.

Fawzi al-Qawuqji tried to continue the struggle long after the other nationalist leaders had given up. Between October 1926 and March 1927 he campaigned tirelessly to resume the revolt, but the fight had gone out of the Syrian people, who had grown cautious in the face of violent French retaliation. In his last campaign, in March 1927, al-Qawuqji managed to raise a band of seventy-four fighters, of which only twenty-seven had horses. They skirted Damascus, taking to the desert, only to be betrayed by desert tribes that formerly had supported the movement. Through guile and deception they managed to retreat to Transjordan, eluding capture but leaving their country secure in French hands.[30]

The Syrian Revolt failed to deliver independence from French rule. The nationalist movement passed to a new leadership of urban elites who eschewed armed struggle to pursue their aims through a political process of negotiation and nonviolent protest. Until 1936 the Syrian nationalists would have little to show for their efforts.

————

Even though French colonial authorities from Morocco to Syria spent much of the 1920s suppressing rebellions, they at least had a party in Algeria to look forward to.

A century had passed since the dey of Algiers sealed the fate of his country with an ill-tempered swish of the fly whisk in 1827. Since landing their first troops at Sidi Ferrush in June 1830, the French had ousted the Ottomans, defeated Amir Abd al-Qadir, and suppressed a number of major rebellions—the last in 1871–1872. By the early twentieth century they had completed their conquest from the Mediterranean to the Sahara.

By the 1920s, over 800,000 settlers had moved from France to Algeria.[31] The French in Algeria were no longer on foreign soil; since 1848, when Algeria had been declared French territory, the three provinces of Oran, Algiers, and Constantine had been converted into *départements* of France, with elected representatives in the French Chamber in Paris. The "Algerian" deputies—or more precisely, the French Algerian deputies, as native Algerians were allowed neither to vote nor to stand for election to national office—enjoyed disproportionate influence in the Chamber and worked as a bloc to protect settler interests.

With the approach of the 1930 centenary, the French Algerians took the opportunity to impress on both the Metropolitan French and the native Algerians the triumph and permanence of the French presence in Algeria. The planning for the celebrations began years in advance. The first step was taken by the governor-general of Algeria in December 1923, when he decreed the creation of a commission "to prepare a program celebrating the centenary of the French seizure of Algiers in 1830." The French parliament authorized a budget of 40 million francs and the convening of a commission charged with the task of organizing events. In the end, the celebrations cost more than 100 million francs.

Algeria was transformed for the year. Artists were commissioned to create monuments celebrating major milestones in the history of French Algeria, to decorate the towns and countryside. Museums were built in the great cities—Algiers, Constantine, Oran. Public works were constructed across the country—schools, hospitals, orphanages and poor houses, agricultural colleges and professional schools, and the world's most powerful broadcasting station to ensure news of the centenary events reached across all Algeria. A major exposition was organized in the western coastal city of Oran, with all the fanfare of a world's fair. Well over fifty international conferences and congresses were held on virtually every subject under the sun. Sporting events, trans-Saharan auto rallies, and yacht races marked the calendar. Cities were lit at night, with prominent buildings outlined in strands of electric lights and exquisite firework displays.

The symbolism of the centenary was best captured in the monuments commissioned to mark the event. In Boufarik, a few miles south of Algiers, a massive stone plinth 45 meters wide and 9 meters high (about 148 feet by 30 feet) celebrated "the glory of the colonising genius of France." The sculptor Henri Bouchard (who designed the Protestant Reformation memorial in Geneva) placed at the center of the monument a cluster of French "pioneering heroes of civilization" headed by General Bugeaud and General de Lamoricière, the military commanders who scorched Algeria to defeat the Amir Abd al-Qadir in the 1830s and 1840s. A group of French nobles, mayors, and "model settlers" stood in proud ranks behind the military men. To the rear, looking over the shoulders of the French men in uniforms and suits, the sculptor included a few Arabs in national dress, representatives of "the first natives whose active fidelity made the task [of French colonization] possible."[32]

The French even managed to insinuate a sympathetic Algerian presence into the 1830 military memorial. The French press had heatedly debated whether the monument proposed to celebrate the landing of French troops at Sidi Ferrush on June 14, 1830, would "upset the natives." "All those who know Algeria," wrote Mercier, the official historian of the centenary, "and who live in daily contact with its Arabo-Berber population, had no apprehensions in this respect." The true feelings of all native Algerians, Mercier insisted, were captured in the remarks of the tribal leader Bouaziz Ben Gana, who claimed: "If the natives had known the French in 1830, they would have loaded their rifles with flowers rather than bullets to greet them." These sentiments were captured in the inscription on the 10-meter-high monument, picturing a cockaded Marianne gazing down into the eyes of a dutiful Arab son: "One hundred years later, the French Republic having given to this country prosperity, civilization and justice, a grateful Algeria pays homage of undying attachment to the Motherland." It was as though the French wished to cast the Algerians in a supporting role in the colonization of their own country.[33]

The centenary celebrations reached their climax at Sidi Ferrush on June 14, 1930. Here again, the organizers sought to present colonial Algeria as a Franco-Arab joint production, officially known as "the celebration of the union of the French and indigenous populations." A massive crowd gathered around the new monument of Sidi Ferrush to watch the military parade and hear the speeches. The governor-general headed a phalanx of colonial officials. The air force made a flyover and dropped flower petals on the crowd surrounding the memorial. Torch bearers, following Olympic example, set off running from the monument to Algiers, some 30 kilometers (about 19 miles) to the east.

The speeches given by the French were predictably triumphalist, but far more astonishing were the comments that came from the Algerian dignitaries who took to the podium. Hadj Hamou, a religious scholar speaking on behalf of the teaching staff of the mosque schools, expressed his gratitude for the freedom he enjoyed to teach Islam without interference. All mosque-goers, he claimed, followed the lead of their imams in "the common love of the secular holy French Republic" (la sainte République Française laïque)—a wonderful oxymoron. M. Belhadj, speaking on behalf of Muslim intellectuals, remarked on the day's celebration of "the profound union of the French and indigenous people" who had transformed into "a single, unique people, living in peace and concord, in the shadow of the same flag and in the same love of the Mother land." M. Ourabah, a leading Arab notable, supplicated: "Instruct us, raise us yet higher, raise us up to your level. And let us join in one voice as in one heart to cry: Long live France, ever greater! Long live Algeria, ever French!"[34]

In an age of burgeoning Arab nationalism, Algeria seemed to be embracing imperialism. Yet the Algerians were not satisfied with their lot. Many of the educated elite recognized they could not beat the French, and so they sought to join them—with the full rights of French citizenship that, down to 1930, had been denied them. Accepting French rule as inevitable, these Algerians opted for a civil rights movement instead of nationalism. Their spokesman was a student of pharmacology at the University of Algiers named Ferhat Abbas.

Ferhat Abbas (1899–1985) was born in a small town in eastern Algeria to a family of provincial administrators and landholders. He was trained in French schools and came to share in French values. What he wanted more than anything else was to enjoy the full privileges of any Frenchman. Yet the laws of France put severe limits on the legal and political rights of Algerian Muslims. These laws divided Algeria geographically, between areas with relatively high European populations, where French common law applied; rural communes with European minorities, where a combination of military and civilian rule applied; and Arab territories, which were under full military administration.

The laws also clearly distinguished between Europeans and Muslims in Algeria. In 1865 the French Senate decreed that all Algerian Muslims were French subjects. Although they could serve in the military and civil service, they were not actually *citizens* of France. To be considered for French citizenship, native Algerians would have to renounce their Muslim civil status and agree to live under French personal status laws. Given that marriage, family law, and the distribution of inheritance is all precisely regulated in Islamic law, this was tantamount to asking Muslims to abandon their faith. Not surprisingly, only 2,000 Algerians applied for citizenship during the eighty years in which this law remained in force.

Unprotected under French law, Algerian Muslims actually came under a host of discriminatory legislation known as the *Code de l'Indigénat* ["Indigenous People's Law Code"]. Like the Jim Crow laws passed after the American Civil War to keep African Americans in a segregated, subordinate status, the code, drafted in the aftermath of the last major Algerian revolt against French rule in 1871, allowed native Algerians to be prosecuted for acts that Europeans could legally perform, such as criticizing the French Republic and its officials. Most of the crimes set out in the code were petty, and the punishments were light—no more than five days in prison, or a fine of fifteen francs. Yet the code was applied all the more regularly because its consequences were so trivial. And, more than any other legal distinction, the code reminded Algerians they were second-class citizens in their own land. To someone like Ferhat Abbas, who had been schooled in French republican thinking, the indignity was unbearable.

Abbas responded to the centenary celebrations with a sharply critical essay, written in French, that captured the disillusionment of a young Algerian after a century of French rule. Entitled *The Young Algerian: From Colony to Province*, Abbas's book was an eloquent plea to replace French colonialism in Algeria with the more enlightened aspects of French republicanism.

> The century which has passed away was the century of tears and blood. And it is we the indigenous people in particular who have cried and bled. . . . The celebrations of the Centenary were but a clumsy reminder of a painful past, an exhibition of the wealth of some before the poverty of others. . . . Understanding between the races will remain but empty words if the new century does not place the different elements of this country on the same social rank and give the weak the means to raise their standing.[35]

We hear in Abbas's writing the echoes of the Muslim notables who spoke at the centenary celebrations in Sidi Ferrush—"raise us yet higher, raise us up to your level." Yet Abbas was more assertive in his demands.

Abbas claimed that the Algerians had earned their rights of citizenship by virtue of their wartime service. France had placed a heavy burden on indigenous Algerians since conscription was first introduced to Algeria in 1913. Over 200,000 Algerian Muslims had been drafted during the First World War, and many never returned. Estimates of Algerian war dead range from 25,000 to 80,000. Many more were wounded.[36]

Even after the war, Algerians were conscripted into the French army. Abbas maintained that he had earned his rights of citizenship through his own military service in 1922. France did not distinguish between soldiers by race and religion in military service, he argued, and should not do so in law. "We are Muslims and we are French," he continued. "We are indigenous and we are French. Here in Algeria there are Europeans and indigenous people, but there are only Frenchmen."[37] Yet native Algerians had been reduced to an underclass in their own country through colonial society and its laws. "What more can be said about the daily insults which the indigenous man suffers in his native land, in the street, in the cafés, in the slightest transaction of daily life? The barber closes the door in his face, the hotel refuses him a room."[38]

Abbas was particularly critical of French naturalization laws that required Muslims to renounce their personal status. "Why should an Algerian seek to be naturalized? To be French? He already is, as his country has been declared French soil." Writing of Algeria's French rulers, he asked rhetorically: "Do they wish to raise this country to a higher level or do they wish to divide and rule?" For Abbas, the answer was self-evident. "What is needed is for the same law to be applied to all, if truly we wish to guide Muslim Algeria towards a higher civilization."[39] Even so, he clung to the cultural rights of Algerians to preserve their religion and to be taught in their own language—Arabic—without prejudice to their rights as French citizens.

Abbas was not the first to set out a claim for full citizenship rights; the Young Algeria movement had pressed for such reforms since the early 1900s. Nor did he speak for all Algerians. The Islamic reform movement, headed by Abd al-Hamid Ben Badis (1889–1940), rejected Abbas's idea of assimilation out of hand. The differences between Abbas and Ben Badis were captured in an exchange of editorials in 1936, when Ferhat Abbas famously declared there was no such thing as the Algerian nation: "Algeria as a father-land is a myth. I have not discovered it. I have questioned history; I have questioned the dead and the living; I have visited the cemeteries: no one has spoken to me of it." Algeria, he claimed, was France and Algerians were French. Indeed, carried away by his rhetoric, Abbas went on to say that he *was* France ("*La France, c'est moi*").[40]

"No, sirs!" Ben Badis retorted:

> We have scrutinized the pages of history and the current situation. And we have found the Algerian Muslim nation. . . . This community has its history, full of great feats. It has its religious and linguistic unity. It has its own culture, its habits and customs, good or bad, like all nations. Moreover, this Algerian and Muslim nation is not France. It would not know how to be France. It does not want to become France. It could not become France, even if it wanted to.

Yet Ben Badis made no more claim for Algerian independence than did Abbas. Whereas Abbas sought equality with the French, Ben Badis wanted Algerian Muslims to be "separate but equal" to the French. He asked the French to grant indigenous Algerians liberty, justice, and equality while respecting their distinctive culture, their Arabic language, and Muslim faith. Ben Badis concluded his essay by insisting that "this Algerian Muslim father land is a faithful friend to France."[41] The differences between the secular assimilationists and the Islamic reformers were hardly insurmountable.

Ironically, the only activists to demand full independence for Algeria came from the expatriate worker community in France. A handful of politically engaged men in the 100,000-strong Algerian workforce in France came to nationalism through the Communist Party. Their leader was Messali Hadj (1898–1974), who founded the workers' nationalist association L'Étoile Nord-Africaine (the North African Star) in 1926. Messali presented the new organization's program to the Congress of the League against Colonial Oppression in Brussels in February 1927. Among the points called for were independence for Algeria, the withdrawal of the French occupation forces, the formation of a national army, confiscation of settler plantations and a redistribution of farmlands to native farmers, and a host of social and economic reforms for independent Algeria.[42] The association's demands were as just as they were unrealistic at that time, and they attracted little support among Algerians at home or abroad.

Of all the Algerian political activists in the 1930s, Ferhat Abbas was the most influential. His writings were widely read by educated Algerians and French policy makers alike. "I read your book with great interest," Maurice Viollette, former governor-general of Algeria, wrote to Abbas in 1931. "I would not have written it in the same way. I regret certain pages in it, but faced with some veritable provocations . . . I recognize that it is difficult for you to retain your composure and I understand." The tone was condescending, but Abbas clearly did not mind (he used the quote as encomia on the dust jacket of his book). He knew that, through Viollette, his arguments would be discussed in the upper echelons of the French administration.

Maurice Viollette had grown yet more influential since the end of his term as governor-general of Algeria and his return to Paris. He was named to the French Senate, where in March 1935 he opened a debate on granting citizenship rights to a select group of Algerians on the basis of their assimilation of French culture and values— referred to in French as *évolués*. The expression, meaning "more highly evolved," was pure Social Darwinism that conceived of Algerians as advancing from a lower to a higher state of civilization as they shed Arab culture in favor of "superior" French values. This "civilizing mission" was one of the principles by which the French justified their imperial project. While playing to the ideals of the "civilizing mission," Viollette argued before the Senate that the enfranchisement of progressive Muslim Algerians would forestall nationalism and encourage assimilation.

The French colonial lobby (comprising settler representatives and their supporters in Paris) was too powerful, however, and defeated Viollette's 1935 motion. They feared that granting full citizenship rights even to a select group of Algerians would only lead to a broader enfranchisement that ultimately would undermine European dominance in Algeria.

Viollette found a more sympathetic hearing for his controversial views in 1936, when he was appointed to a cabinet post in the socialist Popular Front government led by Léon Blum. The Popular Front spoke of a whole new relationship between France and its colonies, and Algeria's political elites knew Viollette to be an ally to their cause. The Islamic reformers led by Ben Badis decided to unite forces with Ferhat Abbas's assimilationists. They met in the first Algerian Muslim Congress in Algiers in June 1936 and endorsed Maurice Viollette's proposal to grant full citizenship to a select group of Francophile Algerians without requiring them to renounce their Muslim civil status. The Congress then dispatched a delegation to Paris to present its political demands to the government. The delegates were received by Blum and Viollette, who promised to satisfy many of the Algerians' demands.

By the end of December 1936, Blum and Viollette had drafted a bill on Algeria and submitted it to parliament. The Blum-Viollette bill, they believed, was enlightened legislation that would secure France's position in Algeria once and for all, through the cooperation of the country's political and economic elites. "It is truly impossible, after so many solemn promises made by so many governments, notably at the time of the centenary (1930), that we should not realize the urgency of this necessary task of assimilation that affects in the highest degree the moral health of Algeria," they wrote in the bill's preamble.[43]

The bill set out the categories of indigenous Algerian Muslims who would be eligible for citizenship. Nine different groups were defined, beginning with those Algerians who served as officers or career master-sergeants in the French army or were soldiers decorated for valor. Those Algerians who had attained diplomas of higher education from either French or Muslim academies, as well as civil servants recruited through competitive examination, were also eligible. Natives elected to chambers of commerce or agriculture, or to administrative positions in the financial, municipal, or regional councils, were named, as were notables holding traditional office such as aghas and qa'ids. Finally, any Algerian awarded such French honors as the Legion of Honor or the Labor Medal would be eligible for full enfranchisement. In all, no more than 25,000 Algerians from a total population of 4.5 million would have qualified for citizenship under the terms of the Blum-Viollette bill.

Given the bill's very limited aims, and its authors' clear intention to perpetuate French rule in Algeria, it is amazing how much opposition the Blum-Viollette reforms encountered. Once again, the colonial lobby went into action to ensure the bill was not even debated, let alone put to a vote. The colonial press savaged the bill as opening the flood gates to the Islamization of France and the end of French Algeria.

The debates in the French Chamber set off disturbances in the streets of Algeria between proponents and opponents of the bill. Indigenous Algerians took to the streets in mass protests and demonstrations to assert their demands for civil rights. The unrest in Algeria only reinforced the arguments of the conservatives and the colonial lobby, who claimed that the troubles were caused by the disastrous policies of the Blum government. French mayors in Algeria went on strike in protest, as did elected Algerian politicians, as the bill passed from one parliamentary committee to another without ever coming to the floor for debate. In the end, the colonial lobby prevailed. The Blum-Viollette bill was abandoned in 1938 without ever having been discussed in the Chamber of the National Assembly.

The centenary was over. In spite of the many solemn promises made, the French government would not concede the urgent task of assimilation. It is hard to capture the depth of disillusionment that set in among Algerian elites, whose expectations had been raised to new heights only to be dashed by the failure of the Blum government to deliver on its promises. Henceforth, the dominant trend in the Algerian opposition movement would be nationalist. France would not get another century in Algeria. Within sixteen years the two countries would be at war.

———————

L eon Blum's Popular Front government had also hoped to resolve differences between France and its mandates in Syria and Lebanon. After years of opposition interspersed with fruitless negotiations, nationalists in Beirut and Damascus responded to the change of government in Paris with a new optimism. The year 1936 seemed to herald a new age of broader Arab independence and reduced imperial controls. Britain, which had conceded independence to Iraq in 1930, was on the verge of concluding a similar agreement with Egypt in 1936. Nationalists in Syria and Lebanon had every reason to believe the Popular Front government, with its enlightened views on empire, would follow suit and conclude treaties that would allow them to follow Egypt and Iraq into the League of Nations as nominally sovereign states.

In the aftermath of the 1925–1927 revolt, Syrian nationalists had pursued the politics of national liberation through nonviolence and negotiation, in a policy known as "honorable cooperation." The National Bloc, headed by wealthy urban notables, became the dominant coalition of parties and factions working toward the common aim of securing Syria's independence. They redoubled their efforts after Iraq secured its nominal independence in 1930. However, faced with the persistent opposition of the conservative French colonial lobby, the National Bloc had made no gains through cooperation. The first treaty the French offered, in November 1933, fell far short of granting independence and was rejected by the Syrian Chamber. Honorable cooperation began to give way to systematic resistance, culminating in a fifty-day general strike called by Syrian nationalists at the start of 1936.

The Popular Front government of Leon Blum seemed both to sympathize with the demands of Syrian nationalists and to place a high priority on restoring peace and stability to their troubled mandate. Shortly after coming to power, the Blum government entered into fresh negotiations with the Syrian National Bloc, in June 1936. The two sides made rapid progress as the French negotiators conceded many of the nationalists' demands. A draft treaty of preferential alliance was concluded between the French and Syrian negotiators in September 1936 and submitted to their respective parliaments for ratification. Syria believed itself on the verge of independence.

In light of Syria's success, the Lebanese pressed the French to draft a similar treaty granting Lebanon its independence. Negotiations were opened in October 1936. Following the model of the Syrian document, a draft Franco-Lebanese treaty was concluded in just twenty-five days and sent on for parliamentary approval in Paris and Beirut.

Nationalists in Syria and Lebanon were very satisfied with the terms of the new treaties with France, as demonstrated by the ease of the ratification process in Beirut and Damascus. The Lebanese Chamber approved its treaty in November, and the Syrian Chamber approved its own at the end of December 1936, by unanimous vote in both countries. However, as with the Blum-Viollette bill, the colonial lobby in France succeeded in blocking any debate or vote on the 1936 treaties with Syria and Lebanon in the French National Assembly until the fall of the Blum government in June 1937. Lebanese and Syrian hopes for independence crashed with Blum's government.

In 1939, with war looming in Europe, the French Assembly refused to ratify the treaties. Adding injury to insult, French colonial authorities took the further step of ceding the northwestern Syrian territory of Alexandretta to Turkey, which had long claimed the region for its 38 percent Turkish minority, in order to secure Turkey's neutrality in the impending war in Europe. Outraged Syrian nationalists organized huge rallies and demonstrations, provoking massive repression by the French authorities, who suspended Syria's constitution and dissolved its parliament.

France was on the verge of a major confrontation with its two Levantine mandates when Nazi Germany occupied the country and overthrew its government in May 1940. A collaborationist French government—the Vichy Regime—was set up under Marshal Philippe Pétain, the same "hero of Verdun" who had displaced Lyautey in Morocco at the height of the Rif War. Under the new regime Syria and Lebanon were to be ruled by a Vichy high commissioner, General Henri Dentz.

The British, already troubled by the pro-Axis leanings of Arab nationalists in Egypt, Iraq, and Palestine, saw the Vichy administration in Syria and Lebanon as a hostile entity. When Commissioner Dentz offered Germany the use of Syrian airbases in May 1941, Britain was quick to intervene. United with the anti-Vichy Free French forces, headed by General Charles de Gaulle, the British occupied Syria and Lebanon in June–July 1941.

With the British occupation of Syria, the Free French promised full independence to Syria and Lebanon. In a proclamation read shortly after the Anglo-French invasion, General Georges Catroux, speaking on behalf of General de Gaulle, announced: "I come to put an end to the mandatory régime and to proclaim you free and independent."[44] The French declaration of Syrian and Lebanese independence was guaranteed by the government of Great Britain. Nationalist celebrations in Syria and Lebanon proved premature. The Free French had not forsaken the hope of retaining their empire after the war. Both Syria and Lebanon would face an uphill battle to secure their independence against tremendous French opposition.

No sooner had the Free French proclaimed an end to the mandates than the Lebanese began to prepare for independence. Nationalist leaders of the different religious communities worked out a power-sharing arrangement in an unwritten agreement known as the National Pact, concluded in 1943. Witnessed by the political heads of all of the communities involved, the Lebanese upheld the National Pact without ever seeing the need to record its terms in an official document. According to the terms of the pact the president of Lebanon would henceforth be a Maronite Christian, the prime minister a Sunni Muslim, and the speaker of the parliament a Shiite Muslim. Other important cabinet posts would be distributed among the Druzes, Orthodox Christians, and other religious communities. Seats in the parliament would be distributed in a ratio of six Christian seats for every five Muslim deputies (for which purposes the Sunnis, Shiites, and Druzes were all considered Muslim).

The National Pact seemed to have resolved the tensions between Lebanon's communities and given them all a stake in their country's political institutions. Yet the pact enshrined the same principle of "confessionalism" upheld by the French, rigidly distributing posts based on religious community, undermining Lebanese politics, and preventing the country from achieving genuine integration. In this way, the French left a legacy of division that long survived their rule in Lebanon.

Once the Lebanese notables had resolved their political differences, they called for fresh parliamentary elections in 1943. In keeping with the country's constitution, the fifty-five new members of parliament assembled to elect the president, and on September 21, 1943, they chose the lawyer and nationalist Bishara al-Khoury to serve as the first president of independent Lebanon.

Al-Khoury was the same lawyer who had once advised General Gouraud and who had been an early critic of the French mandate in Lebanon. He had risen to national prominence in 1934 when he and a like-minded group of politicians formed the Constitutional Bloc, seeking to replace the French mandate with a Franco-Lebanese treaty. Since that time he had worked consistently to bring French rule in Lebanon to a close. The deputies broke out in loud applause when al-Khoury was named president, and white doves were released in the Chamber. "When the final result was announced," al-Khoury recalled, "and I went up to the podium to give my speech, I could barely hear my own voice over the shouts and gunfire from outside. Yet I managed to make myself heard and told how we would cooperate with the Arab states and end Lebanon's isolation."[45]

The Lebanese considered themselves fully independent and saw no grounds to expect any resistance from the French. The Free French had pledged to end the mandate, and the Vichy Regime had been forcibly expelled from the Levant by the British. The Lebanese parliament proceeded to assert its independence by revising the constitution to strip France of any privileged role or right to intervene in Lebanese affairs. However, when the Free French authorities learned of the agenda for the Lebanese parliamentary session of November 9, 1943, they demanded a meeting with al-Khoury. They warned the Lebanese president that General de Gaulle would not tolerate any unilateral measures to redefine Franco-Lebanese relations. It was a tense meeting that ended without a resolution of the two sides' differences.

The Lebanese paid little concern to French warnings. The Free French were a fragmented government in exile whom the Lebanese believed to be in no position to halt their legitimate claim to independence—which Great Britain had guaranteed. The Lebanese deputies met as planned and revised Article 1 of the Constitution, which defined the frontiers of Lebanon as those "the Government of the French Republic officially recognized" to assert their "complete sovereignty" within the country's current and recognized boundaries, which were spelled out in some detail. They established Arabic as the sole official national language, relegating French to a subordinate status. They empowered the president of Lebanon, rather than the government of France, to conclude all foreign agreements, with the parliament's consent. All powers and privileges delegated to France by the League of Nations were formally excised from the Constitution. Finally, the deputies voted to change Article 5 of the Constitution, which defined the national flag: horizontal bands of red, white, and red replaced the French Tricolor, with the national symbol, the cedar tree, still emblazoned in its center. Legally and symbolically, Lebanon had asserted its sovereignty. It remained to secure French agreement to this new order.

The French authorities reacted swiftly and decisively to the revision of the Lebanese Constitution. President al-Khoury was awakened in the early morning hours of November 11 by French marines who burst into his house. His first thought was that they were renegades who had come to assassinate him. He shouted to his neighbors to call the police, but no one answered. The door to his room was flung open by a French captain armed with a pistol, holding his son. "I do not mean to do you harm," the Frenchman said, "but I am carrying orders from the High Commissioner for your arrest."

"I am president of an independent republic," al-Khoury replied. "The High Commissioner has no authority to give me orders."

"I will read the order to you," the captain responded. He then read a typewritten statement that accused al-Khoury of conspiracy against the mandate. The officer refused to give the order to al-Khoury and allowed him only ten minutes to pack his things. He was surrounded by soldiers "armed to the teeth." Al-Khoury was disturbed to see that the soldiers were Lebanese. The French took al-Khoury by motorcar to the fortress of the southern town of Rashayya. They were joined en route by several other cars carrying the prime minister, Riyad al-Solh, and leading members of his cabinet. By that afternoon, six members of the Lebanese government had been taken to Rashayya.

Violent demonstrations broke out in Beirut as word of the arrests spread. Al-Khoury's wife joined the demonstrators to show solidarity with those protesting the injustice done to her husband and the Lebanese government. The Lebanese appealed to the British, in their role as guarantors of the Free French declaration of Lebanon's independence in July 1941, who intervened to force the French to release President al-Khoury and the other Lebanese politicians. The changes to the Lebanese Constitution were preserved, but France clung to its Levantine mandate through its control over the security forces. The government of Lebanon would continue its struggle against the French to secure command of its army and police forces in a tug-of-war that would last another three years.[46]

The Syrians were less sanguine than the Lebanese about their prospects for achieving independence after the July 1941 Free French proclamation. The Free French authorities in Damascus had made clear to the Syrian political leadership that they had no intention of conceding independence to Syria or Lebanon until a new set of treaties had been concluded to secure French interests in both countries. The National Bloc needed to mobilize for a major confrontation with the French to force its demands for independence.

The leader of the National Bloc was Shukri al-Quwatli, a wealthy Damascene from a notable land-owning family. Exiled in 1927 by the French for his nationalist activities, al-Quwatli returned and assumed the leadership of the National Bloc in September 1942. When parliamentary elections were called in Syria in 1943, al-Quwatli's list emerged with a clear majority and elected their leader as president. The National Bloc government pursued conciliatory policies toward France, hoping to persuade the Free French to relinquish increasing authority until Syria might secure its independence. However, as in Lebanon, the Syrians found the French unwilling to make concessions with the country's security forces—the national army, known as the Syrian Legion, and the internal security force, the Sureté Générale.

Al-Quwatli's government in Syria worked closely with the al-Khoury government in Lebanon, seeking international support for their position against France. Large anti-French demonstrations were held in the winter of 1944 and spring of 1945. When France announced it would not surrender control over the Syrian national army until the government of Syria had signed a treaty, the governments of Syria and Lebanon refused further negotiations.

French intransigence led to widespread demonstrations and anti-French protests across Syria in May 1945. Damascus emerged as the center of opposition, as the capital and the seat of national politics. Without sufficient armed forces at their disposal to police a situation rapidly deteriorating beyond their control, the French responded with lethal force to decapitate the government and bombard its citizens into submission.

The first target of the French attack was the Syrian government itself. Khalid al-Azm was a member of the National Bloc who had been elected to parliament in 1943 and was appointed finance minister. On the evening of May 29, 1945, he was in the Government Palace in downtown Damascus discussing the crisis with a group of deputies when they heard the first rounds of artillery at six in the evening.[47] Al-Azm and his colleagues were appalled by the French escalation of the crisis and the severity of the artillery bombardment. They tried to call for help but found that all the telephone lines in the government offices were dead. Al-Azm received reports from messengers that the parliament building had already been stormed and occupied by French troops, who had killed all of the Syrian guards there. Shortly after they had taken the parliament, French soldiers took up positions around the Government Palace. They opened fire on the building, shattering its windows.

The French had cut the electrical power supply to Damascus, and night fell over the darkened city. The politicians and their guards in the Government Palace worked together to barricade the entrance to the building with tables and chairs in a vain attempt to deter the French from entering. Before midnight, al-Azm and his colleagues were tipped off that the French planned to occupy their building, and they slipped out through a back window. They made their way through the back streets of the city, eluding the French forces, and took refuge in al-Azm's spacious house in the center of the Old City of Damascus. His large courtyard was soon filled with over one hundred refugees—government ministers, deputies, and guards. The French discovered their whereabouts when the prime minister, Jamil Mardam, foolishly attempted to use al-Azm's telephone, which was under French surveillance. Once the French knew their whereabouts, they trained their artillery on al-Azm's neighborhood and unleashed a merciless barrage. The government ministers and deputies sought refuge in the most secure rooms of the house. The ground shook beneath their feet with the impact of the artillery and aerial bombardment, showering plaster and masonry onto those sheltered inside. They passed the night in fear and uncertainty, to the sounds of the destruction of their city.

The French redoubled their efforts to reduce the Syrian government to submission the following day. President al-Quwwatli had set up office in the hillside suburb of Salihiyya, where most of the government ministers went to join him. Al-Azm chose to remain with his family in Damascus and share the city's fate. The French attack grew yet more severe. They began to fire incendiary shells into the city's residential quarters, setting fires that blazed out of control. "Terror spread among the residents who feared the entire neighbourhood would be consumed by the flames," al-Azm recalled. "The shells continued to fall, and there was no fire brigade willing or able to fight the fires, as the French soldiers would not allow them to perform their duty." After another day under the artillery barrage, al-Azm decided to abandon his home and take his family to the relative safety of the suburbs with Shukri al-Quwwatli and the rest of the government.

From his safe house in Salihiyya, President al-Quwwatli appealed to British officials to intervene. Invoking the 1941 guarantee of Syrian independence, he formally requested the British to intercede with the French to stop the bombardment of Damascus. The Syrian president's appeal gave Britain legitimate grounds to interfere in French imperial affairs, and they prevailed upon their wartime ally to lift their attack. By the time French guns fell silent, more than four hundred Syrians had been killed, hundreds of private homes had been destroyed, and the building that housed the Syrian parliament had been reduced to rubble by the ferocity of the attack. France's desperate bid to preserve its empire in the Levant had failed, and nothing could persuade the embittered Syrians to compromise on their long-standing demand for total independence.

The French finally admitted defeat in July 1945 and agreed to transfer control of the military and security forces to the independent governments of Syria and Lebanon. There was no question of France imposing a treaty on either state. The international community recognized the independence of Syria and Lebanon when the two Arab states were admitted as founding members of the United Nations, on an equal footing with France, on October 24, 1945. All that remained was for France to withdraw its own troops from the Levant. The French military withdrew from Syria in the spring of 1946 and that August boarded ships in Beirut to return home.

As a young woman, Damascene journalist Siham Tergeman remembered the celebrations in Damascus on "the Night of Evacuation," when the last French soldier withdrew from the capital in April 1946. She described a jubilant city celebrating its first night of true independence as a "wedding of freedom" in which "the happy charming bride" was Damascus herself. "The guests came in carts and in cars big and small, and torches lighted up all the roofs of the city, the hotels and sidewalks, electrical poles, the gardens of Marje and the poles of the Hejaz Railway line, the iron railings of the River Barada, and all the thoroughfares and crossroads." Tergeman and her family celebrated through the night as singers and musicians entertained the crowds that gathered around the central Marje Square. "And the wedding of independence in Syria," she recalled, "continued on until daybreak."[48]

Syrian joy was matched by French bitterness at the end of the mandate. Though France still held its Arab possessions in North Africa, it regretted the loss of influence in the Eastern Mediterranean. After twenty-six years in Beirut and Damascus, the French had nothing to show for their efforts. Worse yet, France suspected its wartime ally and imperial rival, Great Britain, of coming to Syria and Lebanon's assistance only to draw the Levantine states into its own sphere of influence. Even so, the British Empire in the Middle East was under pressure and on the retreat in 1946. Indeed, France's troubles in Syria and Lebanon seem benign in comparison to the crisis Britain faced in Palestine in 1946.

1. Abd al-Aziz ibn Abd al-Rahman Al Saud, better known in the West as Ibn Saud, founder of the modern Kingdom of Saudi Arabia, is pictured here (center with glasses) towering over his advisors in Jidda in 1928. Following his conquest of the Hashemite Kingdom of the Hijaz in 1925, Ibn Saud took the title "Sultan of Najd and King of the Hijaz." In 1932, Ibn Saud renamed his kingdom Saudi Arabia, making it the only modern state named after its ruling family.

2. Fawzi al-Qawuqji (center) among commanders of the 1936–1939 Arab Revolt in Palestine. Qawuqji took part in the most famous Arab revolts against European rule, including the Battle of Maysalun in Syria (1920), the Syrian Revolt (1925–1927), the Arab Revolt in Palestine, and the Rashid Ali Coup in Iraq (1941). He took refuge from the British in Nazi Germany during WWII before returning to lead the Arab Liberation Army in Palestine in 1947–1948.

3. Exemplary punishment: The British Army destroys the homes of Palestinian villagers suspected of supporting the 1936–1939 Arab Revolt. Such collective punishments, conducted without due process, were given legal standing by a series of Emergency Regulations passed by British authorities to combat the Arab insurgency. An estimated 2,000 houses were destroyed between 1936 and 1940.

4. The opening of the Syrian Parliament, August 17, 1943. Following the Free French declaration of Syrian and Lebanese independence in July 1941, the Syrians went to the polls to elect their first independent government. The National Bloc list took a clear majority and, in the first parliamentary session (pictured right), their leader Shukri al-Quwatli was elected president of the republic.

5. The Syrian Parliament in disarray, May 29, 1945. Despite French assurances, De Gaulle's government had no intention of conceding full independence to Syria and refused to transfer control of the country's armed forces to President al-Quwatli's government. When the Syrians rose in nationalist demonstrations in May 1945, the French stormed the Parliament, fired upon government offices, and bombarded residential quarters in Damascus in a vain attempt to impose their authority on the unwilling Syrians. The last French soldier withdrew from Syria in April 1946.

6. This posed propaganda photo portrays a mixed group of regular and irregular soldiers defending the walls of Jerusalem from Jewish attack, under the command of a Muslim cleric distinguished by his turban.

7. In reality, Palestinian fighters were ill-prepared to defend their country in 1948. Poorly armed and trained, none had combat experience to match that of the Jewish forces they faced in 1948. Worse yet, they underestimated their adversary, and suffered total defeat to Jewish forces by the time the British withdrew from Palestine on May 14.

8. The Egyptian Free Officers shortly after taking power in Egypt in July 1952. At 51, General Muhammad Naguib (seated behind the desk) was the elder statesman of the young Free Officers, whose average age was 34. Lieutenant-Colonel Gamal Abdel Nasser (seated to Naguib's right) had Naguib placed under house arrest and assumed the presidency in 1954. Nasser's right-hand man, Major Abd al-Hakim Amer, is standing to Naguib's right. Republican Egypt's third president, Lieutenant-Colonel Anwar al-Sadat, is seated fourth from the left.

9. The leadership of the Algerian National Liberation Front (FLN) is shown here before boarding the Moroccan airliner that would fly them to captivity. Originally destined for Tunis, French warplanes intercepted the DC-3 and forced it to land in the Algerian city of Oran on October 22, 1956, where (from left to right) Ahmed Ben Bella, Mohammed Khider, and Hocine Ait-Ahmad were arrested and held for the remainder of the Algerian War. Prince Moulay Hassan (later King Hassan II, pictured here in uniform), son of Sultan Mohammad V of Morocco, saw off the Algerian revolutionaries.

Civil War in Lebanon, 1958.

10. Christian women, supporters of former president Camille Chamoun, taunted soldiers of the Lebanese Army with broomsticks in popular demonstrations against the government of Prime Minister Rashid Karami and the new president, General Fuad Shihab, in July 1958. Many women were reported wounded in the fighting.

11. Lebanon became the only country to invoke the Eisenhower Doctrine when President Chamoun requested American support against "Communist subversion" in the aftermath of the Iraqi Revolution in July 1958. Within three days, some 6,000 U.S. Marines landed on the shores of Lebanon, where they came under the scrutiny of the residents of Beirut. The force grew to a total strength of 15,000 men, backed by the Sixth Fleet and naval aircraft, before withdrawing on October 25 without having fired a shot in anger. [original caption: Interested Lebanese watch as U.S. marines relax . . .]

12. Colonel Abd al-Salam Arif was one of the leaders of the Iraqi Revolution that overthrew the Hashemite monarchy in July 1958. He seized the national radio station on July 14 to declare the Republic and the death of King Faysal II to the shocked Iraqi nation. The Iraqi people gave their full support to the revolution. Here Arif addressed masses of supporters in the Shiite shrine city of Najaf on the objectives and reforms of the new government. Arif subsequently overthrew President Abd al-Karim Qasim in 1963 to become the second president of the Iraqi republic.

13. The Israeli Air Force initiated the June 1967 War with a series of devastating attacks on Egyptian, Jordanian, and Syrian air bases on the morning of June 5. In less than three hours, the Israelis had destroyed 85 percent of Egypt's fighter aircraft and rendered their air bases unusable. Once they had achieved air superiority, Israeli ground forces swept over the Sinai, the West Bank, and Golan, inflicting total defeat on the armies of Egypt, Jordan, and Syria. Here, Israeli soldiers examine destroyed Egyptian aircraft in a Sinai air base.

14. The Israeli conquest of the West Bank in June 1967 drove over 300,000 Palestinians to seek refuge in the East Bank of Jordan. The journey was made all the more perilous by the destruction of road and bridges between the two banks of the Jordan River. Many of the new refugees fled with only those possessions they could carry.

Palestinian Hijackings.

15. Leila Khaled was a member of the Popular Front for the Liberation of Palestine who successfully hijacked a TWA airliner in 1969 from Rome to Damascus, where all passengers and staff were released unharmed. Her second operation, against an Israeli airliner, was foiled by El-Al security officers who killed her partner and overwhelmed Khaled before making an emergency landing in London, where Khaled was taken into custody by British police. She was released by the British on October 1, 1970, as part of a prisoner exchange.

16. The Popular Front for the Liberation of Palestine took control of a deserted airstrip named Dawson's Field in the desert east of the Jordanian capital Amman and declared it "Revolution Airport." Between September 6 and 9, 1970, the PFLP hijacked an American TWA airliner, a British BOAC jet, and a Swissair flight to "Revolution Airport." All 310 passengers were evacuated from the planes which were destroyed on September 12. The operation succeeded in bringing the Palestinian cause to international attention but provoked King Hussein to drive the Palestinian movement out of Jordan in the violent Black September War of 1970–1971.

CHAPTER 9

The Palestine Disaster and Its Consequences

In January 1944, Jewish extremists in Palestine declared war on Great Britain. "There is no longer any armistice between the Jewish people and the British Administration in Eretz Israel [i.e., the Land of Israel] which hands our brothers over to Hitler," the underground resistance movement asserted. "Our people is at war with this regime—war to the end."[1]

It may seem incredible that Jewish settlers would go to war with the British government, which had turned the Zionist dream of a Jewish national home in Palestine into a reality. However, over the course of the Second World War, Britain had come under increasing attack by the Jewish community of Palestine. The 1939 White Paper, which had imposed strict limits on Jewish immigration and called for Palestinian independence under (Arab) majority rule by 1949, had infuriated the Zionist leadership.

With war looming between Britain and Nazi Germany, David Ben-Gurion had pledged to help the British army fight fascism as if there were no White Paper, while opposing the terms of the White Paper as if there were no war. Most of the Zionists in Palestine fell in line with Ben-Gurion's policy and grudgingly supported the British in their war against the Nazi regime in Germany. But other, more radical Zionist parties saw Britain as the greater threat. They launched an armed insurgency with the stated aim of driving the British out of Palestine.

Two Jewish terrorist organizations, the Irgun and the Stern Gang, were responsible for the worst of the violence. The Irgun (short for Irgun Zvai Leumi, or National Military Organization) had been formed in 1937 to protect Jewish settlements from attack during the 1936–1939 Arab Revolt. After the White Paper was approved by the British Parliament in May 1939, however, Irgun members came to view Britain as the real enemy. The Irgun launched a series of bomb attacks on British government offices and police stations in Palestine before suspending hostilities in June 1940. With Britain at war with Germany, the Irgun leadership decided to comply with Ben-Gurion's policies of working with the British to fight Nazism.

One faction in the Irgun dissented and continued its attacks on the British. The splinter group, which came to be known in Hebrew by the acronym Lehi (for Lohamei Herut Yisrael, or Freedom Fighters of Israel), are better known in the West as the Stern Gang, after the leader of the faction, Abraham Stern. Stern and his followers believed that the Jewish people had an inalienable right to the land of Israel and that it was their duty to redeem the land—by armed force, if necessary. For Stern, the 1939 White Paper cast Britain in the role of an illegitimate occupier. Rather than siding with Britain against Nazi Germany, Stern actively approached the Nazis to make common cause against the British. Like some Arab nationalists, Stern hoped to work with the Germans to liberate Palestine from British rule—Nazi anti-Semitism notwithstanding. In Stern's view, Nazi Germany was but a persecutor of the Jewish people, whereas England was an enemy who would deny the Jews statehood in Palestine.

Toward the end of 1940, Stern sent a representative to meet with German officials in Beirut to argue for a convergence of interests "between the aims of the 'New Order' in Europe as interpreted by the Germans and the true national aspirations of the Jewish people." Through his envoy, Stern offered to use Jewish forces to drive Britain out of Palestine in return for unrestricted Jewish emigration from Germany to Palestine and German recognition of Jewish statehood. He argued that such an alliance would resolve the Jewish question in Europe and Jewish national aspirations while dealing their common British enemy a crucial defeat in the Eastern Mediterranean.[2]

Stern never received a response from the Third Reich. He clearly miscalculated the genocidal nature of Nazi anti-Semitism. For his overtures to the Germans, Stern was roundly condemned by both the Irgun and the Jewish Agency, which provided intelligence to the British to assist them in their crackdown on the Lehi. The mandate authorities were in hot pursuit of the Stern Gang for a string of attacks and bank robberies in Palestine. In February 1942, British officers killed Stern in a raid on a Tel Aviv apartment. Its leadership in disarray after Stern's death, the Lehi lapsed into inactivity. A fragile truce prevailed between the Yishuv and the British between 1942 and 1944, while the Second World War raged.

The Irgun began to reorganize itself as a resistance movement against British rule in 1943. The movement was headed by a dynamic new leader named Menachem Begin. Born in Poland, Begin (1913–1992) joined a Zionist youth movement before fleeing the country during the German invasion of Poland in 1939. He later volunteered for a Polish military unit in the Soviet Union. In 1942 his unit was sent to Palestine, where Begin was recruited to the Irgun. He rapidly rose to lead the organization and made contact with the new leadership of the Lehi, including Yitzhak Shamir. Both men would become prime minister of Israel toward the end of their lives, though they began their political careers in Palestine as terrorists. Continued restrictions on Jewish immigration to Palestine, combined with growing knowledge of the Nazi death camps and the Holocaust, exacerbated tensions between the radical Zionist movements and the British authorities in Palestine. By 1944, the Irgun and Lehi were no longer willing to be bound by the general truce and resumed attacks on the British in Palestine.

The Irgun and the Lehi used very different tactics in their common conflict against the British. Begin's Irgun carried out attacks against the offices of the British mandate and communications infrastructure in Palestine. Shamir's Lehi, in contrast, conducted targeted assassination attacks against British officials. The organization gained particular notoriety when two of its members assassinated the British minister resident in the Middle East, Lord Moyne, outside his home in Cairo on November 6, 1944. Moyne was the highest ranking British official in the Middle East and had upheld the 1939 White Paper's restrictions on Jewish immigration to Palestine. His assassins were caught by Egyptian police and subsequently hanged for their crime. The Jewish Agency and its paramilitary wing, the Haganah, distanced themselves from the Lehi and its acts, for fear of British retaliation.

It was only after the end of the Second World War that the Irgun, the Lehi, and the Haganah combined forces to fight against the British in Palestine. The liberation of the Nazi death camps had revealed the monstrous crime of the Holocaust. The leaders of the Yishuv were determined to bring Jewish survivors of the genocide from displaced person camps in Europe to Palestine. They refused to respect the limits on Jewish immigration imposed by the 1939 White Paper and declared a revolt against the British mandate. For a brief period in 1945–1946, the Haganah secretly coordinated operations with the Lehi and Irgun, to force a change in British policy through violence.

For ten months the Haganah cooperated with the Irgun and Lehi in a series of bank robberies, attacks on infrastructure, and kidnappings of British personnel. The Jewish Agency, led by Ben-Gurion, consistently denied any involvement in these operations and kept the Haganah's participation secret. The British authorities, however, suspected the Yishuv as a whole of complicity in the violence and responded with a massive clampdown. Between June 29 and July 1, 1946, over 2,700 members of the Yishuv were arrested, including several Jewish Agency leaders. The British authorities also seized the papers of the Jewish Agency and took them back to the mandate secretariat, then housed in a wing of the King David Hotel.

The British seizure of its documents amounted to more than an administrative problem for the Jewish Agency. Among the papers were items implicating the agency and the Haganah in attacks on the British.[3] Were the mandate authorities to find the evidence of Haganah and Jewish Agency involvement in terror activities, it would only stiffen British resolve to prevent further Jewish immigration to Palestine, and to concede to Palestinian Arab demands. From the moment these incriminating documents were taken into the mandate secretariat, the fate of the King David Hotel was sealed. The Irgun already had detailed plans for an attack on the high-rise hotel in West Jerusalem, headquarters to both the civil and military administrations of Palestine, but the Haganah had previously restrained it, arguing that such an atrocity would "inflame the British excessively." On July 1, immediately after the British seizure of the Jewish Agency's files, the Haganah sent a command to the Irgun ordering it to carry out the operation against the King David Hotel as soon as possible.

Preparations for the King David Hotel bombing took three weeks. On July 22 a group of Irgun operatives delivered a number of milk cans filled with 500 pounds of high explosives to the basement of the hotel. The "milkmen" were surprised by two British soldiers, and a fire fight ensued. But the terrorists had already managed to set the timers to detonate the explosives thirty minutes later.

"Each minute seemed like a day," Menachem Begin later wrote. "Twelve-thirty-one, thirty-two. Zero hour drew near. The half-hour was almost up. Twelve-thirty-seven. . . . Suddenly, the whole town seemed to shudder."[4]

The British authorities claimed that they had received no advance warning of the attack. The Irgun insisted it had given telephone warnings to both the hotel and other institutions. Whatever the truth of the claims on either side, no attempt had been made to evacuate the King David Hotel. The explosives, detonated beneath a public café at the height of the lunch hour, sheared an entire wing from the hotel and collapsed all six stories into the basement. Ninety-one people were killed and over one hundred wounded in the explosion—Britons, Arabs, and Jews alike.

The atrocity shocked the world and was denounced by the Jewish Agency as a "dastardly crime perpetrated by a group of desperadoes." Yet the British government knew full well that the Haganah was implicated in the terror campaign, and it made the point in a White Paper on terrorism in Palestine published only two days after the King David bombing.

The British recognized they were fighting more than just a radical fringe. The Jewish Agency and the Haganah might differ with the Irgun and Lehi on tactics and methods, but they were united in purpose: the expulsion of the British to achieve Jewish statehood in Palestine.

In the aftermath of the Second World War, Britain had neither the resources nor the resolve to remain in Palestine. The differences between Jews and Arabs in Palestine were irreconcilable. If the British made concessions to the Jews, they feared the Arabs would start a revolt like that of 1936–1939. If they made concessions to the Arabs, it was now clear what the Jews would be capable of. British efforts to convene a meeting of Arab and Jewish leaders in London in September 1946 failed when both sides refused to attend. Subsequent bilateral meetings in London in February 1947 collapsed under the weight of contradictory Arab and Jewish demands for statehood.

The British had reached an impasse, and the fallacy of the Balfour Declaration was now clear: Britain could not deliver a "national home for the Jewish people" without prejudice to "rights of existing non-Jewish communities in Palestine." The British government was out of solutions and had no more leverage over the disputing parties in Palestine. And so, on February 25, 1947, British Foreign Secretary Ernest Bevin referred the Palestine question to the newly created United Nations in the hope that the international community might have more success in solving the problem.

The United Nations assembled an eleven-nation Special Committee on Palestine, known by the acronym UNSCOP. Aside from Iran, none of the UNSCOP members had any particular interest in Middle Eastern affairs: Australia, Canada, Czechoslovakia, Guatemala, India, Iran, the Netherlands, Peru, Sweden, Uruguay, and Yugoslavia. Delegates spent five weeks in Palestine in June and July 1947. Arab political leaders refused to meet with the UNSCOP delegates, whereas the Jewish Agency took the opportunity to put the most persuasive case forward to the international community in support of the creation of a Jewish state in Palestine.

While the UNSCOP delegates were in Palestine, waves of illegal Jewish immigrants were flooding from Europe into Palestine, with Jewish Agency assistance, in derelict steamers. The British authorities made every effort to bar entry to these refugees, most of whom were Holocaust survivors. The most famous of these ships was the *Exodus*, whose 4,500 passengers reached the port of Haifa on July 18. The ship's passengers were denied entry to Palestine and shipped back to France the very next day for subsequent internment in German camps. Britain faced widespread international condemnation for its handling of the Jewish refugee crisis, and for the *Exodus* affair in particular.

Violence between Britain and the Jewish community escalated while the UNSCOP delegates conducted their investigation. The British had condemned three Irgun men to death for terror crimes in July 1947. On July 12 the Irgun seized two British sergeants, Cliff Martin and Mervyn Paice, and held them hostage to prevent the British from hanging the Irgun men. When the British carried out the executions, the Irgun hanged Martin and Paice in retaliation, on July 29. The killers pinned a list of charges to the dead men's bodies in a macabre parody of British legal jargon. Martin and Paice were "British spies" condemned for "criminal anti-Hebrew activities" such as "illegal entry into the Hebrew homeland" and "membership of a British criminal terrorist organisation known as the Army of Occupation."[5]

Worse, the men's bodies were booby-trapped to explode when cut down. The act was designed to provoke maximum outrage and undermine Britain's will to continue the fight in Palestine.

The hanging of the two sergeants made front-page news across Britain. Tabloids stirred anti-Jewish hostility with banner headlines screaming "Hanged Britons: Picture That Will Shock the World." Instantly, a wave of anti-Jewish demonstrations gave way to riots that spread across England and Scotland and raged through the first week of August. The worst of the violence took place in the port city of Liverpool, where in the course of five days more than 300 Jewish properties were attacked and some eighty-eight townspeople arrested by the police. The *Jewish Chronicle* reported attacks on synagogues in London, Glasgow, and Plymouth, and threats to temples in other towns. Only two years after the liberation of the Nazi death camps, swastikas and slogans such as "Hang All Jews" and "Hitler Was Right" stained British cities.[6]

The UNSCOP delegates were thus all too aware of the complexity of the situation in Palestine by the time they drew up their findings for the United Nations in August 1947. The delegates were unanimous in calling for the end of the British mandate, and they recommended the partition of Palestine into Jewish and Arab states by a strong majority of eight to three. Only India, Iran, and Yugoslavia opposed partition, preferring a unified federal state of Palestine.

The British did not even wait for the United Nations to debate the recommendations of the UNSCOP proposals. The *Exodus* scandal, the hanging of the British sergeants, the anti-Semitic riots that followed, and the UNSCOP report, all in quick succession, completely undermined Britain's resolve to remain in Palestine. On September 26, 1947, the British government announced its intention to withdraw unilaterally from Palestine and entrust its mandatory responsibilities to the United Nations. The date for the British withdrawal was set for May 14, 1948.

The terrorists had achieved their first objective: they had forced the British to withdraw from Palestine. Though their methods were publicly denounced by the leaders of the Jewish Agency, the Irgun and Lehi had played a key role in removing a major impediment to Jewish statehood. By using terror tactics to achieve political objectives, they also set a dangerous precedent in Middle Eastern history—one that plagues the region down to the present day.

The UNSCOP report was presented to the General Assembly for debate in November 1947. The terms of debate were shaped by the majority recommendation for the partition of Palestine into a Jewish and an Arab state. The Partition Resolution divided Palestine into a checkerboard of six parts, three Arab and three Jewish, with Jerusalem under international trusteeship. The plan allotted some 55 percent of the area of Palestine to the Jewish state, including all of the Galilee panhandle to the northeast of the country, as well as the strategic Mediterranean coastline from Haifa through Jaffa, and the Araba Desert down to the Gulf of Aqaba.

Zionist activists lobbied UN members assiduously to secure the two-thirds majority required to carry the Partition Resolution and the promise of Jewish statehood. American Zionists played a major role in securing the Truman administration's support for the resolution. In his memoirs, Harry Truman later recalled that he never "had as much pressure and propaganda aimed at the White House as I had in this instance."[7] In the eleventh hour, the United States reversed its position of nonintervention and actively pressured other members to lend their support to partition. On November 29, 1947, the Partition Resolution passed by a vote of 33 to 13, with 10 abstentions.

Having secured international authorization for the creation of a Jewish state in at least part of Palestine, the Zionists had taken another major step toward achieving their goal of statehood. However, the Arab world generally, and the Palestinian Arabs in particular, remained implacably opposed to both partition and to Jewish statehood in Palestine.

It is not hard to understand the Palestinian Arab position. By 1947 the Arabs of Palestine constituted a two-thirds majority with over 1.2 million people, compared to 600,000 Jews in Palestine. Many towns and cities with Palestinian Arab majorities, like Haifa, were allotted to the Jewish state. Jaffa, though nominally part or the Arab state, was an isolated enclave surrounded by the Jewish state. Moreover, Arabs owned 94 percent of the total land area of Palestine and some 80 percent of the arable farmland of the country.[8] Based on these facts, Palestinian Arabs refused to confer on the United Nations the authority to split their country and give half away.

Jamal al-Husayni, a notable of Jerusalem, captured Palestinian frustrations in his response to the UNSCOP proposals in September 1947. "The case of the Arabs of Palestine was based on the principles of international justice; it was that of a people which desired to live in undisturbed possession of the country where Providence and history had placed it. The Arabs of Palestine could not understand why their right to live in freedom and peace, and to develop their country in accordance with their traditions, should be questioned and constantly submitted to investigation." Al-Husayni, addressing his comments to the UN committee on the Palestinian question, continued: "One thing is clear, it was the sacred duty of the Arabs of Palestine to defend their country against all aggression."[9]

No one had any illusions that partition would go unchallenged. The Jews in Palestine would have to fight for the lands allotted them by the UN's Partition Resolution, not to mention any other territories designated for the Arab state to which they might aspire. The Arabs, for their part, would have to defeat the Jews if they hoped to prevent them from taking any part of Palestine.

The morning after the Partition Resolution was announced, Arabs and Jews began to prepare for an inevitable war—a civil war between the rival claimants to Palestine.

For six months Arabs and Jews fought for their rival claims over Palestine. The Jewish community of Palestine was well prepared for battle. The Haganah had gained extensive training and combat experience during the Second World War. They had also stockpiled extensive arms and ammunition. The Palestine Arabs had made no such preparations and placed their trust in the justice of their cause and the support of neighboring Arab states.

The controversial leader of the Palestinian Arab community was Hajj Amin al-Husayni, the exiled grand mufti of Jerusalem. Hajj Amin was a very divisive figure who provoked opposition both in Palestine and abroad. He was reviled by the British and other Western powers for his defection to Nazi Germany during World War II, and he was mistrusted to varying degrees by Arab heads of state. Hajj Amin's leadership was contested by a number of Palestinian notables, dividing the Arab community just as it faced its greatest challenge. As he tried to lead the Palestinian movement from his exile in Egypt, Hajj Amin undermined the prospects for meaningful common action between the Palestinian Arabs themselves, and between the Palestinians and the other Arab states.

The Arab states, many of which had only just gained independence from European colonial rule, were similarly divided and demoralized. They had just suffered their first diplomatic defeat with the passing of the UN Partition Resolution over their impassioned opposition. Faced with the decision to divide Palestine, inter-Arab rivalries rose to the surface.

The only Arab country to support the idea of partition, since it was first mooted in 1937, was Transjordan. King Abdullah (the former amir had been crowned king in May 1946) welcomed the opportunity to append the Arab territories of Palestine to his own nearly landlocked kingdom. Abdullah's support for partition provoked deep resentment from Palestinian political elites and the active hatred of the mufti, Hajj Amin. Abdullah's isolation in the Arab world was almost complete. He could only count on a modicum of support from his Hashemite cousins in Iraq. He suffered the active mistrust of the Syrian government, who feared Abdullah's ambitions in their own lands dating back to the early 1920s; the long-standing hostility of the Hashemites' rivals in Arabia, the House of Saud; and the suspicions of the Egyptian monarchy, who feared any challenge to Egypt's self-declared primacy in Arab affairs.

Rather than coordinate their actions and commit their national armies, the neighboring Arab states preferred to call on irregular volunteers—Arab nationalists and Muslim Brothers determined to save Arab Palestine. Much as Americans and Europeans responded to the call to fight fascism in the Spanish Civil War, these Arab "Lincoln Brigades" came to defeat Zionism. They were called the Arab Liberation Army (ALA), and their most famous commander was Fawzi al-Qawuqji.

Fawzi al-Qawuqji had never missed the opportunity to fight against European imperialism in the Arab world. His every battle had proved a glorious defeat. He was among the forces who retreated from Maysalun on the day the French defeated King Faysal's Arab Kingdom in 1920. He led the revolt against the French in the Syrian town of Hama and played a key role in the Syrian revolt of 1925–1927. He was also a veteran of the Palestinian Arab Revolt of 1936–1939. He sided with the Iraqi military against the British in the Rashid Ali coup of 1941 and, when that movement was crushed, defected to Nazi Germany, where he married his German wife and waited out the rest of the war years.

Al-Qawuqji was impatient to return from Europe to Arab politics. After Germany's defeat, he fled to France, where he and his wife boarded a plane to Cairo under assumed identities with forged passports, in February 1947. That November he made his way to Damascus, where he was hosted by the Syrian government and paid a monthly allowance.

For the Syrian government, al-Qawuqji was a godsend. Unwilling to commit their own small army to war in Palestine, the Syrians threw their full support behind the Arab Liberation Army, for which al-Qawuqji was the ideal commander. He enjoyed a hero's reputation across the Arab world and possessed vast experience in commando warfare. Now aged fifty-seven, the grizzled commander set up camp in Damascus and busily recruited his irregular army.

In February 1948, a Lebanese journalist named Samir Souqi published an interview with al-Qawuqji that captured the atmosphere in his Damascus headquarters during the lead up to war:

> This Arab leader, motivated by utmost resolve, has made of his home a military headquarters guarded by irregulars in American military uniform. Not an hour of the day passes without Bedouins, peasants and young men in modern clothes turning up on his doorstep, demanding to enlist as volunteers in the Arab Liberation Army. He also has headquarters in Qatanah, where volunteers are undergoing military training, waiting to be sent to Palestine.[10]

Working together in a new regional organization known as the Arab League, the Arab states hoped to rely on the ALA to defeat the Jewish forces in Palestine without having to send in their regular armies. They appointed the Iraqi general Ismail Safwat as commander in chief of the ALA and charged him with implementing a coordinated war plan for the volunteer irregular army. Safwat divided Palestine into three main fronts to coordinate operations according to a master plan. He placed al-Qawuqji in charge of the northern front and the Mediterranean coastline; the southern front would fall under Egyptian command. The central front—called the Jerusalem Front—was to be under Hajj Amin's authority, who named the charismatic Abd al-Qadir al-Husayni to lead his forces.

Though a member of the mufti's Husayni family, Abd al-Qadir transcended the factional fighting and was held in respect by Palestinians from all walks of life. Educated in the American University in Cairo, he was a veteran of the Palestinian Arab Revolt, where he earned a reputation for bravery and leadership, and was twice wounded. Like al-Qawuqji, he later fought the British in Iraq in 1941.

The greatest problem facing Arab commanders both in Palestine and the neighboring Arab states was the shortage of arms and ammunitions. Unlike the Jewish soldiers in the Haganah, who had enjoyed British training for over a decade and had gained combat experience fighting with the British in World War II, the Palestinian Arabs had not had the opportunity to build up an indigenous militia. Also, whereas the Jewish Agency had been smuggling arms and ammunition into Palestine, the Palestinian Arabs had no independent access to arms. With no source of resupply, it would not take long for Palestinian fighters to run out of the limited ammunition they held.

The logistical shortcomings did not constrain the Palestinian fighters, however. Sporadic attacks against Jewish settlements began on November 30, 1947, and spread from the cities to the countryside. Arab forces tried to cut roads leading to settlements and to isolate Jewish villages. For most of the winter months of 1948, the Haganah dug in and fortified its positions, working to secure the territory allotted to the Jewish state by the Partition Resolution in advance of the British withdrawal scheduled for mid-May.

In late March 1948, Jewish forces went on the offensive. Their first target was the Tel Aviv–Jerusalem road. The Jewish quarter of Jerusalem was encircled and besieged by Arab forces. The Haganah was determined to open a supply line and relieve Jewish positions in Jerusalem.

The Arab situation in Jerusalem was far weaker than the Jewish commanders realized. Palestinian fighters, commanded by Abd al-Qadir al-Husayni, did not have the weaponry to retain their positions. The Arabs held the strategic town of al-Qastal, which commanded the high ground on the Tel Aviv–Jerusalem road. As Jewish forces advanced toward al-Qastal, al-Husayni made an emergency visit to Damascus in early April to secure the arms his men needed to hold their ground.

Inter-Arab disputes undermined al-Husayni's mission from the outset. The Syrian government was hostile to the mufti, Hajj Amin al-Husayni, and refused all support to Abd al-Qadir, who was the mufti's cousin. A bitter rivalry had developed between the Syrian-backed ALA and the local Palestinian forces headed by Abd al-Qadir al-Husayni that served to further divide Arab ranks. Al-Husayni found himself caught up in these inter-Arab politics as he met with Syrian and Arab League leaders in Damascus.

While Arab leaders and commanders squabbled in Damascus, al-Qastal fell to the elite Palmach units of the Haganah on April 3. Arab attempts to retake the town had failed, and the Jewish forces were consolidating their defenses. Al-Qastal was the first Arab town to be captured by Jewish forces, and the news came as a shock to all those meeting in Damascus. From this strategic position, Haganah forces posed a real threat to Jerusalem. Yet the Arab League commanders remained incapable of meaningful action, seemingly confined to a fantasy world.

General Ismail Safwat, the Iraqi commander in chief of the Arab Liberation Army, turned to Abd al-Qadir al-Husayni and said, "So al-Qastal has fallen. It is your job to get it back, Abd al-Qadir. And if you aren't able to get it back, tell us so that we can entrust the job to [Fawzi] al-Qawuqji."

Al-Husayni was incensed. "Give us the weapons I have requested and we will recover the town. Now the situation has deteriorated, and the Jews have artillery and aircraft and men. I cannot occupy al-Qastal without artillery. Give me what I ask for and I guarantee you victory."

"What is this, Abd al-Qadir, you have no cannons?" Ismail Safwat retorted. He grudgingly promised the Palestinian commander whatever leftover guns and ammunition they had available in Damascus—105 outdated rifles, 21 machine guns, insufficient ammunition, and some mines—for later delivery. In essence, they sent al-Husayni home empty-handed.

Al-Husayni exploded in anger and stormed out of the hall: "You are traitors. You are criminals. History will record that you lost Palestine. I will occupy al-Qastal, and I will die along with my brothers, the *mujahidin*."[11]

Abd al-Qadir al-Husayni left Damascus that very night, on April 6, and reached Jerusalem at dawn the following morning, accompanied by fifty ALA volunteers. After a short rest, he set off for al-Qastal at the head of a force of some three hundred Palestinians and four British soldiers, who had crossed ranks to fight with the Arabs.[12]

The Arab counterattack on al-Qastal began at 11 P.M. on April 7. The Arab forces broke into detachments and approached the village in a three-pronged assault. One of the Arab detachments suffered heavy casualties and nearly ran out of ammunition. As their wounded leader retreated, al-Husayni led a small detachment to take their place and attempted to lay charges under the defenses erected by the Jewish forces. But al-Husayni and his men were pinned down by heavy fire from the Jewish defenders and soon found themselves surrounded by Jewish reinforcements from nearby settlements.

As dawn broke on the morning of April 8, word spread like wildfire among the Arab fighters that al-Husayni and his men were surrounded by the enemy; the battle of al-Qastal looked certain to end in defeat. However, Arab reinforcements rallied to the call, and some five hundred men joined the besieged troops at al-Qastal. They fought through the day and managed to retake the town by the late afternoon. Their joy in recovering al-Qastal was shattered when the Arab fighters found the body of Abd al-Qadir al-Husayn on the eastern periphery of the town. The Palestinian fighters vented their rage by killing their fifty Jewish prisoners. On both sides, the civil war would prove a war of atrocity.

Abd al-Qadir al-Husayni was buried the following day. Ten thousand mourners attended his funeral at the Aqsa Mosque in Jerusalem. "The people wept for him," recalled Arif al-Arif, a native of Jerusalem and historian of 1948. "They called him the hero of al-Qastal."[13] The Palestinians never fully recovered from the loss of Abd al-Qadir al-Husayni. No other local leader rose to command a national resistance to the Jewish forces in Palestine, and his death was a tremendous blow to public morale. Worse yet, his death proved entirely in vain. The demoralized Arab defenders left only forty men to hold al-Qastal. Within forty-eight hours, Jewish forces retook the town—this time for good.

The death of Abd al-Qadir al-Husayni and the loss of al-Qastal were overshadowed by the massacre of the Palestinian villagers of Dayr Yasin on April 9. The massacre, which took place on the same day as al-Husayni's funeral, sent shock waves of fear across Palestine. From that day forward, the Palestinians had lost the will to fight.

Dayr Yasin was a peaceful Arab village of some 750 residents located to the west of Jerusalem. It was a mixed village of farmers, masons, and merchants. There were two mosques and two schools, one for boys and one for girls, and a sporting club. It was the last village in Palestine to expect a Jewish attack, for the residents had concluded a nonaggression pact with the Jewish commanders in Jerusalem. The Irgun and Lehi gave no reason for their unprovoked attack on Dayr Yasin. Palestinian historian Arif al-Arif believed the Jewish terror organizations targeted the village "to give their own people hope and to fill the hearts of the Arabs with terror."[14]

The attack on Dayr Yasin began in the predawn hours of April 9, 1948. With only eighty-five armed men facing a superior Jewish force supported by armored cars and aircraft, panic spread among the villagers. One peasant woman was breastfeeding her baby when the fighting erupted. "I heard the tanks and rifles, and smelled the smoke. I saw them coming. Everybody was yelling to their neighbours, 'If you know how to leave, leave!' Whoever had an uncle tried to get the uncle. Whoever had a wife tried to get the wife." She ran for her life with her baby son in her arms, to the neighboring village of 'Ayn Karam.[15]

Though there were Arab Liberation Army units in Ayn Karam, and British police nearby, no one came to the villagers' rescue. Eyewitnesses reported that the Jewish attackers gathered all of the armed Arab defenders and shot them. Arif al-Arif, the Palestinian chronicler, interviewed a number of survivors of Dayr Yasin soon after these events and catalogued the horrors of the day, naming names and detailing deaths. "Among the atrocities," he recounted,

> they killed al-Haj Jabir Mustafa, a ninety-year-old man, and threw his body from the balcony of his home into the street. They did the same to al-Haj Isma'il 'Atiyya, an old man aged ninety-five, and killed his eighty-year-old wife and their grandchild. They murdered a blind youth named Muhammad Ali Khalil Mustafa and his wife, who tried to protect him, and her eighteen-month-old child. They murdered a school teacher who was tending to the wounded.[16]

In all, over 110 villagers were killed in Dayr Yasin.

According to al-Arif's sources, the killing would have continued in Dayr Yasin had an older Jewish commander not given the order to stop. However, survivors were forced to march to the Jewish quarter of Jerusalem, where they were "publicly reviled before the Jewish people, as if they were criminals," before they were finally released near the Italian hospital near Hayy al-Mismara.[17] Between the massacre of innocent villagers and the brutal humiliation of survivors, Dayr Yasin provoked universal condemnation. The Jewish Agency denounced the atrocity and distanced its Haganah forces from the extremists of the Irgun and Lehi.

The massacre at Dayr Yasin provoked a mass exodus of Palestinian Arabs that continued right up to the British withdrawal on May 15. As word of the killing spread, al-Arif explained, people across Palestine "began to flee their homes, carrying with them different accounts of Jewish atrocities which left people shuddering in horror." The political leadership only exacerbated fears by publishing accounts of Dayr Yasin and other atrocities in the Arab press. Although the Palestinian leaders hoped to force the Arab states to intervene by playing on the humanitarian crisis, their reports only served to reinforce the fear and encourage villagers to abandon their homes.[18] Time and again, contemporary accounts make reference to townspeople and villagers across Palestine taking their loved ones and abandoning their homes and possessions out of fear of another Dayr Yassin.

Palestinians had already begun fleeing the territory earlier in the spring. Between February and March 1948, some 75,000 Arabs had left their homes in the towns that were the center of fighting, such as Jerusalem, Jaffa, and Haifa, for the relative safety of the West Bank or neighboring Arab states.[19] That April, after Dayr Yasin, the stream of refugees became a flood.

Some Palestinians chose to fight horror with horror. Four days after the massacre at Dayr Yasin, on April 13, Palestinian fighters ambushed a Jewish medical convoy heading to Mount Scopus on the edge of Jerusalem. The two ambulances were clearly marked with medical insignia, and the passengers were in fact doctors and nurses of the Hadassah Hospital and employees of the Hebrew University. There were 112 passengers in the convoy. Only 36 survived.

The brutality of the ambush was captured in a series of grisly photographs in which the attackers posed in triumph next to the bodies of their victims. These barbaric photographs were sold commercially in Jerusalem, as if to demonstrate to the Arabs of Palestine that they could destroy the Jewish threat. Yet photographs of atrocity could not dispel the air of defeat that permeated the towns and countryside of Palestine in April 1948.

Palestinian morale had been shattered, and the massacre of Jewish civilians at Mount Scopus only heightened fears of further atrocity and Jewish retribution. Sensing the collapse in public morale, the Haganah stepped up its operations in line with a military plan known as Plan D for the depopulation and destruction of Palestinian towns and villages deemed necessary to establish a viable Jewish state.

Haifa fell to Jewish forces on April 21–23, sending another shock wave through Palestine. Haifa was the economic heart of Palestine, thanks to its port and oil refinery. The total Arab population came to more than 70,000. It was also the administrative center of Northern Palestine.

Because Haifa had been allocated to the Jewish state by the UN Partition Resolution, Jewish forces had been planning to take the city for months. Haifa had first come under attack by Jewish forces in mid-December 1947. "The attacks set off a fearsome emigration from the city," wrote Rashid al-Hajj Ibrahim, a municipal leader in Haifa. "A large part of the population saw the danger that threatened them, as Jewish preparedness revealed how much the Arabs lacked to defend themselves, which drove them to flee their homes."[20] Hajj Ibrahim, chairman of the Haifa National Committee, worked with his colleagues in the municipality to restore calm and restrain the attacks by local and foreign irregulars, many of them ALA volunteers. But their efforts were in vain. Violent exchanges between Arab irregulars and Haganah fighters continued through the winter months and into the spring. By early April, between twenty and thirty thousand residents had left Haifa.

The final onslaught began on April 21. As British troops were withdrawing from their positions in Haifa, the Haganah launched a massive attack to take the city. Over the next forty-eight hours Jewish forces pounded Arab neighborhoods relentlessly with sustained mortar attacks and gunfire. On Friday morning, April 23, Jewish aircraft attacked the city, "provoking terror among the women and children," Hajj Ibrahim wrote, "who were very influenced by the horrors of Dayr Yasin."[21] They flooded to the waterfront, where ships were waiting to evacuate the terrified civilians of Haifa.

Hajj Ibrahim described the tragedy he witnessed on the Haifa waterfront: "Thousands of women, children and men hurried to the port district in a state of chaos and terror without precedent in the history of the Arab nation. They fled their houses to the coast, barefoot and naked, to wait for their turn to travel to Lebanon. They left their homeland, their houses, their possessions, their money, their welfare, and their trades, to surrender their dignity and their souls."[22] By the beginning of May, only three to four thousand Arabs, of an original population exceeding 70,000, remained in Haifa to live under Jewish rule.

Once Haifa had been secured, Jewish forces concentrated on the rest of the coastline that had been awarded to the Jewish state by the United Nations. The Irgun, working independently of the Haganah, initiated hostilities to capture the other major Arab port town of Jaffa, next to the Jewish city of Tel Aviv. Its offensive began at dawn on April 25. Armed with three mortars and twenty tons of bombs, the Irgun took the northern Manshiyya quarter of Jaffa on April 27. From its new position, the Irgun subjected the downtown areas of Jaffa to relentless bombing over the next three days.

The attacks shattered public morale and the resistance of the townspeople of Jaffa. The fact that it was the Irgun attacking raised fears of another Dayr Yasin massacre. The fall of Haifa only a few days earlier had left most of the city's 50,000 remaining residents (already by April some 20,000 residents had sought refuge outside their city) with little hope that Jaffa would withstand the attack. Panic swept the city as its residents fled in a mass exodus. Municipal leaders sought ships to evacuate townspeople to Lebanon, and they negotiated for others to withdraw from the city to the Gaza Strip through Jewish lines. By May 13, there were only 4,000–5,000 inhabitants left to surrender their city to Jewish forces.

With time running out before the British withdrawal would be finalized, Jewish forces concentrated their attacks to secure the northeastern territories conceded to the Jewish state by partition. Safad, a town of 12,000 Arabs and 1,500 Jews, was attacked by elite Palmach units of the Haganah and fell on May 11. Beisan, a town of 6,000, was conquered on May 12 and its inhabitants expelled to Nazareth and Transjordan. At the same time, Haganah operations led to mass evacuations and expulsions of villagers from the Galilee region, the coastal plain, and the Tel Aviv–Jerusalem road. The roads of Palestine were filled with streams of homeless refugees, with only the possessions they could carry, fleeing the terrors of war. One Arab eyewitness de-scribed the human misery of the refugees: "People left their country dazed and direc-tionless, without homes or money, falling ill and dying while wandering from place to place, living in niches and caves, their clothing falling apart, leaving them naked, their food running out, leaving them hungry. The mountains grew colder and they had no one to defend them."[23]

By the end of the war, the Jews of Palestine had secured the main towns of the coastal plain and the Galilee panhandle. In the process, they had driven between 200,000 and 300,000 Palestinians from their homes. The Palestinian refugees in-tended to return when peace had been restored. They were never allowed back. As David Ben-Gurion told his cabinet in June 1948, "We must prevent at all costs their return."[24]

The civil war ended on the last day of the British mandate. The Jews of Palestine declared their statehood on May 14, 1948, and would henceforth be known as Is-raelis. The defeated Arabs had no state to dignify their Palestinian identity. They placed their trust in their Arab neighbors, whose armies were massing on Palestine's borders, awaiting the final British withdrawal.

On May 14, as they had promised, the British played the "Last Post," took down their flag, and boarded ship, turning their backs on the disaster they had made of Palestine.

The day after the British withdrew from Palestine, the armies of the surrounding Arab states invaded. On May 15, 1948, the civil war between Palestinian Arabs and Jews was over, and the first Arab-Israeli war had begun. The governments of Egypt, Transjordan, Iraq, Syria, and Lebanon each committed their armies, osten-sibly to defend Arab Palestine and defeat Israel. In fact, the Arab League only decided to commit the regular armies of the Arab states two days before the British with-drawal from Palestine, on May 12, 1948. Had their intervention enjoyed a modicum of coordination and advance planning, a glimmer of trust and common purpose, the Arab forces might have prevailed. Instead, the Arabs entered Palestine more at war with each other than with the Jewish state.

The Arab states were in complete disarray on the eve of the first Arab-Israeli War. The conflict in Palestine had gone worse than anyone had predicted. For all his blus-ter, Fawzi al-Qawuqji had proved a disaster on the battlefield, his ill-trained and undisciplined troops forced to retreat from every action against the Haganah. The Arab Liberation Army was by all accounts more of a burden than a relief to the be-leaguered Palestinians, and the strategy of relying on Arab volunteers had proven an utter failure. As the date of British withdrawal neared, the neighboring Arab states came to recognize that they would have to commit their regular armies to prevent Jewish forces from conquering all of Palestine.

The Arab states all faced a serious dilemma. They saw the conflict in Palestine as an Arab cause and felt a moral obligation to intervene to protect fellow Arabs in Palestine. This was only reinforced by the fact that the Arab states met under the aegis of the Arab League to coordinate common action. However, the individual Arab states each had their own national interests—they entered the war as Egyptians, Jordanians, and Syrians rather than as Arabs. And they brought their inter-Arab rivalries to the battlefield.

The Arab League convened a cycle of meetings in autumn 1947 and winter 1948 to address the Palestine crisis. The conflict of interests between the new Arab states became increasingly apparent. Each Arab country had its own concerns, and none of the Arab states placed great trust in the others. King Abdullah of Transjordan provoked the most suspicion among his Arab brethren. His support for partition revealed his ambition to annex the Arab territories of Palestine to aggrandize his own state. This earned him the hatred of Palestinian leader Hajj Amin al-Husayni, the rivalry of Egyptian King Farouq, and the suspicion of the Syrians. In Syria, President Shukri al-Quwatli struggled to contain the threat of the "monarchist movement" among some of his officers, who supported King Abdullah of Transjordan and his call for a Greater Syria, uniting Syria and Transjordan under Hashemite rule. Much of what Syria did in the resulting war was calculated to contain Transjordan. The Arab states ultimately went to war to prevent each other from altering the balance of power in the Arab world, rather than to save Arab Palestine.

The cynicism of Arab leaders was lost on Arab citizens, who applauded their governments' intervention to protect Arab Palestine from the Zionist threat. The Arab public, and the soldiers fighting in the Arab armies, were moved by the rhetoric and believed in the justice of their cause. Public disenchantment with their politicians in the aftermath of defeat would lead to great upheaval in the Arab world following the "loss" of Palestine.

In May 1948 the armies of the Arab states were not ready for war, in large part because most of those states had only just secured independence from their colonial rulers. France had retained control over the armed forces of Syria and Lebanon until 1946 and had left little behind in the way of arms and ammunition when its forces grudgingly withdrew. Britain had a monopoly on the supply of weapons to the armed forces of Egypt, Transjordan, and Iraq. The British guarded the flow of supplies to their semi-independent allies to ensure their national armies never posed a threat to British forces in the region.

The Arab armies were also quite small at the time. The whole of the Lebanese army probably did not exceed 3,500 soldiers, and their weapons were hopelessly out of date. The Syrian army did not exceed 6,000 men and was more of a threat than an asset to President al-Quwatli—hardly a month had passed in 1947 without rumors of a plotted military coup. In the end, the Syrians committed fewer than half their total military strength—perhaps 2,500 men—to the struggle in Palestine. The Iraqi army contributed 3,000 men. The Transjordanian Arab Legion was the best trained and most disciplined army in the region, but it could only commit 4,500 of its total strength of 6,000 men at the outset of the war. The Egyptians had the largest force and sent 10,000 troops into Palestine. Yet in spite of these constraints, Arab war planners were predicting a swift victory over Jewish forces within eleven days. If sincere, such an estimate confirms how little the Arab side appreciated the seriousness of the conflict that lay ahead.

Of all the Arab states, only Transjordan had a clear policy and interests in the Palestine conflict. King Abdullah had never been satisfied with the territory the British assigned him in 1921. He had aspired to restore his family's rule over Damascus (hence the call for a "Greater Syria") and since 1937 had supported the idea of a partition of Palestine in which the Arab territory would be annexed to his desert kingdom (hence the animosity between the mufti and King Abdullah).

King Abdullah had enjoyed extensive contacts with the Jewish Agency dating back to the 1920s. These contacts developed into secret negotiations during the UN debate on the partition of Palestine. In November 1947 King Abdullah met with Golda Meyerson (who later changed her name to Meir and rose to be Israel's prime minister) and hammered out a basic nonaggression pact two weeks before the passage of the UN Partition Resolution. Abdullah would not oppose the creation of a Jewish state in the territory authorized by the United Nations; in return, Transjordan would annex the Arab parts of Palestine that it bordered—in essence the West Bank.[25]

Transjordan needed Britain's approval to proceed with its plans to absorb the Arab parts of Palestine. In February 1948, Abdullah sent his premier, Tawfiq Abu al-Huda, to London, accompanied by his British commander, General John Bagot Glubb (better known as Glubb Pasha), to secure British consent for this plan. On February 7, Prime Minister Abu al-Huda set out Transjordan's plans to the British foreign secretary, Ernest Bevin: upon the termination of the Palestine mandate, the government of Transjordan would send the Arab Legion across the Jordan to occupy those Arab lands of Palestine that were contiguous to the frontiers of Transjordan.

"It seems the obvious thing to do," Bevin responded, "but do not go and invade the areas allotted to the Jews."

"We would not have the forces to do so, even if we so desired," Abu al-Huda replied. Bevin thanked the prime minister of Transjordan and expressed his full agreement with his plans for Palestine—essentially giving King Abdullah the green light to invade and annex the West Bank.[26]

Thus, alone among the Arab nations, Transjordan knew precisely why it was entering the Palestine theater of conflict, and what it sought to gain. The problem was that the other Arab states were all too aware of King Abdullah's ambitions, and they dedicated more effort to contain Transjordan than to save Palestine. Syria, Egypt, and Saudi Arabia constituted an undeclared bloc on Jordanian ambitions, and their actions actively hindered the sound conduct of war. Though the Arab League named King Abdullah commander in chief of the Arab forces, the commanders of the individual Arab armies refused to meet with him, let alone to accept any of his orders. Abdullah himself questioned the Arab League's intentions, asking an Egyptian military delegation on the eve of war: "The Arab League appointed me as the commander-in-chief of the Arab armies. Should not this honour be conferred on Egypt the largest of the Arab states? Or is the real purpose behind this appointment to pin the blame and responsibility on us in case of failure?"[27]

If the Arab states were hostile to Abdullah's intentions, they were none the more sympathetic to the Palestinians, given their animosity toward the Palestinian leader, Hajj Amin al-Husayni. The Iraqis begrudged Hajj Amin for the support he gave to Rashid Ali al-Kaylani's coup against the Hashemite monarchy in 1941. King Abdullah of Transjordan had long since fallen out with Hajj Amin over their rival ambitions to rule Arab Palestine. Egypt and Syria gave Hajj Amin only lukewarm support, particularly after the collapse of Palestinian defenses in April and May 1948.

The Arab coalition thus entered the Palestine War with largely negative goals: to prevent the establishment of an alien Jewish state in their midst, to prevent Transjordan from expanding into Palestine, and to keep the mufti from forming a viable Palestinian state. With such war aims, it is no surprise that the Arab forces found themselves overwhelmed by Jewish forces driven by a desperate determination to establish their state.

Jewish superiority in the battlefield was more a matter of manpower and firepower than willpower. The image of a Jewish David surrounded by a hostile Arab Goliath is not reflected in the relative size of Arab and Jewish forces. When five Arab states— Lebanon, Syria, Iraq, Transjordan, and Egypt—all went to war on May 15, total Arab forces did not exceed 25,000 men, whereas the Israel Defense Force (as the army of the new state was designated) numbered 35,000. In the course of the war, both the Arabs and the Israelis reinforced their troops, though the Arabs never came near to matching Israeli forces, which reached 65,000 in mid-July, and peaked at over 96,000 by December 1948.[28]

The Israelis needed their numerical advantage. In the first phase of the war, which ran from May 15 until the initial truce of June 11, they were forced to fight a multifront battle for survival. The army of Transjordan, known as the Arab Legion, crossed into the West Bank at dawn on May 15. Though at first reluctant to enter Jerusalem, which by the terms of the UN Partition Resolution was declared an international zone, the Arab Legion took up positions in the Arab quarters of Jerusalem on May 19 to prevent Israeli forces from overrunning the city. Meanwhile, the army of Iraq secured the northern half of the West Bank on May 22 and secured its positions in Nablus and Jenin without going on the offensive against Israeli forces. Egyptian units swept up from the Sinai into the Gaza Strip and Negev Desert, heading north to meet up with the Arab Legion. Syrian and Lebanese forces invaded Northern Palestine. During this first phase of the conflict, all sides took heavy losses, though the Israeli position was perhaps the most vulnerable of all for having to take on so many armies simultaneously.

With the outbreak of fighting between Israel and the Arab states, the United Nations convened to restore the peace. The UN called for a cease-fire on May 29, which came into effect on June 11. Count Folke Bernadotte, a Swedish diplomat, was appointed as official mediator in the conflict and entrusted with the mission of restoring peace in Palestine. The first truce was set for twenty-eight days, and a total embargo on arms was imposed on the region. The Arab states tried to secure arms for their depleted forces but found the British, French, and Americans scrupulously abiding by the terms of the embargo. The Israelis, in contrast, secured essential arm shipments via Czechoslovakia and increased their troop numbers to over 60,000 soldiers. When the cease-fire came to an end on July 9, Israel was better prepared than its adversaries for the resumption of hostilities.

In the second phase of the war, the Israelis used their superiority of troop numbers and munitions to turn the tide against the Arab armies on every front. They mauled Syrian forces in the Galilee and drove the Lebanese back across their own border. They seized the towns of Lydda and Ramla from the Arab Legion and focused their energies on Egyptian positions in the south. The United Nations, alarmed by the humanitarian crisis in Palestine as tens of thousands of refugees fled the fighting, resumed intensive diplomacy to secure a fresh cease-fire. The UN diplomats found the Arab states—several of which had nearly run out of ammunition—all too willing to support a truce. The second cease-fire came into effect on July 19 and lasted until October 14.

Whatever common aspirations the Arab states might have held before May 15 had been shattered by two disastrous months of war. The divisions between the Arab states, already deep before the start of the war, were seriously exacerbated by the losses their armies had suffered in the first two rounds of the war. Instead of a quick victory as the Arab League planners had optimistically foreseen, the Arab states saw their armies pinned down in a conflict that looked increasingly unwinnable. Nor did any of the Arab states see a clear exit strategy. Arab public opinion looked on in shocked disbelief as they saw their national armies subdued by a foe they had dismissed as mere "Jewish gangs."

Rather than accept the blame for their own lack of preparation and coordination, the Arab states began to pin the blame on each other. The Egyptians and Syrians turned on Transjordan. Hadn't King Abdullah met in secret with the Jews? Wasn't his British commander Glubb Pasha fulfilling Britain's promise to create a Jewish state in Palestine? The fact that the Arab Legion held the West Bank and Arab East Jerusalem against determined Israeli attacks was seen as proof of Jordanian treachery and collusion with the Zionists rather than valor. These squabbles had terrible consequences for the Arab war effort. The more the Arab states alienated each other, and acted in isolation, the easier it was for Israeli forces to pick off their armies one by one.

Count Bernadotte led UN efforts to find a resolution to the Arab-Israeli crises during the three months of cease-fire. On September 16 he proposed a revised partition plan for Palestine in which the Arab territories would be annexed to Transjordan, including the towns of Ramla and Lydda, which had fallen to the Israelis, and the Negev Desert, which had been allocated to the Jewish state by the original UN Partition Resolution. The state of Israel would comprise the Galilee and coastal plain, and Jerusalem would remain in international hands. Although both the Arabs and Israelis were quick to reject Bernadotte's plan, his diplomatic efforts were brutally cut short when terrorists from the Lehi assassinated the Swedish diplomat on September 17. With no prospect of a diplomatic solution, war resumed upon the expiration of the cease-fire on October 14.

In the third round of fighting, between October 15 and November 5, 1948, the Israelis completed the conquest of the Galilee region, driving all Syrian, Lebanese, and Arab Liberation Army forces back into Syrian and Lebanese territory. Thereafter, the Israelis concentrated all of their efforts on defeating the Egyptian forces. The Israeli army surrounded the isolated Egyptian units, and their air force pummeled Egyptian positions for three weeks.

Egyptian losses in Palestine would have serious political implications in Egypt. A large detachment of Egyptian forces was under siege in southern Palestine, in the village of Faluja, some 20 miles northeast of Gaza. Pinned down for weeks with little relief, the Egyptian soldiers felt betrayed. They had been sent to war with inadequate training, arms, and ammunition. The more politically minded officers had plenty of opportunity to meditate on the political bankruptcy of Egypt's monarchy and government. Among the officers trapped in Faluja were Gamal Abdel Nasser, Zakaria Mohi El Din, and Salah Salem—three of the Free Officers who later would plot the overthrow of the Egyptian monarchy. "We were fighting in Palestine but our dreams were in Egypt," Nasser wrote.[29] As a result of their experiences in the Arab-Israeli War, the Free Officers would eventually turn defeat in Palestine into victory in Egypt, vanquishing the very government that had betrayed them.

The Arab states continued to meet in a vain attempt at collective action to stave off disaster. On October 23 the Arab leaders convened in the Jordanian capital, Amman, to discuss a plan to relieve Egyptian forces, but mutual mistrust between Syria, Transjordan, and Iraq prevented any meaningful collaboration. The Egyptians, for their part, were loath to admit to their Arab brothers that they were beaten and refused to coordinate military action even when it would have brought their own besieged forces relief.

Arab division played to Israel's advantage. In December the Israelis not only succeeded in forcing a total Egyptian withdrawal from Palestine—aside from those Egyptian troops still encircled in Faluja—but actually invaded Egyptian territory in the Sinai. King Farouq's government had no choice but to invoke the 1936 Anglo-Egyptian Treaty—much despised by nationalists for the way it perpetuated Britain's influence in Egypt—to request British intervention to force an Israeli withdrawal from the Sinai. On January 7, 1949, a truce was struck between Egypt and Israel. The last Israeli offensive was in the Negev Desert, seizing territory down to Um Rashrash on the Gulf of Aqaba, where the port of Eilat would later be built.

With the conquest of the Negev, the new state of Israel took final shape within 78 percent of the territory of Mandate Palestine. Transjordan had retained the West Bank, and Egypt held the Gaza Strip, as the last territories of Palestine to remain in Arab hands. With the defeat of the Egyptian, Syrian, and Lebanese armies, and the containment of the Arab Legion and the Iraqi army, the Israelis won a comprehensive victory in 1948 and could impose their terms on the Arab states. The UN introduced a new cease-fire and opened armistice negotiations between Israel and its Arab neighbors on the Mediterranean island of Rhodes. Bilateral armistice agreements were concluded between Israel and Egypt (February), Lebanon (March), Transjordan (April), and Syria (July). The first Arab-Israeli War was over.

For the Palestinians, 1948 would be remembered as *al-Nakba*—the Disaster. Between the civil war and the Arab-Israeli War, some 750,000 Palestinians were reduced to refugees. They flooded into Lebanon, Syria, Transjordan, and Egypt, as well as to the surviving Arab territories of Palestine. Only the Gaza Strip and the West Bank, including East Jerusalem, remained in Arab hands. The Gaza Strip came under Egyptian trusteeship as a nominally self-governing territory. The West Bank was annexed to Transjordan, which, now spanning both banks of the River Jordan, shortened its name to Jordan.

At the end of the first Arab-Israeli war, there was no place left on the map called Palestine, only a dispersed Palestinian people living under foreign occupation or in the diaspora, who would spend the rest of their history fighting for recognition of their national rights.

_____

The entire Arab world was stunned by the magnitude of the Palestine disaster. Yet in this moment of crisis, Arab intellectuals proved remarkably clear-sighted about both the causes and the consequences of the loss of Palestine.

Two critical works appeared in the immediate aftermath of the first Arab-Israeli War that set the tone for Arab self-criticism and reform. The first was written by Constantine Zurayk, one of the great Arab intellectuals of the twentieth century. Born in Damascus in 1909, Zurayk had completed his B.A. at the American University of Beirut, his M.A. at the University of Chicago, and his doctorate at Princeton—all by the age of twenty-one. He spent his life between academic and public service in Lebanon and Syria, and wrote a string of hugely influential works on Arab nationalism. It was Zurayk who gave the 1948 war its Arabic name, al-Nakba, with his influential tract *Ma'nat al-Nakba* (or, "The Meaning of the Disaster"), published in Beirut at the height of the war in August 1948.[30]

The second landmark book was written by a Palestinian notable named Musa Alami. The son of a former mayor of Jerusalem, Alami studied law at Cambridge before entering service with the mandate government in Palestine. He rose to the rank of Arab secretary to the high commissioner and crown counsel before resigning in 1937 at the height of the Arab Revolt, to enter private practice and support the nationalist movement. Alami represented Palestinian aspirations in the London conferences of 1939 and 1946–1947 and served as Palestinian representative to the formative meetings of the Arab League. His March 1949 essay *'Ibrat Filastin* ("The Lesson of Palestine"), reflected on the Arabs' total defeat and the route to national regeneration.[31]

Both authors recognized that the loss of Palestine and the creation of Israel opened a dangerous new chapter in Arab history. "The defeat of the Arabs in Palestine," Zurayk warned, "is no simple setback or light, passing evil. It is a disaster in every sense of the word and one of the harshest of the trials and tribulations with which the Arabs have been afflicted throughout their long history—a history marked by numerous trials and tribulations."[32] Arab failure to confront this new danger would condemn them to a future of division and rule, not so unlike the colonial era from which they were only just gaining their independence.

Given the similarities in their diagnoses of Arab ills, it is not surprising that Alami and Zurayk recommended similar cures. The spectacle of Arab divisions impressed on both men the need for Arab unity. The post–World War I settlement, and the

partition of the Arab world between Britain and France, had fragmented and weakened the Arab nation. The Arabs, they argued, would only realize their potential as
a people by overcoming the divisions of the imperial order through Arab unity. They
recognized the contradictions between narrow nation-state nationalism (e.g., the
distinct nationalism of Egyptians or Syrians) and the broader Arab nation to which
they aspired. Zurayk believed formal union was impossible in the short term, given
deeply entrenched national interests among the newly emergent independent Arab
states. So, in the first instance, Zurayk called for "far-reaching, comprehensive
changes" to the existing Arab states in advance of the long-term goal of unity.[33]
Alami placed his hopes in an "Arab Prussia" that might, through force of arms,
achieve the desired unity.[34] The role of Arab Prussia would appeal to a number of
nationalists in the upper ranks of Arab armies, as the military men prepared to take
their place on the political stage in the aftermath of the Palestine disaster.

In their response to the Palestine disaster, Alami and Zurayk both called for nothing short of an Arab renaissance as prelude to Arab unity, and as a prerequisite for
the redemption of Palestine and Arab self-respect in the modern world. Their books
enjoyed wide circulation and were hugely influential, precisely because their analyses
reflected the spirit of their times. Arab citizens had grown deeply disenchanted with
their rulers. The old political elites, who had led the struggle for national independence, had grown tainted by association with their imperial masters. They had been
educated in European universities and spoke their language, they dressed in Western
clothes, they worked through the institutions imposed by colonialism—all in all,
they reeked of collaboration. They bickered over small gains, and their worldview
had been narrowed to the borders of the states the imperialists had imposed on them.

Politicians in the Arab world had lost sight of the greater Arab nation that still
inspired so many of their fellow citizens. The bankruptcy of their politics had been
revealed to all through the disastrous Arab performance in Palestine. Hence the
remedies proposed by Alami and Zurayk, of a greater Arab nation composed of empowered citizens facing the challenges of the modern age with the strength of unity,
struck so many Arabs as the obvious solution to their present weakness. The lesson
of Palestine was that divided, the Arabs were sure to fall, and only if united could
they hope to withstand the challenges of the modern world.

The times were changing. Arab rulers were gravely weakened by their failures in
Palestine. A new generation was rising to the call of Arab nationalism and took their
own governments as their first targets.

Arab defeat in Palestine and the emergence of the state of Israel completely destabilized the newly independent Arab states. The months immediately following

al-Nakba were stained by political assassinations and coups in Egypt, Syria, Lebanon, and Jordan.

Following the Palestine disaster, Egypt was thrown into political chaos. For a new religious party, the loss of Muslim land to create a Jewish state was nothing short of a betrayal of Islam. The Egyptian Muslim Brotherhood had been founded in March 1928 by Hasan al-Banna, a primary school teacher in the Suez Canal city of Ismailiyya. Al-Banna was a charismatic reformer who fought against the Western influences that he believed were undermining Islamic values in Egypt. Between European-inspired reforms and British imperialism, al-Banna argued, the people of Egypt had "departed from the goals of their faith."[35] What began as a movement for the renewal of faith within Egyptian society evolved into a powerful political force that had, by the late 1940s, come to rival in power the established parties, even the Wafd.

The Brotherhood had declared the Palestine War a jihad and dispatched battalions of volunteers into Palestine to fight against the creation of a Jewish state. Like the other Arab volunteers in the Liberation Army, they had underestimated Jewish strength and organization. Unprepared for battle, they were equally unprepared for defeat. They saw the Arab failure in Palestine as a betrayal of religion and pinned the blame on Arab governments generally and on the Egyptian government in particular. They returned to Egypt to organize demonstrations and accused the government of responsibility for the defeat.

The Egyptian government took quick action to suppress the Muslim Brotherhood. In the closing months of 1948, the organization was accused of fomenting riots and plotting the overthrow of the Egyptian government. Prime Minister Mahmud Fahmi al-Nuqrashi, who had declared martial law, approved a decree dissolving the Muslim Brotherhood on December 8, 1948. The assets of the society were frozen, its records seized, and many of its leaders arrested.

The leader of the Muslim Brotherhood, Hasan al-Banna, was left at liberty, and he tried to reconcile extremists inside his own movement with the government. His efforts were undermined by intransigence on both sides. Prime Minister al-Nuqrashi refused to meet with al-Banna or to make any concessions to the Brotherhood. Extremists within the society resorted to violence. On December 28, the Egyptian premier was gunned down while entering the Ministry of Interior, shot at close range by a veterinary student who had been a member of the Brotherhood since 1944. Al-Nuqrashi was the first Arab leader to fall in the tense aftermath of the Palestine disaster.

The government never arrested Hasan al-Banna for al-Nuqrashi's assassination. The leader of the Muslim Brotherhood took little comfort in his freedom, knowing that so long as he was at liberty he would be at risk of a retaliatory assassination. Al-Banna tried to negotiate with al-Nuqrashi's successor but found all government doors closed to him. He protested the Brotherhood's innocence of all attempts to overthrow the political system, but to no avail.

On February 12, 1949, Hasan al-Banna was shot and killed outside the head-quarters of the Young Men's Muslim Association. It was widely assumed that the assassination had been ordered by the government with the support of the palace. The two political murders in the space of six weeks raised political tensions in Egypt to unprecedented levels.

In Syria, the Palestine disaster provoked a military coup d'état. President Shukri al-Quwatli had long feared that his army would overthrow him, and on March 30, 1949, his fears were vindicated. Colonel Husni al-Za'im, army chief of staff, led a bloodless coup described by veteran Syrian political Adil Arslan as "the most significant and strangest event in recent Syrian history." In his diary, Arslan elaborated: "The general public celebrated, and the majority of the students took the opportunity to hold demonstrations in the streets. However, the political elites were struck silent with anxiety over the fate of their country."[36] Syria's political elite were anxious to preserve the young Syrian republic's democratic institutions. They feared military dictatorship, and with good reason. Though al-Za'im's government lasted less than 150 days, his coup marked the entry of the military into Syrian politics. Except for a couple of brief hiatuses, military men would remained in control of Syria for the rest of the century.

One of the strangest aspects of al-Za'im's rule, according to his foreign minister, Adil Arslan, was his willingness to come to terms with Israel so soon after Syria's defeat. The armistice between Syria and Israel was concluded by Husni al-Za'im's government on July 20, 1949. Behind the scenes, al-Za'im was willing to go be-yond an armistice, to pursue a comprehensive peace treaty with Israel. With the full support of the U.S. government, al-Za'im relayed a series of proposals to Israeli prime minister David Ben-Gurion through the Syrian team at the armistice nego-tiations. Al-Za'im offered full normalization of relations between Syria and the Jew-ish state—an exchange of ambassadors, open borders, and full economic relations with Israel.

Al-Za'im's proposal to settle up to 300,000 Palestinian refugees in Syria attracted the attention of both American and UN officials. It was already clear that the refugee problem would prove the greatest humanitarian issue and a major sticking point in resolving the Arab-Israeli conflict. Al-Za'im sought U.S. development assistance for the Jazira District, north of the Euphrates River, where he proposed to settle the Palestinians. He believed that the injection of Palestinian labor and American funds would help modernize his country and develop its economy.[37]

The Israeli prime minister had no interest in al-Za'im's offer. Despite the best efforts of the Truman administration, UN mediator Dr. Ralph Bunche, and the Is-raeli foreign minister, Moshe Sharett, Ben-Gurion refused to meet with al-Za'im or even to discuss his proposals. Ben-Gurion insisted the Syrians sign an armistice first.

He knew that al-Za'im wanted to adjust Syria's boundaries to divide the Lake of Tiberias between Syria and Israel, which Ben-Gurion rejected out of hand. The Israeli prime minister was in no hurry to conclude peace deals with his Arab neighbors, and he certainly did not want to set a precedent of making territorial concessions to secure peace. If anything, Ben-Gurion worried that the boundaries of Israel, as reflected in the armistice agreements with its Arab neighbors, fell well short of the needs of the Jewish state.

When Ben-Gurion refused to meet with al-Za'im, the U.S. administration suggested a meeting between the foreign ministers of Syria and Israel. The U.S. ambassador to Damascus, James Keeley, approached al-Za'im's foreign minister, Adil Arslan, to propose the meeting. Arslan was the scion of a princely Druze family who had entered government under al-Za'im with some misgivings. In his diary he described the colonel as both a friend and a madman, though Keeley's proposal, recorded by Arslan in his diary on June 6, 1949, convinced him that al-Za'im had lost his bearings.

"Why do you want me to agree to hold a meeting with [Israeli foreign minister Moshe] Shertok," Arslan asked the U.S. ambassador, "when you know that I have never been fooled by the bluffs of the Jews, and I am the last among the Arabs to make concessions to them?"

"Your question forces me to give you a candid reply," Keeley responded, "though I am not at liberty to discuss the matter, which remains secret. However, as I know you are an honourable man, I would ask for your word to keep the matter secret."

Arslan gave his word, and Keeley continued. "It was Za'im who suggested he meet with Ben-Gurion . . . who refused, so we [i.e., the U.S. administration] thought a meeting might be held between the foreign ministers of Syria and Israel. Shertok agreed, and put forward the suggestion which you have now rejected."

The astonished Arslan tried to hide his emotions as Keeley exposed al-Za'im's secret diplomacy with the Israelis, and tried to dismiss the overture as a diplomatic ploy by the Syrian president. The American did not force the point and withdrew, leaving Arslan to contemplate his next move.[38]

Arslan stayed in his office late that night. He conferred with a member of the Syrian delegation to the armistice talks, who was convinced al-Za'im intended to meet with Shertok himself. Arslan considered stepping down but decided to stay in office to keep the Israelis from achieving their objective of getting Syria to break ranks with the other Arab states by concluding a separate peace deal. He began to contact other Arab governments to warn them of "a great danger," though he was careful not to reveal what it was.

Arslan's reaction indicates how out of touch al-Za'im had grown with both Syrian public opinion and the views of the political elite. Coming out of a bruising defeat, the Syrians were in no mood to make peace with Israel—the army least of all. Had al-Za'im gone public with his peace plan, he would have faced insurmountable opposition at home. Even so, too many respected international figures, including U.S. Secretary of State Dean Acheson, UN mediator Ralph Bunche, and a host of Israeli political and intelligence agents, were sufficiently persuaded of the merits of al-Za'im's plan at the time for us to dismiss it out of hand today. What does emerge from the story is that it was in fact Ben-Gurion who ruled out the first Arab peace initiative. Faced with a peace plan that had both U.S. and UN backing, Ben-Gurion said no.

Al-Za'im did not head Syria long enough to give peace a chance. His reforms (of which peace overtures with Israel represented but a small part) alienated the different social groups that had originally supported his rise to power, leaving him isolated. Some of the officers who had supported his coup now plotted against him. On August 14, 1949, they repeated the measures taken in the March coup, arresting leading government figures and securing the radio station. A group of six armored cars surrounded al-Za'im's house and, after a brief shootout, arrested the deposed president. Al-Za'im and his premier were taken to a detention center, where they were summarily executed.

The man who arrested and executed Husni al-Za'im was a follower of Antun Sa'ada, one of the most influential nationalist leaders in the Arab world. Sa'ada (1904–1949) was a Christian intellectual who returned to his native Lebanon from Brazil in 1932 to found the Syrian Social Nationalist Party. A lecturer at the American University of Beirut, he opposed the French mandate and its efforts to break up Greater Syria, and he militated for a union of the states of Greater Syria. His political views provided an alternative to pan-Arab nationalism and, with his call for separation of religion from politics, appealed to a wide range of minority groups who feared Sunni Muslim domination in a pan-Arab state.

In July 1949, Antun Sa'ada launched a guerrilla campaign to overturn the Lebanese government. His revolt was short-lived; he was caught by the Syrians within days of launching his campaign and handed over to the Lebanese authorities, who promptly tried and executed the would-be revolutionary on July 8, 1949.

Sa'ada's zealous followers were quick to seek their revenge. On July 16, 1951, a Sa'ada partisan assassinated the former Lebanese premier, Riyad al-Sulh (whose government had executed Sa'ada) while he was on a visit to the Jordanian capital, Amman.

Arab politics were growing increasingly violent as political coups, executions, and assassinations marked the change of leadership in Arab states. Only four days after the assassination of Riyad al-Sulh, King Abdullah of Transjordan was assassinated as he entered the al-Aqsa Mosque in Jerusalem for Friday prayers. His fifteen-year-old grandson Hussein, the future king of Jordan, was with him when he was killed.

"I wonder now," Hussein wrote in his autobiography, "looking back across the years, whether my grandfather had an inner knowledge of the tragedy that was so close." Hussein remembered a conversation with King Abdullah on the morning of his death. The old king spoke words "so prophetic that I would hesitate to repeat them had they not been heard by a dozen men alive today," Hussein recorded. "'When I have to die, I would like to be shot in the head by a nobody,' he said. 'That's the simplest way of dying. I would rather have that than become old and a burden.'" The old king would see his wish granted sooner than he expected.

King Abdullah knew that his life was in danger. He was surrounded by enemies in the Palestinian territories recently annexed to his kingdom. Many Palestinians accused him of striking a bargain with the Jews to expand his country at their expense, and Hajj Amin al-Husayni blamed King Abdullah for betraying Palestine. Yet, no one could have foreseen the new culture of Arab political violence reach right into one of the holiest Muslim places of worship.

The "nobody" who shot King Abdullah was a twenty-one-year-old tailor's apprentice from Jerusalem named Mustafa 'Ashu. More a hired gun than a man with political motives, 'Ashu himself was shot dead instantly by the king's guard. Scores of arrests were made, and ten men were charged with complicity in the assassination, though the trial did little to shed light on who lay behind the king's murder. Four of the ten were acquitted, two condemned to death in absentia (both had defected to Egypt), and four men hanged for their role in the assassination. Three of the men who were executed were common tradesmen—a cattle broker, a butcher, and a café owner—with criminal records. The fourth, Musa al-Husayni, was a distant relative of the mufti's.[39] Both the mufti and King Farouq of Egypt were suspected of bankrolling the assassination, though the truth has now surely been lost forever. Ultimately, King Abdullah was another victim of the Palestine disaster.

After the post–World War I partition of the Middle East, the Palestine disaster stands as the most important turning point in twentieth century Arab history. We are still living its consequences today.

Among the most enduring legacies of the war is the Arab-Israeli conflict that continues today. Between Arab refusal to accept the loss of Palestine and Israeli aspirations for more territory, further Arab-Israeli wars became inevitable and have recurred with deadly frequency over the past six decades.

The human costs of this conflict have been devastating. The Palestinian refugee problem remains unresolved. The original 750,000 displaced persons now exceeds 4.3 million refugees registered with the United Nations, the result of further territorial losses in 1967 and natural growth over sixty years. Over the intervening decades, the

Palestinians have created representative bodies to advance their goal of statehood, but they have also pursued their goals through armed struggle ranging from border raids on Israel to terrorist attacks on Israeli interests abroad, to popular insurrection and armed resistance in the Occupied Gaza Strip and West Bank, and terror attacks against Israel. In spite of—some would argue, because of—these strategies, Palestinian national aspirations have gone unfulfilled.

The Palestine disaster had a terrible impact on Arab politics. The hopes and aspirations of the newly independent Arab states were overshadowed by their failure in 1948. In the aftermath of defeat in Palestine, the Arab world witnessed tremendous political upheaval. The four states bordering Mandate Palestine were wracked with political assassinations, coups, and revolution. A major social revolution was taking place, as the old elites were overthrown by a younger generation of military men, many from rural backgrounds who were more in touch with popular politics than the foreign-educated political elites of the interwar years. Whereas the old-guard politicians struggled for national independence within the boundaries of their own states, the firebrand Free Officers were Arab nationalists who promoted pan-Arab unity. The *ancien regime* spoke European languages; the new vanguard spoke the language of the street.

In a very real sense, the Palestine disaster spelled the end of European influence in the Arab world. Palestine was a problem made in Europe, and Europe's inability to resolve the problem reflected its own weakness in the aftermath of the Second World War. Britain and France emerged from that conflict as second-rate powers. The British economy was in tatters after the war effort, and French morale was shattered by years of German occupation. Both had too much to rebuild at home to invest much abroad. Empire was on the retreat, and new powers dominated the international system.

The young officers who came to power in Syria in 1949, in Egypt in 1952, and in Iraq in 1958 had no ties to Britain or France and looked instead to the new world powers—the United States and its superpower rival, the Soviet Union. It was the end of the imperial age and the beginning of the new age of the Cold War. The Arabs would have to adapt to a new set of rules.

CHAPTER 10

The Rise of Arab Nationalism

The Arab world entered the new era of the Cold War in a state of revolutionary ferment. The anti-imperialism of the interwar years gained renewed vigor at the end of the Second World War. Hostility toward Britain and France was rife in the aftermath of the Palestine War. This complicated Britain's position in Egypt, Jordan, and Iraq, where it still enjoyed preferential alliances with the monarchies it had created.

The old nationalist politicians, and the kings they served, were discredited for their failure to make a clean break from British imperial rule. A host of radical new parties, ranging from the Islamist Muslim Brothers to the Communists, vied for the allegiance of a new generation of nationalists. The young officers in the military were not immune to the political ferment of the age. The younger generation questioned the legitimacy of Arab monarchies and the multiparty parliaments installed by the British, instead showing more enthusiasm for revolutionary republicanism.

The transcendental ideology of the age was Arab nationalism. Liberation from colonial rule was the common wish of all Arab peoples by the 1940s, but they had yet higher political aspirations. Most people in the Arab world believed they were united by a common language, history, and culture grounded in the Islamic past, a culture shared by Muslims and non-Muslims. They wanted to dissolve the frontiers drafted by the imperial powers to divide the Arabs and build a new commonwealth based on the deep historic and cultural ties that bound the Arabs. They believed that Arab greatness in world affairs could only be restored through unity. And they took to the streets, in their thousands, to protest against imperialism, to criticize their governments' failings, and to demand Arab unity.

Egypt was in many ways at the forefront of these developments. Medical doctor and feminist intellectual Nawal El Saadawi entered medical school in Cairo in 1948.

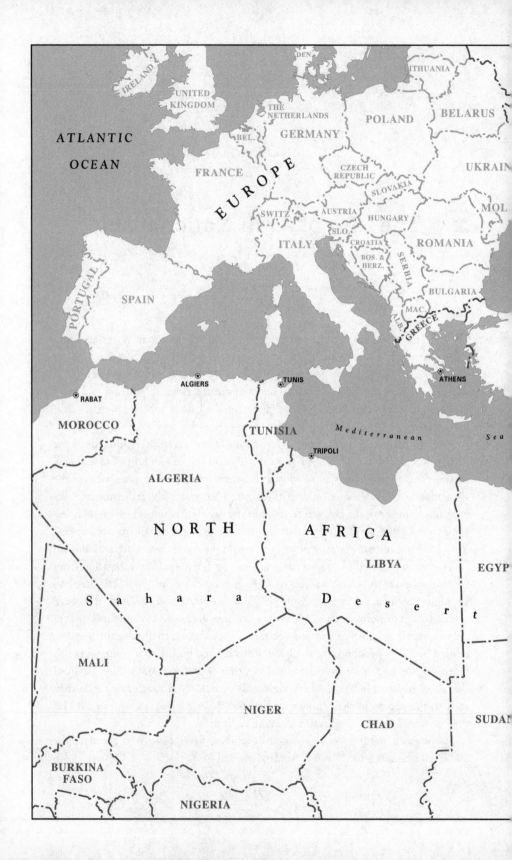

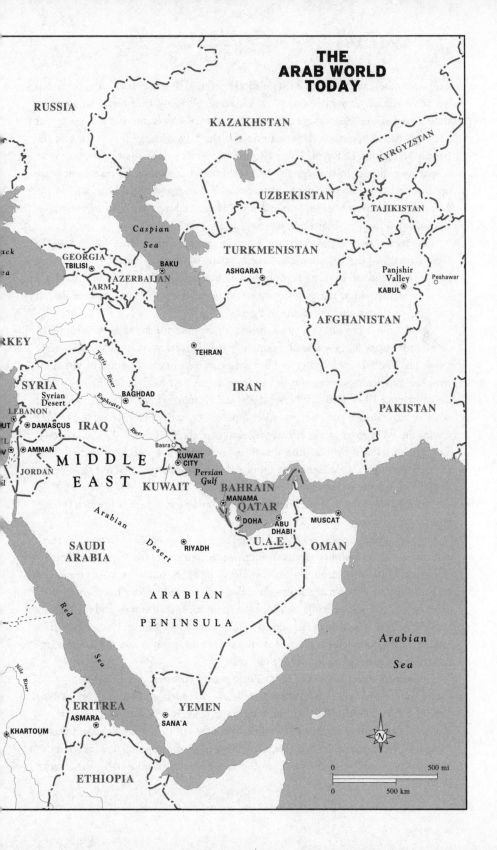

The atmosphere was charged with political tension. "In those days," she recalled in her autobiography, "the university was the scene of almost continuous demonstrations." Saadawi was no stranger to nationalist politics. Her father read the newspaper with her and condemned the corruption of the king, the military class, and the British occupation of Egypt. "It's a chronic triple misery and there's no solution to it without a change in the regime," he would tell his daughter. "People must wake up, must rebel."[1] The younger Saadawi took her father's words to heart and by the time she was a high school student had already begun taking part in the mass demonstrations that brought Cairo to a standstill in the late 1940s.

The demonstrations reflected the Egyptian people's impatience for change. In the aftermath of the Palestine disaster Egyptians were disenchanted with political parties, disillusioned by King Farouq, and increasingly intolerant of the British position in their country. The postwar era was an age of decolonization, and the British had long outstayed their welcome in Egypt.

Egypt went to the polls in 1950 to elect a new government after the turmoil of defeat in Palestine and the assassination of Prime Minister al-Nuqrashi in December 1948. The Wafd secured victory and formed a government that resumed negotiations with the British to achieve the full independence that had eluded Egyptian nationalists since 1919. Between March 1950 and October 1951, the Wafd conducted talks with the British government. After nineteen months of talks failed to produce results, the Wafd government unilaterally abrogated the 1936 Anglo-Egyptian Treaty. The British refused to recognize the abrogation, which would have turned their forces in the Suez Canal Zone into an illegal army of occupation. And though the British Empire was on the retreat—the British had withdrawn from India in 1947— the strategic importance of the Suez Canal remained a cornerstone of British foreign policy.

Having failed to achieve its goals through negotiation, the Wafd stepped up pressure on the British by other means. With the tacit approval of the Wafd government, young men—mostly Muslim Brothers, students, peasants, and workers—volunteered for guerrilla units, known as *fida'iyin* (literally, "fighters ready to sacrifice themselves"). In October 1951 the guerrilla bands began to attack British troops and facilities in the Canal Zone. The British responded to these attacks with force. One of Nawal El Saadawi's classmates left his medical studies to join the fida'iyin and was killed in action against the British, a martyr for the cause.

The armed struggle in the Canal Zone provoked intense political debates in Cairo. Saadawi remembered a student rally she attended at the university in November 1951. She listened with growing impatience to the student politicians— Wafdists, Communists, Muslim Brothers—as they struck heroic poses and waxed rhetorical. Then one of the fida'iyin, a man named Ahmed Helmi, was called to the podium. He was one of the freedom fighters who had taken part in the attacks on British troops occupying the Canal Zone. He appealed to his squabbling class-mates in a quiet voice. "Colleagues," he explained, "the freedom fighters in the Canal Zone need ammunition and rations, their rear lines have to be stable to protect them, there is no time, no room for partisan struggles. We need unity of the people."[2] Saadawi was riveted by the intense young man and later married him.

By January 1952 the British had decided to use military force to assert their con-trol over the Suez Canal Zone. British forces began to occupy Egyptian police sta-tions in the Canal Zone in order to prevent the policemen from lending their support to the fida'iyin. On January 24 the British secured the surrender of 160 po-licemen in their station in one of the canal towns without a fight. The Egyptian government was embarrassed by the ease with which the British had taken over the station, and in response it called on Egyptian policemen in the Canal Zone to resist the British "to the last bullet." The opportunity came the very next day, when 1,500 British troops surrounded the governorate in Ismailiyya and demanded its surrender. The 250 policemen guarding the government offices refused. The British pummeled Egyptian positions with tank and artillery fire for nine hours, as the Egyptians fought until their ammunition was depleted. By the time they finally surrendered, the Egyp-tians had suffered forty-six dead and seventy-two wounded.

News of the British assault provoked outrage across Egypt. A general strike was declared for the next day, Saturday, January 26, 1952. Workers and students con-verged on Cairo in the tens of thousands. The city braced itself for a day of mass demonstrations protesting the British action. Yet nothing had prepared the people or government of Egypt for Black Saturday.

Dark forces were at work in Cairo on Black Saturday. What began as a series of angry demonstrations quickly degenerated into violence in which over fifty Egyptians and seventeen foreigners (including nine Britons) were killed by the crowd. Provoca-teurs and arsonists worked under the cover of the demonstrations to generate maxi-mum disorder. Anouar Abdel Malek, a Communist intellectual who witnessed the events of Black Saturday, described how the demonstrators stood aside to watch in fascination as the arsonists put the richest quarters of central Cairo to the torch. "They watched as they did because the splendid capital belonged not to them but to the rich whose businesses were burning. So they let it go."[3] In the course of the day, crowds torched a British club, a Jewish school, an office of the Muslim Brothers, four hotels (including the famous Shepheard's Hotel), four night clubs, seven department stores, seventeen cafés and restaurants, eighteen cinemas, and seventy other commercial es-tablishments, including banks, automobile display rooms, and airline ticket offices.[4]

The terrible events of January 25–26, 1952, spelled the end of the political order in Egypt. It was clear to all that the arson attacks, unprecedented in Egypt's history, had been planned. Rumors and conspiracy theories swept the capital. The Commu-nists blamed the Socialists and the Muslim Brothers. Some argued it was a plot to undermine the position of King Farouq (who hosted a banquet celebrating the birth of his son on the night Cairo burned). Others maintained the fire was planned by the king and the British to bring down the Wafd and to appoint a caretaker government that would be more responsive to the king's wishes.

Whatever his role in Black Saturday, King Farouq did dismiss the Wafd government of Mustafa Nahhas on January 27 and appointed a series of cabinets headed by independent politicians loyal to the throne. Parliament was dissolved on March 24, and elections for a new assembly were postponed indefinitely. It looked as though Farouq was following in his father's footsteps and repeating the 1930 experiment of palace rule. Public confidence in the government of Egypt plummeted.

Ultimately, it matters little who ordered the burning of Cairo (there never has been a conclusive answer to the question). The rumors and conspiracy theories revealed a crisis of confidence in both the monarchy and the government that presaged the coming revolution in Egypt.

Though many were talking about revolution in Egypt in 1952, only a small group of army officers was actively plotting the overthrow of the government at the time. They called themselves the Free Officers, and their leader was a young colonel named Gamal Abdel Nasser. The Free Officers were united by their patriotism and the firm belief that Egypt's monarchy and parliamentary government had failed the country. Nasser and his colleagues had been appalled by their experiences in the Palestine War, when they were sent to battle without adequate weapons and found themselves besieged by the Israelis for months and ultimately defeated. The Free Officers came together initially to oppose British imperialism in Egypt. In time, they came to see the political system of Egypt as the main obstacle to realizing their aspirations for total independence from Britain.

In the aftermath of the Palestine War, Nasser recruited some of his most trusted colleagues to join a secret political cell of military men. He drew Palestine War veterans like Abd al-Hakim Amer and Salah Salem; men with connections to the Muslim Brothers, like Anwar Sadat; and Communists, like Khaled Mohi El Din, in an effort to secure the broadest support for their actions. They held their first meeting in Nasser's living room in the autumn of 1949. As the Free Officers organization grew, new cells were created independent of each other to evade detection. Members of each cell recruited like-minded officers from across the different branches of the Egyptian armed forces.[5] They issued their first leaflet in fall 1950 to generate support in the officer corps for their anti-imperialist cause.[6]

The events of Black Saturday transformed the Free Officers movement. Until January 1952 their focus had been on combating imperialism, and they had restricted their criticism of the government to issues of corruption and collaboration with the British. After January 1952 the Free Officers began to discuss openly the overthrow of King Farouq and the royalist governments he appointed. They set a target date for their coup in November 1952 and began to escalate their recruitment and mobilization of opposition officers.

The confrontation between the palace and the Free Officers came to a head over the seemingly innocuous elections to the Egyptian Officers' Club executive in December 1951. For Farouq, the Officers' Club served as a barometer of the military's loyalty to the monarchy. The Free Officers decided to use the elections as a means to confront the king and his supporters. Nasser and his colleagues convinced the popular general Muhammad Naguib to run for president of the club at the head of an opposition slate for the board of directors. When Naguib and the opposition slate swept the elections, King Farouq tried by all means to have the results over-turned. Finally, in July 1952, Farouq intervened personally to dismiss Naguib and to dissolve the board of the Officers' Club. The Free Officers recognized that they would lose all credibility if they did not respond to the king's challenge immediately. As Abd al-Hakim Amer, one of Nasser's closest colleagues, warned the other Free Officers, "The King has dealt us a strong blow, and unless we reply in the same manner, our organization will lose its credibility with the officers and no one will agree to join us."[7]

The Free Officers were in total agreement that failure to act quickly and decisively would land them all in jail. Nasser met with the senior statesman of the Free Officers, General Naguib, to plan an immediate coup against the monarchy. "We unanimously agreed that Egypt was now fully ripe for a revolution," Naguib recalled in his memoirs. The king and his cabinet were in their summer residences in Alexandria, leaving Cairo to the military men. "It was so hot and sultry that no one besides ourselves would be thinking in terms of an immediate revolution," Naguib reasoned. "It was therefore the ideal time for us to strike." They resolved to act before the king had time to appoint a new cabinet "and before his spies had time to discover who we were and what we had in mind."[8]

The Free Officers had reached the point of no return. The risks of plotting against the regime were high. The Free Officers knew they would face charges of treason if they failed. They went over their plans very carefully: the simultaneous occupation of the radio station and the military headquarters. The mobilization of loyal military units behind the coup plotters. Measures to ensure public security and to prevent foreign intervention. There were many details to get right in advance of the coup date of July 23, 1952.

The coup plotters were under close government scrutiny, adding to the intense pressures of the last days before the coup. General Naguib was warned by one of his officers on the eve of the coup that he was about to be arrested on suspicion of leading a conspiracy against the government. "I did my best to conceal my alarm,"

Naguib confessed in his memoirs. He decided to stay at home that night, while the coup unfolded, claiming he was under surveillance and feared he might compromise the Free Officers' plans.[9] Anwar Sadat took his wife to the cinema that night, where he got into a very noisy fight with another moviegoer and went to the police station to file a complaint—as good an alibi as a coup plotter could hope for in case of failure.[10] Even Gamal Abdel Nasser and Abd al-Hakim Amer surprised their supporters when they showed up for the coup dressed in civilian clothes (they later changed into uniform).[11]

In spite of their doubts and fears, the Free Officers succeeded in orchestrating a near-bloodless coup. Rebel military units surrounded Egyptian army headquarters and overcame light resistance to occupy the facility by 2:00 A.M. on the morning of July 23. Once the headquarters had been secured, the military units supporting the coup were given the go-ahead to occupy strategic points in Cairo while the city slumbered. When the army had taken its positions, Anwar Sadat went to the national radio station and announced the coup in the name of General Muhammad Naguib, as commander in chief of the armed forces, completing what had been a classic coup d'état.

Nawal El Saadawi was working in the Kasr al-Aini Hospital in central Cairo on July 23, and she described the exultation that followed on from the announcement. "In the wards the patients had been listening to the radio. Suddenly the music broke off for an important announcement which said that the army had taken over control of the country and that Farouk was no longer king." She was astonished by the patients' spontaneous reaction. "Suddenly as we stood there the patients rushed out of the wards shouting 'Long live the revolution!' I could see their mouths wide open, their arms waving in the air, their tattered shirts fluttering around their bodies. It was as though the corpses from the dissecting hall had suddenly risen from the dead and were shouting 'Long live the revolution!'" Indeed, even the dead were stopped in their tracks, as she saw a funeral cortege leaving the hospital brought to a halt by the news. "The men carrying the coffin put it down on the pavement and mixed with the crowd shouting 'Long live the revolution!' and the women who a moment ago had been mourning the defunct started to shrill out [in celebration] instead of shrieks."[12]

King Farouq and his government crumpled on July 23. Yet the Free Officers had little idea of how to proceed now that their movement had succeeded. "It was obvious that we hadn't prepared ourselves, when we carried out our revolution, for taking over government posts," Sadat reflected in his memoirs. "We had no ambition to be government ministers. We had not envisaged that and had not even drawn up a specific government program."[13] They decided to ask veteran politician Ali Maher to form a new government. The Free Officers had no idea what to do with Farouq himself: Arrest him? Execute him? Nasser made the wise decision to secure Farouq's abdication and allow him to go into exile rather than risk tying up the new government with potentially divisive judicial proceedings or turning an unpopular monarch into a martyr through a messy execution. Farouq abdicated in favor of his infant son Ahmed Fuad II, under a regent, and was seen off by General Naguib on July 26 with a twenty-one-gun salute from Alexandria in the royal yacht Mahroussa.

"I saluted him and he returned my salute," Naguib recalled in his memoirs:

> A long and embarrassing pause ensued. Neither of us knew what to say.
> "It was you, *effendim* [My Lord], who forced us to do what we have done."
> Faruk's reply will puzzle me for the rest of my life.
> "I know," he said. "You've done what I always intended to do myself."
> I was so surprised that I could think of nothing more to say. I saluted and the others did likewise. Faruk returned our salutes and we all shook hands.
> "I hope you'll take good care of the Army," he said. "My grandfather, you know, created it."
> "The Egyptian Army," I said, "is in good hands."
> "Your task will be difficult. It isn't easy, you know, to govern Egypt."[14]

General Naguib in fact would be given little chance to govern Egypt. The real leader in Egypt was Nasser, as would soon become apparent.

The Free Officers revolution represented the advent of a newer, younger generation in Egyptian politics. Naguib, at age fifty-one, was the old man in a movement whose average age was thirty-four. All were native-born Egyptians of rural origins who had risen through the military to positions of responsibility—much like the men around Colonel Ahmad Urabi in the 1880s.

Like Urabi, the Free Officers chafed at the privileges and pretensions of the Turco-Circassian elites that had surrounded the royal family. One of their first decrees after taking power was to abolish all Turkish titles such as bey and pasha, which they believed had been conferred by "an abnormal King . . . on people who did not deserve them."[15]

Stripped of its titles, the Egyptian aristocracy was next deprived of its land. The Free Officers initiated a major land reform, passing laws that limited individual land holdings to 200 acres. The vast plantations of the royal family were confiscated by the state, and some 1,700 large landholders saw their estates expropriated by the government, which reimbursed them in thirty-year bonds. In all, some 365,000 acres were seized from Egypt's landed elite. These lands were then redistributed to small holders with no more than five acres of property. The program passed over the strenuous objections of Prime Minister Ali Maher, who represented a civilian elite whose wealth lay in landed property. The Free Officers valued mass support over the wishes of the propertied elite and secured Maher's resignation in September 1952.

The land reform measure secured tangible political benefits for the Free Officers. Although only a fraction of Egypt's farming population actually benefited from the land reform measures of 1952—about 146,000 families in all, out of a total Egyptian population of 21.5 million—it engendered tremendous goodwill among the citizens of Egypt.[16] With the backing of the Egyptian masses, the military men were emboldened to take the reins of power and play a more direct role in politics.

Once the Free Officers entered politics, they proved very decisive. General Naguib agreed to form a new, largely civilian, government in September 1952. Nasser created a committee of military men to oversee the work of the revolution, ostensibly in collaboration with the government, but increasingly in rivalry with Naguib, called the Revolutionary Command Council (RCC). The military men were quick to purge Egyptian politics of party pluralism. In January 1953, in response to pressures from the Wafd and the Muslim Brothers, the RCC banned all parties and expropriated their funds for the state. Working behind the scenes, Colonel Nasser introduced a new state-sponsored party known as the Liberation Rally. Nasser argued that party factionalism was largely responsible for the divisive politics of the interwar years. He hoped the Liberation Rally would serve to mobilize popular support behind the new regime. Nasser made the final break with the old order when the RCC abolished the monarchy, on June 18, 1953. Egypt was declared a republic and Muhammad Naguib named its first president. For the first time since the Pharaonic era, Egypt was ruled by native-born Egyptians. As Nawal El Saadawi put it, Naguib was "the first Egyptian to rule since King Mena in ancient Egypt."[17]

The Egyptian republic was now a government of the people, and it enjoyed the full support of the great mass of the Egyptian people. "The atmosphere in the country changed," Saadawi recalled. "People used to walk along with grim, silent faces. Now the streets had changed. People . . . chatted, smiled, said good morning, shook hands with complete strangers, asked about one another's health, about recent events, congratulated one another for the change of regime, discussed, tried to foretell future events, [and] kept expecting changes to happen every day."

The challenge for the new government would be to meet the high expectations of a people eager for change. It would not be easy. The new Egyptian government inherited an intimidating array of economic problems. The country was over-reliant on agriculture, and agricultural output was constrained by Egypt's desert environment. There was no way to expand the land under cultivation without the water resources for desert reclamation. Egyptian industry remained largely underdeveloped. Whereas agriculture contributed 35 percent of the Egyptian gross domestic product in 1953, industry contributed only 13 percent (with services accounting for the remaining 52 percent of GDP).[18] The slow pace of industrialization was in large part due to low levels of public and private investment. Overall population growth well outstripped the rate of job creation, which meant that fewer Egyptians would get the steady jobs necessary for a significant improvement in their standard of living.

The officers of the Revolutionary Command Council had a radical solution to all their problems: a hydroelectric dam on the Nile. Engineers had identified the ideal place for the dam in Upper Egypt near the town of Aswan. The new Aswan High Dam would store enough water to allow an expansion of land under cultivation from 6 million acres to between 8 and 9.5 million acres, and would generate enough electricity to permit Egypt's industrialization and provide affordable electricity to the country as a whole.[19] Such a project would cost hundreds of millions of dollars—far more than Egypt could raise from its own resources.

To finance the Aswan Dam, and to secure Egypt's economic independence, the ruling officers would have to engage with the international community. Yet Egypt was intensely jealous of its independence, and sought at all costs to secure its aims without compromises to its sovereignty. The Free Officers were soon to discover how hard it was to engage with the rest of the world without making compromises.

In the international arena, the top priority of the new Egyptian government was to secure Britain's complete withdrawal. It was the unfinished business of Egyptian nationalism since half a century before.

In April 1953 Nasser and his men entered into negotiations with the British, brokered by the United States, to secure Britain's complete withdrawal from Egypt. The stakes were very high for both sides. Nasser believed that failure would prove the downfall of the Free Officers, and Britain was very sensitive about its international position in an increasingly postcolonial world. The process dragged out over sixteen months, as negotiations broke down and resumed with some frequency. In the end, the British and Egyptians struck a compromise in which the British would withdraw all military personnel from Egyptian soil within twenty-four months, leaving some 1,200 civilian experts in the Canal Zone for a seven-year transition period. It was not a complete and unconditional British withdrawal: the two-year delay for military withdrawal and the concessions for a seven-year British civilian presence were grounds for criticism from some Egyptian nationalist circles. However, it was independence enough for Nasser to secure the RCC's approval in July 1954. The settlement was concluded between the two governments on October 19, 1954, and the last British soldier left Egypt on June 19, 1956.

The new agreement with Great Britain faced criticism within Egypt. President Muhammad Naguib seized on the shortcomings of the agreement to batter his young rival Gamal Abdel Nasser. No longer satisfied with his role as figurehead, Naguib sought the full powers that he believed were his due as president. Nasser, through his control of the Revolutionary Command Council, was encroaching on the powers of the president. Relations between Nasser and Naguib had deteriorated by early 1954 to what some contemporaries described as hatred, and after Naguib criticized the British withdrawal, Nasser deployed his loyal followers to discredit Naguib and turn public opinion against a man they still revered.

The Muslim Brotherhood also seized upon the incomplete British withdrawal to criticize the Free Officer regime. The Islamist organization, banned along with all the other political parties in 1953, already had its grievances with the new military regime. Early in 1954, Nasser's clampdown on the Brotherhood made him the target of an Islamist splinter group bent on his assassination. They even considered deploying a suicide bomber wearing a dynamite belt who might get close enough to kill Nasser with the blast—one of the earliest suicide bomb plots in Middle Eastern history. However, the tactic did not appeal to the Islamists of 1954, and there were no volunteers.[20]

On October 26, 1954, a member of the Muslim Brotherhood named Mahmoud Abd al-Latif tried to assassinate Nasser using a more traditional method. He fired eight bullets at Nasser during a speech celebrating the evacuation agreement with the British. Abd al-Latif was a very bad shot—none of the bullets so much as grazed their target. But with bullets whizzing around him, Nasser performed heroically. He did not flinch under fire and only briefly paused in his speech. When he resumed with great emotion, he electrified an audience that extended via radio broadcast across Egypt and the Arab world: "My countrymen," Nasser shouted into the microphone, "my blood spills for you and for Egypt. I will live for your sake, die for the sake of your freedom and honor." The crowd roared their approval. "Let them kill me; it does not concern me so long as I have instilled pride, honor, and freedom in you. If Gamal Abdel Nasser should die, each of you shall be Gamal Abdel Nasser."[21]

The moment could not have been more dramatic, and the Egyptian public declared Nasser their champion. With his newfound popularity, Nasser established his primacy over the revolution and now had a free hand to dispose of both President Muhammad Naguib and the Muslim Brotherhood—his two main rivals for the public's allegiance. Thousands of Muslim Brothers were arrested, and in December six of their members were hanged for their role in the assassination attempt. Naguib was implicated in the trials and, though he was never charged of wrong-doing, was dismissed as president on November 15 and confined to house arrest for the next twenty years.

Egypt now had one undisputed master. From the end of 1954 until his death in 1970, Nasser was president of Egypt and the commander in chief of the Arab world.

No Arab leader has exercised such influence on the Arab stage before or since, and few would match Nasser's impact on world affairs. Egypt was on the brink of a remarkable adventure, years of pure adrenaline when anything seemed possible.

Once the evacuation agreement had been concluded with the British, the next item on Egypt's agenda was the unfinished business with the new state of Israel. Tensions ran high along the fragile border between Egypt and the Jewish state. Premier David Ben-Gurion made a number of attempts to sound out the intentions of the Free Officers, but Nasser and his men avoided direct contact with the Israelis (secret exchanges did take place between Israeli and Egyptian diplomats in Paris in 1953, with no result). Ben-Gurion came to the conclusion that Egypt under its new military rulers could turn into the Prussia of the Arab world and as such posed a clear and present danger to Israel. Yet Nasser knew his country was far from the necessary military strength to contain, let alone confront its hostile new neighbor. In order to pose a credible threat to Israel, Egypt needed to acquire materiel from abroad. Nasser quickly discovered, however, that in exchange for arms, foreign governments would inevitably set conditions that would compromise Egypt's newfound independence.

Nasser turned first to the United States, approaching the Americans for assistance in November 1952. In response the Free Officers were invited to send a delegation to the United States to state their needs: aircraft, tanks, artillery, and ships. The Americans were willing to assist in principle but wanted Egypt to commit to a regional defense pact before processing any orders for military hardware.

In May 1953, Secretary of State John Foster Dulles visited Cairo with the dual mission of promoting a peace agreement between Israel and the Arab states, and isolating America's super-power rival, the Soviet Union, in the Middle East. Discussions with the Egyptian government quickly turned to the subject of weapons. Dulles made clear that the United States remained willing to assist Egypt, on condition that it join a new regional defense pact called the Middle East Defense Organization (MEDO) that would bring Egypt into a formal alliance with the United States and Great Britain against the Soviet Union.

Nasser rejected Dulles's suggestion out of hand. MEDO provided a basis for extending the British military presence in Egypt—something no Egyptian leader could permit. What Nasser could not get Dulles to appreciate was that the Egyptians saw no grounds to fear a Soviet menace. The real threat for Egypt was Israel. Mohamed Heikal (b. 1923) was editor of the influential Egyptian daily *Al-Ahram* and a close confidant of Nasser's. He remembered Nasser asking Dulles: "How can I go to my people and tell them I am disregarding a killer with a pistol sixty miles from me at the Suez Canal [i.e., Israel] to worry about somebody who is holding a knife 5,000 miles away?"[22]

Relations between Egypt and Israel deteriorated following the signing of the Anglo-Egyptian Evacuation Agreement in 1954. Ben-Gurion saw the British presence in the Suez Canal Zone as a buffer between the Egyptians and Israel, and the imminent withdrawal of British troops thus spelled disaster. In July 1954, Israeli military intelligence started covert operations in Egypt, planting incendiary devices in British and American institutions in Cairo and Alexandria. They apparently hoped to provoke a crisis in relations between Egypt, Britain, and the United States that might drive Britain to reconsider its withdrawal from the Suez Canal.[23] Much to Israel's embarrassment, however, one of the Israeli spies was caught before planting his device, and the whole ring was exposed. Two of the men in the notorious Lavon Affair (named after the then defense minister Pinhas Lavon, who was blamed for the fiasco) were later executed, one committed suicide in prison, and the others were sentenced to long prison terms.

Tensions between Egypt and Israel reached a new height in the wake of the Lavon Affair and the subsequent execution of the Israeli agents. Ben-Gurion, who had stood down as prime minister for just over a year while the dovish Moshe Sharett headed the government, returned to the premiership in February 1955. He marked his return to office with a devastating attack on Egyptian forces in Gaza on February 28, 1955.

The Gaza Strip was the only part of the Palestine mandate to remain in Egyptian hands at the end of the 1948 war, and it teemed with hundreds of thousands of Palestinian refugees. The border between Gaza and Israel was frequently infiltrated by dispossessed Palestinians, some to recover property from lost homes inside what was now Israel, others to inflict damage on the Jewish state that had displaced them. Two such infiltrations in February 1955 served as the Israeli government's pretext for massive retaliation. Two companies of Israeli paratroopers crossed into Gaza and destroyed the Egyptian army's local headquarters, killing thirty-seven Egyptian soldiers and wounding thirty-one. Israel had displayed its military superiority, and Nasser knew his days would be numbered if he did not provide his army with better weaponry with which to stand up to the Israelis.

Egyptian losses in Gaza placed Nasser in a terrible bind. He needed foreign military assistance more than ever yet could not afford to make concessions to secure such aid. The British and the Americans continued to press Nasser to join a regional alliance before they would consider providing modern weapons to Egypt. The English-speaking powers were now urging Nasser to sign on to a NATO-sponsored alliance called the Baghdad Pact. Turkey and Iraq had concluded a treaty in February 1955 against Soviet expansion, to which Britain, Pakistan, and Iran all acceded in the course of the year. Nasser was bitterly opposed to the Baghdad Pact, which he saw as a British plot to perpetuate its influence over the Middle East and to promote its Hashemite allies in Iraq over the Free Officers in Egypt. Nasser condemned the Baghdad Pact in no uncertain terms and succeeded in preventing any other Arab state from acceding to the pact, despite British and American enticements.

British Prime Minister Anthony Eden began to see Nasser's influence behind every setback to British policy in the Middle East and hardened his line against the Egyptian leadership. In light of the growing antagonism between Nasser and Eden, there was no question of Britain supplying Egypt's military with advanced weapons.

Nasser next sounded out the French as an alternate source of military hardware. But the French, too, had grave misgivings about Nasser due to his support for nationalist movements in North Africa. Nationalists in Tunisia, Morocco, and Algeria were mobilizing to secure their full independence from France, and they looked to Egypt as both a role model and an ally. Nasser in turn sympathized with the North African nationalists and saw their struggle against imperialism as part of the broader Arab world's resistance to foreign domination. Although he had little in the way of financial or military resources to offer, he was only too happy to provide refuge to exiled nationalists and to leave them the freedom to mobilize their independence struggle within Egypt's frontiers.

So long as Nasser provided a free haven to North African nationalists, the French refused to provide him with military assistance. When faced with a choice between the Arabs and the French, Nasser chose the Arabs. The fact that the French were fighting a losing battle with Arab nationalism made them resent Nasser's position all the more.

French authority in North Africa had been dealt a fatal blow by France's defeat by Nazi Germany at the start of World War II. The demoralized colonial officials of the collaborationist Vichy Regime were poor representatives of a once great empire. Nationalist movements in Tunisia, Algeria, and Morocco were encouraged by the perception of French weakness.

In November 1942, American troops easily defeated Vichy forces in Morocco. Two months later, President Franklin Roosevelt and Prime Minister Winston Churchill met in Casablanca to plot the North African campaign. They invited the sultan of Morocco, Mohammed V, to join them for a dinner in which Roosevelt was outspoken in his criticism of French imperialism. The sultan's son Hassan, who would later succeed to the Moroccan throne as King Hassan II, also attended the dinner. He quoted Roosevelt saying "the colonial system was out of date and doomed." Churchill, himself prime minister of an imperial power, disagreed, but Roosevelt warmed to his theme.

According to Hassan, Roosevelt "foresaw the time after the war—which he hoped was not far off—when Morocco would freely gain her independence, according to the principles of the Atlantic Charter." Roosevelt promised U.S. economic aid once Morocco achieved its independence.[24]

Roosevelt's words reached far beyond the dinner table. Two weeks after his visit, a group of nationalists drafted a manifesto and wrote to the U.S. president to request his support for Moroccan independence. The sultan even offered to declare war on Germany and Italy and to enter the war on the Allies' side. However, both the British and the Americans were committed to supporting General Charles de Gaulle's Free French forces and so, rather than accede to Moroccan demands for independence, the Americans handed Morocco over to de Gaulle's Free French in June 1943. The Moroccans would have to achieve their own independence without foreign intervention. And so they did.

The strength of the Moroccan independence movement derived from the partnership between the monarchy and the nationalists. In January 1944 a new nationalist movement calling itself the Istiqlal, or Independence Party, published a manifesto calling for Moroccan independence. The Istiqlal was openly monarchist, and its manifesto proposed that the sultan negotiate with the French on behalf of the Moroccan nation. The party's one condition was that the sultan establish the instruments of a democratic government.

Mohammed V gave his full support to the Istiqlal, which placed him on a collision course with the French colonial authorities. As the nationalist movement spread from the narrow circle of political elites to the labor unions and urban masses in the late 1940s, the sultan increasingly was viewed by the colonial authorities as the head of the nationalist snake that threatened the French empire in North Africa.

The broader Arab world offered moral support to the Moroccan nationalists. Exiled Moroccan militants established the Office of the Arab Maghrib in Cairo in 1947 where they could plan political action and spread propaganda without French intervention. The Maghrib Office made headlines when it freed the leader of the 1920s Rif War against Spain and France, Muhammad Abd al-Krim al-Khattabi, also known as Abd el-Krim, from the French ship that was bringing him back from his exile in the island of Réunion to Paris. Abd el-Krim was given a hero's reception in Cairo and named the chairman of the Committee for the Liberation of North Africa.

The French were growing increasingly concerned that the tide of Arab nationalism might sweep away their North African possessions. Mohammed V began to place great emphasis on Morocco's ties to the Arab world. In April 1947 he delivered a speech in Tangier in which he spoke of Morocco's Arab ties without making any mention of France. In 1951 a hard-line French resident-general presented Mohammed V with an ultimatum: either disavow the Istiqlal or abdicate. Though the sultan conceded to French pressure, he still retained the full support of the nationalists and the Moroccan masses, who began to mobilize in mass demonstrations. Public order in Morocco broke down as the labor unions called for strikes and as nationalist demonstrations turned into riots.

Nationalist demonstrations raged in Tunisia at the same time. In December 1952, the French assassinated a Tunisian labor leader named Farhat Hached. His murder provoked mass demonstrations in both Tunisia and Morocco. The French authorities suppressed the riots that broke out in the main cities of Morocco with such violence that they inadvertently encouraged the nationalist movement. Moroccan writer Leila Abouzeid captured the intense shock provoked by the violence in her autobiographical novel, *The Year of the Elephant*. For Zahra, the book's narrator, the violence of December 1952 marked the moment when she decided to join the underground nationalist movement.

> I did take a position years before actually joining the resistance. I remember the day and the occasion quite clearly. The slaughter that black day in Casablanca can never be forgotten. Whenever I think of it, my body goes numb. I see them, [French] soldiers from the Foreign Legion, emerging from a barracks close to our neighbourhood, their machine guns blasting down passersby.
>
> How long I lived with those shots reverberating in my ears and the sight of women and children falling constantly in my mind. Later I would see many corpses lying like garbage bags on the sidewalk, but they never affected me like the events of that horrible day. . . . That day I lost all affection for life. . . . The situation had to be changed or it was not worth living.[25]

In the aftermath of the December 1952 riots, both the Istiqlal and the Communist Party were banned by the French authorities, and hundreds of political activists were exiled. However, the sultan remained the key rallying point of Moroccan nationalist aspirations, and the French were determined to secure his abdication. Working through a coterie of Moroccan notables loyal to France and opposed to Mohammed V, the French orchestrated an indigenous coup against the sultan. A group of religious leaders and heads of the Muslim mystical brotherhoods, convinced that Mohammed V's nationalist politics were somehow contrary to their religion, declared their allegiance to a member of the royal family named Ben Arafa. The French authorities demanded that the sultan abdicate, and when he refused he was arrested by French police, on August 20, 1953, and flown from the country at gunpoint. For the next two years Mohammed V was held in exile on the East African island of Madagascar.

The exile of Mohammed V did nothing to calm the situation in Morocco. The nationalists went underground and turned to violent tactics now that their right to political self-expression was denied. They attempted to assassinate several French colonial officials, notables collaborating with the French, and even the usurper sultan Ben Arafa. In response, the French settlers established their own terrorist organization, called Présence Française ("the French Presence"), to assassinate nationalist figures and intimidate their supporters. The French police instigated a reign of terror, arresting suspected nationalists and torturing political prisoners.

It was against this background that Zahra, the protagonist in Leila Abouzeid's autobiographical novel, entered the resistance. Her first mission was to help one of the men in her husband's secret cell to flee the French police and escape from Casablanca to the international zone in Tangier. The mission was all the more ironic because the fugitive was a veteran of the French war in Vietnam who had lost his leg in Dien Bien Phu. Yet Zahra managed to see her fellow-resistance fighter safely to the international zone in Tangier.

After her first success, the leaders of the resistance gave Zahra more challenging tasks. She led an arson attack on the shop of a collaborator in the center of Casablanca and ran for her life from the crowded market, with police and tracker dogs in hot pursuit. Zahra took refuge in a courtyard where she found the women of the house cooking. "I'm a guerrilla fighter," she told them, and they gave their protection without asking any questions. Finding herself under the protection of Moroccan women, Zahra mused on how politics had changed her life and the position of women in her country. "If my grandmother had returned from the dead and seen me setting shops ablaze, delivering guns, and smuggling men across borders, she would have died a second death," Zahra reflected.[26]

The turning point for the French Empire in North Africa came in 1954. Protests had been mounting against French rule in Morocco and Tunisia since the late 1940s, prompting the French authorities to reconsider their position in both protectorates. The two states were nominally ruled by indigenous dynasties—the Alaoui sultans in Morocco and the Husaynid Beys in Tunisia. The French believed they could better secure their interests in both countries by coming to an accommodation with the nationalists and conceding independence under friendly governments. Yet French imperial policy was thrown into disarray by two events that spelled the end of the French Empire: the loss of Indochina following the decisive French defeat in the Battle of Dien Bien Phu (March–May 1954), and the outbreak of the Algerian war for independence on November 2, 1954.

The French did not consider Algeria a colony. Unlike Tunisia and Morocco, which were ruled as protectorates, the territory of Algeria had been annexed to the French state and divided into *départments* just like the rest of metropolitan France. One million French citizens lived in Algeria, with their interests actively protected by elected representatives in the French parliament. As far as the French—government and people alike—were concerned, Algeria was French. So when Algerian nationalists declared war, the French responded rapidly and with full force. They sent their troops, already embittered by the defeat in Vietnam and determined never to face surrender again, to "defend" Algeria from the threat of nationalism.

Faced with a war in Algeria, the government of Pierre Mendès-France took decisive action to cut its losses and resolve relations with Tunisia and Morocco. The French premier went to Tunis in person to ask the ruling bey, Muhammad VIII al-Amin (r. 1943–1956) to appoint a new government to negotiate Tunisian independence. The bey, who sought to preserve his own power over the nationalists, tried to exclude the most popular nationalist party, Habib Bourguiba's Neo-Destour. However, by March 1955 he was forced by popular demand to invite Bourguiba to participate in the negotiations.

The charismatic Bourguiba quickly assumed the leadership position of the Tunisian negotiating team and secured agreement for autonomy in April 1955 before concluding the March 20, 1956, protocol in which France recognized Tunisia's independence. Affirming the republican principle that sovereignty lay in the people, Bourguiba moved in July 1957 to abolish the monarchy in Tunisia, which had been compromised by its collaboration with French colonial rule. The Tunisian Republic elected Bourguiba its first president, which post he held for the next thirty years.

In Morocco the French sought to calm the situation by allowing Sultan Mohammed V to return from Madagascar to resume the throne. On November 16, 1955, the sultan landed in Morocco to a rapturous reception. Two days later, Mohammed V addressed the nation from the Royal Palace in Rabat, on the occasion of the Fête du Trône, the Moroccan national day. "What to say that could describe that day?" reflected Zahra, the nationalist freedom fighter of Leila Abouzeid's autobiographical novel. "The whole of Casablanca became one huge celebration connected by stages and loudspeakers. Songs and performances mingled with speeches, and the aroma of tea being prepared on sidewalks filled the air." Zahra, her family, and friends boarded a bus from Casablanca to Rabat to hear the sultan's address. She remembered the "incredible roar" that greeted Mohammed V and his two sons when they appeared on the balcony of the palace. "How many times have I listened to his throne speech delivered that November 18! What a speech! I learned it by heart and can still recite it to this day."

Zahra repeated the sultan's words from memory: "On this joyous day God has blessed us twice over. The blessing of return to our most beloved homeland after a long and sorrowful absence, and the blessing of gathering again with the people we have so missed and to whom we have been unerringly faithful and who have been faithful to us in turn." The sultan's message was clear: Morocco had achieved its independence only because the monarch and the people had supported each other. To Zahra, the events of November 18 revealed nothing so much as the failure of French efforts to split the monarch from his people through exile. "Fantastic what an effect [the sultan] had on our hearts! His exile had wrapped him in a sacred cloak, and for his sake the people had joined the resistance, as if he had become an ideal or a principle. Had the French not exiled him, their presence in Morocco would have continued much longer; I'm certain of that."[27]

On March 2, 1956, Morocco achieved its independence from France.

By the time Morocco and Tunisia had achieved their independence, Algeria had descended to all-out war. What had started as a poorly organized insurgency by a small band (estimates range from 900 to 3,000 fighters on November 1, 1954) of underarmed men had developed into a mass popular uprising in which unarmed civilians—both settlers and native Algerians—were often the target of indiscriminate and murderous violence.

In August 1955, the Algerian National Liberation Front, known by the French acronym, FLN attacked the settler village of Philippeville, killing 123 men, women, and children. The French retaliated with extraordinary brutality, killing thousands of Algerians (official French figures acknowledge 1,273 deaths whereas the FLN claimed 12,000 Algerians killed).[28]

The Philippeville massacres intensified FLN resolve and also strengthened the organization by attracting large numbers of volunteers from those outraged by unmeasured French reprisals against Algerian citizens. The massacres also served as a stark reminder of the FLN's strategic weakness in the face of the French army of occupation, with all of the resources of an industrial power.

The Cairo office of the FLN was an important base for the movement's international operations, and the Egyptian government under Gamal Abdel Nasser had given full public support for the cause of Algerian independence. It was in order to isolate Algerian nationalists and to force Egypt to abandon its support for the FLN that France placed conditions on the sale of any military hardware to Nasser's Egypt—conditions that, true to form, Nasser was unwilling to accept.

By 1955 Nasser had made some influential friends. He was respected by the leaders of the Non-Aligned Movement—men like Yugoslavia's Josip Broz Tito, India's Jawaharlal Nehru, and China's Zhou Enlai. Nonalignment was a natural line for Egypt to adopt, given its aversion to foreign domination. Like the other members of the movement, the Egyptian government wanted to preserve the freedom to enjoy cordial relations with both the United States and the Soviet Union without having to take sides in the Cold War. The organization also provided a forum for the countries of Asia and Africa to advance their goal of decolonization. Nasser, for example, proposed a resolution to the movement's inaugural conference in Bandung, Indonesia, in support of Algerian independence that passed unanimously—much to France's chagrin.

The Egyptian people were delighted as their charismatic young president was recognized as a leader on the world's stage. The Americans, however, were far less pleased. President Dwight Eisenhower rejected the politics of nonalignment out of hand. His administration believed there was no middle position between the United States and the USSR—ultimately, a country could only be with the Americans or against them. Nasser's refusal to join a regional alliance against the Soviet Union had raised American ire, though many in the American administration still hoped to bring Nasser around. They were to be disappointed.

Nasser's pursuit of the arms denied him by the West ultimately led to the Communist bloc. He discussed the problem of securing modern weapons for his army with Chinese Premier Chou En-Lai, who offered to raise the matter with the Soviet Union on Egypt's behalf. In May 1955, the Soviet ambassador in Cairo sought an audience with Nasser, initiating negotiations that ran through the summer months of 1955.

Even as he turned to the Soviets for military assistance, Nasser tried to keep the Americans on his side. The Egyptian president informed the Americans about his communications with the Soviets and told the U.S. Ambassador to Cairo that he had a firm offer of arms from the Soviet Union, but that he would still prefer U.S. military assistance. In Mohamed Heikal's view, Secretary of State John Foster Dulles first thought Nasser was bluffing. It was only after he had incontrovertible evidence that Nasser was about to conclude an agreement with the Soviets that Dulles sent envoys to prevent the deal from going through.

In September 1955 Nasser presented the Americans with a fait accompli when he announced that Egypt would obtain arms from the Soviet satellite state of Czechoslovakia.[29] The magnitude of the arms deal dramatically changed the balance of power in the Middle East as Egypt acquired 275 modern T-34 tanks and a fleet of 200 warplanes, including MiG-15 and MiG-17 fighters and Ilyushin-28 bombers.[30]

Following this first demarche toward the Communist bloc, the Egyptian government further alienated the Eisenhower administration in May 1956 when it extended diplomatic relations to the People's Republic of China. Egypt had gravely undermined U.S. attempts to contain the spread of Communist influence in the Middle East, and the United States was determined to get Egypt to change its policies.

The British, French, and Israelis were more ambitious still: they wanted to change Egypt's government altogether. They saw Nasser as the champion of a dangerous new force known as Arab nationalism, which they believed he could mobilize against their vital interests in the Middle East. Ben-Gurion feared Nasser might rally the Arab states to mount a fatal attack on Israel. Prime Minister Anthony Eden believed Nasser deployed Arab nationalism to strip Britain of its influence in the Middle East. The French saw Nasser as encouraging the Algerians to intensify their war against France. Each of these states had a real reason to seek Nasser's overthrow to advance their national interests.

In the course of the year of 1956 these three states conspired to make war on Egypt in a fiasco dubbed both the Suez Crisis (in the West) and the Tripartite Aggression (by the Arabs).

The road to Suez began in Aswan. Along with the land reform program, the Aswan High Dam remained a central part of the Free Officers' domestic development agenda, as it was expected to provide both the country's energy needs for industrialization and a significant expansion of agricultural area through irrigation.

The Egyptian government could not, however, fund the dam on its own. It was one of the largest civil engineering projects in the world, and the price was astronomical—an estimated $1 billion, of which $400 million would have to be paid in foreign currency. The Egyptian government negotiated a finance package with the World Bank in late 1955 to provide a loan of $200 million, backed by a commitment from the United States and Great Britain to provide the remaining $200 million.

The British and U.S. governments hoped to use the Aswan Dam project as a means to exercise some control over the politics of Nasser's Egypt. According to Heikal, the United States and Britain never intended to give the full amount Egypt needed, pledging only one-third the sum requested—not enough to guarantee the dam but rather just enough to exercise influence over Egypt during the years it would take to build it. Dulles allegedly told the Saudi king Sa'ud in January 1957 that "he had decided to help [Egypt] with the Dam because the project was a long term one," according to Heikal. "It would have tied Egypt to America for ten years, and in that time Nasser would either have learned the danger of co-operating with the Soviet Union or he would have fallen from power."[31]

The U.S. government also tried to make the loan contingent on a commitment from the Egyptian government not to buy more arms from the Soviet Union. The military expenditure would, it argued insincerely, undermine Egypt's ability to pay its part of the dam's construction costs. Nasser had no intention of breaking with the Soviet Union, which was the only power willing to assist his military with no preconditions.

Nasser had come to recognize that the rules of the Cold War precluded cooperation with both the Soviets and the Americans. By April 1956 he suspected that the United States would withdraw its support for the Aswan High Dam. Three months later, on July 19, 1956, Eisenhower announced that he was withdrawing all American financial aid for the project.

Nasser learned of the U.S. announcement in mid-air on his way back to Cairo from a meeting in Yugoslavia. He was irate; Eisenhower had announced the decision to withdraw financial support for the dam before giving the Egyptian government the courtesy of an advance warning, let alone an explanation. "This is not a withdrawal," Nasser said to Heikal, "it is an attack on the regime and an invitation to the people of Egypt to bring it down."[32]

Nasser believed he had to strike a bold response and quickly. Within twenty-four hours he had a plan, and only six days to pull off his most ambitious coup yet.

Nasser was scheduled to give a major speech in Alexandria on July 26 marking the fourth anniversary of the revolution. His theme would be the Aswan Dam. If the Western powers refused to help the Egyptians, he planned to argue, then Egypt would pay for the dam itself by nationalizing the Suez Canal and diverting the canal's revenues to meet the cost of the dam.

Legally, the Egyptian government had every right to nationalize the Suez Canal, so long as it paid shareholders in the Suez Canal Company fair compensation for their stock. However, as a public company listed in France, with the British government as the largest shareholder, Nasser knew that nationalization of the canal would provoke an international crisis. Britain in particular was determined to preserve its influence in the Middle East and would interpret the nationalization as another hostile measure by the Egyptian government. Nasser estimated the likelihood of foreign intervention to run as high as 80 percent.

In the event they opted for war, Nasser calculated that it would take the British and the French at least two months to raise the necessary military force to intervene. The two-month delay would give him crucial time to negotiate a diplomatic settlement. It was quite a gamble, but one Nasser believed he had to take to uphold Egypt's independence from foreign domination.

Nasser tasked a young engineer named Colonel Mahmoud Younes with the actual takeover of the Suez Canal Company's offices. On the evening of July 26, Younes was to tune into Nasser's speech on the radio and launch the operation if and when he heard Nasser say the code words, "Ferdinand de Lesseps"—the architect of the Suez Canal. If Nasser did not mention the name during the speech, Younes was to do nothing and wait for further orders.

As was his habit, Nasser gave his speech from notes and launched into the background of the Aswan Dam crisis. He recounted the history of Egypt's exploitation by the imperial powers, he cited the case of the Suez Canal, and he mentioned Ferdinand de Lesseps—many times over. "The President was so worried [Mahmoud

Younes] would miss it that he kept on repeating the Frenchman's name," Heikal re-called. "It was de Lesseps this and de Lesseps that until he had repeated it about ten times and people began to wonder why he was making such a fuss about de Lesseps, for the Egyptians had no real love for him."

Nasser needn't have worried, as the attentive Colonel Younes had heard the name on the first mention, turned off his radio, and went to work. "I'm sorry," he later confessed to Nasser, "I missed the rest of your speech."

His teams secured the Suez Canal Company branch offices in Cairo, Port Said, and Suez. Younes personally commanded the takeover of the company's headquarters in Ismailiyya. As one of the men who accompanied Younes recalled, "We entered the offices in Ismailia at around 7pm and there was no staff in the offices, except the nightshift. We called the senior staff, foreigners of course because there was no Egyptian in the decision-making level . . . and they were taken by surprise."[33] The occupation of all three offices of the company was accomplished by a team of thirty officers and civil engineers.

By the time Nasser reached the climax of his speech, the canal was securely in Egyptian hands. "We will not allow the Suez Canal to be a state within a state," Nasser told his enchanted audience. "Today the Suez Canal is an Egyptian company." After declaring the nationalization of the canal, Nasser went on to pledge that the £35 million revenues from the canal would henceforth be applied to build the Aswan High Dam project. "The people went wild with excitement," Heikal remembered.[34]

News of the nationalization of the Suez Canal sent shock waves through the international community. Ben-Gurion's first thought was that it would provide the opportunity to topple Nasser. He made overtures to the United States but found the Eisenhower administration noncommittal. He confided to his diary: "The Western powers are furious . . . but I am afraid that they will not do anything. France will not dare to act alone; [British Prime Minister] Eden is not a man of action; Washington will avoid any reaction."[35] Yet Ben-Gurion underestimated the depth of British and French anger over Nasser's move.

The French were the first to react. The day after the nationalization, Maurice Bourgès-Maunoury, the French minister of defense, called Shimon Peres, then serving as director-general of the Israeli Ministry of Defense, to ask him how long it would take the Israel Defense Force to conquer the Sinai Peninsula to the Suez Canal. Peres made a rough guess: two weeks. The French minister came straight to the point: Would Israel agree to take part in a tripartite attack on Egypt, in which Israel's role would be to seize the Sinai, and a joint Anglo-French force would occupy the Suez Canal Zone? Peres was in no position to commit the Israeli government to a war alliance, but he gave the French an encouraging reply and initiated a collusion that would result in the Second Arab-Israeli War.

The French next approached Sir Anthony Eden with the plan, in which an Israeli attack on Egypt in the Sinai would provide the pretext for a joint Anglo-French military intervention to "restore peace" in the Canal Zone. The assumptions were that Nasser's government could not survive such an attack, that Israel would secure its frontiers with Egypt, and that Britain and France could reassert their control over the canal by such improbable means. The whole mad plan reveals nothing so much as a collective lapse in judgment.

To conclude the unlikely tripartite alliance, a meeting was convened in Sèvres, on the outskirts of Paris, attended by Christian Pineau and Selwyn Lloyd—the French and British foreign ministers—and Israeli Prime Minister David Ben-Gurion. It was an uncomfortable conversation marked by deep mistrust between the Israelis and the British, reflecting the bitterness of the end of the Palestine mandate. But the conspirators were held together by their shared hatred of Nasser and their determination to see him destroyed.

After forty-eight hours of intense negotiations, the three parties struck a secret agreement on October 24, 1956. First Israel would invade Egypt, provoking an Arab-Israeli conflict that placed maritime communications through the Suez Canal in jeopardy. Britain and France would insist on a cessation of hostilities, which would of course be ignored. The Anglo-French alliance would then intervene with their own troops to occupy the Canal Zone. So little did the Israeli diplomats trust their French and English counterparts that they insisted that all parties sign a written agreement, lest the Europeans try to back out after Israel's initial invasion.

Britain and France both had good reason to reconsider their collusion with Israel. France had gained widespread hostility for providing arms to the Israelis after 1948, and for denying Algerian demands for independence. Britain's imperial past continued to bedevil its relations with Arab nationalists. For the former imperial powers to side with Israel was a plan destined to poison the European powers' relations to the Arab world. And there was little chance of such a conspiracy long remaining a secret.

Yet the improbable plan went into effect when Israel attacked Egypt on October 29, initiating a war in the Sinai and a rush to the Suez Canal. The next day, Britain and France delivered the agreed ultimatum to both the Egyptians and the Israelis to cease hostilities and withdraw their forces 10 miles from their respective banks of the Suez Canal. The French and British revealed their hand in the crisis by mistiming their announcement. They demanded the withdrawal of all belligerents from the Canal Zone while Israel was still miles from the canal. As Nasser's confidant Mohamed Heikal reasoned, "What justification was there in the demand for a mutual withdrawal ten miles from the Canal when the Israelis at that stage had only one battalion of lightly armed paratroopers still forty miles from the Canal?" The only reason why Britain and France might expect the Israelis to be at the canal was if they had played a role in planning the attack.

As evidence of British collusion in Israel's attack mounted—British surveillance aircraft were spotted flying over the Sinai—the Egyptians were forced to accept the unthinkable. As Heikal recalled, "Nasser just could not bring himself to believe that Eden, with all the knowledge he claimed of the Middle East, would jeopardise the security of all Britain's friends and Britain's own standing in the Arab world by making war alongside Israel on an Arab nation."[36]

The United States was also incredulous as it watched the Suez Crisis unfold. Certainly, the Americans were not above such tactics—the Central Intelligence Agency had itself been plotting a coup against the Syrian government, to be executed on the very day the Israelis began their attack.[37] The Syrians had accepted Soviet economic assistance, and the United States wanted to contain the threat of Soviet expansion into the Middle East. Such an operation was entirely consistent with the U.S. worldview in 1956.

The Eisenhower administration found the Suez conflict incomprehensible. Britain and France were still acting like imperial powers at the height of the Cold War. For the Americans, the containment of Soviet expansion was the only geostrategic game that mattered, in the Middle East as in other critical parts of the world. They could not conceive of their NATO allies Britain and France going to war over a once-strategic waterway that led to their now-defunct empires in South and Southeast Asia. Eisenhower was also furious with his European allies for undertaking such a major military operation without consulting the United States. Had they been consulted, the Americans certainly would have opposed the Suez war. The British and French governments knew perfectly well how the Americans would respond and chose to leave Washington in the dark.

From the American perspective, the Suez Crisis was an unmitigated disaster. The disruption to an American covert operation in Syria was completely overshadowed by events in Hungary. On October 23, just six days before the Israeli attack on Egypt, a revolution had erupted in Hungary. Student demonstrations against the Stalinist regime in Budapest had led to nationwide protests. Within days, the Soviet-supported government fell, and a new cabinet was formed under the leadership of reformer Imre Nagy, who quickly moved to withdraw Hungary from the Warsaw Pact, effectively ending military cooperation with the Soviets and their allies. It was the first crack in the Iron Curtain separating Soviet-controlled Eastern Europe from the West, and the most important development since the start of the Cold War.

Working the halls of the United Nations to protect the movement in Hungary from Soviet retaliation, the Eisenhower administration watched in fury as the British and French began hostilities in Egypt. The Anglo-French intervention provided a better distraction than the Soviets could have dreamed of. After their bombers blitzed Egyptian air bases on October 31, the British and French dropped paratroops into the Canal Zone in early November. Soviet diplomats were able to seize the moral high ground in defending Nasser's Egypt against Western aggression, all the while deploying their own forces in Hungary to restore their authority over Eastern Europe. NATO solidarity was undermined just when the West most needed to provide a solid front to contain the USSR. Eisenhower placed full responsibility for the loss of Hungary on Britain and France.

In Egypt, Nasser found himself fighting a war he could not win against three better-armed enemies. In the opening days of the war he ordered his forces to retreat from Gaza and the Sinai, which fell rapidly to the Israelis, and to concentrate on defending the Canal Zone. Nawal El Saadawi was serving as a doctor in a village clinic in the Delta and remembered hearing Nasser's speech echoing "from thousands of radios in the houses and on the streets: 'We shall go on fighting until the invaders leave. We will never surrender.'" His defiance in the face of an unprovoked attack by superior forces once again electrified the Egyptian people, who volunteered en masse to assist the national effort. "I took off my doctor's coat," Saadawi recalled, "and put on fatigues."

Saadawi, like many other Egyptians, was prepared to go to the war zone to assist the effort, but in the disorder that followed she never got the call; she thus followed events from her village in the Delta. When, on November 6, British and French paratroops laid siege to Port Said, she—like all Egyptians—was horrified. "Rockets and bombs were dropped by thousands from planes, naval ships bombarded it from the sea, tanks roared through the streets, and sharpshooters were parachuted on to the roofs of houses," Saadawi wrote. The Egyptians mounted civilian resistance that fought alongside their army. "Groups of guerrilla fighters, most of them very young, were formed and began to fight with guns, grenades and Molotov cocktails."[38] In all, some 1,100 civilians were killed in the fighting in the Canal Zone.

The Americans placed great pressure on Britain and France to stop fighting and withdraw their troops. American efforts in the Security Council were stymied by Britain and France exercising their vetoes to prevent the passage of any resolutions constraining their actions in Suez. With the Soviets and their allies threatening to intervene in the conflict on Egypt's side, the Eisenhower administration resorted to outright threats against Britain and France to secure compliance with their demands for an immediate cease-fire. Both countries were threatened with expulsion from NATO, and the U.S. Treasury warned it would sell part of its Sterling bond holdings to force a devaluation of the British currency, which would have had a catastrophic impact on the British economy. The threats were effective, and Britain and France conceded to a United Nations cease-fire on November 7. All British and French troops were withdrawn from Egypt by December 22, 1956, and the last Israeli forces withdrew from Egypt in March 1957, to be replaced by a United Nations peacekeeping force.

For Egypt, the Suez Crisis was the classic example of a military defeat turned to a political victory. Nasser's bold rhetoric and defiance were not matched by any military accomplishments. The very act of survival was deemed a major political victory, and the Egyptians—and Nasser's mass following across the Arab world—celebrated as though Nasser had in fact defeated Egypt's enemies. Nasser knew that his nationalization of the Suez Canal would face no further challenge and that Egypt had achieved full sovereignty over all of its territory and resources.

For the Israelis, the Suez war represented a stunning military victory and a political setback. Although Ben-Gurion was embarrassed to have to retreat from territory the IDF had occupied by force of arms, he had demonstrated Israeli military prowess to his Arab neighbors once again. Yet Israeli participation in the Tripartite Aggression reinforced the widespread view in the Arab world that Israel was an extension of imperial policy in the region.

Israel's association with imperialism made it all the more difficult for the Arab world to accept the Jewish state, let alone to extend recognition or to make peace. Rather, the defeat of Israel came to be associated with ridding the Middle East of imperialism, as well as the liberation of Palestine—powerful ideological impediments to any peace process in the 1950s.

France lost a great deal in the Suez Crisis. Its position in Algeria was undermined and its influence in the Arab world more generally decreased. For the remainder of the 1950s, the French gave up on the Arab world and threw their support behind Israel. Indeed, in the immediate aftermath of the Suez Crisis the French armed the Israelis and helped them to establish their nuclear program, providing a reactor in 1957 twice the original capacity promised.

Britain, which had hoped to preserve a major influence in the Arab world, was undoubtedly the greatest loser of the Suez Crisis. The decision to go to war had engendered tremendous domestic opposition in Britain and provoked a number of high-level resignations from both government and Foreign Office officials. Anthony Eden suffered a major breakdown in the aftermath of Suez and resigned his premiership in January 1957. The impact of Suez on Britain's position in the Middle East was even more devastating. As Heikal concluded, "No Arab leader could be Britain's friend and Nasser's enemy after Suez. Suez cost Britain Arabia."[39]

Nasser's remarkable string of successes propelled him to a position of dominance in the Arab world. His anti-imperial credentials and calls for Arab solidarity made him the champion of Arab nationalists across the region. Nasser took his message to the Arab masses across the airwaves, as the power of long-distance radio broadcasting combined with the spread of affordable and portable transistor radios in the course of the 1950s. In an age of widespread adult illiteracy, Nasser was able to reach a vastly broader audience via radio than he ever could have through newspapers.

At the time, the most powerful and widely followed radio station in the Arab world was the Cairo-based Voice of the Arabs (Sawt al-'Arab). Launched in 1953 to promote the ideas of the Egyptian revolution, the Voice of the Arabs combined news, politics, and entertainment. It connected Arabic speakers across national boundaries through a common language and promoted the ideas of pan-Arab action and Arab nationalism. Listeners from across the Arab world were electrified: "People used to have their ears glued to the radio," one contemporary recalled, "particularly when Arab nationalist songs were broadcast calling Arabs to raise their heads and defend their dignity and land from occupation."[40]

Nasser conquered the Arab world by radio. Through the Voice of the Arabs, he was able to pressure other Arab rulers to toe his line, bypassing the heads of Arab governments to address their citizens directly. In a political report on the situation in Lebanon in 1957, the director of intelligence in Lebanon, Amir Farid Chehab, wrote: "Political propaganda in Nasser's favour is what mostly occupies the spirit of the Muslim masses who consider him the only leader of the Arabs. They care for no other leader but him thanks to the influence of Egyptian and Syrian radio stations and his achievements in Egypt."[41]

Some Arab nationalists began to take Nasser's calls for Arab unity more literally than the Egyptian president intended—nowhere more so than in Syria.

Politics in Syria had been relentlessly volatile since Husni al-Zaim overthrew President Shukri al-Quwatli in 1949. Between al-Quwatli's fall in 1949 and his return to power in 1955, Syria had witnessed five changes of leadership, and by the late summer of 1957 the country was on the verge of complete political disintegration. Caught between the Soviet Union and the United States (which were plotting the overthrow of the Quwatli government in 1956), and between inter-Arab rivalries in an age of revolutionary ferment, the country was also being torn from within by deep political divides.[42]

The two most influential parties in Syria in the late 1950s were the Communists and the Arab Renaissance Party, better known as the Ba'th (literally, "Renaissance"). The Ba'th was founded by Michel 'Aflaq and Salah al-Din Bitar in the early 1940s as a secular pan-Arab nationalist party. Their motto was "One Arab nation with an eternal message." The Ba'th eschewed smaller nation-state nationalism in individual countries in favor of a greater Arab nationalism uniting all Arab people. The ideologues of the Ba'th held that the Arabs could only achieve full independence from outside rule and social justice at home through full Arab unity—a utopian vision of a single Arab state freed from the imperial boundaries imposed by the 1919 Versailles settlement. Branches of the party had cropped up in Syria, Lebanon, Jordan, and Iraq in the late 1940s.

Although Ba'thism would become a major political force from the 1960s through the present day, the party was still quite weak in Syria in the 1950s. A middle-class intellectual's party, the Ba'th had no mass support base. In the 1955 elections the party secured fewer than 15 percent of the seats in the Syrian parliament. The party was very much in need of a powerful ally, and its members found it in Egypt's Nasser. They gave their wholehearted backing to Nasser both out of conviction—his anti-imperialism and pan-Arab rhetoric so closely matched their own—and to harness Nasser's massive popularity in Syria to their own cause.

The Communist Party in Syria had less need of Nasser, as its position was growing with the expansion of Soviet influence in the country. The Syrian Communists also were wary of Nasser because he had suppressed the Egyptian Communist Party. Yet they too sought to profit from Nasser's mass appeal in Syria.

By 1957 both the Ba'th and the Communists approached Nasser with proposals to unite Syria and Egypt, with the rival Syrian parties outbidding each other in their efforts to court Nasser's favor. Whereas the Ba'th proposed a federal union, the Communists raised the stakes with the suggestion of a full merger of the two countries into a single state—confident that Nasser would reject the offer. It was all a bit of a game, as neither the Ba'th nor the Communists had the power to conclude a union with Egypt.

The game became serious, however, when the Syrian army got involved in the merger. The army had already staged three coups against the Syrian government, and many of its officers were avowed Ba'thists. They were drawn to the military-led government of Nasser's Egypt and believed that union would favor them as the dominant power in Syrian politics. On January 12, 1958, without prior warning to their own government, the Syrian chief of staff and thirteen of his top officers flew to Cairo to discuss a union with Nasser. A high-ranking Syrian officer called on cabinet ministers—including Khalid al-Azm, then minister of finance—to inform them of the army's actions only after the chief of staff had left for Cairo. "Wouldn't it have been better for you to inform the government of your decision and discuss the matter with them before going to Cairo?" al-Azm asked the officer.

"What's done is done," the officer replied, and withdrew.

Al-Azm was one of the patrician nationalist politicians who had fought for Syria's independence from the French mandate and had withstood the terrible bombardment of Damascus in 1945. He was convinced that the military would bring disaster to Syria. "If Abdel Nasser agrees to this proposal," he reflected in his diary, "Syria will disappear altogether, and if he refuses the Army will occupy the offices of state and bring down both the government and the parliament."[43]

The Syrian government decided to send the foreign minister, Salah al-Din Bitar, who was also one of the co-founders of the Ba'th, to Cairo to sound out Nasser's views and report back to the cabinet. Once in Cairo, Bitar got caught up in the excitement of the moment and traded observer status for that of self-declared negotiator. Bitar entered into direct discussions with Nasser as an official representative of the Syrian government.

Nasser was bemused by the steady stream of Syrian politicians and military men who flocked to Cairo to fling their country at his feet. Although he had always promoted Arab unity, he understood the expression to mean Arab *solidarity*, a unity of purpose and of goals. He had never aspired to formal union with other Arab states. Egypt, he recognized, had a very distinct history from the rest of the Arab world. Prior to the revolution, most Egyptians would not have identified themselves as Arabs, reserving the term either for the residents of the Arabian Peninsula or for the desert Bedouin. The proposal was all the more unlikely given that Egypt and Syria shared no borders but were separated by the iron wall raised by Israel.

Yet Nasser saw how a union with Syria could advance his interests. As head of a union of two major Arab states, Nasser could secure his position as the unrivaled leader of the Arab world. The union would be hugely popular with the Arab masses beyond Egypt and Syria, reinforcing their greater loyalty to Nasser than to their own national rulers. It would also demonstrate to the great powers—the Americans and Soviets, the British and French—that the new political order in the Middle East was being shaped by Egypt. Having overcome imperialism, Nasser was now circumventing the Cold War.

Nasser received his Syrian visitors and imposed his terms: full union, with Syria ruled from Cairo by the same institutions that governed Egypt. The Syrian army would come under Egyptian command and would have to stay out of politics and return to the barracks. All political parties were to be disbanded and replaced with a single state party to be known as the National Union, party pluralism being equated with divisive factionalism.

Nasser's terms came as something of a shock to his Syrian guests. The Ba'th representatives were appalled by the prospect of dissolving their party, but Nasser reassured them that they would dominate the National Union, which would prove their vehicle to shape the political culture of the United Arab Republic (UAR), as the new state was to be called. The name was deliberately open ended, as the union of Syria and Egypt was to be but the first step toward a broader Arab union and toward the Arab renaissance to which the Ba'th aspired. Though Nasser set terms that disenfranchised both the Ba'th and the military in politics, both groups came away from the Cairo discussions under the illusion that they would exercise predominant influence in Syria through the union with Egypt.

After ten days' discussion, Bitar and the officers returned from Cairo to brief the Syrian cabinet on the union scheme they had agreed with Nasser. Khalid al-Azm made no effort to hide his opposition to their proposals, but he found himself in the minority. Al-Azm watched in dismay as the elected leadership of Syria blithely surrendered their country's hard-gained independence on what he saw as an Arab nationalist whim. He mocked President al-Quwatli's opening remarks, using "words like 'Arabness' and 'the Arabs' and 'glory'" to "fill an otherwise empty speech." Al-Quwatli then gave the floor to the foreign minister. Bitar told his colleagues that he and Nasser had agreed to a full union of Syria and Egypt into a single state, and that they proposed to put the matter to a public referendum in both countries—knowing full well that the union would enjoy massive public support in both Syria and Egypt.

When Bitar finished, many of his cabinet colleagues affirmed their support for the union. "When they all had had their say," al-Azm related, "I asked for the session to be adjourned to give those present the opportunity to study the proposal. They all looked astonished by the suggestion. It was now my turn to be amazed. I could not believe that the Cabinet would be presented with so significant a proposal, which entailed nothing less than the dissolution of the Syrian entity, without allowing the ministers sufficient time to study the matter and to sound out the views of their parties, members of parliament, and policy makers in the country."[44] He succeeded only in securing a twenty-four hour adjournment.

Al-Azm prepared an extensive response and put forward a compromise union scheme based on a federation of the two states. His proposal gained enough support in the Syrian cabinet to be sent on to Cairo, but Nasser would have nothing to do with the compromise: it was total union or nothing at all. The Syrian army intervened again, preparing an airplane to take the cabinet to conclude the deal in Cairo. The chief of staff clarified the issue for the undecided politicians. "There are two roads open to you," he is reported to have said. "One leads to Mezze [the notorious political prison outside Damascus]; the other to Cairo."[45] The Syrian government took the road to Cairo and concluded the union agreement with Egypt on February 1, 1958.

It was the beginning of a revolutionary year. The union of Egypt and Syria heralded a new age of Arab unity, generating tremendous public support across the Arab world. Nasser's standing reached new heights, much to the consternation of the other Arab heads of state.

Perhaps the most vulnerable Arab leader in 1958 was the young King Hussein of Jordan, who would celebrate his twenty-third birthday in November of that year. Given Jordan's history of relations with Britain, Hussein had been a particular target of the Nasserist propaganda machine. The Voice of the Arabs broadcast damning criticisms of Hussein and encouraged the Jordanian people to overthrow the monarchy and join the progressive ranks of modern Arab republics.

In response to these external pressures, King Hussein did all he could to distance himself from Britain. He stood up to British pressures and stayed out of the Baghdad Pact. In March 1956 he dismissed the British officers still running his army, including the influential commander Glubb Pasha. He even negotiated the termination of the Anglo-Jordanian treaty in March 1957—effectively ending British influence over the Hashemite Kingdom. These measures were followed by conciliatory efforts toward Egypt and Syria and by efforts to demonstrate Jordan's commitment to Arab nationalism.

Hussein's boldest concession was to open his government to pro-Nasserist forces. In November 1956 Hussein held free and open elections for the first time in Jordan's history, which gave left-leaning Arab nationalists a clear majority in the Jordanian parliament. Hussein took the risk and invited the leader of the largest party, Sulayman al-Nabulsi, to form a government of loyal opposition. The experiment lasted less than six months.

The reform-minded Nabulsi government had a difficult time reconciling the contradictions between loyalty and opposition. Moreover, al-Nabulsi enjoyed greater public support and loyalty from the Nasserist "Free Officer" elements in the Jordanian military than did the king. Hussein came to believe that prolonging the Nabulsi government would shorten his monarchy, and he decided to act. In April 1957 Hussein took a real gamble in demanding al-Nabulsi's resignation, on the pretext of the government's sympathies for communism. Shortly after dismissing al-Nabulsi, Hussein took forceful measures to reassert his hold over the country and its armed forces. By mid-April, King Hussein had orchestrated the arrest or exile of the leading Jordanian Free Officers who threatened his rule and secured oaths of loyalty from his troops.

The pressures on Jordan intensified following the 1958 union of Syria and Egypt.[46] Arab nationalists redoubled their calls for the Hashemite government to step aside and for Jordan to join the progressive Arab ranks through union with the United Arab Republic. Hussein's own vision of Arab nationalism was more dynastic than ideological, and he turned to Iraq, led by his cousin King Faysal II, to shore up Jordan's vulnerable position. Within two weeks, he concluded a unity scheme with Iraq called the Arab Union, launched in Amman on February 14, 1958.

The Arab Union was a federal arrangement that preserved each country's separate national status but called for joint military command and foreign policy. The capital of the new state was to alternate between Amman and Baghdad every six months. The two Hashemite monarchies were connected by blood ties, a shared history under British tutelage, and even had a border in common.

The Arab Union was no match for the United Arab Republic, however. The union of Iraq and Jordan was seen as a rearguard action against the threat of Nasserism. By throwing in his lot with Iraq, host of the Baghdad Pact, whose prime minister Nuri al-Sa'id was reviled as the most anglophile Arab politician of his day, Hussein had exposed his kingdom to even greater pressure from the Nasserists.

Lebanon was another pro-Western state that came under intense pressure from the union of Syria and Egypt. The sectarian division of power agreed to in the 1943

National Pact had begun to unravel. Lebanese Muslims (which term grouped Sunnis, Shiites, and Druzes) were particularly aggrieved. They did not approve of the pro-Western policies pursued by the Maronite Christian president Camille Chamoun and wanted to align Lebanon with more overtly Arab nationalist policies. The Lebanese Muslims in 1958 had reason to believe that they outnumbered the Christians. The fact that the government had not authorized a new census since 1932 only confirmed Muslim suspicions that the Christians refused to recognize demographic reality. Lebanese Muslims began to question the political distribution of power that left them with less political voice than their numbers would warrant under a more proportional system. They knew that under true majority rule, Lebanon would pursue policies in line with the dominant Nasserist politics of the day.

The Lebanese Muslims saw Nasser as the solution to all their problems, a strong Arab and Muslim leader who would unite the Arab world and end the perceived subordination of Lebanon's Muslims in the Christian-dominated Lebanese state. President Chamoun, however, believed Nasser posed a direct threat to Lebanon's independence, and he sought foreign guarantees from outside subversion.

After the Suez Crisis, Chamoun knew he could not count on France or Britain for support. Instead, he turned to America. In March 1957 he agreed to the Eisenhower Doctrine. First presented to the U.S. Congress in January 1957, the doctrine was a major milestone in the Cold War in the Middle East. As a new policy initiative designed to contain Soviet influence in the Middle East, it called for American development aid and military assistance to Middle Eastern states to help them defend their national independence. Most significant, the Eisenhower Doctrine authorized "the employment of the armed forces of the United States to secure and protect the territorial integrity and political independence" of states in the region "against overt armed aggression from any nation controlled by International Communism."

Given the deepening of Soviet-Egyptian relations since the Czech arms deal and the Suez Crisis, the Eisenhower Doctrine seemed to many a policy designed to contain Egyptian as much as Soviet influence in the Arab world. Egypt rejected the new American policy as the Baghdad Pact all over again—another attempt by the Western powers to impose their anti-Soviet priorities on the Arab region, ignoring Arab concerns over Israel. Thus, when the president of Lebanon formally accepted the Eisenhower Doctrine, he entered on a collision course with both the Nasser government and Nasser's many supporters in Lebanon.

Matters came to a head in the Lebanese parliamentary elections, held in the summer of 1957. In Lebanon, the parliament elects the president of the republic for a single six-year term. The parliament resulting from the 1957 elections would thus elect the next Lebanese president in 1958, so the stakes were high.

In the run-up to the elections, Chamoun's opponents—Muslims, Druze, and Christians alike—formed an electoral bloc called the National Front. The front brought together a formidable group of politicians: the Sunni leader from Tripoli, Rashid Karami; the most powerful Druze politician, Kamal Jumblatt; and even Maronites hostile to Camille Chamoun's rule, like Bishara al-Khoury's Constitutional Bloc. The National Front represented a far larger share of the Lebanese public than those supporting the beleaguered President Chamoun.

Lebanon became a battlefield between the Americans, trying to promote regimes sympathetic to the West, and the Nasserists, who were trying to unite Arab ranks against foreign intervention. As parliamentary elections neared, the U.S. government feared Egypt and Syria would promote the National Front and undermine the position of the pro-Western Chamoun. So the Americans subverted the elections themselves. The C.I.A. provided massive funds to underwrite the election campaigns of candidates running in Chamoun's bloc in an operation overseen personally by the American ambassador to Lebanon, who was determined to achieve "a 99.9 percent-pure pro-U.S. parliament." Wilbur Crane Eveland, the C.I.A. agent who hand-delivered the funds to Chamoun in his distinctive gold Chrysler DeSoto convertible, had grave misgivings about the operation. "So obvious was the use of foreign funds by the [Lebanese] president and prime minister that the two pro-government ministers appointed to observe the polling resigned halfway through the election period."[47] Electoral tensions gave rise to large-scale fighting in northern Lebanon, where many civilians were killed and wounded during the voting.

Chamoun won in a landslide. The victory was not so much an endorsement of the Eisenhower Doctrine as evidence of the corruption of the Chamoun government. The opposition press took the election results as proof that Chamoun sought to stack the parliament in his favor in order to amend the Lebanese constitution to allow himself an unlawful second term as president.

With the opposition shut out of the parliament, some of its leaders turned to violence to prevent Chamoun from gaining a second term of office. Bombings and assassinations wracked the capital city of Beirut and the countryside from February to May 1958. The breakdown in order accelerated after the union of Syria and Egypt, as pro-Nasser demonstrations gave way to violence.

On May 8, 1958, Nasib Matni, a pro-Nasser journalist, was assassinated. Opposition forces blamed the government for his death. The National Front held Chamoun's government responsible for the murder and called for country-wide strikes in protest. The first armed disturbance broke out in Tripoli on May 10. By May 12, armed militias were fighting in Beirut as Lebanon dissolved into civil war.

The commander of the Lebanese army, General Fuad Shihab, refused to deploy the army to prop up the discredited Chamoun government. The Americans prepared to intervene in Lebanon as the situation deteriorated and the pro-Western Chamoun government looked in danger of falling to the Nasserists.

––––––––––

At the height of the fighting in Lebanon, Iraqi journalist Yunis Bahri turned to his wife and suggested they leave the turmoil of Beirut for the relative calm of Baghdad. Bahri, a native of the northern Iraqi city of Mosul, was an outspoken critic of British imperialism in the Middle East and had been one of many Arab nationalists drawn to Hitler's Germany. He was renowned in the Arab world as the voice of Radio Berlin's Arab service in the Second World War. "Hail, Arabs, this is Berlin," was his famous call sign. After the war he moved between Beirut and Baghdad, writing for the leading Arab newspapers and working as a radio broadcaster. Fatefully, in 1958 he accepted a commission from the Iraqi prime minister Nuri al-Sa'id to broadcast a series of reports critical of Nasser. When war broke out in Lebanon, Bahri's Beirut home was taken over by popular resistance forces. He told his wife they should go to Baghdad to take refuge from the shelling and shooting.

"But Baghdad is a burning hell at this time of the summer," she replied.

"The flames of Iraq are more comfortable than the bullets of Beirut," he insisted.[48] Little did he know.

Bahri and his wife arrived in Baghdad on July 13, 1958, to a warm reception. The local press had covered their return, and their first night in town was spent in a string of engagements thrown in their honor. They awoke the next morning to a revolution.

A group of military conspirators led by Brigadier Abd al-Karim Qasim and Colonel Abd al-Salam 'Arif had been plotting since 1956 to overthrow the monarchy in Iraq and establish a military-led republic. They called themselves the Free Officers, inspired by the example of the Nasser and his colleagues in Egypt. Driven by Arab nationalism and anti-imperialism, the Iraqi Free Officers condemned the Hashemite monarchy and the government of Nuri al-Sa'id for being too pro-British—a particularly serious charge in the aftermath of the Suez Crisis. The Free Officers sought to sweep away the old order installed by the British in the 1920s and install a new government created by the Iraqi people themselves. They believed the monarchy could only be overthrown by a singular act of revolutionary violence.

The Free Officers' opportunity came when the Iraqi government ordered the deployment of army units to the Jordanian border to reinforce their Arab Union partner state against further threats from Syria and Egypt, on the night of July 13–14. The route from the army base to the Jordanian border took the rebel officers past the capital city. The conspirators decided to divert their troops to central Baghdad and seize power that very night.

After the Free Officers gave instructions to loyal soldiers to divert their trucks from the highway toward the capital, the rebel soldiers took up positions in key points of the city. One detachment made its way to the Royal Palace to execute King Faysal II and all members of the ruling Hashemite family. Others went to the homes of high government officials. Orders were given for the summary execution of Prime Minister Nuri al-Sa'id. Colonel Abd al-Salam 'Arif led a small detachment to take over the radio station to broadcast word of the revolution and to assert the Free Officers' control over Iraq.

"This is Baghdad," 'Arif intoned over the airwaves in the early morning hours of July 14, 1958, "Radio Service of the Iraqi Republic." To the Iraqi listening public, this was the first indication of the end of the monarchy. The edgy 'Arif paced the room between his broadcasts, anxious for word from his co-conspirators on the success of their revolution. Around 7:00 A.M. an officer in a blood-stained uniform burst into the room holding a submachine gun in his right hand and confirmed the death of the king and royal family. 'Arif began to shout *Allahu Akbar! Allahu Akbar!* [God is great!]" at the top of his voice. He then sat at a desk, penned a few lines, and disappeared into the broadcast studio, repeating to himself, "*Allahu Akbar*, the Revolution was victorious!"[49]

Yunis Bahri followed the first reports of the revolution through 'Arif's broadcasts. "We did not know what was happening either inside or outside the capital," Bahri recalled. "The people of Baghdad crouched in their homes, confused by the sudden shock of events." Then 'Arif called the people into the streets to support the revolution and track down its enemies.

Though 'Arif knew that the royal family had already been killed, he called on the Iraqis to attack the royal palace, as though he sought to implicate the Iraqi people in the crime of regicide. He also offered a reward of 10,000 Iraqi dinars for the capture of Nuri al-Sa'id, who had managed to escape his assailants at dawn—only to be caught disguised as a woman and lynched the following day. "When the people of Baghdad heard the incitement to attack the royal palace and Nuri al-Sa'id's palace, they left their homes overcome with the desire to kill, murder, rob and plunder," Bahri recalled. The urban poor leaped at the opportunity to plunder the fabled riches of Baghdad's palaces and to kill anyone who got in their way.

Yunis Bahri took to the streets to witness the Iraqi Revolution firsthand. He was appalled by the carnage that greeted him. "Blood flowed in a violent stream down al-Rashid Street. The people applauded and cheered when they saw men dragged to death behind cars. I saw the mob drag the remains of the body of 'Abd al-Ilah after they had made an example of him, gratifying their thirst for revenge upon him. Then they hanged his body from the gate of the Ministry of Defence." The crowd pulled down the statues of King Faysal I and General Maude, the British commander who first occupied Baghdad in 1917, and set fire to the British Chancery in Baghdad.

In the atmosphere of mass hysteria, anyone could be mistaken for a man of the ancient regime and lynched. "It was sufficient for anyone to point a finger, saying 'That's [cabinet minister] Fadhil al-Jamali!' for the crowd to seize and bind the man's legs and drag him to death without hesitation or mercy, while he screamed in vain and called upon God, the prophets and all the angels and devils protesting [the mistaken identity]." Baghdad was unrecognizable, "ablaze in fires and drenched in blood, the corpses of the victims scattered in the streets."[50]

While the violence raged in the streets of Baghdad, Colonel 'Arif continued to issue statements and orders throughout the day over the national radio station. He ordered the arrest of all former Iraqi cabinet ministers, as well as the ministers of the Arab Union, both Iraqi and Jordanian. As the day wore on, lower-level figures were singled out for arrest, from the mayor of Baghdad to the chief of police. By the afternoon they were calling for broadcasters and journalists who were considered sympathetic to the monarchy. Yunis Bahri, who had assisted Nuri al-Sa'id, was named as a sympathizer of the fallen government and was arrested the following day. He reached the Ministry of Defence just as al-Sa'id's mangled corpse arrived in the back of a jeep.

The men of the old order were rounded up like sheep and led off to a new prison converted from an old hospital in a suburb of Baghdad known as Abu Ghurayb. The prison of Abu Ghurayb would gain notoriety as the torture chamber of Saddam Hussein and, later yet, of U.S. forces following the 2003 invasion of Iraq. Bahri was detained in Abu Ghurayb for seven months before being released without charge. He and his wife returned to Beirut early in 1959 to find a new government and the civil war at an end.

In Lebanon, the opposition forces celebrated the fall of the monarchy in Iraq. They believed the Hashemite monarchy was a British puppet state and that the Free Officers were Arab nationalists in Nasser's mold. They took comfort in the fall of the pro-Western government in Iraq and redoubled their efforts against the Chamoun government in Lebanon. As Chamoun recorded in his memoirs, "In rebel neighbourhoods, men and women had gone into the streets, filled cafes and public places, joyful, dancing with a frenetic joy, threatening legal authority with the fate that had been that of Baghdad leaders. On the other hand, a great fear had spread to those Lebanese committed to a peaceful and independent Lebanon."[51]

The Lebanese state, shaken by civil war, was now threatened with collapse. Chamoun invoked the Eisenhower Doctrine two hours after receiving news of the violent revolution in Iraq (Lebanon had the distinction to be the only country ever to invoke the doctrine). With the U.S. Sixth Fleet on hand in the Eastern Mediterranean, Marines landed in Beirut the very next day.

The United States intervened in Lebanon to prevent the fall of a pro-Western government to Nasserist forces. The American show of force on behalf of its Lebanese ally included 15,000 troops on the ground, dozens of naval vessels off the coast, and 11,000 sorties by naval aircraft that made frequent low-level flights over Beirut to intimidate the warring Lebanese. U.S. troops remained only three months in Beirut (the last American forces were withdrawn on October 25) and left without firing a shot.

Political stability returned to Lebanon under the brief American occupation. The commander of the Lebanese army, General Fuad Shihab, was elected president on July 31, 1958, putting to rest the opposition's concerns of an unconstitutional extension of Chamoun's rule. President Chamoun's term of office ended on schedule, on September 22. That October, President Shihab oversaw the creation of a coalition government combining loyalist and opposition members. Arab nationalist hopes that Lebanon would throw in its lot with Egypt and Syria in the United Arab Republic were dashed, as the new Lebanese government called for national reconciliation under the slogan "no vanquished and no victor."

The Iraqi Revolution left Jordan totally isolated and threatened by the same Arab nationalist forces that had swept away the much stronger monarchy in Baghdad. King Hussein's first reaction was to dispatch his army to put down the revolution and restore his family's rule in Iraq. It was an emotive response rather than a rational calculation. Even if his overstretched, underarmed forces had managed to overpower the stronger Iraqi army, there were no surviving Hashemites in Iraq to restore to the throne (the only surviving member of the family, Prince Zeid, was then serving as Iraq's ambassador to Great Britain and lived in London with his family).

Hussein soon recognized the vulnerability of his own position, and how easy it would be for his enemies in the UAR to overthrow him now that he no longer had Iraq to back him up. As he recalled his own army, which had reached 150 miles inside Iraq, Hussein turned to Britain and the United States on July 16 to request military assistance. As in Lebanon, foreign troops were seen as essential to prevent outside intervention in Jordan. It was a great risk for Hussein to turn to the former imperial power, so discredited by the Suez Crisis. Yet the risks of going it alone were even worse. On July 17, British paratroopers and aircraft began to arrive in Jordan to contain the damage of the Iraqi Revolution.

At the height of the Cold War, when political analysts conceived of whole regions of the world as dominoes at risk of falling, officials in Washington, London, and

Moscow alike believed the Iraqi Revolution would set off an Arab nationalist sweep. They were convinced that the Iraqi coup had been masterminded by Nasser and that he was intent on bringing all the Fertile Crescent under his dominion in the United Arab Republic. This in part explains the speed with which the United States and Britain intervened to prop up the pro-Western states in Lebanon and Jordan.

All eyes now turned to Egypt—to sound out Nasser's views on recent events—and to Iraq, to see what Brigadier Abd al-Karim Qasim intended to do. Would he bring Iraq into union with Syria and Egypt, creating the Arab superstate that would redress the balance of power in the region? Or would the traditional rivalry between Cairo and Baghdad be preserved in the republican era?

According to Nasser's confidant, Mohamed Heikal, the Egyptian president had misgivings about the Iraqi Revolution from the outset. Given the extraordinary volatility of the Arab world in 1958, and the tensions between the Soviets and the Americans, further regional instability could only represent a liability for Egypt.

Nasser was meeting with Tito in Yugoslavia when he first learned of the coup in Baghdad, and he flew directly to Moscow to meet with Soviet leader Nikita Khrushchev on July 17. The Soviets were convinced that Nasser had orchestrated the whole affair and were concerned about the U.S. reaction. Khrushchev admonished Nasser, saying, "Frankly we are not ready for a confrontation. We are not ready for World War Three."[52]

Nasser tried to convince his Soviet ally that he had no part in the events in Baghdad, and he tried to secure Soviet guarantees against U.S. retaliation. The most that Khrushchev was willing to offer was to conduct Soviet-Bulgarian maneuvers on the Turkish border to discourage the United States from deploying Turkish troops in Syria or Iraq. "But I am telling you frankly, don't depend on anything more than that," Khrushchev warned the Egyptian president. Nasser reassured Khrushchev that he had no intention of seeking Iraq's accession to the UAR.

The new Iraqi government was itself divided on whether to seek union with Nasser or preserve the independence of Iraq. The new leader of Iraq, Brigadier Abd al-Karim Qasim, was determined to rule an independent state and had no intention of delivering his country to Nasser's rule. He worked closely with the Iraqi Communist Party, seeking closer ties to the Soviet Union, and was cool toward the Cairo regime that had clamped down upon the Egyptian Communist Party. Qasim's second-in-command, Colonel 'Arif, played to the Arab nationalist gallery in calling for Iraq to join Egypt and Syria in the UAR. Qasim ultimately arrested his co-conspirator and had 'Arif imprisoned, condemned to death, and reprieved (in 1963 'Arif would head the coup that would overthrow and execute Qasim).

For the next five years, Qasim took Iraq down the road of rivalry, rather than unity, with Egypt, and relations between Iraq and the UAR deteriorated in mutual recrimination. Iraq's failure to join the United Arab Republic was a great disappointment to Arab nationalists across the Middle East, who had seen in the bloody revolution the possibility of uniting the three great centers of Arabism—Cairo, Damascus, and Baghdad.

The Arab world had been utterly transformed by the Egyptian Revolution. In the course of the 1950s Egypt had emerged as the most powerful state in the region and Nasser the undisputed leader of the Arab world.

Nasser rose to the peak of his power in 1958 with the union of Egypt and Syria in the United Arab Republic. The union sent shock waves across the Arab world that nearly toppled the fragile governments in neighboring Lebanon and Jordan. Arab nationalists welcomed the prospect of the collapse of the Hashemite monarchy in Jordan and of the pro-Western Christian state in Lebanon in the expectation that both would join the United Arab Republic. The Iraqi Revolution of 1958 that overthrew the Hashemite monarchy in Baghdad seemed the harbinger of a new Arab order, uniting Egypt and the Fertile Crescent and fulfilling the hopes of Arab nationalists in a united, progressive Arab superstate. For one brief, heady moment, it looked as though the Arab world might break the cycle of foreign domination that had marked the Ottoman, imperial, and Cold War eras to enjoy an age of true independence.

Iraq's decision to stay out of the United Arab Republic was a major turning point. Without the excitement and momentum that the accession of Iraq, or indeed of Jordan or Lebanon, might have brought to the UAR, Egypt and Syria were left to the mundane business of making their hybrid state work. They would not succeed. Arab nationalism turned a corner, and Nasser, having reached the pinnacle of success in the course of the 1950s, suffered a string of setbacks and defeats that turned the 1960s into a decade of defeats.

CHAPTER 11

The Decline of Arab Nationalism

In the course of the 1950s, Gamal Abdel Nasser and the Free Officers had led Egypt and the Arab world through a string of improbable triumphs. "Nasserism" had become the dominant expression of Arab nationalism. Men and women across the Arab world believed the Egyptian president had a master plan for unifying the Arab people and leading them to a new age of independence and power. They saw their hopes realized in the union of Syria and Egypt.

Nasser's remarkable run of successes came to an end in the 1960s. The union with Syria unraveled in 1961. The Egyptian army got mired in Yemen's civil war. And Nasser led his nation and its Arab allies into a disastrous war with Israel in 1967. The long-promised liberation of Palestine was yet further set back by Israel's occupation of the remaining Palestinian territories, as well as the Egyptian Sinai Peninsula and Syrian Golan Heights. The hopes of the Arab world in 1960 had been worn down to disillusion and cynicism by the time of Nasser's death in 1970.

The events of the 1960s had a radicalizing impact on the Arab world. With British and French imperialism increasingly a thing of the past, the Arabs found themselves drawn into the politics of the Cold War. By the 1960s the Arab states had divided into pro-Western and pro-Soviet blocs. The influence of the Cold War was most pronounced in the Arab-Israeli conflict, which developed into a proxy war between Soviet and American arms. The Arab experience, it seemed, would continue to be one of divide and rule.

The United Arab Republic would prove more of a challenge than Nasser had ever anticipated. Shukri al-Quwatli, the twice-deposed president of Syria, reportedly warned Nasser that he would find Syria "a difficult country to govern." He explained: "Fifty per cent of the Syrians consider themselves national leaders, twenty-five per cent think they are prophets, and ten per cent imagine they are gods."[1]

The Syrians chafed under Egyptian rule. The Syrian army, which had initially shown such enthusiasm for the union, hated taking orders from Egyptian officers. The Syrian landowning elites were outraged when Egypt's land reform program was applied to Syria. By January 1959 over one million acres of farmland had been confiscated from large landholders for redistribution to Syrian peasants. Syrian businessmen saw their position undermined by socialist decrees that transferred their companies from private to state ownership, as the government expanded its role in economic planning. The average Syrian was crushed under the weight of the notorious paperwork of Egyptian bureaucracy.

The Egyptians alienated the Syrian political elites by excluding them from government. Syrian society was intensely political, and the Syrian politicians resented the dissolution of their parties and their subordination to Egypt's single state party. Nasser named his own right-hand man, Field Marshal Abd al-Hakim Amer, to be his viceroy over the Syrian regional government, relegating his supporters in the Ba'th party to posts of second importance. By the end of 1959, leading Ba'thists had resigned from the UAR cabinet in protest—including some of the architects of the union, such as Salah al-Din Bitar. In August 1961, Nasser decided to dispense with the Syrian regional government altogether and to rule Syria through an expanded cabinet based in Cairo.

Having led its country into union with Egypt in February 1958, the Syrian army now organized a coup to sever ties and take Syria back again. On the morning of September 28, 1961, Syrian army units moved into Damascus before dawn, arrested Field Marshal Amer, and secured the radio station. The Syrian interim government, an entirely civilian cabinet, expelled Amer and ordered the deportation of all Egyptians from Syrian soil on September 30—some 6,000 troops, 5,000 civil servants, and an estimated 10,000–20,000 Egyptian guest workers.

Nasser was perplexed by Syria's bid for secession. His first reaction was to dispatch the Egyptian army to repress the coup with force. He relented hours later and recalled his forces, accepting Syrian secession "so that no Arab blood would be shed." "Nasser was tormented by the breakup of the UAR," journalist Mohamed Heikal recalled. "It had been the first international expression of his dream of Arab Unity and it was not revived in his lifetime."[2]

In the aftermath of the Syrian coup, Nasser initially pinned the blame for the breakup of the UAR on its opponents—the Jordanians, the Saudis, even the Americans. Yet the Syrian secession forced Nasser to ask hard questions about his own political orientations and the direction the Egyptian revolution had taken. He never recognized the obvious problem with the UAR—that Egypt had ruled in a quasi-imperial fashion over the proud Syrians. Instead, Nasser came to the conclusion that Egypt and Syria had failed to achieve the degree of social reform necessary for such an ambitious Arab unity scheme to work. His response to the breakup of the UAR was to introduce a radical reform agenda to strip the "reactionary" elements from Arab society and pave the way for a future "progressive" union of the Arab people.

Starting in 1962, Nasser took the Egyptian revolution down the road of Arab socialism—an ambitious if quixotic reform agenda fusing Arab nationalism and Soviet-inspired socialism. The Egyptian government accelerated the nationalization of private enterprise, which had begun in the aftermath of the 1956 Suez Crisis, to create an entirely state-led economy. Already in 1960 the UAR government had introduced its first Soviet-style five year plan (1960–1965) with overly ambitious targets for economic expansion in industry and agricultural output. In the countryside, the land reform measures begun in 1952 were intensified as new laws lowered the maximum land holding from 200 to 100 acres, with expropriated lands redistributed to landless and smallholder peasants. Egyptian industrial workers and peasants were given new prominence in state institutions.

Egypt's new political orientation was enshrined in the 1962 National Charter, which sought to weave Islam, Arab nationalism, and socialism into a coherent political project. Not only did the National Charter envision a new political culture for Egypt, but it set out ideals for reshaping Arab society at large. And the ideological orientation of the country was entrusted to the official state party, the National Union, which was renamed the Arab Socialist Union.

With his turn to Arab socialism, Nasser gave up trying to subvert the rules of the Cold War and threw in his lot with the Soviet Union, following its model of a state-led economy. Leaving the door open to future unity schemes, Nasser retained the name "United Arab Republic" for his country. It was only in 1971 that the UAR was laid to rest and Nasser's successor renamed the country the Arab Republic of Egypt.

Arab socialism would exercise great influence in Egypt and divide the Arab world. The language of politics in Egypt grew much more doctrinaire. The ultimate target of Nasser's critique after the breakup of the UAR was the "reactionaries," the men of property who put narrow national self-interest before the interests of the Arab nation. By extension, those Arab states that were supported by the West—conservative monarchies like Morocco, Jordan, and Saudi Arabia, and liberal republics like Tunisia and Lebanon—were dismissed as "reactionary" states (in the West they were known as "moderate" states). The revolutionary Arab states all aligned themselves with Moscow and followed its social and economic model. They were known in the Arab world as "progressive" states (dismissed as "radical" Arab states in the West). The list of progressive states was initially quite small—Egypt, Syria, and Iraq—though their ranks would expand with the conclusion of successful revolutions in Algeria, Yemen, and Libya.

Egypt was fairly isolated in this new division of the region, as it had poor relations with the other emerging "progressive" Arab states—Iraq in particular. However, in 1962 Nasser had just gained an important ally. After the bloodiest anticolonial war in the region's history, Algeria had finally secured its independence from France.

The Algerian war of independence raged for nearly eight years, from the first uprising of November 1, 1954, until the establishment of the Democratic and Popular Republic of Algeria in September 1962. The conflict spared no part of Algeria, spreading from the cities to the countryside. By war's end, over one million Algerians and Frenchmen had lost their lives.

When the Algerians launched their bid for independence, they had every reason to expect high casualties. In 1945 French repression of moderate nationalists in the eastern market town of Sétif (the nationalists wished to carry Algerian flags alongside French flags in their local Victory in Europe parade) resulted in riots that left forty Algerians and Europeans dead. The French overreaction to the Sétif demonstrations set off nationwide protests across Algeria through the month of May 1945. The French deployed warships, aircraft, and some 10,000 soldiers to quell the uprising. Whereas about one hundred European men, women, and children had been killed by Algerian insurgents, many more Algerians had been killed by French retaliatory measures. The French government acknowledged some 1,500 Algerian dead, though the army put the figure at 6,000–8,000. Algerians claims ran as high as 45,000 dead. The French intended Sétif as a warning against further nationalist activity. Predictably, their murderous overreaction had the opposite effect intended, driving many Algerians to embrace the nationalist cause. As Algerian nationalists rose up against the French in 1954, they were still haunted by the memory of Sétif.

The heavy casualties of the 1954–1962 Algerian War reflected an implacable logic of violent retribution. The Algerian nationalists of the National Liberation Front (FLN) believed they had to inflict terror on the French that would provoke a terrible retaliation from them, which would force the colonial power from the country. The French, for their part, had no intention of withdrawing from their oldest and most entrenched North African possession. "Algeria *is* France," the French insisted—and they meant it. They believed the nationalists to be a marginal force that could be crushed, leaving the silent majority of complacent Algerians to continue under French rule. The resulting savage war of unspeakable horrors shattered Algeria and France alike.

Atrocities against civilians began with FLN attacks on the French settlers in Philippeville in August 1955, when Algerian fighters killed 123 men, women, and children. After the experience of Sétif, the FLN knew the French would retaliate with a vengeance that would generate broad-based Algerian hatred for the French.

They were right. The French acknowledged killing over 1,200 Algerian civilians in retaliation for the Philippeville massacre. The FLN claimed the French had killed 12,000. Thousands of Algerians volunteered for the FLN as a result. In such a way, the small FLN insurgency of 1954 erupted into total war by the end of 1955.

As thousands of Algerians volunteered to join the national liberation struggle, the FLN managed to consolidate its hold over Algerian politics through a combination of conviction and intimidation. The aggressive tactics of the French military encouraged a number of Algerian political parties and movements to make common cause with the FLN. Early nationalists such as Ferhat Abbas, as well as the parties of the left, like the Communists, folded their own organizations into the National Liberation Front. The FLN was ruthless with its internal opponents. In the first three years of the war of independence it is estimated that the FLN killed six times more Algerians than Frenchmen in their operations. By July 1956, the FLN had secured unrivaled command of the national liberation struggle, which it declared both a war of independence and a social revolution.

The leadership of the FLN was divided between six internal commanders, who organized resistance within five insurrectionary provinces, or *wilayas*, and three external leaders based in Cairo. With the outbreak of the nationalist uprising in November 1954, the French used their extensive intelligence network to clamp down on the internal leadership. During the first six months of operations, the French had killed the commander of Wilaya II and arrested the leaders of Wilayas I and IV. With the internal leadership in disarray, the initiative passed to the external leadership.

Of the three external leaders of the FLN—Ahmed Ben Bella, Hocine Ait Ahmed, and Mohamed Khider—Ben Bella gained the most prominence (he would later become the first president of independent Algeria). Born in a village in western Algeria in 1918, Ben Bella was in every sense a child of French Algeria. French was his first language, he volunteered for the French army in 1936, and he even played for a French soccer team in the late 1930s. His conversion to nationalist politics was provoked by French repression of the 1945 Sétif uprising. He was arrested by the French in 1951 but escaped from prison in Algeria and made his way to Tunisia and Cairo, where he established an FLN office. Following the outbreak of the war, Ben Bella moved between Arab capitals raising funds and political support for Algeria's bid for independence from France.

The French succeeded in decapitating the leadership of the FLN in October 1956. Following reliable intelligence, the French air force intercepted a Moroccan DC-3 carrying Ben Bella, Ait Ahmed, and Khider, as well as the supreme commander of the internal leadership, Mohamed Boudiaf, and forced the plane to land in the western Algerian city of Oran. The FLN leaders were arrested and dispatched to prison in France, where they served out the remaining years of the Algerian War.

The French public celebrated the arrests of the FLN leadership as if this development marked the end of the Algerian War. Mouloud Feraoun, a celebrated author and member of Algeria's Berber community, reflected bitterly that the capture of the leaders of the movement would do nothing to restore peace between Algerians and the French. "They present the seizure [of the FLN leaders] as a great victory, prelude to the final victory," he wrote in his diary. "What final victory? Snuffing the revolt, the death of the rebellion, the renaissance of Franco-Algerian friendship, of confidence, of peace?"[3] Written in a tone of bitter irony, Feraoun recognized that whatever the French might hope, the arrest of Ben Bella and his colleagues was the prelude to more, not less, violence.

By the time of Ben Bella's arrest, the violence had already moved from the countryside to the cities. On a Sunday evening in September 1956, the relative peace of the capital, Algiers, was shattered by three bombs set off in the European quarters of the city. It was the start of a violent campaign known as the Battle of Algiers. The FLN took the war to the capital in a calculated bid to provoke a French reaction that would bolster support for the National Liberation Front inside Algeria and generate international condemnation that would isolate France. Through the autumn of 1956 and the winter of 1957, the FLN organized a number of murderous terror attacks. The French retaliated with mass arrests and extensive torture to expose the FLN's network in Algiers. The Battle of Algiers did attract widespread international attention, and France did face condemnation. But the Algerians paid a terrible price for these gains.

Mouloud Faraoun observed the violence in Algiers with horror and condemned both the French and the FLN for the murder of innocents. "The attacks in the cities are multiplying," he wrote in his diary in October 1956, "stupid, atrocious. Innocents are torn to shreds. But which innocents? Who is innocent? The dozens of peaceful Europeans drinking in a bar? The dozens of Arabs who littered the road near a mangled bus? Terrorism, counter-terrorism," he reflected with ironic bitterness, "desperate cries, atrocious screams of pain, agony. Nothing more. Peace."[4]

The FLN mobilized all segments of the society in the Battle of Algiers. Women in particular played a central role, carrying bombs, running guns, serving as couriers between leaders in hiding, and providing a safe refuge for activists wanted by the French. The role of Djamila Bouhired and other women in the movement was captured with a gritty realism in Gillo Pontecorvo's 1965 film, *The Battle of Algiers*.

Fatiha Bouhired and her twenty-two-year-old niece Djamila played central roles in the Battle of Algiers. Fatiha Bouhired's husband was one of the first men in her quarter of the Casbah, or old city of Algiers, to join the independence movement. He was arrested by the French early in 1957 and killed while trying to escape. Her husband's death redoubled Bouhired's commitment to the liberation struggle, and she allowed the FLN to operate a clandestine bomb factory in her attic. Her niece Djamila served as one of the bomb carriers and delivered correspondence between FLN activists hiding in the Casbah. Both women showed remarkable presence of mind under pressure. Once, Fatiha and Djamila were alerted that soldiers were about to search their house. They made coffee, put classical music on the gramophone, and got dressed up. When the soldiers arrived they were greeted like welcome guests by attractive women with fresh coffee.

"I would be most curious to know what lies behind those beautiful eyes," the captain of the patrol murmured suggestively to Djamila Bouhired.

"Behind my eyes," she replied, rolling her head flirtatiously, "is my hair."[5]

The officers searched the house no further.

The police would soon discover another side of Djamila Bouhired. On April 9, 1957, Djamila was shot in the shoulder while fleeing a French patrol in the Casbah. She was found carrying correspondence addressed to Saadi Yacef and Ali la Pointe, high-level FLN leaders who were at that time the two most wanted men in Algiers. She was taken to a hospital to be treated for the bullet wound, then transferred directly from the operating table to the interrogation chamber.

Over the next seventeen days she was subjected to horrific torture, clinically described in her deposition to the kangaroo court that ultimately condemned her to death. She never cracked. Her only comment in court was that "those who tortured me had no right to inflict such humiliation on a human being, physically upon my person, and morally upon themselves."[6] Her death sentence was later commuted to life imprisonment.

Fatiha Bouhired continued to serve the FLN after her niece was arrested. She bought a house in the Casbah to provide a new refuge for Saadi Yacef and Ali la Pointe. They could trust no one else. "They were at home in my home, not hiding among other people," Bouhired explained. The Casbah was riven with mistrust as the French infiltrated the FLN through collaborators and intelligence obtained by torturing detainees. "I was afraid of those who had sold out," Fatiha Bouhired confided to an interviewer, "and preferred to do everything myself: I did the shopping, I was their intermediary, I helped them move about. I did everything, but that way I felt more at ease."

The French were relentless in their pursuit of the surviving FLN leadership in Algiers. In July 1957, Yacef's sister was arrested. Under torture, she revealed Fatiha Bouhired's role in the movement and her connections to Saadi Yacef and a female bomber named Hassiba. The French authorities immediately arrested Bouhired. "They took me away and tortured me all night," Fatiha Bouhired recalled. "Where is Yacef? Where is Yacef?" they demanded. Fatiha disclaimed any knowledge of Saadi

Yacef and said Hassiba only came to her house to give her financial assistance on behalf of the FLN for the loss of her husband. She stuck to her story through repeated torture and ultimately persuaded the French, who agreed to place agents in her house to catch Hassiba when she next called on Fatiha.

Even with French agents in Fatiha Bouhired's house, Ali la Pointe and Saadi Yacef remained in place. This led to the ironic situation of the French providing security to the FLN's covert command center, with Ali la Pointe safely in the attic and French soldiers on the ground floor. Fatiha would prepare couscous, the Algerian traditional dish, for the French agents downstairs, always allowing Saadi Yacef to spit in the food before serving it to her unwelcome guests. "This time take them their couscous, and next time we'll send them a well-seasoned bomb," growled Yacef.[7]

Fatiha chafed in her new role as make-believe informant to the French, but her play-acting came to a sudden end when the French discovered Yacef's hiding place and arrested him along with Fatiha in September 1957. She spent months in prison— refusing afterward to discuss her tortures—before being placed under house arrest.

With all of the senior leadership of the FLN in the capital dead or imprisoned, the Battle of Algiers came to an end in autumn 1957. But the larger Algerian War raged on.

Buoyed by its hard-fought success in defeating the insurgency in Algiers, the French army renewed its effort to break the National Liberation Front in the countryside. In late 1956 the French initiated a policy of forcing Algerian peasants from their homes and farms into internment camps. The forced resettlement of rural Algerians gained pace after the Battle of Algiers. Hundreds of thousands of men, women, and children were rounded up and forced to live under French surveillance in camps with no access to their farmlands or work. Rather than suffer these French measures, many rural workers fled to the cities, where they congregated in slums. Others sought refuge in Tunisia or Morocco. By war's end in 1962, some three million rural Algerians had been displaced from their homes, many never to return.

The French further isolated the FLN by closing the frontiers between Algeria and its neighbors with electrified fences and mine fields, thus preventing the migration of arms, fighters, and supplies from Morocco and Tunisia.

In military terms, the French had contained and defeated the insurgency in Algeria by 1958. However, the FLN opened new fronts in its war of independence, bringing its cause to the attention of the international community. With support from Egypt and other countries of the Non-Aligned Movement, they succeeded in getting the Algerian question on the agenda of the United Nations General Assembly in 1957. The following year, the FLN declared a provisional government in exile based in its Cairo office, with veteran nationalist leader Ferhat Abbas as president.

And in December 1958 the provisional government of Algeria was invited to send a delegation to the People's Republic of China. Algerian nationalists were gaining international attention and support that served to isolate France politically even as it seemed to have won the war militarily.

France itself was increasingly divided over the Algeria question by 1958. French taxpayers were beginning to feel the enormous cost of war. The French force in Algeria, only 60,000 men in 1954, had expanded ninefold to over 500,000 by 1956.[8] This massive occupation force could only be sustained through conscription and extended national service—always unpopular measures. The young conscripts found themselves caught up in a war of unspeakable horror. Many returned home appalled by what they had witnessed and traumatized by what they had done: violations of human rights, forced resettlement, house demolitions, but worst of all, the systematic use of torture against men and women.[9] French public opinion was shocked by reports of French soldiers resorting to methods associated with the brutal Nazi repression of the French Resistance in the Second World War. Leading French intellectuals like Jean-Paul Sartre grew increasingly outspoken against the war at home, while France suffered isolation in the international arena for the violence of an imperial war during an age of decolonization.

The army and the settler community in Algeria were alarmed by the wavering French support for the Algerian colony. In May 1958 a group of French settlers rose in rebellion against the anemic government of French Premier Pierre Pflimlin, whom they suspected of seeking accommodation with the FLN enemy. Their slogan was "the Army to Power!" On May 13 the settlers overran the governor-general's offices in Algiers to declare effective self-rule under a revolutionary "committee of public safety" with General Jacques Massu, commander of the elite paratrooper units, as its president.

The French military in Algeria was in full sympathy with the settlers' movement. General Raoul Salan, commander in chief of French forces in Algeria, had dispatched a long telegram to his superiors in Paris on May 9. Salan conveyed his officers' concerns that "diplomatic processes" might lead to "the abandonment of Algeria." He continued: "The army in Algeria is troubled by the recognition of its responsibility towards the men who are fighting and risking a useless sacrifice if the representatives of the nation are not determined to maintain *Algérie française*."[10] Salan warned that only determined government action to preserve French Algeria would prevent a military putsch—not just in Algeria, but in metropolitan France as well. The crisis in Algeria risked toppling the French republic itself.

The settler insurrection sent shock waves through Algiers. Mouloud Feraoun captured the fear and uncertainty in his diary on May 14: "Atmosphere of revolution. People barricaded in their homes. Demonstrators march up and down the major arteries of the city, shops closed. The radio speaks of a Committee of Public Health that has taken all in hand and occupies the Governor General's office and controls broadcasts." The Muslims of Algiers recognized that this was a fight between the French that did not involve them. Feraoun questioned the Fourth Republic's ability to withstand the pressure. "At base, the Algeria War will prove a very hard blow for France, perhaps a mortal blow to the Republic. After which, no doubt, this blow will bring the remedy to Algeria and Algerians."[11]

Soon after, Pfimlin's government fell, and the hero of the French resistance in World War II, General Charles de Gaulle, was returned to power by public acclaim in June 1958. Within three months, de Gaulle submitted a new constitution to plebiscite and in September 1958 launched the Fifth Republic.

One of de Gaulle's first acts was to fly to Algeria to face the rebellious settler community. In a famous speech delivered in Algiers, de Gaulle calmed the restive army and settlers by promising that Algeria would remain French. "I have understood you!" de Gaulle reassured the rapturous crowds. He put forward an ambitious reform platform to develop Algeria and integrate its Arab citizens into the commonwealth of France through industrial development, land distribution, and the creation of 400,000 new jobs.

De Gaulle's proposals were clearly intended to reassure the army and settlers in Algeria and bring an end to General Salan's Committee of Public Safety. However, his comments demonstrated how little he understood the nationalist movement behind the FLN's war. Reflecting on de Gaulle's pronouncements, Mouloud Feraoun wrote bitterly: "Algerian nationalism? It doesn't exist. Integration? You've got it." It was as though de Gaulle were going back to the idea of assimilation as first set out in the Blum-Viollette proposals of 1930. Assimilation might have held some appeal even as late as 1945. By 1958 it was an irrelevance. To Feraoun, it was as if de Gaulle were saying: "You are French, old man. Nothing else. Don't give us any more headaches."

In the face of stubborn FLN resistance, de Gaulle was forced to come to terms with Algerian demands for total independence. In spite of his early promises, de Gaulle reversed his position and began to prepare his countrymen for Algeria's secession from France. In September 1959 he spoke for the first time of Algerian self-determination, provoking a round of violent demonstrations by settlers in Algeria in January 1960. De Gaulle persisted and in June 1960 convened the first direct negotiations with the provisional government of the Algerian Republic in Evian.

Hard-liners in the settler movement and their allies in the army began to see de Gaulle as a traitor. They formed terrorist organizations, like the Front of French Algeria and the notorious Secret Armed Organization, better known by its French acronym, the OAS, and actively plotted de Gaulle's assassination. The OAS also unleashed a violent terror campaign within Algeria that inflicted random violence on Arab civilians.

The Evian negotiations, combined with the breakdown in public security, provoked a political crisis among the settlers and military in Algeria. In January 1961 the French government held a referendum on self-determination in Algeria, which carried with a resounding 75 percent vote in favor. In April 1961 the Foreign Legion parachute regiment in Algiers mutinied in protest against the French government's moves to concede Algerian independence. However, the mutiny did not gain wider support among the French military, which remained faithful to de Gaulle, and the coup leaders were forced to surrender after only four days.

As the settlers' position in Algeria grew more tenuous in 1961 and early 1962, the OAS stepped up its terrorist violence inside Algeria. "Now it seems that the OAS doesn't warn anyone," Mouloud Feraoun noted in one of his last journal entries, in February 1962. "They murder in cars, on motorcycle, with grenades, with machine-gun fire, with knives. They attack cashiers in banks, post offices, companies . . . with the complicity of some and the cowardice of all."[12] Feraoun's brave voice of reason was silenced by OAS guns on March 15, just three days before the signing of the Evian Accords.

While violence continued to rage in Algeria, the FLN and de Gaulle's government made steady progress in their negotiations in Evian. On March 18, 1962, the two sides signed the Evian Accords, conferring full independence on Algeria. The terms of the accords were put to public vote in a plebiscite held in Algeria on July 1. Algerians voted in near unanimity for independence (the vote was 5.9 million in favor, 16,000 opposed). On July 3, de Gaulle proclaimed the independence of Algeria. Celebrations in Algiers were delayed for two days to coincide with the anniversary of the French occupation of the city on July 5, 1830. After 132 years, the Algerians had finally driven the French from their lands.

Ongoing terror and an uncertain future drove the French community from Algeria in massive waves—300,000 left in the month of June 1962 alone. Many settler families had lived for generations in North Africa. By the end of the year, only some 30,000 European settlers remained in Algeria.

But most destructive was the bitter fighting that swiftly broke out between the internal and external leadership of the National Liberation Front in a desperate bid to seize power in the country they had fought so hard and sacrificed so much to win. For the battle-weary Algerian people it was too much. The women of Algiers took to the streets to protest the fighting between their own freedom fighters, chanting "Seven years, enough is enough!"

It was not until Ahmed Ben Bella and Houari Boumedienne secured Algiers in September 1962 that the fighting came to an end. Ben Bella took his place at the head of government; a year later, after the ratification of the constitution in September 1963, he was elected president. Three years later, Boumedienne displaced him in a bloodless coup, reflecting the continued factionalism within the FLN leadership.

For many, independence proved a hollow victory—particularly for Algerian women. After their courage and sacrifice, they were appalled to hear FLN leader Mohamed Khider insist that women should "return to their couscous." Baya Hocine, one of the veterans of the Battle of Algiers who suffered torture and years in prison, reflected on the mixed emotions that came with independence:

> 1962 was a black hole. Before then it was a great adventure and then . . . you found yourself all alone. I don't know how the other sisters felt, but I had no immediate political objectives in mind. 1962 was the greatest comfort, the end of the war, but at the same time it was the great fear. In prison, we so believed we would . . . get out, that we would make a socialist Algeria. . . . And then we saw an Algeria made practically without us . . . without anyone thinking about us. For us, it was worse than before, because we had broken all of the barriers and it was very difficult for us to go back to that. In 1962, all of the barriers were restored, but in a terrible way for us. They were put back in place to exclude us.[13]

Algeria had achieved independence—but at a high price. Its population had suffered death and dislocation on a scale unprecedented in Arab history. Its economy was shattered by war and willful destruction by the departing settlers. Its political leadership was divided by factionalism. And its society was divided by the different expectations of what roles men and women should play in the building of independent Algeria. Yet Algeria quickly set about forming a government and took its place among the progressive Arab states as a republic born of revolutionary struggle against imperialism.

With the success of the Algerian revolution, Nasser had a new ally in his battle against Arab "reaction." Egypt, still known as the United Arab Republic after the Syrian secession, had set its sights on wholescale reform of the Arab world as the prelude to achieving Arab unity. Revolutionary Algeria, with its emphasis on anti-imperialism, Arab identity politics, and socialist reform, was a natural partner. Nasser's new state party, the Arab Socialist Union, drafted a joint communiqué with the FLN in June 1964 to assert their unity of purpose to promote Arab socialism.[14]

Nasser took some credit for having supported the Algerian revolution from inception to independence. He was moving away from an earlier role as standard bearer of Arab nationalism and now sought to present himself as the champion of progres-

sive revolutionary values. Carried away by his rhetoric, Nasser found himself providing unquestioning support to Arab revolutionary movements wherever they occurred. When a group of officers toppled the monarchy in Yemen, Nasser gave
immediate support—in his own words: "We had to back the Yemeni revolution,
even without knowing who was behind it."[15]

Yemen, long autonomous within the Ottoman Empire, had secured its independence as a kingdom in 1918. The first ruler of independent Yemen was the
Imam Yahya (1869–1948), who as head of the Zaydi sect, a small Shiite community
found only in Yemen, provided both religious and political leadership to his country.
In the 1920s and 1930s, Yahya extended his rule by dint of conquest over tribal lands
across the territory of northern Yemen, much of it inhabited by Sunni Muslims.

Throughout his reign, Yahya faced pressures from Saudi Arabia to the north,
which seized 'Asir and Najran from what Yahya considered "historic Yemen," and
from the British in the south, who had held the port city of Aden and its hinterlands
as a colony since the 1830s. Nevertheless, Yahya's ongoing military conquests gave
the illusion of unity to a society deeply divided along regional, tribal, and sectarian
lines. Under his rule, Yemen had very little exchange with the outside world, remaining focused on pursuing policies that preserved the country's isolation.

Yemen's isolation came to an end with Imam Yahya's rule. Yahya was assassinated
by a tribal shaykh in 1948 and was succeeded by his son, the Imam Ahmad (r. 1948–
1962). Ahmad had a reputation for ruthlessness that was reinforced when he ascended to power and had his rivals imprisoned and executed. He departed from
Yahya's xenophobia and established diplomatic relations with both the Soviet Union
and the People's Republic of China in his search for development assistance and
military aid.

Yet Ahmad was not secure on his throne. An attempted coup in 1955 made him
increasingly suspicious of domestic rivals and threats from abroad—particularly
Nasser and his relentless calls for overturning "feudal" regimes. The Egypt-based
Voice of the Arabs reached as far as Yemen, carrying its electrifying message of Arab
Nationalism and anti-imperialism.[16] In Yemen as elsewhere in the Arab world,
Nasser's direct radio appeal to the people placed Imam Ahmad under pressure and
was a source of tension between Yemen and Egypt.

Yet Nasser was not consistently hostile to the Yemenis. In 1956 Yemen, Egypt,
and Saudi Arabia concluded an anti-British pact in Jiddah, and in 1958 Imam
Ahmad gave his full support to the union of Egypt and Syria, joining a federation
scheme with the UAR known as the United Arab States. However, Ahmad opposed

Nasser's vision of Arab socialism, with its state-led economy and nationalization of private companies, which he condemned in verse as "taking property by forbidden means" that was "a crime against Islamic law."[17]

Coming right after Syria's secession from the UAR in 1961, Ahmad's lecture on Islamic law infuriated Nasser. Egypt severed ties to Yemen, and the Voice of the Arabs stepped up its rhetoric, putting pressure on the Yemenis to topple their "reactionary" monarchy.

The opportunity arose the following year. Imam Ahmad died in his sleep in September 1962, putting the kingdom in the hands of his son and successor Imam Badr. One week later, Badr was overthrown in an officer's coup, and the Yemen Arab Republic was declared.

Supporters of the Yemeni royal family challenged the coup, with support from the neighboring Kingdom of Saudi Arabia. Egypt threw its full weight behind the new republic and its military rulers as part of what Nasser saw as the larger battle between progressives and reactionaries in the Arab world.

The Yemeni revolution quickly devolved into a civil war within Yemen itself, and an inter-Arab war between the Egyptians and the Saudis, between the "progressive" republican order and the "conservative" monarchies in a battle for the future of the Arab world. There were no Egyptian interests at stake, only a confusion between rhetoric and *realpolitik*. This was Nasser's first war of choice, and it proved to be his Viet Nam.

Egyptian troops began to flood into Yemen after the September 1962 coup. Over the next three years the total deployment swelled from 30,000 at the end of 1963 to a peak of 70,000 in 1965—nearly half the Egyptian army.

From the start, the war in Yemen was unwinnable. The Egyptians faced tribal guerrillas fighting on their own terrain, and more than 10,000 soldiers and officers were killed over the course of five years of war. High casualties and few successes took their toll on troop morale, as the Egyptians failed to advance their lines much beyond the capital city, Sanaa. Whereas the Saudis bankrolled the royalists, and the British gave them covert assistance, the Egyptians had no surplus wealth to underwrite the huge expense of a foreign war. Yet such practical concerns had no impact on Nasser, who was blinded by his mission to promote revolutionary reform in the Arab world. "Withdrawal is impossible," Nasser told his commander in Yemen. "It would mean the disintegration of the revolution in Yemen."[18]

Nasser readily acknowledged that he saw the Yemen War as "more a political operation than a military one." What he failed to appreciate was the Yemen War's impact on Egypt's military preparedness to confront the more immediate threat of Israel.

In the decade since the Suez Crisis, Israel and its Arab neighbors had been engaged in an arms race in preparation for the inevitable next round of war. The United States began to overtake France as the primary source of military hardware for Israel, Britain supplied the Jordanians, and the Soviets armed Syria and Egypt. The Soviets were not above using their position in Egypt and Syria to pressure their rival, the United States, in an area of strategic interest to both superpowers.

War was inevitable because Israel and the surrounding Arab states were dissatisfied with the status quo and unwilling to consider peace on the basis of the status quo. The Arabs were so unreconciled to Israel that they refused to refer to the country by name, preferring to speak of "the Zionist entity." Having lost wars to the Israeli army in 1948 and 1956, the Arabs were determined to settle the score. The Palestinian refugees in Lebanon, Syria, Jordan, and the Gaza Strip served as a daily reminder of the Arabs' failure to live up to their promises to liberate Palestine.

The Israelis were also intent on war. They feared that the country's narrow waist between the coastline and the West Bank—at points only 7.5 miles, or 12 kilometers, wide—left Israel vulnerable to a hostile thrust dividing the north from the south of the country. In addition, the Israelis had no access to the Western Wall and the Jewish Quarter of the old city of Jerusalem, which remained in Jordanian hands. And Syria held the strategic Golan Heights overlooking the Galilee. Moreover, the Israelis believed that their strategic advantage—holding more and better quality weapons than their Arab neighbors—would diminish over time as the Soviets provided weapons systems of the latest technology to the Egyptians and Syrians. The Israelis needed one good war to secure defensible boundaries and inflict a decisive defeat on the Arabs to impose peace on terms with which Israel could live.

In the spring of 1967 the Israelis began to complain of Palestinian infiltrators crossing from Syria to attack Israel, and tensions between the two countries escalated rapidly. The Israelis and Syrians put their armed forces on alert. Prime Minister Levi Eshkol threatened offensive action against Damascus if the Syrian provocations did not stop. Threats gave way to hostilities in April, when Israeli jets engaged the Syrian air force in dogfights over Syrian airspace. The Israeli air force downed six Syrian MiG fighters. Two of the planes crashed in the suburbs of Damascus. As Egyptian journalist Mohamed Heikal recalled, "The situation between Syria and Israel became very dangerous."[19] The sudden escalation of hostilities placed the whole region on a war footing.

At this moment of heightened tension, the Soviet Union chose to leak a false intelligence report to the Egyptian authorities alleging a massing of Israeli troops on the Syrian frontier. The Soviets no doubt were smarting from the ease with which the Israelis with their French Mirage fighters had downed the state-of-the-art MiG 21s the USSR had provided the Syrian air force. Egypt had a mutual defense pact with the Syrians, which meant that if the Israelis initiated hostilities with Syria, Egypt would have to go to war. Perhaps the Soviets hoped to mobilize the Egyptians with false intelligence and contain the Israelis with the prospect of a two-front conflict.

Although Nasser was in possession of good intelligence, including aerial photographs, suggesting that the Israelis were not in fact mobilizing on the Syrian frontier, he continued to act publicly as though there were an imminent threat of war. Perhaps Nasser hoped to claim a victory over Israel without having to fire a shot: first, by circulating the Soviet intelligence of an Israeli threat to Syria, then by deploying his troops to the Israeli frontiers as a deterrent, subsequently claiming the absence of Israeli troops on the Syrian frontier as proof the Israelis had withdrawn in the face of Egyptian pressure. Whatever his reasoning, Nasser continued to act on the basis of the false Soviet intelligence and ordered his army across the Suez Canal on May 16 to mass in the Sinai near the Israeli frontier. This miscalculation would prove the initial step to war.

The first challenge Nasser faced was to mount a credible threat to the Israelis. With 50,000 of his best troops still tied down in the Yemen War, Nasser was forced to call up all his reservists to muster the necessary manpower. He needed to make his soldiers appear more formidable than they actually were, both to generate enthusiasm among the Egyptian people and to pose a credible threat to the Israelis. Nasser gave his troop deployment a dramatic twist by parading soldiers and tanks through central Cairo for the benefit of the cheering crowds and the international press. "Our troops were deliberately marched through the streets of Cairo on their way to Sinai," General Abd al-Ghani al-Gamasy complained, "in full view and for all to see—citizens and foreigners alike. The mass media covered these movements, contrary to all principles and measures of security."[20]

The constant stream of soldiers to the front raised public expectations of an imminent war that might redeem Arab honor and liberate Palestine. None of Nasser's millions of supporters doubted for a moment that the Egyptian army would lead its Arab allies to victory over Israel. However, the Egyptian forces were sent into the Sinai with no clear military objective, as though their sheer mass would intimidate the Israelis. Meanwhile, al-Gamasy reflected, "Israel quietly prepared for war under optimal circumstances." Its strategists had full knowledge of the numbers and equipment of the Egyptian deployment. Not only had they spent the previous months gathering detailed intelligence, but they had seen it all on TV.

When the Egyptian units reached the Sinai, they came face-to-face with the United Nations Emergency Force. The UNEF had been posted to the Sinai in the aftermath of the 1956 Suez War to keep the peace between Egypt and Israel. It was comprised of 4,500 international soldiers posted to forty-one observation points in the Gaza Strip, along the Israeli-Egyptian frontier, and at Sharm al-Shaykh at the southern tip of the Sinai.

1. As a young captain, Muammar al-Qadhafi led a military coup that toppled the Libyan monarchy in 1969 and established a novel "republic of the masses" in its place. In 1970 he took on the oil industry and asserted his government's control over production, pricing, and profits of its petroleum resources. The other Arab oil producers followed his lead, enhancing their global economic power.

2. On the afternoon of October 6, 1973, Egyptian troops crossed the Suez Canal and overran Israeli defences along the formidable sand ramparts of the Bar Lev Line. Attacking on the Jewish holiday of Yom Kippur, the Egyptians caught the Israelis by surprise and, within minutes of launching their attack, succeeded in raising their flag over Sinai territory lost in the June 1967 War. It was the Arab world's first victory in arms against the Jewish state in two decades of war.

3. Within one week of intense combat, the Israelis had regrouped and gone on the offensive against Syria and Egypt. They used the same breaches opened in the earthworks of the Bar Lev Line by Egyptian water cannons on October 6 to cross the Suez Canal and besiege Egyptian forces on the west bank of the Canal. The war ended in a military stalemate that Egyptian president Anwar al-Sadat turned to political advantage.

4. The Arab oil states deployed oil as a weapon at the height of the October 1973 War with devastating consequences for the world economy. The United States faced a total Arab oil embargo for its support of Israel's war effort. U.S. secretary of state Henry Kissinger called on Saudi king Faisal on a tour of Arab capitals in December 1973 in an unsuccessful bid to get the Saudis to lift their embargo on oil shipments to the U.S. The Arab oil states finally raised the embargo in March 1974.

5. PLO chairman Yasser Arafat enjoyed head of state treatment when invited to address the United Nations General Assembly on November 13, 1974. The Israeli delegation vacated their front-row seats in protest. "Today I have come bearing an olive branch and a freedom fighter's gun," he told the packed hall. "Do not let the olive branch fall from my hand."

6. Whole neighbourhoods of Beirut were laid waste by the violence of civil war in 1975–1976. Yet this was only the first stage of a conflict that would drag on for fifteen years, in which no quarter was spared.

The assassination of Anwar Sadat, 6 October 1981

7. Egyptian president Anwar Sadat was assassinated October 6, 1981. Sadat made a point of attending the October 6 military parade in full dress uniform to celebrate the high point of his presidency in the 1973 War. Isolated for breaking Arab ranks to conclude a separate peace treaty with Israel, the annual military parade took on added significance for Sadat after 1979. The Egyptian president traveled in an open limousine to attend his last October 6 parade in 1981.

8. The predictable drone of the military parade was suddenly shattered when one artillery truck fell out of line and armed men opened fire on the review stand. President Sadat was killed almost instantly. His assassin was an Islamist named Khalid al-Islambuli. "I have killed Pharoah," he shouted, "and I do not fear death."

9. The Israeli siege of West Beirut in July 1982, to drive PLO fighters from the Lebanese capital, introduced an unprecedented level of violence to war-torn Beirut. The Israelis only lifted their siege in August when U.S. president Ronald Reagan intervened to broker a withdrawal of PLO combatants under the supervision of an international force of U.S., French, and Italian peacekeepers.

10. On August 22, 1982, Palestinian fighters mounted trucks to make the short drive to the port of Beirut where they boarded ship for exile. Beirut had served as the center of the Palestinian armed struggle against Israel since the PLO was expelled from Jordan in 1970–1971. The PLO fighters claimed victory for having survived Israel's siege and withdrew from Beirut under Palestinian flags and portraits of Arafat carrying their weapons.

11. Palestinian refugees of the 1948 War, still living in camps, were vulnerable to Lebanese Christian militias who blamed the Palestinians for some of the worst violence of the civil war. Following the withdrawal of foreign troops and the assassination of the Maronite president-elect Bashir Gemayel in September 1982, Christian militiamen entered the Palestinian camps under Israeli guard and massacred the unarmed civilians of Sabra and Shatila. Here a survivor walks among the debris of the Sabra camp immediately after the massacre.

12. The atrocities in Sabra and Shatila forced the return of American, French, and Italian forces to Lebanon. They entered as peacekeepers but found themselves caught up in the fighting in a bid to uphold the Lebanese government of President Amin Gemayel. On October 23, 1983, coordinated suicide bombings levelled the French and American compounds, killing 241 American servicemen and 58 French paratroopers in an instant. Here, U.S. Marines help the rescue operation among the rubble of their headquarters near the Beirut International Airport.

13. The Shiites of Lebanon emerged as a new power in the 1980s. They were linked to the attacks on the French and American headquarters in 1983 and to a string of devastating attacks on Israeli forces in Lebanon. In 1985, a new Iranian-supported organization emerged called Hizbullah. As a militia, Hizbullah made Israel's position in South Lebanon untenable, forcing a unilateral withdrawal in 2000. Here, a group of clerics lead Hizbullah members in Ashura celebrations commemorating the death of Imam Husayn ibn Ali in West Beirut, 1989.

14. The 1990 Iraqi invasion of Kuwait was repelled by the 1991 Desert Storm Gulf War. After suffering weeks of aerial bombardment, on the eve of the ground war, Iraqi forces detonated charges on 700 of Kuwait's oil wells in an act of environmental and economic warfare against Kuwait and its supporters.

15. Retreating before the savagery of the ground war, Iraqi troops commandeered trucks and cars in a desperate bid to flee Kuwait. Thousands of vehicles were destroyed by American aircraft in an exposed stretch of Highway 80 leading north from Kuwait to Iraq. Dubbed the "Highway of Death," the disproportionate killing provoked international condemnation and put pressure on U.S. president George H. W. Bush to bring the Desert Storm War to an end on February 28, 1991.

16. One of the unintended consequences of the liberation of Kuwait was the initiation of the first meaningful peace process between Israel and the Palestinians. Secret track two diplomacy conducted under the auspices of the Norwegian foreign ministry resulted in the Oslo Accords, which were signed by Israel and the PLO and sealed with a historic handshake between aged adversaries Yasser Arafat and Yitzhak Rabin brokered by U.S. president Bill Clinton at the White House on September 13, 1993.

17. The Oslo Accords transferred authority over the Gaza Strip and a small West Bank enclave surrounding the town of Jericho to Palestinian self-rule. For the residents of Gaza, the
Peace Accords promised an end to Israeli occupation, and thousands took to the streets to
celebrate in September 1993.

18. The failure of the Oslo Accords to produce a viable two-state solution to the Israel-Palestine conflict
generated support for the Islamic Resistance Movement, Hamas. Hamas supporters organized a mass
rally in the West Bank city of Nablus in March 2005 to mark the first anniversary of Israel's assassination
of their founder and spiritual leader, Shaykh Ahmad Yasin (pictured above). By 2006, Hamas had overtaken Fatah and secured an overwhelming majority of seats in the Palestinian Legislative Council.

The UN forces were now an inconvenience, coming between the Egyptian troops and the Israeli frontiers. How could the Egyptian army pose a credible threat to the Israelis so long as there was a buffer force between them? The Egyptian chief of staff wrote to the commander of the UNEF to request the withdrawal of UN troops from the eastern frontiers between Egypt and Israel. The UN commander relayed the request to the secretary-general, U Thant, who responded that it was within Egypt's sovereign rights to request the withdrawal of UN troops from its territory, but that he would only approve a total withdrawal of UN forces. The UNEF, U Thant argued, was an integral unit, and it made no sense to withdraw part of the force from the eastern frontier while preserving peacekeepers in the Gaza Strip and the Strait of Tiran. Egypt reflected on the secretary-general's response and, on May 18, requested a total pullout of all UN troops from the Sinai. The last UNEF unit withdrew on May 31. Suddenly there was no buffer between the Egyptians and Israelis at all, heightening tensions between the two countries to fever pitch. This was Nasser's second miscalculation, which took him much closer to war.

The withdrawal of UN forces created an unforeseen diplomatic problem for Nasser. Since 1957 the UN had kept the Strait of Tiran open to all shipping, regardless of the flag or destination of vessels. This had given Israel a decade of free access to the Red Sea from its port of Eilat. Once the UN had been withdrawn, the strait returned to Egyptian sovereignty. Egypt came under tremendous pressure from its Arab neighbors to close the strait to all Israeli shipping, as well as to vessels destined for Eilat. As Anwar Sadat recalled, "Many Arab brothers criticized Egypt for leaving the Tiran Strait . . . open to international, particularly Israeli, navigation."

In the heated climate of May 1967, Nasser succumbed to the pressure. He convened a meeting of the Supreme Executive Committee that brought together the commander in chief of the armed forces, Field Marshal Abd al-Hakim Amer; Prime Minister Sidqi Sulayman; Speaker of the National Assembly Anwar Sadat; and other leading Free Officers. "Now with our concentrations in Sinai," Nasser reflected, "the chances of war are fifty-fifty. But if we close the Strait [of Tiran], war will be a one hundred percent certainty." Nasser turned to the commander of his armed forces and asked, "Are the armed forces ready, Abdel Hakim [Amer]?" Amer was positive: "On my own head be it, boss! Everything's in tiptop shape."[21]

On May 22 Egypt declared the closure of the Strait of Tiran to Israeli shipping and to all oil tankers destined for Eilat. Nasser was correct in his assessment of the probability of conflict. For Israel, this threat to its maritime routes was grounds for war.

By late May, the Arab world had abandoned any effort to avoid war. Arab public opinion, still smarting from the lost wars of 1948 and 1956 and a string of lesser attacks, was impatient to see Israel dealt a decisive defeat. The well-televised mobilization of Egyptian troops had raised expectations that the moment of reckoning was at hand. And inter-Arab cooperation meant that Israel would face attacks on three fronts. Syria and Egypt were already bound by a mutual defense pact, and on May 30, King Hussein of Jordan flew to Cairo to throw in his lot with Nasser. Modern weapons, unity of purpose, strong leadership: surely the Arabs had all they needed to deal the Israelis a comprehensive defeat. Yet behind all the bluster, the Arabs were less prepared for war than ever.

Egypt and the other Arab states had not learned the lessons of 1948. They had undertaken no meaningful war planning, and despite their mutual defense pacts, there was no military coordination between Egypt, Syria, and Jordan, let alone a strategy for defeating so determined a foe as Israel. To make matters worse, Egypt had squandered its wealth and military resources on an unwinnable war in Yemen, where one-third of its armed forces remained pinned down in May 1967. It was as though Egypt were going to war with one arm tied behind its back.

War with Israel must have been the last thing Nasser wanted in 1967, yet he was hostage to his own success. The people of Egypt and the Arab world at large had responded to his propaganda and believed in him. They had every confidence in his stewardship and felt confident that he would deliver. Nasser's credibility and his claim to leadership in the Arab world were at stake. As each of his miscalculations took him closer to war, he had ever less room for maneuver to avoid conflict.

The military mobilization in Egypt provoked a deep crisis in Israel. The Israeli public, increasingly fearful of encirclement by Arab enemies, looked to their government for reassurance—and grew yet more anxious. Israeli prime minister Levi Eshkol wanted to exhaust all diplomatic means before risking all-out war. His generals, headed by chief of staff Yitzhak Rabin, disagreed. They were confident they could prevail over each of the Arab armies if they acted quickly, before their adversaries could establish secure positions and coordinate a plan of attack. Cabinet meetings grew increasingly divided. Eshkol feared entering a three-front war with Egypt, Syria, and Jordan. Even the hawkish former premier, David Ben-Gurion, now retired, expressed reservations to Rabin over his mobilization for war. "You have led the state into a grave situation," he admonished Rabin. "We must not go to war. We are isolated. You bear the responsibility."[22]

The two weeks between the closure of the Strait of Tiran and the outbreak of war were a period of great tension, known as the "waiting period" in Israel. The Israeli public feared for the very existence of their state and had no confidence in their prime minister, whom they saw as indecisive.

The turning point came at the end of May. Isolated within his own coalition government, Eshkol was forced to bring the belligerent retired general Moshe Dayan into his cabinet as defense minister. Dayan's entry into the government tipped the scales in favor of the war party. With reassurances from the United States that it would stand by Israel in the event of war, the Israeli cabinet met on June 4 and made the decision to go to war. The generals swung into immediate action.

At 8:00 A.M. on June 5, 1967, an early-warning radar station in 'Ajlun, Jordan, detected waves of aircraft setting off from Israeli air bases and heading to the southwest. The Jordanian operator immediately broadcast a warning to the Egyptian air defense operations center in Cairo and to the Egyptian Ministry of War. His warning fell on deaf ears. The corporal on duty in the main receiving station had set his radio to the wrong station, and the duty officer in the ministry failed to inform the minister. Israel went to war with the advantage of total surprise.

While waves of Israeli bombers were heading toward Egyptian airspace, the commander in chief of Egyptian forces, Field Marshal Amer, was in a transport plane with several senior officers, flying to the Sinai to review air force and infantry positions. The head of the advanced command center in Sinai, General Abd al-Muhsin Murtagi, was waiting on the ground at Tamada Air Base to receive the Egyptian military's top brass. "At forty-five minutes past eight," he recalled, "Israeli planes attacked the airport, destroying all aircraft and bombing runways to render them inoperational." Incapable of landing, Amer's plane was forced to return to Cairo, as all of the Sinai air bases were under simultaneous attack.[23]

At exactly the same time, Vice President Husayn al-Shaf'i of Egypt was taking the Iraqi prime minister, Tahir Yahya, on a tour of the Suez Canal Zone. They touched down in the Fayed airport at 8:45, just as the first wave of Israeli planes attacked. "Our plane was able to land," Shaf'i wrote,

> and two bombs exploded nearby. We came down, scattered, taking shelter on the ground, and watched events unfold minute by minute. Enemy planes came at ten- to fifteen-minute intervals in groups of three to four planes, targeting specifically the planes which stood motionless on the ground, their wings touching each other as though carefully arranged to be destroyed in the shortest time possible, with no effort or trouble. Every sortie ended with one or two planes going up in flames.[24]

As the delegation made its way back to Cairo by car, columns of smoke were seen rising above each of the air bases it passed.

In less than three hours the Israeli air force had achieved air supremacy over Egypt, eliminating all of its bombers and 85 percent of its fighter aircraft, and inflicting such damage on radar systems and runways as to prevent other aircraft from using Egyptian airspace. Indeed, Nasser requested that the Algerian government lend its MiGs to his air force before he realized that the extent of the damage to Egypt's air bases prevented their deployment.

With the Egyptian air force out of commission, the Israelis went to work next on Jordan and Syria. King Hussein had put his armed forces under Egyptian command in keeping with the defense agreement he had concluded with Nasser six days earlier. The Egyptian commander now ordered Jordanian artillery and the Jordanian air force to attack Israeli air bases. The small Jordanian air force had made its first sorties and returned to base to refuel when it was struck by Israeli jets shortly after noon. In two waves, the Israelis eliminated the entire Jordanian air force—planes, runways, and bases. They turned next to attack the Syrians, eliminating two-thirds of Syria's air force in the course of the afternoon.

Once they had achieved control of the skies, the Israelis dispatched their ground forces in a bid to eliminate their Arab adversaries—Egypt, Jordan, and Syria—in quick succession so as to avoid fighting on more than one front at a time. They began in the Sinai, deploying some 70,000 infantry and 700 tanks against a total Egyptian force of 100,000 in the Sinai. After intensive fighting on June 5, the Israelis had captured large parts of the Gaza Strip, broken through Egyptian lines on the Mediterranean coast, and seized the strategic crossroads of Abu 'Uwigla in eastern Sinai by nightfall.

The Egyptians fought back. The next morning the Egyptian commanders ordered one of their armored divisions to retake Abu 'Uwigla. General El-Gamasy was a witness. "I saw one of our armoured brigades under attack. It was heartbreaking. The Israeli planes had complete freedom of the skies. The tanks were moving across open desert in daylight, which made them easy targets with no effective means of defense."[25] By afternoon, the Egyptian assault was abandoned. Field Marshal Amer, without consulting his officers on the ground, gave orders for a general retreat from the Sinai to regroup his forces on the west bank of the Suez Canal. Disorganized and uncoordinated, this retreat turned Egypt's defeat into a rout. El-Gamasy recalled watching the troops "withdraw in the most pathetic way . . . under continuous enemy air attacks, which had turned the Mitla Pass into an enormous graveyard of scattered corpses, burning equipment, and exploding ammunition."[26]

Now that Egypt's military had been neutralized, the Israelis turned to the Jordanian front. After the successful air strikes of June 5, the Israelis used their air supremacy to good effect, bombing the Jordanian armored units that had mounted a serious defense of the West Bank. Concerted Israeli attacks on Jordanian positions in Jerusalem and Jenin continued through the night before the air force could resume its strikes at dawn. By June 6 the Jordanian ground forces were besieged in the Old City of Jerusalem and on the retreat from Jenin. King Hussein went to the front to assess the situation for himself. "I will never forget the hallucinating sight of that defeat. Roads clogged with trucks, jeeps, and all kinds of vehicles twisted, disembowelled, dented, still smoking," he recalled. "In the midst of this charnel house were men. In groups of thirty or two, wounded, exhausted, they were trying to clear a path under the monstrous coup de grace being dealt them by a horde of Israeli Mirages screaming in a cloudless blue sky seared with sun."[27]

Hussein continued to hold out, both to avoid incrimination from his fellow Arabs for breaking ranks and in hopes of a UN cease-fire, which might save his position in Jerusalem and the West Bank. But the cease-fire came too late for Jordan. The Old City of Jerusalem fell on the morning of June 7, and Jordanian positions in the rest of the West Bank crumbled before the Israelis agreed to a cease-fire with the Jordanians. Syria and Egypt agreed to a cease-fire with Israel on June 8, but the Israelis pressed their advantage and attacked Syria, occupying the Golan Heights, before bringing the Six Day War to an end on June 10, 1967.

Stunned by their losses, the Egyptian commanders resorted to fantasy to buy time. On the first day of fighting, Cairo reported the downing of 161 Israeli planes.[28] The Syrians followed suit, claiming to have shot down 61 Israeli aircraft in the opening hours of the war. It was the beginning of a concerted disinformation campaign broadcast over the radio waves and reproduced in the state-controlled newspapers that led the Arab world to believe that Israel was on the verge of total defeat. "We heard about the war from the radio," one Egyptian intelligence officer recalled. "The whole world thought that our forces were at the outskirts of Tel Aviv."[29]

To the extent the Arab leadership was willing to acknowledge setbacks, they blamed them on American collusion with the Israelis. On the first day of the war, the Voice of the Arabs broadcast the accusation that "the United States is the enemy. The United States is the hostile force behind Israel. The United States, oh Arabs, is the enemy of all peoples, the killer of life, the shedder of blood, that is preventing you from liquidating Israel."[30] Nasser actually contacted King Hussein of Jordan, notorious in progressive Arab circles for his close relations with both Britain and the United States, to coordinate statements pinning the blame for Israeli gains on an Anglo-American collusion. In an indiscrete telephone conversation intercepted by Israeli intelligence, Nasser was delighted by Hussein's acquiescence. "I will make an announcement," Nasser explained, "and you will make an announcement and we will see to it that the Syrians will make an announcement that American and British airplanes are taking part against us from aircraft carriers. We will stress the matter."[31] The fact that Britain and France had gone to war with Israel against Egypt in 1956 only gave credence to the rumors of conspiracy.

The disinformation campaign perpetrated by the Arab leadership did nothing but postpone the awful day of reckoning when they would have to present their citizens with the magnitude of their losses: the total defeat of the armies and air forces of Egypt, Jordan, and Syria, and the occupation of vast Arab territory: the whole of

Egypt's Sinai Peninsula; the Palestinian Gaza Strip; the West Bank, including Arab East Jerusalem; and the Syrian Golan Heights.

Yet during the first week of June, the deluded Arab masses were still celebrating. Jubilant crowds organized victory celebrations across the Arab world, never once suspecting that their leaders were lying to them. Anwar Sadat recalled his sense of despair as he watched the spontaneous parades "applauding the faked-up victory reports which our mass media put out hourly. The fact that they were rejoicing in an imaginary victory—rejoicing in what was in effect *defeat*—made me feel sorry for them, pity them, and deeply hate those who had deceived them and Egypt as a whole." Sadat dreaded the inevitable moment of truth when the Egyptian people "realized that the victory they had been sold was in fact a terrible disaster."[32]

That moment came on June 9, when Nasser took to the airwaves to assume full responsibility for the "reversal"—Nasser gave the war its Arabic name, *al-Naksa*—and to tender his resignation. He maintained the accusation of Anglo-American collusion with Israel. The war, he argued, was but the latest chapter in a long history of imperialist domination of Egypt and the Arab world, with the United States now taking the lead. As Sadat recalled, Nasser argued that the United States "wanted to be in sole control of the world and to 'rule' Egypt into the bargain. As Nasser could not grant this wish, he had no option but to step down and hand over power."[33]

Immediately after this broadcast, the streets of Cairo filled with demonstrators, "men, women, and children from all classes and walks of life," Sadat recalled in his memoirs, "united by their sense of crisis into one solid mass, moving in unison and speaking with the same tongue, calling on Nasser to stay on." It was enough for the people of Egypt to come to terms with the shock of defeat. They did not want to do so without Nasser. For the Egyptians, keeping their leader was part of resisting defeat and foreign domination—"the United States this time, not Britain." For seventeen hours, Sadat claimed, the people refused to leave the streets until Nasser agreed to rescind his resignation.[34] Though he agreed to remain in office, Nasser never recovered from "the setback."

The losses of 1967 ushered in a radical new age of Arab politics. The magnitude of the defeat, combined with the deliberate deception of the Arab public, set off a crisis of confidence in Arab political leaders. Even Nasser, back by popular acclaim, was not spared public scorn. Sadat, not always generous to his predecessor, recalled how after the defeat of 1967, "people everywhere sneered at [Nasser] and made him a laughing stock." The other Arab leaders enjoyed a moment of respite as Nasser, the Arab colossus, was knocked off his plinth. They no longer had to fear the tirades of Nasser's propaganda machine broadcast over the Voice of the Arabs when they failed to toe Egypt's line. Nevertheless the moment did not last long. Internal threats swiftly mounted against Arab leaders in the aftermath of "the setback."

Public disenchantment set off a wave of coups and revolutions against governments across the Arab world, just as had happened after the 1948 war. President Abd al-Rahman 'Arif of Iraq was toppled by a coup led by the Ba'th in 1968. King Idris of Libya was overthrown by a Free Officers coup headed by Colonel Muammar al-Qadhafi, and Ja'far al-Numayri wrested power from the Sudanese president in 1969. In 1970, Syrian president Nur al-Din Atassi fell to a military coup that brought Hafiz al-Asad to power. Each of these new governments adopted a radical Arab nationalist platform as the basis of their legitimacy, calling for the destruction of Israel, the liberation of Palestine, and triumph over imperialism—this time epitomized by the United States.

The 1967 war would utterly transform America's position in the Middle East. It was then that the special relationship between the United States and Israel began, commensurate with Arab antagonism toward the United States. The split was bound to happen, given the differences in their respective geostrategic priorities. The Americans could not convince the Arabs to take their side against the Soviet menace, and the Arabs could not get the Americans to respect their views of the Zionist threat.

During the 1967 war, U.S. president Lyndon Johnson's administration abandoned neutrality in the Arab-Israeli conflict and tilted in favor of Israel. Believing that Nasser and his Arab socialism were taking the Arab world into the Soviet camp, they were pleased to see him discredited in defeat. Nasser, for his part, came to believe his own disinformation. What had started as a smokescreen to deflect domestic criticism— the claim of U.S. participation in the war on Israel's side—grew into a conviction that America was using Israel to advance its own domination over the region in a new wave of imperialism. Throughout the Arab world, the alleged collusion between Israel and the United States served to explain a defeat that none could have imagined. All but four Arab countries (Tunisia, Lebanon, Kuwait, and Saudi Arabia) severed relations with the United States for its alleged role in the 1967 war.

With hindsight we know Nasser's claims that the United States actually took part in the war on Israel's side were unfounded. In fact, the very opposite was true. On the fourth day of the war, Israeli air and naval forces attacked a surveillance ship, the U.S.S. *Liberty*, killing thirty-four U.S. servicemen and wounding 171. The Israelis never provided a public explanation for their attack, though it is apparent that they wanted to disable the ship to keep the Americans from monitoring Israeli communications from the battlefield. The fact that such an unprovoked attack, incurring so many American casualties, could so easily be forgiven reflected the nature of the new special relationship between Israel and the United States.

Arab attitudes toward Israel also underwent significant hardening in the aftermath of the Six Day War. There had been some overtures by Arab states over the two decades since the creation of the Jewish state in 1948, and some secret diplomacy between Arab and Israeli leaders. Nasser had engaged in secret exchanges with the Israelis in 1954, and King Hussein opened direct channels with the Jewish state in 1963.[35] The Arab defeat in 1967 put an end to all covert negotiations with Israel. Nasser and Hussein, who had lost the most in the war, hoped to recover Arab territory through a postwar negotiated settlement with Israel. However, they were marginalized by the hard line adopted during the meeting of Arab heads of state in late August and early September 1967. Held in Khartoum, Sudan, the Khartoum Summit is best known for the adoption of the "three nos" of Arab diplomacy: no recognition of the Jewish state, no negotiation with Israeli officials, and no peace between Arab states and Israel. Henceforth the moral high ground in Arab politics would be defined in terms of adherence to the resolutions of the summit.

The international community still hoped to bring Israel and the Arabs together to conclude a just and enduring peace. When the United Nations debated the issue in November 1967, it found the Arab world divided over the possibility of a diplomatic solution. Resolution 242, unanimously approved by the UN Security Council on November 22, 1967, provided the legal framework for a resolution of the Arab-Israeli conflict based on an exchange of land for peace. The resolution called for the "withdrawal of Israel armed forces from territories occupied in the recent conflict" in return for "respect for and acknowledgment of the sovereignty, territorial integrity and political independence of every State in the area and their right to live in peace within secure and recognized boundaries." Resolution 242 has remained the basis of all subsequent "land for peace" initiatives in the Arab-Israel conflict.

The resolution gained the support of Egypt and Jordan, but not of Syria or the other Arab states. For them, the three nos of Khartoum ruled out the diplomatic solution implied by Resolution 242. It was an intransigent stance, but after losing three wars to Israel—in 1948, 1956, and 1967—most Arab leaders were only willing to negotiate with the Jewish state from a position of strength. After 1967, those leaders were convinced that the Arabs were in no position to negotiate.

The Palestinian people themselves had the most to lose from the postwar diplomacy. During the two decades since they had been driven from their homeland, the Palestinians had never gained international recognition as a distinct people with national rights. Since mandate times, they had been referred to as the Arabs of Palestine, rather than as Palestinians. In 1948 the Jews of Palestine took on a national identity as Israelis, whereas the Palestinian Arabs remained just "Arabs"—either "Israeli Arabs," the minority who remained in their homes upon the creation of the state of Israel, or "Arab refugees," those who took refuge from the fighting in neighboring Arab states. As far as Western public opinion was concerned, the displaced Arabs of Palestine were no different than Arabs in Lebanon, Syria, Jordan, or Egypt and would be absorbed by their host countries in due course.

Between 1948 and 1967, the Palestinians disappeared as a political community. When Israeli premier Golda Meir claimed there were no Palestinians, few in the international community disputed her admittedly self-interested remark. This lack of awareness of Palestinian national aspirations was reflected in the UN debates of autumn 1967. Reasonable though Resolution 242 may sound to us now, at the time it represented the end of all Palestinian national aspirations. The principle of "land for peace" would confirm Israel's permanence among the community of nations, returning what little territory remained of Arab Palestine to Egyptian or Jordanian trusteeship. The country formerly known as Palestine would disappear from the atlas forever, and there would be no state for all the Palestinians driven from their homes as refugees by the two wars of 1948 and 1967. It was not enough for Palestinians to reject Resolution 242. They also had to bring the justice of their cause to the attention of the international community by all possible means.

For twenty years the Palestinians had entrusted their cause to their Arab brethren in the hopes that combined Arab action would achieve the liberation of their lost homeland. The collective Arab defeat in 1967 convinced Palestinian nationalists to take matters in their own hands. Inspired by Third World revolutionaries, Palestinian national groups launched their own armed struggle not only against Israel but also against those Arab states that got in their way.

The founders of the Palestinian armed struggle first met in Cairo in the early 1950s. A Palestinian engineering student named Yasser Arafat (1929–2004), a veteran of the 1948 war, was elected president of the Palestinian Student Union in Cairo in 1952. He used the position to motivate a generation of young Palestinians to dedicate their lives to the liberation of their homeland.

One of Arafat's closest collaborators was Salah Khalaf, who came to be known by his nom de guerre, Abu Iyad. During the Arab-Israeli War of 1948, the fifteen-year-old Khalaf had been forced to leave his hometown of Jaffa for Gaza. He went on to study in Cairo at the teacher training college Dar al-'Ulum, where he met Arafat at a meeting of the Palestinian Student Union in the autumn of 1951. "He was four years older than myself," Khalaf recalled, "and I was immediately taken by his energy, enthusiasm, and enterprising spirit." Khalaf and Arafat were united by their mistrust of the Arab regimes in the aftermath of the 1948 disaster, though with the advent of Nasser and the Free Officers, Khalaf recalled, "Everything seemed possible, even the liberation of Palestine."[36]

Revolutionary Egypt proved a difficult place for Palestinian politics. Though Nasser promised the restoration of Palestinian national rights, his government kept Palestinian nationalist activity under tight controls. Over the ensuing years, the Palestinian students fanned out across the Arab world, establishing footholds in various nations that would eventually become organized cells. Arafat moved to Kuwait in 1957, where

Khalaf joined him two years later. Others, like Mahmud Abbas, the current president of the Palestinian Authority, found jobs in Qatar. The well-educated Palestinians were successful in their new jobs and channeled their resources toward their national cause—the liberation of Palestine.

The Palestinians only began to create distinct political organs in the late 1950s. In October 1959, Arafat and Khalaf convened a series of meetings with twenty other Palestinian activists in Kuwait to establish Fatah. The organization's name was doubly significant. It is both the Arabic word for "conquest" and a reverse acronym for *Harakat Tahrir Filastin*—the Palestine Liberation Movement. The movement advocated armed struggle to transcend factionalism and achieve Palestinian national rights, and it would aggressively recruit and organize new members over the ensuing five years. Fatah began to publish a magazine—*Filastinuna*, or "Our Palestine"—to circulate its views. Its editor, Khalil al-Wazir (Abu Jihad), would emerge as Fatah's official spokesman.

The Arab states decided to create an official organ to represent Palestinian aspirations. In 1964 the first summit of Arab leaders met in Cairo and called for a new organization to enable the Palestinian people "to play their role in the liberation of their country and their self determination." Arafat and his colleagues had grave misgivings about the new organ, dubbed the Palestine Liberation Organization (PLO). The Palestinians had not been consulted in the establishment of their own liberation organization, and Nasser had imposed a lawyer named Ahmad Shuqayri to head the PLO. Shuqayri's Palestinian credentials were slim at best. Born in Lebanon of mixed Egyptian, Hijazi, and Turkish descent, the eloquent Shuqayri had served until 1963 as the Saudi representative to the United Nations. Arafat and the Fatah activists were convinced that the PLO had been created by the Arab regimes to control the Palestinians rather than to involve them in the liberation of their homeland.

At first, Fatah tried to cooperate with the PLO. Arafat and Khalaf met with Shuqayri when he visited Kuwait, and they sent delegates to the first Palestinian National Congress, convened in Jerusalem in May 1964. The PLO was formally established at the Jerusalem Congress. The 422 invited delegates, drawn mostly from elite families, reconstituted themselves as the Palestinian National Council, a sort of parliament in exile, and ratified a set of objectives enshrined in the Palestinian National Charter. The new organization even called for the creation of a Palestinian national army, which would come to be called the Palestine Liberation Army. Fatah was marginalized at the congress and left Jerusalem determined to upstage the new official Palestinian organ. To seize the initiative, Fatah decided to launch an armed struggle against Israel.

Fatah's first operation against Israel was a military failure but a propaganda success. Three commando teams were scheduled to attack Israel from Gaza, Jordan, and Lebanon on December 31, 1964. However, the governments of Egypt, Lebanon, and Jordan were keen to prevent the Palestinians from antagonizing the Israelis, knowing they would face severe reprisals against their own territory. The Egyptian authorities apprehended the Fatah squad in Gaza one week before the operation was due to take place. Lebanese security forces arrested the second group before they reached the Lebanese frontier with Israel. A third team crossed into Israel from the West Bank on January 3, 1965, and left dynamite charges in an irrigation pumping station, though the Israelis found the explosives and disarmed them before they could go off. As the Palestinian commandos returned to Jordanian territory, they were arrested by Jordanian authorities and one guerrilla was killed resisting arrest. Fatah had its first martyr, though tellingly he was killed by fellow Arabs.

The symbolism of the ultimately unsuccessful attacks was far more significant than Fatah's military objectives. On New Year's Day 1965, Fatah issued a military communiqué under an assumed name—*al-Asifa*, or "the Storm"—claiming "our revolutionary vanguards burst out, believing in the armed revolution as the way to Return and to Liberty, in order to stress to the colonialists and their henchmen, and to world Zionism and its financers, that the Palestinian people remains in the field; that it has not died and will not die."[37]

Palestinians around the world were electrified by the news. "On January 1, 1965, Fatah opened a new era in modern Palestinian history," wrote Leila Khaled, a soldier of the armed struggle whose family had been driven from Haifa in 1948. To her, the attacks represented the beginning of the Palestinian revolution and the first step toward the liberation of her homeland. "The Palestinian people had spent seventeen years in exile living on hopes fostered by the Arab leadership. In 1965 they decided they must liberate themselves rather than wait for God's help."[38]

In its first eighteen months, the Palestinian armed struggle remained a marginal movement easily contained by Israel and its Arab neighbors. Salah Khalaf claimed Fatah carried out "about 200 raids" between January 1965 and June 1967, though he acknowledged such attacks were "limited in scope and not the sort that could endanger Israeli state security or stability."

The Arab defeat in 1967 was, ironically, a moment of liberation for the Palestinian armed struggle. With Gaza and the West Bank now under Israeli occupation rather than under Egyptian and Jordanian rule, as they had been between 1948 and 1967, the Palestinian movement could claim to speak on behalf of Palestinians in the occupied territories for the first time. Moreover, the Palestinian movement gained its freedom from the defeated Arab states. Nasser and the other Arab leaders had imposed stringent restrictions on Fatah and the other Palestinian factions. The chastened Nasser could no longer stand in the way of the Palestinian movement but used his diminished authority to pressure the other Arab states bordering Israel to allow the Palestinians to launch attacks from their territory.

Jordan became the primary center of Palestinian operations in the immediate aftermath of the Six Day War. Weakened by the destruction of his armed forces and the loss of the West Bank, King Hussein turned a blind eye to Fatah operations against Israel. The armed Palestinian factions set up their headquarters in the Jordan Valley, in the village of Karamah. The Israelis took note of Fatah's preparations. In March 1968, Fatah was warned by Jordanian authorities of an imminent Israeli strike on its base in Karamah. The Palestinians decided to hold their ground and make a stand rather than retreat before superior Israeli forces. The Jordanians agreed to provide artillery support from the highlands overlooking the Jordan Valley.

On March 21 a major Israeli expedition force crossed the Jordan River in an attempt to destroy Fatah's headquarters. Some 15,000 Israeli infantry and armor attacked both the village of Karamah and the Fatah training camps. Mahmoud Issa, a 1948 refugee from Acre, was there. "We were given orders not to intervene through the first part of the operation," Issa recalled. "Abu Amar [Yasser Arafat's nom de guerre] came in person to explain that we could only survive such a desperate situation by ruse. He had no difficulty in convincing us. We were materially incapable of defending Karamah." Indeed, it is now estimated that there were only 250 Fatah guerrillas and administrative staff, and perhaps 80 members of the Palestine Liberation Army, based at Karamah at the time. "Our only option," Issa continued, "was to ambush the Israelis, and to choose the right moment to do so."[39]

Issa and his comrades took up positions outside the camp to strike their counterattack at sunset. "The day wore on," Issa related in his memoirs. "There was nothing left of Karamah. Only ruins. Many women, men and children had been taken prisoner. There were also many dead." After completing their mission under heavy Jordanian artillery fire, the Israelis began their withdrawal. It was the moment for which Issa and his comrades had been waiting.

> The moment the tanks passed our positions, the signal was given for us to attack. It was a great relief for me and my comrades. It was as though we had held our breath for too long. We ran straight ahead and wanted to run faster yet. We could imagine the surprise of the Israelis, seeing commandos they believed buried under the rubble now racing towards them. The light failed. The bridges over the Jordan had been blown. The tanks were stopped in their tracks, and with the help of [Jordanian] artillery cover, a new battle took place.

The Palestinians disabled a number of Israeli vehicles with rifle-propelled grenades and inflicted a number of casualties with small arms before the Israelis completed their withdrawal across the Jordan.

For the Palestinians, Karamah was a victory of survival against superior forces and a moment of dignity (significantly, the word *karama* means "dignity" or "respect" in Arabic) when the Israelis were forced to withdraw under fire. Dignity came at a high price, however. Though inflated casualty figures were reported in the Arab press, at least 28 Israelis, 61 Jordanians, and 116 Palestinian fighters were killed in action.[40] Yet the battle of Karamah was treated as an outright Palestinian victory across the Arab world. For the first time since 1948, an Arab army had stood up to the Israelis and shown that the enemy was not invincible.

Fatah was the prime beneficiary of the battle. As Leila Khaled recalled with some critical detachment, "Arab news media inflated the incident to make it appear as if the liberation of Palestine was just around the corner. Thousands of volunteers poured in; gold was collected in kilos, arms came by the ton. Fatah, a movement of a few hundred semi-trained guerrillas, suddenly appeared to the Arabs like the Chinese liberation army on the eve of October, 1949. Even King Hussein declared that he was a commando!"[41] Salah Khalaf, one of Fatah's founders, claimed that their offices were flooded with volunteers—some 5,000 in the first forty-eight hours following the battle. And Fatah operations expanded accordingly: 55 operations in 1968 grew to 199 operations in 1969 and peaked at 279 operations against Israel in the first eight months of 1970.[42]

Public support for the Palestinian armed struggle, and Fatah in particular, masked the factionalism and deep political rifts that fragmented the Palestinian national movement. Differences in ideology gave rise to a variety of tactics that would lead the Palestinian armed struggle from guerrilla warfare to terrorism.

The PLO underwent a major transformation in the aftermath of the 1967 war. Ahmad Shuqayri, who had never succeeded in establishing his leadership over the broader Palestinian movement, tendered his resignation as chairman of the PLO in December 1967. Though Arafat's Fatah movement was in a strong position to take over the PLO, its followers chose instead to preserve the organization as a front for all Palestinian factions. Yet Fatah emerged as the dominant party under the PLO's umbrella, and in February 1969 Yasser Arafat was elected chairman of the PLO, a title he would hold until his death in 2004.

Not all Palestinian groups accepted Fatah's leadership. The Popular Front for the Liberation of Palestine (PFLP), headed by medical doctor George Habash (1926–2008), had deep ideological differences with Fatah. The PFLP believed that according to the Chinese and Vietnamese models, the armed struggle for national liberation could only occur after a social revolution; Fatah, in contrast, put the struggle for national liberation first. The PFLP leader was dismissive of Fatah, believing the rival organization ideologically bankrupt and tainted by association with Arab governments he deemed corrupt.

When Fatah took control of the PLO, the Popular Front leadership decided to follow their own path to the Palestinian revolution and to raise international awareness of the Palestinian cause. They left Fatah to pursue the armed struggle through guerrilla raids in Israeli territory—a strategy that looked increasingly quixotic given the high casualties the Palestinians suffered (1,350 guerrillas killed and 2,800 taken prisoner by the end of 1969, according to Israeli records).[43] The Popular Front opted instead for high-profile operations against Israeli and U.S. targets abroad designed to raise international awareness of the Palestinian issue.

The Popular Front was the first Palestinian organization to engage in air piracy. In July 1968, three PFLP commandos hijacked a passenger jet of the Israeli national carrier, El Al, and ordered the pilot to land the plane in Algiers. The hijackers released all the passengers unharmed, preferring to hold a press conference rather than hostages. In December 1968, Mahmoud Issa, the veteran of Karamah, evacuated and sabotaged another El Al plane in Athens. He had been instructed by his superiors to surrender to the Greek authorities, in the expectation that his trial would generate wide press interest and serve as a platform to put the Palestinian cause to a global audience. Issa carried out his mission to the letter, seizing and evacuating the plane before detonating grenades in the empty aircraft and surrendering to the puzzled Greek authorities.

The Israelis responded to Palestinian attacks on their airliners by bombing the Beirut International Airport, where they destroyed thirteen Boeing aircraft of the Lebanese national carrier Middle East Airlines. "We thanked the Israelis for enlisting Lebanese support for the [Palestinian] revolution," Leila Khaled remarked ironically, "and admired their audacity in blowing up planes that were seventy to eighty percent American owned!"[44]

The PFLP believed its strategy was producing results and that it had focused international attention on the Palestinian cause. "The world was at last forced to take notice of Palestinian actions. The Arab press couldn't ignore them, nor could the Zionists conceal them," Khaled concluded.[45] In the international press, however, the Palestinians were gaining a reputation for terrorism that would undermine the legitimacy of their movement in Western public opinion.

As in the Algerian revolution, women played an important role in the Palestinian armed struggle. Amina Dhahbour became the first Palestinian woman to take part in a hijacking operation when she commandeered an El Al jet in Zurich in February 1969. Dhahbour's involvement was an inspiration for women in the movement. Leila Khaled heard the news on the BBC World Service and immediately told her women comrades. "Within a few minutes we were all celebrating the liberation of Palestine and the liberation of women," she recalled.[46]

Khaled, who had recently joined the Popular Front, volunteered for the Special Operations Squad and was sent to Amman for training. In August 1969, Khaled was given her first mission. "Leila," her superiors told her, "you are going to hijack a TWA plane." She was thrilled by the assignment, which she saw as a mission against American imperialism.[47] She was firmly convinced that the strategy of hijacking Israeli and American aircraft advanced the strategic objectives of the movement to liberate Palestine. "Generally," Khaled wrote, "we act not with a view to crippling the enemy—because we lack the power to do so—but with a view to disseminating revolutionary propaganda, sowing terror in the heart of the enemy, mobilising our masses, making our cause international, rallying the forces of progress on our side, and underscoring our grievances before an unresponsive Zionist-inspired and Zionist informed Western public opinion."[48] The hijacking of the TWA plane was timed to coincide with an address by President Richard Nixon to the annual meeting of the Zionist Organization of America in Los Angeles, California, on August 29, 1969.

Given the extensive security measures applied by airports today, it seems incredible how easily Leila Khaled and her associate smuggled pistols and hand grenades onto TWA Flight 840 in Rome's Fiumicino Airport. Shortly after takeoff, her accomplice forced his way onto the flight deck and announced the plane was under a "new captain." Leila then assumed command of the aircraft. "To demonstrate my credibility, I immediately offered [the pilot] Captain Carter the safety pin from the grenade as a souvenir. He respectfully declined it. I dropped it at his feet and made my speech. 'If you obey my orders, all will be well; if not, you will be responsible for the safety of passengers and aircraft.'"[49]

Once she had secured control over the plane, Khaled enjoyed her command enormously. She ordered the pilot to fly to Israel. She communicated directly with air traffic controllers en route, and particularly relished forcing the Israeli authorities to address the aircraft not as "TWA Flight 840" but as "Popular Front, Free Arab Palestine." She had the pilot circle over her native city, Haifa, which she saw for the first time since 1948, shadowed by three Israeli fighters. Finally, she instructed the pilot to land in Damascus, where all of the passengers were ultimately released unharmed. Leila and her associate were held under house arrest by the Syrian authorities for forty-five days before they were allowed to return to Lebanon. They had enjoyed complete success in their mission and escaped with impunity.

The late 1960s were the heyday of the Palestinian commando movement. Fatah's operations in Israel and the Popular Front's hijackings brought the Palestinian cause to the world's attention and gave hope to exiled Palestinians the world over. However, relations between the Arab host states and the Palestinian revolution soon began to deteriorate. The tensions were most pronounced in Lebanon and Jordan.

Palestinian guerrillas enjoyed significant public support in Lebanon, particularly among Leftist and Muslim groups disenchanted with the conservative Maronite-dominated political order. The Lebanese government, however, saw the Palestinian movement as a direct threat to its sovereignty and a risk to the country's security. When Israeli commandos attacked Beirut Airport in 1968, the Lebanese authorities attempted to crack down on the Palestinians. Clashes erupted between the Lebanese security forces and Palestinian guerrillas in the course of 1969. Egyptian president Nasser intervened to broker a deal between the Lebanese government and the Palestinian factions. The Cairo Accord of November 1969 set the ground rules for the conduct of the Palestinian movement in Lebanese territory. It permitted Palestinian guerrillas to operate from Lebanese territory and gave the Palestinian factions full control over the 300,000 Palestinians living in refugee camps in Lebanon. The Cairo Accord provided a tenuous truce between the Lebanese government and the Palestinian movement that would be stretched to the breaking point over the next six years.

Relations with the Kingdom of Jordan were even more volatile. Some of the Palestinian factions openly called for the overthrow of the "reactionary" Hashemite monarchy to mobilize Palestinian and Arab masses through social revolution, which they saw as the necessary first step for the liberation of Palestine. Salah Khalaf acknowledged that the guerrillas were in part to blame for the breakdown in relations. "It's true that our own behaviour wasn't terribly consistent," he wrote. "Proud of their force and exploits, the fedayeen [Palestinian commandos] often displayed a sense of superiority, sometimes even arrogance, without taking into consideration the sensibilities or interests of the native Jordanians. Still more serious was their attitude toward the Jordanian army, which they treated more as an enemy than as a potential ally."[50] But all the Palestinian factions believed King Hussein behaved duplicitously toward them and that he had thrown in his lot with the Americans and even the Israelis against the Palestinian cause.

By 1970 the Jordanians and the Palestinians were on a collision course. In June, the Popular Front took the first secretary of the American Embassy in Jordan hostage and seized the two largest hotels in Amman—the Intercontinental and the Philadelphia, taking more than eighty guests as hostages. King Hussein responded by sending his army to attack Palestinian positions in the refugee camps of Amman. The fighting raged for a week before a truce was struck and all the hostages were released. Leila Khaled regretted that the Popular Front had not continued fighting. "We missed the opportunity to depose Hussein when we had the confidence of the people and the power to defeat his fragmented forces," she later reflected.[51]

The Popular Front struck again in September 1970 when it hijacked another plane to Athens and demanded the release of Mahmoud Issa. Since his own attack on an El Al passenger plane in Athens in December 1968, Issa had been held in a squalid Greek jail cell, forgotten by the outside world. The show trial he had hoped for in Greece, to focus international attention on the Palestinian cause, never materialized. As a result of its bold and successful hijacking, the PFLP was able to seize headlines and forced the Greek government to release Issa.

Mahmoud Issa returned to Jordan to a hero's welcome, and within two months he had his next assignment. He was to prepare a landing strip for a spectacular PFLP operation—a synchronized three-plane hijacking that would bring Israeli and Western aircraft to the deserts of Jordan. The Popular Front hoped by these means to secure the front pages of the world's press and to assert the authority of the Palestinian revolution over Jordan. It was a deliberate provocation, a challenge to both King Hussein and his army. Issa went to work on a disused airstrip to the east of the Jordanian capital Amman known as Dawson's Field, renamed for the occasion "Revolution Airport."

On September 6, 1970, commandos of the Popular Front boarded an American TWA airliner en route from Frankfurt to New York, and a Swissair flight from Zurich to New York, and forced both planes to land in Jordan.

The PFLP also assigned four commandos to seize an Israeli passenger plane that same day. The El Al ground staff refused boarding passes to two of the would-be hijackers, who chose to hijack an American Pan Am airliner instead. The Pan Am pilot refused to land his aircraft at Dawson's Field, claiming the runway was not long enough to accommodate his massive Boeing 747 aircraft. He flew to Beirut, where Popular Front explosive teams wired the first-class cabin, and then directed the plane on to Cairo. The hijackers told the passengers and crew they would have only eight minutes to evacuate the aircraft once the plane landed. In fact, the explosives went off only three minutes after the plane touched down. Remarkably, all 175 passengers and crew managed to get off safely before the aircraft exploded.

The other two PFLP operatives succeeded in boarding the El Al flight from Amsterdam to New York. In command was Leila Khaled, the hijacker of TWA 840. Having suffered a string of attacks since 1968, El Al had intensified its security measures: cockpit doors had been reinforced, and air marshals were now posted on all flights. Shortly after takeoff, Leila and her comrade attempted to seize control of the aircraft. They met with determined resistance from the Israeli air marshals and crew. Some fourteen shots were fired, leaving an Israeli steward critically wounded and hijacker Patrick Arguello dead (Leila Khaled claimed he was summarily executed on the plane). Khaled was overpowered and disarmed. The pilot made an emergency landing in London to evacuate the wounded steward. The British authorities took the dying Arguello off the plane and arrested Leila Khaled. The Popular Front was quick to respond, hijacking a British BOAC airliner in Bahrain on September 9, where it joined the Swissair and TWA aircraft in Jordan's "Revolution Airport."

The multiple hijackings, combined with the destruction of the Pan Am aircraft in Cairo, captivated the international media. In terms of air piracy, the events of September 1970 would not be surpassed until September 2001. With three aircraft in Jordan still under its control, the PFLP began to make its demands: the release of Leila Khaled, three guerrillas held in West Germany, three other guerrillas held in Switzerland, and an unspecified number of Palestinians held by Israel. If its demands were not met within three days, all hijacked aircraft—which held a total 310 passengers and crew—would be destroyed. In fact, the Popular Front was still loath to alienate international public opinion by killing hostages, and it began to release women and children. Accounts of the hostages' experiences dominated the front pages of the world's press. On September 12, the remaining passengers were taken from the aircraft by armed PFLP guards and held hostage in a hotel commandeered by the Popular Front in central Amman. Charges were laid in the empty aircraft, which were destroyed in a series of spectacular explosions, captured by the television cameras of the world press.

A bigger explosion would follow five days later, when the Jordanian army declared war on the Palestinian revolution. For King Hussein and his army, the Palestinian factions had outstayed their welcome. The euphoria of Karamah had given way to Black September (as the war to drive the Palestinian revolution from Jordanian soil came to be called). The Popular Front had made no attempt to hide its wish to overthrow the monarchy and turn Jordan into the launching pad for the liberation of Palestine, and its decision to stage its hijacking outrage on Jordanian soil was the final straw. Fatah denounced the actions of the Popular Front, but the Jordanians no longer drew distinctions between Palestinian factions. There was not room for both the Palestinian revolution and the Hashemite monarchy in Jordan.

Both King Hussein and his army were outraged by the PFLP's audacity in seizing Jordanian territory for its terror operations. When segments of Jordan's army attempted to intervene in the hijackings at Dawson's Field, the Palestinian guerrillas countered with threats to the hostages. The Jordanian soldiers withdrew and held their fire, waiting for the hostage crisis to be resolved before taking action. This inaction in the face of Palestinian threats seemed to strip the Jordanian soldiers of their sense of manhood, taking them to the verge of mutiny against their monarch. One anecdote that gained wide circulation at the time was that when King Hussein reviewed his armored units, they flew women's lingerie from their antennae in protest. "It's we who are the women now," a tank commander told his monarch.[52]

On September 17, Hussein ordered his army into action. Black September was all-out war. For ten days Palestinian guerrillas fought the Jordanian army in a conflict that threatened to broaden into a regional conflagration. As head of a conservative monarchy in a divided Middle East, Hussein came under threat by his "progressive" Arab neighbors who wished to intervene on behalf of the Palestinians. Hussein faced a serious threat from Iraqi troops that had been posted to Jordan since the Six Day War, and an actual invasion of his northern provinces by Syrian tanks flying the colors of the Palestine Liberation Army.

With his army overstretched by what was now a two-front war—against the Palestinians and the invading Syrians—Hussein invoked his friendship with the United States and Britain and even sought Israeli assistance to protect Jordanian airspace from outside attack. Western intervention, however, risked provoking a Soviet response in defense of its own regional allies. Nasser called on the other Arab states to broker a resolution to the conflict before it spiraled out of control.

It took Nasser's authority to bring Arafat and Hussein together in Cairo on September 28 to resolve their differences. In a deal negotiated by the Arab heads of state, the Jordanians and Palestinians agreed to a total cease-fire. The remaining Western hostages from the hijack drama were released from the hotel and the different holding rooms to which they had been taken by the PFLP. The British authorities released Leila Khaled and a number of Palestinian guerrillas in a covert operation. But the damage done could not be repaired—even by Gamal Abdel Nasser. An estimated 3,000 Palestinian fighters and civilians had been killed in the Black September war; the Jordanians had also suffered hundreds of casualties. The city of Amman had been shattered by the ten days of fighting, and the Palestinian camps in the city had been reduced to ruins.

The days of intense negotiation had taken their toll on the Egyptian president. After seeing off Hussein and Arafat on September 28, 1970, Nasser returned home, where he suffered a massive heart attack and died at 5:00 P.M. that very evening.

Cairo Radio interrupted its regular programs to broadcast a solemn recital of verses from the Qur'an. After a suitable delay, Vice President Anwar Sadat announced the death of Gamal Abdel Nasser. "The effect was both instantaneous and fantastic," Mohamed Heikal recalled.

> People poured out of their houses into the night and made their way to the broadcasting station on the banks of the Nile to find out if what they had heard was true. . . . First there were little groups to be seen in the streets, then hundreds, then thousands, then tens of thousands and then the streets were black with people and it was impossible for anybody to move. A group of women outside the broadcasting station were screaming. "The Lion is dead," they cried, "The Lion is dead." It was a cry that came to echo round Cairo and it spread through the villages until it filled Egypt. That night and in the days to come he was mourned with a wild and passionate grief. Soon people began to move into Cairo from all parts of Egypt until there were ten million in the city. The authorities stopped the trains running for there was nowhere for the people to stay and food supplies were running short. But still they came, by car, by donkey, and on foot.[53]

The grief over-spilled Egypt's borders to spread across the Arab world. Mass demonstrations filled the major cities of the Arab world. Nasser, more than any other leader before or since, embodied the hopes and aspirations of Arab nationalists across the Middle East. Yet Arab nationalism had already died before Nasser. Syrian secession from the United Arab Republic, the inter-Arab war in the Yemen, and the massive defeat of 1967 and the loss of all of Palestine had dealt Pan-Arab aspirations successive blows from which it would not recover. The events of Black September cast the deep divisions between Arab states in sharp relief. Only Nasser seemed to transcend the fault lines growing between the Arab states, increasingly divided along Cold War lines into allies of the United States and partisans of the Soviet Union.

By 1970 the Arab world was firmly divided into distinct states with their own interests to uphold. There would be further high-profile unity schemes between Arab states after 1970, but none ever challenged the integrity of the states involved, and none endured. The unity schemes of the 1970s and 1980s were public relations exercises designed to confer legitimacy on Arab governments that knew that Arab nationalism still held a strong appeal to their citizens. Governments continued to pay lip service to common Arab themes of fighting the Zionist enemy and liberating the Palestinian homeland. But they were all looking out for their own interests. And a new force was taking hold of the Middle East, as the region's oil resources began to generate tremendous wealth and give the Arabs influence over the world economy.

CHAPTER 12

The Age of Oil

The Arab world was shaped by the power of oil in the eventful years of the 1970s. Nature spread oil unevenly among the Arab states. With the exception of Iraq, where the mighty Tigris and Euphrates rivers have supported large agrarian populations for millennia, the greatest oil reserves are to be found in the least densely populated Arab states: Saudi Arabia, Kuwait, and the other Persian Gulf states, Libya, and Algeria in North Africa. Token discoveries have been made in Egypt, Syria, and Jordan, though not enough to meet local demand.

Oil was first discovered in the Arab world in the late 1920s and early 1930s. For four decades, Western oil companies enjoyed unfettered control over the production and marketing of Arab hydrocarbons. Rulers in oil-producing states grew wealthy and in the 1950s and 1960s initiated development schemes to bring the benefits of oil wealth to their impoverished populations.

It was only in the 1970s, however, that a convergence of factors turned oil into a source of power for the Arab world. Growing global dependence on petroleum, the decline of American oil production, and the political crises that jeopardized the export of oil from the Middle East to the industrial world combined to generate unprecedented oil prices in the 1970s. Increasingly over the course of that decade, the Arab states took control of their oil, and the power that came with it, from the Western oil companies.

Oil more than any other commodity has come to define Arab wealth and power in the modern age. Yet oil represents an illusive sort of power. The great wealth that oil confers also makes a state more vulnerable to outside threats. The wealth of oil can be used for development, or, through arms races and regional conflicts, for destruction. Ultimately, oil conferred little security on the Arab states to enjoy its mixed blessing, and even less on the region as a whole, during the tumultuous 1970s.

Since the beginning of the twentieth century, when oil exploration in the Middle East began in earnest, relations between oil companies and oil-producing states had been governed by concessions—licenses issued by governments to companies to explore for and exploit petroleum resources in return for a fee. Commercial quantities of oil were discovered in Iran (1908) and Iraq (1927); beginning in 1931, Western oil men turned to the Arab shores of the Persian Gulf. Initially, cash-strapped local rulers sold rights to British and American firms that assumed the full risk and expense of prospecting for oil.

The risks were very real for the oil pioneers in the Persian Gulf. Some companies drilled for years without so much as an oily rag to show for their efforts. Yet, increasingly in the 1930s the oil men struck it big in Arabia. Standard Oil of California discovered oil in Bahrain in 1932. CalTex found major reserves in Kuwait in 1938, and Standard Oil of California had its first strike after six years of disappointment in the Eastern Province of Saudi Arabia, also in 1938.

When they did strike oil, the companies paid royalties to the host nation and kept the rest of the profit for themselves. Arab rulers had no complaints, for oil money came without any toil on their part. Revenues from petroleum soon exceeded all other sources of national income in the Gulf states, while the oil companies themselves bore the enormous costs of transporting and refining Arabian oil for global markets. Extracting oil from the Arabian Peninsula was a massively expensive undertaking, particularly in the early years: pipelines had to be laid and fleets of tankers had to be commissioned to carry the oil, while new refineries had to be built to convert Arabian crude to marketable products. It seemed perfectly fair to the oil companies that they should enjoy full control over the production (how much oil to extract) and marketing (setting the price in an increasingly competitive market) of a resource that they and they alone had extracted at great risk, expense, and effort.

By 1950, however, the oil-producing states had grown increasingly dissatisfied with the terms of the original concessions. Now that the infrastructure for extraction, transport, and refining was in place, the oil companies reaped tremendous profits from their investment. Aramco, the consortium of four American firms (Exxon, Mobil, Chevron, and Texaco) that enjoyed exclusive rights to Saudi oil, reaped three times the profits enjoyed by the Saudi government in 1949. Worse yet, the taxes Aramco paid to the federal government exceeded the Saudi take by some $4 million—meaning the U.S. government made more off Saudi oil than did the Saudis themselves.[1]

The Arab Gulf states demanded a greater share of those profits. After all, it was *their* oil and the main source of wealth for their growing economies. The oil men had recouped their original outlay and had been handsomely rewarded. Arab leaders now felt it was time the producing states got their fair share of the profits—both for their increasingly ambitious development plans and to provide for the future in anticipation of the day when oil would run out. There was precedent for their demands: in South America, Venezuela had managed to secure a 50:50 division of oil returns with its concession holders in 1943. The Arab states were determined to achieve the same division of oil revenues. The Saudis negotiated a 50:50 deal with the Aramco consortium in December 1950, and the other Arab oil states were quick to follow suit. There was a tidiness about this division of royalties, suggesting an equal partnership that both sides were willing to accept. But the oil companies resisted any effort to break the 50-50 split for fear that the producing nations would gain the upper hand over them.

The oil producing states of the Arab world would gain increasing power by dint of their massive oil reserves. Over the 1950s and 1960s, the Persian Gulf eclipsed the United States as the greatest oil-producing region in the world. Middle Eastern output expanded from 1.1 million to 18.2 million barrels per day between 1948 and 1972.[2] Though the oil-producing states now enjoyed an equal share of revenues with the oil companies, the oil companies remained sovereign in all matters relating to production and pricing. In the early days of oil exploration, the Western oil men could rightly claim to have a better understanding of the geology, chemistry, and economics of oil than their Arab interlocutors. But by the 1960s this was no longer the case. The oil states were now sending their best and brightest to study geology, petroleum engineering, and management in leading Western universities. A new generation of Arab technocrats returned with advanced university degrees to government jobs and chafed at the power exercised by the foreign oil companies over their natural resources and national economy.

Abdullah al-Turayqi was one of the first Arab oil experts. Born in Saudi Arabia in 1920, al-Turayqi spent twelve years in school in Nasser's Egypt, where he also received an education in Arab nationalism. He went on to study chemistry and geology at the University of Texas, returning to Saudi Arabia in 1948. He was placed in charge of the Directorate of Oil and Mining Affairs in 1955, which made him the highest-ranked Saudi in the oil industry. From this position, al-Turayqi had privileged access to the decision makers from other oil-producing states. He pressed his fellow Arab oil men to protect their interests through collective action.[3]

Most of the other Arab oil ministers were reluctant to rock the boat. They faced an oil glut, as Soviet oil began to flood the market in the 1950s. If the Arab producers put too many demands on the oil companies, the companies might simply extract their oil elsewhere. After all, the major oil companies were global giants with extensive reserves in the Americas and Africa, as well as in the Middle East. Having recently extracted a 50:50 division of oil rents from the oil companies, most Arab oil states remained cautious about pressing for more.

The Arab oil producers were rocked out of their complacency in 1959, when British Petroleum (BP) took the fateful decision to cut the posted price of oil by 10 percent. The glut of Soviet oil had put real pressure on the international price for oil, and BP's decision simply reflected market realities. The problem with this seemingly rational decision was that BP had failed to give advance notice of its decision to the oil-producing states. Because oil revenues for both companies and producing states were based on the posted price of oil, this unilateral decision meant that the oil company had imposed a cut on the revenues—and thus the national budgets—of the oil-producing states without consultation or obtaining their consent. BP had inadvertently demonstrated how unequal the partnership really was between the companies and the states.

The oil-producing states were furious. In the wake of the cut Abdullah al-Turayqi found his fellow oil ministers more open to the idea of collective action. In April 1959, on the sidelines of the first Arab oil congress, al-Turayqi met in secret with government representatives from Kuwait, Iran, and Iraq at a sailing club in the Cairo suburb of Maadi. The Arab oil men concluded a "gentlemen's agreement" to form a commission to defend oil prices and establish national oil companies. Their goal was to break through the 50:50 barrier to achieve a 60:40 division of revenues with the Western oil companies, securing the principle of national sovereignty over oil resources.

The resolve of Arab oil producers was stiffened in August 1960, when Standard Oil of New Jersey repeated BP's mistake and unilaterally cut the posted price of oil by 7 percent. The move provoked outrage among oil states and convinced even the most cautious that the Arabs would be controlled by the oil companies until they asserted control over their own oil resources. Al-Turayqi went to Iraq to suggest making common cause with Venezuela against the oil companies. The Saudi oil minister suggested the creation of a global cartel to protect the rights of oil-producing states from arbitrary action by the oil companies. Muhammad Hadid, then the Iraqi finance minister, recalled al-Turayqi's visit: "The Iraqi government welcomed the suggestion and convened a meeting of the oil producing states in Baghdad in which they agreed to establish this organization." On September 14, 1960, Iran, Iraq, Kuwait, Saudi Arabia, and Venezuela announced the formation of the Organization of Petroleum Exporting Countries, better known as OPEC.[4]

By 1960, two new Arab oil states had emerged in North Africa. Oil had only been discovered in commercial quantities in Algeria in 1956 and in Libya in 1959. The advantages of late entry meant that the North African states could learn from the experiences of their Arab colleagues in the Persian Gulf and secure the best terms for exploration and export of their petroleum products.

Libya was a poor and underdeveloped kingdom when oil was first discovered. Under Italian colonial administration until 1943, the Libyan territories passed under joint British and French rule following the Allied occupation of Italy. The three territories of Tripolitania, Cyrenaica, and Fezzan were consolidated into the United Kingdom of Libya, which gained its independence in 1951. The British rewarded Sayyid Muhammad Idris al-Sanussi (1889–1983), leader of the powerful Sanussi religious brotherhood, with the Libyan throne for his wartime services against Axis forces. He ruled as King Idris I from 1951until 1969 and saw his country pass from poverty to wealth through the discovery of oil.

Even at the prospecting stage before any oil had been discovered, the Libyans were keen to make the most of their petroleum resources. Unlike the other Arab states, which had given concessions over vast expanses of territory to major oil companies, King Idris's government decided to break up the target exploration areas into numerous small concessions and to favor independent oil companies. The Libyans reasoned that independent companies, with fewer alternative sources of petroleum, would have more incentive to discover and bring Libyan crude to market than the majors with their worldwide operations. Their strategy worked. By 1965, only six years after the discovery of oil, Libya had already emerged as the sixth largest oil exporter in the non-Soviet world, responsible for 10 percent of all petroleum exports. By 1969 the country's petroleum exports had reached parity with Saudi Arabia.[5]

While King Idris ruled over a newly prosperous country, he faced strong domestic criticism as a conservative, pro-Western monarch. A group of Arab nationalist officers in the Libyan army, headed by a young captain named Muammar al-Qadhafi (b. 1942), saw the king as a British agent. They believed they needed to overthrow King Idris for Libya to achieve its complete independence from foreign domination. In the early morning hours of September 1, 1969, they toppled the monarchy in a bloodless coup while the elderly king was abroad for medical treatment.

In his first communiqué to the Libyan nation, broadcast by radio at 6:30 that morning, Qadhafi announced the fall of the monarchy and declared the establishment of the Libyan Arab Republic. "People of Libya! Your armed forces have undertaken the overthrow of the corrupt regime, the stench of which has sickened and horrified us all." His message was replete with historical allusions. "By a single stroke [the army] has lightened the long dark night in which the Turkish domination was followed first by Italian rule, then by this reactionary and decadent regime, which was no more than a hotbed of extortion, faction, treachery and treason." He promised the Libyan people a new age "where all will be free, brothers within a society in which, with God's help, prosperity and equality will be seen to rule us all."[6]

Libya's new ruler was a devoted admirer of Gamal Abdel Nasser. Upon seizing leadership of Libya, Qadhafi assumed the rank of colonel (Nasser's rank at the time of the 1952 revolution in Egypt) and, following the Egyptian model, established a Revolutionary Command Council to oversee the government in the new Libyan Republic.

"Tell President Nasser we made this revolution for him," Qadhafi told Mohamed Heikal in the immediate aftermath of the coup.[7]

Upon Nasser's death in September 1970, Qadhafi declared himself Nasser's ideological successor. Henceforth, anti-imperialism and Arab unity would be the hallmark of Libyan foreign policy. The new Libyan government promoted the Arabic language (foreign street names were Arabized), imposed Islamic strictures (alcohol was prohibited and churches closed), and advanced the "Libyanization" of the economy by expropriating foreign-owned property in the name of the Libyan people. British and U.S. military bases were closed and all foreign troops expelled. It was in this spirit that the new Libyan regime took on the Western oil companies, believing the control they exercised over petroleum production and marketing to represent the greatest threat to Libyan sovereignty and independence.

For advice on oil policy, Colonel Qadhafi turned to the Arab nationalist oil expert Abdullah al-Turayqi (who had lost his job as Saudi oil minister to a bright new technocrat named Ahmad Zaki al-Yamani upon King Faysal's succession to the throne in 1962). Al-Turayqi, who argued in 1967 that "it is only just that those oil producing countries who rely on oil as their primary source of revenues have the right to set the fair price for its prime natural resource," shared Qadhafi's determination to break the power of oil companies over the Arab oil-producing states.[8] In 1970 Qadhafi embarked on a series of policies to assert Libya's full sovereignty over its oil resources—at the oil companies' expense.

In January 1970, Qadhafi summoned the heads of the twenty-one oil companies working in Libya to a meeting to renegotiate the terms of their contracts. The Western oil men sat uneasily in their chairs. They were still coming to terms with the new military rulers of Libya. The executives declared their resistance to any change in the way they did business in Libya. Qadhafi rounded on the oil men and made it clear that he would sooner cut oil production altogether than let his country be exploited by Western interests. "People who have lived without oil for 5,000 years," he warned, "can live without it again for a few years in order to attain their legitimate rights." The Western oil men shifted uncomfortably under Qadhafi's baleful gaze.[9]

Qadhafi decided to force the issue and to impose his price on the oil companies. That April the Libyan government requested an unprecedented 20 percent increase ($0.43) in the price per barrel of oil, which was then trading at $2.20 per barrel. The oil major Esso (the European affiliate of Exxon) responded with an offer of only five cents a barrel and held firm. With all their alternate sources of petroleum, Esso and Exxon were immune to Qadhafi's threats.

In response, Libyans put the squeeze on the smaller independent companies. As Libyan oil expert Ali Attiga recalled, "The government of Libya learned to use—and to use very well—the independents to raise the price of oil." The Libyans chose their target carefully. Occidental Petroleum had emerged from total obscurity to become one of the largest oil firms in the West on the strength of its discoveries in the Libyan desert. The only problem for Occidental was that it had no other source of oil outside Libya and so was entirely reliant on Libyan oil to meet its contracts. The Libyans imposed massive production cuts on Occidental. As the government-imposed reductions began to take effect, Occidental scrambled to find alternate sources to cover its commitments to its European customers. Yet none of the oil majors would extend a helping hand to the vulnerable independent as its daily production was trimmed by the Libyan authorities from 845,000 to 465,000 barrels. Cuts were imposed on the other oil companies as well, but none was so adversely affected as Occidental. "Now the cut in production contributed to two things," Attiga claimed. "It made the independents accept the increase in price because they had no alternative supply sources from which to meet their commitments, and it contributed to the beginning of a shortage in oil supply," which exerted an upward pressure on oil prices.[10]

Libya's strategy met with full success, and Qadhafi's young regime could claim victory over the oil companies. In the end, the chairman of Occidental Petroleum, Armand Hammer, was forced to accept Libyan terms in a landmark deal concluded in September 1970. Occidental agreed to raise the posted price of Libyan oil by an unprecedented thirty cents to $2.53 per barrel. More significant yet was Occidental's agreement to concede a majority of profits to Libya, breaking the 50:50 agreements that had prevailed for the past twenty years and introducing a new ratio of 55 percent profit to the producing state and only 45 percent to the oil companies. For the first time in the history of petroleum, a producing state gained the majority share of its oil revenues.

The Occidental precedent was applied on all of the oil companies working in Libya, and the Libyan precedent was followed by Iran and the Arab oil-producing states. In February 1971 Iran, Iraq, and Saudi Arabia concluded the Tehran Agreement, which secured a minimum 55 percent of profit for the oil states and raised the posted price of oil a further $0.35. On the back of the Tehran Agreement, the Libyans and Algerians negotiated a further hike in oil prices of $0.90 per barrel in Mediterranean markets in April 1971. These agreements set two trends in motion: regular increases by the oil-producing states in the posted price of oil, and regular decreases in the oil companies' share in profits. It was the end of the era of the Western oil barons and the beginning of the age of the Arab oil shaykhs.

The year 1971 marked the last of the Gulf states' emergence from British protection to full independence. The Trucial States had preserved their special treaty relationship to Great Britain through all the turmoil of decolonization and Arab nationalism. Independence for Bahrain and Qatar and the establishment of the United Arab Emirates represented the end of the British Empire in the Middle East, which had begun in the Persian Gulf in 1820, finally coming to an end in the same region a century and a half later.

The Gulf shaykhdoms were not technically British colonies, but independent ministates whose relations to Britain were governed by nineteenth-century treaties. The external relations of the shaykhdoms had remained under British control in return for British protection from external threats—primarily from the Ottoman Empire, which sought to extend its influence over the Arab Gulf states at the end of the nineteenth century.

In 1968 there remained nine Gulf states under the British protectorate: Bahrain, which since 1946 had served as the seat of the British Political Residency for the Gulf, Qatar, Abu Dhabi, Dubai, Sharjah, Ras al-Khaima, Um al-Qaiwain, Fujayra, and 'Ajman. Britain had exploited its privileged position in the Gulf to secure valuable oil concessions for British companies, particularly in Abu Dhabi and Dubai, and continued to exercise influence in that region transcending its reduced global status. The rulers of the Gulf states were perfectly happy with the arrangement, which enabled them to survive as ministates against the menace of powerful neighbors like Saudi Arabia and Iran with ambitions on their oil-rich lands.

It was the British rather than the ruling shaykhs of the Trucial States who initiated the process of decolonization in the Gulf. In January 1968, Harold Wilson's Labour government caught the Gulf rulers completely by surprise when they announced their intention to withdraw from Britain's commitments East of Suez by the end of 1971. Britain's decision to withdraw from the Gulf was prompted by domestic economic troubles. In November 1967 Wilson had been forced to devalue the pound to address trade and balance-of-payment deficits. Against such austerity measures, the government could not justify the cost of maintaining British military bases in the Persian Gulf. These economic concerns were compounded by the culture of the ruling Labour Party, which was openly hostile to the practice of Empire twenty years after the withdrawal from India.

The shaykhs' first reaction was to refuse to allow the British to go—or more precisely, they refused to discharge Britain from its treaty commitments to protect the region from outside aggression. They had good grounds for concern. Saudi Arabia laid claim to most of oil-rich Abu Dhabi, and Iran declared sovereignty over the island state Bahrain and a number of smaller islands straddling major offshore oil fields. Over the next three years Britain applied all its diplomatic acumen to resolve the different claims on Gulf territories and to encourage a union of the Trucial States that would give them the critical mass to survive the treacherous waters of the Persian Gulf.

In 1970 the Shah of Iran relinquished his claim over Bahrain. Shaykh 'Isa bin Salman, the ruler of Bahrain, withdrew from union discussions with the other Trucial

States and declared his country's independence on August 14, 1971. Bahrain's neighbor and long-time rival, the peninsular state of Qatar, quickly followed suit on September 3, 1971. The differences between the remaining seven states were significant but not insurmountable, and as the deadline for the British withdrawal approached, six of the states came to an agreement to form a Union of Arab Emirates (later the United Arab Emirates) on November 25, 1971.

The odd country out was Ras al-Khaima, which refused to join the union in protest against Iranian claims to two of its islands, the Greater and Lesser Tunbs. Ras al-Khaima did not want to release Britain from its duty to preserve what it held to be its sovereign territory in the disputed islands. Britain, in contrast, was convinced that it needed Iranian goodwill to preserve the territorial integrity of the Gulf states and was willing to sacrifice two of Ras al-Khaima's smaller islands in the interest of preserving the independence of the union as a whole. The British had brokered an agreement between Sharjah and Iran to divide another disputed island, Abu Musa, between them and saw such concessions as a necessary evil to keep the shah from doing worse. In the end, Ras al-Khaima joined the United Arab Emirates, which was admitted to the Arab League on December 6 and to the United Nations on December 9, 1971.

Ironically, Britain's withdrawal from the Gulf strained relations with two of the states most committed to the ideals of Arab nationalism and anti-imperialism. Iraq severed relations with Britain in protest against British complicity in the Iranian occupation of Arab territory—Abu Musa and the Tunbs. Libya went a step further and nationalized Britain's oil interests on December 7, to punish the British for delivering Arab lands to Iranian rule. The West's growing dependence on Arab oil made it vulnerable to such punitive action, and the Arabs began to view their oil as a weapon to attain their political objectives. It was not long before the Arab world began to consider ways to deploy the oil weapon in its conflict with Israel and its Western allies.

———————————

Colonel Qadhafi's oil advisor, Abdullah al-Turayqi, saw early on how useful oil could be in reshaping geopolitics. Months after the June 1967 War, he published an essay with the PLO research center in Beirut in which he described Arab petroleum as "a weapon in the battle." Setting out the just grounds for deploying oil strategically against Israel's allies, al-Turayqi argued, "It is generally agreed that every state has the right to use all available means to apply pressure on its enemies. And the Arab states possess one of the most powerful economic weapons that might be used against its enemies." The Arabs, he claimed, held no less than 58.5 percent of the world's known petroleum resources, and the industrial world was increasingly dependent on the Arab world for its energy supplies. Why should the Arabs continue to supply the West while the United States, Britain, Germany, Italy, and the Netherlands supported their enemy, Israel? "The Arab peoples call for the use of the oil weapon and it is the responsibility of each government to satisfy the will of its people," al-Turayqi concluded.[11]

Using oil as a weapon was easier said than done. Al-Turayqi knew better than most how ineffectual the oil weapon had proven in the June 1967 War. Arab oil ministers had met on June 6, the day war broke out, and agreed to ban shipments to the United States, Britain, and West Germany for their support of Israel. Within forty-eight hours both Saudi Arabia and Libya had closed down their production entirely. Arab output was reduced by 60 percent, putting tremendous pressure on Western markets.

Yet the industrial world withstood this first use of the oil weapon. It is nearly impossible to track oil once it has entered the international market, allowing embargoed states to circumvent the ban on direct sales by purchasing oil through intermediaries not affected by the embargo. The United States and other non-Arab oil producers expanded production to make up the difference, and the Japanese deployed fleets of massive new "supertankers" to transport oil to global markets. Within a month, the industrial states were back to full supply, demonstrating the futility of a gesture that had in the meantime deprived the Arab oil producers of vital revenues. By the end of August 1967, the defeated Arab states—Egypt, Syria, and Jordan—called on their oil-producing brethren to resume production to help them meet the terrible burden of postwar reconstruction.

Not only had the oil weapon proven ineffectual in the 1967 War, but it harmed Arab economies long after the guns fell silent. The return of Arab oil to international markets produced a glut that drove prices down. The oil weapon had backfired and hurt the Arab states far more than Israel and its Western supporters. Yet such was the lack of confidence in Arab armies, in the aftermath of the 1967 defeat, that many policymakers still believed the Arab world more likely to achieve its objectives against Israel by economic than by military means.

The post-1967 malaise affected Egypt worse than any other Arab state. The crushing defeat of its army and the loss of the entire Sinai Peninsula were compounded by the economic effects of the war. Egypt faced a massive postwar reconstruction bill, exacerbated by the closure of the Suez Canal and the collapse in the tourist trade, Egypt's two most important sources of external revenue.

The prospects for a peaceful resolution to the Arab-Israeli conflict were more remote after the 1967 War than at any point since the creation of the state of Israel.

International efforts to broker a resolution between Egypt and Israel were undermined by the positions taken by the two antagonists: Israel wanted to retain all of the Sinai as a bargaining chip to force Egypt to conclude a full peace treaty, whereas the Egyptian government demanded the return of the Sinai as a precondition for any peace talks.

For Egypt, the longer Israel remained in the Sinai, the greater the risk of the international community accepting the Israeli occupation of Egyptian territory. President Gamal Abdel Nasser was determined to prevent the Israelis from turning the Suez Canal into a de facto border between the two states, and engaged Israel in an undeclared War of Attrition that lasted from March 1969 to August 1970. The Egyptians used commando raids, heavy artillery, and air attacks in a bid to wear down Israeli positions along the Suez Canal. The Israelis responded by building a series of fortifications along the canal, dubbed the Bar-Lev Line after the serving chief of staff, General Chaim Bar-Lev, and by unleashing air raids deep into Egyptian territory.

The Israelis proved their continued military superiority over the Egyptians through the months of the War of Attrition. The Egyptians had no effective air defense, leaving Israeli planes free to strike the suburbs of Cairo and the cities of the Nile Delta. "The aim was to put the Egyptian people under heavy psychological pressure and make the political leadership appear weak, forcing it to halt the War of Attrition," Egypt's General Abd al-Ghani El-Gamasy reasoned. "The raids carried the implicit message that since the Egyptian armed forces could not see the futility of fighting, the raids might demonstrate this directly to the Egyptian people."[12]

Although the Israeli raids did not turn the Egyptian public against its government, the War of Attrition was hurting Egypt far more than Israel. Nasser was increasingly open to American mediation, and in August 1970 he agreed to a cease-fire with Israel as part of a still-born peace plan brokered by the U.S. secretary of state, William Rogers. Nasser died the following month, leaving Egypt and Israel no closer to resolving their differences.

Nasser's successor was his vice president, Anwar Sadat. Though he was one of the founders of the Free Officers movement, had taken part in the 1952 revolution, and was one of the original members of the Revolutionary Command Council, Sadat remained something of an unknown quantity at home and abroad. He had none of Nasser's charm or public appeal and had to prove himself if he hoped to remain in power.

Sadat faced an inauspicious international setting when he took office. The Nixon administration was pursuing a policy of détente with Egypt's ally, the Soviet Union. As tensions between the superpowers diminished, regional disputes such as the Arab-Israeli conflict took on less urgency in Moscow and Washington. The Soviets and the Americans were willing to live with the status quo, a policy of "no war, no peace" between the Arabs and Israel, until the disputing parties showed a more pragmatic attitude toward resolving their differences. Sadat knew the status quo favored Israel. With each passing year, the international community would come to accept Israel's hold over Arab territories occupied in 1967.

To break the impasse, Sadat had to take the initiative. He needed to force America to reengage with the Arab-Israeli conflict, to push the Soviets to provide high-tech weapons to the Egyptian military, and to present the Israelis with a credible threat to recover the Sinai. In order to achieve his goals, he would need to go to war—a limited war to achieve specific political objectives.

Sadat took his first step to war by expelling all of the 21,000 Soviet military advisors in Egypt in July 1972. It was a counterintuitive move, but one designed to force both the Americans and the Soviets to reengage with the Arab-Israeli conflict. The Americans began to question Egypt's ties to the Soviet Union and the possibility of diverting the most powerful Arab state to the pro-Western camp. It was precisely this threat that stirred the Soviets from their complacency toward their Egyptian client. Sadat had pressed the Soviet leadership to reequip Egypt's devastated armed forces in the years after the Six Day War and the war of attrition. Moscow had prevaricated, delaying delivery of arms and withholding the more sophisticated Soviet arms needed to counter the high-tech arms the United States was providing Israel. Although Sadat expelled the Soviet military advisors, he was careful not to cut relations with the Soviet Union. Instead, he preserved Egypt's Treaty of Friendship with the USSR and continued to extend base privileges to Soviet forces, thereby demonstrating his alliance. Sadat's strategy proved brilliantly successful: between December 1972 and June 1973 the Soviets exported more advanced weapons to Egypt than in the previous two years combined.

Sadat's next objective was to prepare his military for war. He called the heads of the Egyptian armed forces to a meeting at his home on October 24, 1972, to confront them with his decision to initiate a war against Israel. "This is not a matter about which I'm taking your advice," he warned the Egyptian top brass.

The generals were aghast. They believed Israel was much better prepared for a war than the Arab states. Egypt was entirely dependent on the Soviet Union for advanced weaponry, and the Soviets still lagged well behind the Americans in supplying their allies in the Arab-Israeli conflict. As far as the generals were concerned, this was no time to be talking of war. General El-Gamasy, who attended the meeting, described the atmosphere as "exceptionally stormy and agitated," with Sadat growing increasingly angry with his generals' rebuttals. "By the end of the meeting, it was clear that President Sadat was not pleased with what had taken place—not with the reports presented, the opinions expressed, or the forecasts."[13] Nor had he changed his mind. Following the meeting, Sadat reshuffled his military to relieve the doubters of their commands. El-Gamasy was named chief of operations and tasked with planning the war.

General el-Gamasy was determined not to repeat the mistakes of the Six Day War. He knew from firsthand experience how unprepared Egypt was in 1967 and how poorly the Arab armies had coordinated their war efforts. The first priority for the Egyptian war planners was to conclude a deal with Syria to launch a two-front attack on the Israelis. The Syrians were as determined to redeem their losses in the Golan Heights as the Egyptians were in the Sinai, and they struck a top secret agreement to unify the command of their armed forces with the Egyptians in January 1973.

Next, the planners had to decide on the ideal date to launch their attack to achieve the greatest degree of surprise. El-Gamasy and his colleagues pored over their almanacs to find the ideal moonlight and tidal conditions for crossing the Suez Canal. They considered the Jewish religious holidays, as well as the political calendar, to find a time when the military and the general public might be distracted. "We discovered that Yom Kippur fell on a Saturday and, what was more important, that it was the only day throughout the year in which radio and television stopped broadcasting as part of the religious observance and traditions of that feast. In other words, a speedy recall of the reserve forces using public means could not be made."[14] Taking all these factors into consideration, el-Gamasy and his officers recommended beginning operations on Saturday, October 6, 1973.

While the general prepared Egypt's military for war, Sadat traveled to Riyadh to persuade the Saudis to deploy an entirely different weapon: oil. Sadat made an unannounced visit to Saudi Arabia in late August 1973 to brief King Faysal on his secret war plans and to ask for Saudi support and cooperation. Sadat needed to be persuasive, for the Saudis had consistently refused Arab requests to deploy the oil weapon since the disastrous experience of 1967.

Fortunately for Sadat, the world was far more dependent on Arab oil in 1973 than it had been in 1967. American oil production had reached its peak in 1970 and was now falling each year. Saudi Arabia had replaced Texas as the swing producer that could fill shortfalls in global supplies simply by pumping more oil. As a result, the United States and the industrial powers were more vulnerable to the oil weapon than ever before. Arab analysts estimated in 1973 that the United States imported some 28 percent, Japan some 44 percent, and the European states as much as 70–75 percent of their oil from the Arab world.[15] The Saudi king, a committed Arab nationalist, believed his country could use its oil resources effectively and promised Sadat his support if Egypt went to war against Israel. "But give us time," Faysal reportedly told Sadat. "We don't want to use our oil as a weapon in a battle which only goes on for two or three days, and then stops. We want to see a battle which goes on for long enough time for world opinion to be mobilized."[16] There was no point in deploying a weapon after war was over, as the Saudis learned in 1967. The Saudi king wanted to be sure the next war would last long enough for the oil weapon to be effective.

War broke out minutes past two on the afternoon of Saturday, October 6, 1973, as the Syrian and Egyptian armies simultaneously attacked Israel to the north and south. In spite of Egyptian precautions to maintain secrecy, Israeli intelligence was convinced that an attack was imminent, though they assumed that a more limited assault would come toward sunset. An all-out, two-front war was but the first surprise for the Israeli military.

Under a blistering artillery attack—el-Gamasy claimed the Egyptians fired over 10,000 rounds in the first minutes of conflict—waves of Egyptian commandoes crossed the Suez Canal in dinghies and stormed the sand ramparts of the Bar-Lev Line, shouting "Allahu Akbar" ("God is Great"). The Egyptian troops suffered very light casualties in overcoming what were widely believed impregnable Israeli positions. "At five minutes past two the first news of the battle started coming in to Centre Number Ten [central command]," journalist Mohamed Heikal recalled. "President Sadat and [Commander-in-Chief] Ahmad Ismail listened with astonishment. It seemed as though what they were watching was a training exercise: 'Mission accomplished . . . mission accomplished.' It all sounded too good to be true."[17]

Israeli commanders listened with no less disbelief as their soldiers in the Bar-Lev fortifications, their guard down during Yom Kippur observances, sounded the alert and declared their positions untenable in the face of superior enemy forces. Syrian tanks overran Israeli positions and pressed deeply into the Golan Heights. Both the Egyptian and Syrian air forces swept deep inside Israel to attack key military positions.

When the Israelis scrambled their own air force, their fighter jets were intercepted by Soviet SAM 6 missiles as soon as they reached the fronts. Gone was the air supremacy of the 1967 War, as the Israelis lost twenty-seven planes over the Egyptian front alone in the opening hours of the war and were forced to hold their aircraft fifteen miles behind the Canal Zone. Israeli tanks sent to relieve their troops along the Bar-Lev Line faced a similar shock, encountering Egyptian infantrymen armed with Soviet wire-guided antitank missiles that knocked out scores of Israeli armor.

With both the Israeli ground and air forces held in check, Egyptian military engineers set up high-pressure water pumps and literally washed away the sand ramparts of the Bar-Lev Line, opening the way for Egyptian forces to pass through Israeli front lines into the Sinai Peninsula beyond. Pontoon bridges were laid across the canal for Egyptian troops and armor to cross over to the east bank and into the Sinai.

At the end of the first day of fighting, some 80,000 Egyptian soldiers had crossed through the Bar-Lev Line and were dug into positions up to 4 kilometers (about

2.5 miles) inside the Sinai Peninsula. On the northern front, Syrian troops broke through Israeli defenses in the Golan Heights, inflicting heavy losses on Israeli tanks and aircraft in a concerted press toward Lake Tiberias. With the benefit of near total surprise, the initiative was squarely in the hands of Egypt and Syria in the opening hours of the war, as the Israelis scrambled to respond to the gravest threat the Jewish state had ever faced.

The Israeli military regrouped and went on the offensive. Within forty-eight hours reserves were called and deployed, holding positions in the Sinai and concentrating their offensive on the Golan, in the hopes of defeating Syria first before concentrating on the larger Egyptian army. In response, Iraqi, Saudi, and Jordanian infantry and armor units were dispatched to Syria to resist the Israeli counterattack in the Golan. Israel and the Arabs were suffering heavy casualties and running down their reserves of arms and ammunition in the fiercest fighting yet witnessed in the Arab-Israeli conflict.

By the end of the first week of the war, both sides were in need of resupply.[18] On October 10 the Soviets began airlifting weapons to Syria and Egypt, and on October 14 the Americans initiated their own secret airlift of arms and ammunition to the Israelis. Armed with new American tanks and artillery, the Israelis mounted a successful counterattack that by October 16 had overwhelmed the Syrian front and led to the encirclement of Egyptian forces on the west bank of the Suez Canal. The military situation was grinding to a stalemate with Israeli troops consolidating their advantage over their Arab adversaries.

It was at this point that the Arab states decided to deploy the oil weapon. On October 16, Arab oil ministers gathered in Kuwait. They had a new sense of confidence and self-respect in light of Egyptian and Syrian gains in the first days of the war. The leaders of the Arab oil states were also buoyed by the knowledge that the industrial world was dependent on them. This meant that when the Arabs raised the price of their oil, they were able to inflict immediate punishment on those industrial countries that supported Israel.

On the first day of their meeting in Kuwait, the Arab oil ministers imposed a 17 percent price hike without so much as a phone call to the now powerless Western oil companies. "This is a moment for which I have been waiting a long time," Saudi oil minister Shaykh Ahmad Zaki Yamani told one of the delegates. "The moment has come. We are masters of our own commodity."[19] The impact on oil markets was immediate and provoked widespread panic. By the end of the day, oil traders had raised the posted price of a barrel of oil to $5.11, up 70 percent over the trading price of $2.90 in June 1973.

The price hike was but the first crack of the whip to get the world's attention. The following day the Arab oil ministers released a communiqué outlining a series of production cuts and embargoes to force the industrial powers to modify their policies toward the Arab-Israeli conflict. "All Arab oil exporting countries shall forthwith cut their production respectively by no less than five percent of the September production," it read, "and maintain the same rate of reduction each month thereafter until the Israeli forces are fully withdrawn from all Arab territories occupied during the June 1967 War, and the legitimate rights of the Palestinian people are restored."[20]

The oil ministers reassured friendly states that they would not be affected by these measures. Only "countries which demonstrate moral and material support to the Israeli enemy," the oil ministers explained, "will be subjected to severe and progressive reduction in Arab oil supplies, leading to a complete halt." The United States and the Netherlands, given their traditional friendship for Israel, were threatened with a complete embargo "until such time as the Governments of the USA and Holland or any other country that takes a stand of active support to the Israeli aggressors reverse their positions and add their weight behind the world community's consensus to end the Israeli occupation of Arab lands and bring about the full restoration of the legitimate rights of the Palestinian people."

After demonstrating their strength on the battlefield and over the oil markets, the Arab states opened a diplomatic front. The very day that the Arab oil states sent out their communiqué, the foreign ministers of Saudi Arabia, Kuwait, Morocco, and Algeria met with President Nixon and his secretary of state, Henry Kissinger, in the White House. The Arab ministers found the American administration amenable to the implementation of UN Security Council Resolution 242, calling for Israeli withdrawal from Arab territory occupied in June 1967 in return for full peace between Israel and the Arab states. The Algerian foreign minister asked why the resolution had never been implemented in the first place. "Kissinger said that, quite frankly, the reason was the complete military superiority of Israel. The weak, he said, don't negotiate. The Arabs had been weak; now they were strong. The Arabs had achieved more than anyone, including themselves, had believed possible."[21] To the Arabs, it seemed that the Americans only understood force.

The Nixon administration found itself in an unusually difficult position. It wanted to placate the Arab world but not at the expense of Israel's security. This went beyond American loyalty to the Jewish state. In Cold War terms, the Americans were determined that Israel, with its American-supplied arms, should prevail over the Arabs with their Soviet weapons. When Israel turned to the United States with an emergency request to restore its depleted arsenal, President Nixon approved legislation on October 18 for a $2.2 billion arms package for the Jewish state.

The blatant U.S. support for Israel's war effort outraged the Arab world. One by one, the Arab oil states imposed a complete embargo on the United States. Arab oil output dropped by 25 percent, and oil prices spiked, eventually reaching a peak of

$11.65 a barrel by December 1973. In six months, the price of oil had quadrupled, radically unsettling Western economies and hurting consumers. As reserves diminished, drivers faced long lines at the gas pumps and rationing of scarce petroleum resources.

Western governments faced growing pressure from their citizens to bring the oil embargo to a close. The only way to resolve the oil crisis was to address the Arab-Israeli conflict. Sadat had fulfilled his strategic objectives and forced the United States to reengage with regional diplomacy. With Egyptian forces still dug in on the east bank of the Suez Canal, there was no longer any question of the international community coming to accept the canal as the de facto border between Egypt and Israel. The Egyptian leader now looked for the opportune moment to end the war and consolidate his gains.

Sadat's military position was growing weaker the longer the war went on. By the third week of October, Israel had gone on the offensive, its troops surging deep into Arab territory to within 60 miles of Cairo and only 20 miles of Damascus. These gains had come at a tremendous cost, with over 2,800 Israelis killed and 8,800 wounded—much higher casualties in proportion to Israel's population than the 8,500 Arab soldiers killed and nearly 20,000 wounded in the war.[22]

The Israeli counterattack raised new tensions between the superpowers. As the Israelis threatened the encircled Egyptian Third Army on the west bank of the Suez Canal, Soviet premier Leonid Brezhnev sent a letter to U.S. president Richard Nixon calling for joint diplomatic action. Brezhnev warned that the Soviet Union might otherwise be forced to intervene unilaterally to protect its Egyptian allies. With the Red Army and the Soviet Navy on alert, U.S. intelligence feared the Soviets might introduce a nuclear deterrent in the conflict zone. U.S. security officials responded by placing their military on high nuclear alert for the first time since the Cuban missile crisis. After a few hours of heightened tension, the superpowers agreed to combine forces to seek a diplomatic end to the October War.

The Egyptians and the Israelis were also impatient to bring the devastating armed conflict to an end. After sixteen days of intensive warfare, both sides were ready to lay down their arms, and a cease-fire was negotiated through the UN Security Council on October 22. That same day, the Security Council passed Resolution 338, which reaffirmed the earlier Resolution 242 calling for the convening of a peace conference and a resolution of Arab-Israeli differences through an exchange of land for peace. That December the United Nations convened an international conference in Geneva to address the issue of Arab land occupied by Israel in 1967 as a first step toward a just and enduring resolution to the Arab-Israeli conflict.

Kurt Waldheim, the secretary-general of the United Nations, opened the conference on December 21, 1973. Cosponsored by the United States and the USSR, the conference was attended by delegations from Israel, Egypt, and Jordan. President

Hafiz al-Asad of Syria refused to attend when he could not obtain a guarantee that the conference would restore all occupied territory to the Arab states. There was no Palestinian representation. The Israelis vetoed PLO participation, and the Jordanians were not keen to have a rival representing the Palestinians in the occupied West Bank.

The conference in Geneva proved inconclusive. The Arab delegations failed to co-ordinate before the conference, and their presentations revealed deep divisions in Arab ranks. The Egyptians referred to the West Bank as Palestinian territory, undermining Jordan's negotiating position. The Jordanians felt the Egyptians were punishing them for not having taken part in the 1973 War. The Jordanian foreign minister, Samir al-Rifa'i, called for a complete Israeli withdrawal from all occupied Arab territories, including East Jerusalem. Abba Eban, Israel's foreign minister, insisted Israel would never return to the 1967 lines and declared Jerusalem the undivided capital of Israel. The only significant result of the conference was the creation of a joint Egyptian-Israeli military working group to negotiate a disengagement of Egyptian and Israeli forces in the Sinai.

In the aftermath of the failed conference, U.S. secretary of state Henry Kissinger embarked on several rounds of intensive shuttle diplomacy to secure disengagement agreements between Israel and its Arab neighbors. Agreements were concluded between Egypt and Israel on January 18, 1974, and between Syria and Israel in May 1974. By these agreements, Egypt regained the whole of the eastern bank of the Suez Canal, with a UN-controlled buffer zone between Egyptian and Israeli lines in the Sinai. The Syrians too regained a slice of Golan territory lost in the June 1967 War, again with a UN buffer force between Syrian and Israeli lines in the Golan. With the war over and diplomacy in full swing, the Arab oil producers declared their objectives met and brought the oil embargo to a close on March 18, 1974.

Yet the events of 1973 were not seen as an unqualified success by all Arab analysts. Mohamed Heikal believed Egypt and the Arab oil states conceded too much, too soon. Having imposed an embargo with specific political objectives—the evacuation of all Arab territories occupied in June 1967—the Arabs had lifted the embargo before any of their objectives had actually been met. "All that can be said on the credit side," Heikal concluded, "is that the world saw the Arabs acting for once in unison and oil being used, even if clumsily, as a political weapon."[23]

Nevertheless, the Arab world did make significant gains in 1973. The display of discipline and unity of purpose impressed the international community and forced the superpowers to take the Arab world more seriously. On an economic level, the events of 1973 led to full Arab independence from the Western oil companies. In Shaykh Yamani's words, the Arab oil states had asserted mastery over their own commodity and came out of the oil crisis immensely wealthier. Oil, which had traded at less than $3 a barrel before the 1973 crisis, stabilized at prices ranging from $11–13 for most of the 1970s. If Western cartoonists vilified the oil shaykh as a greedy hook-nosed character holding the world to ransom, Western businessmen were quick to flock to an emerging market of seemingly limitless resources. Even the Western oil companies had reaped enormous profits from the crisis, as their vast oil reserves appreciated with the spike in prices. Yet the events of October 1973 dealt the final blow to the oil concessions that had governed relations between Western companies and the Arab oil-producing states. Kuwait and Saudi Arabia followed Iraq and Libya in buying out the assets of Western oil companies for their national oil industries, bringing the age of the Western influence over Arab oil to a close by 1976.

The October War was also a diplomatic success. Sadat had succeeded in using the war to break the deadlock with Israel. Concerted Arab military action had proved a credible threat to Israel, and the war had raised dangerous tensions between the Soviets and Americans. The international community now gave a high priority to resolving the Arab-Israeli conflict through diplomacy based on UN Security Council Resolutions 242 and 338.

Through his bold initiatives in 1973, Anwar Sadat had secured Egypt's interests—and placed Palestinian national aspirations in dire jeopardy. Although the UN resolutions upheld the territorial integrity of all the states in the region, they made no mention of the stateless Palestinians, other than to promise "a just settlement of the refugee problem." The Palestine Liberation Organization, the effective government-in-exile of the Palestinian people, faced a stark choice: engage in the new diplomacy, or see Jordan and Egypt regain the West Bank and Gaza Strip through a comprehensive peace deal that would spell the end of Palestinian hopes for an independent state.

A helicopter cut swiftly through the predawn gloom along the East River to the United Nations headquarters in Manhattan. At 4:00 A.M. on November 13, 1974, the helicopter touched down, and anxious security men rushed PLO Chairman Yasser Arafat to a secure suite inside the UN building. Arriving without warning in the dark of night, Arafat was spared the indignity of driving through the thousands of demonstrators who gathered later that morning at the UN Plaza to protest his appearance, carrying banners proclaiming the "PLO is Murder International" and the "UN Becomes a Forum of Terrorism." He was also protected from assassins.

Arafat's visit to the United Nations was the culmination of a remarkable year for Palestinian politics. The Soviet Union, the Eastern Bloc states, the countries of the Non-Aligned Movement, and the Arab world had combined forces to secure an invitation for the PLO chief to open the UN debate on "The Question of Palestine." It was his opportunity to present Palestinian aspirations to the community of nations.

The UN appearance also marked Arafat's transition from guerrilla leader to statesman—a role for which he had little preparation. "Why don't you go?" he had asked Khalid al-Hasan, the chairman of the Foreign Relations Committee of the Palestine National Council (PNC), the Palestinian parliament in exile. Hasan dismissed the suggestion out of hand, insisting that only Arafat could speak on behalf of Palestinian aspirations. "You're our Chairman. You're our symbol. You're Mr. Palestine. It's you or there's no show."[24]

The show had changed dramatically in the course of 1974.

In the aftermath of the October War, the guerrilla chief had made a strategic decision to turn away from the armed struggle, and the terror tactics this involved, to negotiate a two-state solution to the Palestinian-Israeli conflict. For two and a half decades the Palestinian national movement had been more or less unanimous in seeking the liberation of the whole of historic Palestine and the destruction of the state of Israel. After the October War, Arafat recognized that the Jewish state, then twenty-five years old, was the military superpower of the region, enjoying the full support of the United States and the recognition of nearly all the international community. Israel was here to stay.

In the postwar diplomacy, Arafat rightly predicted, the neighboring Arab states would eventually accept this reality and negotiate peace treaties with Israel under U.S. and Soviet sponsorship, based on Resolution 242. The Palestinians would be pushed to the side. "What does 242 offer the Palestinians?" Arafat asked a British journalist in the 1980s. "Some compensation for the refugees and perhaps, I say only perhaps, the return of some few refugees to their homes in Palestine. But what else? Nothing. We would have been finished. The chance for us Palestinians to be a nation again, even on some small part of our homeland, would have passed. Finished. No more a Palestinian people. End of story."[25]

Arafat's solution was to settle for a ministate based in the Gaza Strip and West Bank. There were, however, a number of barriers that Arafat would have to overcome before he could hope to achieve even ministatehood for the Palestinians.

The first obstacle was Palestinian public opinion. Arafat recognized that he needed to persuade the Palestinian people to relinquish their claims to the 78 percent of Palestine lost in 1948. "When a people is claiming the return of 100 percent of its land," Arafat explained, "it's not so easy for leadership to say, 'No, you can take only thirty per cent.'"[26]

Nor was Arafat's claim to even 30 percent of Palestine universally recognized. The Gaza Strip had been under Egyptian administration from 1948 until occupied by Israel in the June 1967 War, and the West Bank had been formally annexed to the Hashemite Kingdom of Jordan in 1950. Though the Egyptians had no interest in absorbing the Gaza Strip, King Hussein of Jordan was determined to recover the

West Bank and the Arab quarters of East Jerusalem, Islam's third-holiest city, for Jordanian rule. Arafat needed to wrest the West Bank from King Hussein's grasp.

The hard-line factions within the PLO were unwilling to concede recognition to Israel, which meant Arafat would have to overcome their opposition to a two-state solution. The Democratic Front for the Liberation of Palestine and the Popular Front, whose notorious hijackings had precipitated the Black September war in Jordan in 1970, remained committed to the armed struggle for the liberation of all of Palestine. Had Arafat openly acknowledged the compromise he was willing to make to achieve limited statehood for the Palestinians, the more militant Palestinian factions would have demanded his head.

Finally, Arafat had to overcome international abhorrence to the PLO as an organization, and to his leadership of the PLO. Gone were the days of "humane" terrorism, in which airplanes were destroyed and hostages released unharmed. By 1974 the PLO was associated with a string of heinous crimes against civilians in Europe and Israel: an attack on El-Al offices in Athens in November 1969 that left one child dead and thirty-one people wounded; a mid-air bomb that destroyed a Swissair jet in February 1970, killing all forty-seven aboard; and the notorious attack on the 1972 Munich Olympics that led to the death of eleven Israeli athletes. Israel and its Western supporters saw the PLO as a terror organization and refused to meet with its leaders; Arafat needed to persuade Western policymakers that the PLO would forego violence for diplomacy to achieve Palestinian self-determination.

Arafat had set himself high goals for 1974: securing Palestinian public support for a two-state solution, containing the hard-liners within the PLO, trumping King Hussein's claim to the West Bank, and gaining international recognition within a single year would not be easy.

Given the constraints, Arafat had to proceed slowly and secure a constituency for the change in policy. He could not come out openly with the idea of a two-state solution, as this would entail ending the armed struggle, which enjoyed widespread Palestinian support. Negotiating for a two-state solution would have meant conferring some degree of recognition to Israel, which most Palestinians would have rejected. Instead, Arafat couched the new policy, first issued in a working paper in February 1974, in terms of establishing a "national authority" to be established "on any lands that can be wrested from Zionist occupation."

Next, he had to gain the support of the Palestinian National Council, the parliament in exile, for his new policy. When the PNC met in Cairo in June 1974, Arafat tabled a ten-point platform that committed the PLO to the "national authority" framework. However, to get past the hard-liners in the PLO, the platform reaffirmed the role of the armed struggle and the right of national self-determination, and it ruled out any recognition of Israel. The PNC adopted Arafat's platform, but Palestinians knew that change was afoot. However, to the rest of the world the PLO still looked like a guerrilla organization committed to the armed struggle.

The PLO clearly needed to present a new face to the international community if the organization were to gain recognition as a government in exile. In 1973 Arafat named Said Hammami as the PLO's representative to London. A native of the coastal city of Jaffa, Hammami had been driven out of Palestine with his family in 1948 and grew up in Syria, earning a degree in English literature at Damascus University. Hammami was both a committed Palestinian nationalist and a political moderate who quickly established good relations with journalists and policymakers in London.

In November 1973, Hammami published an article in the *Times* of London calling for a two-state solution to the Israel-Palestine conflict. "Many Palestinians," he wrote, "believe that a Palestinian state on the Gaza Strip and the West Bank . . . is a necessary part of any peace package." He was the first PLO representative ever to make such a proposal. "It is no small thing for a people who have been wronged as we have to take the first step towards reconciliation for the sake of a just peace that should satisfy all parties"—which, by implication, included Israel. The editor of the paper added a note to the article stressing that Hammami was "known to be very close to the PLO chairman, Mr. Yasser Arafat," and that Hammami's decision to state such views publicly was thus "of considerable significance."[27] Through his London representative, Arafat had succeeded in opening a channel not only to the West but also to Israel itself.

An Israeli journalist and peace activist named Uri Avnery was electrified by what he had read in Hammami's article. Avnery had immigrated to Palestine during the mandate and joined the Irgun in the late 1930s, when still just a teenager. He would later silence those who criticized him for speaking with Palestinian "terrorists," saying, "You can't talk to me about terrorism, I was a terrorist." Avnery was wounded in the 1948 war and went on to serve three terms in the Knesset as an independent. Though a committed Zionist, Avnery had always advocated a two-state solution, long before anyone in the Arab world would support the idea. Menachem Begin used to deride him in Knesset debates, asking, "Where are the Arab Avnerys?"[28] In reading Hammami's articles, Uri Avnery immediately recognized he had found his Palestinian counterpart.

In December 1973, Hammami penned a second column for the *Times*, this time calling for mutual recognition between Israel and the Palestinians. "The Israeli Jews and the Palestinian Arabs should recognize one another as peoples, with all the rights to which a people is entitled. This recognition should be followed by the realization of . . . a Palestinian state, an independent, fully-fledged member state of the United Nations."[29] With this second article, Avnery recognized that Hammami's views must have reflected a conscious change of policy within the PLO. A diplomat might make one indiscretion and keep his job, but a repeat offender would certainly get the sack. Hammami could only suggest such things as mutual recognition between Israelis and Palestinians with the support of Yasser Arafat.

Avnery was determined to make contact with Said Hammami. While attending the Geneva peace conference in December 1973, Avnery met a journalist with the *Times* and asked him to arrange a meeting with the PLO representative. The meeting carried great risks for both men. In the climate of terrorist violence of the early 1970s, both the hard-line Palestinian factions and the Israeli secret service, the Mossad, were actively assassinating their enemies. Hammami and Avnery were willing to take the risk of meeting, for both men were convinced that a two-state solution held the only prospect for a peaceful resolution of the Arab-Israeli conflict.

They had their first meeting in Avnery's London hotel room on January 27, 1974, during which Hammami set out his views. Avnery summarized them as follows:

The two peoples, the Palestinian and the Israeli, exist.

He did not like the way the new Israeli nation in Palestine came into being. He rejected Zionism. But he accepted the fact that the Israeli nation does exist.

Since the Israeli nation exists it has the right to national self-determination, much as the Palestinians have this right. At present, the only realistic solution is to allow each of the two peoples to have a state of its own.

He did not like Itzhak Rabin and understood that the Israelis did not have to like Yassir Arafat. Each people must accept the leaders chosen by the other side.

We must make peace without the intervention of either of the superpowers. Peace must come from the peoples in the region itself.[30]

Avnery stressed to Hammami that Israel was a democracy of its Jewish citizens, and that in order to change Israeli government policy, they would have to change Israeli public opinion. "One does not change public opinion by words, statements, diplomatic formulas," he later recalled telling Hammami. "One changes public opinion with the impact of dramatic events, which speak directly to the heart of everyone, events which a person can see with his own eyes on television, hear on the radio, read in the headlines of his paper."[31]

For the moment, neither Arafat nor Hammami could go further to win over Israeli public opinion than to argue for the two-state solution in the Western press. In the climate of the times, this represented a more radical shift in policy than the PLO leadership dared to express more openly. While the meetings between Avnery and the PLO's London representative continued to be kept in strictest secrecy, Hammami's moderate message no doubt played a part in Arafat's invitation to address the United Nations. Through his articles in the *Times*, Hammami showed the Western world that the PLO was ready to engage in a negotiated settlement with the Israelis. Arafat's speech would provide the opportunity for the sort of "dramatic event" Avnery believed necessary to force a shift in Israeli policy.

The next major breakthrough for Arafat in 1974 came in the inter-Arab arena. At the Rabat Summit of Arab leaders, Arafat defeated his old rival King Hussein of Jordan in securing Arab recognition for the PLO as the sole legitimate representative of the Palestinian people. On October 29, 1974, the meeting of Arab heads of state gave its unanimous support to the PLO and affirmed the right of the Palestinian people to establish a "national authority" on "any liberated Palestinian land" under PLO leadership. The resolution dealt a terrible blow to King Hussein's claims to represent the Palestinians and to Jordan's sovereignty over the West Bank. Arafat left Rabat with the PLO's claims as a government-in-exile greatly strengthened.

Fifteen days after his triumph in Rabat, Arafat landed at the United Nations to secure international support for Palestinian self-determination. Lina Tabbara, a Lebanese diplomat who was half Palestinian, was in his entourage to assist with the translation of his speech into English and French. Tabbara was overwhelmed by the drama of the moment. "I entered through the main door of the glass building right behind Yasser Arafat, who received the reception accorded to a head of state except for a few details of protocol," Tabbara recalled. "It was the climax of the [Palestinian] resistance movement, a moment of triumph for the disinherited, and one of the most beautiful days of my life." Seeing Arafat take to the rostrum and receive a standing ovation from the General Assembly awakened her "feelings of pride at having Palestinian blood."[32]

Arafat gave a long speech—101 minutes in all. "It was a real committee job," Khalid al-Hasan later recalled. "Drafts, drafts and more drafts. When we thought we'd got it about right, we asked one of our most celebrated poets to put the finishing touch to it."[33] It was a rousing speech, a call for justice, but ultimately a speech targeting a Palestinian audience, and those who supported the Palestinian revolutionary struggle. It was not a speech intended to sway the Israeli public and force a change in Israeli government policy. Arafat did not enjoy enough support within his own movement to suggest any accommodation with Israel. And the Israelis weren't listening: the Israeli delegation boycotted Arafat's speech in protest against the PLO chairman's appearance.

Instead of reinforcing Hammami's appeal for a two-state solution, Arafat reverted to his long-standing "revolutionary dream" of "one democratic State where Christian, Jew and Moslem live in justice, equality, fraternity and progress" in the whole of Palestine. To the Israelis, and their American supporters, this still sounded like the familiar old call for the destruction of the Jewish state. Even worse, instead of using the UN podium to extend his hand to the Israelis, Arafat famously ended with a rhetorical threat. "Today I have come bearing an olive branch and a freedom-fighter's gun. Do not let the olive branch fall from my hand. I repeat: do not let the olive branch fall from my hand."[34]

Arafat departed the hall to another standing ovation. The PLO chairman's call for justice and statehood for the Palestinian people enjoyed widespread support in the international community. Arafat had more need for supporters than for bold gestures. When Lina Tabbara next saw Arafat, the PLO chairman would be fighting for his political survival in Civil War Lebanon, just two years later.

So much had been achieved by the Palestinian movement in 1974. Khalid al-Hasan, chairman of the PNC Foreign Relations Committee, declared 1974 "such an important year," when the PLO leadership was "committed to an accommodation with Israel." But no further progress was made on Palestinian-Israeli negotiations after Arafat's UN speech. Hammami and Avnery continued to meet in secret in London, with Hammami briefing Arafat and Avnery periodically meeting with Itzhak Rabin to update their respective leaders on their conversations. "It is impossible to exaggerate the importance of Said Hammami's work," Khalid al-Hasan insisted. "If the Israeli Government of Yitzhak Rabin had responded to the signals we were sending through Hammami, we could have had a just peace in a very few years."[35] But Arafat did not dare make any concessions to Israel, and Rabin did not want to do anything that might encourage the creation of a Palestinian state, to which he was adamantly opposed.

With both the Palestinians and the Israelis hardening their positions after 1974, both Hammami and Avnery faced growing danger from extremists within their own societies. In December 1975, a mad Israeli attacked Avnery with a knife and severely wounded him near his Tel Aviv home. And in January 1978 Hammami was gunned down in his London office, executed by the Palestinian rejectionist Abu Nidal Group for his meetings with Israelis. The gunman fired a single shot to Hammami's head, spat on him, and called him a traitor before slipping away through the streets of London with impunity.[36]

The window of opportunity for peace between the Israelis and Palestinians was now closed. On April 13, 1975, Christian militiamen ambushed a busload of Palestinians in the Beirut suburb of Ain Rummaneh, killing all twenty-eight on board. It was the start of a civil war that over the next fifteen years would lay waste to Lebanon and drive the Palestinian movement to the brink of extermination.

———————

Political stability in Lebanon was placed under growing pressure as the demographic balance of the country changed. The French had carved the biggest possible country out of the Syrian mandate so as to create a state in which their Christian protégés would represent a majority. However, the Muslim communities of Lebanon (which included the Druzes along with the Sunnis and Shiites) experienced a higher rate of population growth and by the 1950s began to overtake the Christians (which included the dominant Maronites, along with Greek Orthodox, Armenians, Protestants, and a number of smaller sects) in sheer numbers. The 1932 census, which showed the Christians with a small majority over the Muslims, was to prove the last formal head count: to this day, there still are no accurate figures for the population breakdown of Lebanon.

By the time Lebanon achieved independence in 1943 the Muslims population was willing to concede political predominance to the Christians in exchange for a Christian commitment to integrate Lebanon in the Arab world and to distance themselves from their former colonial power and protector, France. The power-sharing formula they struck in the 1943 National Pact was a "confessional" or sectarian system, in which the top government posts were apportioned to Lebanon's communities—e.g., a Maronite president, a Sunni prime minister, a Shiite speaker of parliament. Seats in the parliament were distributed among Christians and Muslims by a ratio that marginally favored the Christians 6:5.

This power-sharing agreement was first challenged in the 1958 civil war. U.S. military intervention and the election of a reformist president, Fuad Chehab, in September 1958 restored the status quo in Lebanon and preserved the confessional system for another decade. The advent of the Palestinian revolution on Lebanese soil in the late 1960s catalyzed the next assault on the confessional system.

The Palestinians disrupted the political and demographic balance in Lebanon in specific ways. The number of registered Palestinian refugees had grown from 127,600 in 1950 to 197,000 by 1975, though the true Palestinian presence was closer to 350,000 by 1975.[37] The Palestinian refugees were overwhelmingly Muslim. Though they were never integrated into the Lebanese population or given citizenship, their presence on Lebanese soil meant a major increase in the country's Muslim population. They had been politically quiescent until 1969, when Egyptian president Gamal Abdel Nasser had negotiated terms with the Lebanese government for Palestinian guerrillas to operate from Lebanese soil against northern Israel. Lebanon became the operational headquarters of the PLO after the expulsion of Palestinian militias from Jordan following Black September. The Palestinian refugee camps became increasingly militarized and politically militant. They challenged the sovereignty of the Lebanese government in ways that led some to accuse the Palestinian revolution of constituting a state within a state in Lebanon.

There were many in Lebanon who placed the blame for the 1975 civil war squarely on the shoulders of the Palestinians. To former president Camille Chamoun, still one of the most influential Maronite leaders in the mid-1970s, the conflict was never a civil war: "It began and continued to be a war between Lebanese and Palestinians" that, he argued, was harnessed by Lebanese Muslims to help them "seize the supreme authority over the whole of the country."[38] Chamoun was being economical with the truth. Differences between the Lebanese had grown so profound that the Palestinians were no more than a catalyst in a conflict to redefine politics in Lebanon.

In the early 1970s, Muslims, Druzes, Pan-Arabs, and Leftist organizations, including some Christians, forged a political coalition called the National Movement. Their goal was to overturn Lebanon's outdated sectarian system and replace it with a secular democracy of one citizen, one vote. The head of this coalition was Druze leader Kamal Jumblatt. Born in 1917 in his family's stronghold in the village of Moukhtara, Jumblatt studied law and philosophy in Paris and at the Jesuit University in Beirut before entering the Lebanese parliament in 1946 at the age of twenty-nine. "Only a secular, progressive Lebanon freed of confessionalism," he maintained, "could ever hope to survive."[39] To his critics, Jumblatt's call for a secular Lebanon was nothing less than a bid for Muslim majority rule—by the mid-1970s, Lebanese Muslims were estimated to outnumber Christians by a ratio of 55:45—and the end of Lebanon's identity as a Christian state in the Middle East.

The Palestinians, in Jumblatt's view, were but a contributing factor in a war that was fundamentally between the Lebanese. "If the Lebanese had not been ready for an explosion," he reasoned, "there would have been no explosion." The differences between Chamoun's and Jumblatt's views of Lebanon could not be more profound. The Maronite leader Chamoun was wedded to preserving the National Pact distribution of power—and through it the privileged position of Christians in Lebanon. Jumblatt and the National Movement called for a new order based on equal rights of citizenship that would advantage Lebanon's Muslim majority. At root it was a power struggle over who would rule Lebanon, with both sides claiming the moral high ground. One contemporary described Chamoun and Jumblatt as "paragons to their supporters and monsters to their opponents" who "detest and cold shoulder one another, both entrenched in their palaces and in their certainties."[40]

Conflict between defenders of the status quo and proponents of social revolution came to a head in the spring of 1975. That March, Muslim fishermen in the southern city of Sidon went on strike to protest a new fishing monopoly they feared would destroy their livelihood. The consortium was run by Camille Chamoun and a number of other Maronites, making a sectarian issue of what was at heart industrial action. The fishermen mounted demonstrations, which the Maronite-commanded Lebanese army was dispatched to quell. The National Movement condemned the military intervention as a Maronite army defending Maronite big business. The army fired on protesters and killed Ma'ruf Sa'd, a Sunni Muslim leader of a left-wing Nasserist party, on March 6. Sa'd's death sparked a popular uprising in Sidon in which Palestinian commandos joined forces with Leftist Lebanese militiamen in pitched battles against the Lebanese army.

The conflict spread from Sidon to Beirut when a carload of gunmen made an unprovoked attack on Maronite leader Pierre Gemayel as he was leaving church on Sunday, April 13. Gemayel was the founder of the right-wing Maronite Phalangist Party, the single largest militia in Lebanon, with an estimated 15,000 armed members. The gunmen killed three people, including one of Gemayel's bodyguards. Bent on revenge, the outraged Phalangists ambushed a busload of Palestinians that same day as they drove through the Christian suburb of Ain al-Rummaneh, killing all twenty-eight people on board. As news of the massacre spread, the Lebanese populace knew immediately that the sudden escalation of violence spelled war. The following day, no one went to work, schools closed, and the streets were empty as the people of Beirut followed events anxiously from their homes, reading the newspapers, listening to the radio, and relaying local news by telephone against the staccato background of gunfire.

Lina Tabbara was working in Beirut when the civil war began. After completing her tour of duty at the United Nations, where she had assisted Yasser Arafat with his 1974 speech, Tabbara had returned to Lebanon to work at the Ministry of Foreign Affairs. In many ways she typified the affluent, cosmopolitan Lebanese: well-educated; fluent in English, French, and Arabic; married to an architect; and living in one of the most elegant neighborhoods of downtown Beirut. She was thirty-four years old with two young daughters, ages two and four, at the outbreak of the war.

With her auburn hair and blue eyes, Tabarra could pass for a Christian, though she was in fact a Muslim of mixed Palestinian and Lebanese parentage. She wore her mixed identities with pride, and in the opening months of the war she refused to take sides, even as she watched society around her divide into two deeply entrenched camps. It was not an easy position to maintain. From its opening moments, the Lebanese civil war was marked by sectarian murder and the brutal reciprocity of revenge killings.

On May 31, after seven weeks of fighting between militias, Beirut witnessed the first sectarian massacres in which unarmed civilians were killed simply on the grounds of their religion. A friend called Lina Tabbara to warn her that Muslims were rounding up Christians in the Bashoura quarter of West Beirut. "There's a barricade and an identity checkpoint," Tabbara's friend exclaimed. "The Christians have to get down. They are dragged off to the cemetery." Ten Christians were executed in Beirut that day. The newspapers called it Black Friday. Much worse was to follow.[41]

Throughout the summer of 1975, life in Beirut took on an unnatural normalcy as the city's residents adapted to the constraints imposed by the war. One of the most popular radio programs provided listeners with periodic updates on safe routes and no-go zones. "Dear listeners," the reassuring presenter would announce, "we advise you to avoid this area and to take that route instead." As the conflict deepened over the summer and into the autumn of 1975, his tone grew increasingly urgent. "Ladies and gentlemen, good evening. Today, Sunday, 20th October, you've all had a good time, haven't you? Now you must go back home very quickly, very quickly!"[42] The radio alert marked the start of a new battle in central Beirut in which rival militias fought over the tallest buildings as platforms from which to observe and bombard their enemies. The incomplete shell of a skyscraper called the Murr Tower, overlooking the commercial center of Beirut, became a stronghold of the Sunni Leftist Murabitun militia. The high-rise Holiday Inn, in the heart of the Beirut hotel district, was seized by the Maronite Phalangist militia.

Missiles and artillery shells were exchanged between the two towers in all-night battles, causing massive destruction to surrounding areas. National Movement forces—Tabbara called them the "Islamo-Progressives"—laid siege to the hotel district and trapped the Maronite forces in October 1975. The Christian militiamen were rescued by Camille Chamoun, who, as minister of the interior, had the authority to deploy 2,000 soldiers from the Lebanese army around the hotel district as a buffer between the combatants. Another cease-fire followed in November, but no one had any illusions that the fighting was over.

In December, the barricades were back in place and the mindless killing of innocents resumed. Four Phalangists were kidnapped and later found dead. Maronite militiamen retaliated by killing 300–400 civilians whose identity cards betrayed them as Muslims. Muslim militiamen responded in kind, killing hundreds of Christians. The day came to be known as Black Saturday. For Lina Tabbara, it was the day she finally took sides. "It's no longer possible to ignore the yawning gulf separating Christians and Moslems; things have gone too far with this Black Saturday." Henceforth, Lina identified with the Muslim cause. "I feel the seeds of hatred and the desire for revenge taking root in my very depths. At this moment I want the Mourabitouns or anybody else to give the Phalangists back twice as good as we got."[43]

By the beginning of 1976 outside powers began to play an active role in the war between the Lebanese. The months of intense fighting consumed a great deal of guns and ammunition, jeeps and uniforms, and rockets and artillery, all of which were enormously costly. Lebanese militias sought arms from neighboring countries that were awash in weapons. One of the consequences of the oil boom was the rapid expansion of arms sales to the Middle East, and Lebanon's neighbors seized on the deepening civil war to exercise influence over the country through arming its militias.

The Soviets and the Americans had long provided weapons systems to their allies in the region. Other states were quick to enter the lucrative market, with European producers competing with the Americans for sales of heavy weapons to West-leaning "moderate" Arab states. Saudi defense spending, for instance, increased from $171 million in 1968 to over $13 billion by 1978.[44] Surplus weapons began to make their way to supply the warring Lebanese militias, as regional powers sought to influence developments in Lebanon. Lina Tabbara reported rumors of Saudi support for Christian militias "as the regime in Riyadh prefers to support the opponents of Islam for fear of a hypothetical takeover by the Communists."[45] The Maronites also received arms and ammunition from the Israelis, to assist in their fight against Palestinian militias. The Left-leaning National Movement secured arms from the Soviet Union and through Soviet client states like Iraq and Libya. The internal conflict between Lebanese was getting dragged into the Cold War, the Arab-Israeli conflict, and the struggle between revolutionary and conservative regimes in the Arab world.

The Lebanese war dissolved into an exterminationist conflict in the course of 1976, in which massacre begat retaliatory massacre. Christian forces overran the Muslim shantytown of the Karantina in January 1976, killing hundreds and using bulldozers to obliterate the slum quarter from the map. The National Movement and Palestinian forces retaliated by laying siege to Camille Chamoun's stronghold at Damour, a major Christian town on the coast to the south of Beirut. Five hundred Maronites were killed when Damour fell to the Palestinians and Muslim militias on January 20. Five months later, Maronite forces laid siege to the isolated Palestinian refugee camp at Tal al-Za'tar, set in the midst of Christian neighborhoods. The camp's 30,000 inhabitants suffered a fifty-three-day campaign of relentless violence before surrendering, after weeks without medical relief, fresh water, and dwindling food supplies. No reliable casualty figures were available for the siege, though an estimated 3,000 died in Tal al-Za'tar.[46] In all, some 30,000 people were killed and nearly 70,000 wounded between the outbreak of the war in April 1975 and the cessation of general hostilities in October 1976—an enormous toll in a population of 3.25 million.[47]

The end of the first stage of the Lebanese civil war, in October 1976, came as a result of a political crisis. In March 1976 the Lebanese parliament passed a vote of no confidence in the president of the republic, Suleiman Franjieh, and asked for his resignation. When Franjieh refused, Kamal Jumblatt threatened all-out war, and dissident army units began to shell the Presidential Palace in the Beirut suburbs. The Syrian president, Hafiz al-Asad, sent his troops into Lebanon to protect Franjieh and to secure a cease-fire.

The Lebanese parliament met again under Syrian protection and agreed to hold early elections to resolve the political deadlock. The Lebanese president was, and still is, elected by the members of parliament, who assembled in May 1976 to cast their votes for a new leader. There were two candidates—Elias Sarkis, who was supported by conservative Christians and the Maronite militias; and Raymond Eddé, the preferred choice of the reformists and the National Movement. Much to the surprise of the Muslim forces in Lebanon, Asad of Syria put his full support behind Elias Sarkis and ensured his victory over Eddé. It was a critical turning point, as Syria began to intervene directly in Lebanese politics and to secure its influence over the country by deploying its troops in strategic points in Beirut and across Lebanon.

In giving their support to Elias Sarkis, the Syrians were in effect taking sides against Jumblatt's National Movement and the Palestinians. It was an astonishing reversal of positions, for the Syrians had always stood for Pan-Arabism and the Palestinian cause. Yet here they were coming to the defense of the West-leaning, anti-Arabist Maronites. For Lina Tabbara, the reality of the situation was brought home when she watched Syrian forces in the Beirut Airport "using Soviet-made Grad ground-to-ground missiles bought with Soviet aid to shell Palestinian refugee camps and the Beiruti areas held by the [Muslim] Progressives."[48] Lina quickly recognized that the Syrians were not supporting the Maronites in their own right so much as using the Maronites as a means to extend their own domination over Lebanon.

Syria's intervention in Lebanon provoked concern among the other Arab states, which did not wish to see Damascus take advantage of the Lebanon conflict to absorb its once prosperous neighbor. King Khalid of Saudi Arabia (r. 1975–1982) convened a minisummit of Arab leaders in Riyadh attended by Lebanese president Sarkis, PLO chairman Yasser Arafat, and representatives of Kuwait, Egypt, and Syria.

The Arab leaders announced their plans for Lebanon on October 18, 1976, with a call for total disengagement by all armed elements and a permanent cease-fire to take effect in ten days' time. The Arab states were to create a 30,000-man peacekeeping force to be placed under the command of the president of Lebanon. The Arab peacekeepers would have the authority to disarm combatants and to confiscate weapons from all who violated the cease-fire. The Riyadh summit called on the PLO to respect Lebanese sovereignty and to withdraw to the areas allotted the Palestinian fighters in the 1969 Cairo Agreement. The summit resolution concluded with a call for political dialogue between all the parties in Lebanon to achieve national reconciliation.

Despite their concerns for Syria's intentions, the Riyadh resolutions had done little to lessen Damascus's grasp over Lebanon. With other Arab states unwilling to commit significant numbers of troops to Lebanon, the Syrian army dominated the Arab multinational force: of the 30,000 Arab troops sent to keep the peace in Lebanon, some 26,500 were Syrian. The token contingents from Saudi Arabia, Sudan, and Libya did not stay in Lebanon for long before delegating the task wholly to the Syrians. In mid-November, some 6,000 Syrian troops occupied Beirut, reinforced by 200 tanks. The Riyadh summit resolutions thus proved little more than a formula to legitimize the Syrian occupation of Lebanon.

Though President Sarkis called on the Lebanese to greet the Syrians "in love and brotherhood," Muslim and Progressive parties had grave doubts. Kamal Jumblatt recorded one of his conversations with Hafez al-Asad in his memoirs: "I beg you to

withdraw the troops you have sent into Lebanon. Carry on with your political intervention, your mediation, your arbitration. . . . But I must advise you against military means. We do not want to be a satellite state."[49] Lina Tabbara was appalled to
see the Syrian army spread all over Beirut, but what annoyed her most was that
"nearly everybody is apparently satisfied with this state of affairs."

In the wake of the Riyadh summit, the fifty-sixth cease-fire since the start of the
war took effect. If the Lebanese people had hoped that the Syrian occupation would
bring them peace after nearly two years of war, they were soon disappointed. Shortly
after the Syrians entered Beirut, Tabbara witnessed one of the first car bombs that
were to become a hallmark of the violence in Lebanon. "Loud cries and screams can
be heard off-stage," she wrote, describing the carnage before her eyes. "Look out,
it's a booby-trapped car, there may be another, someone exclaims. This kind of attack
has increased during the past few days, but no one knows who is behind them. Many
badly wounded people are lying on the road." Tabbara reflected grim satisfaction
on seeing "the triumphant placidity of the Lebanese under the Syrian peace shattered."[50] She and her family had witnessed enough blood and destruction. They
left Beirut to the Syrians and joined the hundreds of thousands of Lebanese in foreign exile.

Yet as far as the international community was concerned, the conflict in Lebanon
had been resolved—at least for the moment. The focus of the global media had shifted
from war-torn Lebanon to Jerusalem, where, on Sunday, November 20, 1977, Egyptian President Anwar Sadat was about to address the Knesset, the parliament of the
state of Israel, to propose an end to the Arab-Israeli conflict.

In January 1977, Sadat was giving an interview to a Lebanese journalist in his va-
cation home in the town of Aswan on the upper Nile. The journalist broke off
her questioning as a column of thick smoke rose from the center of the town. "Mr.
President," she said, "something strange is happening behind you." Sadat turned
and saw fires in Aswan and a mob crossing the bridge over the Nile toward his house.
Sadat had just ordered the cash-strapped Egyptian government to lift a number of
crucial subsidies on bread and other staples. Egypt's poor saw their subsistence placed
in jeopardy and rose in nationwide bread riots that left 171 dead and hundreds injured before the subsidies, and calm, were restored.[51]

Something strange indeed was happening behind Sadat. The Egyptian public,
who once hailed him as the "Hero of the Crossing" for Egypt's successes on the Suez
Canal in the October War, were losing confidence in their president. Sadat did not
have Nasser's charisma or mass appeal. He needed to deliver on his promises of pros-

perity or face deposal. Sadat grew increasingly convinced that prosperity could only be achieved through American support—and peace with Israel.

In the immediate aftermath of the 1973 War, Sadat had leveraged Egypt's credible military performance and the successful deployment of the Arab oil weapon to secure U.S. support for a partial Israeli withdrawal from the Sinai. U.S. Secretary of State Henry Kissinger initiated his signature shuttle diplomacy, making frequent negotiating trips between Cairo and Jerusalem to secure the two Sinai Disengagement Accords (January 1974 and September 1975) that restored both the Suez Canal and some of the Sinai oil fields to Egypt.

The recovery of the Suez Canal was a major accomplishment for Sadat, first because he had succeeded where Nasser had failed—in ensuring the canal did not become the de facto boundary between Egypt and Israel—and second, because the canal was a major revenue source for cash-strapped Egypt. With American assistance, the Egyptians cleared the wrecks of ships destroyed in the course of the Arab-Israeli War of 1967 from the canal, and on June 5, 1975, Sadat reopened the strategic waterway to international shipping. The first ships to exit the canal were some of the fourteen vessels of the "Yellow Fleet," a group of international steamers trapped in the Great Bitter Lakes by the 1967 War that had spent eight years gathering the yellow dust for which the fleet was named. Though Egypt celebrated these gains, the Sinai Accords left Israel in control of most of the Sinai Peninsula (Egyptian territory occupied by Israel in the Six Day War) and the Egyptian treasury still struggling to make ends meet.

Sadat was growing increasingly desperate for new funds for his treasury, and he revealed a willingness to turn against his Arab neighbors to reinforce his own position. In his desperation to increase Egypt's revenues, in the summer of 1977 Sadat attempted to seize oil fields belonging to Libya. According to contemporary estimates, Libya generated some $5 billion in oil revenues each year, a vast sum for a population that was a fraction the size of Egypt's—protected by an army that was also a fraction the size of Egypt's. In a moment of mad opportunism, Sadat considered the Soviet arms deliveries to his wealthy neighbor a pretext to invade—as though the Libyan arsenal represented a threat to Egypt's security.

Sadat withdrew his forces on the Israeli front in the Sinai to attack the Libyans in the Western Desert on July 16. The Egyptian air force bombed Libyan bases and provided air cover for the invasion of Libya. "Almost immediately it became clear that Sadat had miscalculated," veteran analyst Mohamed Heikal recalled. "Neither the [Egyptian] public nor the army saw any logic in disengaging forces with an enemy, Israel, only to attack an Arab neighbour."

The Egyptian attack on Libya went on for nine days. Egyptian public was unenthusiastic, and Washington was openly hostile to Egypt's unprovoked aggression. The

U.S. ambassador in Cairo made clear Washington's opposition to any invasion of Libya, and Sadat was forced to back down. On July 25, Egyptian troops withdrew from Libya, bringing the conflict to an end. "Thus it was," Heikal concluded, "that the food riots in January and a botched foreign adventure . . . led Sadat to the conclusion by mid-1977 that Egypt would have to negotiate a new relationship with Israel."[52] If Sadat failed to increase his revenues, he would face further food riots. He could not secure the funding from his Arab brethren—by persuasion or coercion. Yet by being the first Arab state to conclude peace with Israel, Egypt could attract substantial U.S. development aid and foreign investment. It was a high-risk strategy, given Arab intransigence toward Israel. Yet Sadat had taken high risks before and succeeded.

The obstacles to peace with Israel had never appeared higher. In May 1977, Menachem Begin led the right-wing Likud Party to victory, shattering the Labour Party's monopoly of government since the founding of the state of Israel. Under Begin's leadership, the Likud Party was committed to establishing Jewish settlements to retain the Arab territories Israel occupied in the June 1967 War. It would be hard to imagine a more intransigent negotiating partner than the ex-terrorist proponent of Greater Israel. And yet it was Begin who made the first contact, sending conciliatory messages to the Egyptian president through King Hassan II of Morocco and Romanian president Nicolae Ceausescu. The latter persuaded Sadat that "a peace treaty would have been impossible with Labour in power and Begin in opposition, but with the roles reversed the prospects were better," for the Labour Party was less likely to stand in the way of a peace deal with Egypt.[53]

Sadat returned to Egypt and began to contemplate the unthinkable: direct negotiations with the Israelis to secure an Arab-Israeli peace treaty. He had demonstrated Egypt's military leadership in the October War and would secure Egypt's leadership over the Arab world by leading the peace. Just as his generals had been resistant to making war with Israel when he first broached the subject in 1972, so he knew his politicians would resist his peace plans. He would need to reshuffle his political team and bring in some new talent less resistant to change. He chose a complete outsider to help plan his peace campaign.

Boutros Boutros-Ghali (b. 1922) was a professor of political science at Cairo University. His grandfather had served as prime minister and his uncle as foreign minister under Egypt's monarchy. Members of the landed aristocracy, the Boutros-Ghali family saw their agricultural estates confiscated by the new government's land reform measures following the 1952 revolution.

In a country that was overwhelmingly Muslim, Boutros-Ghali was a Coptic Christian and his wife a member of a prominent Egyptian Jewish family. Yet these very qualities, which had marginalized Boutros-Ghali from Egyptian politics since the 1952 revolution, now recommended him for government service when Sadat decided to attempt a peace settlement with Israel. On October 25, 1977, the professor who would later become secretary-general of the United Nations was astonished to learn that he had been appointed minister of state in a cabinet reshuffle.

Shortly after entering government, Boutros-Ghali attended Sadat's November 9 speech to the People's Assembly, in which the president first intimated his willingness to work with Israel. "I am ready to travel to the ends of the earth if this will in any way protect an Egyptian boy, soldier, or officer from being killed or wounded," Sadat told the legislators. Speaking of the Israelis, he continued: "I am ready to go to their country, even to the Knesset itself and talk with them."

Boutros-Ghali recalled that PLO chairman Yasir Arafat, who attended the session to hear Sadat's speech, "was the first to burst into applause at these words. Neither Arafat nor my colleagues nor I understood the implications of what the president had said." None of them had a clue that Sadat actually contemplated imminent travel to Israel.[54] But one week later, Boutros-Ghali understood the full significance of Sadat's words, when the then vice president Husni Mubarak asked him to draft the outline of a speech "that the president will give next Sunday—in Israel!" Boutros-Ghali was excited to find himself "at the heart of this historic event."

As Sadat expected, many of his politicians rejected his plans. Foreign Minister Ismail Fahmi and Muhammad Riyad, the minister of state for foreign affairs, both resigned rather than accompany Sadat to Jerusalem. Two days before Sadat was scheduled to depart, Boutros-Ghali was appointed acting foreign minister and invited to join the presidential delegation to Jerusalem. His friends warned him not to go. "The fear in the air was palpable," Boutros-Ghali recalled. "The Arab press was vicious. No Muslim, they wrote, would agree to accompany Sadat, so he chose the Christian Boutros-Ghali, who has a Jewish wife."[55] Yet the new acting foreign minister found himself "attracted by the extraordinary challenge" of shattering the taboos set out in the 1967 Khartoum Summit, which had bound all Arab states to a common position of no recognition of the Jewish state, no negotiation with Israeli officials, and no peace between Arab states and Israel.

The Egyptian president annoyed his fellow Arab heads of state by announcing his plans and only then seeking their support for his initiative. Eager to avoid a break with Syria, Sadat flew to Damascus to brief President Hafiz al-Asad on his plans to visit Israel. Al-Asad was quick to remind Sadat of the common Arab position. "Brother Anwar, you are always in a hurry," Asad told him. "I understand your impatience, but please understand that you cannot go to Jerusalem. This is treason," he warned. "The Egyptian people will not take it. The Arab nation will never forgive you."[56]

Yet Sadat was not to be deterred, and on November 19, with Boutros-Ghali in tow, he boarded a government plane for the forty-five-minute flight to Tel Aviv. "I had not realized the distance was so short!" Boutros-Ghali exclaimed. "Israel seemed as strange to me as a land in outer space."[57] After so many years of war and enmity, it was as though the Egyptian people were looking at Israel as a real country for the first time. They had very mixed feelings. Veteran Egyptian journalist Mohamed Heikal captured the moment as Sadat emerged from his airplane at Lod Airport: "As television cameras followed him down the steps the guilt felt by millions of Egyptians was replaced by a sense of participation. Right or wrong, Sadat's political and physical courage was beyond dispute. His arrival on forbidden territory enthralled many Egyptians and appalled the rest of the Arab world."[58]

The following day, Sunday, November 20, 1977, Egypt's President Anwar Sadat addressed the Israeli Knesset in Arabic (much to Boutros-Ghali's chagrin, the English text on which he had worked so long was not used). This was exactly the bold gesture that Uri Avnery had always pressed the PLO to make—a gesture calculated to convince the Israeli public that there was an Arab partner for peace. "Allow me to address my call from this rostrum to the people of Israel," Sadat said to the television cameras. "I convey to you the message of peace of the Egyptian people," he declared, "a message of security, safety, and peace to every man, woman, and child in Israel." Sadat went right over the heads of the Israeli lawmakers to exhort the Israeli electorate to "encourage your leadership to struggle for peace."

"Let us be frank with each other," Sadat continued to his audience both within and beyond the Knesset. "How can we achieve permanent peace based on justice?" Sadat made clear his view that for peace to endure, it had to bring a just solution to the Palestinian problem. "Nobody in the world could accept today slogans propagated here in Israel, ignoring the existence of a Palestinian people and questioning even their whereabouts," he chided his hosts. Peace, he continued, was also incompatible with the occupation of other countries' land. He called for the return of all Arab territory occupied in 1967—including East Jerusalem. In return, Israel would enjoy the full acceptance and recognition of all its Arab neighbors. "As we really and truly seek peace we really and truly welcome you to live among us in peace and security," Sadat insisted.

Sadat's visit to Jerusalem proved a remarkable diplomatic coup—it began the first serious peace process between Israel and its Arab neighbors. However, the road to peace proved long, arduous, and full of hazards. The Egyptians and Israelis came to the negotiating table with very different expectations. Sadat hoped to lead the rest of the Arab world to conclude peace with Israel, on the basis of a complete Israeli withdrawal from all territories occupied in 1967 and the establishment of a Palestinian state in East Jerusalem, the West Bank, and the Gaza Strip. Begin had no intention of making such concessions, and he undermined Sadat's credibility within the Arab world when, in his response to Sadat at the Knesset, he asserted, "President Sadat knows, *as he knew from us before he came to Jerusalem,* that our position concerning permanent borders between us and our neighbors differs from his."[59] In the course of their subsequent negotiations, Begin declared his willingness to restore most of the Sinai Peninsula to Egypt and most of the Golan Heights to Syria in exchange for a full normalization of relations, but he categorically refused to make concessions to the Palestinians.

Israel's position on a comprehensive Arab-Israeli peace deal was far too restrictive to attract broader Arab involvement. Begin was intent on preserving Jewish settlements and retaining parts of occupied Syrian and Egyptian land for strategic reasons. The most the Israelis were willing to concede the Palestinians was a degree of self-rule in Gaza and the West Bank, which Begin consistently referred to by the Biblical names of Judea and Samaria. The Israelis refused to meet with the PLO, and there was no question of Palestinian independence, or statehood, or of Israel returning any part of Jerusalem, which the Knesset had declared the eternal, indivisible capital of the Jewish state (which claim has yet to gain international recognition).

Having embarked on his bold peace initiative, Sadat found himself caught between intransigence on both the Arab and the Israeli sides. None of the Arab rulers was inclined to follow Egypt's lead, and Prime Minister Begin gave them little incentive to do so. He was convinced that peace with Egypt was in Israel's strategic interests, for no other Arab country would be able to mount a credible threat to the Jewish state without Egypt. Peace with other Arab states was a secondary priority, and he was unwilling to make any concessions that might draw them into serious negotiations. Sadat was left to go it alone in negotiating with Israel against widespread Arab hostility.

U.S. president Jimmy Carter exerted every effort to shepherd the beleaguered Egyptian-Israeli initiative toward peace. He convened a meeting at the presidential retreat in Camp David, Maryland, in September 1978. Once again, Boutros Boutros-Ghali was in the Egyptian delegation. Flying with Sadat to the Camp David meeting, Boutros-Ghali listened to the Egyptian president's game plan with mounting concern. Sadat naively believed he could win over American public opinion to Egypt's negotiating position, that President Carter would take his side and force the necessary concessions from Israel to deliver what Sadat wanted. Boutros-Ghali did not think it would prove so simple. "I feared that the Americans would not pressure Israel and that Sadat would then make concessions."[60]

Sadat was not entirely wrong. Egypt's position enjoyed wide support in the United States, and President Carter did exert tremendous efforts to force concessions from Prime Minister Begin. It took thirteen days of bitter negotiations and twenty-two drafts before Carter brought the two sides to agreement. Begin agreed to retreat from the whole of the Sinai (where he had planned to spend his retirement); however, Sadat was forced to make concessions as well. Crucially, the agreement did not secure Palestinian rights to self-determination. The framework document provided for a five-year transitional period in the West Bank and Gaza Strip, an Israeli military withdrawal, and a freely elected self-governing authority in the Palestinian territories. However, it left open the final status of the occupied Palestinian territories to future negotiations between Egypt, Israel, Jordan, and the elected representatives of the Palestinian territories. And it contained no penalty for Israel's failure to fulfill these commitments.

The new Egyptian foreign minister, Muhammad Ibrahim Kamil, resigned in protest of Sadat's betrayal of Palestinian rights. Yet Sadat would not be deterred and went to Washington to sign the "Framework for the Conclusion of a Peace Treaty" in a formal ceremony at the White House on September 17, 1978.

The Arab world was appalled by Sadat's decision to break ranks and pursue a separate peace with Israel. In November 1978, the Arab heads of state convened a summit conference in Baghdad to address the crisis. The oil states pledged to provide Egypt with an annual allocation of $5 billion for a ten-year period, to undermine any material incentive Sadat might have had in seeking peace with Israel. They also threatened Egypt with expulsion from the Arab League, and to move the league's headquarters from Cairo to Tunis, should Sadat make peace with Israel.

Yet Sadat had come too far to be deterred by Arab threats. After six months of further negotiations, Carter, Begin, and Sadat returned to the White House lawn to sign the final peace treaty between Egypt and Israel, on March 26, 1979. After Egypt had fought five wars against Israel, the most powerful Arab state put down its sword. Without Egypt, Arabs could never prevail over Israel militarily. The Palestinians and the other Arab states would have to secure their national and territorial ambitions by negotiation. Yet the Arab states would never enjoy sufficient leverage to pressure an intransigent Israel to return their lands, nor would they forgive Egypt for breaking Arab ranks to secure its own territory at their expense. Through collective action, the other Arab states argued, the Arabs could have secured a better peace deal for all.

Immediately after the signing of the peace treaty in March 1979, the Arab states acted on their threats and severed ties with Egypt. It would take over twenty years for Egypt to return fully to the Arab fold. Sadat feigned indifference, but the Egyptian people, proud of their country's leadership of Arab affairs, were shaken by their isolation. They watched in dismay as the colors of Arab states were struck from the flag poles of the Arab League headquarters and embassy buildings across downtown Cairo in 1979, and viewed with no less concern the Star of David raised over the new Israeli Embassy in Cairo, with the conclusion of full diplomatic relations in February 1980.

The Egyptian people were not averse to peace with Israel; they just did not want peace at the price of Egypt's ties to the Arab world. Egypt and Israel were now at peace, but it brought little joy to the people of either country.

At the end of the 1970s, Arab-Israel peacemaking was overtaken by one of the most momentous events in modern Middle Eastern history. Though Iran lies outside the Arab world, the impact of the Islamic Revolution was felt across the Arab Middle East.

In January 1979, the American-supported shah of Iran was toppled by a popular revolution headed by Islamic clerics. The Islamic Revolution was one of the most significant events of the Cold War era, for it profoundly altered the balance of power in the Middle East as the United States lost one of its pillars of influence in the region. The Iranian revolution also had a profound impact on oil prices. In the turmoil of the revolution, Iranian oil production—the second largest in the world—had ground to a virtual halt. In the panic following the fall of the shah, global markets experienced the second oil shock of the decade. Prices nearly tripled, from $13 to $34 per barrel.

While consumers around the world suffered, the oil-producing states enjoyed a new age of prosperity. Saudi Arabia, the world's largest hydrocarbons exporter, was the oil-rich state par excellence. Its revenues from oil rose from $1.2 billion in 1970 to $22.5 billion at the height of the 1973–1974 oil embargo. Following the second oil shock provoked by Iran's revolution, Saudi revenues leaped to $70 billion in 1979—nearly a sixty-fold increase over the course of the 1970s. The other Arab oil producers, including Libya, Kuwait, Qatar, and the United Arab Emirates, enjoyed similar rates of growth. The Saudis responded with the most ambitious public expenditure program in the Arab world, with annual spending on development leaping from $2.5 billion in 1970 to $57 billion in 1980.[61]

Yet Saudi Arabia, like the other oil states, lacked the manpower to realize its development objectives on its own and was forced to recruit labor from the rest of the Arab world. Egypt was the premier labor-exporting state, though Tunisia, Jordan, Lebanon, Syria, and Yemen, as well as the stateless Palestinians, were all active in Arab labor migration. In the course of the 1970s, the number of Arab migrant workers in the oil states rose from some 680,000 in 1970 to 1.3 million in the aftermath of the 1973 oil embargo, to an estimated 3 million by 1980. These Arab labor migrants contributed enormously to their national economies. Egyptian workers in the oil states sent home $10 million in 1970, $189 million in 1974, and an estimated $2 billion in 1980—a 200-fold increase in the course of one decade.

Egyptian sociologist Saad Eddin Ibrahim identified a "new Arab social order" that resulted from this exchange of labor and capital between oil-rich and oil-poor states. At a time of deep political divides, the Arabs were enjoying growing interdependence at the economic level. The new order was resilient enough to withstand inter-Arab hostilities: when Egypt went to war with Libya in the summer of 1977, none of the 400,000 Egyptian workers was expelled in retaliation. Such pragmatism prevailed even when Sadat broke Arab ranks to make peace with Israel; demand for

Egyptian manpower in the oil states only increased in the years following the Camp David Accords. As Ibrahim concluded, oil had made the Arab world more closely linked socioeconomically by the end of the 1970s than at any time in its modern history.[62]

The impact of the Iranian revolution went much further than just the oil markets. The fall of one of the longest-ruling autocrats in the Middle East, backed by one of the most powerful armed forces in the region and enjoying the full support of the United States, made Arab politicians sit up and take notice. Nervous Arab rulers began to consider Islamic parties within their own boundaries with growing concern. "Is there a risk that the Iranian revolution can spread to Egypt?" Boutros Boutros-Ghali later recalled asking an Egyptian journalist. "The Iranian revolution is a sickness that cannot spread to Egypt," the journalist assured him.[63] Iran is a Shiite state, he argued, whereas Egypt and the Arab states were overwhelmingly Sunni Muslim. And Egypt was protected from the contagion of Iran by another Islamic state—the Kingdom of Saudi Arabia. Events would soon prove the journalist wrong. Islamic politics would rise to challenge every political leadership in the Arab world in the coming decade—starting in Saudi Arabia.

The Islamic challenge to the Saudi Kingdom came on November 20, 1979, when a little-known organization calling itself the Movement of the Muslim Revolutionaries of the Arabian Peninsula occupied the Great Mosque of Mecca, the very nerve center of Islam. The leader of the movement called for the purification of Islam, the rejection of Western values, and the liberation of the country from the Saudi monarchy, which he accused of hypocrisy and corruption. The standoff lasted more than two weeks, with some 1,000 rebels holding Islam's holiest shrine hostage. The Saudis were forced to send in their national guard to put down the rebellion. Official figures put the death toll in the dozens; unofficial observers claimed that hundreds were killed. The leader of the movement was captured and later executed, along with sixty-three of his followers, many of whom were from Egypt, Yemen, Kuwait, and other Arab countries.

While the Great Mosque was still under siege, Saudi Arabia's Shiite community in the Eastern Province rose in violent demonstrations on November 27, carrying portraits of the spiritual leader of Iran's revolution, Ayatollah Khomeini, and distributing leaflets calling for the overthrow of the "despotic" Saudi regime. The overstretched Saudi national guard took three days to put down the pro-Iranian demonstrations, leaving dozens dead and wounded.[64]

Suddenly even the wealthiest, most powerful oil state looked vulnerable to the rising force of political Islam. A new generation was emerging in the Arab world that no longer believed in the rhetoric of Arab nationalism. They were disenchanted with their political leaders, seeing the Arab kings and presidents building palaces on corruption and putting their personal power over the common Arab good. They did not like the communism or the atheism of the Soviet Union. They believed the United States represented a new imperial power playing divide-and-rule politics among the Arab states and promoting Israel's interests over Palestinian rights. The lesson they took from Iran's revolution was that Islam was stronger than all their enemies combined. United behind the eternal truth of their religion, Muslims could overthrow autocrats and stand up to superpowers. The Arab world was entering a new age of political and social change inspired by the power of Islam.

CHAPTER 13

The Power of Islam

Each year the Egyptian armed forces hold a parade on the sixth of October, a national holiday marking the anniversary of the 1973 War. The Cairo parade ground is set against the dramatic backdrop of a modern pyramid commissioned by President Anwar Sadat to honor the fallen of the October War. This monument also serves as the tomb of Egypt's unknown soldier.

The Armed Forces Day parade celebrates the high point of Sadat's presidency, when he became the "Hero of the Crossing" of the Suez Canal. The parade commemorates Egypt's military leadership of the Arab world against Israel in 1973, before Egypt's separate peace with the Jewish state severely compromised its standing.

Sadat did his utmost to focus public attention on the Armed Forces Day parade, which he attended in person in the full glare of the Egyptian and international press. At least for a day, he could ignore the fact of Egypt's isolation: in response to the Camp David Accords, the other Arab states had severed their ties to Egypt, and the Arab League had relocated its headquarters from Cairo to Tunis. These measures only stiffened the Egyptian government's resolve to celebrate the accomplishments of the 1973 War as a matter of national honor.

On October 6, 1981, Sadat took his seat in the review stand with full state pomp, dressed in his ceremonial uniform, surrounded by his cabinet, clerics, foreign dignitaries, and the military's top brass. Row upon row of tanks, armored personnel carriers, and missile launchers filed between the pyramid-shaped cenotaph and the review stand. A tight formation of air force fighters screamed overhead, trailing colored smoke. "Now comes the artillery," the commentator announced, as the dull tan-colored trucks pulling howitzers approached the review stand.

One of the trucks swerved violently and came to a sudden halt. A soldier leaped from the cab and lobbed a number of stun grenades into the review stand, while his three accomplices opened fire on the assembled dignitaries from the back of the flatbed truck. They had achieved total surprise, and the renegade soldiers enjoyed thirty seconds of unimpeded carnage. They probably killed Sadat with their opening shots.

The leader of the band ran to the front of the reviewing stand and fired point blank at the prone body of President Sadat until finally one of the presidential guards shot and wounded him. "I am Khalid al-Islambuli," the assassin shouted to the chaos in the review stand. "I have killed Pharaoh, and I do not fear death."[1]

The assassination of Sadat, broadcast live on television, sent shock waves around the world. A minor Islamist, acting almost entirely on his own, had assassinated the president of Egypt, the most powerful Arab state. The prospect of an Islamic revolution could no longer be confined to Iran, as Islamist movements cropped up across the Arab world to challenge secular governments.

When Khalid al-Islambuli shouted, "I have killed Pharoah," he was condemning Sadat for being a secular ruler who placed man's law before religion. The Islamists were united by their belief that Muslim societies had to be ruled in accordance with "God's law," the body of Islamic law derived from the Qur'an, the wisdom of the Prophet Muhammad, and the jurisprudence of Islamic theologians collectively known as sharia. They saw their own secular governments as the enemy and referred to their rulers as "pharaohs." The Qur'an, like the Hebrew Bible, is very critical of the pharaohs of ancient Egypt, portraying them as despots who promoted man's law over God's commandments. There are no fewer than seventy-nine verses of the Qur'an condemning pharaohs. The more extreme Islamists advocate violence against the latter-day pharaohs ruling the Arab world as a necessary measure to overturn secular governments and build Islamic states in their place. Khalid al-Islambuli was one of their ranks, and he declared the assassination of Sadat legitimate by denouncing the fallen president as pharaoh.

The Islamists were not Sadat's only critics. Anwar Sadat was laid to rest on October 10, 1981, in a state funeral attended by a number of international leaders but few representatives from the Arab states. Attendees included Richard Nixon, Gerald Ford, and Jimmy Carter, the three American presidents with whom Sadat had worked closely. Prime Minister Menachem Begin, who had shared the 1978 Nobel Peace Prize with Sadat for the Egypt-Israel peace treaty, led a prominent Israeli delegation. Among Arab League members, only Sudan, Oman, and Somalia sent representatives to the funeral.

More striking, perhaps, was the paucity of prominent Egyptians at their president's funeral. Mohamed Heikal, the veteran journalist and political analyst who nurtured his own grievances against Sadat (Heikal had been arrested and imprisoned in a roundup of opposition figures one month before the assassination), reflected on how "a man who was mourned as a heroic and far-seeing statesman in the West found hardly any mourners among his fellow-countrymen."[2]

Yet both his critics and his admirers were satisfied with the choice of Sadat's final resting place. To those who honored the "Hero of the Crossing" it was most appropriate that Sadat was buried in the grounds of the 1973 War memorial, facing the review stand where he had been gunned down. Sadat's Islamist enemies took satisfaction in the fact that the pharaoh had been buried in the shadow of his pyramid.

The Islamists had managed to kill the president of Egypt, but they lacked the resources and planning to topple the government of Egypt. Vice President Husni Mubarak, who had been rushed from the parade grounds with minor wounds, was declared president shortly after the announcement of Sadat's death. The Egyptian security forces rounded up hundreds of suspects and allegedly subjected many of them to torture.

Six months later, in April 1982, five of the defendants were sentenced to death for their role in the assassination of Sadat: Khalid al-Islambuli, his three accomplices, and their ideological guide, an electrician named 'Abd al-Salam Faraj who had written a tract advocating jihad against "un-Islamic" (i.e., secular) Arab rulers. Their executions made martyrs of Sadat's assassins, and throughout the 1980s, Islamist groups continued to wage an often violent campaign against the Egyptian government in their ongoing bid to turn the secular nationalist Arab Republic of Egypt into the Islamic Republic of Egypt.

———————

Given the prominence of Islam in public life across much of the Arab world today, it is easy to forget just how secular the Middle East was in 1981. In all but the most conservative Arab Gulf states, Western fashions were preferred over traditional dress. Many people drank alcohol openly, in disregard of Islamic prohibition. Men and women mixed freely both in public and in the work place, as more and more women were entering higher education and professional life. For some, the freedoms of the modern age marked a high point in Arab progress. Others viewed these developments with unease, fearing that the rapid pace of change was leading the Arab world to abandon its own culture and values.

The debates over Islam and modernity have deep roots in the Arab world. Hassan al-Banna had created the Muslim Brotherhood in 1928 to fight against Western influences and the erosion of Islamic values in Egypt. Over the decades the Muslim Brothers had faced increasing repression, banned by the Egyptian monarchy in December 1948, and then by Nasser's regime in 1954. In the course of the 1950s and

1960s, Islamic politics were driven underground across the Arab world, and Islamic values were undermined by secular states that increasingly drew their inspiration from either Soviet socialism or Western free-market democracy. Yet repression only strengthened the will of the Muslim Brothers to fight secularism and promote their own vision of Islamic values.

A radical new trend emerged from the Muslim Brotherhood in the 1960s, led by a charismatic Egyptian thinker named Sayyid Qutb. He was to prove one of the most influential Islamic reformers of the century. Born in a village in Upper Egypt in 1906, Qutb moved to Cairo in the 1920s to study in the teachers' college, Dar al-'Ulum. Upon graduation, he worked for the Ministry of Education as a teacher and an inspector. He was also active in the literary circles of the 1930s and 1940s as both an author and a critic.

In 1948 Qutb was sent on a two-year government scholarship to study in the United States. He took his masters in education from the University of Northern Colorado's Teachers' College, with periods of study in both Washington, D.C., and Stanford, California. Though he crossed the United States from east to west, Qutb came away with none of the typical exchange student's affection for the country. In 1951 Qutb published his reflections, "The America I Have Seen," in an Islamist magazine. Condemning the materialism and dearth of spiritual values he encountered in the United States, Qutb was appalled by what he saw as moral laxity and unbridled competitiveness in American society. He was particularly shocked to find these vices in American churches. "In most churches," Qutb wrote, "there are clubs that join the two sexes, and every minister attempts to attract to his church as many people as possible, especially since there is a tremendous competition between churches of different denominations." Qutb found such behavior, of trying to pack in the crowds, more appropriate for a theater manager than a spiritual leader.

In his essay Qutb told the story of how one night he had attended a church service followed by a dance. He was appalled to see the lengths to which the pastor went to make the church hall look "more romantic and passionate." The pastor even chose a sultry record to set the mood. Qutb's description of the tune—"a famous American song called 'But Baby, It's Cold Outside,'" captures the gulf that separated him from American popular culture. "[The song] is composed of a dialogue between a boy and a girl returning from their evening date. The boy took the girl to his home and kept her from leaving. She entreated him to let her return home, for it was getting late, and her mother was waiting but every time she would make an excuse, he would reply to her with this line: but baby, it's cold outside!"[3] Qutb clearly found the song distasteful, but he was even more shocked that a man of religion would choose such an inappropriate tune for his young parishioners to dance to. Nothing could be further from the social role of mosques, in which the sexes are separated and modesty is the rule in dress and behavior.

Qutb returned to Egypt determined to snap his fellow countrymen out of their complacent admiration for the modern values that America embodied. "I fear that a balance may not exist between America's material greatness and the quality of its people," he argued. "And I fear that the wheel of life will have turned and the book of time will have closed and America will have added nothing, or next to nothing, to the account of morals that distinguishes man from object, and indeed, mankind from animals."[4] Qutb did not want to change America; rather, he wanted to protect Egypt, and the Islamic world generally, from the moral degeneration he had witnessed in America.

Shortly after his return from the United States, in 1952 Sayyid Qutb joined the Muslim Brotherhood. Because of his background in publishing, he was placed in charge of the society's press and publications office. The ardent Islamist had gained a wide readership through his provocative essays. Following Egypt's 1952 revolution, Qutb enjoyed good relations with the Free Officers. Nasser reportedly invited Qutb to draft the constitution of the new official party, the Liberation Rally. Presumably, Nasser did so less out of admiration for the Islamist reformer himself than as a calculated bid to harness Qutb's support for the new official organ into which all political parties—the Muslim Brotherhood included—were to be dissolved.

The new regime's goodwill toward the Muslim Brotherhood proved short lived. Qutb was arrested in the general clampdown on the organization after a member of the Brotherhood attempted to assassinate Nasser in October 1954. Like many other Muslim Brothers, Qutb claimed he had been subjected to horrific torture and interrogation while under arrest. Convicted on charges of subversive activity, Qutb was sentenced to fifteen years' hard labor.

From prison, Qutb continued to inspire fellow Islamists. Ill health often confined him to the hospital wing, where he wrote some of the most influential works of the twentieth century on Islam and politics, including a radical commentary on the Qur'an and his clarion call for the promotion of a genuine Islamic society, titled *Milestones*.

Milestones represents the culmination of Qutb's views on both the bankruptcy of Western materialism and the authoritarianism of secular Arab nationalism. The social and political systems that defined the modern age, he argued, were man-made and had failed for that very reason. Instead of opening a new age of science and knowledge, they had resulted in ignorance of divine guidance, or *jahiliyya*. The word has particular resonance in Islam, as it refers to the pre-Islamic dark ages. Twentieth-century jahiliyya, Qutb argued, "takes the form of claiming that the right to create values, to legislate rules of collective behaviour, and to choose any way of life rests with men, without regard to what God has prescribed." By implication, the remarkable advances in science and technology of the twentieth century had not led humanity into a modern age; rather, the abandonment of God's eternal message had taken society back to the seventh century. This was as true for the non-Islamic West, Qutb believed, as it was for the Arab world. The result, he argued, was tyranny. Arab regimes did not bring their citizens freedom and human rights, but repression and torture—as Qutb knew from painful firsthand experience.

Qutb believed that Islam, as the perfect statement of God's order for mankind, was the only route to human freedom, a true liberation theology. By extension, the only valid and legitimate laws were God's laws, as enshrined in Islamic sharia. He believed that a Muslim vanguard was needed to restore Islam to "the role of the leader of mankind." The vanguard would use "preaching and persuasion for reforming ideas and beliefs" and would deploy "physical power and jihad for abolishing the organizations and authorities of the Jahili system which prevents people from reforming their ideas and beliefs but forces them to obey their erroneous ways and make them serve human lords instead of the Almighty Lord." Qutb wrote his book to guide the vanguard who would lead the revival of Islamic values, through which Muslims would once again achieve personal freedom and world leadership.[5]

The power of Qutb's message lay in its simplicity and directness. He identified a problem—jahiliyya—and a clear Islamic solution that was grounded in the values that many Arab Muslims held dear. His critique applied equally to imperial powers and to autocratic Arab governments, and his response was a message of hope grounded in the assumption of Muslim superiority:

> Conditions change, the Muslim loses his physical power and is conquered; yet the consciousness does not depart from him that he is the most superior. If he remains a Believer, he looks upon his conqueror from a superior position. He remains certain that this is a temporary condition which will pass away and that faith will turn the tide from which there is no escape. Even if death is his portion, he will never bow his head. Death comes to all, but for him there is martyrdom. He will proceed to the Garden [i.e., heaven], while his conquerors go to the Fire [i.e., hell].[6]

However much Qutb disapproved of Western imperial powers, his first target was always the authoritarian regimes of the Arab world, and Nasser's government in particular. In his exegesis of the Qur'anic verses on the "Makers of the Pit," Qutb draws a thinly veiled allegory of the struggle between the Muslim Brothers and the Free Officers. In the Qur'anic story, a community of Believers was condemned for their faith and burned alive by tyrants who gathered to watch their righteous victims die. "Doomed were the makers of the pit," the Qur'an relates (85:1–16). In Qutb's commentary, the persecutors—"arrogant, mischievous, criminal and degraded people"—took sadistic pleasure in witnessing the pain of the martyrs. "And when some young man or woman, some child or old man from among these righteous Believers was thrown in to the fire," Qutb wrote, "their diabolical pleasure would reach a new height, and shouts of mad joy would escape their lips at the sight of blood and pieces of flesh"—graphic scenes absent from the Qur'anic tale, but perhaps inspired by Qutb's experiences, and those of his fellow Muslim Brothers, at the hands of their torturers in prison. "The struggle between the Believers and their enemies," he concluded, was essentially "a struggle between beliefs—either unbelief or faith, either Jahiliyya or Islam." Qutb's message was clear: the government of Egypt was incompatible with his vision of an Islamic state. One would have to go.

Qutb was released from prison in 1964, the year *Milestones* was published. His standing enhanced by his prison writings, he quickly reestablished contact with comrades from the banned Muslim Brotherhood. Yet Qutb must have known that his every movement would be followed by Nasser's secret police. The Islamist author had gained such prominence across the Muslim world for his radical new thoughts that he would be a danger to the Egyptian state at home and abroad.

Qutb's followers faced the same surveillance and risks as the reformer himself. One of Qutb's most influential disciples was Zaynab al-Ghazali (1917–2005), the pioneer of the Islamist women's movement. When only twenty years old, al-Ghazali founded the Muslim Ladies' Society. Her activities had brought her to the attention of Hasan al-Banna, the founder of the Muslim Brotherhood, who tried to persuade her to join forces with the Muslim Sisterhood he had just launched. Though the two Islamist women's movements followed their separate courses, al-Ghazali became a loyal follower of Hasan al-Banna.

In the 1950s al-Ghazali met the sisters of the imprisoned Sayyid Qutb, who gave her draft chapters of *Milestones* before the book had been published. Inspired by what she read, al-Ghazali devoted herself to the vanguard role envisaged by Qutb's manifesto—preparing Egyptian society to embrace Islamic law. Just as the Prophet Muhammad spent thirteen years in Mecca before migrating to Medina to found the first Islamic community, so the followers of Qutb allowed thirteen years to transform Egyptian society as a whole into an ideal Islamic society. "It was decided," she wrote, "that after thirteen years of Islamic training of our youth, elders, women and children, we would make an exhaustive survey of the state. If this survey revealed that at least 75% of the followers believed that Islam is a complete way of life and are convinced about establishing an Islamic state, then we would call for the establishment of such a state." If the poll results suggested a lower level of support, al-Ghazali and her colleagues would work for another thirteen years to try to convert Egyptian society.[7] In the long run, their aim was nothing less than the overthrow of the Free Officers' regime and its replacement with a true Islamic state. Nasser and his government were determined to eliminate the Islamist threat before it gained ground.

The Egyptian authorities released Sayyid Qutb from prison at the end of 1964, after a decade's imprisonment. Zaynab al-Ghazali and his other supporters celebrated Qutb's release and met frequently with him, under the watchful gaze of Egyptian police surveillance. Many believed that Qutb had been released only to lead the authorities to like-minded Islamists. In August 1965, after only eight months' liberty, Qutb was rearrested, along with al-Ghazali and all their associates. They were charged with conspiracy to assassinate President Nasser and overthrow the Egyptian government. Although their long-term aim was certainly to replace the Egyptian government with an Islamic system, the defendants insisted they were innocent of any plot against the life of the president.

Al-Ghazali spent the next six years in prison and later wrote an account of her ordeal, capturing in graphic horror the tortures to which the Islamists, men and women alike, were subjected by the Nasserist state. She was confronted with the violence from her first day in prison. "Almost unable to believe my eyes and not wanting to accept such inhumanity, I silently watched as members of the *Ikhwan* [i.e., the Muslim Brothers] were suspended in the air and their naked bodies ferociously flogged. Some were left to the mercy of savage dogs which tore at their bodies. Others, with their face to the wall awaited their turn."[8]

Al-Ghazali was not spared these atrocities; she faced whipping, beatings, attacks with dogs, isolation, sleep deprivation, and regular death threats, all in a vain attempt to secure a statement implicating Qutb and the other leaders of the Muslim Brotherhood in the alleged conspiracy. When two newly arrested young women were admitted to share al-Ghazali's cell, after she had suffered eighteen days of abuse, she could not convey the horrors in her own words but read them the Qur'anic verses on "The Makers of the Pit" instead. Upon hearing these verses, one of the women began crying silently; the other asked, disbelievingly: "Does this really happen to ladies?"[9]

The trial against Sayyid Qutb and his followers opened in April 1966. In all, forty-three Islamists—Qutb and al-Ghazali among them—were formally charged with conspiring against the Egyptian state. The state prosecutors used Qutb's writings as evidence against Qutb and charged him with promoting the violent overthrow of the Egyptian government. In August 1966, Qutb and two other defendants were found guilty and sentenced to death. Zaynab al-Ghazali was given twenty-five years with hard labor.

By executing Qutb, the Egyptian authorities not only made him a martyr of the Islamist cause but confirmed to many the truth of Qutb's writings, which became yet more influential after his death than they had been during his own lifetime. His commentary on the Qur'an, and *Milestones*, his charter for political action, were reprinted and distributed across the Muslim world. A new generation, coming of age in the 1960s and 1970s, was electrified by Qutb's message of Islamic regenera-

tion and justice. Its members dedicated themselves to achieve his vision—by all possible means, peaceful and violent alike.

———————

The Islamist challenge spread from Egypt to Syria in the 1960s. The influence
of the Muslim Brotherhood, and Sayyid Qutb's radical critique of secular government, combined to create a revolutionary Islamic movement bent on the overthrow of Syria's praetorian republic. The conflict took Syria to the brink of civil war
and claimed tens of thousands of lives before reaching its brutal climax in the Syrian
town of Hama.

The founder of the Syrian branch of the Muslim Brotherhood, Mustafa al-Siba'i
(1915–1964), was himself a native of Hums. He studied in Egypt in the 1930s, where
he came under the influence of Hasan al-Banna. Upon his return to Syria, Siba'i
brought together a network of Muslim youth associations to create the Muslim Brotherhood in Syria. Siba'i drew on the Muslim Brotherhood's network to win a seat in
the Syrian parliament in the 1943 elections. From that point onward, the Syrian
Muslim Brothers were too strong to be ignored by the political elite, even if they were
not powerful enough in their own right to exercise much influence on the increasingly
secular and Arab nationalist political discourse in Syria in the 1940s and 1950s.

When the Ba'th party seized power in Syria in 1963, the Muslim Brothers went
on the offensive. The politics of the Ba'th were intensely secular, calling for a strict
separation of religion and state. This was only natural, given the sectarian diversity
of the party. Whereas the population of Syria was overwhelmingly Sunni Muslim
(about 70 percent of the total), the Ba'th had also attracted many Christian members
as well as secular Sunni Muslims. It had also had substantial support among the
Alawites. An offshoot of Shiite Islam, the Alawites were the largest of Syria's minority
groups, representing about 12 percent of the population. After years of marginal-
ization by Syria's Sunni majority, the Alawites had risen through the military and
the Ba'th to new prominence in Syrian politics by the 1960s.

As the Ba'th tended toward secular, even atheist views, it provoked growing resistance from the Muslim Brotherhood, which claimed to be Syria's "moral majority."
The Muslim Brotherhood saw the rise of the Alawites to political prominence as a
distinct threat to the Sunni Muslim culture of Syria, and its members were determined to undermine their government through violent means if necessary.

In the mid-1960s, the Brotherhood formed an underground resistance movement
in Hama and the northern city of Aleppo. The Islamist militants began to stockpile
weapons and train young recruits drawn from high schools and universities across
Syria. One of Hama's most charismatic imams (mosque prayer leaders), Shaykh

Marwan Hadid, was particularly successful in recruiting students to the Islamic underground movement. For many of the young Islamists, Hadid was an inspiration and a role model for Islamic activism.[10]

Confrontation between the Islamist underground and the Syrian government became inevitable when the Ba'thist commander of the Syrian air force, General Hafiz al-Asad, came to power in the coup of November 16, 1970. As a member of the Alawite minority community, al-Asad was Syria's first non-Sunni Muslim leader. He made efforts to placate Sunni Muslim sensitivities in his early years in office, but to no avail. The introduction of a new constitution in 1973, which for the first time did not stipulate that the president of Syria would be a Muslim, revived questions of religion and state. The constitution sparked violent demonstrations in the Sunni Muslim heartland of Hama. Further Islamist violence followed al-Asad's decision to intervene in the Lebanese civil war on the side of the Maronite Christians and against the progressive Muslim forces and the Palestinian movement in April 1976.

Al-Asad's intervention in the Lebanon War raised grave concerns among Syria's Muslim majority. Many disgruntled Sunnis, who had found themselves marginalized by the Alawite-dominated government since al-Asad came to power in 1970, suspected the new regime of promoting a "minority alliance" that bound Syria's ruling Alawites with the Lebanese Maronites to subjugate the Muslim majority of Syria and Lebanon. With tensions growing between the government and the Sunni community, al-Asad ordered a crackdown on the Syrian Muslim Brothers. In 1976 the authorities arrested Hama's radical imam, Shaykh Marwan Hadid. The Islamist recruiter immediately went on a hunger strike, and he died in June 1976. The authorities insisted that Hadid had taken his own life by starvation, but the Islamists accused the government of his murder and promised to avenge Marwan Hadid's death.

It took three years for Syria's Islamists to organize their retaliatory blow against the Asad regime. In June 1979, the Islamist guerrillas attacked a military academy in Aleppo, the majority of whose students—some 260 of the 320 cadets—were from the Alawite community. The terrorists killed 83 cadets, all of them from the Alawite minority.

The attack on the military academy was the opening volley in an all-out war between the Muslim Brotherhood and the regime of Hafiz al-Asad that was to rage for the next two and one-half years, dragging Syria into a hellish daily back-and-forth of terrorism and counterterrorism.

The Muslim Brothers in Syria, convinced of the righteousness of their cause, refused to negotiate or compromise with the Asad regime. "We reject all forms of despotism, out of respect for the very principles of Islam, and do not seek the fall of the Pharaoh so that another might take his place," they announced in a leaflet distributed across the towns and cities of Syria in mid-1979.[11] Their language echoed the Islamist militants in Egypt, who were similarly bent on overthrowing the Sadat government by violence, and who gave moral support to their Brothers in Hama in their revolt against Syria's pharaoh.

With no scope for reconciliation, the hard-liners in the Syrian government, headed by the president's brother, Rifa'at al-Asad, were given a free hand to suppress the Islamic insurgency by force. In March 1980, Syrian commandos descended by helicopter on a rebel village between Aleppo and Latakia and placed the entire village under martial rule. According to official figures, more than two hundred villagers were killed in the operation.

Emboldened by its success in the countryside, the Syrian government sent 25,000 troops to invade the city of Aleppo, scene of the cadet massacre one year earlier. Soldiers searched every house in those quarters known to support the Islamist insurgency and arrested more than 8,000 suspects. Rifa'at al-Asad warned the townspeople from the turret of his tank that he was ready to execute 1,000 a day until the city was cleansed of the Muslim Brotherhood.

The Muslim Brothers struck back on June 26, 1980, with an assassination attempt against President al-Asad. Militants threw hand grenades and fired machine guns at the president while he received a visiting African dignitary. Al-Asad was shielded by his bodyguards and narrowly escaped death. The following day, Rifa'at al-Asad sent his commandos to the notorious Tadmur Prison, where Muslim Brother prisoners were detained, to exact a terrible revenge.

'Isa Ibrahim Fayyad, a young Alawite commando, would never forget his first mission, when he was ordered to massacre unarmed prisoners at Tadmur. The Syrian soldiers were flown by helicopter to the prison at 6:30 A.M. There were perhaps seventy commandos in all, divided into seven platoons, each dispatched to a different cell block. Fayyad and his men took up their positions and went to work. "They opened the gates of a cell block for us. Six or seven of us entered and killed all those we found inside, some 60 or 70 people in all. I must have gunned down fifteen myself." The cells echoed with machine-gun fire and the screams of the dying shouting "*Allahu Akbar.*" Fayyad had no compassion for his victims. "Altogether some 550 of those Muslim Brother bastards must have been killed," he reflected grimly. Other participants estimated as many as 700–1,100 Muslim Brothers were gunned down in their cells. The unarmed prisoners made desperate attacks on the commandos, killing one and wounding two others in the melee. When the commandos were finished, they had to wash the blood from their hands and feet.[12]

Having exterminated the Muslim Brothers in Tadmur Prison, al-Asad took the initiative to eliminate the Brotherhood from Syrian society. On July 7, 1980, the Syrian government passed a law that made membership in the Muslim Brotherhood an offense punishable by death. Undaunted, the Islamist opposition movement embarked on a series of assassinations against prominent Syrian officials, including some of President al-Asad's personal friends.

The Syrian government responded in April 1981 by sending the army into the Muslim Brothers' stronghold in Hama. The fourth-largest city in Syria, with a population at the time of about 180,000, Hama had been the center of Islamist opposition since the 1960s. When the troops arrived, the townspeople put up no resistance, assuming this would be a raid like those in the past, in which people were detained for questioning and intimidated by the commandos before being released. They were wrong.

The Syrian army decided to make an example of the civilians of Hama, killing children and adults indiscriminately. One eyewitness described the carnage to a Western journalist: "I walked a few steps before coming on a pile of bodies, then another. There must have been 10 or 15. I walked by them, one after the other. I looked at them a long time, without believing my eyes. . . . In each pile there were 15 bodies, 25, 30 bodies. The faces were totally unrecognizable. . . . There were bodies of all ages, 14 and up, in pyjamas, *gelebiyehs* [native robes], in sandals or barefoot."[13] Estimates ranged from 150 to several hundred killed in the attack. The total death toll in two years of hostilities between government forces and Islamists already exceeded 2,500.

The Muslim Brothers responded to the army's Hama atrocity in kind, initiating a terror campaign against innocent civilians in the major towns and cities of Syria. The Islamists shifted the battlefield from the northern towns of Aleppo, Latakia, and Hama to the capital city of Damascus. The Muslim Brothers planted a series of explosive devices that shook the Syrian capital between August and November of that year, culminating in a massive car bomb in the city center on November 29 that killed 200 and wounded up to 500—the largest casualty toll of any single bomb the Arab world had witnessed up to that point.

Anwar Sadat's assassination in October 1981 coincided with President Asad's fifty-first birthday; Syrian Islamists circulated leaflets threatening him with the same fate. Al-Asad authorized his brother Rifa'at to conduct an extermination campaign against the Muslim Brothers in their stronghold in Hama, to defeat the movement once and for all.

The Syrian government went to war against the Muslim Brotherhood in their stronghold of Hama in the early morning hours of February 2, 1982. Helicopter gunships ferried platoons of commandos to the hills outside the city. After the government's murderous raid in April 1981, the townspeople were on high alert, and the vigilant Islamists were quick to react when they heard the incoming helicopters. Shouting "*Allahu akbar*," the Muslim Brothers rose in armed revolt against the Syrian state.

The call to jihad, or holy war, was made over the loudspeakers of the city's mosques, normally used for the daily calls to prayer. The leader of the Muslim Brothers urged the townspeople to drive the "infidel" Asad regime from power once and for all.

By dawn, the first wave of soldiers was in retreat and the Islamist fighters went on the attack, killing government officials and Ba'th members in Hama. Early success gave the insurgents a false hope of victory. For behind the first wave of army commandos lay tens of thousands of soldiers, supported by tanks and aircraft. It was a battle the government could not afford to lose and that the insurgents lacked the means to win.

For the first week, the Muslim Brothers managed to fight off the Syrian army onslaught. Yet the government's superior firepower took its toll, as tanks and artillery leveled whole city blocks, burying their defenders under the rubble. When the town finally fell, government agents exacted a bloody toll of the survivors, arresting, torturing, and arbitrarily killing the townspeople of Hama for the slightest suspicion of support for the Muslim Brothers. *New York Times* correspondent Thomas Friedman, who entered Hama two months after the violence, found a city in which whole quarters had been destroyed and leveled by bulldozers and steamrollers. The human toll was far more terrible. "Virtually the entire Muslim leadership in Hama—from sheiks to teachers to mosque caretakers—who survived the battle for the city were liquidated afterward in one fashion or another; most anti-government union leaders suffered the same fate," Friedman reported.[14]

To this day, no one knows how many people died in Hama in February 1982. Journalists and analysts have estimated a death toll ranging somewhere between 10,000–20,000, but Rifa'at al-Asad boasted of having killed as many as 38,000. The Asad brothers wanted the world to know they had crushed their adversaries and dealt the Muslim Brotherhood in Syria a blow from which it would never recover.

The stakes were now higher than ever in the conflict between Islamists and pharaohs. Whereas the Egyptian authorities had resorted to widespread torture and selective execution of its Islamist opponents, the Syrian regime engaged in mass extermination. A higher degree of training, planning, and discipline were required for the Islamists to topple such powerful adversaries.

The experiences of Islamists in Syria and Egypt had shown that Arab states were too strong to be toppled by assassination or subversion. Those Islamists who hoped to overturn secularism and establish Islamic states would have to look elsewhere. The conflict in civil war Lebanon provided one opportunity for Islamist parties to promote their ideal vision of an Islamic society. Afghanistan after the 1979 Soviet invasion presented a different option. In both cases, Islamist parties took their struggle to the international arena, broadening the scope of their battle to combat regional and global superpowers like Israel, the United States, and the Soviet Union. What had begun as a domestic security struggle for individual states was becoming a global security issue.

Two nearly simultaneous bombs shook the very foundations of Beirut on Sunday morning, October 23, 1983. Within seconds, over 300 people had perished: 241 U.S. servicemen, 58 French paratroopers, 6 Lebanese civilians, and 2 suicide bombers. The U.S. Marines faced the highest single-day death toll since Iwo Jima, the French had absorbed the greatest single day's casualties since the Algerian war, and the suicide bombers had transformed the conflict in Lebanon.

The bombers approached their targets in trucks laden with tons of high explosives. One approached the U.S. Marines' barracks, a concrete building in the Beirut International Airport compound, through a service entrance at 6:20 A.M. He gathered speed and smashed through the metal gates. The shocked sentries did not have time even to load their weapons to stop him. One survivor watched the truck speed by. All he could remember after the blast was that "the man was smiling as he drove past."[15] The driver was clearly delighted that he had penetrated the American compound, no doubt believing that his violent death would open the Gates of Paradise before him.

The blast was so strong that it severed the building from its foundation; the compound collapsed like a house of cards. The ruins were rocked by secondary explosions as the Marines' ammunition stores in the basement were detonated by the heat.

Three miles to the north, another suicide bomber drove his truck into the underground parking garage of the high-rise building that served as headquarters to the French paratroopers. He detonated his bomb, leveling the building and killing fifty-eight French soldiers. Journalist Robert Fisk, who reached the ruins of the French compound moments after the explosion, could not grasp the enormity of the destruction. "I run up to a smoking crater, 20 feet deep and 40 wide. Piled beside it, like an obscene sandwich, are the nine floors of the building. . . . *The bomb lifted the nine-storey building into the air and moved it 20 feet. The whole building became airborne. The crater is where the building was.* How could this be done?"[16]

Even for war-shattered Beirut, the devastation wrought by the attacks of October 23, 1983, was shocking. The operations also revealed an unprecedented and deeply troubling degree of planning and discipline. Today we would say it bore the hallmark of an al-Qaida operation—a decade before that movement's first attacks.

No one knows precisely who was responsible for the attacks on the U.S. Marines and the French paratroopers in Beirut, but the prime suspect was a shadowy new group that called itself Islamic Jihad. In one of its earliest operations, in July 1982, members of the Islamic Jihad kidnapped the acting president of the American University of Beirut, an American academic named David Dodge. They also claimed responsibility for the massive car bomb that sheared a wing off the United States Embassy in downtown Beirut in April 1983, killing 63 and wounding over 100.

Radical new forces were at work in the Lebanese civil war. Islamic Jihad revealed itself to be a Lebanese Shiite organization collaborating with Iran. In an anonymous telephone call to a foreign press agency, Islamic Jihad claimed its July bombing of the U.S. Embassy was "part of the Iranian revolution's campaign against the imperialist presence throughout the world." Iran had dangerous friends in Lebanon, it seemed. "We will continue to strike at the imperialist presence in Lebanon," the Islamic Jihad spokesman continued, "including the multi-national force." Following the October bombings, Islamic Jihad once again claimed responsibility. "We are the soldiers of God and we are fond of death. We are neither Iranians nor Syrians nor Palestinians," they insisted. "We are Lebanese Muslims who follow the principles of the Koran."[17]

The conflict in Lebanon had grown infinitely more complex in the six years between the Syrian intervention in 1977 and the suicide bombings of 1983. Though it had started as an internal war between Lebanese factions with Palestinian involvement in 1975, the war was by 1983 a regional conflict that drew in Syria, Israel, Iran, Europe, and the United States directly—and many more countries indirectly, such as Iraq, Libya, Saudi Arabia, and the Soviet Union, which bankrolled different militias and provided them with weaponry.

The war had also led to significant shifts in the balance of power among the different Lebanese communities. The Syrian army, which entered Lebanon in 1976 as part of an Arab League peacekeeping force, had first sided with the beleaguered Maronite Christians to prevent the victory of the Leftist Muslim factions headed by Kamal Jumblatt. Syria was jealous of its dominant position in Lebanon and acted quickly to prevent any one group from gaining a clear victory in that country's civil war. This led Syria to change its alliances with some frequency. No sooner had Syria's army defeated the leftist Muslim militias than it turned against the Maronites and sided with the rising new power of Lebanon's Shiite Muslim community.

Long marginalized by the political elites, the Shiites had emerged as a distinct political community in Lebanon only since the onset of the Lebanese civil war. By the 1970s the Shiites had become the largest Lebanese community in terms of numbers, though they remained the poorest and most politically disenfranchised of the country's sects. The traditional centers of Lebanon's Shiite communities were in the poorest parts of the country—South Lebanon and the northern Bekaa Valley. Increasingly, Shiites fled the relative deprivation of the countryside, moving to the southern slums of Beirut in search of jobs.

In the 1960s and 1970s, many Lebanese Shiites had been drawn to secular parties promising social reform, like the Ba'th, the Lebanese Communist Party, and the Syrian Social Nationalist Party. It was only in the 1970s that a charismatic Iranian cleric of Lebanese ancestry named Musa al-Sadr drew the Shiites together into a distinct communal party known as the Movement of the Dispossessed (Harakat al-Mahrumin) and began to compete with the leftist parties for the loyalty of the Lebanese Shiites. Upon the outbreak of the civil war in 1975, the Movement of the Dispossessed created its own militia, known as Amal.

In the first stages of the Lebanese civil war, Amal sided with the leftist Muslim parties of the National Movement, headed by Kamal Jumblatt. But Musa al-Sadr soon grew disenchanted with Jumblatt's leadership, accusing the Druze leader of using the Shiites as cannon-fodder—in al-Sadr's words, "to combat the Christians to the last Shi'i."[18] Tensions had also emerged between Amal and the Palestinian movement, which since 1969 had used South Lebanon as a base for its operations against Israel. Not only did the Shiite community suffer great hardship from Israeli retaliatory strikes provoked by Palestinian operations from the south, but it grew to resent the control the Palestinians exercised over South Lebanon.

By 1976 Amal had broken with Jumblatt's coalition and the Palestinian movement to side with the Syrians, whom its followers saw as the only counterweight to Palestinian influence in the south. It was the beginning of an enduring alliance between Syria and the Shiites of Lebanon that has survived until today.

The Iranian Revolution and the creation of the Islamic Republic in 1979 transformed Shiite politics in Lebanon. The Shiites of Lebanon were bound to Iran by common religious and cultural ties that spanned the centuries. Musa al-Sadr was himself an Iranian of Lebanese origins, and he promoted political activism very much in line with the thinking of the Islamic revolutionaries in Iran.

Al-Sadr never lived to see the Iranian Revolution. He disappeared on a trip to Libya in 1978 and is widely assumed to have been murdered there. The 1979 revolution galvanized the Shiites of South Lebanon by giving them a host of new leaders to rally behind at a crucial moment when they were still coming to terms with the recent disappearance of their leader. Portraits of Ayatollah Khomeini flanked those of Musa al-Sadr in the southern slums of Beirut and the Roman ruins of Baalbek. The Iranians did all they could to encourage the enthusiasm of Lebanese Shiites, as part of their early bid to export their revolution, and to extend their influence to the traditional centers of Shiite Arab culture in southern Iraq, the Eastern Province of Saudi Arabia, Bahrain, and Lebanon. Through this network, Iran could put pressure on its rivals and enemies—particularly the United States, Israel, and Iraq.

American-Iranian relations deteriorated rapidly after the Islamic Revolution in 1979. The new Iranian government mistrusted the American administration because of its past support for the shah, Mohamed Reza Pahlavi. When the U.S. government allowed the deposed shah into the United States for medical treatment (he was terminally ill with cancer), a group of Iranian students overran the American Embassy in Tehran and took fifty-two American diplomats hostage on November 4, 1979. U.S. president Jimmy Carter froze Iranian assets, applied economic and political sanctions on the Islamic Republic, and even attempted an aborted military rescue mission to relieve the hostage crisis—to no avail. The American government was powerless and humiliated as its diplomats were held captive for 444 days. In a calculated swipe at Jimmy Carter, whose reelection campaign had been derailed by the hostage crisis, the American diplomats were released only after Ronald Reagan had been sworn in as president, in January 1981. The gesture did not endear the Iranian government to the Reagan administration, and the damage caused by the hostage crisis has troubled American-Iranian relations ever since. The new Iranian regime denounced the United States as the Great Satan and the enemy of all Muslims. The Reagan administration—and those that followed—branded the Islamic Republic a rogue state and sought all means to isolate Iran and bring down its government.

The outbreak of the Iran-Iraq War in 1980 exacerbated the antagonism between the Islamic Republic and the United States, with dire consequences for Lebanon. Headed since 1978 by President Saddam Hussein, Iraq invaded its eastern neighbor without warning on September 22, 1980. Hussein attempted to take advantage of the political turmoil within revolutionary Iran and the country's international isolation during the hostage crisis to seize disputed waterways and rich oil fields in Iranian territory. By far the most violent conflict in the history of the modern Middle East, the Iran-Iraq War lasted eight years (1980–1988) and claimed an estimated 500,000–1,000,000 lives amid tactics reminiscent of the World Wars—trench warfare, gas and chemical weapons, and aerial bombardment and rocket attacks on urban centers.

It took the Iranians two years to drive the Iraqis from their soil and go on the offensive. As the war turned to Iran's advantage, the United States gave its open support to Iraq, in spite of that country's close ties to the Soviet Union. Starting in 1982, the Reagan administration began to provide arms, intelligence, and economic assistance to Saddam Hussein for his war against Iran. This compounded Iranian hostility toward the United States, and the Iranians took every opportunity to strike at American interests in the region. Lebanon soon emerged as an arena for the Iranian-American confrontation.

Iran enjoyed two allies in Lebanon—the Shiite community, and Syria. The Iranian-Syrian alliance was in many ways counterintuitive. As an overtly Arab nationalist, secular state engaged in a violent struggle with its own Islamic movement, Syria was an unlikely ally for the non-Arab Islamic Republic of Iran. What bound the two countries together were pragmatic interests—primarily their mutual antagonism toward Iraq, Israel, and the United States.

In the 1970s Iraq and Syria had been engaged in an intense competition for leadership of the Arab world. Both countries were governed as single-party states under rival variants of the Arab nationalist Ba'th party. As a result, Ba'thism actually served to undermine unity of action or common purpose between Iraq and Syria. So deep was the antagonism between the two Ba'thi states that Syria broke ranks with the other Arab countries to side with Iran in its war with Iraq. In return, Iran provided Syria with arms and economic aid, and reinforcements in Syria's conflict with Israel. And the Syrian-Iranian alliance completed a triangle of relations binding Syria and Iran to the Lebanese Shiite community. The catalyst for activating this fateful triangle was the Israeli invasion of Lebanon in the summer of 1982.

Israel's 1982 invasion of Lebanon opened a new phase in the conflict in Lebanon. Violence and destruction reached unprecedented levels. And, by invading Lebanon, Israel came to be drawn into the factional politics as an outright participant in the Lebanese conflict. The Israelis were to remain in Lebanon for over eighteen years, with enduring consequences for both countries.

The Israeli invasion of Lebanon was triggered by an attack on British soil. On June 3, 1982, the Abu Nidal terror group—the same organization that murdered the PLO's London diplomat Said Hammami in 1978—attempted to assassinate Israeli ambassador Shlomo Argov outside a London hotel. Though Abu Nidal was a renegade group violently opposed to Yasser Arafat and the PLO, and though the PLO had observed a year-long cease-fire with Israel, the Israeli government nonetheless took the assassination attempt as grounds for war against the PLO in Lebanon.

Israel's prime minister, Menachem Begin, and his militant defense minister, General Ariel Sharon, had ambitious plans to reshape the Middle East by driving the PLO and Syria out of Lebanon. Begin believed the Christians in Lebanon were a natural ally for the Jewish state, and, since coming to power in 1977, his Likud government had developed an increasingly open alliance with the right-wing Maronite Phalangist Party (with predictably adverse consequences for Syrian-Maronite relations).[19] Phalangist militiamen were brought to Israel for training, and the Israelis provided over $100 million in arms, ammunition, and uniforms to the Christian fighters.

Begin believed Israel could secure a full peace treaty with Lebanon if both the PLO and Syria were driven from the country and Bashir Gemayel, son of Pierre Gemayel, founder of the Phalangist Party, were to become president. Peace with Lebanon, following the peace with Egypt, would isolate Syria and leave Israel a free hand to annex the Palestinian territories in the West Bank, occupied by Israel in the June 1967 War. For both strategic and ideological reasons, the Likud government was determined to integrate the West Bank, which it consistently referred to by the Biblical names Judea and Samaria, into the modern state of Israel. However, although Israel's government sought the territory of the West Bank, it did not want to absorb its Arab population. Sharon's solution was to drive the Palestinians out of the West Bank and to encourage them to fulfill their national aspirations by overthrowing King Hussein and taking over Jordan, a country whose population was already 60 percent Palestinian. This represented what Sharon liked to call the "Jordan option."[20]

These were ambitious plans that could only be achieved by military means and—upon reflection—a callous indifference to human life. The first step would be to destroy the PLO presence in Lebanon, and the Likud used the assassination attempt in London as the grounds on which to initiate hostilities. The very next day, on June 4, 1982, Israeli aircraft and naval vessels began a murderous bombardment of South Lebanon and West Beirut. On June 6, Israeli ground forces swept across the Lebanese border in a campaign dubbed "Operation Peace for Galilee." Over the next ten weeks, UN figures reported more than 17,000 Lebanese and Palestinians killed and 30,000 wounded by the Israeli invasion, the overwhelming majority of them civilians.

The Israelis unleashed the full force of their military on Lebanon. While Lebanese towns and cities were bombed from the air and sea, the Israeli army advanced rapidly through South Lebanon to lay siege to Beirut, where the PLO had its headquarters in the southern suburb of Fakhani. The residents of Beirut became the helpless victims of a conflict between Israel, the Palestinians, and the Syrians. The Israelis targeted the leadership of the PLO in particular, hoping to decapitate the movement by killing Yasser Arafat and his top lieutenants. Arafat was forced to change residence daily to avoid assassination. The buildings in which he was reported to take shelter were quickly targeted by Israeli bombers.

Lina Tabbara, who assisted Arafat with his 1974 speech at the UN General Assembly, had survived the first phase of the Lebanese civil war with her family in Muslim West Beirut. Her marriage, however, did not, and she reverted to her maiden name, Lina Mikdadi. Living in West Beirut during the 1982 siege, Mikdadi witnessed the leveling of an apartment building that Arafat had left only minutes earlier. "I noticed a space where a building had been, right behind the public gardens. . . . I ran to the spot. An eight-story building had disappeared. People ran around half-crazed, women screamed their children's names."[21] The destruction of that one building in which Arafat had been taking refuge claimed 250 civilian lives, according to Mikdadi. One of Arafat's commanders said the raid had left Arafat distraught. "What crime has been committed by these children, now buried under the rubble?" Arafat asked. "All they are guilty of is having been in a building I visited a couple of times." Thereafter, Arafat slept in his car, away from built-up areas.[22]

For ten weeks of unspeakable violence the siege continued. Survivors reported hundreds of raids conducted within a single day. There was no safe haven, no place to take refuge. As casualty figures spiraled into the tens of thousands, international pressure mounted on Israel to bring its siege of Beirut to a close. The violence reached its peak in August 1982. On August 12 the Israelis carried out eleven hours of nonstop air raids, dropping thousands of tons of ordnance on West Beirut. An estimated 800 homes were destroyed, with 500 casualties. In Washington, President Ronald Reagan placed a call to Prime Minister Begin in Israel and convinced him to stop the fighting. "President Reagan," Mikdadi asked rhetorically, "why didn't you make your phone call earlier?"[23]

Begin relented under U.S. pressure, and the Reagan administration brokered a complex cease-fire agreement between the Israelis and the Palestinians. The PLO combatants would withdraw from Beirut by sea, and a multinational force composed of U.S., French, and Italian troops would be deployed to take up positions vacated by the Israelis.

The first stage of the disengagement plan went very smoothly. French troops arrived on August 21 to take control of the Beirut International Airport. The next day, the first of the PLO forces began their withdrawal from Beirut's sea port. There was a great deal of concern for the security of the departing Palestinians. Many Lebanese had grown hostile to the Palestinian movement, blaming the PLO for causing the civil war in the first place and for provoking the Israeli invasions of 1978 and 1982. Yet when Lina Mikdadi, herself half-Palestinian, went to the assembly point to bid the Palestinian men farewell, she found that many citizens of West Beirut had done the same. "Women lean out of windows that no longer have any panes to throw rice; they wave from half-destroyed balconies. Many cry as they watch the trucks go by. The Palestinians have already said goodbye to their children, wives and parents at the municipal stadium."[24]

The departing Palestinian fighters were to be scattered among a number of Arab countries—Yemen, Iraq, Algeria, Sudan, and Tunisia, where the PLO established its new headquarters. Their expulsion from Beirut marked the end of the PLO as a coherent fighting force. Yasser Arafat was the last to leave, on August 30, and with his departure the siege of Beirut was effectively over. The whole process had gone so smoothly that the international forces, originally deployed for thirty days, withdrew ten days early, believing their mission accomplished. The last French contingent left Lebanon on September 13.

The retreating Palestinian fighters left behind their parents, wives, and children. The Palestinian civilians that remained were left completely defenseless. One of the main tasks of the multinational forces was to ensure the security of the families of Palestinian combatants who were vulnerable in a hostile country. As those forces began to withdraw, no one was left to protect the Palestinian refugee camps from their many enemies.

At the same time the PLO was withdrawing from Lebanon, the Lebanese parliament was scheduled to meet on August 23 to elect a new president. Due to the civil war, there had not been a parliamentary election since 1972. The parliamentarians' numbers had been reduced by mortality from 99 to 92, of which only 45 were actually in Lebanon. Only one candidate had declared his intention to run for office: Israel's ally Bashir Gemayel of the right-wing Maronite Phalangist Party. To this Lebanon's vaunted democracy had been reduced. Yet for the war-weary and pragmatic Lebanese, Gemayel was a consensus candidate. His connections to Israel and the West might just win the Lebanese some much-needed peace. There was genuine celebration across Lebanon when Gemayel's election was confirmed.

Bashir Gemayel's presidency proved short lived—as did Lebanon's peace. On September 14, a bomb destroyed the Phalangist Party headquarters in East Beirut, killing Gemayel. There is no evidence of any Palestinian involvement in the assassination; in fact, a young Maronite named Habib Shartouni, a member of the pro-Damascus Syrian Socialist National Party, was arrested two days later and confessed to the crime, denouncing Gemayel as a traitor for his dealings with Israel. Yet the Phalangist militiamen harbored such deep hatred for the Palestinians, cultivated over seven years of civil war, that they sought revenge for the assassination of their leader in the Palestinian camps.

Had the American, French, and Italian troops of the multinational force seen out their full thirty-day mandate, they might have been able to provide the necessary protection for the unarmed Palestinian refugees. Instead, the Palestinian camps had come under the protection of the Israeli army, which reoccupied Beirut immediately after Gemayel's assassination was announced. On the night of September 16, Israeli defense minister Ariel Sharon and chief of staff Raphael Eitan authorized the deployment of Phalangist militiamen into the Palestinian refugee camps. What followed was a massacre of innocent, unarmed civilians—a crime against humanity.

Though the massacres at Sabra and Shatila were conducted by Maronite militiamen, they were given full access to the camps by the Israeli forces, which had secured all points of entry to the area. The Israelis knew their Maronite allies well enough to know the danger they posed to the Palestinians. Any doubts about Maronite intentions were dispelled when Israeli officers overheard the radio exchanges between the Phalangists shortly after they entered the Palestinian camps. One Israeli lieutenant followed an exchange between a Phalangist militiaman and Maronite commander Elie Hobeika. Hobeika had lost his fiancée and many family members in the Palestinian siege of the Christian stronghold of Damour in January 1976—his hatred of Palestinians was legendary. The militiaman reported to Hobeika in Arabic that he had found fifty women and children and asked what he should do with them. Hobeika's reply over the radio, the Israeli lieutenant recounted, was: "This is the last time you're going to ask me a question like that, you know exactly what to do." Raucous laughter broke out among the Phalangist militiamen following the radio exchange. The Israeli lieutenant confirmed he "understood that what was involved was the murder of the women and children."[25] Because of their complicity in the massacre, the Israeli armed forces—and General Ariel Sharon in particular—were stained by the Maronite crimes against the Palestinians of Sabra and Shatila.

Over a thirty-six-hour period, the Phalangists systematically murdered hundreds of Palestinians in the Sabra and Shatila camps. Maronite militiamen made their way through the fetid alleys of the camps, killing every man, woman, and child they found. Jamal, a twenty-eight-year-old member of Arafat's Fatah movement, had remained in Beirut after the PLO's withdrawal and was an eyewitness to the massacres. "On Thursday the flares over the camp began at 5.30 P.M. . . . There were aircraft dropping light bombs too. The night was like day. The next few hours were terrible. I saw people running in panic to the small mosque, Chatila Mosque. They were taking shelter there because apart from being a sanctuary it was also built with a strong steel structure. Inside were 26 women and children—some of them had horrible injuries." These may well have been the refugees that Hobeika had condemned over the radio.

While the killing was going on, the Phalangists set to work leveling the refugee camp with bulldozers, often killing the people sheltering inside. "They killed everyone they found, but the point is the *way* they killed them," Jamal recounted. The old were cut down, the young were raped and murdered, family members were forced to witness the murder of their loved ones. The Israelis estimated 800 were killed, but the Palestinian Red Cross reported that over 2,000 died. "They must have been crazed to do things like that," Jamal concluded. He spoke of these events with some detachment and saw the massacre as part of a bigger plan. "Psychologically it is clear what they were trying to do to us. We were trapped like animals in that camp, and that is how they have always tried to show us to the world. They wanted us to believe it ourselves."[26]

The massacre in the Sabra and Shatila camps provoked widespread condemnation across the world—not least in Israel, where opposition to the Lebanon War had grown increasingly vocal over the course of the summer. On September 25, some 300,000 Israelis, representing 10 percent of the total population of the country, gathered in a mass demonstration in Tel Aviv to protest Israel's role in the atrocity. In response, the Likud government was forced to convene an official commission of inquiry—the Kahan Commission—that in 1983 would charge the most powerful Israeli officials involved—Prime Minister Begin, Foreign Minister Yitzhak Shamir, Chief of Staff General Eitan—with responsibility for the massacre. The commission also called for the resignation of Defense Minister Ariel Sharon.

More immediately, the international outcry led to the return of the multinational forces and American engagement in resolving the crisis in Lebanon. U.S. Marines, French paratroopers, and Italian soldiers returned to Beirut on September 29, too late to provide the security they had promised the families of the deported PLO fighters.

If at first they had been deployed to see out the Palestinian fighters, the multinational forces were now sent in as a buffer for the Israeli withdrawal from Beirut. The Israelis, for their part, did not want to move until they had concluded a political agreement with Lebanon. First a replacement president had to be elected. On September 23, the day Bashir Gemayel had been due to take up office, Lebanon's parliament reconvened to elect his older brother Amin as president. Whereas Bashir had worked closely with the Israelis, Amin Gemayel had better relations with Damascus and showed none of his brother's enthusiasm for close cooperation with Tel Aviv. However, with nearly half his country under Israeli occupation, the new President Gemayel had no choice but to enter into negotiations with Begin's government. Talks opened on December 28, 1982, and shifted between Khalde, in Israeli-occupied Lebanon, and the northern Israeli town of Kiryat Shimona. Thirty-five rounds of intense negotiations were conducted over the next five months, facilitated by American officials. U.S. secretary of state George Shultz spent ten days in shuttle diplomacy to help conclude the Israeli-Lebanese agreement on May 17, 1983.

The May 17 Agreement was condemned across the Arab world as a travesty of justice, in which the American superpower forced the powerless Lebanese to reward its Israeli ally for invading and destroying their country. Less than the full peace treaty the Israelis initially hoped for, the agreement nevertheless represented more normalization with the Israeli occupier than most Lebanese could accept. It terminated the state of war between Lebanon and Israel and placed the Lebanese government in the difficult position of ensuring the security of Israel's northern border from the Jewish state's many enemies. Lebanon's army was to be deployed in the south to create a "security region" covering approximately one-third the territory of Lebanon, extending from the town of Sidon south to the Israeli border. The Lebanese government also agreed to integrate the South Lebanon army, an Israeli-funded Christian militia that had gained notoriety as collaborators, into the Lebanese army. It was, in the words of one Shiite official, a "humiliating accord" concluded "under the Israeli bayonet."[27]

The Syrian government was particularly aggrieved by the terms of the May 17 Agreement, which would only isolate Syria and alter the regional balance of power in Israel's favor. In the course of the negotiations, the United States had deliberately bypassed Syria's president, Hafiz al-Asad, knowing he would obstruct negotiations between Israel and Lebanon. Nor did the May 17 Agreement include any concessions for the Syrians. Article 6 of the agreement would have required the withdrawal of all Syrian troops from Lebanon as a precondition for Israel's withdrawal. Syria had invested too much political capital in Lebanon in the six years since it first intervened in the civil war to permit the country to pass into Israel's sphere of influence under U.S. auspices.

Syria quickly mobilized its allies in Lebanon to reject the May 17 Agreement. Fighting resumed as the opposition forces began to shell Christian areas of Beirut, underlining the weakness of the Gemayel government. They also fired on the American troops of the multinational forces, whose role as disinterested peacekeepers had been fatally compromised by the regional politics of the United States. When American forces returned fire—often very heavy fire from the massive guns of U.S. warships—they went from being intermediaries above the fray to participants mired in the Lebanon conflict.

Though a superpower, the United States was at a disadvantage in Lebanon. Its local allies, the isolated government of Amin Gemayel and the Israeli occupation forces, were more vulnerable than its enemies: Soviet-backed Syria, Iran, and the Shiite Islamic resistance movements. Like the Israelis, the Americans believed they could achieve their objectives in Lebanon through use of overwhelming force. They were soon to discover how the deployment of their military to Lebanon left the superpower exposed and vulnerable to its many regional enemies.

More than any other event in the years of conflict, the Israeli invasion brought the Islamic movement to Lebanon. Islamist parties had faced isolation and condemnation for their actions against their own governments and societies in Egypt and Syria. However, the Lebanon conflict provided external enemies for the Islamist movement to fight. Any party that inflicted pain and humiliation on the United States and Israel would gain mass support in Lebanon and the broader Arab world. These were perfect conditions for the emergence of a new Shiite Islamist movement that would develop into the scourge of Israel and the United States—a militia that called itself the Party of God, or Hizbullah.

Hizbullah emerged from the training camps set up by the Iranian revolutionary guards in the largely Shiite town of Baalbek in the central Bekaa Valley in the early 1980s. Hundreds of young Lebanese Shiites flocked to Baalbek for religious and political education and advanced military training. They came to share the ideology of the Islamic Revolution and grew to hate Iran's enemies as their own.

Ironically, Hizbullah owes its creation as much to Israel as to Iran. The Shiites of South Lebanon had not felt particularly hostile toward Israel in June 1982. PLO operations against Israel since 1969 had brought untold suffering to the inhabitants of the south, and by 1982 the Shiites of South Lebanon were glad to see the backs of the PLO fighters and initially received the invading Israeli forces as liberators. "As a reaction to the hostility towards Palestinians that had engulfed some inhabitants of South Lebanon," Hizbullah deputy secretary general Naim Qassem recalled, "the [Israeli] invaders were welcomed with trilling cries of joy and the spraying of rice."[28]

Shiite opposition to Israel intensified, however, in response to the siege of Beirut, the enormity of the casualty toll, and the arrogance of Israeli occupation troops in South Lebanon. Iranian propaganda exacerbated this emerging hostility, nurturing rage against Israel and the United States, and their common project in Lebanon, the May 17 Agreement.

From its very inception, Hizbullah was an organization distinguished by the courage of its convictions. Its members were united in their unswerving faith in the message of Islam and their willingness to make any sacrifice to achieve God's will on earth. Their role model was Imam Husayn, the grandson of the Prophet Muhammad, whose death in the southern Iraqi town of Karbala fighting the ruling Umayyad dynasty in A.D. 680 still stands for Shiite Muslims as the ultimate example of martyrdom against tyranny. The example of Imam Husayn gave rise to a culture of martyrdom within Hizbullah that it turned into a lethal weapon against its enemies. Hizbullah's prolific use of suicide bombers has led many analysts to try to link Islamic Jihad, the shadowy organization that claimed responsibility for the suicide bombing of the American and French barracks, to the embryonic Hizbullah movement that took shape between 1982 and 1985—though Hizbullah itself has always denied any involvement in those attacks.

The struggle against Israel and the United States was but the means to a greater end. Ultimately, Hizbullah's goal was to create an Islamic state in Lebanon. However, the party has always maintained its unwillingness to impose such a government against the will of the diverse population of Lebanon. "We do not want Islam to rule in Lebanon by force, as the political Maronism is ruling at present," Hizbullah leaders asserted in the February 1985 Open Letter declaring the establishment of the party. "But we stress that we are convinced of Islam as a faith, system, thought, and rule and we urge all to recognize it and to resort to its law."[29] Like the Muslim Brotherhood in Egypt and Syria, Hizbullah hoped to replace man's law with God's law. The leaders of Hizbullah were convinced that the vast majority of the people of Lebanon—even the country's large Christian communities—would willingly opt for the greater justice of God's law once the Islamic system of government had proven its superiority to secular nationalism. The Hizbullah leadership believed that nothing could better demonstrate the superiority of Islamic government than a victory over Israel and the United States. Young Shiite men were willing to sacrifice their lives, like their role model the Imam Husayn, to achieve this goal.

The first Shiite suicide bombing in Lebanon was organized by the Islamic Resistance, a progenitor of Hizbullah, in November 1982. A young man named Ahmad Qasir conducted the first "martyrdom operation" when he drove a car laden with explosives into the Israeli army headquarters in the southern Lebanese city of Tyre, killing seventy-five Israelis and wounding many others. Journalist Robert Fisk went to Tyre to investigate the bombing. He was shocked by the number of Israeli casualties pulled from the wreckage of the eight-story building, but it was the method of the bombing that he found hardest to accept. "A *suicide* bomber? The idea seemed inconceivable."[30] A number of attacks following the bombing of the Israeli head-quarters confirmed suicide bombing as a dangerous new weapon in the arsenal of the enemies of America and Israel: the U.S. Embassy bombing in April 1983, the attacks on the American and French barracks in October 1983, and a second attack on Israeli headquarters in Tyre in November 1983, killing sixty more Israelis.

Israeli intelligence was quick to identify the threat posed by the Islamic Resistance and struck back with targeted assassinations against Shiite clerics. Far from subduing the Shiite resistance, the assassinations only served to escalate the violence. "By 1984," one analyst noted, "the pace of [Shiite] attacks was so intense that an Israeli soldier was dying every third day" in Lebanon.[31] In the course of that year, the Shiite militias also diversified their tactics and began to kidnap Westerners in a bid to drive the foreigners out of Lebanon. By the time Hizbullah emerged on the scene in 1985, their enemies were already on the retreat.

The first defeat the Shiite insurgency dealt Israel was the destruction of the May 17 Agreement. The besieged government of Amin Gemayel had been unable to im-plement any part of the agreement and, within a year of its signing, the Lebanese Council of Ministers abrogated the treaty with Israel. The Islamic Resistance's next victory was to drive the U.S. and European armies out of Lebanon. As American ca-sualties in Lebanon mounted, President Reagan came under growing pressure to with-draw his troops. Italian and American troops evacuated Lebanon in February 1984, and the last French soldiers pulled out at the end of March. The Israelis also found their position in Lebanon increasingly untenable, and in January 1985 Prime Minister Yitzhak Shamir's cabinet agreed to withdraw from the urban centers in South Lebanon to what they termed the South Lebanon Security Zone, a strip of land along the Israel-Lebanon border that ranged from 5–25 kilometers (3–15 miles) in depth.

The Security Zone was to prove the most enduring legacy of the 1982 Israeli in-vasion of Lebanon. The idea behind the South Lebanon Security Zone was to create a buffer to protect northern Israel from attack. Instead, it created a shooting gallery for Hizbullah and other Lebanese militias to carry on the fight against the Israeli occupier. For the next fifteen years, Hizbullah gained support from Lebanese of all religions, if not for an Islamic state, then at least as the national resistance movement against a much-hated occupation.

For Israel, the 1982 invasion ultimately replaced one enemy—the PLO—with a yet more determined adversary. Unlike the Palestinian fighters in Lebanon, Hizbul-lah and the Shiites of South Lebanon were fighting for their own land.

In Cold War terms, the Lebanon conflict had proved a major defeat for the United States in its rivalry with the Soviet Union. However, the Soviets were in no position to celebrate. Their 1979 invasion of Afghanistan had provoked a sustained insurgency, attracting a growing number of devout Muslims to join the ranks of the

Afghan mujahidin fighting to expel the "atheist Communists." If Lebanon was the Shiite school for jihad, Afghanistan became the training ground for a new generation of Sunni Muslim militants.

———————

In 1983, a twenty-four-year-old Algerian named Abdullah Anas took the bus from his native village of Ben Badis to the market town of Sidi Bel Abbès, where there was a newsstand, so that he could catch up on world events.[32] Anas had been one of the founders of the Islamist movement in western Algeria, and he continued to follow political developments in the Islamic world with great interest.

On that day, Anas remembered buying a copy of a Kuwaiti magazine that had captured his attention with a fatwa (legal opinion by Islamic scholars) signed by a number of religious scholars. It declared that support for the jihad in Afghanistan was a personal duty for all Muslims. Anas went to a nearby coffee house and settled down to read the fatwa in detail. He was impressed by the long list of famous clerics who had signed the declaration, including leading muftis from the Arab Gulf states and Egypt. One name in particular stood out: Shaykh Abdullah 'Azzam, whose publications and tape-recorded sermons circulated widely in Islamist circles.

Born to a conservative religious family in a village near the Palestinian town of Jenin in 1941, Abdullah 'Azzam had joined the Muslim Brotherhood as a teenager in the mid-1950s.[33] After completing his high school studies, he went on to study Islamic law at the University of Damascus. Following the June 1967 War, 'Azzam spent a year and a half fighting against the Israeli occupation in the West Bank in what he called his "Palestinian jihad." He then moved to Cairo, where he took his masters and doctorate from al-Azhar University. While in Egypt, 'Azzam came to know Muhammad and Amina Qutb, the brother and sister of the late Sayyid Qutb, who had been executed by Nasser's government in 1966. 'Azzam was profoundly influenced by the writings of Qutb.

With his academic credentials, 'Azzam joined the faculty of Islamic studies at the University of Jordan in Amman, where he taught for seven years before his inflammatory publications and sermons landed him in trouble with the Jordanian authorities. He left Jordan for Saudi Arabia in 1980, taking a post at the King Abdulaziz University in Jeddah.

Just before 'Azzam moved to Jeddah, the Soviets invaded Afghanistan. The Communist government in Afghanistan and its Soviet ally had proven their hostility to Islam, and the Afghans were fighting "in the path of God." 'Azzam gave their cause his full support, confident that victory in Afghanistan would revive the spirit of jihad in Islam.

As his later writings attest, 'Azzam saw victory in Afghanistan as a way to mobilize Muslims to action in other conflict zones. A native of Palestine, he saw Afghanistan as the training ground for future action against Israel. "Do not think we forget Palestine," he wrote:

> Liberating Palestine is an integral part of our religion. It is in our blood. We never forget Palestine. But I am certain that working in Afghanistan constitutes a revival of the spirit of jihad and a renewal of allegiance to God, no matter how great the sacrifices are. We have been deprived from waging jihad in Palestine because of the borders, restraints and prisons. But this doesn't mean that we abandon jihad. It does not mean either that we have forgotten our country. We must prepare for jihad in any spot of the earth we can.[34]

'Azzam's message of jihad and sacrifice gained wide circulation both through his writings and recordings of his fiery sermons. He awakened the spirit of jihad in Muslim men across the world, reaching even remote market towns like Sidi Bel Abbès in Algeria.

The more Anas read the text of the fatwa 'Azzam had signed, and weighed its arguments, the more he was convinced that Afghanistan's fight against Soviet occupation was the responsibility of all Muslims. "If a stretch of Muslim territory is attacked, jihad is an individual duty for those who inhabit that territory and those who are neighbours," the fatwa asserted. "If there are too few of them, or if they are incapable or reticent, then this duty is incumbent upon those who are nearby, and so on until it spreads throughout the world."[35] Given the gravity of the situation in Afghanistan, Anas felt that the duty of jihad had reached him in rural Algeria. This was all the more remarkable for, as Anas confessed, he didn't know a thing about Afghanistan at the time—he couldn't even place it on the map.

As Anas would soon learn, Afghanistan is a country of rich cultural diversity and a tragic modern history. Its population is composed of seven main ethnic groups, the largest of which are the Pashtun (roughly 40 percent of the population) and the Tajiks (30 percent), with a Sunni Muslim majority, a large Shiite minority, and two official languages (Persian and Pashto). The country's diversity reflects its geographic location, situated between Iran in the west, Pakistan to the south and east, and China and the (then Soviet) Central Asian republics of Turkmenistan, Uzbekistan, and Tajikistan to the north. Diversity and geography have not afforded much stability to land-locked Afghanistan, and since 1973 the country has been wracked with political turmoil and wars.

The origins of the Soviet-Afghan war date to the 1973 military coup that toppled the monarchy of King Zahir Shah and brought a left-leaning government to power. The republican regime of President Mohammed Daoud Khan was in turn toppled

by a violent Communist coup in April 1978. The Communists declared the establishment of the Democratic Republic of Afghanistan, a single-party state allied to
the Soviet Union, bent on rapid social and economic reforms. The new Afghan government was openly hostile to Islam and promoted state atheism, provoking widespread opposition within the largely religious Afghan population.

With Soviet backing, the Communist regime instigated a reign of terror against
all opponents, arresting and executing thousands of political prisoners. However,
the ruling Communists were themselves split by factionalism and succumbed to in-
fighting. After a spate of assassinations, the Soviet Union intervened in Afghanistan
on Christmas Eve 1979, sending an invasion force of 25,000 men to secure the capital city of Kabul and to install its Afghan ally Babrak Karmal as president.

The Soviet invasion of Afghanistan provoked international condemnation, but no
country was in a position to intervene directly to force a Soviet withdrawal. It fell to
the Afghan resistance movements to repel the Red Army, and the Islamist parties led
the fight. They received extensive covert assistance from the United States, which saw
the conflict strictly in Cold War terms, in which the anticommunism of the Islamist
fighters made them natural allies against the Soviets. The United States provided the
Afghan resistance with military supplies and sophisticated hand-fired antiaircraft missiles through Pakistan. During the Carter administration, the United States gave some
$200 million in aid to the Afghan resistance. Ronald Reagan stepped up American
support, providing $250 million in assistance in 1985 alone.[36]

The government of Pakistan served as an intermediary between the Americans
and the Afghan resistance and aided with intelligence and training facilities for the
Afghan mujahidin (literally, "holy warriors," Islamic guerrillas). The Islamic world
provided significant financial assistance and, starting in 1983, began to recruit volunteers to fight in the Afghan jihad.

Abdullah 'Azzam led the call to recruit Arab volunteers to fight in Afghanistan,
and Abdullah Anas was one of the first to respond. The two men met by chance
while on pilgrimage in Mecca in 1983. Among the millions who gathered for the
rituals of the pilgrimage, Anas recognized the distinctive face of Abdullah 'Azzam,
with his long beard and broad face, and went up to introduce himself.

"I read the fatwa that you and a group of clerics published on the duty of jihad
in Afghanistan, and I am convinced by it, but I don't know how to get to Afghanistan," Anas said.

"It is very simple," 'Azzam replied. "This is my telephone number in Islamabad.
I will return to Pakistan at the end of the Hajj. If you get there, call me and I will
take you to our Afghan colleagues in Peshawar."[37]

Within two weeks, Anas was on a plane to Islamabad. Never having been outside
the Arab world, the young Algerian was disoriented in Pakistan. He went straight to
a public telephone and was relieved when 'Azzam answered and invited him over for

dinner. "He received me with a human warmth that touched me," Anas recalled. Welcoming Anas into his home, 'Azzam introduced him to his other dinner guests. "His house was full of the students he taught in the International Islamic University in Islamabad. He asked me to stay with him until he went to Peshawar because I would not be able to meet with the Afghan colleagues if I went to Peshawar on my own."

Anas spent three days as a guest in 'Azzam's home. It was the beginning of a profound friendship and political partnership, sealed when Anas later married 'Azzam's daughter. While at 'Azzam's home, Anas got to meet the first of the Arab men to respond to 'Azzam's call to volunteer for the Afghan jihad. There were no more than a dozen Arab volunteers in the Afghan jihad when Anas arrived in 1983. Before their departure for Peshawar, 'Azzam introduced Anas to another Arab volunteer.

"I present you Brother Osama bin Ladin," 'Azzam said by way of introduction. "He is one of the Saudi youths who love the Afghan jihad."

"He struck me as very shy, a man of few words," Anas recollected. "Shaykh Abdullah explained that Osama visited him from time to time in Islamabad." Anas did not get to know bin Ladin well, as they served in different parts of Afghanistan. But he never forgot that first encounter.[38]

While still in Pakistan, Anas was sent with two other Arab volunteers to a training camp. Having done his national service in Algeria, he was already proficient with a Kalashnikov submachine gun. After two months, the volunteers were given their first opportunity to enter Afghanistan.

Before they set off from their camp in Pakistan to join the Afghan mujahidin, 'Azzam explained to his Arab protégés that the Afghan resistance was divided into seven factions. The largest were the Pashtun-dominated Hezb-e Islami (the Islamic Party) of Gulbuddin Hekmatyar, and the Jamiat-e Islami (the Islamic Society) headed by the Tajik Burhanuddin Rabbani. 'Azzam warned the Arab volunteers to avoid taking sides in Afghan factionalism and to see themselves as "guests of the entire Afghan people."

Yet as the Arabs volunteered for service in the different Afghan provinces, they came under the command of specific parties and inevitably gave their loyalty to the men with whom they served. Anas volunteered to serve in the northern province of Mazar-e Sharif, under the command of Rabbani's men of the Jamiat-e Islami. The handful of Arab volunteers set off with their Afghan commanders in the depth of winter, crossing territory under Soviet control, in a caravan of 300 armed men, all on foot. The perilous journey took forty days.

Once he reached Mazar-e Sharif, Anas was discouraged by his first experiences of the Afghan jihad. The local commander in Mazar had just died in a suicide operation against the Soviets, and three of his subordinates were vying with one another to control the resistance forces in the strategic town. Anas recognized he was out of his depth. "We were young men with no information, training or money," Anas wrote of himself and the two other Arabs who were with him on the journey. "I realized that participation in the jihad required a much higher standard [of preparation] than we had reached."

Within a month of his arrival in Mazar, Anas decided to leave the "explosive situation" and return to Peshawar as soon as possible. His first impression of Afghanistan was that its problems were too big to be solved by a handful of well-intentioned volunteers. "Inevitably the Islamic world would have to be called upon to assume its responsibility. The Afghan problem is bigger than five Arab men, or twenty-five Arabs or fifty Arabs." He believed it was essential to brief Abdullah 'Azzam of the political situation inside Afghanistan "so that he could present the situation to the Arab and Islamic worlds, and request more assistance for the Afghan problem."[39]

The frontier town of Peshawar had undergone significant changes over the months Anas had spent in Afghanistan. There were now many more Arab volunteers, their numbers swelling from a dozen, when Anas first arrived, to seventy or eighty by the beginning of 1985. Abdullah 'Azzam had created a reception facility for the growing number of Arabs who were responding to his call. "While you were away," 'Azzam explained to Anas, "Osama bin Ladin and I established the Services Office [Maktab al-khadamat] with a group of brothers. We established the Office to organize Arab participation in the Afghan Jihad."[40] 'Azzam saw the Services Office as an independent center where Arab volunteers could meet and train without the risk of getting caught up in the political divisions of the Afghans. The Services Office had three objectives: to provide aid, to assist in reform, and to promote Islam. The office began to open schools and institutes inside Afghanistan, as well as among the swelling Afghan refugee camps in Pakistan. It provided aid to orphans and widows of the conflict. At the same time, it engaged in active propaganda to attract new recruits to the Afghan jihad.

As part of its propaganda effort, the Services Office published a popular magazine, distributed across the Arab world, called *al-Jihad*. The pages of *al-Jihad* were replete with stories of heroism and sacrifice intended to inspire Muslims young and old. Leading Islamist thinkers contributed articles. Zaynab al-Ghazali, who had been imprisoned by Nasser for her Islamist activities in the 1960s, gave an interview to *al-Jihad* while on a visit to Pakistan. Now in her seventies, al-Ghazali had lost none of her zeal for the Islamist cause. "The time I spent in prison is not equal to one moment in the field of jihad in Afghanistan," she told her interviewer. "I wish I could live with the women fighters in Afghanistan, and I ask God to give victory to the mujahidin and to forgive us [i.e., the international community of Islam] our shortcomings in bringing justice to Afghanistan."[41] Al-Ghazali idealized the Afghan jihad as "a return to the age of the companions of the Prophet, peace be upon him, a return to the era of the rightly guided Caliphs."

The magazine *al-Jihad* reinforced this heroic narrative of the Afghan war against the Soviets, publishing accounts of miracles reminiscent of the Prophet Muhammad's times. Among them were articles describing a group of mujahidin that killed 700 Soviets, losing only seven of their own men to martyrdom; a young man who single-handedly shot down five Soviet aircraft; even flocks of heavenly birds that created an avian curtain shielding mujahidin from the enemy. The magazine sought to convince readers of divine intervention, in which God rewarded faith with victory against impossible odds.

Abdullah Anas was a pragmatist, however, and he'd been on the ground in Afghanistan. There were no miracles in his own dry-eyed account of the war. He returned to Mazar-e Sharif in 1985, where he served under the commander of Jamiat-e Islami forces in the northern Panjshir Valley region, Ahmad Shah Massoud. Massoud was a born leader, a charismatic guerrilla commander in the mold of Che Guevara. He regularly withdrew with his forces to the forbidding terrain of the Hindu Kush, creating bases in the deep mountain caves where he could withstand weeks of punishing bombardment, only to emerge from the rubble to inflict heavy casualties on Soviet forces. Yet his men suffered too. On one occasion, Massoud was retreating through a narrow valley with one of his units when they were surprised by Soviet rocket fire. "In less than five minutes, more than ten of our men fell as martyrs," Anas recalled. "It was an unimaginable sight."[42] Anas described another battle, in which Massoud led 300 of his men (including fifteen Arab volunteers) to victory over the Soviets. The engagement lasted a full day and night, and Massoud suffered eighteen dead (including four Arabs) and many more wounded.[43]

The Afghan mujahidin and their Arab supporters fought a desperate and ultimately successful battle against superior forces. A decade of occupation had proven very costly to the Soviet Union in men and materiel. At least 15,000 Red Army soldiers died in Afghanistan, and 50,000 were wounded in action. The Afghan resistance managed to shoot down over 100 aircraft and 300 helicopters with antiaircraft missiles provided by the United States. By the end of 1988, the Soviets came to recognize that they could not impose their will on Afghanistan with an invasion army of 100,000 men. The Kremlin decided to cut its losses and withdraw. On February 15, 1989, the last Soviet units withdrew from Afghanistan. Yet this great victory of Muslim arms over a nuclear superpower was ultimately a disappointment for the men who volunteered to fight in Afghanistan.

The Afghan resistance's victory over the Soviets did not lead to the ultimate Islamist objective—the creation of an Islamic state. Once the Soviet enemy was outside their frontiers, the Afghan factions turned against each other in a power struggle that quickly degenerated into civil war. Despite Abdullah 'Azzam's best efforts, many

Arab volunteers divided along Afghan factional lines, taking sides with the party they knew. Others chose to leave Afghanistan. The violent turf battles between rival warlords did not constitute jihad, and they had no wish to fight fellow Muslims.

The Arab volunteers did not make much of an impact in the Afghan war against the Soviet Union. In retrospect, Abdullah Anas declared that the Arab contribution to the Afghan war amounted to no more than "a drop in the ocean." The group of volunteers who came to be known as the "Afghan Arabs" probably never exceeded a maximum of two thousand men, and of those, "only a very small proportion entered Afghanistan and took part in the fighting with the mujahidin," Anas claimed. The remainder stayed in Peshawar and volunteered their services "as doctors and drivers, cooks and accountants and engineers."[44]

Yet the Afghan jihad had an enduring influence over the Arab world. Many of those who answered the call to jihad returned to their native lands intent on realizing the ideal Islamic order that had eluded them in Afghanistan. Anas estimated some 300 Algerian volunteers served in Afghanistan; many of them would return home to play an active part in a new Islamist political party, the Islamic Salvation Front (more commonly known by the French acronym, the FIS). Others gathered around Osama bin Ladin, who established a rival institution to Abdullah 'Azzam's Services Office. Bin Ladin called his new organization "the Base," but it has come to be better known by its Arabic name, al-Qaida. Some of the Arabs who served with Anas in the Panjshir Valley chose to remain in Pakistan and became founding members of al-Qaida.

The man who inspired the Arab Afghans was himself laid to rest in Pakistan. Abdullah 'Azzam was killed on November 24, 1989, with two of his sons when a car bomb detonated as they approached a mosque in Peshawar for Friday prayers. There have been many theories, none conclusive, about who might have ordered the killing of Abdullah 'Azzam: rival Afghan factions; the circle of Osama bin Ladin; even the Israelis, who saw 'Azzam as the spiritual leader of a new Palestinian Islamist movement called Hamas.

By December 1987, the people of Gaza had spent twenty years under Israeli occupation. The Gaza Strip is a narrow finger of coastland 25 miles long and 6 miles wide, then populated by about 625,000 Palestinians. The residents of Gaza, three-quarters of whom were refugees from those parts of Palestine conquered by the new state of Israel in 1948, had suffered great isolation between 1948 and 1967. Gazans were confined to their enclave by the Egyptian authorities and cut off from their lost homeland by the hostile frontier with Israel.

With the Israeli occupation of 1967 came new opportunities for Gazans to cross into the rest of historic Palestine and meet the other Palestinians who had remained on the land—in the towns and cities of Israel and the occupied West Bank. Gaza also enjoyed something of an economic boom after 1967. Under the occupation, Gazans were able to secure jobs in Israel and moved back and forth across the border with relative ease. Israelis shopped in Gaza to take advantage of tax-free prices. In many ways, life for the residents of Gaza had improved under Israeli rule.

Yet no people is happy under occupation, and the Palestinians aspired to independence in their own land. But their hopes for deliverance by the other Arab states were dashed when Egypt concluded a peace treaty with Israel in 1979, and their hopes for liberation at the hands of the PLO collapsed after the 1982 Israeli invasion of Lebanon dispersed Palestinian fighting units across the Arab world.

Increasingly, over the course of the late 1970s and early 1980s, Palestinians within Gaza and the West Bank began to confront the occupation themselves. The Israeli government recorded an escalation of "illegal acts" in the West Bank alone, rising from 656 "disturbances" in 1977 to 1,556 in 1981 and 2,663 in 1984.[45]

Resistance within the occupied territory provoked heavy Israeli reprisals: mass arrests, intimidation, torture, humiliation. A proud people, the Palestinians found the humiliation hardest to bear. The loss of dignity and self-respect was compounded by the knowledge that their occupier saw them, in the words of the Islamist intellectual Azzam Tamimi, as "sub-human and not worthy of respect."[46]

Worse yet, Palestinians felt complicit in their own subjugation through their cooperation with the Israeli occupation. The fact that Palestinians in Gaza and the West Bank were taking jobs in Israel and attracting Israeli customers to their shops implicated them in the occupation. Given that the Israelis were engaged in land confiscation and settlement building on occupied Palestinian land, cooperation with the Israelis felt more like collaboration. As the Palestinian scholar and activist Sari Nusseibeh explained, "The contradiction of using Israeli paint to scribble our anti-occupation graffiti was becoming so insufferable as to make an explosion inevitable."[47]

The explosion finally came in December 1987, sparked by a traffic accident near the Erez checkpoint in northern Gaza. On December 8 an Israeli army truck drove into two minivans carrying Palestinian workers home from Israel, killing four and wounding seven. Rumors spread throughout the Palestinian community that the killing was deliberate, raising tension in the territories. The funerals were held the next day and were followed by major demonstrations, which Israel troops dispersed with live fire, killing demonstrators.

The killings on December 9 sparked riots that spread like wildfire across Gaza and into the West Bank, rapidly transforming into a popular uprising against twenty years of Israeli occupation. The Palestinians called their movement the "Intifada," an Arabic word that means both an uprising and a dusting off, as though the Palestinians were shaking off the decades of accumulated humiliation through direct confrontation with the occupation.

The Intifada began as an uncoordinated series of confrontations with the Israeli authorities. The demonstrators ruled out the use of weapons and declared their movement nonviolent, stone-throwing notwithstanding. The Israeli authorities responded with rubber bullets and tear gas. Israeli forces killed twenty-two demonstrators before the end of December 1987. Instead of quelling the violence, Israeli repression only served to accelerate the cycle of ad hoc protests and confrontations.

In the opening weeks of the Intifada, there was no central leadership. Instead, the movement developed through a series of spontaneous demonstrations across the Gaza Strip and the West Bank. As Sari Nusseibeh recalled, it was a grass-roots movement in which "every demonstrator did what he thought best, and the more established leaders raced to catch up with him."[48]

Two underground organizations emerged to give direction to the Intifada. In the West Bank, the local branches of the PLO factions, including Yasser Arafat's Fatah movement, the Popular and the Democratic Fronts for the Liberation of Palestine, and the Communists, combined to create an underground leadership that called itself the United National Command (UNC). In Gaza, Islamists associated with the Muslim Brotherhood created the Islamic Resistance Movement, better known by its Arabic acronym, Hamas. The strength of Israeli repression made it impossible for these underground leaderships to meet or exercise their authority in open. Instead, they each published periodic leaflets—one series of leaflets by Hamas, and a totally independent series of communiqués by the UNC—to set out their objectives and to guide public action. The leaflets of the United National Command and Hamas were calls to action and news sheets. They also captured the increasingly bitter struggle between the secular nationalist forces of the PLO and the rising Islamist movement for control of the Palestinian national movement within the Occupied Territories.

The Muslim Brotherhood was the best-organized political movement in the Gaza Strip and was the first to respond to the popular uprising. Its leader was a paraplegic activist in his mid-fifties named Shaykh Ahmad Yassin. Like so many of its residents, Yassin had come to Gaza as a refugee in 1948. Paralyzed in a work accident as a teenager, he had continued his education to become a school teacher and religious leader. He joined the Muslim Brotherhood in the 1960s, becoming a great admirer of Sayyid Qutb, whose works he reprinted and circulated to reach the widest possible readership in Gaza. In the mid-1970s he established a charitable organization named the Islamic Center, through which he funded new mosques, schools, and clinics across Gaza that provided a network for the spread of Islamist values.

On December 9, 1987, the night the troubles broke out, Yassin convened a meeting of the leaders of the Brotherhood to coordinate action. They decided to transform the Muslim Brotherhood in Gaza into a resistance movement, and Hamas was launched with their first leaflet on December 14.

The novelty of Hamas was to articulate Palestinian aspirations in strictly Islamist terms. From its first communiqué, Hamas set out an intransigent message that combined confrontation with the Jewish state and a rejection of secular Arab nationalism. "Only Islam can break the Jews and destroy their dream," Hamas insisted. Following the arguments of Abdullah 'Azzam, who made the case for jihad in both Afghanistan and Palestine, the Palestinian Islamists declared their resistance against the foreign occupier on Islamic land rather than against authoritarian Arab leaders, as Sayyid Qutb advocated. "When an enemy occupies some of the Muslim lands," Hamas asserted in its 1988 charter, "Jihad becomes obligatory for every Muslim. In the struggle against the Jewish occupation of Palestine, the banner of Jihad must be raised."[49]

Though they were secular nationalists as had dominated Palestinian politics since the 1960s, there was something new about the Unified National Command as well. For the first time, local activists in the West Bank were putting forward their own views without consulting Arafat and the leadership in exile. In the West Bank, the UNC issued its first communiqué shortly after the Hamas leaflet was released. Sari Nusseibeh recalled that the first UNC leaflet was authored by "two local PLO activists" who "were already in jail by the time their flyers hit the streets," arrested by the Israeli authorities in a massive clampdown. The leaflet called for a three-day general strike—a total economic close-down of the Occupied Territories—and warned against attempts to break the strike or cooperate with the Israelis.

The UNC continued to issue newsletters every couple of weeks (it issued thirty-one in the first year of the Intifada alone) in which the group began to articulate a series of demands: an end to land expropriation and to the creation of Israeli settlements on occupied land, the release of Palestinians from Israeli prisons, and the withdrawal of the Israeli army from Palestinian towns and villages. The leaflets encouraged people to fly the Palestinian flag, which the Israelis had long forbidden, and to chant "Down with the occupation!" and "Long live free Arab Palestine!" The UNC's ultimate objective was an independent Palestinian state with its capital in East Jerusalem.[50] The Intifada was quickly turning into an independence movement.

The outbreak of the Intifada caught the PLO leadership in Tunis completely by surprise. Recognized by all Palestinians as their "sole legitimate representative," the PLO had long monopolized the Palestinian national movement. Now the initiative had passed from the "outside" leadership in Tunis to "inside" PLO activists working in the Occupied Palestinian Territories. The distinction between "insiders" and "outsiders" put the PLO leadership at a distinct disadvantage. Suddenly, Arafat and his lieutenants looked redundant as the residents of Gaza and the West Bank launched their own bid for an independent Palestinian state.

In January 1988 Arafat moved to bring the Intifada under the PLO's authority. He dispatched one of Fatah's highest-ranking commanders, Khalil al-Wazir (better known by his nom de guerre Abu Jihad), to coordinate action between Tunis and the West Bank. The UNC's third leaflet of January 18, 1988, was the first to be authorized by the Fatah leadership in Tunis. Within a matter of hours, over 100,000 copies of the leaflet were distributed across Gaza and the West Bank. The residents of the Occupied Territories responded to the authoritative voice of Arafat's political machine with alacrity. As Sari Nusseibeh observed, "it was like watching musicians take cues from a conductor."[51] Henceforth the Intifada would be managed by Arafat and his officials.

The Israeli government was determined to prevent the PLO from taking advantage of the Intifada to make political gains at Israel's expense. Abu Jihad's mission was cut short by Israeli assassins, who gunned down the PLO official at his home in Tunisia on April 16, 1988. Yet once the link between the UNC and PLO had been forged, Tunis was able to preserve its control over the secular forces of the Intifada.

The cycle of strikes and demonstrations, called in response to leaflets issued by the UNC and Hamas, continued unabated. The Israeli authorities had expected the movement to run out of steam. Instead, it seemed to be gaining in strength and posed a genuine challenge to Israeli control in the Occupied Territories. As the Intifada entered its third month, the Israeli authorities turned to extra-legal means to quell the uprising. Drawing on the Emergency Regulations drafted by British mandate officials long before the Geneva Conventions established international legal standards for the treatment of civilians under occupation, the Israeli army resorted to collective punishments such as mass arrests, detention without charge, and house demolitions.

International public opinion was appalled by the image of heavily armed soldiers responding to stone-throwing demonstrators with live fire, prompting Yitzhak Rabin, then Israel's defense minister, to order the use of "might, force and beatings" instead of lethal fire. The brutality of this seemingly benign policy was exposed when the CBS television network in the United States broadcast images of Israeli soldiers meting out horrific beatings to Palestinian youths near Nablus in February 1988. In one particularly graphic segment, a soldier was seen to extend a prisoner's arm and pound it repeatedly from above with a large rock to break the bone.[52] Israel's attorney general admonished Rabin to warn his soldiers of the illegality of such acts, but the Israeli army continued to subject Palestinian demonstrators to violent beatings. Over thirty Palestinians were beaten to death in the first year of the Intifada.[53]

Against this background of Israeli violence, it is remarkable that the Palestinians preserved the tactics of nonviolent resistance. Palestinian claims to nonviolence were challenged by Israeli authorities, who noted that protestors threw iron bars and Molotov cocktails as well as stones—missiles capable of inflicting serious injury or death. Yet the Palestinians never resorted to firearms in their confrontations with the Israelis, which did much to reverse decades of Western public opinion that had portrayed the Palestinians as terrorists and Israel as a beleaguered David figure. Israel found itself in the unaccustomed position of dispelling a distinct Goliath image in the international press.

Nonviolence made the Intifada the most inclusive of Palestinian movements. Rather than privileging young men with military training, the demonstrations and civil disobedience of the Intifada mobilized the whole of the population of the Occupied Territories—men and women, young and old—in a common liberation struggle. The underground leaflets of Hamas and the UNC provided a wide range of resistance strategies—strikes, boycotts of Israeli products, home teaching to subvert school closures, garden plots to increase food self-reliance—that empowered Palestinians under occupation and instilled a deep sense of common purpose that kept the Intifada going in spite of heavy Israeli repression.

Tensions emerged between the secular United National Command and Hamas as the Intifada ran through the spring and into the summer of 1988. Both organizations claimed to represent the Palestinian resistance. In its leaflets, Hamas referred to itself as "your movement, the Islamic Resistance Movement, Hamas," and the UNC claimed leadership of the Palestinian masses, "this people that heeded the call of the PLO and of the United National Command of the Uprising."[54] The secular and Islamist rivals read each other's leaflets and vied for control over popular actions in the streets. When Hamas called for a national strike in its leaflet of August 18—a prerogative the PLO claimed for itself in the Occupied Territories—the UNC issued its first direct criticism of the Islamist organization, claiming "every blow to the unity of ranks is tantamount to doing the enemy a significant service and harms the uprising."

Such jostling for ascendancy masked the fundamental differences that divided Hamas from the PLO: whereas Hamas sought the destruction of the Jewish state, the PLO and the UNC wanted to establish a Palestinian state alongside Israel. Hamas viewed the whole of Palestine as inalienable Muslim land that needed to be liberated from non-Muslim rule through jihad. Its confrontation with Israel would be long-term, for its ultimate objective was the creation of an Islamic state in the whole of Palestine. The PLO, in comparison, had been moving toward a two-state solution since 1974. Yasser Arafat seized on the Intifada as a vehicle to achieve independent statehood for the Palestinians in the Gaza Strip and the West Bank, with its capital in East Jerusalem—even if this meant conferring recognition on Israel and conceding the 78 percent of Palestine lost in 1948 to the Jewish state. The positions of the two resistance movements could not be reconciled, and so the PLO proceeded down the path of the two-state solution without consideration for the views of the Islamic Resistance Movement.

Palestinian resistance and Israeli repression had placed the Intifada squarely on the front pages of the international press—and nowhere more so than in the Arab world. In June 1988, the Arab League convened an emergency summit in Algiers to address the Intifada. The PLO took the opportunity to present a position paper that called for mutual recognition of the right of the Palestinians and the Israelis to live in peace and security. Hamas rejected the PLO's position outright and reasserted its claim for Muslim rights to the whole of Palestine. Its leaders made their views known in Hamas's leaflet of August 18, in which the Islamic Resistance insisted that "the Muslims have had a full—not partial—right to Palestine for generations, in the past, present and future."

Undeterred by Islamist opposition, the PLO proceeded to use the Intifada to legitimize its call for a two-state solution to the Israeli-Palestinian conflict. In September 1988 the PLO announced plans to convene a meeting of the Palestine National Council (PNC), the Palestinian parliament in exile, to consolidate the gains of the Intifada and secure the Palestinian people's "national rights of return, self-determination, and the establishment of an independent state on our national soil under the leadership of the PLO."[55] Again Hamas rejected and condemned the PLO position. Its leaflet of October 5 read, in part: "We are against conceding so much as an inch of our land which is steeped in the blood of the Companions of the Prophet and their followers." Hamas insisted that "we shall continue the uprising on the road to the liberation of our whole land from the contamination of the Jews (with the help of God)." The lines of confrontation between the PLO and the Islamic Resistance could not have been clearer.

Arafat's agenda for the meeting of the PNC, which had been set for November 1988, was nothing less than a Palestinian declaration of statehood in the Occupied Territories. For many in Gaza and the West Bank, worn down by eleven months of the Intifada and violent Israeli reprisals, statehood held the promise of independence and an end to the occupation, which seemed sufficient gains for their sacrifices, and they looked forward to the November meeting of the PNC with growing anticipation.

Though Sari Nusseibeh had some reservations about the PLO's policies, he saw the impending declaration of independence as "an important milestone, and like everyone else, I looked forward to its unveiling." Nusseibeh, who had received an advance copy of Arafat's text, wanted the Palestinian declaration of independence to be a moment that people would remember, and he hoped to read the text to "tens of thousands of people" in the Haram al-Sharif, the mosque complex atop the Temple Mount in the Old City of Jerusalem. "I wanted a people under occupation, the people of the intifada, to congregate at the center of our universe, and to celebrate our independence."

It was not to be. On November 15, 1988, the day Arafat addressed the PNC, Israel imposed a draconian curfew over the territories and East Jerusalem, banning cars and civilians from the streets. Nusseibeh chose to disregard the curfew and made his way through the backstreets to the Al-Aqsa Mosque, where a handful of political activists had gathered, milling about with religious clerics. "Together, we all walked into Al-Aqsa mosque. At the appointed hour, as the bells from the [church of the]

Holy Sepulchre swung, and calls wailed out from the minarets, we all solemnly read our declaration of independence."[56]

The declaration, which Arafat read to the nineteenth session of the Palestine National Council in Algiers, represented a radical departure from past PLO policies. The declaration endorsed the UN partition plan of 1947 that provided for the creation of Arab and Jewish states in Palestine, and it approved UN Security Council Resolutions 242 and 338, drafted after the 1967 and 1973 Wars, that established the principle of the return of occupied land for peace. The declaration committed the PLO to peaceful coexistence with Israel.

The PLO had come a very long way since its London diplomat Said Hammami's first attempts to broach the two-state solution in 1974. No longer a guerrilla organization—Arafat now categorically renounced "all forms of terrorism, including individual, group and state terrorism"—the PLO presented itself to the international community as the provisional government of a state in waiting.

International recognition was quick to follow. Eighty-four countries extended full recognition to the new state of Palestine, including most Arab states, a number of European, African, and Asian countries, and such traditional supporters of the Palestinian liberation movement as China and the Soviet Union. Most West European states granted a diplomatic status to Palestine that fell short of full recognition, but the United States and Canada withheld recognition altogether. In mid-January 1989 the PLO scored another symbolic victory by gaining the right to address the UN Security Council on equal footing with member states.[57]

The PNC declaration did not meet with the Israeli government's approval. Prime Minister Yitzhak Shamir responded in a written statement on November 15 to denounce the declaration as "a deceptive propaganda exercise, intended to create an impression of moderation and of achievements for those carrying out violent acts in the territories of Judea and Samaria," and the Israeli cabinet dismissed it as "disinformation meant to mislead world public opinion."[58]

Hamas too was unimpressed by the statement. The Islamic resistance issued a communiqué in which it stressed "the right of the Palestinian people to establish an independent state on all the soil of Palestine," not just in the Occupied Territories: "Do not heed the U.N. resolutions which try to accord the Zionist entity legitimacy over any part of the soil of Palestine . . . for it is the property of the Islamic nation and not of the U.N."[59]

For all the excitement surrounding the PNC declaration of independence, the initiative brought no tangible benefits to the residents of Gaza and the West Bank. Israel showed no more willingness to relinquish the Occupied Territories after November 15, 1988, than it had before the PNC declaration. After a year of excitement and high expectations, nothing seemed to change. And yet the Palestinians had paid an enormous price for such small results. By the first anniversary of the Intifada, in December 1988, an estimated 626 Palestinians had been killed, 37,000 Palestinians had been injured, and over 35,000 Palestinians had been arrested in the course of the year—many of them still behind bars at the start of the second year of the uprising.[60]

By 1989 the early idealism of the Intifada had given way to cynicism, and the unity of purpose to factionalism. Hamas supporters broke out in open fights with Fatah members. Vigilantes within Palestinian society began to intimidate, beat, and even murder fellow Palestinians suspected of collaboration with the Israeli authorities. And still the communiqués were issued, the demonstrations held, the rocks thrown, and the casualties mounted as the Intifada continued toward no discernable end, the latest phase of a decades-old Arab-Israeli conflict for which the international community seemed to have no solution.

Over the course of the 1980s, a number of Islamic movements launched armed struggles to overthrow secular rulers or to repel foreign invaders. The Islamists hoped to establish an Islamic state ruled in accordance with sharia law, which they firmly believed to be God's law. They took their inspiration from the success of the Iranian Revolution of 1979 and the creation of the Islamic Republic of Iran. In Egypt a splinter movement managed to assassinate President Anwar Sadat. In Syria, the Muslim Brotherhood mounted a civil war against the Ba'thist government of Hafiz al-Asad. The Lebanese Shiite militant movement Hizbullah, heavily influenced by the Islamic Republic of Iran, viewed the United States and Israel as two sides of the same coin and sought to deal both a massive defeat in Lebanon. Jihad in Afghanistan was directed against both internal and external enemies, targeting the Soviet occupation forces and the Communist government in Afghanistan that was openly hostile to Islam. Islamists in Gaza and the West Bank called for a long-term jihad against the Jewish state to restore Palestine to the Islamic world under an Islamic government. The military successes enjoyed by Hizbullah in forcing a total U.S. withdrawal and an Israeli redeployment, and by the Afghan mujahidin by forcing the Soviets to evacuate their country in 1989, did not lead to the ideal Islamic states that their ideologues had hoped for. Both Lebanon and Afghanistan remained mired in civil wars long after their external enemies had been forced into retreat.

Islamists across the Arab world adopted a long-term approach to the ultimate goal of an Islamic state. The Egyptian Islamist Zaynab al-Ghazali spoke in terms of a thirteen-year cycle of preparation, to be repeated until a significant majority of the Egyptians supported an Islamic government. Hamas vowed to struggle for the liberation of all of Palestine "however long it takes." The ultimate triumph of the Islamic state was a protracted project and required patience.

If the Islamists had lost some battles in the "struggle in the path of God," they remained confident that they would ultimately prevail. In the meantime, Islamist groups chalked up a number of successes in reshaping Arab society. Islamist organizations emerged across the Arab world, attracting growing numbers of adherents in the 1980s and 1990s. Islamist values were spreading in Arab society, as more young men began to grow beards and women increasingly took to head scarves and modest body-covering fashions. Islamic publications dominated bookshops. Secular culture was driven into retreat before an Islamic resurgence that continues ever stronger down to the present day.

The Islamists took courage from major changes in world politics at the end of 1989. The certainties of the Cold War were crumbling as quickly as the Berlin Wall, which fell on November 9, marking the end of U.S.-Soviet rivalry and ushering in a new world order. Many Islamists interpreted the collapse of Soviet power as proof of the bankruptcy of atheist communism and a harbinger of a new Islamic age. Instead, they found themselves faced with a unipolar world dominated by the last surviving superpower, the United States of America.

CHAPTER 14

After the Cold War

After nearly a half-century of superpower rivalry, the Cold War came to an abrupt end in 1989. Soviet president Mikhail Gorbachev's policies of greater openness (glasnost) and internal reform (perestroika) wrought permanent change to the political culture of the Soviet Union during the mid-1980s. By the time the Berlin Wall was formally breached in November 1989, the Iron Curtain separating Eastern and Western Europe already lay in tatters. Starting with the defeat of the Communist Party in the Polish elections in June 1989, the governments of the Soviet bloc fell one by one: in Hungary, Czechoslovakia, Bulgaria. The once all-powerful dictator of East Germany, Erich Honecker, tendered his resignation that autumn, and Nicolae Ceausescu, who had ruled Romania with an iron fist for over twenty-two years, was summarily executed by revolutionaries on Christmas Day 1989.

The international system was transformed as the balance-of-power politics of the two superpowers gave way to a unipolar age of American dominance. Gorbachev and U.S. president George H. W. Bush captured the sense of hope engendered by the end of the Soviet-American antagonism, promising a "new world order." For the Arab world, one of the central theatres of the Cold War, the new era of American ascendancy held great uncertainties. Once again, Arab leaders were forced to come to terms with new rules in the international arena.

The conservative Arab monarchies were disconcerted by the specter of popular movements overturning long-standing governments, but they did not mourn the collapse of communism: Morocco, Jordan, Saudi Arabia, and the other Gulf states had placed their trust in the West, and, fortunately for them, the West had emerged victorious from the Cold War.

Not so the left-leaning Arab republics like Syria, Iraq, Libya, and Algeria, which had more in common with the Communist regimes of Eastern Europe: single-party states, they were all headed by long-term dictators with large armies and centrally planned economies. The video images of Ceausescu's corpse broadcast around the world provoked deep disquiet in some Arab capitals. If it could happen in Romania, what was to prevent similar events in Baghdad or Damascus?

Clearly, the Soviet Union could no longer be counted on to stand up for its Arab allies. For the past four decades, Arab republics had turned to the Soviet Union for military hardware, development assistance, and diplomatic support to counterbalance the forces of Western domination. Those days were finished. In autumn 1989 Syria's president, Hafiz al-Asad, pressed Gorbachev for more advanced weapons to help Syria achieve strategic parity with Israel. The Soviet president rebuffed him, saying: "Your problems are not going to be solved through any such strategic points—and anyway, we're no longer in that game." Al-Asad returned to Damascus devastated.

The factions of the PLO were also worried. George Habash, leader of the Popular Front for the Liberation of Palestine, criticized Gorbachev's policies on a visit to Moscow in October 1989. "If you go on like this you are going to hurt us all," he warned. Veteran analyst Mohamed Heikal witnessed the confusion among the Arab leadership. "Everyone sensed that a shift from one phase of international relations to another was taking place, but they still clung to the old familiar rules. On all sides there was a failure to anticipate the new ones correctly."[1]

The old Arab conflicts of the Cold War-era burst to the fore in the new unipolar age of American dominance. Iraq, weakened economically by its eight-year war with Iran (1980–1988), still had sufficient military resources to assert its bid for regional ascendance. The 1990 Iraqi invasion of Kuwait proved the first crisis of the post–Cold War world. The invasion of one Arab state by another polarized the entire Arab world, with some countries opposing foreign intervention and others participating in an American-led coalition to liberate Kuwait from Iraqi rule. The Kuwait crisis also divided citizens from their governments, as Iraqi president Saddam Hussein emerged as a popular hero across the Arab world for standing up to America and for his cynical promises to liberate Palestine from Israeli rule.

It was not enough to drive Iraq from Kuwait to restore order in the Arab region. Saddam Hussein had linked Iraq's occupation of Kuwait to Syria's position in Lebanon and Israel's longstanding occupation of Palestinian territory. In the aftermath of the war to liberate Kuwait, the Arab world was forced to address the Lebanese Civil War, then in its fifteenth year. The United States for its part convened in Madrid the first meeting of Arabs and Israelis to address their differences since the 1973 Geneva Peace Conference. It was unclear to contemporary observers if Iraq's invasion and subsequent expulsion from Kuwait was the harbinger of a new age of conflict resolution, or just an escalation in a long history of regional disputes.

One of the first Arab leaders to recognize the realities of the post–Cold War world was the president of Iraq, Saddam Hussein. As early as March 1990, Hussein had warned his fellow Arab leaders that "for the next five years there would be only one true superpower"—the United States.[2]

In many ways, Iraq was better positioned than the other Arab republics to make the transition from the old rivalries of the Cold War to the new realities of American predominance. Although Iraq had enjoyed particularly close relations with the Soviet Union, confirmed in their 1972 Treaty of Friendship and Cooperation, the eight-year Iran-Iraq War (1980–1988) had led to a thaw in U.S.-Iraqi relations. American hostility to the Islamic Republic of Iran drove the Reagan administration to support Iraq in order to prevent an outright Iranian victory. Even after the war ended in stalemate, Washington had continued its rapprochement with Baghdad.

The new American president, George H. W. Bush, had every intention of building better relations with Iraq when he came to office in January 1989. In October of that year the Bush administration issued a national security directive that set out U.S. policies toward the Persian Gulf that put a high premium on closer ties to Iraq. "Normal relations between the United States and Iraq would serve our longer-term interests and promote stability in both the Gulf and the Middle East," it read. "The United States should propose economic and political incentives for Iraq to moderate its behavior and to increase our influence with Iraq." The directive also encouraged an opening of the Iraqi market to American companies. "We should pursue, and seek to facilitate, opportunities for U.S. firms to participate in the reconstruction of the Iraqi economy." This extended to "non-lethal forms of military assistance" to enhance American influence over the Iraqi defense establishment.[3] Saddam Hussein could be forgiven for believing he had guided his country well through the turmoil of the end of the Cold War.

Yet Saddam Hussein still faced daunting challenges ruling his country—challenges stemming from disastrous decisions taken since he came to power in 1978. The Iraqi president's unprovoked and ultimately fruitless war with Iran had taken a terrible toll on the country—and his own support base among the Iraqi populace. Half a million Iraqi men died in the course of the eight-year conflict, provoking domestic opposition to Hussein's rule. As the war dragged on, the opposition to Saddam Hussein grew violent. In 1982 Hussein survived an assassination attempt in the village of Dujail to the north of Baghdad. The Iraqi president responded with overwhelming violence, ordering his security forces to kill nearly 150 villagers in retaliation.

In northern Iraq, Kurdish factions took advantage of the war with Iran to make a bid for autonomy. The Iraqi government responded with an extermination campaign dubbed *al-Anfal*, or "the spoils." Between 1986 and 1989, thousands of Iraqi Kurds were forcibly resettled, 2,000 villages were destroyed, and an estimated 100,000 men, women, and children were killed in Anfal operations. In one of the most notorious incidents, the Iraqi government used nerve gas against the village of Halabja in March 1988, killing 5,000 Kurdish civilians.[4]

Along with the Kurds, the Sunni and Shiite communities of Iraq also faced intense repression—arbitrary arrest, widespread torture, and summary executions—to stifle dissent. Only confirmed members of the ruling Ba'th Party were to enjoy confidence and advancement within Saddam Hussein's Iraq. Once celebrated for its secular values, high literacy rates, and gender equality, by 1989 Iraq had degenerated into a republic of fear.[5]

Besides a restive populace, the most immediate challenge facing Saddam Hussein at the end of the Iran-Iraq War was the reconstruction of his country's shattered economy. Iraq's wealth derived from its massive petroleum resources. For eight years, the country's vital lifeline of oil had been cut by attacks on pipelines and port facilities, and a ruthless tanker war that took the Iran-Iraq conflict to the Gulf's international shipping lanes. Deprived of oil revenues, Iraq had been forced to borrow billions of dollars from its Arab Gulf neighbors to sustain its war effort. By the war's end in 1988, Iraq owed some $40 billion to the other Gulf states, and debt repayment consumed over 50 percent of Iraq's oil income in 1990.[6]

Compounding Iraq's difficulties was the steady decline in the price of oil. To pay off his country's debts Saddam Hussein needed oil prices to remain in the range of $25 a barrel (at the height of the Iran-Iraq War, prices had reached as high as $35 a barrel). He watched in despair as the international price slumped to $14 by July 1990. The Gulf, at peace once again, was now able to export all the oil the world needed. To make matters worse, some Gulf states were producing well beyond their OPEC quotas. Kuwait was one of the worst offenders. Kuwait had its own reasons for breaking ranks with OPEC over production quotas. Earlier in the 1980s, the Kuwaiti government had diversified its economy by investing heavily in Western refineries and opening thousands of gasoline stations across Europe under the new brand name "Q-8," a homonym for "Kuwait." Kuwait's crude oil exports increasingly went to its own facilities in the West. The more crude oil the Kuwaitis sold to their Western refineries, the higher their profits in Europe.[7] These refining and marketing outlets generated higher profit margins than the export of crude and insulated Kuwait from variations in the price of crude oil. Kuwait was more interested in generating maximum output than seeking the highest price per barrel by hewing to OPEC's guidelines.

Iraq, in contrast, had no such external outlets, and its revenues were inextricably linked to the price of crude oil. Every drop of one dollar in the price of a barrel of oil represented a net loss of $1 billion to Iraq's annual revenues. In OPEC meetings, Iraq and Kuwait found themselves on the opposite side of the table, with Iraq pressing to reduce output and drive up the price of oil while Kuwait called for greater output. The Kuwaitis paid little attention to Iraqi concerns. In June 1989 Kuwait simply refused to be bound by the quota it was assigned by the other OPEC members. Having supported Iraq's war effort against Iran with loans totaling $14 billion, the Kuwaitis felt justified in putting their own economic interests first now that the war was over.

Saddam Hussein began to pin the blame for Iraq's economic woes on Kuwait, and he responded by applying pressure and threats to the small Gulf shaykhdom. He called on Kuwait not only to forgive Iraq's $14 billion debt but to make a further loan of $10 billion for Iraq's reconstruction. He accused Kuwait of stealing Iraqi oil from their shared Rumaila oil field. He also claimed that Kuwait had seized Iraqi territory during the Iran-Iraq War, and he demanded the "return" of the strategic islands of Warba and Bubiyan at the head of the Gulf both for military facilities and to provide Iraq with a deep-water port.

Hussein's assertions, though unfounded, reopened Iraq's long-standing challenge to Kuwait's frontiers and independence. Iraq had already claimed Kuwait as part of its territory twice in the twentieth century—in 1937, and upon Kuwaiti independence in 1961. Yet Iraq's Arab neighbors took these new claims and threats to be no more than empty rhetoric.

The Arab states were mistaken: in July 1990, Hussein backed up his words with actions when he deployed large numbers of troops and tanks to Iraq's border with Kuwait. The other Arab states were forced into action, now aware that a serious crisis was brewing.

Egypt and Saudi Arabia responded to the growing crisis by trying to broker a diplomatic solution. King Fahd of Saudi Arabia and President Mubarak of Egypt arranged a meeting between the Kuwaitis and Iraqis in the Saudi Red Sea port of Jidda, scheduled for August 1. Saddam Hussein promised the Arab leaders before the meeting that all differences between Iraq and its neighbors would be settled in a "brotherly manner."

Saddam Hussein had already made up his mind to invade Kuwait. Before sending his vice president to meet with the Kuwaiti crown prince in Jidda, Hussein requested a meeting on July 25 with the U.S. ambassador to Baghdad, April Glaspie, to sound out Washington's position on the crisis. Glaspie assured the Iraqi president that the United States had "no opinion on the Arab-Arab conflicts, like your border disagreement with Kuwait."[8] It appears that Hussein interpreted Ambassador Glaspie's remarks to mean the United States would not intervene in an inter-Arab conflict, and shortly after the meeting, he changed the scope of his invasion plans. Initially he had envisaged a limited incursion into Kuwait to seize the two islands and the Rumaila oil field. Now he called for a total occupation of the country. In a meeting with the governing Revolutionary Command Council, Hussein argued that if he were to leave the ruling al-Sabah family in charge of part of Kuwait, they would mobilize international—particularly American—pressure to force Iraq to withdraw. A quick and decisive invasion that toppled the al-Sabah before they had a chance to call for American intervention would give Iraq the best chance for success. Moreover, were Iraq to absorb its oil-rich neighbor entirely, it could solve all its economic problems at once.

When Saddam Hussein sent his Vice President to meet with the Kuwaiti Crown in Jidda on August 1, he was using diplomacy to achieve total surprise for his military plans. The meeting between Ezzat Ibrahim and Shaykh Saad al-Sabah was conducted amiably, without any hit of threats. The two men parted on good terms and agreed to hold their next meeting in Baghdad. By the time they left Jidda at midnight, Iraqi troops were already moving across the border into Kuwait.

In the early morning hours of August 2, tens of thousands of Iraqi troops crossed into Kuwait in a dash to occupy the oil-rich state. The shocked residents of Kuwait were the first to find out. Jehan Rajab, a school administrator in Kuwait City, recalled: "At 6:00 A.M. on 2 August I got out of bed as usual, opened the window and looked outside. To my consternation I heard the sharp staccato sounds of gunfire, not a shot or two but sustained firing, which was being answered back. The sounds resonated off the walls of the mosque beside us and it immediately and horrifyingly became obvious what was happening. Kuwait was being invaded by Iraq."[9]

Telephones began to ring across the Arab capitals. King Fahd was awakened with the news at 5:00 A.M. Having just seen off the Iraqi and Kuwaiti negotiators in Jidda the night before, the Saudi king could scarcely believe that Iraqi troops had invaded Kuwait. He immediately tried to contact Saddam Hussein but could not reach him. His next call was to King Hussein of Jordan, who was known to be closest to the Iraqi leader.

An hour later, aides woke the Egyptian president, Husni Mubarak, to report that Iraqi troops had occupied the amir's palace and key ministries in the Kuwaiti capital. The Arab leaders had to wait until mid-morning for the first explanation from Baghdad: "This is just part of Iraq returning to Iraq," Saddam's political envoy explained to the incredulous Arab heads of state.[10]

The international community now faced the first crisis of the post–Cold War era. News of the invasion reached the White House at 9:00 P.M. on August 1; the Bush administration issued a robust condemnation of the Iraqi invasion that same night. The next morning it referred the matter to the UN Security Council, which swiftly passed Resolution 660, calling for an immediate and unconditional withdrawal of Iraqi forces.

Undaunted, Iraqi forces sped into the capital, Kuwait City, in a bid to seize Kuwait's amir, Shaykh Jabar al-Ahmad al-Sabah, and his family. Had they successfully captured the ruling family, the Iraqis would have enjoyed far more control over the country, holding the amir and his family hostage to secure their objectives. However, the amir had been warned that the Iraqis were on the move and left with his family to take refuge in neighboring Saudi Arabia.

The Kuwaiti crown prince, Shaykh Saad, returned from his Jidda meeting with the Iraqi vice president to learn that the invasion was already underway. He immediately called the U.S. ambassador in Kuwait and officially requested American military support to repel the Iraqi invasion, before joining the rest of the royal family in exile in Saudi Arabia. By these two simple acts—the request for American assistance, and taking exile—al-Sabah managed to foil Saddam's invasion just as it was starting. Yet the Kuwaiti people would face seven months of horror before the ordeal of occupation would end.

Given the authoritarianism and political double-talk of the Ba'thist regime, the first days of the occupation seemed to emanate straight from the pages of George Orwell's *1984*. The Iraqis preposterously claimed to have entered Kuwait on the invitation of a popular revolution to overthrow the ruling al-Sabah family. "God helped the free people from the pure ranks in Kuwait," a communiqué issued by the Iraqi government explained. "They have swept away the old order and brought about a new order and have asked for the brotherly help of the great Iraqi people."[11] The Iraqi regime then installed what it called the Provisional Free Kuwait Government.

With no obvious Kuwaiti revolutionaries to support Iraq's claims, however, Saddam Hussein's government quickly abandoned the pretense of liberation and announced the annexation of Kuwait. On August 8 it was declared the nineteenth province of Iraq. The Iraqis went to work erasing Kuwait from the maps, and even redesignated the capital Kuwait City by a name of their own coining—Kazimah.

By October, new decrees were issued that required all Kuwaitis to change their identity papers, as well as the license plates on their cars, to standard Iraqi issue. The Iraqis tried to force compliance by denying services to Kuwaitis without Iraqi papers. Ration cards for basic foods like milk, sugar, rice, flour, and cooking oil were only issued to people with Iraqi papers. People had to present Iraqi identification to get medical service. Gas stations would only serve cars with Iraqi license plates. Yet the majority of Kuwaitis resisted these pressures and refused to take Iraqi citizenship, preferring to trade for essentials on the black market.[12]

The invasion of Kuwait was accompanied by the wholesale looting of shops, offices, and residences by Iraqi forces, much of it for reshipment to Baghdad. Watching the truckloads of stolen goods depart for Baghdad, one Kuwaiti official questioned an Iraqi officer:

"If you are saying that this is part of Iraq, why are you taking everything away?"
"Because no province can be better than the capital," the officer replied.[13]

The brutality of the occupation grew more intense with each passing day. Toward the end of August, Saddam Hussein appointed his notorious cousin Ali Hasan al-Majid, grimly nicknamed "Chemical Ali" for his use of gas warfare against the Kurds in the Anfal campaign, as military governor of Kuwait. "After the arrival in Kuwait of Ali Hassan Al Majeed," Kuwait resident Jehan Rajab noted in her journal, "the reign of terror intensified, as did the rumours of possible chemical attacks." Those who could, fled. "Escape was on everyone's mind," reflected Kuwaiti banker Mohammed al-Yahya. He described cars from Kuwait four abreast at the Saudi border, backed up for 30 kilometers (about 19 miles). Al-Yahya, however, chose to remain in Kuwait.[14]

As the full repression of Iraq's political system took root in Kuwait, its people rose up in nonviolent resistance. "Within the first week of the invasion," Jehan Rajab wrote, "Kuwaiti women decided to demonstrate on the streets against what had happened." The first demonstration was held on August 6, just four days after the invasion. "There was a feeling of tension and expectancy: it was almost as if the crowd subconsciously realized that even peaceful demonstrations would not be countenanced by the Iraqis." As many as 300 people took part in the march, carrying banners, posters of the exiled amir and crown prince, and Kuwaiti flags.

The protesters combined chants in honor of Kuwait and the amir with condemnations of Saddam Hussein: "Death to Saddam" and, incongruously, "Saddam is a Zionist." The first two demonstrations met with no Iraqi reaction, but by the third consecutive day of protests, the swelling mass came face to face with armed Iraqi soldiers who fired straight into the crowd. "Pandemonium broke out," Rajab recorded. "Car engines roared as they tried to back wildly down the road, people screamed and the shooting continued." Dead and wounded demonstrators littered the ground outside the police station in downtown Kuwait City. "That was the last of such marches in our district, and probably the last anywhere, for the Iraqis shot to kill or maim. Kuwaitis were beginning to understand just how ruthless the invaders were."[15]

Yet nonviolent resistance activities continued throughout the Iraqi occupation. The resistance movement changed tactics to avoid the risk of Iraqi gunfire. On September 2, the Kuwaitis marked the end of the first month of the occupation with a show of defiance. The plan spread by word of mouth for all residents of Kuwait City to climb to their roofs at midnight and cry out "Allahu akbar," or "God is great." At the appointed hour, thousands joined in a chorus of protest against the occupation. For Jehan Rajab, it was a shout of "defiance and fury at what had taken place—at the invasion, the brutality that had followed, the killings, and the torture centres that had been set up in various places around Kuwait." Iraqi soldiers fired warning shots to the rooftops to silence to protest, but for one hour the people of Kuwait successfully defied the occupation. "Some say Kuwait was born anew that night," the banker al-Yahya claimed.[16]

Many Kuwaitis mounted armed resistance against the Iraqis as well, led by former police and soldiers who were trained in the use of firearms. They ambushed Iraqi troops and ammunition stores. The road that ran past Jehan Rajab's school was a main thoroughfare for Iraqi military vehicles and became the focus of many resistance attacks. In late August, Rajab was shocked by an enormous explosion from the main road, followed by a random volley of rocket fire. She soon realized that the resistance had struck Iraqi ammunition trucks and detonated the ordnance they were carrying. She only dared to leave her apartment when the explosions died down. She found fire engines dousing the flaming wreckage of the Iraqi army trucks. "There was little left to be seen other than scattered and blackened skeletal remains," she noted in her journal. "Anything human must have been blasted into infinity."

The attacks placed the residents of her neighborhood at grave risk, both from the fallout of the attacks and from the retaliation of the Iraqis. "After this particular incident," she noted, "in which a few houses had been hit and, worse, the Iraqis had threatened to kill everyone in the area if anything like it happened again, the Resistance tried to protect ordinary civilians by keeping its explosions further away from residential districts."[17]

The residents of Kuwait took Iraqi threats very seriously. The stench of death hung heavy over the occupied country. Death had literally come to the doorsteps of many Kuwaitis: one of the Iraqis' tactics was to return a detainee to his home and gun him down before his family. To compound the horror, the authorities threatened to kill all members of the household if the body was moved. The dead were often left for two or three days in the heat of summer to serve as a grisly warning to others who dared to resist.

Yet in spite of Iraqi efforts to intimidate the Kuwaitis into submission, resistance continued unabated throughout the seven months of occupation. Jehan Rajab's claims of "continued resistance during the long months" of the occupation are corroborated by Iraqi intelligence documents, seized after the liberation of Kuwait, that tracked resistance activities through the seven months of the occupation.[18]

In the early days of the occupation, there was no reason to believe that Iraq would confine its ambitions to Kuwait. None of the Arab Gulf countries had sufficient military strength to repel an Iraqi invasion, and following the fall of Kuwait, both the Americans and the Saudis were concerned that Saddam Hussein might attempt to occupy nearby Saudi oil fields.

The Bush administration believed a large American presence to be the only deterrent against Saddam Hussein's ambitions. It wanted base rights for U.S. troops in the event of military action to displace the Iraqis; however, the administration would need a formal request from the Saudi government for military support before any troops could be dispatched. King Fahd demurred, fearing a negative domestic public reaction. As the birthplace of Islam, Saudi Arabia has always been particularly uncomfortable with a non-Muslim presence on its soil. Furthermore, never having been subject to foreign imperial control, the Saudis guard their independence from the West jealously.

The prospect of American troops flooding into Saudi Arabia rallied the country's Islamists to action. Saudi veterans of the Afghan conflict, flushed with their successes against the Soviets, were adamantly opposed to an American intervention in Kuwait. Osama bin Ladin had returned from the Afghan jihad and had been placed under house arrest by the Saudi government for his outspoken speeches, which were enjoying wide circulation by cassette recording.

When Saddam Hussein's forces invaded Kuwait, Bin Ladin wrote to the Saudi minister of interior, Prince Nayef bin Abdul Aziz, to suggest mobilizing the mujahidin network that he believed had been so effective in driving the Soviets from Afghanistan. "He claimed he could muster an army of 100,000 men," recalled Abdul Bari Atwan, one of the few journalists to interview Bin Ladin in his hideout in the Tora Bora Mountains of Afghanistan. "This letter was ignored."

On balance, the Saudis believed the Iraqis to pose the greater threat to their country's stability, and opted for American protection in spite of domestic Saudi opposition. Bin Ladin denounced the move as a betrayal of Islam. "Bin Laden told me that the Saudi government's decision to invite U.S. troops to defend the kingdom and liberate Kuwait was the biggest shock of his entire life," Atwan recorded.

> He could not believe that the House of Al Saud could welcome the deployment of "infidel" forces on Arabian Peninsula soil, within the proximity of the Holy Places [i.e., Mecca and Medina], for the first time since the inception of Islam. Bin Ladin also feared that by welcoming U.S. troops onto Arab land the Saudi government would be subjecting the country to foreign occupation—in an exact replay of the course of events in Afghanistan, when the Communist government in Kabul invited Russian troops into the country. Just as bin Laden had taken up arms to fight the Soviet troops in Afghanistan, he now decided to take up arms to confront U.S. troops on the Arabian Peninsula.[19]

His passport confiscated by the Saudi authorities, Bin Ladin had to exploit his family's close ties with the Saudi monarchy to secure travel documents and go into permanent exile. In 1996 he declared jihad against the United States and declared the Saudi monarchy "outside the religious community" for "acts against Islam."[20] Yet his alienation from the United States and the Saudi monarchy, his former allies in the Afghan jihad, dated to the events of August 1990.

The Kuwait crisis opened a new chapter of Soviet-American cooperation in international diplomacy. For the first time in its history, the Security Council was able to take decisive action without being undermined by Cold War politics. Over the four months following the swift passage of Resolution 660 on August 2, the Security Council passed a total of twelve resolutions as the crisis deepened without the risk of a veto. On August 6 it imposed trade and economic sanctions on Iraq and froze all Iraqi assets abroad (Res. 661); the UN tightened the sanction regime again on September 25 (Res. 670). On August 9 the Security Council declared the Iraqi annexation of Kuwait "null and void" (Res. 662). A number of resolutions condemned Iraqi violations of diplomatic immunity in Kuwait and upheld the rights of third-state nationals to leave Iraq and Kuwait. When on November 29 the Soviets joined with the Americans in passing Resolution 678, authorizing member states "to use all necessary means" against Iraq unless it withdrew fully from Kuwait by January 15, 1991, the Cold War in the Middle East came to a formal end.

What most surprised Arab statesmen—and the Iraqis in particular—was the Soviet position. "Many in the Arab world assumed that even if Moscow refused to help Iraq after the invasion it would at least remain neutral, and they were surprised when the Soviet Union helped the Americans to pass resolution after resolution through the UN Security Council," Egyptian analyst Mohamed Heikal recalled. What the Arab world had not reckoned on was the weakened state of the Soviet Union and its concern to preserve good relations with Washington. Given America's geostrategic interests in the Gulf, the Soviets knew they could either support the U.S. or confront it, but they could not deter it from action. With nothing to be gained from confrontation, the Soviets opted for cooperation with the United States and left their former Arab ally totally exposed.

The Arab world was slow to recognize the reorientation of Moscow's policies in the post–Cold War age. As Iraq turned a deaf ear to the UN, and as the United States began to mobilize a war coalition, the Arab world still expected the Soviet Union to prevent the United States from taking military action against its ally Iraq. Instead, Soviet foreign minister Eduard Shevardnadze worked closely with U.S. secretary of state James Baker in drafting the very resolution that authorized military action. "To the amazement of Arab delegations," Heikal claimed, "it became clear that Moscow would give Washington a license to act."[21]

Whereas the Americans and the Soviets enjoyed a moment of unprecedented cooperation over the Kuwait crisis, the Arab world had never been so fragmented. The invasion of one Arab state by another, and the threat of outside intervention, provoked deep divisions among Arab leaders.

Egypt, recently rehabilitated after a decade's isolation for its peace treaty with Israel, took the lead in organizing an Arab response to the Kuwait crisis. President Mubarak convened a snap Arab summit, the first to be held in Cairo since the Camp

David Accords, on August 10. The Iraqis and Kuwaitis faced each other for the first time since the invasion. It was a tense moment. The amir of Kuwait gave a conciliatory speech, trying to mollify the Iraqis and to advance a diplomatic resolution to the crisis. He hoped to return to where negotiations had left off in the August 1 meeting in Jidda. The Iraqis, however, took an intransigent line. When the amir finished his speech and sat down, the Iraqi delegate Taha Yassin Ramadan protested: "I don't know on what basis the sheikh is addressing us. Kuwait does not exist any more."[22] The amir stormed out of the hall in protest.

For some Arab leaders, the threat of American intervention was more serious yet than the Iraqi invasion of Kuwait. President Chadli Benjedid of Algeria admonished the assembly: "We have fought all our lives to get rid of imperialism and imperialist forces, but now we see that our endeavours are wasted and the Arab nation . . . is inviting foreigners to intervene."[23] The leaders of Libya, Sudan, Jordan, Yemen, and the PLO all shared Benjedid's concerns, and they pressed for concerted Arab action to resolve the crisis. They hoped to negotiate an Iraqi withdrawal from Kuwait on terms that both sides could accept without further armed conflict or foreign intervention.

When it came to the vote on the final resolution of the Cairo summit, the divisions within the Arab world were most apparent. The resolution condemned the invasion, disavowed Iraq's annexation, and called for an immediate withdrawal of all Iraqi forces from Kuwait. It also endorsed Saudi Arabia's request for Arab military support against Iraq's threats to its territory. Mubarak curtailed the debate on the resolution after just two hours and put the text to a vote that split the Arab world into two deeply divided camps, with ten in favor and nine opposed to the final resolution. "It had taken just under two hours to create the deepest divisions the Arab world had ever seen," Mohamed Heikal wrote. "The last slender chance for an Arab solution had been lost."[24]

The American government believed nothing short of a credible threat could force the Iraqis to withdraw from Kuwait. They had no confidence in Arab diplomacy and instead began to recruit Arab allies for military action. The first American forces had already landed in Saudi Arabia on August 8, where they were joined by Egyptian and Moroccan units. The Syrians, long-time enemies of Iraq and interested in rapprochement with the United States since the Soviets had withdrawn their support, were leaning toward joining the coalition and confirmed their participation on September 12. The other Gulf states—Qatar, the United Arab Emirates, and Oman—also sided with the Saudis and offered troops and facilities to the American-led coalition.

Having split the Arab states into irreconcilable camps by his actions, Saddam Hussein next played to Arab public opinion to turn citizens against their governments in Arab states. He presented himself as a man of action who stood up to the Americans and the Israelis. He condemned the United States of double standards, of enforcing U.N. Security Council resolutions on behalf of oil-rich Kuwait while turning a blind eye to Israel's repeated violations of UN resolutions calling for withdrawal from occupied Arab lands. By his actions, Saddam Hussein put added pressure on Arab regimes by making them out to be lackeys of the Western powers who sacrificed Arab interests to preserve good relations with the United States. Hussein openly accused his fellow Arab leaders of playing by America's rules in the new post–Cold War age. And the Arab masses rallied to the one leader who refused to bow to American pressure. Violent demonstrations broke out in Morocco, Egypt, and Syria in protest of their leaders' decision to join the coalition. Large rallies were held in Jordan and the Palestinian territories in support of the Iraqis—much to the chagrin of the exiled Kuwaitis, who for years had provided generous support to both the Hashemite monarchy and the PLO.

King Hussein of Jordan and PLO chairman Yasser Arafat, who had once enjoyed cordial relations with the Iraqi regime, now found themselves caught between Arab public opinion in support of Saddam Hussein and the international community's demand that they side with the U.S.-led coalition against the Iraqi invasion of Kuwait. Arafat openly threw in his lot with Saddam Hussein, whereas Jordan's monarch limited himself to refusing to condemn the Iraqis as he pursued an increasingly unlikely "Arab solution" to the Kuwait crisis. For failing to condemn the Iraqis, King Hussein was accused by both the Bush administration and the Arab Gulf leaders of supporting the invasion of Kuwait. In the aftermath of the crisis, Jordan faced isolation from both the Arab Gulf states and the West. However, King Hussein retained the support of the Jordanian people, averting a crisis that could well have cost him his crown.

Ultimately, Saddam Hussein became a prisoner of his popularity with the Arab street. Once he had claimed the moral high ground on issues like the Israeli occupation of Palestine or withstanding American pressure, he left himself no room for compromise. Nor did arguments that generated Arab public support carry much weight with the American government. The Bush administration refused to broaden the discussion from the immediate context of the Iraqi invasion of Kuwait. And Saddam Hussein could not afford to withdraw without some face-saving concession on the Palestine-Israel track that the Americans were unwilling to concede. Unwilling to play by America's rules, Saddam Hussein grew increasingly fatalistic about the prospect of war.

By the time the January 15, 1991, deadline set by UN Security Council Resolution 678 had passed, the United States had mobilized a massive international coalition to force Iraq out of Kuwait. American forces accounted for over two-thirds the total, with 650,000 soldiers. The Arab world contributed nearly 185,000 soldiers, with

100,000 Saudi troops reinforced by units from Egypt, Syria, Morocco, Kuwait, Oman, the United Arab Emirates, Qatar, and Bahrain. Britain and France headed the European contribution to the coalition, though Italy and eight other European states also contributed. In all, some thirty-four countries from six continents combined to make a world war against Iraq.

The world held its breath as January 15 passed without incident. The next day, the United States launched Operation Desert Storm with a massive aerial bombardment of Baghdad and of Iraqi army positions in both Kuwait and Iraq. Saddam Hussein remained defiant, threatening his adversaries with the "mother of all battles." The greatest uncertainty facing the coalition was if Iraq might use chemical or biological weapons, as it had done against the Kurds in the Anfal campaign. U.S. commanders hoped to beat Iraq from the air without exposing their infantry to the risk of gas warfare.

The Iraqis responded to the air war by firing long-range Scud missiles at Israel and against American positions in Saudi Arabia. Without warning, eight Scuds struck Haifa and Tel Aviv in the early morning hours of January 18, inflicting material damage but no fatalities. As sirens blared, Israeli radio stations advised citizens to don gas masks and take shelter in sealed rooms for fear that the Iraqis might deploy chemical warheads on the Scuds.

Yitzhak Shamir's government met in emergency session to decide how to retaliate, but the Bush administration managed to persuade the Israelis to stay out of the war. Saddam Hussein clearly hoped to transform the war for Kuwait into a broader Arab-Israeli conflict that would confound the American-led coalition. Mohamed Heikal recounted how Iraq's missile strikes against Israel confused the loyalties of Arab soldiers in the coalition. When a group of Egyptian and Syrian soldiers encamped in Saudi Arabia heard that Iraq had fired Scud missiles at Israel, they celebrated with shouts of *Allahu Akbar*—"only to remember an instant later that they were supposed to be against Iraq. Too late—seven Egyptians and several Syrians were disciplined."[25]

In all, some forty-two missiles were fired at Israel, some falling short and striking Jordan and the West Bank, others intercepted by Patriot missiles. The Scuds provoked more fear than casualties. Many Palestinians in the Occupied Territories cheered Saddam Hussein's strikes against Israel. Frustrated by the stalemate of the Intifada and Israeli iron-fist policies to break the popular uprising, and now confined to home by a strict twenty-four-hour curfew, the Palestinians were glad to see the Israelis under attack for a change. When journalists filmed Palestinians dancing on their rooftops, cheering on the Scuds, Palestinian academic Sari Nusseibeh explained their reaction to a British newspaper: "If Palestinians are happy when they see a missile going from east to west, it is because, figuratively speaking, they have seen missiles going from west to east for the last 40 years." Nusseibeh was to pay for his missile-spotting comments; a few days later he was arrested on the spurious grounds of helping the Iraqis guide their Scuds against Israeli targets, for which he was given three months in Ramle Prison.[26]

The Iraqis fired forty-six Scuds against Saudi Arabia. Most were intercepted by Patriot missiles, though one Scud struck a warehouse in Dhahran used as a barracks for American soldiers, killing 28 and injuring over 100, the highest number of casualties sustained by American forces in any single incident in the war.

Analysis of missile wreckage reassured American commanders that the Iraqis were not using biological or chemical agents. The failure to deploy unconventional weapons emboldened coalition forces to take their war from the air to the ground, and on February 22, President George H. W. Bush gave Saddam Hussein a final ultimatum to withdraw from Kuwait by noon the following day or face a ground war.

By February, Iraq and its army had suffered more than five weeks of unprecedented aerial bombardment, which dwarfed the impact of its crude Scuds on Israel and Saudi Arabia. Coalition aircraft sustained a rate of up to 1,000 sorties a day, deploying laser-guided precision weapons with high explosives and cruise missiles against Iraqi targets. Baghdad and the cities of southern Iraq endured extensive bombing raids that destroyed power stations, communications, roads and bridges, factories, and residential quarters.

Though there are no official statistics for civilian deaths in the Desert Storm Gulf War—estimates range from 5,000 to 200,000—there is no doubt that thousands of Iraqi civilians were killed and wounded by the intense bombardment. In the worst single incident of the war, the U.S. Air Force dropped two 2,000-pound "smart bombs" on an air-raid shelter in the Amiriya district of Baghdad, killing over 400 civilians, most of them women and children taking refuge from the intense bombardment of the city. The Iraqi army too had suffered heavy casualties from the sustained bombardment, and morale was low by the third week of February.

Facing imminent eviction from Kuwait, the Iraqi government responded with acts of environmental warfare intended to punish Kuwait and the neighboring Gulf states. Already in late January, Iraqi forces deliberately pumped four million barrels of oil into the waters of the Persian Gulf, creating the world's greatest oil slick, a lethal mass 35 miles long and 15 miles wide (56 kilometers long by 24 kilometers wide). Given the fragility of the Gulf as an ecosystem, and coming after years of damage inflicted by the Iran-Iraq War, the oil slick was an environmental catastrophe of unprecedented scale.

On the eve of the ground war, the Iraqis detonated charges in 700 Kuwaiti oil wells, creating an inferno. Jehan Rajab witnessed the explosions from the roof of her home in Kuwait. "We can hear for ourselves that the Iraqis have been setting off more of the dynamite placed around the well heads," she recorded in her journal. "The sky is a throbbing, burning red. Some of the flames rise and fall steadily, others shoot straight into the air to a great height and, I imagine, let out a mighty roar of theatrical proportions. Yet others are almost palpably alive: they spurt out in a swollen ball that pulsates steadily with evil intensity." The next morning, the blue skies of Kuwait had been blotted out by the smoke of 700 burning oil wells. "The entire sky this morning was black. It blotted out the sun."[27]

The Iraqis' environmental war added urgency to the ground campaign, which began in the early morning hours of Sunday, February 24, 1991. The ground war proved brief and brutally decisive. Coalition forces swept into Kuwait and forced a complete Iraqi withdrawal within 100 hours. The intense fighting was terrifying for the inhabitants of Kuwait and the Iraqi invaders alike. Jehan Rajab described massive explosions and heavy fires across Kuwait City, against the background noise of blazing oil wells and hundreds of aircraft crowding the skies. "What an unbelievable night!" she wrote on February 26, two days into the ground assault. "The barrage lit up the lower sky with a blinding white light and blood red flashes."

The panicked Iraqi forces began a disorganized retreat. Soldiers sought rides on trucks and jeeps heading north to the Iraqi border, and commandeered whatever vehicles were still in running order (the Kuwaitis had sabotaged their own cars to deter theft). Many of those who found a ride out of Kuwait perished at Mutla Ridge, an exposed stretch of Highway 80 running from Kuwait north to the Iraqi border. Thousands of Iraqi soldiers in army trucks, buses, and stolen civilian vehicles caused a massive traffic jam on Highway 80. Coalition aircraft bombed the front and rear of the retreating column, trapping thousands of vehicles in between. Some 2,000 vehicles were destroyed in the ensuing carnage. It is not known how many Iraqis managed to flee their vehicles and how many were killed. Yet the images of the "Highway of Death" exposed the American-led coalition to accusations of using disproportionate force, even of war crimes. Concerned lest such atrocities jeopardize the international support they had built for their campaign, the Bush administration pressed for a complete cease-fire on February 28, bringing the Gulf War to an end.

Liberation came at a high price. The Kuwaitis expressed profound joy at the restoration of their independence, but their country had been utterly destroyed by the Iraqi invasion and the war. Hundreds of oil wells burned out of control, infrastructure had been shattered, and much of the country had to be rebuilt from scratch. The population of Kuwait was deeply traumatized by occupation and war, with thousands killed, displaced, or missing.

The wider Arab world also came out of the conflict divided and traumatized. Arab citizens strongly opposed their governments' decision to side with the coalition and fight against a fellow Arab state. Those governments that joined the coalition ostracized those who did not. Jordan, Yemen, and the PLO were condemned for having been too supportive of Saddam Hussein's regime. All three were heavily reliant on financial support from the Gulf, and they suffered economically for the stance they had taken. Many Arab analysts expressed deep mistrust for the United States and concerns for American intentions in the new unipolar world. America's single-minded pursuit of a military solution, and perceived obstruction of efforts to secure a diplomatic resolution to the Gulf crisis, led many to believe that the United States used the war to establish its military presence in the Gulf and to dominate the region's oil resources. The fact that thousands of American troops remained in Saudi Arabia and the other Gulf states years after the liberation of Kuwait only deepened these concerns.

Withdrawal from Kuwait brought no respite to Iraq. The Bush administration, believing it had destroyed Saddam Hussein's prestige along with his military, encouraged the people of Iraq to rise up and overthrow their dictator in early February, 1991. American radio stations broadcast messages into Iraq promising U.S. support for popular uprisings. Their message fell on receptive ears in both the Kurdish districts of northern Iraq and the Shiite regions of the south that had suffered most from Saddam Hussein's rule. Uprisings broke out in both regions in early March 1991.

It was not the outcome the United States had hoped to achieve with its propaganda. The Americans wanted to see a military coup in Baghdad overthrow Saddam Hussein. The Kurdish and Shiite uprisings both threatened American interests. Turkey, which was an ally to the United States under the North Atlantic Treaty Organization (NATO), had been combating a bitter separatist insurgency led by the Kurdistan Workers' Party (known by the Kurdish acronym, the PKK) since 1984 and opposed any measure that might give rise to an Iraqi Kurdish state on Turkey's eastern frontier. The Americans for their part feared that a successful Shiite revolt would only strengthen the regional influence of the Islamic Republic of Iran.

The Americans offered no support to either the Shiites or Kurds, despite having encouraged the Iraqis to rise up. Instead, the Bush administration turned a blind eye while Saddam Hussein reassembled the remnants of his forces to suppress the rebellions with ruthless brutality. Tens of thousands of Iraqi Shiites are believed to have been killed in the suppression of their revolt, and hundreds of thousands of Kurds fled Iraqi retaliation to take refuge in Turkey and Iran.

Faced with a massive humanitarian catastrophe of its own making, the United States responded by imposing a no-fly zone over northern Iraq. U.S. aircraft patrolled the region north of the 36th Parallel to protect the Kurds from Saddam Hussein's forces, while British planes imposed a no-fly zone over Southern Iraq. Ironically, the no-fly zone created precisely the sort of autonomous Kurdish enclave that Turkey had most opposed. Elections to a regional assembly independent of Saddam Hussein's state were held in May 1992, setting in motion the creation of what would become the Kurdish Regional Government in Iraq.

Having failed to unseat Hussein by military means or domestic uprising, the Bush administration returned to the United Nations to secure a resolution stripping Iraq of its weapons of mass destruction, establishing Iraq's responsibility to pay wartime reparations, and reinforcing economic sanctions imposed by earlier resolutions. Saddam Hussein recognized that these measures were designed to provoke his overthrow, and he responded with defiance. He commissioned a mosaic portrait of George H. W. Bush in the entrance of the Al-Rashid Hotel in Baghdad so that all its customers would tread on the face of his adversary. In November 1992, Hussein celebrated Bush's defeat in the presidential elections. Bush had fallen; Saddam was still in power.

The Americans could claim an outright military victory in the Gulf War, but only a partial political victory. The survival of Saddam Hussein meant Iraq remained a source of instability in a region of heightened volatility. And, much against the wishes of the Bush administration, Saddam set the agenda for regional politics after the Desert Storm Gulf War. By drawing parallels between Iraq's position in Kuwait to the Syrian occupation of Lebanon, and the Israeli occupation of Palestinian territory, the Iraqi leader forced the international community to address some of the outstanding conflicts in the Middle East.

———————

By the end of the 1980s, the prospects for peace in Lebanon had never seemed more remote. Ninety percent of the country was under foreign occupation, with Israel in control of the so-called South Lebanon Security Zone, and Syrian troops everywhere else. Foreign funds flooded the country, arming a host of rival militias whose power struggles laid waste to towns and cities in all parts of Lebanon. A whole generation had grown up in the shadow of war, denied an education or the prospect of a earning an honest living. The once-prosperous model democracy of the Middle East had disintegrated into a failed state over which Syria exercised a tenuous control.

The breakdown of the Lebanese state under the duress of communal fighting had put into question the very bases of Lebanon's sectarian system of politics as set out in the 1943 National Pact. Many veteran politicians held Lebanon's volatile mix of religion and politics responsible for the civil war and were determined to impose a root and branch reform as part of any peace settlement. Rashid Karami, a Sunni Muslim who served ten times as prime minister, had long called for a major reform of the Lebanese government to establish political equality between Muslims and Christians. Karami, who again held the premiership between 1984 and 1987, believed that all Lebanese citizens, regardless of their faith, should have an equal right to run for any office. Other reformist members of the cabinet shared Karami's views. Nabih Berri, head of the Shiite Amal Party and minister of justice, dismissed the National Pact as "a sterile system incapable of revision or improvement" and called for a new political system.[28]

Amin Gemayel, whose six-year term as president represented the nadir of Lebanese politics (1982–1988), became the focus of the reformers' attacks. The Druze transport minister, Walid Jumblatt, suggested Gemayel should be driven from office at gunpoint. Many ministers refused to attend the cabinet sessions that he chaired. Karami joined the boycott, and the cabinet ceased to meet, bringing the government to a complete standstill.

Karami escalated the confrontation with Gemayel in May 1987, when the premier tendered his resignation. Many observers believed Karami had resigned to make a bid for the presidency in the upcoming1988 elections. The Sunni politician had tried once before, in 1970, and had been barred from running for a post that was reserved for Maronite Christians. Karami was a respected public figure with powerful supporters in the reformist camp. Perhaps, given the breakdown in Lebanese politics, he might have stood a better chance in 1988 than he had in 1970. However, he never got the chance to declare his candidacy. Four weeks after resigning as prime minister, Rashid Karami was assassinated by a bomb planted in his helicopter. Though Karami's assassins were never found, the message behind his killing was widely understood: the National Pact was not open for negotiation.

The isolated President Gemayel could not find a credible Sunni politician who was willing to serve as prime minister following Karami's assassination. He designated the Sunni minister of education in Karami's defunct cabinet, Selim al-Hoss, as acting premier. From June 1987 until the end of Gemayel's term on September 22, 1988, Lebanon went without a functioning government. The challenge facing Lebanon in 1988 was to agree on a new president when the warring political elites could not agree on anything.

Only one candidate stood for the presidency in 1988: former president Suleiman Franjieh. The public had no confidence in the seventy-eight-year-old warlord who had proved ineffectual in preventing civil war in his previous term of office (1970–1976). No one believed he would be any more effective at achieving national reconciliation twelve years later.

The lack of presidential candidates proved a moot point, for by election day there were not even enough electors present to select a new president. In Lebanon, the president is elected by the parliament, and as no parliamentary elections had been held since the outbreak of civil war, the aging survivors of the 1972 parliament were summoned on August 18 to fulfill their constitutional duty for the third time. Many of the seventy-six surviving deputies had fled their war-torn country for a safer life abroad, and on election day only thirty-eight managed to take their seats. The parliament inquorate, Lebanon went without a president for the first time in the country's history.

According to the Lebanese constitution, in the absence of an elected president, the prime minister and his cabinet are empowered to exercise executive authority until a new president is installed. As President Gemayel's term came to an end, this constitutional provision posed grave dangers to the Maronite guardians of the political status quo. As Lebanon had never gone without a president, no Sunni had ever exercised executive authority. Conservative Maronites feared that if al-Hoss were to assume such power, inevitably he would seek to reform the political system and dispense with the National Pact in the interest of (Muslim) majority rule. And that would mean the end of Lebanon as a Christian state in the Middle East.

As the end of Gemayel's term approached, at midnight on September 22, the Maronite commander in chief of Lebanon's army, General Michel Aoun, took matters in his own hands. A native of the mixed Christian-Shiite village of Haret Hreik in Beirut's southern suburbs, the fifty-three-year-old general demanded that Gemayel dismiss the caretaker al-Hoss government before it achieved executive powers by default. "Mr. President," General Aoun warned him, "it is your constitutional right either to form a new government or not. Should you choose to do the latter [i.e., *not* form a government], we will consider you a traitor from midnight."[29]

In trying to prevent one crisis Aoun's coup was creating another. As a Maronite Christian, he was ineligible for the premiership, which under the terms of the National Pact was reserved for Sunni Muslims. The man who claimed to be upholding the National Pact was actually undermining the foundations of Lebanon's sectarian system. Yet at the eleventh hour—at a quarter to midnight, to be precise—Amin Gemayel succumbed to Aoun's pressures and signed his last two executive orders. The first dismissed the caretaker cabinet of Selim al-Hoss, and the second appointed General Michel Aoun as head of an interim government. Al-Hoss and his supporters rejected Gemayel's last-minute decrees and claimed the right to rule Lebanon.

Overnight, Lebanon went from being a country with no government to a country with two governments, with mutually incompatible agendas: al-Hoss sought to replace Lebanon's confessional system with an open democracy that would favor the country's Muslim majority, under Syrian trusteeship; Aoun hoped to reestablish the Lebanese state on the basis of the National Pact, preserving its Christian dominance, with total independence from Syria.

The rival governments split Lebanon into Christian and Muslim statelets. Few Christians were willing to serve in the al-Hoss cabinet, and no Muslims would participate in the Aoun government. Al-Hoss ruled over the Sunni and Shiite heartlands, and Aoun over the Christian districts of Lebanon. There was an element of farce in the rivalry, as both leaders appointed their own heads of the military, security apparatus, and civil service. Only the Lebanese Central Bank withstood the pressures of duplication, though it found itself financing the expenditures of both governments.

The real danger came from outside patrons. Al-Hoss's cabinet was openly supportive of Syria's role in Lebanon and enjoyed the full backing of Damascus. Aoun condemned the Syrian presence in Lebanon as a threat to the sovereignty and independence of the country, and he gained Iraq's full support. Baghdad was intent on settling scores with Damascus for having broken Arab ranks to side with Iran in the 1980–1988 Iran-Iraq War. Lebanon's many feuds provided the Iraqi government with ample opportunity to punish Syria. With massive stores of weapons and ammunition, the Iraqi government was able to provide military assistance to Aoun in his opposition to Syria's presence in Lebanon, especially after the Iran-Iraq War came to an end in August 1988.

So emboldened, Aoun declared a war of liberation against Syria on March 14, 1989. Syria's army responded by imposing a total blockade over the Christian regions under Aoun's rule. The two sides began to exchange lethal volleys of heavy artillery, causing massive destruction to Muslim and Christian districts of Lebanon and displacing tens of thousands of civilians in what proved the heaviest bombardment since the 1982 Israeli siege of Beirut.

Two months of horrific fighting and heavy civilian casualties galvanized the Arab states into action. In May 1989, an Arab summit was convened in Casablanca, Morocco, to address the new crisis in Lebanon. The conference gave a mandate to three Arab heads of state, King Fahd of Saudi Arabia, King Hassan II of Morocco, and President Chadli Benjedid of Algeria, to negotiate an end to the violence and set in process the restoration of stable government in Lebanon.

The three rulers, dubbed "the troika," ordered Syria to respect a cease-fire and demanded that Iraq stop arms shipments to Aoun and the Lebanese Forces militia. The troika's efforts met with little success at first. The Syrians ignored the troika's demands and stepped up their bombardment of the Christian enclave, and Iraq continued to supply its allies through ports under the control of Syria's Maronite opponents.

After six months of fighting, the troika finally persuaded all sides to observe a cease-fire in September 1989. The Arab leaders invited Lebanon's parliamentarians to a meeting in the Saudi city of Taif to initiate a process of national reconciliation on neutral ground. The Lebanese deputies, all survivors of the election of 1972, ventured from their places of exile in France, Switzerland, and Iraq, or from their safe houses in Lebanon, to assemble in Taif to decide the future of their country. Sixty-two deputies attended the meeting—half of them Christians, the rest Muslims—providing the necessary quorum to make decisions on behalf of the Lebanese state. The Saudi foreign minister, Prince Saud al-Faisal, convened the opening meeting on October 1, 1989, warning that "failure was forbidden."

Success took longer than expected. What had been planned as a three-day conference turned into a twenty-three-day marathon that produced nothing less than the blueprint for Lebanon's Second Republic. The terms of Lebanon's political reconstruction, enshrined in the Taif Accord, preserved many of the elements of the confessional system set out in the National Pact but modified the structure to reflect the demographic realities of modern Lebanon. Thus, seats in parliament were still distributed among the different religious communities, but the distribution had been changed from a 6:5 ratio that favored the Christian communities to an equal division of seats between Muslims and Christians. The number of seats in parliament was increased from 99 to 108 so that the expansion of Muslim representatives could be achieved without any decrease in Christian seats.

The reformers failed in their primary objective of opening political office to all citizens without distinction by religion. It soon became apparent that such an assault on the confessional order would not gain consensus. The compromise solution was to preserve the distribution of offices as set out in the National Pact but to redistribute the *powers* of those offices. The president would remain a Maronite Christian, but the office was reduced to the more ceremonial role of "head of state and symbol of unity." The prime minister and the cabinet, known as the Council of Ministers, were the main beneficiaries of the redistribution of power. Executive authority would now lie with the Sunni premier, who would chair the cabinet meetings and was charged with implementation of policy. Moreover, although the president still named the prime minister, only the parliament had the power to dismiss the premier. The speaker of the parliament, the highest post allowed for a Shiite Muslim, was also given important new powers by the Taif reforms, including a "kingmaker" role in advising the president on the appointment of the prime minister. With these changes, the Maronites could claim to have preserved their key offices, while Muslims could claim to hold more powers than the Christians. As a reform measure, the Taif Accord provided a compromise that all parties could accept, even if it left all dissatisfied.

Aoun's supporters failed in their bid to force Syria from Lebanon through the Taif Accords. The troika found Hafiz al-Asad unwilling to compromise on Syria's position in Lebanon, and recognized that an accord would be meaningless without Syria's support. The Taif Accord gave formal thanks to the Syrian army for past services rendered, legal recognition to Syrian troops currently stationed in Lebanon, and left it to the Lebanese and Syrian governments to agree among themselves when to terminate the Syrian military presence in Lebanon at some unspecified point in the future. The Taif Accord also called on the governments of Lebanon and Syria to formalize their "privileged relationships in all fields" through bilateral treaties. In short, the accord gave legal sanction to Syria's position in Lebanon and bound the two countries closer together. The Lebanese politicians assembled in Saudi Arabia recognized the realities of their position and accepted a compromise solution in the hope of achieving better in the future. The final draft of the accord was approved by the Lebanese deputies in Taif without opposition.

The announcement of the Taif Accord set off the final round of fighting in war-torn Lebanon. From his battered enclave in the Christian highlands, General Aoun persisted in his claim to be the sole legitimate government of Lebanon. He rejected the accord outright for the legal cover it gave to Syria's presence in Lebanon. He issued a presidential decree dissolving the Lebanese parliament in a bid to prevent the implementation of the Taif Accord, but to no avail. Aoun was now isolated at home and abroad as both the Lebanese and the international community put their support behind the framework for national reconciliation in Lebanon.

In a bid to forestall Aoun's challenge, the deputies hastened back to Beirut to ratify the Taif Accord. On November 5 the Lebanese parliament formally approved the accord and proceeded to elect the sixty-four-year-old deputy from Zghorta, René Moawad, as president of the republic. Scion of a respected Maronite family from the north, Moawad was a consensus candidate who enjoyed the support of both Lebanese nationalists and the Syrians. Yet Moawad had dangerous enemies. On his seventeenth day in office, the new president of Lebanon was assassinated by a powerful roadside bomb detonated as he returned home from Lebanese Independence Day celebrations. Syria, Iraq, Israel, and Michel Aoun were all accused of the murder, but those responsible for Moawad's assassination have never been brought to justice.

Moawad's brutal murder risked provoking the collapse of the Taif process—as his assassins no doubt intended. The Lebanese parliament reconvened within forty-eight hours to elect a replacement before Moawad's death could set back the reconstruction process agreed to in Taif. The Syrian authorities were even quicker than the Lebanese parliamentarians in finding a replacement for Moawad. Radio Damascus announced Elias Hrawi as the new president before the Lebanese deputies had put his nomination to the vote.[30] By this deliberate gaffe, the Asad regime made clear to all that ultimate authority over Lebanon in the Taif era remained with Syria.

One of President Hrawi's first acts would be to take on Michel Aoun, now widely recognized as a renegade and an impediment to Lebanon's political reconciliation. The day after his election, Hrawi dismissed Aoun as commander of the army and ordered him to withdraw from the presidential palace in Baabda within forty-eight hours. Ignoring Hrawi's command, Aoun turned to his Iraqi patrons for resupply, securing arms, ammunition, and antiaircraft defenses through his own port near

Beirut to reinforce his position against outside attack. The human shield surrounding Aoun—thousands of his civilian supporters camped out around the presidential palace in Baabda in a festival atmosphere—proved the greatest deterrent to Hrawi in facing down Aoun's defiance.

The Lebanese president did not have to take any action. Rivalries between Aoun and the Maronite Lebanese Forces militia turned into open conflict when the Lebanese Forces commander Samir Geagea declared his support for the Taif Accord in December 1989. Geagea, like Aoun, was supplied by the Iraqis. In January 1990, the rival factions went to war in fighting more intense than at any time since the outbreak of the civil war. Iraqi rockets, tanks, and heavy artillery were deployed with utter disregard for the safety of noncombatants in heavily populated neighborhoods, inflicting heavy civilian casualties. The fighting continued for five months before a tenuous cease-fire between the rival Christian factions was mediated by the Vatican, in May 1990.

Though he faced isolation and growing opposition, Michel Aoun took some satisfaction in knowing that his battle with the Lebanese Forces had, for the moment at least, derailed the Taif Accord.

The Iraqi invasion of Kuwait in August 1990 proved the watershed in the Lebanese conflict. At war once again, Iraq could no longer afford to arm its Lebanese clients. Moreover, Saddam Hussein's attempt to link Iraq's withdrawal from Kuwait to a general resolution of regional problems, including the Syrian "occupation" of Lebanon, was a transparent bid to divert international pressure onto Syria to withdraw from Lebanon.

The Syrians were far too adept at regional politics to succumb to Saddam Hussein's ploy. Hafiz al-Asad was using the Kuwait crisis to improve Syrian relations with Washington, and Washington fully supported the Taif Accord. Al-Asad thus decided to give his government's full support to implementing the Taif framework and cast Iraq's ally Michel Aoun as the main obstacle to peace. The Lebanese and Syrians conferred, and on October 11 President Hrawi formally requested Syrian military assistance, under the terms of the Taif Accord, to oust General Aoun. Two days later, Syrian aircraft began the bombardment of Aoun's positions while Syrian and Lebanese Army tanks advanced into territory held by Aoun's forces. Within three hours, General Aoun had capitulated and sought asylum in the French Embassy while his partisans continued the struggle. The fighting—often very intense—was over within eight hours. When the smoke cleared over the empty presidential palace in Baabda on October 13, the people of Lebanon enjoyed their first glimpse of a postwar world, if still under Syrian occupation.

It was only after the defeat of Michel Aoun that the postwar reconstruction envisaged by the Taif Accord could begin in earnest. In November 1990 the government ordered all militias out of the capital, Beirut, and in December the army cleared the barricades separating Muslim West Beirut from Christian East Beirut, reuniting the city for the first time since 1984.

On Christmas Eve 1990, Omar Karami, brother of the assassinated reformist premier Rashid Karami, announced a new government of national unity. With thirty ministers, the cabinet was the largest in Lebanon's history, and it integrated the leaders of nearly all the country's main militias. The advantages of forming a government from the very warlords responsible for the worst atrocities of the conflict soon became apparent when the government decreed the disarmament of the militias—again, in accordance with the Taif Accord. The militias were given to the end of April 1991 to disband and surrender their weapons; in return, the government promised to integrate those militiamen who wished to serve in Lebanon's army. However much the militia leaders might have objected, they did not oppose the government or resign from the cabinet.[31]

Only one militia was allowed to continue military operations: Hizbullah, which enjoyed Iranian and Syrian support, retained its weapons so that it could continue its resistance to the Israeli occupation in the south of Lebanon. The Shiite militia agreed to confine its operations to the territory Israel claimed as part of its South Lebanon "security zone," which at any rate lay beyond the writ of the Lebanese government. Hizbullah would continue its jihad against the Israeli occupier, with growing sophistication and lethal effect.

The fighting finally at an end, Lebanon faced the nearly insurmountable task of reconstruction after fifteen years of civil war. Between 1975 and 1990 an estimated 100,000–200,000 people died, many more were wounded and disabled, and hundreds of thousands were driven to exile. No city had been spared, as whole quarters were reduced to silent streets of shattered buildings. Squatters—refugees from later battles—had taken over habitable buildings abandoned in earlier battles. Utilities had completely broken down in many parts of the country. Private generators provided electricity, running water was sporadic and unhealthy, and raw sewage flowed through the streets, encouraging luxuriant plant growth among the ruins of the war.

The social fabric of Lebanon was no less damaged. Memories of atrocities and of injustices that would never be redressed divided Lebanon's many communities long after peace had been declared. A combination of reconciliation, amnesia, and a fierce drive to get on with life enabled the Lebanese to act like a nation again. Some have argued that the Lebanese have emerged stronger in their commitment to their nation as a consequence.[32] Yet Lebanon remains a volatile country in which the threat of renewed conflict is never far from consciousness.

Saddam Hussein's invasion, and the American-led war to liberate Kuwait, had the unintended consequence of forcing America to address the long-simmering Israeli-Palestinian conflict. The American government recognized that the Kuwait crisis had placed its Arab allies under tremendous pressure. However cynical, Saddam Hussein's frequent references to liberating Palestine had earned him widespread popular support across the Arab world and exposed other Arab governments to public condemnation. Arab citizens believed their governments had lost the plot: they should be fighting Israel to liberate Palestine, not fighting Iraq on America's behalf to liberate Kuwaiti wealth and oil.

America too came under widespread condemnation in the Arab press and public opinion. For years the Americans had supported Israel while it flaunted U.N. resolutions calling for the restoration of occupied Arab lands. In 1990, Israel remained in occupation of the Gaza Strip, the West Bank, the Golan Heights, and parts of southern Lebanon. Yet when Iraq invaded Kuwait, America invoked UN Security Council resolutions as though they were sacrosanct. Occupation was either right or wrong, and UN resolutions either were binding or they weren't. The double standard in treatment of Iraq and Israel as occupiers was self-evident.

President George H. W. Bush rejected Saddam Hussein's attempts to link an Iraqi withdrawal from Kuwait to an Israeli withdrawal from the occupied Palestinian territories. But he could not escape the logic of the Iraqi demand. No sooner had the Iraq conflict ended than the Bush administration announced a new Arab-Israeli peace initiative, in March 1991. It was a transparent bid to regain the initiative and demonstrate that, in the New World Order, America could use its power as effectively in peace as in war.

Palestinians greeted the news of the American initiative to restart the peace process with some relief. Their support for Saddam Hussein and his occupation of Kuwait had cost the Palestinians dearly. The international community shunned the PLO, and the Arab Gulf states cut all funding to the Palestinians. Though the Bush administration made clear they had no intention of rewarding the PLO for its stance in the recent conflict, the new peace initiative could only serve to break the Palestinians out of their isolation.

Palestinian activist Sari Nusseibeh celebrated the Bush initiative in his cell in Ramle Prison. Nusseibeh was coming to the end of his three-month sentence, ostensibly for guiding Iraqi Scuds against Israeli targets, when Bush made his announcement in March 1991. The American initiative came as a total surprise to Nusseibeh. "Out of the blue George Bush, Sr., made a stunning policy statement: 'A comprehensive peace must be grounded in resolution 242 and 338 and the principle of territory for peace.'" Bush went on to link Israeli security to Palestinian rights. And his secretary of state, James Baker, declared Israeli settlements in the West Bank the greatest obstacle to peace. "I was dancing in my tiny cage after hearing this," Nusseibeh recalled in his memoirs.[33]

Some Palestinians were more skeptical of American intentions. Hanan Ashrawi, one of Nusseibeh's colleagues at Bir Zeit University and a leading Palestinian political activist, dissected the language of Bush's statement. "The claim was that [Bush] would 'invest the credibility that the United States had gained in the war in order to bring peace to the region.' We read that as claiming the spoils of war." Ashrawi saw the whole peace initiative as an American effort to subordinate the Middle East to its rules. "The claim was that a 'New World Order' was emerging with the end of the Cold War and that we were part of it. We read that as a reorganization of our world according to the American blueprint. The claim was that a window of opportunity was opening up for a Middle East reconciliation. We read that as a peephole, a long tunnel, or a trap."[34]

The first thing the Americans made clear to the Palestinians was that they would not allow the PLO to play any role in the negotiations. The Israeli government categorically refused to attend any meeting with the PLO, and the Americans were intent on sidelining Yasser Arafat in retribution for his support of Saddam Hussein.

U.S. secretary of state James Baker went to Jerusalem in March 1991 to invite Palestinian leaders from the West Bank and Gaza Strip to take part in a peace conference and negotiate on behalf of the Palestinians in the Occupied Territories. The Palestinians saw the Baker initiative as a blatant attempt to create an alternative Palestinian leadership. They wanted no part in undermining the PLO's internationally recognized position as the sole legitimate representative of the Palestinian people. The "insider" political activists wrote to Tunis for official approval from Arafat before agreeing to meet with Baker on March 13.

Eleven Palestinians attended the first meeting, chaired by the Jerusalemite Faisal al-Husseini. The son of Abd al-Qadir al-Husayni, whose death in the 1948 battle of al-Qastal marked the defeat of Palestinian resistance to Zionism, Faisal al-Husseini was the scion of one of Jerusalem's oldest and most respected families. He was also a loyal Fatah member with close ties to Yasser Arafat.

"We are here at the behest of the PLO, our sole legitimate leadership," al-Husseini began.

"Whom you choose as your leadership is your own business," Baker responded. "I am looking for Palestinians from the Occupied Territories who are not PLO members and who are willing to enter into direct bilateral two-phased negotiations on the basis of UNSC resolutions 242 and 338 and the principle of land for peace, and who are willing to live in peace with Israel. Are there any in this room?" Baker looked the eleven Palestinians in the face, but they were not to be rushed.

"We must remind you, Mr. Secretary, that we are a people with dignity and pride. We are not defeated, and this is not Safwan Tent," said Saeb Erakat, referring to the tent set up by the Americans to negotiate the terms of Iraq's surrender at the end of the Gulf War. The burly Erakat was an English-trained professor of political science at al-Najah University in Nablus.

"It's not my fault you backed the losing side," Baker retorted. "You should tell your leadership not to back the wrong horse; that was absolutely stupid. There's a big price to be paid."

"I've agreed to come to this meeting to talk about one thing only," said Haidar Abdel Shafi. A physician and president of the Gaza Medical Association, Abdel Shafi was the senior statesman in the Occupied Territories and had served as speaker of the Palestinian parliament while Gaza was under Egyptian rule, from 1948 to 1967. "Israeli settlement activities in the Occupied Territories must stop. There will be no peace process while the settlements continue. You can count on hearing this from me all the time."

"Begin negotiations, and the settlements will stop," Baker responded.

"They must stop before, or we can't enter the process," the Palestinian activists replied in chorus.

Secretary Baker recognized that the conversation was turning to negotiation, and that he had found a credible group to represent Palestine at the peace conference. "Now you're talking business," he said with some satisfaction.[35]

That first exchange initiated six months of negotiations between the Americans and the Palestinians that ultimately framed the agenda for the peace conference held in Madrid in October 1992. The Americans moved between the Israelis and Palestinians, trying to bridge nearly irreconcilable positions to ensure a successful conference.

The Israeli government proved a far greater impediment to American peace plans than the Palestinians. Prime Minister Yitzhak Shamir headed a right-wing Likud coalition that was committed to retaining all of the Occupied Territories, especially East Jerusalem. With the end of the Cold War, Soviet Jews enjoyed the liberty to emigrate to Israel, and the Israeli government was determined to reserve its options on all the land under its control to accommodate the new wave of immigrants. Israel was stepping up its settlement activity both to extend its claim to West Bank territory and to provide new housing for Russian immigrants.

For the Palestinian negotiators, East Jerusalem and the settlements were red line issues: If the Israelis retained all of Jerusalem and allowed continued construction on occupied land in the West Bank, there would be nothing left to discuss. The Palestinians saw the two issues as inextricably linked. "It couldn't have been an accident that the Israelis wanted to bracket out the settlements and East Jerusalem," Sari Nusseibeh reflected. "Of the two, the issue of East Jerusalem bothered me most. The fight over Jerusalem was existential, not because it is a magical city but because it was, and is, the center of our culture, national identity, and memory—things the Israelis had to extirpate if they were to have their way throughout what they called Judea and Samaria [i.e., the West Bank]. As long as we held on to Jerusalem," Nusseibeh concluded, "I was certain we could resist them everywhere else."[36]

The Bush administration showed sympathy for the Palestinian position, and was clearly irritated by the intransigence of Shamir and his Likud government in the lead-up to the Madrid Conference. Nevertheless, in many ways, the United States continued to privilege Israeli demands over Palestinian arguments. The Israelis insisted on the total exclusion of the PLO from the process, that the Palestinians only be allowed to attend the conference as junior partners in a joint Jordanian-Palestinian delegation, and that no resident of East Jerusalem be accredited to the negotiations. This meant that some of the most influential Palestinians, like Faisal al-Husseini, Hanan Ashrawi, and Sari Nusseibeh, were barred from an official role in the Madrid negotiations. Instead, on Arafat's suggestion, Husseini and Ashrawi accompanied the official Palestinian delegation, headed by Dr Abdul Shafi, as an unofficial "Guidance Committee."

In spite of the restrictions, the Palestinian delegation that accompanied the Jordanians to Madrid were the most eloquent and persuasive spokespeople ever to represent their national aspirations on the international stage. Hanan Ashrawi was designated the official spokesperson for the Palestinian delegation. Ashrawi had studied at the American University of Beirut and took her doctorate in English literature from the University of Virginia before returning to teach at Bir Zeit University in the West Bank. A brilliant woman of great eloquence from a Christian family, Ashrawi was the antithesis of the stereotype of a terrorist that many in the West associated with the Palestinian cause.

Once in Madrid, Ashrawi devoted herself to wooing the media, so as to swing coverage in the Palestinians' favor. Strategically, she knew how important it was for the Palestinian delegation to win over the international press to compensate for their weak position at the negotiating table. Ashrawi showed great ingenuity at putting the Palestinians' message across in Madrid. When denied access to the official press center, Ashrawi created chaos by convening impromptu press conferences in public spaces that attracted more journalists than any other delegation at Madrid. When Spanish security measures proved too stringent, she took over a municipal park where camera crews could set up beyond the restrictions of the security forces. In one day alone she gave twenty-seven extensive interviews to international television networks. The Israeli delegation's spokesman, Benjamin Netanyahu, struggled to keep up with the charismatic Palestinian woman who consistently stole the show.

Ashrawi's most enduring contribution to the Madrid conference was the speech she drafted for Haidar Abdul Shafi to deliver on behalf of the Palestinian delegation on October 31, 1991. With his grave demeanor and deep, rich voice, Abdul Shafi matched in dignity what Ashrawi's text conveyed in eloquence. He began with greetings to the assembled dignitaries before launching into the heart of his text, fixing the global audience with his penetrating gaze. "We meet in Madrid, a city with the rich texture of history, to weave together the fabric which joins our past with the future," he intoned before the assembled Israelis, Arabs, and members of the international community. "Once again, Christian, Moslem, and Jew face the challenge of heralding a new era enshrined in global values of democracy, human rights, freedom, justice, and security. From Madrid we launch this quest for peace, a quest to place the sanctity of human life at the center of our world and to redirect our energies and resources from the pursuit of mutual destruction to the pursuit of joint prosperity, progress, and happiness."[37] Abdul Shafi took care to speak on behalf of all Palestinians, in exile as well as under occupation. "We are here together seeking a just and lasting peace whose cornerstone is freedom for Palestine, justice for the Palestinians, and an end to the occupation of all Palestinian and Arab lands. Only then can we really enjoy together the fruits of peace: prosperity, security and human dignity and freedom." It was a brilliant debut performance for the Palestinian delegation, making their first appearance on the stage of world diplomacy.

Abdul Shafi's speech provoked divided reactions from Palestinians in the Occupied Territories. The Islamist Hamas movement, unreconciled to a two-state solution, had announced its opposition to participation in the conference from the outset. Secular Palestinians were fearful that their delegation might come under such pressure from the United States and Israel as to make concessions inconsistent with Palestinian national aspirations. After four years of the Intifada, all Palestinians wanted to see some concrete results for their years of struggle and sacrifice.

As the Palestinians had most to gain from Madrid, their speech was the most forward-looking. The other delegations paid lip service to the historic nature of the conference but otherwise used the occasion to review past grievances. The Lebanese focused on the ongoing Israeli occupation of South Lebanon, the Israeli premier catalogued Arab efforts to destroy the Jewish state, and the Syrian foreign minister provided a list of "inhuman Israeli practices" to make clear his distaste at having to meet with the Israelis at all.

After three days together, the delegates took off their gloves and openly brawled in their closing speeches. Prime Minister Shamir set a vituperative tone; he lambasted the Syrians, offering to "recite a litany of facts that demonstrate the extent to which Syria merits the dubious honor of being one of the most oppressive, tyrannical regimes in the world." He patronized the Palestinians, claiming Abdul Shafi "made a valiant effort at recounting the sufferings of his people," though he accused the

Palestinian of "twisting history and perversion of fact." At his speech's conclusion, Shamir stormed out of the conference hall with his delegation, ostensibly to observe the Jewish Sabbath.

Abdul Shafi responded angrily, addressing his words to the empty seats vacated by the Israeli delegation. "The Palestinians are a people with legitimate national rights. We are not 'the inhabitants of territories' or an accident of history or an obstacle to Israel's expansionist plans, or an abstract demographic problem. You may wish to close your eyes to this fact, Mr. Shamir, but we are here in the sight of the world, before your very eyes, and we shall not be denied."

The exchange of insults reached its climax when the outraged Syrian foreign minister pulled out a British "Wanted" poster for Yitzhak Shamir dating back to his days in the Stern Gang fighting the British mandate in Palestine. "Let me show you an old picture of Shamir, when he was 32 years old," Farouk al-Shara'a said, brandishing the poster and pausing to note Shamir's diminutive stature—"165 cm," he sneered. Warming to his theme, Shara'a continued: "This picture was distributed because he was wanted. He himself confessed he was a terrorist. He confessed he . . . participated in murdering U.N. mediator Count Bernadotte in 1948, as far as I remember. He kills peace mediators and talks about Syria, Lebanon, terrorism."[38]

Shara'a's tirade was an unedifying spectacle that bode ill for the prospect of Arab-Israeli peace. On that sour note, the Madrid conference came to an end. Yet with the conclusion of the formal conference, a new phase of Arab-Israeli peace negotiations opened under American auspices: bilateral negotiations to resolve the differences between Israel and its Arab neighbors, and multilateral talks involving over forty states and international organizations to address issues of global concern such as water, the environment, arms control, refugees, and economic development. Though ultimately unsuccessful, the Madrid process initiated the most extensive peace negotiations between Israel and its Arab neighbors in over forty years of conflict.

The bilateral negotiations were intended to resolve the Arab-Israeli conflict by returning occupied land in exchange for peace, in line with UN Security Council Resolutions 242 and 338. But the divergent ways in which the Arabs and Israelis interpreted these resolutions bedeviled negotiations from the outset. The Arab states seized on the principle of the "inadmissibility of the acquisition of territory by war" set out in the preamble of the resolution to argue for a full Israeli withdrawal from all Arab territory occupied in the June 1967 War as a prerequisite for peace. The Israelis, in contrast, claimed that the resolution only required "withdrawal of Israeli armed forces from territories occupied" in the 1967 War—not *all* territories, just "territories"—and insisted they had already fulfilled their commitments to Resolution 242 by withdrawing from the Sinai Peninsula following the peace treaty with Egypt. The Israelis argued that the Arab parties had to sue for peace for its own sake and negotiate a mutually acceptable territorial solution without preconditions. No progress was achieved in talks between Israel, Lebanon, Syria, and Jordan.

Talks between Israel and the Palestinians had a different focus. The two sides agreed to negotiate the terms of a five-year interim period of Palestinian self-rule, after which they would enter into final negotiations to conclude the Israeli-Palestinian conflict. But once the negotiations began, the Shamir government did everything in its power to prevent meaningful progress with the Palestinians, and it stepped up settlement activity to deepen Israel's hold over the West Bank. In an interview after his electoral defeat in 1992, Shamir confirmed his government had obstructed negotiations to prevent Palestinian statehood and retain the West Bank for Israeli settlements. "I would have carried on autonomy talks for ten years, and meanwhile we would have reached half a million people in Judea and Samaria."[39]

Shamir's stonewalling came to an end when his government was defeated at the polls. The Israeli elections of 1992 brought Yitzhak Rabin to power at the head of a left-leaning Labor coalition. Rabin's reputation as the man who had authorized physical violence against Intifada demonstrators gave the Palestinian negotiators little grounds for confidence that "Rabin the bone-breaker" could "become Rabin the peacemaker."[40]

In his first months in office, Rabin delivered more continuity than change in the deadlocked bilateral negotiations. In December 1992, Hamas activists kidnapped and murdered an Israeli border guard. Rabin retaliated by ordering the roundup and deportation to Lebanon of 416 suspects without charge or trial. All Arab delegations suspended negotiations in protest. If anything, Rabin appeared to be even more of a hard-liner than Shamir.

Bill Clinton's surprise defeat of George H. W. Bush in the American presidential elections in 1992 raised concerns among the Arab negotiation teams. During the presidential campaign, Clinton had made clear his unconditional support for Israel. The Arab delegations did not believe the change in presidents bode well for them. Although negotiations did resume in April 1993, the Clinton administration took a hands-off approach to the negotiations, and in the absence of strong American leadership the framework launched by the Madrid conference reached a dead end.

The breakthrough in Palestinian-Israeli negotiations came from a change in Israeli policy. Foreign Minister Shimon Peres and his deputy, Yossi Beilin, were convinced that a settlement with the Palestinians was in Israel's national interest. They also recognized that a settlement could only be reached through direct negotiations with the PLO. Yet since 1986, Israelis had been forbidden by law to meet with members of the PLO. By 1992, the number of Israeli journalists and politicians who had violated the ban had grown to such an extent as to make the law irrelevant. Yet the Israeli government could not knowingly break Israeli law. Rabin was not enthusiastic about dealing with the PLO, but he agreed to overturn the law banning contact between Israeli citizens and the PLO in December 1992.

The following month, Yossi Beilin gave the green light for two Israeli academics, Yair Hirschfeld and Ron Pundak, to meet in secret with the PLO treasurer, Ahmad Qurie, in Oslo, Norway. It was the beginning of an intense and fruitful negotiation conducted through fourteen meetings under the auspices of the Norwegian foreign ministry.

The Norwegians were impartial brokers who provided the neutral terrain and discretion to allow the Palestinians and Israelis to work out their differences with minimal interference. The Norwegian facilitator, Terje Roed Larsen, set out his country's role as the Palestinians and Israelis began the first round of secret diplomacy. "If you want to live together, you have to solve your own problems," Larsen insisted. "It is your problem. We are here to give you the assistance you might need, the place, the practicalities, and so on. We can be facilitators . . . but nothing more. I will wait outside and will not interfere unless you come to blows. Then I will interfere." Larsen's humor helped break the ice between the two delegations. "This made us all laugh," PLO official Ahmed Qurie recalled, "as it was meant to."[41]

Qurie, better known by his nom de guerre, Abu Ala, had never met an Israeli prior to his first encounter with Professor Yair Hirschfeld, and he brought to the table all of the dread and mistrust accumulated over years of mutual hostility between Palestinians and Israelis. Yet in the isolation of the Norwegian winter, the five men—three Palestinians and two Israelis—began to break down barriers. "The atmosphere in the house became more relaxed, and though we still felt on our side some mistrust of the Israelis, we nonetheless began somewhat to warm to them." In their first meeting, the delegates set a pattern they were to follow through future rounds. Putting recriminations over the past behind them, Abu Ala recalled, "we focused our attention on the present and the future, trying to gauge the extent to which we had common ground, to identify such points of agreement as we might reach, and to estimate the distance which separated us on the various issues."[42]

Behind closed doors, in total secrecy, Palestinians and Israelis discussed their differences and secured their governments' backing for a framework to resolve them—in eight brief months. They experienced breakdowns, and the Norwegians occasionally had to play a more active role. Foreign Minister Johan Joergen Holst even engaged in a bit of discreet telephone diplomacy between Tunis and Tel Aviv to help overcome deadlocks. Yet by August 1993, the two sides had concluded an agreement they were willing to take public.

When Israel and the PLO announced their agreement on Palestinian interim self-rule in Gaza and Jericho, they caught the world by surprise—and faced predictable criticism. The Clinton administration was nonplussed to see the Norwegians succeed where the Americans had failed in Arab-Israeli peacemaking. In Israel, the opposition Likud Party accused the Rabin government of betrayal and promised to annul the accord when it returned to power. The Arab world criticized the PLO for breaking Arab ranks to conclude a secret deal with the Israelis, and Palestinian dissident groups condemned their leadership for extending recognition to Israel.

Oslo was a desperate gamble for Yasser Arafat, but the PLO chairman was running out of options. The Palestinian movement faced imminent financial and institutional collapse in 1993. The oil states of the Gulf had severed all financial support to the PLO in retribution for Arafat's support of Saddam Hussein in the Gulf crisis. By December 1991 the PLO's budget had been halved. Thousands of fighters and employees were made redundant or went months without pay; by March 1993, up to one-third of all PLO personnel received no pay at all. The financial crisis led to charges of corruption and maladministration that split PLO ranks.[43] The PLO as a government in exile would not long survive the pressures. A peace deal with Israel stood the chance of opening new sources of financial support and would give the PLO a toehold in Palestine on which it could realize the elusive goal of a two-state solution.

The Oslo Accords offered the Palestinians little more than a toe-hold. The deal provided for a provisional Palestinian authority over the Gaza Strip and an enclave surrounding the West Bank town of Jericho. For many Palestinians these seemed small territorial gains for such important Palestinian concessions to Israel. Arafat confided his strategy to Hanan Ashrawi shortly before the Oslo Accords were announced: "I will get full withdrawal from Gaza and Jericho as the first step of disengagement, and there I will exercise sovereignty. I want Jericho because it will get me to Jerusalem and link up Gaza with the West Bank." Ashrawi looked unconvinced. "Trust me, we will soon have our own telephone country code, stamps, and television station. This will be the beginning of the Palestinian state."[44]

The "Gaza-Jericho First" plan became a reality with the signing of the Declaration of Principles on the White House lawn on September 13, 1993. Before a global television audience, Yitzhak Rabin overcame his reluctance and shook Yasser Arafat's hand, sealing the deal. "All Arab television stations carried the ceremony live," Abu Ala recalled. "Many people around the Arab world could scarcely believe what was happening."[45]

The PLO and Israel had agreed to what was effectively a partition plan for Palestine. The document called for the withdrawal of Israeli military administration from Jericho and the Gaza Strip and its replacement with a Palestinian civil administration for a five-year interim period. It also provided for the creation of an elected council so that the people of Palestine would be governed "according to democratic principles." The Palestinian Authority would gain control over education and culture, health, social welfare, taxation, and tourism. Palestinian police would provide security for the areas under Palestinian control.

The agreement deferred discussion of the most controversial issues. The future of Jerusalem, the rights of refugees, the status of settlements, borders, and security arrangements were all to be addressed in final status negotiations set to begin three years into the interim period. The Palestinians expected more from the permanent settlement than the Israelis were likely to concede: an independent Palestinian state in the whole of the West Bank and Gaza Strip, with East Jerusalem as its capital. The Israelis anticipated a disengagement from unessential Arab territory leading to a demilitarized Palestinian entity. Leaving such fundamental disagreement to future negotiations, the Israeli Knesset ratified the Declaration of Principles with a comfortable majority, and the eighty-member Palestinian Central Council gave its overwhelming approval (sixty-three in favor, eight opposed, with nine abstentions) on October 11.

By May 1994 the technical details surrounding the withdrawal of Israeli troops and the establishment of Palestinian rule in Gaza and Jericho had been ironed out. Yasser Arafat made his triumphant return to Gaza to oversee the running of the Palestinian Authority on July 1. In September, Arafat and Rabin returned to Washington to sign the Israeli-Palestinian Interim Agreement on the West Bank and the Gaza Strip, known as Oslo II. Middle Eastern politics had entered the Oslo Era.

The Oslo Accords gained Israel unprecedented acceptance in the Arab world. Once the Palestinians had struck a unilateral deal with the Israelis, the other Arab countries felt free to pursue their own interests toward the Jewish state without risking accusations of betraying the Palestinian cause. For the most part, the Arab world had grown weary of the Arab-Israel conflict and was pragmatic in its views of Israel. The Jordanians were the first to respond to the new realities.

Once the Oslo Accords had been announced, the Jordanians did not hesitate. King Hussein saw peace with Israel as the best way for Jordan to break from the isolation it had suffered since the Iraqi invasion of Kuwait. King Hussein also believed that Jordan would be rewarded for making peace by substantial U.S. aid and international investment into his country. The day after the White House signing of the Declaration of Principles, representatives of Israel and Jordan met in the offices of the U.S. State Department to sign an agenda for peace that the two sides had worked out over the course of bilateral negotiations in Madrid.

On July 25, 1994, King Hussein and Prime Minister Rabin were invited back to Washington to sign a preliminary peace agreement, ending the belligerency between the two states, agreeing to settle all territorial issues in accordance with UN Security Council Resolutions 242 and 338, and recognizing a special role for the Hashemite monarchy in the Muslim holy places of Jerusalem. The final Jordan-Israel peace treaty was signed on the border between the two countries in the Araba Desert on October 26, 1994. Jordan became the second Arab state after Egypt to exchange ambassadors and normalize relations with the Jewish state.

The deals with the PLO and Jordan paved the way for other Arab governments to establish ties with Israel. In October 1994, Morocco and Israel agreed to open liaison offices in each other's capital, and Tunisia followed suit in January 1996. Both countries have significant Jewish minority communities with long-standing ties to Israel. Mauritania, a member state of the Arab League in northwest Africa, established formal relations with Israel and exchanged ambassadors in November 1999. Two of the Arab Gulf states established trade offices with Israel—the Sultanate of Oman, in January 1996; and Qatar in April of the same year. Confounding those who had long argued that the Arab world could never live in peace with the Jewish state, the Oslo Era demonstrated widespread Arab acceptance of Israel from North Africa through the Gulf.

Yet the Oslo process continued to face strong opposition in some quarters— nowhere more intensely than in Israel and the occupied Palestinian territories. Extremists from both Israel and the Palestinian territories resorted to violence in a bid to derail the peace agreements. Hamas and Islamic Jihad claimed responsibility for a number of lethal attacks on Israelis in the immediate aftermath of the signing of the Declaration of Principles in September 1993. Israeli extremists stepped up their own attacks on Palestinians as well. In February 1994 Baruch Goldstein entered the Ibrahimi Mosque in Hebron dressed in his Israeli army reserves uniform and opened fire on the worshipers gathered for dawn prayers, killing 29 and wounding 150 before being overwhelmed and killed by survivors of the attack. Goldstein was a medical doctor and resident of Kiryat Arba, a militant settlement neighboring Hebron that posthumously honored Goldstein for his act of mass murder with a graveside plaque reading: "To the holy Baruch Goldstein, who gave his life for the Jewish people, the Torah and the nation of Israel."

The gulf between Palestinian and Israeli extremists was growing wider. Outrage over the Hebron massacre led to an escalation of Palestinian attacks and an increase in suicide bombings designed to inflict maximum casualties. In April 1994, suicide bombings on buses in Afula and Hadera claimed thirteen lives, and twenty-two people were killed by a suicide attack on a bus in Tel Aviv in October 1994. The Israelis responded by assassinating Islamist leaders. Israeli agents killed Islamic Jihad leader Fathi Shiqaqi in Malta in October 1995 and used a booby-trapped mobile phone to kill Hamas leader Yahya 'Ayyash in January 1996. Israelis and Palestinians found themselves locked in a cycle of violence and retaliation that gravely undermined confidence in the Oslo process.

One murder presaged the end of the Oslo process. On November 4, 1995, Yitzhak Rabin addressed a mass peace rally in downtown Tel Aviv. The Israeli premier was visibly moved by the sea of faces 150,000-strong, united by their common belief in Palestinian-Israeli peace. "This rally must send a message to the Israeli public, to the Jews of the world, to the multitudes in the Arab lands and in the world at large, that the nation of Israel wants peace, support[s] peace," Rabin intoned, "and for this I thank you."[46] Rabin then led the crowd in a peace song before taking his leave.

One man came to the rally to put an end to the peace process. As Rabin was escorted from the podium back to his car, an Israeli law student named Yigal Amir broke through a gap in the prime minister's security cordon and shot him dead. In his trial, Amir openly confessed to the assassination, explaining that he had killed Rabin to put a stop to the peace process. Convinced of the Jewish people's divine right to the whole of the Land of Israel, Amir believed it his duty as a religious Jew to prevent any exchange of land for peace. In an instant, a process that had withstood many acts of violence between Palestinians and Israelis fell to a single act of violence between Israelis.

Rabin was the indispensable man for the Oslo process. His immediate successor as prime minister was his old rival Shimon Peres. Though an architect of Oslo, Peres did not enjoy the same degree of public confidence as Rabin. The Israeli voters did not place the trust in Peres that an enduring land-for-peace settlement required.

Deemed weak on security, Peres tried to confound his critics by launching a military campaign against Hizbullah in retaliation for its attacks on Israeli positions in South Lebanon and missile attacks on northern Israel. The April 1996 initiative, Operation Grapes of Wrath, confirmed voters' doubts about Peres's judgment on security issues. The massive incursion into Lebanon displaced 400,000 Lebanese civilians and provoked widespread international condemnation when the Israeli air force bombed a UN base in the southern Lebanese village of Qana, killing 102 refugees who were seeking shelter from the assault. The operation was brought to an ignominious end by American mediation, with no visible benefit to Israel's security. Peres was punished by voters in the May 1996 election, when Likud leader Benjamin Netanyahu won the premiership by the slenderest of margins.

Netanyahu's election set Israel on a collision course with its Oslo commitments. Netanyahu and his party had consistently opposed the principle of exchanging land for peace. Although he did succumb to American pressure to conclude a redeployment scheme from the West Bank town of Hebron, Netanyahu's minor land for peace deal left Israel in full control of more than 71 percent of the West Bank, and in control of security over 23 percent of the other territories. This was a far cry from the 90 percent transfer the Palestinians expected from the Oslo II agreement.

In his battle for Jerusalem, Netanyahu used the settlement movement to create unalterable facts on the ground. He commissioned 6,500 housing units on Jabal Abu Ghunaym to create a new settlement called Har Homa, which would complete the encirclement of Arab East Jerusalem with Israeli settlements. By encircling Jerusalem with Jewish settlements, Netanyahu intended to preempt any pressure to surrender the Arab parts of the city occupied in June 1967 to the Palestinian Authority. Har Homa was the latest of an escalating settlement policy that, more than any other factor, led to the collapse in Palestinian confidence in the Oslo process.

After three years in office, Netanyahu lost the confidence of his own party and, dogged by corruption scandals, was forced to call for new elections in May 1999. He was defeated, and the Labor Party returned to power under another retired general, Ehud Barak. One of Barak's campaign promises had been to end Israel's occupation of South Lebanon and withdraw all Israeli troops within one year if elected. The occupation of South Lebanon had grown increasingly unpopular in Israel, as persistent attacks by Hizbullah inflicted regular casualties on Israeli forces.

Having won a landslide victory over Netanyahu, Barak made the Lebanon withdrawal one of his first priorities. However, efforts to effect a smooth transfer of power from the departing Israeli forces to their local proxies of the South Lebanon army collapsed as the collaborators surrendered to Hizbullah units. Israel's unilateral withdrawal degenerated into an unseemly retreat under fire, leaving Hizbullah to claim victory in its eighteen-year campaign to drive the Israelis from Lebanon. Israel's top brass chafed, eagerly awaiting the next opportunity to settle the score with the Shiite militia.

The opportunity for future conflict was preserved in a territorial anomaly. Israel withdrew from all of Lebanon except the disputed "Shiba' Farms" enclave, a strip of land 22 square kilometers (8 square miles) in area along Lebanon's frontier with the occupied Golan Heights. Israel claims to this day that it is occupied Syrian territory, whereas Syria and Lebanon insist it is Lebanese territory. Hizbullah takes Shiba' Farms as a pretext for continuing its armed resistance against Israeli occupation of Lebanese territory.

Once out of Lebanon, Prime Minister Barak resumed negotiations with the PLO. In view of Israel's actions under Netanyahu, there was little trust or goodwill between the two sides. Yasser Arafat accused the Israelis of failing to meet their treaty obligations under the Oslo Accords and pressed Barak to respect unfulfilled commitments under the interim agreements. Barak, in comparison, wanted to proceed directly to discuss a permanent settlement. The Israeli premier believed that negotiations with the Palestinians had been undermined through endless disputes over interim details, and he wanted to take advantage of the closing months of the Clinton presidency to secure a permanent settlement.

Bill Clinton invited Barak and Arafat to a summit meeting at the presidential retreat in Camp David, Maryland. The three leaders met for two weeks in July 2000,
and though bold new ideas were put on the table, the summit ended without any
substantive progress toward a settlement. A second summit was held in the Egyptian
resort of Taba in January 2001. There, the Israelis offered the most generous terms
yet tabled; even so, the Taba proposals still left too much of the proposed Palestinian
state under Israeli control to serve as a permanent settlement. The failure of the Camp
David and Taba summits led to bitter recriminations and finger pointing, as both
the American and the Israeli teams wrongly placed the blame for failure on Arafat
and the Palestinian delegation. The trust and goodwill necessary for Palestinian-Israeli
peacemaking had evaporated.

The Oslo framework had been flawed, but it brought Israel and the Arab world
closer to peace than at any point since the founding of the Jewish state in 1948. The
gains of Oslo were very significant. Israel and the PLO had overcome decades of
mutual hostility to exchange recognition and enter into meaningful negotiations toward a two-state solution. The Palestinian leadership left exile in Tunisia to begin
building its own state in the Palestinian territories. Israel broke its isolation within
the Middle East, establishing formal ties with a number of Arab countries for the
first time, and overcoming an Arab League economic boycott that had been in place
since 1948. These were important foundations upon which to build an enduring
peace.

Unfortunately, the process was inextricably linked to building confidence between
the two sides and to generating sufficient economic prosperity that Palestinians and
Israelis would be willing to make the difficult compromises necessary for a permanent settlement. Whereas the Oslo years were a period of economic growth for Israel,
the Palestinian economy suffered recession and stagnation. The World Bank
recorded a significant decline in living standards over the Oslo years and estimated
that one in four residents of the West Bank and Gaza had been reduced to poverty
by 2000. Unemployment rates reached 22 percent.[47] The decline in living standards
between 1993 and 2000 produced widespread disillusion with the Oslo process.

Israel's decision to expand the settlements was also a key factor in dooming the
Oslo accords. As far as the Palestinians were concerned, settlements were illegal in
international law and their continued expansion contravened the terms of the Oslo
II Accords.[48] Yet the Oslo years witnessed the greatest expansion of Israeli settlements
since 1967. The number of settlers in the West Bank and East Jerusalem rose from
247,000 in 1993 to 375,000 in 2000—a 52 percent increase.[49] Settlements were
built in areas Israel wanted to retain either because of their proximity to urban centers
within Israel or to crucial aquifers, providing control over scarce water resources in

the West Bank. Palestinians accused the Israelis of forsaking land-for-peace for a land grab, while the guarantor of the process, the United States, turned a blind eye.

The Palestinians expected nothing less of the Oslo process than an independent state on all of the territory of the West Bank and Gaza Strip with East Jerusalem as its capital. The Palestinians knew their position was supported by international law and believed it was reinforced by the demographic reality that the territories were almost exclusively inhabited by Palestinians. The PLO had come to recognize the state of Israel in the 78 percent of Palestine conquered in 1948, and the Palestinians held to their rights over the remaining 22 percent of the land. With so little space on which to build a viable Palestinian state, there was no room for further concessions.

The expansion of settlements contributed significantly to public anger at a process Palestinians believed failed to deliver statehood, security of property, or prosperity. That anger boiled over in a series of violent demonstrations that broke out in September 2000 and developed into a new popular uprising. Whereas the First Intifada (1987–1993) had been marked by civil disobedience and nonviolence, the second uprising was very violent indeed.

The outbreak of the Second Intifada followed a visit by Ariel Sharon, who had risen to lead the right-wing Likud Party, to East Jerusalem on September 28, 2000. At the Camp David summit, Prime Minister Ehud Barak had raised the possibility of relinquishing East Jerusalem to Palestinian control and for Jerusalem to serve as the capital of both Israel and Palestine. The proposal was enormously controversial in Israel, prompting some of the members of Barak's coalition to withdraw from the government in protest, which in turn required a new election.

For Sharon, Jerusalem was a vote winner. He chose to visit the Temple Mount in East Jerusalem to reinforce his party's claim to preserve Jerusalem as the undivided capital of Israel and to launch his campaign to unseat Barak as prime minister. The Temple Mount, known in Arabic as the Haram al-Sharif (Noble Sanctuary), was the site of Judaism's Second Temple, destroyed by the Romans in A.D. 70, and, since the seventh century, home to the Aqsa Mosque, Islam's third-holiest site after Mecca and Medina. Because of its significance to both Judaism and Islam, the Temple Mount is politically charged territory.

Sharon arrived in Arab East Jerusalem on September 28, 2000, with an escort of 1,500 armed police and toured the Haram al-Sharif. In his comments to the press pack that followed the Likud leader, Sharon asserted his commitment to preserve Israeli rule over all of Jerusalem. A group of Palestinian dignitaries, on hand to protest Sharon's presence, were dispersed by Sharon's security detachment. Television cameras captured Israeli police rough-handling the Aqsa Mosque's highest-ranking Muslim cleric. "As chance would have it, his turban, a symbol of his exalted spiritual status, got knocked off his head and tumbled into the dust," Sari Nusseibeh recalled. "Viewers saw the highest Muslim cleric of this highly charged Muslim site standing bareheaded." This insult to a respected Muslim official in Islam's third holiest site was enough to provoke a massive turnout the next day for Friday prayers in the Haram. "Armed and nervous [Israeli] border police marched into the Old City by the hundreds, while hundreds of thousands of Muslims poured through the gates from neighborhoods and villages."

Prayers were conducted without an incident, but as the angry crowd withdrew from the mosque a violent demonstration erupted. Teenagers threw stones from the Haram complex onto Israeli soldiers posted to the Western Wall below. The Israeli border police stormed the Haram complex while soldiers opened fire on the pro- testers. Within minutes, eight rioters were shot dead and dozens fell wounded. "The 'Al-Aqsa intifada' had begun," Sari Nusseibeh recorded.[50]

The deterioration in public order played to Sharon's advantage, given his repu- tation for being tough on security, and he swept to power in February 2001. Israel's bellicose new prime minister was more interested in land than peace, and his election only exacerbated volatility between Israelis and Palestinians. At the start of a new millennium, the Middle East was further from peace than ever.

As the twentieth century came to a close, the Arab world witnessed a number of important transitions. Three leaders who had been pillars of Arab politics for decades died and were succeeded by their sons. The Middle East had been static under a group of long-term rulers. The successions brought a new generation to power, raising hopes for reforms and change. Yet the fact that both monarchies and republics tended to single-family rule weighed against substantial changes.

On February 7, 1999, King Hussein of Jordan died after a prolonged battle with cancer. With nearly forty-seven years on the throne, he was the longest-serving Arab ruler of his generation. Celebrated at home and abroad as a peacemaker, Hussein caused turmoil in his family and country with a last-minute change in his choice of successor. Hussein's brother Hassan had served as crown prince since 1965. With no warning, Hussein relieved Hassan of his duties and named his eldest son, Ab- dullah, as his heir and successor less than two weeks before his death. Not only was Abdullah relatively young—he had just turned thirty-seven—but he had spent his entire career in the military, with little preparation to rule. Worse yet was King Hus- sein's handling of the change in succession. The dying monarch published a long and angry letter to Prince Hassan in the Jordanian press that was nothing less than a character assassination of his younger brother. Many close to the king explained the letter as a cruel but necessary measure to ensure that Hassan could never mount a challenge to the change in succession. The Jordanians experienced two seismic shocks of the change in succession and the death of their long-ruling monarch within two weeks. Many feared for the future of their precarious country, left in young and inexperienced hands.

Five months later, on July 23, 1999, King Hassan II of Morocco died, ending thirty-eight years on the throne. He was succeeded by his son, Mohammed VI, who was only thirty-six and, like King Abdullah II of Jordan, represented a new generation of Arab leaders. He had trained in politics and law and had spent time in Brussels to familiarize himself with the institutions of the European Union, and his father had been expanding his official duties in the years before his succession. Even so, he remained an unknown quantity to most people at home and abroad, and all were left to wonder how the new king would strike the balance between continuation of his father's policies and making his own mark on the kingdom.

Dynastic succession was not confined to the Arab monarchies. On June 10, 2000, Syria's President Hafiz al-Asad died after nearly thirty years in power. The elder Asad had been grooming his son Basil to succeed him until Basil's untimely death in a car accident in 1994. The grieving president summoned his younger son, Bashar, interrupting Bashar's medical studies in ophthalmology in London, to prepare him for the succession. Bashar al-Asad entered the military academy in Syria and saw his official duties expanded in the last six years of his father's life. Bashar assumed office at age thirty-four on the promise of reform. Though many in Syria expected the new president to face serious challenges from within the political establishment, and from the many enemies his father had created in three decades of authoritarian rule, the succession from the strong man of Damascus to his novice son passed without incident.

Other aging leaders around the Arab world were grooming their sons for succession. In Iraq, Saddam Hussein had originally promoted his son Uday as heir apparent. Uday headed a television station and a newspaper in Iraq. Notorious for his homicidal cruelty, Uday Hussein was critically wounded in an assassination attempt in 1996 that left a bullet lodged in his spine. As the limits of Uday's recovery became apparent, Saddam Hussein began to promote his second son, Qusay, for the leadership role. The leader of Libya, Muammar al-Qadhafi, was rumored to be preparing his sons to inherit power. And in Egypt, Husni Mubarak was promoting his son Gamal and refusing to name a vice president, leading many to assume Gamal would in time assume the presidency.

The most significant succession of 2000, however, took place in the United States. Pundits in the Arab world made jokes at America's expense as the U.S. Supreme Court awarded an Electoral College victory to George W. Bush, son of former president George H. W. Bush. The fact that the popular vote had slightly favored Bush's

Democratic opponent Al Gore—and that the outcome hinged on faulty ballots and contested recounts in the state of Florida, where Bush's brother was governor— suggested the Americans were no less dynastic than the Arabs.

In fact, most Arab observers celebrated the victory of George W. Bush in 2000. They saw the Bush family as Texas oil men with good ties to the Arab world. The fact that Al Gore had chosen Senator Joe Lieberman of Connecticut as his vice presidential running mate, the first Jewish candidate on a major U.S. political party presidential ticket, led many in the Arab world to assume that the Democrats would be yet more pro-Israel than the Republicans. And they placed their trust in Bush.

The new President Bush took little interest in the Middle East. He was not a foreign affairs president, and his priorities lay elsewhere. One week before his inauguration, Bush had a meeting with the Director of Central Intelligence, George Tenet. As part of his intelligence briefing, Tenet presented the president-elect with the three top threats facing the United States: weapons of mass destruction (WMD), Osama bin Ladin, and the emergence of China as a military and economic power.[51]

Though a number of Arab states were believed to have dangerous weapons programs, including Libya and Syria, the international community was most concerned with Iraq's WMD. The government of Iraq had been under sustained pressure by the United Nations and the international community to surrender its weapons of mass destruction since the passage of UN Security Council Resolution 687 in April 1991. The resolution called for the destruction of all chemical, nuclear, and biological weapons, as well as all ballistic missiles capable of reaching beyond 150 kilometers (93 miles). Saddam Hussein, suspecting the Americans of using the weapons inspection regime as a means to subvert his government, obstructed the work of UN weapons inspectors, who withdrew from Iraq in 1998.

The Clinton administration was determined to topple the government of Saddam Hussein. They upheld stringent trade sanctions on Iraq that had been in place since the invasion of Kuwait, and had caused a humanitarian crisis without weakening Hussein's grip on government. They maintained strict control over Iraqi airspace by regular British and American air patrols over northern and southern Iraq. In 1998, the Clinton administration introduced legislation—the Iraq Liberation Act— that committed U.S. government funds to support regime change in Iraq. And in December, 1998, after UN weapons inspectors had left Iraq, President Clinton authorized a four-day bombing campaign to "degrade" Iraq's capacity to produce and use weapons of mass destruction.

George W. Bush preserved Clinton's policies to contain Iraq and the WMD threat it was believed to pose to the United States.

The American intelligence community was far more concerned about the deepening conflict with Osama bin Ladin's al-Qaida network than any threat from Iraq.

Bin Ladin had invested a great deal of time and energy in al-Qaida's stated goals of driving the United States out of Saudi Arabia and the Muslim world more broadly. In August 1998 the U.S. embassies in Tanzania and Kenya were targeted by simultaneous suicide bombings that left over 220 dead and hundreds more wounded—nearly all of them local citizens (only twelve of the fatalities were American citizens). For his role in the embassy bombings, Bin Ladin was placed on the FBI list of ten most wanted criminals. In October 2000, a suicide bomb attack on the USS *Cole* in the Yemeni port of Aden left seventeen American sailors dead and thirty-nine wounded.

Al-Qaida's ability to strike at vulnerable points in America's armor had raised real concerns in White House circles. CIA Director Tenet warned Bush in January 2001 that Bin Ladin and his network posed a "tremendous threat" to the U.S. that was "immediate." However, unlike Saddam Hussein in Iraq, Bin Ladin was a mobile and elusive threat. It was not clear what policy measures the president might authorize to address the Bin Ladin threat.

Bush entered the Oval Office convinced that the threat of Iraqi WMD had been contained, and seems not to have been particularly concerned by the terror threat posed by Bin Ladin and his network. In his first nine months in office Bush made China his top priority.

Extraordinary events on September 11, 2001, would change Bush's priorities, opening a period of the greatest American engagement with the Middle East in its modern history. It would also prove the moment of greatest tension in modern Arab history.

CHAPTER 15

The Arabs in the Twenty-First Century

For many in the Arab world, the opening decades of the third millennium felt like a century in their own right. In the previous century, the major turning points occurred once in a lifetime: World War I from 1914 to 1918, marking the end of the Ottoman age and the introduction of the modern state system under European imperialism; the Palestine War in 1948, initiating both the Arab-Israeli conflict and the Cold War in the Middle East; and the 1991 Gulf War, ushering in the end of the Cold War and a new era of American hegemony.

The new millennium has already witnessed two transformative moments in the Middle East: the September 11, 2001, attacks, initiating an American-led war on terror, and the Arab Spring revolutions of 2011. These two milestones have come to define the Middle East in the twenty-first century. We are living with their consequences still. Between the pressures of the war on terror and the Arab Spring, the claim that the years since September 11, 2001, have been the worst in modern Arab history would be no exaggeration.

On the morning of Tuesday, September 11, 2001, terrorist teams commandeered four jetliners departing from airports in Boston, Washington, D.C., and Newark, New Jersey. Within forty minutes, they had flown two aircraft into the Twin Towers of Manhattan's World Trade Center and a third into the Pentagon, in precisely planned suicide attacks. A fourth jet, believed to have been intended for the U.S. Capitol or the White House, crashed in a field in Pennsylvania. In all, besides the nineteen hijackers, some 2,974 people perished in the four attacks: 2,603 in the World Trade Center, 125 in the Pentagon, and all 246 passengers and crew on the four planes.

The terrorists gave no warning and made no demands. They aimed to inflict maximum damage on the United States and to set change in motion. Though no organization claimed credit for the attacks, the U.S. intelligence services suspected Osama bin Ladin's al-Qaida group from the outset. Within days of 9/11, the Federal Bureau of Investigation had identified the nineteen hijackers. All were Muslim Arab men—fifteen from Saudi Arabia, two from the United Arab Emirates, one from Egypt, and one from Lebanon—with connections to al-Qaida. We can only surmise from subsequent statements by that organization what kinds of changes the suicide hijackers had in mind: to drive America from the Muslim world and to destabilize pro-Western regimes there and replace them with an Islamic state.

The United States responded to the worst attack on American soil since the Japanese raid on Pearl Harbor in 1941 by declaring war on a largely unknown enemy. In a televised address to a joint session of Congress on September 20, 2001, President George W. Bush declared a "war on terror" beginning with al-Qaida and continuing "until every terrorist group of global reach has been found, stopped and defeated." He prepared Americans for a long and unconventional conflict and promised them that America would prevail.

The September 11 attacks and the war on terror placed the United States and the Arab world on a collision course. Many—certainly not all, but many—in the Arab world were glad to see America suffer. To Arab observers, the United States seemed indifferent to Arab suffering—the plight of Palestinians under Israeli occupation or of Iraqis under a decade of stringent sanctions. In his public pronouncements, Osama bin Ladin played on this Arab anger. "What the United States tastes today is a very small thing compared to what we have tasted for tens of years," bin Ladin claimed in October 2001. "Our nation has been tasting this humiliation and contempt for more than 80 years."[1]

Bin Ladin's statements from his clandestine Afghan mountain stronghold added greatly to Arab-American tensions. Admiration for the al-Qaida leader was widespread throughout the Arab and Muslim world. People were impressed by al-Qaida's ingenuity in striking such a devastating blow against the United States on its own soil. Bin Ladin became an overnight cult symbol, the stencil of his face an icon of Islamic resistance to American domination. Americans found such views incomprehensible and reviled bin Ladin as a figure of unqualified evil.

Frightened, confused, and extremely angry after the September 11 attacks, the American people felt threatened at home and unsafe abroad. They demanded that their government strike back swiftly and decisively against their enemies. The Bush administration responded with covert action against jihadi terror networks and by taking America into two wars of choice that confirmed the impression in the Arab world that the war on terror was a war against Islam.

America's war in Afghanistan began on October 7, 2001, backed by a UN-sanctioned and North Atlantic Treaty Organization (NATO)–supported coalition. Its aims were to topple the rigid Islamist Taliban regime, which had hosted bin Ladin and his organization, and to arrest al-Qaida's leadership and destroy its training facilities in Afghanistan. The war was quick and largely successful—the Afghan Northern Alliance and its American allies drove the Taliban from the capital, Kabul, by mid-November, and the last Taliban and al-Qaida strongholds fell by mid-December 2001—and involved a minimum of U.S. ground troops.

Despite its operational successes, key failures marred the Afghanistan War and exacerbated the war on terror. Most immediately, Osama bin Ladin and Taliban leader Mullah Omar eluded capture. Both men escaped from Afghanistan to regroup their forces and resume their fight against the United States from neighboring Pakistan. For bin Ladin's supporters, survival against the Americans was victory enough.

Other al-Qaida members, captured in the course of the Afghanistan War, were designated "enemy combatants" and denied both their rights as prisoners of war under the Geneva Conventions and due process under the U.S. legal system. They were incarcerated in an extraterritorial U.S. military facility on Cuba known as the Guantánamo Bay Detention Camp. Beginning in October 2001, nearly 800 detainees would be sent to Guantánamo, all of them Muslim. Over the years, most of the detainees have been released without charge—by January 2017 the number was down to forty-two—and returned home to tell of their experiences. Ranging from humiliation to torture, the mistreatment of Guantánamo detainees provoked international condemnation and outrage in the Arab world.

Within Afghanistan, the Americans worked with local leaders to create a new political structure for the war-torn country that had suffered over twenty years of conflict since the Soviet invasion in 1979. However, the Americans needed to invest a great deal in economic development and state-building to ensure the stability of President Hamid Karzai's new government. Instead, by 2002 the Bush administration had diverted its energies and resources to planning the Iraq War, leaving the fragile Afghan state vulnerable to reconquest by the Taliban. As a result, a war that began in October 2001 with a handful of foreign ground forces expanded into a major conflict involving over 120,000 Western troops fighting the Taliban at its peak in 2011. The Americans and their coalition allies only declared their combat operations at an end in December 2014, by which time over 100,000 civilians had been killed in the fighting and millions displaced. The Afghan people, innocent of al-Qaida's crimes, paid a heavy price for 9/11.

Most Arab states were uncomfortable with an expanded U.S. military presence in the Muslim world. Their lukewarm support for America's war on terror made the

United States doubt a number of its longtime allies in the region—none more so than Saudi Arabia. The fact that bin Ladin and fifteen of the suicide hijackers in the September 11 attacks were Saudi citizens and that private Saudi funds had bankrolled al-Qaida only worsened relations between the Saudis and the Americans. Other countries came under new scrutiny as well. Washington saw Egypt as soft on terror, labeled Iran and Iraq as part of an "axis of evil," and moved Syria to the top of its list of countries supporting terrorism.

The Arab states found themselves under irreconcilable pressures after 9/11. If they opposed America's war on terror, they risked sanctions that might range from economic isolation to outright calls for regime change by the world's sole superpower. If they took America's side, they opened their own territories to the threat of attacks by local jihadi cells inspired by bin Ladin's example. Between May and November 2003, multiple bomb attacks by domestic Islamists rocked cities in Saudi Arabia, Morocco, and Turkey, leaving 125 dead and nearly 1,000 wounded. In November 2005, coordinated bombs ripped apart three hotels in Amman, Jordan, killing fifty-seven and wounding hundreds—nearly all of them Jordanians. The Arab world faced tremendously difficult choices as it managed its relations with the United States.

The same pressures that drove America and the Arabs apart drew Israel and America closer. Prime Minister Ariel Sharon persuaded President George W. Bush that the United States and Israel faced a common war on terror. The Second Intifada, which erupted in September 2000, had grown increasingly violent by the time of the 9/11 attacks. The use of suicide bombings by Islamist groups to target Israeli civilians convinced President Bush that the United States and the Jewish state were fighting the same enemy. The United States then turned a blind eye to Israeli actions against both its Islamist foes—Islamic Jihad and Hamas in Palestine and Hizbullah in Lebanon—and the internationally recognized Palestinian Authority. Israel took full advantage of American complacency to unleash disproportionate attacks against the Palestinian government and society that heightened tensions in the Arab world enormously.

In June 2002, Prime Minister Sharon ordered the reoccupation of the West Bank. Though he justified the measure in terms of assuring Israel's security from terror attacks, Sharon clearly intended to isolate Yasser Arafat and weaken the Palestinian Authority. As Israeli forces seized Palestinian cities under self-rule since the Oslo Accords—Bethlehem, Jenin, Ramallah, Nablus, Tulkarm, and Qalqiliya—they stepped up attacks against the Palestinian resistance. In total, some 3,200 Palestinians and 950 Israelis met violent deaths in the course of the Second Intifada (September 2000–February 2005).[2]

As the Israeli military struggled to contain the Second Intifada, the Sharon government exacerbated tensions with the Palestinians through measures designed to seize more territory in the West Bank. Israeli settlements expanded in the Occupied Territories. And in June 2002 the Israeli government began construction of a 720-

kilometer (450-mile) wall, ostensibly to insulate Israel from Palestinian terror attacks. The Separation Barrier (dubbed the Apartheid Wall by Palestinians) cuts a path deep into the West Bank and represents a de facto annexation of nearly 9 percent of the Palestinian territory in the West Bank, adversely affecting the lives and livelihoods of nearly 500,000 Palestinians.[3]

Israel's repression of the Second Intifada proved a clear liability to America's war on terror. The images of Palestinian suffering, broadcast live via Arab satellite television, provoked fury across the Middle East. Israeli actions and U.S. inaction served as valuable recruiting devices for al-Qaida and other terrorist organizations. The Bush administration found it necessary to engage in Palestinian-Israeli peacemaking to try to defuse regional tensions.

George W. Bush became the first American president to support a two-state solution to the Palestinian-Israeli conflict. In a major White House address delivered on June 24, 2002, Bush held out a vision of a Palestinian state "living side by side in peace and security" with Israel. However, the Bush vision required the Palestinians to "elect new leaders, leaders not compromised by terror"—a deliberate swipe at the democratically elected president of the Palestinian Authority, Yasser Arafat.

To advance the goal of securing a two-state solution to the Palestinian-Israeli conflict, the Bush administration entered into partnership with Russia, the European Union, and the United Nations. This new grouping, known as the Middle East Quartet, sought to shape an international consensus on resolving the conflict. Crucially, Palestinians saw the Quartet as a way to counterbalance America's support for Israel with states and organizations historically more sympathetic to Palestinian aspirations—Russia and the United Nations in particular.

In April 2003, the Quartet published a "road map to peace in the Middle East" to give direction to the Bush vision of a two-state solution. The road map laid out an ambitious three-phase plan that called for an end to violence between Palestinians and Israelis, leading to the creation of a provisional Palestinian state within temporary borders, followed by a third and final stage in which the Israelis and Palestinians would resolve the most complex issues of borders, the future of Jerusalem, the status of refugees, and the future of Israeli settlements in the West Bank and Gaza Strip. By the end of 2005 the states of Israel and Palestine were to exchange recognition and declare their conflict at an end.

Yet people in the Arab world remained skeptical about America's intentions and the road map's likelihood of leading to a just and enduring peace between Israel and the Palestinians. For in the months between Bush's speech and the publication of the road map, the United States had invaded Iraq in March 2003.

The United States presented its case against Iraq in terms of the global war on terror. The Bush administration alleged that Saddam Hussein's government had amassed a large arsenal of weapons of mass destruction, including chemical and biological agents, and precursors for a nuclear weapon. British prime minister Tony Blair echoed Bush's concerns and aligned the United Kingdom with America's stance on Iraq. The White House also suggested that Hussein's government had connections to Osama bin Ladin's al-Qaida that might see weapons of mass destruction transferred to the terror organization. The Bush administration argued for a preemptive war against Iraq to prevent the most dangerous weapons from falling into the hands of the most dangerous terrorists.[4]

The Arab world was unconvinced by President Bush's accusations. Arab governments believed—erroneously—that Saddam Hussein probably did hold an arsenal of chemical and biological agents. After all, he had used chemical weapons against both the Iranians and the Iraqi Kurds in the 1980s. Even the United Nations' top weapons inspector, Dr. Hans Blix, believed Iraq held such weapons. However, the Arab states knew that Iraq had played no role in the September 11 attacks and strongly doubted any connection between the Islamist al-Qaida movement and the secular Iraqi Ba'th party. Saddam Hussein headed precisely the type of government that Osama bin Ladin sought to overturn. The Arab world simply did not accept what the Bush administration was saying and suspected the United States of ulterior motives—of coveting Iraq's oil and seeking to extend its domination over the oil-rich Persian Gulf.

The invasion of Iraq, which began on March 20, 2003, met with wide condemnation internationally and across the Arab world. The United States, seconded by Great Britain, had invaded an Arab state without provocation or UN sanction. Saddam Hussein remained defiant in the face of superior Western forces, and, as it had during the Gulf War in 1991, his stance generated widespread Arab public support. All twenty-two members of the Arab League except Kuwait supported a resolution condemning the invasion as a violation of the UN Charter and demanding a complete withdrawal of all U.S. and British troops from Iraqi soil on March 23. Yet no one seriously expected the Bush administration to pay heed to the concerns of the United Nations, let alone of the Arab world.

Though the Iraqis put up stiff resistance, superior British and American forces, enjoying unchallenged control of the skies over Iraq, completely overpowered them. On April 9, the Americans secured Baghdad, signaling the fall of Saddam Hussein's government within three weeks of the start of hostilities. The Iraqi people had mixed feelings, celebrating the overthrow of a reviled dictator while resenting the Americans and British for invading their country.

The overthrow of Hussein's government left the United States in control of Iraq. The Bush administration established a governing body called the Coalition Provisional Authority (CPA). Two early decisions by the CPA in May 2003 transformed the chaos of postwar Iraq into an armed insurgency against American rule. The first outlawed Saddam Hussein's Iraqi Ba'th party, barring former Ba'th members from public office. The second disbanded the 500,000-member Iraqi military and intelligence services. Taken together, these measures came to be known as "de-Ba'thification."

The American authorities pursued de-Ba'thification to purge Iraq of Saddam Hussein's malign influence. They took their inspiration from the denazification policies pursued by the Allied occupation authorities in Germany after World War II. They hoped by these measures to enjoy a free hand to build up a new, democratic Iraqi state that would respect human rights. In fact, the CPA had made a great number of well-armed men unemployed and stripped Iraq's Sunni Muslim political elites of any interest in cooperating with America's new democratic Iraq, which became increasingly dominated by the country's Shiite Muslim majority. An insurgency against the American occupation and sectarian conflict between Iraqi communities ensued.

Iraq quickly became a recruiting ground for anti-American and anti-Western activists. New organizations emerged, such as al-Qaida in Iraq, a jihadist group with only nominal ties to Osama bin Ladin's organization, which deployed suicide bombers against foreign and domestic targets. Al-Qaida in Iraq drove the United Nations to close its offices in Baghdad after targeted bombings killed the senior UN envoy to Iraq, Sergio Vieira de Mello, and over twenty of his staff on August 19, 2003. Westerners were taken hostage, and many were brutally murdered. Military patrols became the target of increasingly sophisticated attacks. A war with remarkably few British and American casualties gave way to an occupation in which the allies suffered heavy losses. By the final American withdrawal in 2011, the insurgents had killed nearly 4,500 Americans and over 170 Britons and wounded over 32,000 foreign soldiers.[5]

The spread of democracy was a recurrent theme in America's war on terror. President Bush and his neoconservative advisors believed that democratic values and participatory politics were incompatible with terrorism. A key advocate of these views was Deputy Secretary of Defense Paul Wolfowitz. In a speech to a foreign policy forum in California in May 2002, Wolfowitz asserted, "To win the war against terrorism . . . we must speak to the hundreds of millions of moderate and tolerant people in the Muslim world . . . who aspire to enjoy the blessings of freedom and democracy and free enterprise."[6] Secretary of State Colin Powell launched his own stillborn Middle East Partnership Initiative in December 2002 to bring "democracy and free markets" to the Middle East.[7] The Bush administration argued that a democratic Iraq would prove a beacon to the rest of the Arab states and set off a wave of democratization that would sweep the Arab world.

Iraq was already deeply divided by the time its citizens went to the polls in January 2005 to elect a national assembly to draft a new constitution. Composing between 50 and 60 percent of the total population of Iraq, the Shiites were the prime beneficiaries of the new democratic system and turned out to vote in strength, with Shiite areas reporting up to 80 percent turnout. The Kurds, a non-Arab ethnic group and a minority in Iraq as a whole, hold an outright majority in their own provinces and were yet more enthusiastic supporters of Iraq's new democratic system, with up to 90 percent turnout. The Sunni Arab population, the prime target of de-Ba'thification, largely boycotted elections. Turnout among Sunnis in Mosul was as low as 10 percent.[8]

The December 2005 elections, held under the terms of the new constitution, confirmed the new political realities in Iraq. The United Iraqi Alliance, the leading Shiite bloc, secured a plurality of 128 seats in the 275-seat national assembly. The Kurdish list emerged as the second largest bloc with fifty-three seats. The Iraqi Accord Front, a coalition of Sunni politicians, came in third with forty-four seats. The Kurdish leader Jalal Talabani was named president of Iraq, and the Shiite politician Nouri al-Maliki was appointed prime minister. After centuries of dominating Iraqi politics, the Sunni Arab elites were out of power and, given their relative demographic weight, would never return through the ballot box. Where they couldn't win by democratic means, Sunni militants turned to violence. Insurgent groups shifted their target from the occupation forces to their Shiite fellow citizens as Iraq descended into a devastating sectarian conflict.

The Iraqi security forces and the American military were powerless to contain the communal violence. Suicide bombers wrought daily carnage in the markets and mosques of Iraq's cities. Satellite TV broadcast graphic images of death and devastation across the Arab world. Though the casualty figures for Iraqi civilians since the invasion are widely disputed, the Iraqi government estimated that between 100,000 and 150,000 civilians perished between 2003 and 2011. As in Afghanistan, Iraqi civilians bore the true cost of the war on terror, their security, values, and way of life shattered by the invasion and its violent aftermath.[9]

The rise of the Shiites to power in Iraq after the fall of Saddam Hussein also transformed the regional balance of power in the Arab world. Until 2003, Iraq stood as one of the most powerful Sunni Arab states and a buffer to contain the perceived threat of the Islamic Republic of Iran. After 2005, Iraq under its Shiite-led government came to be perceived as an ally of Iran. Neighboring Sunni states, led by Saudi Arabia and Jordan, spoke ominously of a "Shiite Crescent" extending from Iran through Iraq to Syria (an Iranian ally since 1980) and Lebanon, where the Shiite militias Amal and Hizbullah had come to play a dominant role in national politics. New tensions emerged between Sunnis and Shiites that would grow to destabilize the Arab world as a whole.

The Bush administration's initiatives to promote democracy met with no more success in the rest of the Arab world than they did in Iraq. Popular resentment of its neoconservative foreign policy made Islamist parties advocating resistance to America more attractive to voters than moderates seeking accommodation with the West. Elections in Lebanon in 2005 and in the Palestinian territories in 2006 demonstrated an inconvenient truth about democracy in the Arab world: in any free and fair election, those parties most hostile to the United States were most likely to win.

On November 11, 2004, Yasser Arafat, the historic leader of the Palestinian national struggle and besieged president of the Palestinian Authority, died of medical complications in a Paris hospital. The Bush administration insisted that, though the Palestinians mourned Arafat, his death opened opportunities for them to elect new leaders "not compromised by terror." On January 9, 2005, the Palestinians voted for a new president. Fatah leader Mahmoud Abbas won an outright majority of 63 percent to succeed Arafat. The Bush administration applauded the result and declared Abbas a man it could work with. Israeli prime minister Ariel Sharon, on the other hand, refused to deal with him.

In 2005, Sharon announced his intention to withdraw all Israeli troops and settlers from the Gaza Strip. Israel's position in Gaza was untenable, with thousands of soldiers providing security for 8,000 settlers within a hostile population of 1.4 million Palestinians. Withdrawal from Gaza was popular with the Israeli army and voters. It also allowed Sharon greater freedom to ignore the Road Map, claiming to be pursuing his own peace initiative with the Palestinians. Yet Sharon refused to negotiate with the Palestinian Authority to ensure a smooth handover in Gaza. As a result, when the Israelis completed their withdrawal in August 2005, they created a dangerous power vacuum in the strip and handed Hamas an important victory. The Islamist party naturally took credit for driving Israel from Gaza through its years of resistance.

The true extent of Hamas's gains only emerged in the January 2006 elections for the Palestinian Legislative Council (PLC). The two leading parties were Arafat's Fatah, under Mahmoud Abbas's leadership, and Hamas, led by Ismail Haniya. The press and policymakers in the West fully expected Hamas to gain strong support and reduce Fatah's majority in the PLC. However, the magnitude of Hamas's victory shocked Palestinians and foreign observers alike. Hamas gained an outright majority with 74 of the 132 seats in the PLC; Fatah managed to retain only 45 seats. The Palestinian territories, divided between the West Bank and the Gaza Strip, came under a divided authority, with a Fatah executive and a Hamas parliament. To further complicate matters, a party officially boycotted by the United States and the European Union as a terrorist organization, having won an election deemed free and fair by international monitors, formed the next government of Palestine. It was a shattering reversal for America's war on terror. And the Palestinian people would pay the price.

The new Hamas government of Prime Minister Haniya openly rejected the Quartet's policies. Haniya refused to recognize Israel, to end armed resistance, or to accept the terms of the Road Map. Consequently, the Quartet cut all assistance to the Palestinian Authority. Until Hamas proved willing to "renounce terror" in the West's terms, neither the European Union nor the United States would support a Hamas-led Palestinian Authority—even a democratically elected one.

In Lebanon, the Islamist Hizbullah party also proved its appeal to voters for its politics of resistance against Israel and the United States. Hizbullah's strength came as a surprise to the Bush administration, which upheld Lebanon as an example of citizens' successfully preserving their democratic rights—in this case from Syrian oppression.

The assassination of former Lebanese prime minister Rafik Hariri on February 14, 2005, stirred Lebanon's democracy movement to action. Having resigned his office just four months earlier in protest of Syrian interference in Lebanon's politics, Hariri was a marked man. Yet the intense violence of his murder shocked even the war-calloused Lebanese. Assassins detonated a one-ton car bomb as Hariri's motorcade passed through the waterfront hotel district on his daily drive home from the parliament. Twenty-one people died with Hariri—politicians, bodyguards, and drivers, along with innocent bystanders.

Hariri's son Saad led the nation in mourning and made clear his belief that Syria was responsible for his father's violent death. The assassination set off waves of mass demonstrations that brought politics in Lebanon to a standstill. On March 14, 1 million Lebanese descended on downtown Beirut to demand Syria's complete withdrawal from Lebanon. It was the first instance of the popular mass demonstrations that would come to be associated with the Arab Spring revolutions six years later. The movement met with the full support of the United States, which accused Syria of sponsoring terrorism. Under intense international pressure, the Syrian government agreed to withdraw its soldiers and intelligence forces from Lebanon after an occupation that had lasted nearly three decades. The last Syrian troops crossed out of Lebanon on April 26.

In May and June 2005, the Lebanese public voted to elect a new parliament. The Bush administration lauded the elections as a vindication of America's policies promoting democracy in the Arab world. The anti-Syrian coalition, headed by Saad Hariri, won 72 of the 128 seats in the parliament. However, the political wing of the Shiite militia Hizbullah won a solid bloc of fourteen parliamentary seats and, combined with a group of pro-Syrian parties, emerged as a powerful opposition force in Lebanese politics. Even in Lebanon, parties explicitly hostile to the United States fared well at the polls.

For Islamist parties, resistance against Israel paid political dividends. Indeed, so long as they persisted in striking boldly against the Jewish state, Hamas in Palestine and Hizbullah in Lebanon could count on broad-based political support. They also believed that fighting against Israel to liberate Muslim lands was a religious duty. In the summer of 2006, both parties escalated their attacks on Israel—with disastrous consequences for both the Gaza Strip and Lebanon.

On June 25, 2006, a group of Hamas activists crossed from Gaza to Israel through a tunnel near the Egyptian frontier and attacked an Israeli army post. They killed two soldiers and wounded four others before escaping back to Gaza with a young conscript named Gilad Shalit as their prisoner. On June 28 Israeli soldiers entered Gaza and the next day arrested sixty-four Hamas officials, including eight members of the Palestinian cabinet and twenty democratically elected members of the PLC. Hamas responded by firing homemade rockets into Israel, and the Israelis in turn deployed their air force to bomb Palestinian targets. Eleven Israelis and more than 400 Palestinians died before a cease-fire in November 2006.

Hizbullah's war with Israel provoked a massively disproportionate response against Lebanon. On July 12, 2006, a group of Hizbullah fighters crossed into Israel and attacked two jeeps patrolling the border with Lebanon. They killed three soldiers, wounded two, and took two others prisoner. This unprovoked attack set off a thirty-four-day conflict in which Israeli ground forces invaded South Lebanon. The Israeli air force bombed key infrastructure and leveled whole neighborhoods in the Shiite southern suburbs of Beirut, displacing an estimated 1 million civilians. Hizbullah fighters fought fierce battles with Israeli troops in the hills of South Lebanon and kept up a constant barrage of missiles fired into Israel, forcing thousands of Israelis to evacuate the conflict zone.

The Lebanese government turned to the United States for assistance. After all, the Bush administration had touted democratic Lebanon as an example to the Middle East and had given its full support to Lebanese demands for Syria to withdraw in 2005. Yet America was unwilling to intervene with the Israelis even to call for a cease-fire in 2006. Because Israel was fighting against Hizbullah, which the United States had branded a terrorist organization, the Bush administration refused to restrain its Israeli ally. In fact, the U.S. government resupplied the Israelis with laser-guided weapons and cluster bombs as the intensive bombing campaign against Lebanon depleted the Israeli arsenal. By the end of the thirty-four-day conflict on August 14, over 1,100 Lebanese and 43 Israeli civilians had died under the aerial bombardment. Among combatants, the United Nations estimated 500 Hizbullah militiamen killed, and the Israeli army reported 117 of its soldiers dead.

The summer conflicts in 2006 demonstrated the limits of America's support for Arab democracy and its unlimited support for Israel. In effect, the Bush administration would only recognize election results that brought pro-Western parties to power. And the United States would support any Israeli action, no matter how disproportionate, against parties it associated with terrorism. The very fact that America and Israel condemned Hamas and Hizbullah further strengthened the parties' domestic standing. Far from facing censure for provoking devastating wars with Israel, the Islamic resistance movements enjoyed even greater support at home and across the Arab world for standing up against Bush, Israel, and the U.S.-led war on terror.

With the election of Barack Obama in November 2008, the United States entered a new era of constructive engagement with the Arab and Islamic world. In his first 100 days, the new president initiated a number of policies intended to reduce the regional tensions generated by seven years of the war on terror. President Obama set in motion the reduction of the U.S. troop presence in Iraq. He signaled that the Palestinian-Israeli peace process was a first-term priority. He renewed engagement with states shunned by the Bush administration, such as Syria and Iran.

The clearest expression of this new policy of constructive engagement with the Arab and Islamic world came in Obama's address to Cairo University in June 2009: "I have come here to seek a new beginning between the United States and Muslims around the world, one based upon mutual interest and mutual respect," Obama told his attentive audience. "There must be a sustained effort to listen to each other; to learn from each other; to respect one another; and to seek common ground." While many in the Arab world reserved judgment, waiting to see if Obama's actions lived up to his rhetoric, his message nonetheless came as a welcome relief to a region that had suffered years of strain at the epicenter of the war on terror.

Though awarded the Nobel Peace Prize in 2009, Obama remained at war in the Muslim world throughout his eight years in office. While drawing down troop numbers in Iraq—the last American units departed Baghdad in December 2011—he stepped up the U.S. military presence in Afghanistan to peak at 100,000 and only declared an end of operations there in 2014, making Afghanistan (2001–2014) the longest war in America's history. Most controversially, Obama stepped up the use of lethal drone attacks in Pakistan, Somalia, Yemen, and Libya. Whereas President Bush had authorized some 50 drone strikes, killing 296 combatants and 195 civilians, Obama approved over 500 drone attacks that claimed the lives of 3,040 combatants and hundreds of civilians.[10] The most significant targeted killing authorized by the Obama White House came on May 2, 2011, when U.S. commandos shot Osama bin Ladin dead in his secret compound in Abbotabad, Pakistan, and buried his body at sea. After the 9/11 attacks President Bush had invoked the justice of the Wild West and claimed he wanted bin Ladin "dead or alive." The Nobel Peace laureate succeeded where the architect of the war on terror had failed.

The Arab world's response to bin Ladin's killing was remarkably muted, given the prominence the al-Qaida leader had attained in his conflict with the West. Events across the region in 2011 had eclipsed that conflict and the significance of the West. For, with the fall of Tunisian president Zine el-Abidine Ben Ali and Egyptian president Husni Mubarak, the Arab world had entered a transformative moment of hope and danger that came to be known in the West as the Arab Spring.

The revolutions in Tunisia and Egypt, in January and February 2011, created the Arab Spring. They provided a language and strategy of popular revolt that inspired copycat movements across the Arab world. The same slogans first deployed in Tunisia were repeated in Egypt, followed by Libya, Bahrain, Yemen, and Syria: the imperative "Go!" directed at autocratic rulers who had outlasted their utility and the ubiquitous "The people want the fall of the regime!" The strategy included mass mobilization via social networking websites that allowed organizers to circumvent security forces and enabled demonstrators to occupy central urban public spaces, like Tunis's Avenue Bourguiba and Cairo's Tahrir Square, and mount round-the-clock protests until the fall of the dictator. The size of the demonstrations gave Arab citizens the confidence to sustain their challenge against repressive autocrats. Protestors in capitals across the Arab world insisted they no longer feared their governments. The assumption was that every country that mounted an Arab Spring uprising could repeat the success achieved by protestors in Tunisia and Egypt.

The notion that all Arab states were homogeneous and that one revolutionary template would fit them all proved the fallacy of the Arab Spring. It soon became apparent that Muammar al-Qadhafi's Libya, with its near total absence of state institutions, differed completely from Bahrain, with its Sunni-Shiite sectarian issues, which differed again from Yemen with its long history of regionalism, which bore no resemblance to Syria under the minority rule of its Alawite community. Domestic constraints and intervention by regional powers led to very different outcomes in each of the six countries that experienced revolutions in 2011: counterrevolution, civil war, regional conflict, and the emergence of a transnational caliphate. What began as a liberation movement rapidly degenerated into the worst political and humanitarian crisis to afflict the Middle East in modern times.

Within weeks of the successful revolutions in Tunisia and Egypt, the forces of counterrevolution had turned back the Arab Spring in Bahrain.

Young Bahrainis followed developments in Tunisia and Egypt with mounting excitement. They interacted on Bahrain Online, a social media website that provided a virtual meeting place for the safe, anonymous exchange of political views. By 2011, Bahrain Online had hundreds of thousands of followers. On January 26, 2011, the day after Egyptians massed in Tahrir Square, a contributor to Bahrain Online posted a suggestion: "Let's choose a specific day to begin the popular revolution in Bahrain." The obvious choice, readers concurred, was February 14, a date associated with both heightened expectations and dashed hopes in the island kingdom.[11]

Ten years earlier, on February 14, 2001, the government of Bahrain had held a referendum on a National Action Charter to resolve years of political protest with the promise of reforms. The charter pledged to restore Bahrain's elected parliament, reinforce the country's 1973 constitution, and endow Bahrain with the higher level of democracy associated with a constitutional monarchy. Many in Bahrain took its approval by 98.4 percent of voters to demonstrate a high degree of unity between the kingdom's Shiite and Sunni communities.

The high hopes raised by the National Action Charter were betrayed exactly one year later. On February 14, 2002, the ruler, Shaykh Hamad bin Isa Al Khalifa (r. 1999–), approved by decree a repressive new constitution that established an appointed upper chamber and a virtually powerless elected chamber. The new constitution transformed the state of Bahrain into a monarchy, and its ruler became a king. The opposition condemned the move as a constitutional coup imposing the will of the ruling Al Khalifa family on the people.

Tensions built in Bahrain between 2002 and 2011. Though there are no official figures for the island kingdom's population by religion, the Shiites are widely believed to represent an outright majority of 60 percent or more, with the Sunnis accounting for the balance of the country's 600,000 citizens (over half of the 1.3 million population of Bahrain consists of foreigners). Many in Bahrain saw the new constitutional order as bringing disproportionate benefit to the ruling Sunni minority. Growing inequality and repression of political dissent engendered mounting opposition to the new monarchical regime.

By January 2011, the list of Bahraini dissidents' grievances was long: an unaccountable government that played on sectarianism to divide Bahrainis; corruption, the plunder of the nation's wealth by the ruling elite, and the expropriation of land; brutal repression of dissent, censorship, and constraints on free expression; and the use of foreign security forces against citizens (Shiites did not serve in the security forces). "Anger and frustration is boiling amongst us all," a contributor wrote in a post to Bahrain Online, as February 14 was declared a "day of rage" for popular protest of the ills of the regime. The organizers called themselves the February 14 Youth Movement.

Bahraini protestors took to the streets for the day of rage just two days after Husni Mubarak abdicated power in Egypt. Security forces fired tear gas and live gunfire to disperse the crowds, killing one demonstrator and wounding many more. The funeral for the fallen demonstrator the following day provoked renewed protests, which led to another death. The crowds began to march from surrounding suburbs and villages onto the capital city, Manama, toward a location designated by contributors to Bahrain Online as ideally placed to serve as Bahrain's Tahrir Square: the Pearl Roundabout.

The Pearl Roundabout was a monument created to mark the 1982 meeting of the Gulf Cooperation Council (GCC) hosted by Bahrain. The monument consisted of six arcing sails, one for each of the member states of the GCC (Bahrain, Kuwait, Oman, Qatar, Saudi Arabia, and the United Arab Emirates), upon whose mastheads rested a massive pearl that hearkened back to the country's pearl-diving economy from pre-oil times. Given the roundabout's accessibility, centrality, and proximity to villages neighboring Manama, Pearl was the natural meeting point for Bahrain's protestors.

The demonstrators flooded into Pearl Roundabout on February 15, shouting, "Peaceful! Peaceful!" to discourage the police from firing on them. "The people and the land are furious," they chanted. "Our demand is a binding constitution."[12] For two days they camped in Pearl before the security forces moved in to expel the demonstrators by force on February 17, killing four and wounding scores more. The growing death toll only fed the fury of the protestors, who flooded back to Pearl immediately after the security forces had withdrawn on February 19. They knew that scores had died in Tunisia and hundreds in Egypt before their movements succeeded, and they believed that through their sacrifice they too would secure their legitimate political rights. But the government's repression led to a hardening of the protestors' demands. No longer satisfied with reforms, the people began to demand the king's abdication—the fall of the regime.

For over three weeks Pearl Roundabout served as the nerve center of Bahrain's popular uprising. The protestors had raised tents, screens, makeshift kitchens, medical centers, and a stage for speakers. A media office was opened to feed the international press's insatiable demand for Arab Spring stories. Crowds continued to gather at Pearl, bringing together men and women, Sunnis and Shiites, veteran opposition politicians and the February 14 Youth Movement. However, the carnival atmosphere did little to mask the threat to the monarchy. According to the Arab Spring playbook, this sort of public occupation of a central meeting place only ended in the fall of the regime.

King Hamad and his government were divided on how to respond. Hard-liners led by the prime minister, Prince Khalifa bin Salman Al Khalifa (who, holding the post continuously since 1970, is the world's longest-serving unelected head of government), wanted to clamp down. The crown prince, Salman bin Hamad Al Khalifa, engaged in secret negotiations with the seven recognized opposition movements to propose constitutional reforms that might satisfy the protestors and resolve the crisis.[13] Bahrain's Gulf neighbors sided with the prime minister. For Saudi leaders, the uprising in Bahrain posed existential threats to their own ruling orders. They believed a revolution in any one of the conservative Gulf monarchies would threaten the political stability of all, and they saw Iran's malign influence in a largely Shiite Muslim protest movement. Were Iran to succeed in Bahrain, the Saudis reasoned, they would inevitably rouse the Shiite population of the oil-rich Eastern Province of Saudi Arabia to rise in rebellion. The Saudis were determined to contain and eliminate the dual threats of revolution and Iranian influence in Bahrain before they could take root and spread.

Saudi Arabia and the United Arab Emirates led the intervention to put down the Pearl Roundabout revolution. On March 14, operating under the banner of the GCC Peninsula Shield Force, a joint force based in Saudi Arabia, the Gulf states sent 2,000 troops and 150 armored cars across the 25-kilometer (15-mile) causeway linking Saudi Arabia to Bahrain. The Saudis and their allies justified the intervention in terms that reflected their own fears: they claimed to be protecting Bahraini sovereignty from Iranian influence. King Hamad declared a "State of National Safety," which gave the Bahraini authorities powers to "evacuate or isolate certain areas to maintain security and public order" and to search, arrest, withdraw citizenship, and deport aliens deemed a threat to public security.[14]

Reinforced by their Gulf allies, the Bahraini security forces set about dismantling the demonstrators' camp at Pearl Roundabout. Not only did they tear down the temporary structures erected at Pearl, but the authorities demolished the monument itself, the sails and concrete pearl crushed into rubble and trucked away. The Bahraini foreign minister, Khalid bin Ahmad Al Khalifa, described the operation as the "removal of a bad memory."[15] Then followed a crackdown on all those associated with the protest movement that included mass arrests, allegations of torture, trials by special security courts, and the handing out of harsh prison sentences. The regime took full advantage of the measures decreed by the State of National Safety.

King Hamad's one concession to international criticism of the crackdown was to authorize an independent commission of inquiry into the Bahraini uprising and its suppression. Headed by a distinguished Egyptian American law professor, Cherif Bassiouni, the commission subjected the Gulf state to an unprecedented degree of legal scrutiny. Its detailed, 500-page report, published in November 2011, documented hundreds of unjust convictions and disproportionate sentences, allegations of "forced disappearances" in which detainees were denied access to their families or lawyers for weeks, sixty accounts of torture, and the deaths of five detainees under torture.[16] The king promised to punish those responsible for the abuses, to implement reforms, and to work for national reconciliation after the deeply divisive events of 2011. Ultimately, the recommendations of the Bassiouni Report have gone unfulfilled, the regime resorting to repression to avoid reforms.

The government's victory over the Pearl Roundabout protesters in Bahrain marked the end of the Arab Spring as conceived in Tunisia and Egypt. It would no longer be enough for the people to mass in sufficient numbers to secure the fall of the regime, and the triumph of the people was no longer inevitable. The small Gulf state demonstrated how the regime could survive a revolution if its armed forces remained loyal to the ruler and willing to fire on demonstrators. The counterrevolution began in Bahrain in March 2011 and would culminate in Egypt in July 2013. If the Arab Spring was about citizens losing their fear of governments, the counterrevolution was all about the use of violence to restore fear. It would turn all subsequent uprisings—in Libya, Yemen, and Syria—into bloodbaths.

The Arab Spring came to Libya days after the outbreak of the Bahraini uprising. Muammar al-Qadhafi, Libya's self-styled "Brother Leader" since 1969 (he always rejected the title "president"), had survived in power through brutal repression rather than the consent of the Libyan people. Inspired by the revolutions in Tunisia and Egypt, Libyans rose in rebellion against their dictator of forty-one years, opening a violent new chapter in the Arab awakening of 2011.

Demonstrations erupted in the eastern city of Benghazi on February 15 and were met with force by security agents, who beat demonstrators and wounded dozens. Following the example of Egyptian and Bahraini organizers, Libyan activists called for a "day of rage" on February 17. Protests spread across the country and reached the Libyan capital, Tripoli. Angry crowds set fire to government buildings and police stations. Security forces used live ammunition against the demonstrators, killing over eighty of them. The dictator's son and presumed successor, Seif al-Islam Qadhafi, took to the airwaves in a TV broadcast on February 20 to threaten the Libyan rebels. "'Instead of crying over eighty-four deaths,' he said with contempt, wagging his finger at the camera, 'you will be crying over hundreds of thousands of deaths. There will be rivers of blood.' He spoke of Libya as if it were his family's private property. 'This country belongs to us.'"[17]

The situation rapidly spun out of government control. Opponents of the Qadhafi regime made Libya's second city, Benghazi, their home base and established their ruling National Transitional Council (NTC) there on February 27. Members of the armed forces and security services in the eastern half of the country rebelled against the Libyan government and joined an increasingly organized insurgency seeking the overthrow of Qadhafi. However, that left a large part of the armed forces loyal to the regime. The Libyan revolution, armed from the start, quickly took on the appearance of a civil war.

In the early days of the rebellion, the insurgents were on the ascendant. They consolidated their position in Benghazi and the eastern coastal regions of Libya, under the prerevolutionary Libyan flag in red, black, and green with a white Islamic

star and crescent. Thousands of civilian volunteers, with enthusiasm in inverse proportion to their discipline and training, reinforced the ranks of dissident soldiers.
Driving customized pickup trucks armed with heavy machine guns, they pressed
forward from their base in Benghazi to occupy key coastal cities, including the refinery ports of Brega and Ras Lanuf. By the end of February, the insurgents had extended their hold over the entire coast to the east of Benghazi and over major towns
near Tripoli such as Misurata. Defiant billboards posted around Benghazi proclaimed
"No foreign intervention" in bold red letters surrounded by stark stencils of the instruments of war. "Libyan people can do it alone." Yet predictions that Qadhafi
looked set to follow Ben Ali and Mubarak into retirement proved premature.

The Libyan dictator showed anger but no fear at the growing challenge to his
rule. He imposed a total clampdown in Tripoli. The regime organized pro-Qadhafi
rallies in central Green Square, where thousands of Libyans chanted their support
for the Brother Leader and defiance against the rebels. Qadhafi retained control over
the best-armed and best-trained units in his army. On February 22 he gave a long
and rambling speech that dismissed the rebels as "rats and cockroaches" and vowed
to hunt them down "inch by inch, room by room, house by house, alley by alley."
It was the beginning of Qadhafi's counterrevolution.

Government forces engaged and defeated the rebels in a number of decisive engagements in the first weeks of March. As Qadhafi's troops approached the rebel
stronghold in Benghazi, the international community feared a massacre was imminent. Gone was the defiance of February, as rebel fighters openly called on the international community to intervene. On March 12, the Arab League took the
extraordinary decision to support the insurgents against the recognized government
by requesting that the United Nations authorize a no-fly zone over rebel-held regions
of Libya. On the basis of the Arab League decision, the UN Security Council passed
Resolution 1973 on March 17, imposing a no-fly zone over all of Libya and authorizing "all necessary measures" to protect Libyan civilians.

The UN resolution internationalized the Libyan revolution. Almost immediately,
a NATO-led intervention force struck key targets in the country, with France,
Britain, and the United States taking the lead. Qadhafi's troops were forced back
from Benghazi under lethal fire from NATO aircraft, backed by Arab air force units
from Jordan, Qatar, and the United Arab Emirates. The initiative had shifted from
Libyan to Western hands, and the mission crept from creating a no-fly zone to provoking the fall of Qadhafi. For the first time in the Arab Spring uprisings, it was the
international community that pursued the fall of the regime.

Through the spring and summer of 2011, Qadhafi retained his grip on power
despite thousands of NATO sorties. The breakthrough for the opposition came in
a major offensive on August 20 that breached Qadhafi's defenses in Tripoli. By Au-

gust 23, the Libyan dictator and his sons had fled the capital as the insurgents celebrated victory. The NTC gained international recognition as the provisional government of Libya and promised a quick transition to constitutional government. Fireworks lit public celebrations as Libyans marked the liberation of Tripoli.

Yet the war continued after the fall of the capital. Qadhafi loyalists continued to fight against NTC forces in the fallen leader's hometown of Sirte and the loyalist stronghold of Bani Walid. After a prolonged siege, Sirte fell to NTC forces on October 20, 2011, where Qadhafi and his son Mutassim were captured and lynched. Horrific videos of Qadhafi's death were posted to the Internet, and his body was put on public display in the city of Misurata, which had suffered for months under government siege, to demonstrate to Libyans that the tyrant was truly dead—the latest casualty in a conflict estimated to have claimed over 15,000 lives.

The fall of the regime created a power vacuum rather than leading to a new democratic order. Qadhafi had bequeathed to his people a peculiarly institution-free form of government, which had allowed him to rule for years without checks or balances to his power. When many of Libya's best-educated and worldliest citizens returned home from exile to help rebuild their nation, they found a dangerous chaos, for men with guns fill power vacuums more easily than people with ideas.

The transition to democracy began with promise in Libya. On July 7, 2012, some 2.8 million Libyan citizens turned out enthusiastically to elect a 200-seat General National Congress to replace the National Transitional Council. Yet, from the start, factional divisions between Islamists and secularists, together with tribal and regional cleavages that made politics in Libya very local, hindered the work of the congress. Elected politicians in Tripoli had no control over provinces ruled by tribal militias. By August 2013, armed conflict had broken out between rival militias, which wrested whole towns, port cities, and oil facilities from government control.

In 2014, Libya snapped in two under the pressure of irreconcilable political forces. Islamist factions that had come to dominate the General National Congress secured control over the national capital, Tripoli, and all of western Libya. The House of Representatives, the newly elected parliament created to replace the General National Congress, and the recognized government of Libya, headed by Prime Minister Abdullah al-Thinni, were driven into exile in eastern Libya. The Libyan National Army, headed by one of Qadhafi's former generals, Khalifa Haftar, threw its support behind the House of Representatives in eastern Libya, while powerful militias reinforced the Islamist-dominated General National Congress in western Libya.

The war in Libya has had a devastating impact on the country. Between 2011 and 2015, the conflict killed an estimated 25,000 people and drove over 100,000 from their homes. In terms of human misery and political division, the Libyan revolution has most in common with Yemen's experiences since 2011.

One month after the death of Qadhafi, on November 23, 2011, Yemeni president Ali Abdullah Saleh became the fourth Arab autocrat to fall, after thirty-three years in power.

The revolution in Yemen seemed destined for stalemate almost from the outset. The country was fragmented internally along the lines of the formerly separate states of North and South Yemen (unified in 1990), was host to one of the more active al-Qaida franchises known as al-Qaida in the Arabian Peninsula, and was embroiled in an armed insurgency with the Shiite Houthi community in the frontier regions bordering Saudi Arabia. President Ali Abdullah Saleh had ruled over North Yemen from 1978 to 1990 and became president of the united Republic of Yemen in 1990. In keeping with Arab autocratic practice, he was grooming his son Ahmed to succeed him. With the lowest levels of human development in the Arab world, the people of Yemen viewed the prospect of a father-son succession perpetuating Saleh misrule with grave misgivings. Adopting the slogan of the Arab revolutions of 2011, the Yemeni people wanted the fall of their regime.

Large demonstrations numbering in the tens of thousands gathered in Sana'a, Aden, and Ta'iz in February 2011. Democracy activists set up a tent city near the university in Sana'a and called it Change Square on the model of Cairo's Tahrir Square. Emblazoned with banners reading, "No to Corruption, No to Tyranny, the People Demand the Fall of the Regime," Change Square "took on a distinctly Yemeni feel," *New York Times* journalist Robert Worth remembered. "It may have been inspired by Cairo's Tahrir Square, but it was unmistakably different: larger, dirtier, wilder. It stretched on for blocks in several directions, an unbroken mass of canvas tents pitched on the pavement with a big central stage for speeches."[18]

Support for the president began to break down as key military and tribal leaders joined the ranks of the opposition. However, what began as a peaceful protest movement in Yemen turned increasingly violent. On March 18 elements of the army loyal to the president fired on demonstrators, killing over fifty unarmed civilians. Many of the president's supporters resigned from their posts and joined the opposition. Whole units of the Yemeni army defected to side with the demonstrators. Ali Abdullah Saleh's isolation increased as the international community called on the Yemeni president to step down.

After ten months of political instability, Ali Abdullah Saleh finally signed an agreement brokered by the Gulf Cooperation Council, with the support of the United States and European powers, for the Yemeni president to relinquish power with immediate effect in return for immunity from prosecution. With little advance warning, Saleh transferred power to his vice president, Abed Rabbo Mansour al-Hadi, on November 23. Yet the deal fell well short of protestors' demands for regime change and did little to address the factional rifts that had emerged among Yemen's political elites in the course of the revolution. Activists who wanted to see Ali Abdullah Saleh held responsible for the deaths of demonstrators—nearly 2,000 in all—did not believe he deserved legal immunity. There was little celebration in Yemen when President Ali Abdullah Saleh stood down because the Yemenis remained unconvinced that he had really relinquished power.

Elections were held in Yemen in February 2012, but many Yemenis questioned the point of voting when there was only one name on the ballot: Abed Rabbo Mansour al-Hadi. Yet the 65 percent of voters who did turn out gave President Hadi a mandate to reform the government of Yemen and reconcile the country's fractious communities. His efforts met with some success. The National Dialogue Conference struck agreement on a new federal structure for Yemen and the terms of a new constitution for the country by January 2014. Yet the political transition created instability. The Houthi tribesmen resumed their insurgency in the north of the country, supported by army units formerly loyal to ousted president Ali Abdullah Saleh. Many speculated openly that Saleh was now in league with the same Houthi militants that as president he had sought to crush.

In September 2014 the Houthi militiamen entered the Yemeni capital, Sana'a, unopposed. The Houthis were no strangers to the city. They belong to the Zaydi community, a variant of Shiism whose communal leaders, or imams, had ruled Yemen from Sana'a for centuries until the republican revolution in 1962. Historically, the Zaydis had little contact with mainstream Shiism in Iran and, though a religious minority in Arabia, had never faced sectarian conflict in Yemen. Yet these historic distinctions are easily overlooked in the virulent sectarianism afflicting the Arab world in the twenty-first century.

After months of uncomfortable cohabitation, the Houthis appointed a ruling council in February 2015 to replace President Hadi, who fled to his hometown of Aden with leading members of his government. Unwilling to transfer power to the Houthis, Hadi remained the internationally recognized leader of Yemen. The Houthis advanced on Aden to silence the exiled president, but Hadi fled to Saudi Arabia to rally support for his fallen government. The Saudis viewed the crisis in Yemen with mounting concern, seeing the hand of Iran behind a Shiite movement destabilizing South Arabia. As in Bahrain, they were determined to act decisively to deny Iran a foothold in the Arabian Peninsula.

In March 2015, the Saudis led a ten-nation coalition to war against the Houthi insurgency in Yemen.[19] The Saudi navy imposed a strict embargo on the coastline to prevent Iran from resupplying the Houthis by sea. As in Libya and Bahrain, what started as an internal uprising had evolved into an international conflict. By September 2015 Yemeni government forces, backed by their Arab allies' airpower, had succeeded in recovering Aden. President Hadi returned to the southern port city to head a powerless government, confirming the division of Yemen into a Houthi-dominated north and Hadi-governed south. All the while, the Arab coalition prosecuted a devastating air campaign, leveling residential buildings and infrastructure in the Arab world's poorest country.

Revolution, war, and naval embargo combined to create a humanitarian crisis in Yemen in the years immediately following 2011. By the end of 2015, the war had internally displaced some 2.5 million Yemenis; by 2017 it had left an estimated 10,000 dead and 40,000 wounded. Those who survived faced the onset of famine as the naval blockade closed Yemen, which imports 90 percent of its food, to international shipping. Worse than a failed state, Yemen had degenerated into two failed states at war with each other.[20]

Dreadful though developments proved in Libya and Yemen, the most tragic chapter in the history of the Arab Spring unfolded in Syria.

Syria was one of the last Arab countries to face a popular uprising in 2011. When Facebook activists first attempted to mobilize mass protests in Damascus, the security forces so outnumbered the demonstrators that they were too intimidated to press their case. Moreover, President Bashar al-Asad, who succeeded his late father Hafez al-Asad in 2000, enjoyed a degree of legitimacy and public support that set him apart from other Arab autocrats. He was a relative newcomer after eleven years in power and still had a reputation as a reformer—however undeserved. The regime's spring 2011 arrest and torture of a group of teenagers in the farming town of Deraa, on the Syrian-Jordanian border, shattered that image.

One day in March, a group of rebellious youths painted slogans from the Arab revolutions of 2011 on a wall in Deraa. "The People Want the Fall of the Regime," they proclaimed. This small act of defiance, unremarkable in the Arab world in the spring of that year, provoked a response from the regime that would spark a revolution.

Alarmed by developments across the Arab world, the Asad regime refused to tolerate the least expression of dissent. The secret police arrested fifteen boys aged between ten and fifteen for the dissident graffiti. Their desperate parents petitioned the government for their release and then marched in open protest. The security forces responded with live fire, killing demonstrators in Deraa before finally agreeing to free the detained teens to restore calm. When discharged, the boys bore clear marks of torture. Most of their fingernails had been torn out.

Instead of calming the situation, the release of the abused children of Deraa sparked outrage. The townspeople rose up in their thousands to tear down all symbols associated with the Asad regime in mass protests unprecedented in recent Syrian history. The army responded with increased repression, storming a mosque in the town's center that had served as a base for the protesters, killing five. The size of the protests multiplied as crowds gathered to bury the dead. In the last week of March alone, over fifty-five townspeople of Deraa died.

Syrians all across the land followed the events in Deraa closely. Citizens in many economically depressed small towns like Deraa felt forgotten by their government but didn't dare protest for fear of retribution. In the revolutionary atmosphere of the spring of 2011, the Syrian people felt emboldened to express their dissent and demand change. They began to organize protests, giving each day a distinct name. Samar Yazbek, a single mother in Damascus, began her diary of the Syrian revolution on March 25, 2011—the "Friday of Dignity"—and captured the intense violence that accompanied the uprising from the start:

> Today, on the Friday of Dignity, the Syrian cities come out to demonstrate. More than two hundred thousand demonstrators mourn their dead in Dar'a. Entire villages outside Dar'a march toward the southern cemetery. Fifteen people are killed. In Homs three are killed. People are killed and wounded in Latakia. . . . Army forces surround Dar'a and open fire on any creature that moves. In al-Sanamayn the military security commits a massacre, killing twenty people.[21]

In hindsight, Yazbek's support for the uprising seems all the more surprising, given that she is a member of President Asad's Alawite religious community. Yet, in the opening months of the revolution, Syrians of all communities—Muslims, Christians, Alawites, and Druzes—made common cause to demand reform. Only when the revolution degenerated into civil war did sectarianism come into play.

In the first phase of the Syrian revolution, the protesters were nonviolent. They called for the repeal of the Emergency Law, in place since 1963, to regain their political and human rights. They rallied under the flag used by Syrian nationalists against the French mandate, with three horizontal bars of green, white, and red and three red stars across the center (the official Syrian flag mirrors that used during the union with Egypt between 1958 and 1961, with three horizontal bars of red, white, and black and two green stars in the center). They started in small towns but urged compatriots in the big cities to take up their banner and demands for reform.

However peaceful the demonstrators, the regime responded from the outset with gunfire. As in the other counterrevolutionary states (Bahrain, Libya, and Yemen), a large part of the army remained loyal to the president and proved willing to fire on fellow citizens. A growing number of dissident soldiers deserted in protest of their commanders' orders to fire on unarmed civilians. In July 2011, a group of military defectors formed the Free Syrian Army to lead an armed insurrection against the regime. The shift from nonviolent to armed protest transformed the revolution into a full-scale civil war.

The death toll of Syria's conflict reflects the full meaning of that transformation. Already by the end of the first year of the war, the United Nations reported over 5,000 dead in Syria. By the end of 2012 the figure had risen to 40,000. The United Nations estimated the death toll at 191,000 by the summer of 2014 and in 2016, after five years of war, put the figure in excess of 400,000. While the death toll is shocking, it reflects only a fraction of total Syrian suffering. By 2016 the conflict had uprooted over half the population of Syria. Some 6.1 million Syrians were internally displaced and another 4.8 million had sought refuge outside Syria's borders—in Jordan, Lebanon, Turkey, and the European Union.[22] The Syrian people and the international community have struggled to explain how an Arab Spring revolution could have gone so badly wrong.

The demonstrators and the international community overlooked a number of domestic constraints that prevented the fall of the regime in Syria. However reviled by his opponents, Bashar al-Asad has always enjoyed a large margin of support in Syria. Syria's minority communities—the Alawites, Druze, Ismailis, and Christians—make up some 25 percent of the total population of 22 million. The vast majority of Syrians are Sunni Muslims, estimated to represent 75 percent of the population. Many in the minority communities believe Bashar al-Asad, with his Alawite-dominated government, stands as a bulwark against a conservative Sunni Muslim order that would discriminate against them. Asad also has significant support from more nationalist, secular Sunni Muslims who are members of the ruling Ba'th party. Add to those groups all the members of the army and security forces who have fought for the regime, and Asad's support base appears ever larger, with Syria emerging as far more internally divided than many foreign analysts have acknowledged.

Moreover, the regime has always enjoyed a higher degree of unity than the opposition it is fighting. In the course of the Syrian war, dozens of opposition militias have emerged to challenge the regime, ranging from civil society groups calling for democratic reform to hardline Salafis intent on creating an Islamic state. These rebel groups often work at cross purposes and fight among themselves for territory. The regime, on the other hand, is far more cohesive than the forces it opposes. The more the regime is threatened, the more its core is reinforced. For the Asad regime and its partisans, victory is a matter of survival. The conflict is not just a matter of winner takes all: it has degenerated into one in which the loser must die. This fear, literally of a genocidal retaliation against the Alawites and Ba'thists and others associated with the Asad regime, goes some way to explaining the grim determination with which the regime retains power and its willingness to lay waste to the country as a whole rather than surrender.

Finally, the Syrian conflict rapidly became internationalized, as regional and global powers intervened to protect their own interests. Iran has enjoyed a special relationship with Syria since 1980 when, at the start of the Iran-Iraq War, the Syrian regime broke Arab ranks to side with Iran. Tehran gave the Asad regime unqualified support from the outset, reinforced by the Lebanese Shiite militia Hizbullah. Iranian Revolutionary Guards and Hizbullah fighters have assisted war-weary Syrian regular soldiers in the multifront conflict in Syria. Saudi Arabia and its Gulf allies have sought to diminish Iran's influence by throwing their support behind conservative Sunni Muslim militias, providing them with arms and ammunition. Turkey has provided a base for the Free Syrian Army and Syrian political parties working to bring down the regime, while sending its army across the border into Syria to contain gains made by Syrian Kurdish militias against the Asad regime. The United States and its European allies have provided limited support to a select group of opposition parties and militias, more or less in line with Turkey and the Gulf states.

In September 2015 Russian deployment of aircraft to support the Asad regime laid bare the limits of Western intervention in the Syrian conflict. Russia had clear interests in Syria and acted decisively to protect them. Syria provides Russia with its only naval base in the eastern Mediterranean and a platform for monitoring signals intelligence in the Middle East. It is also Russia's last ally in the Arab world. Were Asad to fall, Russia would lose all influence in Syria, greatly diminishing its standing in the region.

Russia's airstrikes against opposition positions provided strategic as well as moral support to the Syrian military. The government of Vladimir Putin was serving notice that it would not allow the Asad regime to fall. The Western powers condemned the Russian intervention, but neither the United States nor the European powers were willing to confront Russia directly; nor would they put their own forces into the Syrian conflict. Western support for the Syrian opposition thus eclipsed, the Asad regime pursued a strategy of fighting with Russia and Iran against its domestic opposition and leaving America and its allies to deal with yet another contender for mastery over Syria—the Islamic State.

The Islamic State emerged in Iraq among Sunni Muslim groups fighting the American occupation after 2003—particularly al-Qaida in Iraq. Under the leadership of Abu Musab al-Zarqawi, al-Qaida in Iraq developed a reputation for extreme violence against both Westerners and Shiites. Following Zarqawi's death in 2006, his successors rebranded the organization as the Islamic State in Iraq. The Islamic State took advantage of the breakdown of government control in both Iraq, where Sunni opposition to the Shiite-dominated government became entrenched, and in Syria, where the beleaguered Asad regime struggled to retain core territory under its control, to pose the greatest challenge to the regional state system in a century.[23]

Starting in 2011, the Islamic State in Iraq entered into an alliance with one of the al-Qaida affiliates fighting in the Syrian civil war, which emerged in January 2012 as the Nusra Front. In 2013 the al-Qaida leadership rejected a hostile takeover bid of the Nusra Front by the Islamic State. Undeterred, the Islamic State movement changed its name to the Islamic State in Iraq and al-Sham (ISIS). *Al-Sham* is the Arabic word for both the city of Damascus and the Greater Syrian lands (the territory combining the modern states of Lebanon, Syria, Jordan, and Israel/Palestine) dominated by Damascus in early Islam.[24] On June 29, 2014, after seizing key Iraqi cities in the Sunni heartland of Anbar Province and Iraq's second city, Mosul, Abu Bakr al-Baghdadi, the leader of ISIS, proclaimed himself caliph, or spiritual head of the global community of Sunni Muslims. His forces then drove bulldozers through the border between Iraq and Syria and declared that their caliphate no longer recognized state boundaries. ISIS established its capital in the eastern Syrian city of Raqqa and extended its control over a vast if thinly inhabited expanse of territory straddling Iraq and Syria.

The advent of ISIS further internationalized Syria's civil war. The movement quickly established a reputation for extreme violence against its enemies and those it deemed infidels. Graphic videos of beheadings carried out by ISIS fighters against foreign captives and genocidal measures against the Yezidi minority community horrified the global public. ISIS also proved successful in recruiting to its cause radicalized Muslim activists from around the world, raising security concerns from Washington to Beijing. ISIS began to claim terror attacks conducted in Europe and the United States. ISIS franchises in Asia and Africa began to declare their allegiance to the self-declared caliphate. The West's struggle to contain ISIS opened a whole new chapter in the war on terror, with a central focus on Syria and Iraq.

The territory of Syria was fragmented, coming under the control of the Asad regime, the opposition movements, the Kurds in the northeast, and ISIS. The new enemy also served to divide the warring parties, with America and its European allies concentrating their efforts on defeating ISIS, Turkey increasingly focused on containing the Syrian Kurds, and Russia and Iran working with the regime to defeat its opposition. A convergence of forces explains why Syria emerged as the most violent conflict of the counterrevolution.

The decisive chapter in the counterrevolution against the Arab Spring came in Egypt.

The January 25 Movement, which succeeded in toppling Husni Mubarak after three decades in power, raised hopes in Egypt and across the Arab world of a new age of citizens' rights and accountable government. No sooner had Mubarak stepped down than Egypt entered a period of feverish political development. The Egyptian military assumed trusteeship over the government, laying out an ambitious six-month timetable to draft constitutional amendments to guide elections for a new government.

The Muslim Brotherhood, Egypt's longest-running opposition party, had emerged as the country's most powerful political organization. The youth organizers who had been so effective in mobilizing mass protests had no institutional base and no political experience. They created dozens of political parties, none with any critical mass, leaving the better-organized Islamist parties to dominate politics in the transitional period. In order not to provoke alarm from more secular Egyptians, who suspected the Muslim Brotherhood of operating as a secretive cabal intent on transforming Egypt into an Islamic state, the leadership of the Brotherhood pledged not to seek a parliamentary majority or to run a candidate for the presidency. On this basis, the other Tahrir Square movements embraced the Muslim Brotherhood as a constructive partner in the political reform of Egypt.

In fact, when Egyptians went to the polls in November 2011, the Muslim Brotherhood emerged with the largest share of seats—40 percent—followed by the yet more conservative Salafi Islamist "Enlightenment Party" (Hizb al-Nur). With a majority of seats in the elected body going to Islamists, secular Egyptians began to fear that instead of a liberal constitution they would get an Islamist charter that replaced Egypt's civil laws with Islamic law.

Doubts about the Muslim Brotherhood's intentions deepened when, in violation of its earlier pledge, Mohamed Morsi stood for the presidency. A long-standing Muslim Brother, Morsi was an American-educated engineer. He stood against former prime minister Ahmed Shafik, a man closely associated with Mubarak. It was the worst possible choice for liberal Egyptians, having to decide between a Muslim Brother and a member of the ancien régime. They chose change over secularism, and on June 30, 2012, Mohamed Morsi was sworn in as Egypt's fifth president—the first to be democratically elected.

Morsi's presidency lasted only one year. His increasingly authoritarian tendencies alienated large parts of the Egyptian electorate. In November 2012 Morsi issued a presidential decree granting himself powers above the courts as the self-proclaimed guardian of the Egyptian revolution. He oversaw a constitutional assembly from which Coptic Christians as well as secular and liberal Egyptians withdrew in protest of its illiberal and Islamist tendencies. The remaining members of the Constituent Assembly, who were almost exclusively Islamist men, approved the draft constitution on November 30, 2012, and rushed it through a national referendum for approval between December 15 and 22. Liberal Egyptians called for a boycott of the referendum, which was effective to the extent that only 33 percent turned out. Those who did approved the constitution with a majority of 64 percent in favor. When President Morsi signed the new constitution into law on December 26, he confirmed the fears of liberal reformers that the Muslim Brotherhood had hijacked their revolution.

Opposition to President Morsi intensified in the early months of 2013. A new movement calling itself Tamarod ("Rebellion") had launched a nationwide petition campaign calling on Morsi to step down. Setting itself a target of securing fifteen million signatures by the first anniversary of Morsi's inauguration, by June 29 it had reportedly exceeded its own ambitions and claimed more than twenty-two million signatories united in demanding Morsi's resignation. The figure was never confirmed, and news reports quoted some individuals who boasted they had signed the petition twenty times or more. Regardless of potential fraudulence, the petition campaign rallied liberals, who descended on Tahrir Square in a massive demonstration calling for the fall of the Morsi regime.

The Egyptian military seized on the Tamarod movement to intervene in Egypt's political disorder. Many analysts believe the army was active in instigating the petition campaign. From the Free Officer Revolution in 1952 until Morsi's election, a military regime had ruled Egypt, and each of its presidents had been a military man: Gamal Abdel Nasser and Anwar Sadat from the army, Mubarak from the air force. For sixty years, the military had deepened its control over the politics and economy of Egypt. The Morsi administration and its Muslim Brother supporters posed a real threat to the military's interests, and the top brass moved quickly to reassert control and defend their interests from the chaos of Egypt's democracy experiment.

The Egyptian military delivered an ultimatum to Morsi to address the legitimate concerns of the Egyptian people within forty-eight hours or face a military intervention. It was an impossible request, which Morsi rejected. On the night of July 3, Minister of Defense General Abdel Fattah el-Sisi went on live TV to announce Morsi's deposal and the provisional assumption of his duties by the head of the constitutional court, Adly Mansour. Morsi and several of his leading officials were arrested and held in secret locations. It was a classic military coup, though the armed forces and their supporters rejected the label angrily. In Cairo and across the country, Egyptians came out in mass demonstrations, celebrating the army's actions as a show of respect for the legitimate demands of the people—a second revolution.

The coup of July 3 was in fact the beginning of Egypt's violent counterrevolution. Overnight, the ruling Muslim Brotherhood went from party in government to banned organization, its leaders under arrest or on the run. The Brotherhood's support base in Egypt was vast, and the army's unconstitutional and, in their view, illegitimate seizure of power from a democratically elected president outraged its partisans. They massed in mosque demonstrations in Cairo and Alexandria, applying in vain the Arab Spring formula of holding a central location until the people's wishes were respected.

The army and its supporters simply outnumbered the Brotherhood. The majority of Egyptians were disillusioned by the Brotherhood's failure to respect its preelection pledges and alarmed by Morsi's clumsy authoritarianism. Moreover, the average Egyptian was tired of revolutionary chaos. The people wanted a return to normalcy, they wanted the economy to recover, and they wanted to go back to work and earn a living—all aspects of life disrupted by two years of revolutionary upheaval. The people believed the army could deliver order and placed their trust in the military men.

The most violent chapter in modern Egypt's political history ensued. After six weeks of protests, on August 14, 2013, the military assaulted two Muslim Brother protest sites in Cairo: Rabaa al-Adawiya and al-Nahda Square. Using live fire against civilian demonstrators, the security forces massacred as many as 1,000 supporters of the deposed president in a single day.[25] The military authorities declared a state of emergency and imposed a curfew. The law thus suspended, the authorities redoubled their clampdown on the Muslim Brotherhood, arresting thousands. In September the government banned the Muslim Brotherhood and froze its assets, and in December the authorities declared the Brotherhood a terrorist organization. The courts sentenced to death ex-president Mohamed Morsi, Brotherhood supreme guide Mohamed Badie, and hundreds of lower-ranking cadres; more than 20,000 Islamists were arrested and imprisoned.[26]

While the Egyptian army broke the power of the Muslim Brotherhood, General Abdel Fattah el-Sisi, the commander in chief, soared in popularity. His admirers compared him to Nasser and encouraged his political ambitions. In March 2014 Sisi resigned his commission, freeing him to run for the presidency. Challenged only by Hamdeen Sabahi, an opposition activist during the Sadat and Mubarak eras, Sisi won the presidential election in May 2014 by a crushing majority of 96 percent of the vote. Though now in civilian clothes, Sisi undoubtedly represented the restoration of the military's control over Egyptian politics.

The counterrevolution in Egypt was complete. For many, it was as though the January 25 Movement in 2011 had never happened. Gone were the demands for citizens' rights and accountable government as the Arab people abandoned their hopes for political freedom in a desperate bid for stability. Against the background of political turmoil in Egypt and Bahrain and the spiral into civil war in Libya, Yemen, and Syria, the price of revolutionary change has proven too high for the Arab people to bear—except in Tunisia, the one surviving Arab Spring success story.

Tunisia is the only Arab state to negotiate a peaceful political transition to a new constitutional order following an Arab Spring revolution. A unity government combining members of the opposition with holdovers from the Ben Ali era assumed power. In October 2011, Tunisians flocked to the polls to elect a constituent assembly to rewrite the Tunisian constitution. The Islamist party Ennahda, banned under Ben Ali, secured the largest share of the vote (41 percent) but, unlike the Muslim Brotherhood in Egypt, did not attempt to use its power at the polls to dominate Tunisian politics. In Tunisia, the Islamists chose to work in coalition with two centrist and secular parties, preserving a higher degree of national cohesion. The process of drafting a new constitution was lengthy but characterized by consensus building rather than coercion. The new constitution, adopted in January 2014, enshrines the gains of the revolutionary movement in citizen rights and the rule of law.

The transition to a new constitutional era in Tunisia concluded when voters returned to the polls between October and December 2014 to elect a parliament and president by the new rules governing their country—rules hammered out by Tunisians, elected by Tunisians, rather than imposed by foreign agents; rules that resolved the centuries-old struggle to constrain the autocratic powers of rulers. The election results in 2014 gave grounds for optimism. The secular Nidaa Tounes ("Tunisia's Call") party won a plurality, the Islamist Ennahda coming in second, and the two parties agreed to form a coalition government. Nidaa Tounes's leader, Beji Caid Essebsi, was elected president.

Yet Tunisia's gains are fragile. The country has suffered terror attacks that have crippled the crucial tourist industry, and foreign investors have yet to reward Tunisia with their trust. Until the terror threat is contained and economic growth is restored, Tunisia's postrevolutionary gains will remain at risk. Yet the success of Tunisia's fragile experiment in democracy is in the interest of the Arab world and the world at large. For as the Arab world emerges from the violence and devastation of the 2010s, the Arab peoples will inevitably resume their legitimate demands for accountable government. Tunisia will stand as a beacon of what the Arabs can aspire to in the twenty-first century.

Acknowledgments

In writing this modern history of the Arab world I have been privileged to be part of a remarkable intellectual community in the Middle East Centre of St. Antony's College in the University of Oxford.

The late Albert Hourani, one of the greatest historians of the Arab world, assembled an innovative group of scholars who made the Middle East Centre Europe's leading university institute for the study of the modern Middle East. From that original fellowship, my emeritus colleagues Mustafa Badawi, Derek Hopwood, Robert Mabro, and Roger Owen have been my mentors since 1991. I have taken full advantage of their deep knowledge of the Middle East, discussing the arguments of this book with them and imposing draft chapters on them for comment. They have been unstinting in their encouragement and constructive criticisms.

The current Fellowship of the Middle East Centre has in every way preserved the magic of Albert Hourani's original community. In Ahmed Al-Shahi, Walter Armbrust, Raffaella Del Sarto, Homa Katouzian, Celia Kerslake, Philip Robins, and Michael Willis, I have generous friends and colleagues who have made daily contributions to this project—in casual conversation over coffee each morning at the Centre, in suggested readings, and in comments on draft chapters. I owe a particular debt of friendship and gratitude to Avi Shlaim, a brilliant and innovative historian of Israel's troubled history with the Arabs. Avi read every chapter and met with me over lunches in College to give me the most detailed and constructive feedback. His insightful comments have made their impact on every part of the book.

I wish to thank the Middle East Centre's archivist, Debbie Usher, for her generous support for my research in the archive's rich collections of private papers and historic photographs. I am most grateful to the Middle East Centre's Librarian, Mastan Ebtehaj, and to the Centre's administrator, Julia Cook.

I have used material from the book-in-progress for my lectures in modern Arab history at Oxford and am very grateful to our astute students for their feedback. I would like to thank Reem Abou El Fadl, Nick Kardahji, and Nadia Oweidat for their help with research for the book.

Over the years of writing this book I have exploited family and friends, specialists and nonspecialists alike, to read and comment on draft chapters along the way. Their encouragement and critiques did more to see the book through to completion than they might believe. I wish to acknowledge my debt to Peter Airey, Tui Clark, Foulath Hadid—my tutor in Iraqi history, Tim Kennedy, Dina Khoury, Joshua Landis, Ronald Nettler, Tom Orde, Thomas Philipp—who first inspired me to study the history of the Arabs, Gabi Piterberg, Tariq Ramadan, my brother Grant Rogan, Kevin Watkins, and my brilliant wife Ngaire Woods.

I wish to give special thanks to my most persistent and dedicated reader—Margaret Rogan, my mother. She read every chapter of the book from beginning to end without letting a mother's love blind her to the mistakes that she, a life-long student of the Middle East, found along the way.

Since the book was first published, a number of readers have written with suggestions and corrections, many of which have been incorporated into this edition. I wish to thank Ali Allawi, Sir Mark Allen, Mouzaffar H. Al Barazi, Seth Frantzman, Ivor Lucas, Michel Lutfalla, Rick Messick, Max Pieper, Francis Robinson, Azzam Saad, and Richard Underland.

I am indebted to Serge Fouchard of the Musée départemental Albert-Kahn in Boulogne-Billancourt for making copies of the extraordinary autochromes from the Albert Kahn collection available for publication. I am also most grateful to Victoria Hogarth of the Bridgeman Art Library and Jeff Spurr of the Harvard Fine Arts Library for their help with images for the book.

The book would never have happened without the particular genius of my literary agent Felicity Bryan. I am especially grateful to Felicity for breaking her own rule not to represent her friends. I will ever be indebted to George Lucas for agreeing to represent me in New York and for treating me to an unforgettable introduction to New York's publishing world. Together they found the very best publishing houses for this book.

My deepest thanks at Basic Books go to my editor, Lara Heimert, who through humor and insight has cajoled a better book from me than ever I could have written on my own. Brandon Proia has shared his editorial talents and helped with finding the right images for the book. Kay Mariea and Michelle Asakawa were heroic at copyediting at break-neck speed. At Penguin, I have benefited throughout the writing of the book from Simon Winder's deep knowledge and penetrating engagement with the manuscript.

My family have been my strength and inspiration at every point in writing this book. To Ngaire, our son Richard and daughter Isabelle, I owe the sanity that counterbalances the madness of taking on such a project. Thank you.

Permissions

Section One (between pages 184–185)

1. Private collection. Photo © Christie's Images/ The Bridgeman Art Library
2. Private collection. Photo © Christie's Images/ The Bridgeman Art Library
3. Photograph by Bonfils. Harvard College Library, Fine Arts Library, HSM 664
4. Chateau de Versailles, France/ Giraudon/ The Bridgeman Art Library
5. Private collection/ © The Fine Art Society, London, UK/ The Bridgeman Art Library
6. Harvard College Library, Fine Arts Library, HSM 620
7. Chateau de Versailles, Fra   nce/ Lauros/ Giraudon/ The Bridgeman Art Library
8. Musée Condé, Chantilly, France/ Giraudon/ The Bridgeman Art Library
9. Musée Albert-Kahn – Département des Hauts-de-Seine, A15488
10. Musée Albert-Kahn – Département des Hauts-de-Seine, A15562
11. Musée Albert-Kahn – Département des Hauts-de-Seine, A51046
12. Private Collection/Archives Charmet/The Bridgeman Art Library. All best efforts have been made to contact the copyright holder of this anonymous Moroccan work.
13. Musée Albert-Kahn – Département des Hauts-de-Seine, A19031
14. Frédéric Gadmer, Musée Albert-Kahn – Département des Hauts-de-Seine, A19747
15. Owen Tweedy Collection, PA 7/216, Middle East Centre Archive, St. Antony's College, Oxford
16. Sir Edmund Allenby Collection, PA 5/8, Middle East Centre Archive, St Antony's College, Oxford
17. Bibliotheque Nationale, Paris, France/ Archives Charmet/ The Bridgeman Art Library

Section Two (between pages 246–247)

1. Norman Mayers Collection album 1/40, Middle East Centre Archive, St. Antony's College, Oxford

2. John Poole Collection 11/5/5, Middle East Centre Archive, St. Antony's College, Oxford

3. John Poole Collection 11/4/16, Middle East Centre Archive, St. Antony's College, Oxford

4. Sir Edward Spears Collection, Album 8/28, Middle East Centre Archive, St. Antony's College, Oxford

5. Sir Edward Spears Collection, Album 9/75, Middle East Centre Archive, St. Antony's College, Oxford

6. Desmond Morton Collection, 13/1/1, Middle East Centre Archive, St. Antony's College, Oxford

7. Desmond Morton Collection, 13/1/2, Middle East Centre Archive, St. Antony's College, Oxford

8. AP Images

9. © Bettmann/Corbis

10. © Bettmann/Corbis

11. © Bettmann/Corbis

12. © Bettmann/Corbis

13. © Hulton-Deutsch Collection/Corbis

14. © Hulton-Deutsch Collection/Corbis

15. © Bettmann/Corbis

16. © Bettmann/Corbis

Section Three (between pages 336–337)

1. © Genevieve Chauvel/Sygma/Corbis

2. © Bride Lane Library/Popperfoto/Getty Images

3. © Christian Simonpietri/Sygma/Corbis

4. © Bettmann/Corbis

5. © Bettmann/Corbis

6. © Alain DeJean/Sygma/Corbis

7. © Kevin Fleming/Corbis

8. © AFP/Getty Images

9. © Dominique Faget/epa/Corbis

10. © Gérard Rancinan/Sygma/Corbis

11. © Michel Philippot/Sygma/Corbis

12. © Françoise de Mulder/Corbis

13. © Françoise de Mulder/Corbis

14. © Peter Turnley/Corbis

15. © Reuters/Corbis

16. © Reuters/Corbis

17. © Peter Turnley/Corbis

18. © Abed Omar Qusini/Reuters/Corbis

Notes

Introduction

1. Basma Bouazizi, Mohamed's sister, quoted in "Controversy over 'the Slap' That Brought Down a Government," *Asharq Al-Awsat*, February 2, 2011; Fayda Hamdy quoted in Karem Yehia, "Tunisian Policewoman Who 'Slapped' Bouazizi Says 'I Was Scapegoated by Ben Ali,'" *Ahram Online*, December 16, 2014. See also Yasmine Ryan, "The Tragic Life of a Street Vendor: Al-Jazeera Travels to the Birthplace of Tunisia's Uprising and Speaks to Mohamed Bouazizi's Family," AlJazeera.com, January 20, 2011; Kareem Fahim, "Slap to a Man's Pride Set Off Tumult in Tunisia," *New York Times*, January 21, 2011.

2. Fayda Hamdi has given her account of events in a number of interviews. See Yehia, "Tunisian Policewoman Who 'Slapped' Bouazizi," and Radhouane Addala and Richard Spencer, "I Started the Arab Spring. Now Death Is Everywhere, and Extremism Is Blooming," *Daily Telegraph*, December 17, 2015.

3. Roger Owen, *The Rise and Fall of Arab Presidents for Life* (Cambridge, MA: Harvard University Press, 2012); Joseph Sassoon, *Anatomy of Authoritarianism in the Arab Republics* (Cambridge: Cambridge University Press, 2016).

4. Samir Kassir, *Being Arab* (London: Verso, 2006), from the author's introduction.

5. Fayda Hamdi discussed her donning of the head scarf in "Interview with Fadia [*sic*] Hamdi," video posted by CorrespondentsDotOrg on YouTube, July 11, 2012, https://www.youtube.com/watch?v=JSeRkT5A8rQ.

6. George Will, "Take Time to Understand Mideast Asia," *Washington Post*, October 29, 2001.

7. Eugene Rogan, *The Fall of the Ottomans: The Great War in the Middle East, 1914–1920* (New York: Basic Books, 2015).

Chapter 1

1. The death of the Prophet Muhammad gave rise to one of the earliest splits in Islam as his followers disagreed over how to choose his successor, or caliph, to head the Muslim community. One group of Muslims argued for succession within the family of the Prophet and championed the candidacy of Ali ibn Abu Talib, who, as first cousin and son-in-law of the Prophet, was his closest relative. This faction came to be known in Arabic as *Shi'at 'Ali*, or "the Party of Ali," from which the word Shiite is derived. The majority of Muslims, however, argued that the caliph should be the most pious Muslim best able to uphold the *sunna*, or practices and beliefs of the Prophet Muhammad; these came to be known as the Sunnis. For most of Islamic history, the Sunnis have been the dominant majority of the community of believers, particularly in the Arab and Turkish world, with variants of Shi'ite Islam taking root in South Arabia, Persia, and South Asia.

2. The chronicles of Muhammad ibn Ahmad Ibn Iyas (c. 1448–1524), *Bada'i' al-zuhur fi waqa'i' al-duhur* [The most remarkable blossoms among the events of the age], were first published in Cairo in 1893–1894. There is an English translation of excerpts relating to the Ottoman conquest of Syria and Egypt: W. H. Salmon, *An Account of the Ottoman Conquest of Egypt in the Year A.H. 922 (A.D. 1516)* (London: Royal Asiatic Society, 1921); and a full translation by Gaston Wiet, *Journal d'un bourgeois du Caire: Chronique d'Ibn Iyâs*, vol. 2 (Paris: S.E.V.P.E.N., 1960). This account is found in Salmon, *Account of the Ottoman Conquest*, pp. 41–46, and in Wiet, *Journal d'un bourgeois du Caire*, pp. 65–67.

3. Salmon, *Account of the Ottoman Conquest*, pp. 92–95; Wiet, *Journal d'un bourgeois du Caire*, pp. 117–120.

4. Salmon, *Account of the Ottoman Conquest*, pp. 111–113; Wiet, *Journal d'un bourgeois du Caire*, pp. 137–139.

5. Salmon, *Account of the Ottoman Conquest*, pp. 114–117; Wiet, *Journal d'un bourgeois du Caire*, pp. 140–43.

6. Wiet, *Journal d'un bourgeois du Caire*, pp. 171–172.

7. Ibid., p. 187.

8. The Rightly Guided Caliphs were the first four successors of the Prophet Muhammad—Abu Bakr, 'Umar, 'Uthman, and 'Ali—who ruled the early Islamic community in the seventh century. They were followed by the Umayyad dynasty, which ruled from Damascus between 661–750 CE.

9. Thomas Philipp and Moshe Perlmann, eds., *'Abd al-Rahman al-Jabarti's History of Egypt*, vol. 1 (Stuttgart: Franz Steiner, 1994), p. 33.

10. Salmon, *Account of the Ottoman Conquest*, pp. 46–49; Wiet, *Journal d'un bourgeois du Caire*, pp. 69–72.

11. The chronicle of Shams al-Din Muhammad ibn 'Ali Ibn Tulun (c. 1485–1546), "Background Information on the Turkish Governors of Greater Damascus," has been edited and translated by Henri Laoust, *Les Gouverneurs de Damas sous les Mamlouks et les premiers Ottomans (658–1156/1260–1744)* (Damascus: Institut Français de Damas, 1952).

12. Bruce Masters, *The Origins of Western Economic Dominance in the Middle East: Mercantilism and the Islamic Economy in Aleppo, 1600–1750* (New York: New York University Press, 1988).

13. Laoust, *Les Gouverneurs de Damas*, p. 151.

14. Salmon, *Account of the Ottoman Conquest*, p. 49; Wiet, *Journal d'un bourgeois du Caire*, p. 72.

15. Laoust, *Les Gouverneurs de Damas*, pp. 154–157.

16. From the chronicle of Ibn Jum'a (d. after 1744), in Laoust, *Les Gouverneurs de Damas*, p. 172.

17. The accounts of Ibn Jum'a and Ibn Tulun are almost identical, the later chronicler repeating almost verbatim points of Ibn Tulun's narrative. Laoust, *Les Gouverneurs de Damas*, pp. 154–159 and 171–174.

18. Amnon Cohen and Bernard Lewis, *Population and Revenue in the Towns of Palestine in the Sixteenth Century* (Princeton, NJ: Princeton University Press, 1978), pp. 3–18.

19. Muhammad Adnan Bakhit, *The Ottoman Province of Damascus in the Sixteenth Century* (Beirut: Librairie du Liban, 1982), pp. 91–118.

20. I. Metin Kunt, *The Sultan's Servants: The Transformation of Ottoman Provincial Government, 1550–1650* (New York: Columbia University Press, 1983), pp. 32–33.

21. Philipp and Perlmann, *Al-Jabarti's History of Egypt*, vol. 1, p. 33.

22. Michael Winter, *Egyptian Society Under Ottoman Rule, 1517–1798* (London: Routledge, 1992), pp. 16–17.

23. Bakhit, *Ottoman Province of Damascus*, pp. 105–106.

24. Sayyid Murad's sixteenth-century manuscript *Ghazawat-i Khayr al-Din Pasha* [Conquests of Khayr al-Din Pasha] has been published in an abridged French translation by Sander Rang and Ferdinand Denis, *Fondation de la régence d'Alger: Histoire de Barberousse* (Paris: J. Angé, 1837). This account is found in vol. 1, p. 306.

25. John B. Wolf, *The Barbary Coast: Algeria Under the Turks* (New York: W. W. Norton, 1979), p. 20.

26. Cited in ibid., p. 27.

27. Ahmad b. Muhammad al-Khalidi al-Safadi, *Kitab tarikh al-Amir Fakhr al-Din al-Ma'ni* [The book of history of the Amir Fakhr al-Din al-Ma'ni], edited and published by Asad Rustum and Fuad al-Bustani under the title *Lubnan fi 'ahd al-Amir Fakhr al-Din al-Ma'ni al-Thani* [Lebanon in the age of Amir Fakhr al-Din II al-Ma'ni] (Beirut: Editions St. Paul, 1936, reprinted 1985).

28. Abdul-Rahim Abu-Husayn, *Provincial Leaderships in Syria, 1575–1650* (Beirut: American University in Beirut Press, 1985) pp. 81–87.

29. Al-Khalidi al-Safadi, *Amir Fakhr al-Din*, pp. 17–19.

30. Ibid., pp. 214–215.

31. Ibid., pp. 150–154.

32. Daniel Crecelius and 'Abd al-Wahhab Bakr, trans., *Al-Damurdashi's Chronicle of Egypt, 1688–1755* (Leiden: E. J. Brill, 1991), p. 286.

33. Ibid., p. 291.

34. Ibid., p. 296.

35. Ibid., pp. 310–312.

36. Winter, *Egyptian Society Under Ottoman Rule*, p. 24.

Chapter 2

1. Ahmad al-Budayri al-Hallaq, *Hawadith Dimashq al-Yawmiyya* [Daily events of Damascus] *1741–1762* (Cairo: Egyptian Association for Historical Studies, 1959), p. 184; and George M. Haddad, "The Interests of an Eighteenth Century Chronicler of Damascus," *Der Islam* 38 (June 1963): 258–271.

2. Budayri, *Hawadith Dimashq*, p. 202.

3. Ibid., p. 129.

4. Ibid., p. 219.

5. Ibid., p. 57.

6. Ibid., p. 112.

7. Quoted by Albert Hourani, "The Fertile Crescent in the Eighteenth Century," *A Vision of History* (Beirut: Khayats, 1961), p. 42.

8. Thomas Philipp and Moshe Perlmann, eds., *'Abd al-Rahman al-Jabarti's History of Egypt*, vol. 1 (Stuttgart: Franz Steiner, 1994), p. 6.

9. On the Shihabs of Mount Lebanon see Kamal Salibi, *The Modern History of Lebanon* (London: Weidenfeld and Nicholson, 1965). On the Jalilis of Mosul, see Dina Rizk Khoury, *State and Provincial Society in the Ottoman Empire: Mosul, 1540–1830* (Cambridge: Cambridge University Press, 1997).

10. Roger Owen, *The Middle East in the World Economy, 1800–1914* (London: Methuen, 1981), p. 7.

11. Budayri, *Hawadith Dimashq*, pp. 27–29.

12. Ibid., pp. 42–45.

13. Amnon Cohen, *Palestine in the Eighteenth Century* (Jerusalem: Magnes Press, 1973), p. 15.

14. Thomas Philipp, *Acre: The Rise and Fall of a Palestinian City, 1730–1831* (New York: Columbia University Press, 2001), p. 36.

15. Philipp and Perlmann, *Abd al-Rahman al-Jabarti's History of Egypt*, vol. 1, p. 636. On 'Ali Bey al-Kabir see Daniel Crecelius, *The Roots of Modern Egypt: A Study of the Regimes of 'Ali Bey al-Kabir and Muhammad Bey Abu al-Dhahab, 1760–1775* (Minneapolis and Chicago: University of Minnesota Press, 1981).

16. Philipp and Perlmann, *Abd al-Rahman al-Jabarti's History of Egypt*, vol. 1, p. 639.

17. Ibid., p. 638.

18. Ibid., p. 639.

19. This account is from the chronicle of al-Amir Haydar Ahmad al-Shihab of Mount Lebanon (1761–1835), *Al-Ghurar al-Hisan fi akhbar abna' al-zaman* [Exemplars in the chronicles of the sons of the age]. Shihab's chronicles were edited and published by Asad

Rustum and Fuad al-Bustani under the title *Lubnan fi 'ahd al-umara' al-Shihabiyin* [Lebanon in the era of the Shihabi Amirs], vol. 1 (Beirut: Editions St. Paul, 1984), p. 79.

20. Shihab, *Lubnan fi 'ahd al-umara' al-Shihabiyin*, vol. 1, pp. 86–87.

21. Philipp and Perlmann, *Abd al-Rahman al-Jabarti's History of Egypt*, vol. 1, p. 639.

22. Philipp, citing Ahmad al-Shihab's *Tarikh Ahmad Pasha al-Jazzar*, in *Acre*, p. 45.

23. This dramatic account of Zahir al-'Umar's death is found in the chronicle of Mikha'il al-Sabbagh (c. 1784–1816), *Tarikh al-Shaykh Zahir al-'Umar al-Zaydani* [The history of Shaykh Zahir al-Umar al-Zaydani] (Harisa, Lebanon: Editions St. Paul, 1935), pp. 148–158.

24. Cited in Alexei Vassiliev, *The History of Saudi Arabia* (London: Saqi, 2000), p. 98.

25. Philipp and Perlmann, *Abd al-Rahman al-Jabarti's History of Egypt*, vol. 4, p. 23.

26. Mikhayil Mishaqa, *Murder, Mayhem, Pillage, and Plunder: The History of Lebanon in the Eighteenth and Nineteenth Centuries* (Albany: SUNY Press, 1988), p. 62.

Chapter 3

1. Thomas Philipp and Moshe Perlmann, eds., *'Abd al-Rahman al-Jabarti's History of Egypt*, vol. 3 (Stuttgart: Franz Steiner, 1994), p. 2.

2. Ibid., p. 13.

3. Ibid., p. 8.

4. Ibid., p. 51.

5. M. de Bourienne, *Mémoires sur Napoléon*, 2 vols. (Paris, 1831), cited in ibid., p. 57, n. 63.

6. Philipp and Perlmann, *'Abd al-Rahman al-Jabarti's History of Egypt*, vol. 3, pp. 56–57.

7. Afaf Lutfi al-Sayyid Marsot, *Egypt in the Reign of Muhammad Ali* (Cambridge: Cambridge University Press, 1984), p. 37. See also Darrell Dykstra, "The French Occupation of Egypt," in M. W. Daly, ed., *The Cambridge History of Egypt*, vol. 2 (Cambridge: Cambridge University Press, 1998), pp. 113–138.

8. Philipp and Perlmann, *'Abd al-Rahman al-Jabarti's History of Egypt*, vol. 3, pp. 505–506.

9. Ibid., vol. 4, pp. 179–180.

10. Marsot, *Egypt in the Reign of Muhammad Ali*, p. 72.

11. Ibid., p. 201. One purse equaled 500 piasters, and the exchange rate in the 1820s was approximately U.S. $1 = 12.6 piasters.

12. The account of the execution of the Wahhabi leadership was given by the Russian ambassador to the Ottoman Empire, cited in Alexei Vassiliev, *The History of Saudi Arabia* (London: Saqi, 2000), p. 155.

13. Khaled Fahmy, *All the Pasha's Men: Mehmed Ali, His Army, and the Making of Modern Egypt* (Cambridge: Cambridge University Press, 1997), p. 92.

14. Mustafa Rashid Celebi Efendi, cited in ibid., p. 81.

15. Letter from Muhammad 'Ali to his agent Najib Efendi dated October 6, 1827, translated by Fahmy in *All the Pasha's Men*, pp. 59–60.

16. Mikhayil Mishaqa's 1873 chronicle, *al-Jawab 'ala iqtirah al-ahbab* [The response to the suggestion of the loved ones] was translated by Wheeler Thackston and published under the title *Murder, Mayhem, Pillage, and Plunder: The History of the Lebanon in the Eighteenth and Nineteenth Centuries* (Albany: SUNY Press, 1988), pp. 165–169.

17. Ibid., pp. 172–174.

18. Ibid., pp. 178–187.

19. Palmerston's letter of July 20, 1838, cited in Marsot, *Egypt in the Reign of Muhammad Ali*, p. 238.

20. Mishaqa, *Murder, Mayham, Pillage, and Plunder*, p. 216.

21. London Convention for the Pacification of the Levant, 15–17 September 1840, reproduced in J. C. Hurewitz, *The Middle East and North Africa in World Politics*, vol. 1 (New Haven, CT: Yale University Press, 1975), pp. 271–275.

Chapter 4

1. For a complete English translation and study of al-Tahtawi's work, *Takhlis al-Ibriz fi Talkhis Bariz* [The extraction of pure gold in the abridgement of Paris], see Daniel L. Newman, *An Imam in Paris: Al-Tahtawi's Visit to France (1826–1831)* (London: Saqi, 2004).

2. Ibid., pp. 99, 249.

3. Ibid., pp. 105, 161.

4. The analysis of the constitution is reproduced in ibid., pp. 194–213.

5. Al-Tahtawi's analysis of the July Revolution of 1830 may be found in ibid., pp. 303–330.

6. A translation of the 1839 Reform Decree is reproduced in J. C. Hurewitz, *The Middle East and North Africa in World Politics*, vol. 1 (New Haven, CT: Yale University Press, 1975), pp. 269–271.

7. The text of the 1856 Decree is reproduced in ibid., pp. 315–318.

8. The diary of Muhammad Sa'id al-Ustuwana, the Ottoman judge of Damascus, was edited and published by As'ad al-Ustuwana, *Mashahid wa ahdath dimishqiyya fi muntasif al-qarn al-tasi' 'ashar (1840–1861)* [Eyewitness to Damascene events in the mid-nineteenth century, 1840–1861] (Damascus: Dar al-Jumhuriyya, 1993), p. 162.

9. Jonathan Frankel, *The Damascus Affair: "Ritual Murder," Politics, and the Jews in 1840* (Cambridge: Cambridge University Press, 1997).

10. Bruce Masters, "The 1850 Events in Aleppo: An Aftershock of Syria's Incorporation into the Capitalist World System," *International Journal of Middle East Studies* 22 (1990): 3–20.

11. Leila Fawaz, *An Occasion for War: Civil Conflict in Lebanon and Damascus in 1860* (London: I. B. Tauris, 1994); and Ussama Makdisi, *The Culture of Sectarianism: Com-*

munity, History, and Violence in Nineteenth-Century Ottoman Lebanon (Berkeley and Los Angeles: University of California Press, 2000).

12. The memoirs of Abu al-Sa'ud al-Hasibi, Muslim notable of Damascus, as quoted by Kamal Salibi in "The 1860 Upheaval in Damascus as Seen by al-Sayyid Muhammad Abu'l-Su'ud al-Hasibi, Notable and Later *Naqib al-Ashraf* of the City," in William Polk and Richard Chambers, eds., *Beginnings of Modernization in the Middle East: The Nineteenth Century* (Chicago: University of Chicago Press, 1968), p. 190.

13. Wheeler Thackston Jr. has translated Mikhayil Mishaqa's 1873 history under the title *Murder, Mayhem, Pillage, and Plunder: The History of the Lebanon in the Eighteenth and Nineteenth Centuries* (Albany: SUNY Press, 1988), p. 244.

14. Mishaqa's report to the U.S. Consul in Beirut of September 27, 1860, in Arabic, is held in the National Archives, College Park, Maryland.

15. Y. Hakan Erdem, *Slavery in the Ottoman Empire and Its Demise, 1800–1909* (Basingstoke, UK: 1996).

16. Roger Owen, *The Middle East in the World Economy, 1800–1914* (London: Methuen, 1981), p. 123.

17. David Landes, *Bankers and Pashas: International Finance and Economic Imperialism in Egypt* (Cambridge, MA: Harvard University Press, 1979), pp. 91–92.

18. Owen, *Middle East in the World Economy*, pp. 126–127.

19. Janet Abu Lughod, *Cairo: 1001 Years of the City Victorious* (Princeton, NJ: Princeton University Press, 1971), pp. 98–113.

20. The autobiography of Khayr al-Din, "À mes enfants" [To my children], was edited by M. S. Mzali and J. Pignon and published under the title "Documents sur Kheredine," *Revue Tunisienne* (1934): 177–225, 347–396. Passage cited appears on p. 183.

21. Khayr al-Din's political treatise, *Aqwam al-masalik li ma'rifat ahwal al-mamalik* [The surest path to knowledge concerning the conditions of countries], was translated and edited by Leon Carl Brown, *The Surest Path: The Political Treatise of a Nineteenth-Century Muslim Statesman* (Cambridge, MA: Harvard University Press, 1967).

22. Ibid., pp. 77–78.

23. Jean Ganiage, *Les Origines du Protectorat francaise en Tunisie (1861–1881)* (Paris: Presses Universitaires de France, 1959); L. Carl Brown, *The Tunisia of Ahmad Bey (1837–1855)* (Princeton: Princeton University Press, 1974); and Lisa Anderson, *The State and Social Transformation in Tunisia and Libya, 1830–1980* (Princeton, NJ: Princeton University Press, 1986).

24. Quoted in Brown, *The Surest Path*, p. 134.

25. Mzali and Pignon, "Documents sur Kheredine," pp. 186–187.

26. P. J. Vatikiotis, *The History of Egypt from Muhammad Ali to Sadat* (London: Johns Hopkins University Press, 1980).

27. Niyazi Berkes, *The Emergence of Secularism in Turkey* (London: Routledge, 1998), p. 207.

28. Ahmet Cevdet Pasha in Charles Issawi, *The Economic History of Turkey, 1800–1914* (Chicago: University of Chicago Press, 1980), pp. 349–351; and Roderic Davison,

Reform in the Ottoman Empire, 1856–1876 (Princeton, NJ: Princeton University Press, 1963), p. 112.

29. Mzali and Pignon, "Documents sur Kheredine," pp. 189–190.

30. Owen, *Middle East in the World Economy*, pp. 100–121.

31. Ibid., pp. 122–152.

Chapter 5

1. Both texts are reproduced in Hurewitz, *The Middle East and North Africa in World Politics*, vol. 1 (New Haven, CT: Yale University Press, 1975), pp. 227–231.

2. Rifa'a Rafi' al-Tahtawi, *An Imam in Paris* (London: Saqi, 2004), pp. 326–327.

3. Alexandre Bellemare, *Abd-el-Kader: Sa Vie politique et militaire* (Paris: Hachette, 1863), p. 120.

4. The original texts of both agreements, with English translation, are reproduced in Raphael Danziger, *Abd al-Qadir and the Algerians: Resistance to the French and Internal Consolidation* (New York: Holmes & Meier, 1977), pp. 241–260. For maps showing the territories allotted France and Algeria under these treaties, see ibid., between pp. 95–96 and between pp. 157–158.

5. Reproduced in Bellemare, *Abd-el-Kader*, p. 260.

6. Ibid., p. 223.

7. A. de France, *Abd-El-Kader's Prisoners; or Five Months' Captivity Among the Arabs* (London: Smith, Elder and Co., n.d.), pp. 108–110.

8. Bellemare, *Abd-el-Kader*, pp. 286–289. Abd al-Qadir's son wrote on the impact of the capture of the zimala on his soldiers' morale in *Tuhfat al-za'ir fi tarikh al-Jaza'ir wa'l-Amir 'Abd al-Qadir* (Beirut: Dar al-Yaqiza al-'Arabiyya, 1964), pp. 428–431.

9. Tangier Convention for the Restoration of Friendly Relations: France and Morocco, September 10, 1844, reproduced in Hurewitz, *Middle East and North Africa in World Politics*, pp. 286–287.

10. Bellemare, *Abd-el-Kader*, p. 242.

11. Stanford J. Shaw and Ezel Kural Shaw, *History of the Ottoman Empire and Modern Turkey*, vol. 2 (Cambridge: Cambridge University Press, 1985), pp. 190–191. Note that French francs converted to pounds sterling at FF25 = £1, and the Turkish pound converted at the rate of £T1 = £0.909.

12. Urabi contributed an autobiographical essay to Jurji Zaydan's biographical dictionary, *Tarajim Mashahir al-Sharq fi'l-qarn al-tasi' 'ashar* [Biographies of famous people of the East in the nineteenth century], vol. 1 (Cairo: Dar al-Hilal, 1910), pp. 254–280 (hereafter Urabi memoirs).

13. Ibid., p. 261.

14. Urabi recounted these events to Wilfrid Scawen Blunt in 1903, who reproduced the account in his *Secret History of the British Occupation of Egypt* (New York: Howard Fertig, 1967, reprint of 1922 ed.), p. 369.

15. Urabi memoirs, p. 269.

16. Ibid., p. 270.

17. Ibid., p. 272.

18. Blunt asked Muhammad Abdu to comment on Urabi's account of events; Blunt, *Secret History*, p. 376.

19. Urabi memoirs, p. 274.

20. Blunt, *Secret History*, p. 372.

21. A. M. Broadley, *How We Defended Arabi and His Friends* (London: Chapman and Hall, 1884), p. 232.

22. Ibid., pp. 375–376.

23. Blunt, *Secret History*, p. 299.

24. *Mudhakkirat 'Urabi* [Memoirs of Urabi], vol. 1 (Cairo: Dar al-Hilal, 1954), pp. 7–8.

25. On the "scramble for Africa" and the Fashoda Incident see Ronald Robinson and John Gallagher, *Africa and the Victorians: The Official Mind of Imperialism,* 2nd ed. (Houndmills, UK: Macmillan, 1981).

26. Hurewitz, *Middle East and North Africa,* vol. 1, p. 477.

27. Ibid., pp. 508–510.

28. Ahmad Amin, *My Life,* translated by Issa Boullata (Leiden: E. J. Brill, 1978), p. 59.

29. Cited by Ami Ayalon in his *The Press in the Arab Middle East: A History* (New York and Oxford: Oxford University Press, 1995), p. 15.

30. Cited in ibid., p. 30.

31. Cited in ibid., p. 31.

32. Martin Hartmann, *The Arabic Press of Egypt* (London, Luzac, 1899), pp. 52–85, cited in Roger Owen, *Lord Cromer: Victorian Imperialist, Edwardian Proconsul* (Oxford: Oxford University Press, 2004), p. 251.

33. Albert Hourani, *Arabic Thought in the Liberal Age, 1798–1939* (London: Oxford University Press, 1962), p. 113.

34. Ahmad Amin, *My Life,* pp. 48–49.

35. Thomas Philipp and Moshe Perlmann, trans. and eds., *'Abd al-Rahman al-Jabarti's History of Egypt,* vol. 3 (Stuttgart: Franz Steiner, 1994), pp. 252–253.

36. Daniel L. Newman, *An Imam in Paris: Al-Tahtawi's Visit to France (1826–1831)* (London: Saqi, 2004), p. 177.

37. Ahmad Amin, *My Life,* p. 19.

38. Judith Tucker, *Women in Nineteenth Century Egypt* (Cambridge: Cambridge University Press, 1985), p. 129.

39. Qasim Amin, *The Liberation of Women,* trans. Samiha Sidhom Peterson (Cairo: American University at Cairo Press, 1992), p. 12.

40. Ibid., p. 15.

41. Ibid., p. 72.

42. Ibid., p. 75.

43. Ahmad Amin, *My Life*, p. 90.

44. Ibid., p. 60.

45. Ibid., pp. 60–61. The translator here used the term *upset* where the Arabic term is stronger, meaning "grief."

Chapter 6

1. "De Bunsen Committee Report," in J. C. Hurewitz, ed., *The Middle East and North Africa in World Politics*, vol. 2 (New Haven, CT: Yale University Press, 1979), pp. 26–46.

2. The Husayn-McMahon Correspondence has been reproduced in ibid., pp. 46–56.

3. Quote from the unpublished memoirs of the resident of Karak, 'Uda al-Qusus, cited in Eugene Rogan, *Frontiers of the State in the Late Ottoman Empire: Transjordan, 1851–1921* (Cambridge: Cambridge University Press, 1999), pp. 232–233.

4. The Sykes-Picot Agreement is reproduced in Hurewitz, *Middle East and North Africa*, vol. 2, pp. 60–64.

5. George Antonius, *The Arab Awakening: The Story of the Arab National Movement* (London: Hamish Hamilton, 1938), p. 248.

6. The Basle Program of the First Zionist Congress is reproduced in Paul R. Mendes-Flohr and Jehuda Reinharz, *The Jew in the Modern World: A Documentary History* (New York: Oxford University Press, 1980), p. 429.

7. Tom Segev, *One Palestine, Complete* (London: Abacus, 2001) p. 44.

8. The Balfour Declaration is reproduced in Hurewitz, *Middle East and North Africa*, vol. 2, pp. 101–106.

9. Cemal Pasha's remarks were published in *al-Sharq* newspaper, cited in Antonius, *Arab Awakening*, pp. 255–256.

10. Anglo-French Declaration of November 7, 1918, cited in ibid., pp. 435–436; Hurewitz, *Middle East and North Africa*, vol. 2, p. 112.

11. The Faysal-Weizmann Agreement is reproduced in Walter Laqueur and Barry Rubin, eds., *The Israel-Arab Reader: A Documentary History of the Middle East Conflict* (New York: Penguin, 1985), pp. 19–20.

12. Faysal's memo is reproduced in Hurewitz, *Middle East and North Africa*, vol. 2, pp. 130–32.

13. Harry N. Howard, *The King-Crane Commission* (Beirut: Khayyat, 1963), p. 35.

14. The King-Crane Report was first published in *Editor & Publisher* 55, 27, 2nd section, December 2, 1922. An abridged version of their recommendations is reproduced in Hurewitz, *Middle East and North Africa*, vol. 2, pp. 191–99.

15. Abu Khaldun Sati' al-Husri, *The day of Maysalun: A Page from the Modern History of the Arabs* (Washington, DC: Middle East Institute, 1966), pp. 107–108.

16. Reproduced in the Arabic edition of Sati' al-Husri, *Yawm Maysalun* (Beirut: Maktabat al-Kishaf, 1947), plate 25. On the political use of slogans, see James L. Gelvin, *Divided Loyalties: Nationalism and Mass Politics in Syria at the Close of Empire* (Los Angeles and Berkeley: University of California Press, 1998).

17. Al-Husri, *Day of Maysalun*, p. 130; this is confirmed in the confidential appendix of the King-Crane Report, written for the American delegation at Paris.

18. Yusif al-Hakim, *Suriyya wa'l-'ahd al-Faysali* [Syria and the Faysali era] (Beirut: Dar An-Nahar, 1986), p. 102.

19. "Resolution of the General Syrian Congress at Damascus," reproduced in Hurewitz, *Middle East and North Africa*, vol. 2, pp. 180–182.

20. "King-Crane Recommendations," in ibid., p. 195.

21. Al-Husri, *Day of Maysalun*, p. 79.

22. Elie Kedourie, "Sa'ad Zaghlul and the British," *St. Antony's Papers* 11, 2 (1961): 148–149.

23. McPherson's letters on the 1919 Revolution are reproduced in Barry Carman and John McPherson, eds., *The Man Who Loved Egypt: Bimbashi McPherson* (London: Ariel Books, 1985), pp. 204–221.

24. Huda Shaarawi, *Harem Years: The Memoirs of an Egyptian Feminist*, trans. and ed. Margot Badran (New York: The Feminist Press, 1986), p. 34.

25. Ibid., pp. 39–40.

26. Ibid., p. 55.

27. Ibid., pp. 92–94.

28. *Al-Istiqlal,* October 6, 1920, reproduced in Abd al-Razzaq al-Hasani, *al-'Iraq fi dawray al-ihtilal wa'l intidab* [Iraq in the occupation and mandate eras] (Sidon: al-'Irfan, 1935), pp. 117–118.

29. Charles Tripp, *A History of Iraq* (Cambridge: Cambridge University Press, 2000), pp. 36–45.

30. Published by Shaykh Muhammad Baqr al-Shabibi in Najaf, July 30, 1920. Reproduced in al-Hasani, *al-'Iraq*, pp. 167–168.

31. Ghassan R. Atiyya, *Iraq, 1908–1921: A Political Study* (Beirut: Arab Institute for Research and Publishing, 1973).

32. Muhammad Abd al-Husayn, writing in the Najaf newspaper *al-Istiqlal*, October 6, 1920, reproduced in al-Hasani, *al-'Iraq*, pp. 117–118.

33. Aylmer L. Haldane, *The Insurrection in Mesopotamia, 1920* (Edinburgh and London: William Blackwood and Sons, 1922), p. 331.

Chapter 7

1. Charles E. Davies, *The Blood-Red Arab Flag: An Investigation into Qasimi Piracy, 1797–1820* (Exeter: Exeter University Press, 1997), pp. 5–8, 190. See also Sultan Muhammad al-Qasimi, *The Myth of Arab Piracy in the Gulf* (London: Croom Helm, 1986).

2. Agreement between Britain and the Shaykh of Bahrain signed December 22, 1880, in J. C. Hurewitz, *The Middle East and North Africa in World Affairs*, vol. 1 (New Haven, CT: Yale University Press, 1975), p. 432.

3. From the Exclusive Agreement between Bahrain and Britain signed March 13, 1892, in ibid., p. 466.

4. Great Britain, *Parliamentary Debates, Commons*, 5th ser., vol. 55, cols. 1465–1466, cited in ibid., p. 570.

5. De Bunsen Report of June 30, 1915, reprinted in Hurewitz, *Middle East and North Africa*, vol. 2, pp. 28–29.

6. Middle East Centre Archives, St. Antony's College, Oxford (hereafter MECA), Philby Papers 15/5/241, letter from Sharif Husayn to Ibn Saud dated February 8, 1918.

7. MECA, Philby Papers 15/5/261, letter from Sharif Husayn to Ibn Saud dated May 7, 1918.

8. King Abdullah of Transjordan, *Memoirs* (New York: Philosophical Library, 1950), p. 181.

9. Documents captured by Saudi forces in the second battle of Khurma (June 23–July 9, 1918) showed Hashemite forces numbered 1,689 infantry and some 900 cavalry and other troops, for a total of 2,636 troops. MECA, Philby Papers 15/5/264.

10. MECA, Philby Papers 15/2/9 and 15/2/30, two copies of Ibn Saud's letter to Sharif Husayn dated August 14, 1918.

11. MECA, Philby Papers 15/2/276, letter from Sharif Husayn to Shakir bin Zayd dated August 29, 1918.

12. King Abdullah, *Memoirs*, p. 181.

13. Ibid., p. 183; Mary Wilson, *King Abdullah, Britain, and the Making of Jordan* (Cambridge: Cambridge University Press, 1987), p. 37.

14. King Abdullah, *Memoirs*, p. 183.

15. Alexei Vassiliev, *The History of Saudi Arabia* (London: Saqi, 2000), p. 249.

16. Cited in Timothy J. Paris, *Britain, the Hashemites, and Arab Rule, 1920–1925* (London: Frank Cass, 2003), p. 1.

17. Cited in Wilson, *King Abdullah, Britain, and the Making of Jordan*, p. 53.

18. The memoirs of Awda al-Qusus (1877–1943), a Christian from the southern town of al-Karak, have never been published. All passages quoted here are from the ninth chapter of the Arabic typescript on Amir Abdullah in Transjordan.

19. Awda al-Qusus reproduced the indictment, dated November 1, 1923, in his memoirs, p. 163. A copy of the indictment reached him in Jidda on January 9, 1924.

20. Uriel Dann, *Studies in the History of Transjordan, 1920–1949: The Making of a State* (Boulder, CO: Westview Press, 1984), pp. 81–92.

21. Letter of July 8, 1921. The letters of Gertrude Bell have been made accessible on the Internet by the University of Newcastle upon Tyne Library's Gertrude Bell Project, http://www.gerty.ncl.ac.uk/.

22. Sulayman Faydi, *Mudhakkirat [Memoirs of] Sulayman Faydi* (London: Saqi, 1998), pp. 302–303.

23. Gertrude Bell, letter of August 28, 1921.

24. Muhammad Mahdi Kubba, *Mudhakkirati fi samim al-ahdath, 1918–1958* [My memoirs at the center of events, 1918–1958] (Beirut: Dar al-Tali'a, 1965), pp. 22–25.

25. The text of the 1922 treaty is reproduced in Hurewitz, *Middle East and North Africa*, vol. 2, pp. 310–312.

26. Kubba, *Mudhakkirati*, pp. 26–27.

27. Faysal's confidential memo was cited in Hanna Batatu, *The Old Social Classes and the Revolutionary Movements of Iraq* (Princeton, NJ: Princeton University Press, 1978), pp. 25–26.

28. Zaghlul's comments quoted in "Bitter Harvest," *Al-Ahram Weekly Online*, October 12–18, 2000, http://weekly.ahram.org.eg/.

29. Ismail Sidqi, *Mudhakkirati* [My memoirs] (Cairo: Madbuli, 1996), p. 85.

30. Ibid., p. 87. The casualty figures are from a sympathetic political biography of Sidqi by Malak Badrawi, *Isma'il Sidqi, 1875–1950: Pragmatism and Vision in Twentieth-Century Egypt* (Richmond, UK: Curzon, 1996), p. 61.

31. Sidqi, *Mudhakkirati*, p. 97.

32. Population figures for the Ottoman period are particularly unreliable. This has been compounded by the highly politicized nature of demography in the Palestinian-Israeli conflict. The most reliable source is Justin McCarthy, *The Population of Palestine* (New York: Columbia University Press, 1990). These figures are from table 1.4D, p. 10.

33. Ibid., p. 224.

34. Neville J. Mandel, *The Arabs and Zionism Before World War I* (Berkeley and Los Angeles: University of California Press, 1976); Hasan Kayali, *Arabs and Young Turks: Ottomanism, Arabism, and Islamism in the Ottoman Empire, 1908–1918* (Berkeley and Los Angeles: University of California Press, 1997), pp. 103–106.

35. Immigration figures from McCarthy, *Population of Palestine*, p. 224; casualty figures from Charles Smith, *Palestine and the Arab-Israeli Conflict*, 4th ed. (Boston and New York: Bedford/St Martin's, 2001), pp. 113, 130.

36. Churchill's memorandum is reproduced in Hurewitz, *Middle East and North Africa*, vol. 2, pp. 301–305. Emphasis in the original.

37. Matiel E. T. Mogannam, *The Arab Woman and the Palestine Problem* (London: Herbert Joseph, 1937), pp. 70–73.

38. Ibid., p. 99.

39. McCarthy, *Population of Palestine*, pp. 34–35.

40. Akram Zuaytir, *Yawmiyat Akram Zu'aytir: al-haraka al-wataniyya al-filastiniyya, 1935–1939* [The diaries of Akram Zuaytir: The Palestinian national movement, 1935–1939] (Beirut: Institute for Palestine Studies, 1980), pp. 27–30.

41. Ibid., p. 29.

42. Ibid., pp. 32–33.

43. Quoted in Wilson, *King Abdullah, Britain, and the Making of Jordan*, p. 119.

44. Abu Salman's poem was reproduced by Palestinian novelist Ghassan Kanafani in his essay "Palestine, the 1936–1939 Revolt" (London: 1982).

45. Ben-Gurion diaries cited in Tom Segev, *One Palestine, Complete* (London: Abacus, 2001), pp. 403–404.

46. Tom Segev details these and other repressive measures undertaken by the British to combat the Arab Revolt in *One Palestine, Complete*, pp. 415–443. See also Matthew

Hughes, "The Banality of Brutality: British Armed Forces and the Repression of the Arab Revolt in Palestine, 1936–39," *English Historical Review* 124 (2009): 313–354.

47. Harrie Arrigonie, *British Colonialism: 30 Years Serving Democracy or Hypocrisy* (Devon: Edward Gaskell, 1998), described these events, which took place the week before he arrived in Bassa. Arrigonie also reproduced photographs of the destroyed bus and the bodies of the villagers. An Arab account of the massacre is given by Eid Haddad, whose father witnessed the atrocity as a fifteen-year-old, though he dates the event to September 1936; "Painful memories from Al Bassa," http://www.palestineremembered.com. A similar account was told to Ted Swedenburg from the village of Kuwaykat; *Memories of Revolt: The 1936–1939 Rebellion and the Palestinian National Past* (Fayetteville: University of Arkansas Press, 2003), pp. 107–108.

48. The 1939 White Paper is reproduced in Hurewitz, *Middle East and North Africa*, vol. 2, pp. 531–538.

Chapter 8

1. Meir Zamir, *The Formation of Modern Lebanon* (London: Croom Helm, 1985), p. 15.

2. Ammoun was accompanied by another Maronite, a Sunni Muslim, a Greek Orthodox Christian, and a Druze. Lyne Lohéac, *Daoud Ammoun et la Création de l'État libanais* (Paris: Klincksieck, 1978), p. 73.

3. Ammoun's presentation was reported in the influential Paris daily, *Le Temps*, January 29, 1919, and reproduced in George Samné, *La Syrie* (Paris: Editions Bossard, 1920), pp. 231–232.

4. Ghanim's introduction in Samné, *La Syrie*, pp. xviii–xix.

5. Muhammad Jamil Bayhum, *Al-'Ahd al-Mukhdaram fi Suriya wa Lubnan, 1918–1922* [The era of transition in Syria and Lebanon] (Beirut: Dar al-Tali'a, n.d. [1968]), p. 109.

6. Ibid., p. 110.

7. Lohéac, *Daoud Ammoun*, pp. 84–85.

8. Bishara Khalil al-Khoury, *Haqa'iq Lubnaniyya* [Lebanese realities], vol. 1 (Harisa, Lebanon: Basil Brothers, 1960), p. 106.

9. Lohéac, *Daoud Ammoun*, pp. 91–92.

10. Alphonse Zenié, quoted in ibid., p. 96.

11. Yusif Sawda, resident in Alexandria, cited in ibid., p. 139.

12. Bayhum, *al-'Ahd al-Mukhdaram*, pp. 136–140.

13. Si Madani El Glaoui, cited in C. R. Pennell, *Morocco Since 1830: A History* (London: Hurst, 2000), p. 176.

14. Pennell, *Morocco Since 1830*, p. 190.

15. Muhammad ibn Abd al-Karim (Abd el-Krim) published a statement of his political views after his capture by the French in Rashid Rida's influential magazine, *al-Manar* 27, 1344–1345 (1926–1927): 630–634. For a translation see C. R. Pennell, *A Country*

with a Government and a Flag: The Rif War in Morocco, 1921–1926 (Wisbech: MENAS Press, 1986), pp. 256–259.

16. Quoted in Pennell, *Country with a Government*, from French interviews with tribesmen after Abd el-Krim's defeat, p. 186.

17. Ibid., pp. 189–190.

18. Ibid., pp. 256–259.

19. Fawzi al-Qawuqji, *Mudhakkirat* [Memoirs of] *Fawzi al-Qawuqji*, vol. 1, 1914–1932 (Beirut: Dar al-Quds, 1975), p. 81.

20. Edmund Burke III, "A Comparative View of French Native Policy in Morocco and Syria, 1912–1925," *Middle Eastern Studies* 9 (1973): 175–186.

21. Philip S. Khoury, *Syria and the French Mandate: The Politics of Arab Nationalism, 1920–1945* (Princeton, NJ: Princeton University Press, 1987), pp. 102–108.

22. Burke, "Comparative View," pp. 179–180.

23. Abd al-Rahman Shahbandar, *Mudhakkirat* [Memoirs] (Beirut: Dar al-Irshad, 1967), p. 154.

24. Al-Qawuqji, *Mudhakkirat*, p. 84.

25. Shahbandar, *Mudhakkirat*, pp. 156–157.

26. Al-Qawuqji, *Mudhakkirat*, pp. 86–87.

27. Ibid., p. 89; Michael Provence, *The Great Syrian Revolt and the Rise of Arab Nationalism* (Austin: University of Texas Press, 2005), pp. 95–100.

28. Siham Tergeman, *Daughter of Damascus* (Austin: University of Texas Press, 1994), p. 97.

29. Shahbandar, *Mudhakkirat*, pp. 186–189.

30. Al-Qawuqji, *Mudhakkirat*, pp. 109–112.

31. John Ruedy, *Modern Algeria: The Origins and Development of a Nation*, 2nd ed. (Bloomington and Indianapolis: University of Indiana Press, 2005), p. 69.

32. Gustave Mercier, *Le Centenaire de l'Algérie*, vol. 1 (Algiers: P & G Soubiron, 1931), pp. 278–281.

33. Ibid., vol. 1, pp. 296–300.

34. Ibid., vol. 2, pp. 298–304.

35. Ferhat Abbas, *Le jeune Algérien: De la colonie vers la province* [The young Algerian: From the colony toward the province] (Paris: Editions de la Jeune Parque, 1931), p. 8.

36. According to Ruedy's figures, 206,000 Algerians were drafted, of which 26,000 were killed and 72,000 wounded; p. 111. Abbas claimed 250,000 Algerians were drafted, of which 80,000 died; p. 16.

37. Abbas, *Le jeune Algérien*, p. 24.

38. Ibid., p. 119.

39. Ibid., pp. 91–93.

40. Claude Collot and Jean-Robert Henry, *Le Mouvement national algérien: Textes 1912–1954* [The Algerian national movement: Texts 1912–1954] (Paris: L'Harmattan, 1978), pp. 66–67.

41. Ibid., pp. 68–69.

42. Ibid., pp. 38–39. On Messali, see Benjamin Stora, *Messali Hadj (1898–1974): pionnier du nationalism algérien* [Messali Hadj (1898–1974): Pioneer of Algerian nationalism] (Paris: L'Harmattan, 1986).

43. A full translation of the bill is reproduced in J. C. Hurewitz, *The Middle East and North Africa in World Affairs*, vol. 2 (New Haven, CT: Yale University Press, 1975), pp. 504–508.

44. Al-Khoury, *Syria and the French Mandate*, p. 592.

45. Bishara al-Khoury, *Haqa'iq Lubnaniyya* [Lebanese realities], vol. 2 (Beirut: Awraq Lubnaniyya, 1960), pp. 15–16.

46. Ibid., pp. 33–52.

47. Khalid al-Azm, *Mudhakkirat* [Memoirs of] *Khalid al-'Azm*, vol. 1 (Beirut: Dar al-Muttahida, 1972), pp. 294–299.

48. Tergeman, *Daughter of Damascus*, pp. 97–98.

Chapter 9

1. Communiqué of the Jewish Underground Resistance in Palestine, cited in Menachem Begin, *The Revolt* (London: W. H. Allen, 1951), pp. 42–43.

2. Stern's words were reproduced by Joseph Heller, *The Stern Gang: Ideology, Politics and Terror, 1940–1949* (London: Frank Cass, 1995), pp. 85–87.

3. Begin, *The Revolt*, p. 215.

4. Ibid., pp. 212–230.

5. *Manchester Guardian*, August 1, 1947, p. 5, cited in Paul Bagon, "The Impact of the Jewish Underground upon Anglo Jewry: 1945–1947" (M.Phil. thesis, Oxford, 2003), pp. 118–119.

6. *Jewish Chronicle*, August 8, 1947, p. 1, cited in Bagon, "Impact of the Jewish Underground," p. 122.

7. Cited in William Roger Louis, *The British Empire in the Middle East, 1945–1951* (Oxford: Oxford University Press, 1985), p. 485.

8. Charles D. Smith, *Palestine and the Arab-Israeli Conflict*, 4th ed. (Boston and New York: Bedford/St. Martin's, 2001) pp. 190–192.

9. Reproduced in T. G. Fraser, *The Middle East, 1914–1979* (London: E. Arnold, 1980), pp. 49–51.

10. *Al-Ahram*, February 2, 1948.

11. Qasim al-Rimawi accompanied Abd al-Qadir al-Husayni to Damascus and gave his account to the Palestinian historian of the 1948 Palestinian "Catastrophe," Arif al-Arif; see al-Arif, *al-Nakba: Nakbat Bayt al-Maqdis wa'l-Firdaws al-Mafqud* [The catastrophe: The catastrophe of Jerusalem and the lost paradise], vol. 1 (Sidon and Beirut: al-Maktaba al-'Asriyya, 1951), pp. 159–161.

12. Ibid., p. 161. In a footnote, Arif reminded his readers that other British soldiers had joined forces with the Haganah.

13. Ibid., p. 168.

14. Ibid., pp. 171 and 170.

15. Testimony of Ahmad Ayesh Khalil, son of a factory owner, and of Aisha Jima Ziday (Zaydan), from a family of small farmers who was seventeen at the time, reproduced in Staughton Lynd, Sam Bahour, and Alice Lynd, eds., *Homeland: Oral Histories of Palestine and Palestinians* (New York: Olive Branch Press, 1994), pp. 24–26.

16. Arif, *al-Nakba*, p. 173.

17. Ibid., pp. 173–174.

18. Ibid., pp. 174–175.

19. Benny Morris, *The Birth of the Palestinian Refugee Problem, 1947–1949* (Cambridge: Cambridge University Press, 1987), p. 30.

20. Rashid al-Hajj Ibrahim, *al-Difa' 'an Hayfa wa qadiyyat filastin* [The defense of Haifa and the Palestine problem] (Beirut: Institute for Palestine Studies, 2005), p. 44.

21. Ibid., p. 104.

22. Ibid., pp. 109–112.

23. From the diary of Khalil al-Sakakini, quoted in Tom Segev, *One Palestine, Complete* (London: Abacus, 2000), p. 508.

24. Morris, *Birth of the Palestinian Refugee Problem*, p. 141.

25. Avi Shlaim, *The Politics of Partition: King Abdullah, the Zionists, and Palestine, 1921–1951* (Oxford: Oxford University Press, 1998).

26. John Bagot Glubb, *A Soldier with the Arabs* (New York: Harper & Brothers, 1957), p. 66.

27. Quoted in Fawaz Gerges, "Egypt and the 1948 War," in Eugene Rogan and Avi Shlaim, eds., *The War for Palestine: Rewriting the History of 1948* (Cambridge: Cambridge University Press, 2001), p. 159.

28. Avi Shlaim, "Israel and the Arab Coalition in 1948," in ibid., p. 81. Only the Egyptian army expanded its numbers significantly in the course of the war, from an initial deployment of 10,000 to a maximum of 45,000 by the end of the war. Gerges, "Egypt and the 1948 War," p. 166.

29. Gamal Abdel Nasser, *The Philosophy of the Revolution* (Buffalo, NY: Economica Books, 1959), pp. 28–29.

30. Constantine K. Zurayk, *The Meaning of the Disaster*, trans. R. Bayly Winder (Beirut: Khayat, 1956).

31. Musa Alami, "The Lesson of Palestine," *Middle East Journal* 3 (October 1949): 373–405.

32. Zurayk, *Meaning of the Disaster*, p. 2.

33. Ibid., p. 24.

34. Alami, "Lesson of Palestine," p. 390.

35. Richard P. Mitchell, *The Society of the Muslim Brothers* (Oxford: Oxford University Press, 1993), p. 6.

36. 'Adil Arslan, *Mudhakkirat al-Amir 'Adil Arslan* [The memoirs of Amir 'Adil Arslan], vol. 2 (Beirut: Dar al-Taqaddumiya, 1983), p. 806.

37. Avi Shlaim, "Husni Za'im and the Plan to Resettle Palestinian Refugees in Syria," *Journal of Palestine Studies* 15 (Summer 1986): 68–80.

38. Arslan, *Mudhakkirat*, p. 846.

39. Mary Wilson, *King Abdullah, Britain, and the Making of Jordan* (Cambridge: Cambridge University Press, 1987), pp. 209–213.

Chapter 10

1. Nawal El Saadawi, *A Daughter of Isis: The Autobiography of Nawal El Saadawi* (London: Zed Books, 2000), pp. 260–261.

2. Nawal El Saadawi, *Walking Through Fire: A Life of Nawal El Saadawi* (London: Zed Books, 2002), p. 33.

3. Anouar Abdel-Malek, *Egypt: Military Society* (New York: Random House, 1968), p. 36.

4. Mohammed Naguib, *Egypt's Destiny* (London: Gollancz, 1955), p. 101.

5. Anwar el-Sadat, *In Search of Identity* (London: Collins, 1978), pp. 100–101.

6. Khaled Mohi El Din, *Memories of a Revolution: Egypt 1952* (Cairo: American University in Cairo Press, 1995), pp. 41–52.

7. Ibid., p. 81.

8. Naguib, *Egypt's Destiny*, p. 110.

9. Ibid., pp. 112–113.

10. Sadat, *In Search of Identity*, p. 107, notes he was at the cinema when the coup began; Mohi El Din, *Memories of a Revolution*, notes the fight and police report.

11. Mohi El Din, *Memories of a Revolution*, pp. 103–104.

12. El Saadawi, *Walking Through Fire*, p. 51.

13. Sadat, *In Search of Identity*, p. 121.

14. Naguib, *Egypt's Destiny*, pp. 139–140.

15. Ibid., p. 148.

16. Alan Richards, *Egypt's Agricultural Development, 1800–1980* (Boulder, CO: Westview Press, 1982), p. 178.

17. El Saadawi, *Walking Through Fire*, pp. 53–54.

18. Charles Issawi, *An Economic History of the Middle East and North Africa* (New York: Columbia University Press, 1982), table A.3, p. 231.

19. Figures in Naguib, *Egypt's Destiny*, p. 168.

20. Richard P. Mitchell, *The Society of the Muslim Brothers* (New York: Oxford University Press, 1993), p. 149.

21. Joel Gordon, *Nasser's Blessed Movement: Egypt's Free Officers and the July Revolution* (New York and Oxford: Oxford University Press, 1992), p. 179.

22. Mohamed Heikal, *Nasser: The Cairo Documents* (London: New English Library, 1972), p. 51.

23. Avi Shlaim, *The Iron Wall: Israel and the Arab World* (New York: W. W. Norton, 2000), p. 112.

24. Hassan II, *The Challenge* (London, 1978), p. 31, cited in C. R. Pennell, *Morocco Since 1830: A History* (London: Hurst, 2000), p. 263.

25. Leila Abouzeid, *Year of the Elephant: A Moroccan Woman's Journey Toward Independence* (Austin: University of Texas Press, 1989), pp. 20–21. Abouzeid first published her novel in Arabic in the early 1980s.

26. Ibid., pp. 36–38. In the preface of her English translation she wrote: "The main events and characters throughout the whole collection are real. I have not created these stories. I have simply told them as they are. And, Morocco is full of untold stories."

27. Ibid., pp. 49–50.

28. John Ruedy, *Modern Algeria: The Origins and Development of a Nation* (Bloomington and Indianapolis: University of Indiana Press, 2005), p. 163.

29. Heikal, *The Cairo Documents*, pp. 57–63.

30. Motti Golani, "The Historical Place of the Czech-Egyptian Arms Deal, Fall 1995," *Middle Eastern Studies* 31 (1995): 803–827.

31. Heikal, *The Cairo Documents*, p. 68.

32. Ibid., p. 74.

33. Ezzet Adel, quoted by the BBC, "The Day Nasser Nationalized the Canal," July 21, 2006, http://news.bbc.co.uk/1/hi/world/middle_east/5168698.stm.

34. Heikal, *The Cairo Documents*, pp. 92–95.

35. Quoted in Shlaim, *The Iron Wall*, p. 166.

36. Heikal, *The Cairo Documents*, p. 107.

37. For details of the CIA coup plot see Wilbur Crane Eveland, *Ropes of Sand: America's Failure in the Middle East* (New York: W. W. Norton, 1980).

38. El Saadawi, *Walking Through Fire*, pp. 89–99. The casualty figure is from Heikal, *Cairo Documents*, p. 115.

39. Heikal, *Cairo Documents*, p. 118.

40. Abdullah Sennawi, quoted by Laura James, "Whose Voice? Nasser, the Arabs, and 'Sawt al-Arab' Radio," *Transnational Broadcasting Studies* 16 (2006), http://www.tbs journal.com/James.html.

41. Youmna Asseily and Ahmad Asfahani, eds., *A Face in the Crowd: The Secret Papers of Emir Farid Chehab, 1942–1972* (London: Stacey International, 2007), p. 166.

42. Patrick Seale, *The Struggle for Syria: A Study of Post-War Arab Politics, 1945–1958* (New Haven, CT: Yale University Press, 1986), p. 307.

43. Khalid al-Azm, *Mudhakkirat* [Memoirs of] *Khalid al-Azm*, vol. 3 (Beirut: Dar al-Muttahida, 1972), pp. 125–126.

44. Ibid., pp. 127–128.

45. Seale, *The Struggle for Syria*, p. 323.

46. Avi Shlaim, *Lion of Jordan: The Life of King Hussein in War and Peace* (London: Allen Lane, 2007), pp. 129–152; Lawrence Tal, *Politics, the Military, and National Security in Jordan, 1955–1967* (Houndmills, UK: Macmillan, 2002), pp. 43–53.

47. Eveland, *Ropes of Sand*, pp. 250–253.

48. Yunis Bahri, *Mudhakkirat al-rahala Yunis Bahri fi sijn Abu Ghurayb ma' rijal al-'ahd al-maliki ba'd majzara Qasr al-Rihab 'am 1958 fi'l-'Iraq* [Memoirs of the traveler Yunis Bahri in Abu Ghurayb Prison with the men of the Monarchy era after the

1958 Rihab Palace Massacre in Iraq] (Beirut: Dar al-Arabiyya li'l-Mawsu'at, 2005), p. 17.

49. This account was told to Yunis Bahri by an eyewitness while both were in prison in Abu Ghurayb. Bahri, *Mudhakkirat*, pp. 131–134.

50. Ibid., pp. 136–138.

51. Camille Chamoun, *La Crise au Moyen Orient* (Paris, 1963), p. 423, cited in Irene L. Gendzier, *Notes from the Minefield: United States Intervention in Lebanon and the Middle East, 1945–1958* (New York: Columbia University Press, 1997), p. 297–298.

52. Heikal, *Cairo Documents*, p. 131.

Chapter 11

1. Quoted by Malcolm Kerr, *The Arab Cold War: Gamal 'Abd al-Nasir and His Rivals, 1958–1970*, 3rd ed. (New York: Oxford University Press, 1971), p. 21.

2. Mohamed Heikal, *Nasser: The Cairo Documents* (London: New English Library, 1972), p. 187.

3. Mouloud Feraoun, *Journal 1955–1962* (Paris: Éditions du Seuil, 1962), p. 156.

4. Ibid., pp. 151–152.

5. The story was told by Zohra Drif, another woman veteran of the Battle of Algiers, in Danièle Djamila Amrane-Minne, *Des Femmes dans la guerre d'Algérie* [Women in the Algerian War] (Paris: Karthala, 1994), p. 139.

6. Georges Arnaud and Jacques Vergès, *Pour* [For] *Djamila Bouhired* (Paris: Minuit, 1961), p. 10. Djamila Bouhired was the subject of a feature film by Egyptian filmmaker Youssef Chahine.

7. Amrane-Minne, *Femmes dans la guerre d'Algérie*, pp. 134–135.

8. Alistair Horne, *A Savage War of Peace: Algeria, 1954–1962* (New York: New York Review Books, 2006), p. 151.

9. The controversy in France surrounding the use of torture in Algeria was reawakened with the publication in 2001 of General Paul Aussaresses' memoirs of the Battle of Algiers in which he openly acknowledged the extent of torture. The book was published in English under the title *The Battle of the Casbah: Terrorism and Counter-terrorism in Algeria, 1955–1957* (New York: Enigma, 2002).

10. Horne, *Savage War of Peace*, p. 282.

11. Feraoun, *Journal*, p. 274.

12. Ibid., pp. 345–346.

13. Amrane-Minne, *Femmes dans la guerre d'Algérie*, pp. 319–320.

14. Anouar Abdel-Malek, *Egypt: Military Society* (New York: Random House, 1968), p. 287.

15. Quoted in Laura M. James, *Nasser at War: Arab Images of the Enemy* (Houndmills, UK: Palgrave, 2006), p. 56.

16. "There is no doubt that northern tribesmen . . . were listening regularly to Cairo by the mid-1950s." Paul Dresch, *A History of Modern Yemen* (Cambridge: Cambridge University Press, 2000), p. 77.

17. Ibid., p. 86.

18. Quoted in Mohamed Abdel Ghani El-Gamasy, *The October War: Memoirs of Field Marshal El-Gamasy of Egypt* (Cairo: American University in Cairo Press, 1993), p. 18.

19. Heikal, *Cairo Documents*, p. 217.

20. Gamasy, *The October War*, p. 28.

21. Anwar el-Sadat, *In Search of Identity* (London: Collins, 1978), p. 172.

22. Avi Shlaim, *The Iron Wall: Israel and the Arab World* (New York: W. W. Norton, 2000), p. 239.

23. Cited in Gamasy, *The October War*, p. 53.

24. Ibid., p. 54.

25. Ibid., p. 62.

26. Ibid., p. 65.

27. Hussein of Jordan, *My "War" with Israel* (New York: Peter Owen, 1969), pp. 89–91.

28. Michael B. Oren, *Six Days of War: June 1967 and the Making of the Modern Middle East* (London: Penguin, 2003), p. 178.

29. Hasan Bahgat, cited in Oren, *Six Days of War*, p. 201.

30. BBC Monitoring Service, cited in ibid., p. 209.

31. Ibid., p. 226.

32. Sadat, *In Search of Identity*, pp. 175–176.

33. Ibid., p. 179.

34. Ibid.

35. On Nasser's diplomacy see Shlaim, *The Iron Wall*, pp. 117–123; on the initiation of Hussein's meetings with Israeli officials see Avi Shlaim, *The Lion of Jordan: The Life of King Hussein in War and Peace* (London: Allen Lane, 2007), pp. 192–201.

36. Salah Khalaf wrote his memoirs under his nom de guerre, Abu Iyad (with Eric Rouleau), *My Home, My Land: A Narrative of the Palestinian Struggle* (New York: Times Books, 1981), pp. 19–23.

37. Cited in Helena Cobban, *The Palestinian Liberation Organisation: People, Power, and Politics* (Cambridge: Cambridge University Press, 1984), p. 33.

38. Leila Khaled, *My People Shall Live* (London: Hodder and Stoughton, 1973), pp. 85, 88.

39. Mahmoud Issa, *Je suis un Fedayin* [I am a Fedayin] (Paris: Stock, 1976), pp. 60–62.

40. Figures from Yezid Sayigh, *Armed Struggle and the Search for Peace: The Palestinian National Movement, 1949–1993* (Oxford: Oxford University Press, 1997), pp. 178–179.

41. Khaled, *My People Shall Live*, p. 107.

42. Abu Iyad, *My Home, My Land*, p. 60.

43. Sayigh, *Armed Struggle*, p. 203.

44. Khaled, *My People Shall Live*, p. 112.

45. Ibid.

46. Ibid., p. 116.

47. Ibid., p. 124.

48. Ibid., p. 126.

49. Ibid., pp. 136–143.

50. Khalaf, *My Home, My Land*, p. 76.

51. Khaled, *My People Shall Live*, p. 174.

52. Cited in Peter Snow and David Phillips, *Leila's Hijack War* (London: Pan Books, 1970), p. 41.

53. Heikal, *Cairo Documents*, pp. 21–22.

Chapter 12

1. Daniel Yergin, *The Prize: The Epic Quest for Oil, Money, and Power* (New York: Free Press, 1991), p. 446.

2. Ibid., p. 500.

3. See for instance al-Turayqi's arguments for an Arab oil pipeline; *Naql al-batrul al-'arabi* [Transport of Arab petroleum] (Cairo: League of Arab States, Institute of Arab Studies, 1961), pp. 114–122.

4. Muhammad Hadid, *Mudhakkirati: al-sira' min ajli al-dimuqtratiyya fi'l-Iraq* [My memoirs: The struggle for democracy in Iraq] (London: Saqi, 2006), p. 428; Yergin, *The Prize*, pp. 518–523.

5. Yergin, *The Prize*, pp. 528–529.

6. Cited in Mirella Bianco, *Gadhafi: Voice from the Desert* (London: Longman, 1975), pp. 67–68.

7. Mohammed Heikal, *The Road to Ramadan* (London: Collins, 1975), p. 70.

8. Abdullah al-Turayqi, *Al-bitrul al-'Arabi: Silah fi'l-ma'raka* [Arab petroleum: A weapon in the battle] (Beirut: PLO Research Center, 1967), p. 48.

9. Jonathan Bearman, *Qadhafi's Libya* (London: Zed, 1986), p. 81; Frank C. Waddams, *The Libyan Oil Industry* (London: Croom Helm, 1980), p. 230; Yergin, *The Prize*, p. 578.

10. Ali A. Attiga, *The Arabs and the Oil Crisis, 1973–1986* (Kuwait: OAPEC, 1987), pp. 9–11.

11. Al-Turayqi, *al-Bitrul al-'Arabi*, pp. 7, 68.

12. Mohamed Abdel Ghani El-Gamasy, *The October War: Memoirs of Field Marshal El-Gamasy of Egypt* (Cairo: American University in Cairo Press, 1993), p. 114.

13. Ibid., pp. 149–151.

14. Ibid., pp. 180–181.

15. Riad N. El-Rayyes and Dunia Nahas, eds., *The October War: Documents, Personalities, Analyses, and Maps* (Beirut: An-Nahar, 1973), p. 63.

16. Cited in Yergin, *The Prize*, p. 597. Khalid al-Hasan repeated the same story to Alan Hart: "Feisal said: 'The condition is that you will fight for a long time and that you won't ask for a cease-fire after a few days. You must fight for not less than three months.'" Alan Hart, *Arafat: Terrorist or Peacemaker?* (London: Sidgwick and Jackson, 1984), p. 370.

17. Heikal, *The Road to Ramadan*, p. 40.

18. El-Gamasy claimed that 27 Israeli aircraft were shot down on October 6 and that 48 aircraft were downed on October 7, for a total of 75 Israeli planes in the first two days of fighting; p. 234. He put Israel's armored losses at more than 120 tanks destroyed on October 6 and 170 tanks on October 7; pp. 217, 233. These figures seem credible when compared to the official figures for the war as a whole, in which Israel lost a total of 103 aircraft and 840 tanks and Arab forces lost 329 aircraft and 2,554 tanks. Avi Shlaim, *The Iron Wall: Israel and the Arab World* (New York: W. W. Norton, 2000), p. 321.

19. Cited in Yergin, *The Prize*, pp. 601–606.

20. El-Rayyes and Nahas, *The October War*, pp. 71–73.

21. Heikal, *Road to Ramadan*, p. 234.

22. Official Israeli figures cited by Shlaim, *Iron Wall*, p. 321.

23. Heikal, *Road to Ramadan*, p. 275.

24. Cited in Hart, *Arafat*, p. 411.

25. Ibid., p. 383.

26. Ibid., p. 379.

27. Uri Avnery, *My Friend, the Enemy* (London: Zed, 1986), p. 35.

28. Ibid., p. 52.

29. Ibid., p. 36.

30. Ibid., p. 43.

31. Ibid., p. 44.

32. Lina Mikdadi Tabbara, *Survival in Beirut* (London: Onyx Press, 1979), pp. 3–4, 116.

33. Hart, *Arafat*, p. 411.

34. The full text of Arafat's speech is reproduced in Walter Laqueur and Barry Rubin, eds., *The Israel-Arab Reader: A Documentary History of the Middle East Conflict* (New York: Penguin, 1985).

35. Hart, *Arafat*, p. 392.

36. Patrick Seale, *Abu Nidal: A Gun for Hire* (London: Arrow, 1993), pp. 162–163.

37. United Nations Relief Works Agency statistics for numbers of registered refugees. As UNRWA notes, registration is voluntary and the number of registered refugees is not an accurate population figure, but would be less than the actual total. Robert Fisk gave the 1975 figure at 350,000 in *Pity the Nation: Lebanon at War* (Oxford: Oxford University Press, 1990), p. 73. Refugee statistics posted to the UNRWA website, http://www.un.org /unrwa/publications/index.html.

38. Camille Chamoun, *Crise au Liban* [Crisis in Lebanon] (Beirut: 1977), pp. 5–8.

39. Kamal Joumblatt, *I Speak for Lebanon* (London: Zed Press, 1982), pp. 46, 47.

40. Tabbara, *Survival in Beirut*, p. 25.

41. Ibid., p. 19.

42. Ibid., pp. 20, 29.

43. Ibid., pp. 53–54.

44. Saad Eddin Ibrahim, "Oil, Migration, and the New Arab Social Order," in Malcolm Kerr and El Sayed Yasin, eds., *Rich and Poor States in the Middle East* (Boulder, CO: Westview Press, 1982), p. 55.

45. Tabbara, *Survival in Beirut*, p. 66.

46. Walid Khalidi, *Conflict and Violence in Lebanon: Confrontation in the Middle East* (Cambridge, MA: Harvard University Press, 1979), pp. 60–62.

47. Ibid., p. 104.

48. Tabbara, *Survival in Beirut*, p. 114.

49. Jumblatt, *I Speak for Lebanon*, p. 19.

50. Tabbara, *Survival in Beirut*, p. 178.

51. The bread riots took place on January 18–19, 1977. Mohamed Heikal, *Secret Channels: The Inside Story of Arab-Israeli Peace Negotiations* (London: Harper Collins, 1996), p. 245.

52. Ibid., p. 247–248. For the Libyan perspective of the attack, see Bearman, *Qadhafi's Libya*, pp. 170–171.

53. Heikal, *Secret Channels*, pp. 252–254. Sadat gives a similar account in his own memoirs: see Anwar el-Sadat, *In Search of Identity* (London: Collins, 1978), p. 306.

54. Boutros Boutros-Ghali, *Egypt's Road to Jerusalem* (New York: Random House, 1997), pp. 11–12.

55. Ibid., p. 16.

56. Heikal, *Secret Channels*, p. 259.

57. Boutros-Ghali, *Egypt's Road to Jerusalem*, p. 17.

58. Heikal, *Secret Channels*, p. 262.

59. Doc. 74, Statement to the Knesset by Prime Minister Begin, November 20, 1977, in *Israel's Foreign Relations: Selected Documents, vols. 4–5: 1977–1979*, posted to the Israeli Ministry of Foreign Affairs website, www.mfa.gov.il/MFA/Foreign+Relations/Israels+Foreign+Relations+since+1947/1977–1979/. Emphasis added by the author.

60. Boutros-Ghali, *Egypt's Road to Jerusalem*, pp. 134–135.

61. The statistics are drawn from Saad Eddin Ibrahim, "Oil, Migration, and the New Arab Social Order," pp. 53, 55.

62. Ibid., pp. 62–65.

63. Boutros-Ghali, *Egypt's Road to Jerusalem*, pp. 181–182, 189.

64. Alexei Vassiliev, *The History of Saudi Arabia* (London: Saqi, 2000), pp. 395–396.

Chapter 13

1. Gilles Kepel, *The Prophet and the Pharaoh: Muslim Extremism in Egypt* (London: Saqi, 1985), p. 192.

2. Mohamed Heikal, *Autumn of Fury: The Assassination of Sadat* (London: Deutsch, 1983), pp. xi–xii.

3. Sayyid Qutb, "The America I Have Seen," in Kamal Abdel-Malek, ed., *America in an Arab Mirror: Images of America in Arabic Travel Literature* (New York: St Martin's Press, 2000), pp. 26–27.

4. Ibid., p. 10.

5. Sayyid Qutb, Ma'alim fi'l-tariq [lit. "Signposts along the road," often translated under the title *Milestones*] (Cairo: Maktabat Wahba, 1964). There are many English editions of Qutb's *Milestones*. The edition I cite was published in Damascus by Dar al-Ilm (no date). These arguments from the introduction, pp. 8–11; ch. 4, "Jihad in the Cause of God," p. 55; ch. 7, "Islam Is the Real Civilization," p. 93.

6. Ibid., ch. 11, "The Faith Triumphant," p. 145.

7. Zaynab al-Ghazali, *Return of the Pharaoh: Memoir in Nasir's Prison* (Leicester, UK: The Islamic Foundation, n.d.), pp. 40–41.

8. Ibid., pp. 48–49.

9. Ibid., p. 67.

10. One of Hadid's recruits recounted his experiences to a Syrian judge, reproduced in translation in Olivier Carré and Gérard Michaud, *Les frères musulmans* [The Muslim brothers] *(1928–1982)* (Paris: Gallimard, 1983), p. 152.

11. Ibid., p. 139.

12. Isa Ibrahim Fayyad had been arrested in Jordan and accused of being part of a Syrian assassination squad sent to kill the Jordanian prime minister. His account of the massacre in the Tadmur Prison was reproduced in ibid., pp. 147–148.

13. The anonymous eyewitness account was recorded by a *Washington Post* correspondent and reproduced in the article "Syrian Troops Massacre Scores of Assad's Foes," June 25, 1981.

14. Thomas Friedman, *From Beirut to Jerusalem* (London: Collins, 1990), p. 86.

15. Quoted in Robert Fisk, *Pity the Nation: Lebanon at War* (Oxford: Oxford University Press, 1991), p. 518.

16. Emphasis in the original; ibid., p. 512.

17. Quoted in ibid., pp. 480, 520.

18. Quoted in Augustus Richard Norton, *Hezbollah* (Princeton, NJ: Princeton University Press, 2007), p. 19.

19. On the Maronite-Israel alliance, see Kirsten E. Schulze, *Israel's Covert Diplomacy in Lebanon* (London: Macmillan, 1998), pp. 104–124.

20. On Sharon's plans for the restructuring of the Middle East, see Avi Shlaim, *The Iron Wall: Israel and the Arab World* (New York: W. W. Norton, 2000), pp. 395–400.

21. Lina Mikdadi, *Surviving the Siege of Beirut: A Personal Account* (London: Onyx Press, 1983), pp. 107–108.

22. Colonel Abu Attayib, *Flashback Beirut 1982* (Nicosia: Sabah Press, 1985), p. 213.

23. Mikdadi, *Surviving the Siege of Beirut*, p. 121.

24. Ibid., pp. 132–133.

25. From the official translation of the Final Report of "The Commission of Inquiry into the Events at the Refugee Camps in Beirut, 1983," chaired by the president of the Israeli Supreme Court, Yitzhak Kahan, pp. 12, 22.

26. Selim Nassib with Caroline Tisdall, *Beirut: Frontline Story* (London: Pluto, 1983), pp. 148–158.

27. Naim Qassem, *Hizbullah: The Story from Within* (London: Saqi, 2005), pp. 92–93.

28. Ibid., pp. 88–89.

29. The full text of this foundation document, "Open Letter Addressed by Hizbullah to the Downtrodden in Lebanon and in the World" of February 16, 1985, is reproduced in Augustus Richard Norton, *Amal and the Shi'a: Struggle for the Soul of Lebanon* (Austin: University of Texas Press, 1987). Passage quoted on pp. 174–175.

30. Fisk, *Pity the Nation*, p. 460.

31. Norton, *Hezbollah*, p. 81.

32. Abdullah Anas, *Wiladat "al-Afghan al-'Arab": Sirat Abdullah Anas bayn Mas'ud wa 'Abdullah 'Azzam* [The birth of the "Arab Afghans": The autobiography of Abdullah Anas between Mas'ud and Abdullah 'Azzam] (London: Saqi, 2002), p. 14. Born Bou Jouma'a, he adopted the alias Anas as his surname after joining the Afghan jihad.

33. For a brief biography, see Thomas Hegghammer, "Abdallah Azzam, the Imam of Jihad," in Gilles Kepel and Jean-Pierre Milelli, eds., *Al Qaeda in Its Own Words* (Cambridge, MA: Harvard University Press, 2008), pp. 81–101.

34. Abdullah 'Azzam, "To Every Muslim on Earth," published in Arabic in the magazine he edited from Afghanistan, *Jihad*, March 1985, p. 25.

35. Abdullah 'Azzam, "The Defense of Muslim Territories Constitutes the First Individual Duty," in Keppel and Milelli, pp. 106–107.

36. The full record of U.S. support for the Afghan mujahidin is provided by Steve Coll in *Ghost Wars* (New York: Penguin, 2004); figures for the Carter years p. 89; for 1985, p. 102.

37. Anas, *Wiladat "al-Afghan al-'Arab,"* p. 15.

38. Ibid., pp. 16–17.

39. Ibid., pp. 25–29.

40. Ibid., pp. 33–34.

41. Interview with Zaynab al-Ghazali, *Jihad*, December 13, 1985, pp. 38–40.

42. Anas, *Wiladat "al-Afghan al-'Arab,"* p. 58.

43. Ibid., p. 67.

44. Ibid., p. 87.

45. Shaul Mishal and Reuben Aharoni, *Speaking Stones: Communiqués from the Intifada Underground* (Syracuse, NY: Syracuse University Press, 1994), p. 21.

46. Azzam Tamimi, *Hamas: Unwritten Chapters* (London: Hurst, 2007), pp. 11–12.

47. Sari Nusseibeh with Anthony David, *Once Upon a Country: A Palestinian Life* (London: Halban, 2007), p. 265.

48. Ibid., p. 269.

49. The charter was published on August 18, 1988; quote from art. 15. "Charter of the Islamic Resistance Movement (Hamas) of Palestine," *Journal of Palestine Studies* 22, 4 (Summer 1993): 122–134.

50. Communiqués 1 and 2, in Mishal and Aharoni, *Speaking Stones*, pp. 53–58.

51. Nusseibeh, *Once Upon a Country*, p. 272.

52. M. Cherif Bassiouni and Louise Cainkar, eds., *The Palestinian Intifada—December 9, 1987–December 8, 1988: A Record of Israeli Repression* (Chicago: Database Project on Palestinian Human Rights, 1989), pp. 19–20.

53. Ibid., pp. 92–94.

54. Hamas Communiqué No. 33, December 23, 1988, and UNC Communiqué No. 25, September 6, 1988, in Mishal and Aharoni, *Speaking Stones*, pp. 125–126, 255.

55. UNC Communiqué No. 25, September 6, 1988, in Mishal and Aharoni, *Speaking Stones*, p. 125.

56. Nusseibeh, *Once Upon a Country*, pp. 296–297.

57. Yezid Sayigh, *Armed Struggle and the Search for State: The Palestinian National Movement, 1949–1993* (Oxford: Oxford University Press, 1997), p. 624.

58. Cited in Avi Shlaim, *The Iron Wall*, p. 466.

59. Communiqué No. 33, December 23, 1988, in Mishal and Aharoni, *Speaking Stones*, p. 255.

60. Robert Hunter, *The Palestinian Uprising: A War by Other Means* (Berkeley and Los Angeles: University of California Press, 1991), p. 215.

Chapter 14

1. Mohamed Heikal, *Illusion of Triumph: An Arab View of the Gulf War* (London: Harper Collins, 1992), pp. 14–17, for both Habash and Asad quotes. See also Christopher Andrew and Vasili Mitrokhin, *The World Was Going Our Way: The KGB and the Battle for the Third World* (New York: Basic Books, 2005), pp. 212–213.

2. Mohamed Heikal, *Illusion of Triumph*, pp. 16–17.

3. Quoted in Zachary Karabell, "Backfire: U.S. Policy Toward Iraq, 1988–2 August 1990," *Middle East Journal* (Winter 1995): 32–33.

4. Human Rights Watch, *Genocide in Iraq: The Anfal Campaign Against the Kurds* (New York and Washington, DC: Human Rights Watch, 1993).

5. Samir al-Khalil, the alias used by Iraqi author Kanan Makiya, provided a graphic description of political repression in Saddam Hussein's Iraq in his 1989 study, *The Republic of Fear* (Berkeley and Los Angeles: University of California Press, 1989).

6. Charles Tripp, *A History of Iraq* (Cambridge: Cambridge University Press, 2000), p. 251.

7. Daniel Yergin, *The Prize* (New York: Free Press, 1991), p. 767.

8. A transcript of the Glaspie-Hussein interview is reproduced in Phyllis Bennis and Michel Moushabeck, eds., *Beyond the Storm: A Gulf Crisis Reader* (New York: Olive Branch, 1991), pp. 391–396.

9. Jehan S. Rajab, *Invasion Kuwait: An English Woman's Tale* (London: Radcliffe Press, 1993), p. 1.

10. Heikal, *Illusion of Triumph*, pp. 196–198.

11. Ibid., p. 207.

12. Rajab, *Invasion Kuwait*, pp. 55, 99–100.

13. Heikal, *Illusion of Triumph*, p. 250.

14. Mohammed Abdulrahman Al-Yahya, *Kuwait: Fall and Rebirth* (London: Kegan Paul International, 1993), p. 86.

15. Rajab, *Invasion Kuwait*, pp. 14–19.

16. Ibid., pp. 73–74; Al-Yahya, *Kuwait: Fall and Rebirth*, pp. 87–88.

17. Rajab, *Invasion Kuwait*, pp. 43–45.

18. Ibrahim al-Marashi, "The Nineteenth Province: The Invasion of Kuwait and the 1991 Gulf War from the Iraqi Perspective" (D.Phil. thesis, Oxford, 2004), p. 92.

19. Abdul Bari Atwan, *The Secret History of Al-Qa'ida* (London: Abacus, 2006), pp. 37–38.

20. "Declaration of Jihad Against the Americans Occupying the Land of the Two Holy Sanctuaries," reprinted in Gilles Kepel and Jean-Pierre Milelli, eds., *Al-Qaeda in Its Own Words* (Cambridge, MA: Harvard University Press, 2008), pp. 47–50. See also Bin Ladin's CNN interview in ibid., pp. 51–52.

21. Heikal, *Illusion of Triumph*, pp. 15–16.

22. Ibid., p. 230.

23. Ibid.

24. Ibid., p. 234.

25. Ibid., p. 13.

26. Sari Nusseibeh, *Once Upon a Country: A Palestinian Life* (London: Halban, 2007), p. 318.

27. Rajab, *Invasion Kuwait*, p. 181.

28. Theodor Hanf, *Coexistence in Wartime Lebanon: Decline of a State and Rise of a Nation* (London: I. B. Tauris, 1993), p. 319.

29. Ibid., p. 570.

30. Ibid., p. 595.

31. Ibid., p. 616.

32. Kamal Salibi, *A House of Many Mansions* (London: I. B. Tauris, 1988).

33. Nusseibeh, *Once Upon a Country*, p. 337.

34. Hanan Ashrawi, *This Side of Peace: A Personal Account* (New York: Simon & Schuster, 1995), p. 75.

35. Ibid., pp. 82–84.

36. Nusseibeh, *Once Upon a Country*, p. 342.

37. The full text of Haidar Abdul Shafi's lecture is reproduced on the Jerusalem Media and Communications Center website, http://www.jmcc.org/documents/haidarmad.htm.

38. Transcriptions of all opening and closing speeches by heads of delegations to Madrid are reproduced on the Israeli Ministry of Foreign Affairs website, http://www

.mfa.gov.il/MFA/Archive/. Israeli historian Amitzur Ilan attributes "true responsibility for the murder" of Bernadotte to Shamir and two other Lehi leaders; Ilan, *Bernadotte in Palestine, 1948* (Houndmills, UK, and London: Macmillan, 1989), p. 233.

39. Avi Shlaim, *The Iron Wall*, p. 500.

40. Ashrawi, *This Side of Peace*, p. 212.

41. Ahmed Qurie ('Abu Ala'), *From Oslo to Jerusalem: The Palestinian Story of the Secret Negotiations* (London: I. B. Tauris, 2006), p. 58.

42. Ibid., p. 59.

43. Yezid Sayigh, *Armed Struggle and the Search for State: The Palestinian National Movement, 1949–1993* (Oxford: Oxford University Press, 1997), pp. 656–658.

44. Ashrawi, *This Side of Peace*, p. 259.

45. Qurie, *From Oslo to Jerusalem*, p. 279.

46. Avi Shlaim, *The Iron Wall: Israel and the Arab World* (New York: W. W. Norton, 2000), p. 547.

47. World Bank, "Poverty in the West Bank and Gaza," Report No. 22312-GZ, June 18, 2001.

48. The construction of new settlements violated Art. 31 of the Oslo II accords, which stipulated: "Neither side shall initiate or take any step that will change the status of the West Bank and the Gaza Strip pending the outcome of the permanent status negotiations."

49. B'tselem, the Israeli Information Center for Human Rights in the Occupied Territories, "Land Grab: Israel's Settlement Policy in the West Bank," May 2002, p. 8.

50. Ibid., pp. 433–444.

51. Bob Woodward, *Bush at War* (New York: Simon & Schuster, 2002), p. 35.

Chapter 15

1. Osama bin Ladin's television statement was broadcast on Al-Jazeera on October 7, 2001. An English transcription of his statement is posted on the BBC website: "Bin Laden's Warning: Full Text," BBC, October 7, 2001, http://news.bbc.co.uk/1/hi/world/south_asia/1585636.stm.

2. Figures from the Israeli human rights organization B'tselem, quoted by the BBC: "Intifada Toll 2000–2005," BBC, last updated February 8, 2005, http://news.bbc.co.uk/1/hi/world/middle_east/3694350.stm.

3. All statistics relating to administrative detention, house demolition, and the Separation Barrier can be found at "List of Topics," B'tselem.org, http://www.btselem.org/english/list_of_Topics.asp.

4. It is worth noting that British intelligence did not share the Bush administration's assessment. As the 2016 Chilcot Report noted, "The Joint Intelligence Committee continued to judge that cooperation between Iraq and Al Qaida was 'unlikely,' and that there was no 'credible evidence' of Iraqi transfers of WMD-related technology and expertise to terrorist groups." *Iraq Inquiry*, executive summary, paragraph 504, p. 70.

5. American casualty figures in Iraq are available on the Department of Defense website: www.defense.gov/casualty.pdf.

6. "Bridging the Dangerous Gap Between the West and the Muslim World" (remarks prepared for delivery by Deputy Secretary Paul Wolfowitz at the World Affairs Council, Monterey, California, May 3, 2002).

7. Secretary Colin L. Powell, "The U.S.–Middle East Partnership Initiative: Building Hope for the Years Ahead" (lecture delivered to the Heritage Foundation, Washington, DC, 2002).

8. Gareth Stansfield, *Iraq*, 2nd ed. (Cambridge, MA: Polity Press, 2016), pp. 185–194. There are no official figures on the 33-million-strong population of Iraq. In 2011, the CIA estimated Shiites to number as much as 60 to 65 percent of the population, with Sunni Arabs and Kurds splitting the difference, while surveys conducted by the Pew Research Center in late 2011 found 51 percent of Iraqi Muslims claimed to be Shiite.

9. Iraq Body Count, a nongovernmental organization that tallies fatalities listed by media and official sources, reported nearly 120,000 civilian deaths between 2003 and 2011; see "Documented Civilian Deaths from Violence," www.iraqbodycount.org/database. The UN-backed Iraq Family Health Survey Study Group estimated 151,000 violent deaths between March 2003 and June 2006 alone; see "Violence-Related Mortality in Iraq from 2002 to 2006," *New England Journal of Medicine* 358 (2008): 484–493.

10. Micah Zenko, "Obama's Embrace of Drone Strikes Will Be a Lasting Legacy," *New York Times*, January 12, 2016. The official number of civilian casualties, given as 64 to 116, has been challenged; Jack Serle cites a range of 380 to 801 civilian casualties from drone strikes. Jack Serle, "Obama Drone Casualties Number a Fraction of Those Recorded by the Bureau," *Bureau of Investigative Journalism*, July 1, 2016.

11. Ala'a Shehabi and Marc Owen Jones, eds., *Bahrain's Uprising: Resistance and Repression in the Gulf* (London: Zed Books, 2015), pp. 1–2.

12. Shehabi and Jones, *Bahrain's Uprising*, p. 4.

13. Toby Matthiesen, *Sectarian Gulf: Bahrain, Saudi Arabia, and the Arab Spring That Wasn't* (Stanford, CA: Stanford University Press, 2013), pp. 36–48.

14. Cited in "Report of the Bahrain Independent Commission of Inquiry," originally delivered November 23, 2011, final revised version December 10, 2011, accessed online at http://www.bici.org.bh/BICIreportEN.pdf, pp. 47–48.

15. Shehabi and Jones, *Bahrain's Uprising*, p. 84.

16. "Report of the Bahrain Independent Commission of Inquiry."

17. Quoted by exiled Libyan novelist Hisham Matar in *The Return: Fathers, Sons and the Land in Between* (London: Penguin Viking, 2016), p. 235. Matar's father was kidnapped by Libyan security forces in 1990 for his political opposition to the regime and was imprisoned in Libya, where he disappeared without a trace.

18. Robert F. Worth, *A Rage for Order: The Middle East in Turmoil, from Tahrir Square to ISIS* (New York: Farrar, Straus and Giroux, 2016), p. 107.

19. The ten nations were Bahrain, Egypt, Jordan, Kuwait, Morocco, Qatar, Saudi Arabia, Senegal, Sudan, and the United Arab Emirates.

20. Internal Displacement Monitoring Centre, "Global Report on Internal Displacement 2016" (May 2016); Ahmad al-Haj, "Yemeni Civil War: 10,000 Civilians Killed and 40,000 Injured in Conflict, UN Reveals," *Independent*, January 17, 2017.

21. Samar Yazbek, *A Woman in the Crossfire: Diaries of the Syrian Revolution* (London: Haus, 2012), p. 4.

22. Human Rights Watch, in its *World Report 2017*, quoted the Syrian Center for Policy Research's claim of 470,000 dead by February 2016, as well as the figures for displaced persons; see "Syria: Events of 2016," Human Rights Watch, https://www.hrw.org/world-report/2017/country-chapters/syria.

23. Jean-Pierre Filiu, *From Deep State to Islamic State: The Arab Counter-revolution and Its Jihadi Legacy* (London: Hurst, 2015); Fawaz Gerges, *Isis: A History* (Princeton, NJ: Princeton University Press, 2016).

24. Known in Arabic as *Da'ish*, the Arabic acronym for "Islamic State in Iraq and al-Sham," the Western world, confused by the word *al-Sham*, cannot agree on an English acronym, alternating between "ISIS" (IS in Iraq and Syria) and "ISIL" (IS in Iraq and the Levant).

25. The Egyptian Ministry of Health reported 638 deaths in Rabaa Square; Human Rights Watch claimed a minimum of 817 people were killed, and the Muslim Brotherhood claimed 2,600 were killed.

26. Ashraf El-Sherif, "The Muslim Brotherhood and the Future of Political Islam in Egypt" (paper published by the Carnegie Endowment for International Peace, October 21, 2014).

Index

Eugene Rogan is a professor of modern Middle Eastern history at the University of Oxford. The author of numerous books, including the international bestseller *The Fall of the Ottomans*, Rogan is the recipient of the Albert Hourani Prize. He lives in Oxford, England.